University Casebook Series

December, 1982

ACCOUNTING AND THE LAW, Fourth Edition (1978), with Problems Pamphlet (Successor to Dohr, Phillips, Thompson & Warren)

George C. Thompson, Professor, Columbia University Graduate School of Business.
Robert Whitman, Professor of Law, University of Connecticut.
Ellis L. Phillips, Jr., Member of the New York Bar.
William C. Warren, Professor of Law Emeritus, Columbia University.

ACCOUNTING FOR LAWYERS, MATERIALS ON (1980)

David R. Herwitz, Professor of Law, Harvard University.

ADMINISTRATIVE LAW, Seventh Edition (1979), with 1983 Problems Supplement (Supplement edited in association with Paul R. Verkuil, Dean and Professor of Law, Tulane University)

Walter Gellhorn, University Professor Emeritus, Columbia University.
Clark Byse, Professor of Law, Harvard University.
Peter L. Strauss, Professor of Law, Columbia University.

DMIRALTY, Second Edition (1978), with Statute and Rule Supplement

Jo Desha Lucas, Professor of Law, University of Chicago.

ADVOCACY, see also Lawyering Process

AGENCY, see also Enterprise Organization

AGENCY—PARTNERSHIPS, Third Edition (1982)

Abridgement from Conard, Knauss & Siegel's Enterprise Organization, Third Edition.

ANTITRUST AND REGULATORY ALTERNATIVES (1977), Fifth Edition

Louis B. Schwartz, Professor of Law, University of Pennsylvania.
John J. Flynn, Professor of Law, University of Utah.

ANTITRUST SUPPLEMENT—SELECTED STATUTES AND RELATED MATERIALS (1977)

John J. Flynn, Professor of Law, University of Utah.

BUSINESS ORGANIZATION, see also Enterprise Organization

BUSINESS PLANNING (1966), with 1982 Supplement

David R. Herwitz, Professor of Law, Harvard University.

BUSINESS TORTS (1972)

Milton Handler, Professor of Law Emeritus, Columbia University.

CHILDREN IN THE LEGAL SYSTEM (1983)

Walter Wadlington, Professor of Law, University of Virginia.
Charles H. Whitebread, Professor of Law, University of Southern California.
Samuel Davis, Professor of Law, University of Georgia.

UNIVERSITY CASEBOOK SERIES—Continued

CIVIL PROCEDURE, see Procedure

CLINIC, see also Lawyering Process

COMMERCIAL AND CONSUMER TRANSACTIONS, Second Edition (1978)

> William D. Warren, Dean of the School of Law, University of California, Los Angeles.
> William E. Hogan, Professor of Law, Cornell University.
> Robert L. Jordan, Professor of Law, University of California, Los Angeles.

COMMERCIAL LAW, CASES & MATERIALS ON, Third Edition (1976), with 1982 Supplement

> E. Allan Farnsworth, Professor of Law, Columbia University.
> John Honnold, Professor of Law, University of Pennsylvania.

COMMERCIAL PAPER, Second Edition (1976)

> E. Allan Farnsworth, Professor of Law, Columbia University.

COMMERCIAL PAPER AND BANK DEPOSITS AND COLLECTIONS (1967), with Statutory Supplement

> William D. Hawkland, Professor of Law, University of Illinois.

COMMERCIAL TRANSACTIONS—Principles and Policies (1982)

> Alan Schwartz, Professor of Law, University of Southern California.
> Robert E. Scott, Professor of Law, University of Virginia.

COMPARATIVE LAW, Fourth Edition (1980)

> Rudolf B. Schlesinger, Professor of Law, Hastings College of the Law.

COMPETITIVE PROCESS, LEGAL REGULATION OF THE, Second Edition (1979), with Statutory Supplement and 1982 Case Supplement

> Edmund W. Kitch, Professor of Law, University of Chicago.
> Harvey S. Perlman, Professor of Law, University of Virginia.

CONFLICT OF LAWS, Seventh Edition (1978), with 1982 Supplement

> Willis L. M. Reese, Professor of Law, Columbia University,
> Maurice Rosenberg, Professor of Law, Columbia University.

CONSTITUTIONAL LAW, Sixth Edition (1981), with 1982 Supplement

> Edward L. Barrett, Jr., Professor of Law, University of California, Davis.
> William Cohen, Professor of Law, Stanford University.

CONSTITUTIONAL LAW: THE STRUCTURE OF GOVERNMENT (Reprinted from CONSTITUTIONAL LAW, Sixth Edition), with 1982 Supplement

> Edward L. Barrett, Jr., Professor of Law, University of California, Davis.
> William Cohen, Professor of Law, Stanford University.

CONSTITUTIONAL LAW, CIVIL LIBERTY AND INDIVIDUAL RIGHTS, Second Edition (1982)

> William Cohen, Professor of Law, Stanford Law School.
> John Kaplan, Professor of Law, Stanford Law School.

CONSTITUTIONAL LAW, Tenth Edition (1980), with 1982 Supplement

> Gerald Gunther, Professor of Law, Stanford University.

CONSTITUTIONAL LAW, INDIVIDUAL RIGHTS IN, Third Edition (1981), with 1982 Supplement (Reprinted from CONSTITUTIONAL LAW, Tenth Edition)

> Gerald Gunther, Professor of Law, Stanford University.

UNIVERSITY CASEBOOK SERIES—Continued

CORPORATIONS, Second Edition (1982)

Alfred F. Conard, Professor of Law, University of Michigan.
Robert N. Knauss, Dean of the Law School, University of Houston.
Stanley Siegel, Professor of Law, University of California, Los Angeles.

CORPORATIONS, THE LAW OF: WHAT CORPORATE LAWYERS DO (1976)

Jan G. Deutsch, Professor of Law, Yale University.
Joseph J. Bianco, Professor of Law, Yeshiva University.

CORPORATIONS COURSE GAME PLAN (1975)

David R. Herwitz, Professor of Law, Harvard University.

CORRECTIONS, SEE SENTENCING

CREDIT TRANSACTIONS AND CONSUMER PROTECTION (1976)

John Honnold, Professor of Law, University of Pennsylvania.

CREDITORS' RIGHTS, see also Debtor-Creditor Law

CRIMINAL JUSTICE, THE ADMINISTRATION OF, Second Edition (1969)

Francis C. Sullivan, Professor of Law, Louisiana State University.
Paul Hardin III, Professor of Law, Duke University.
John Huston, Professor of Law, University of Washington.
Frank R. Lacy, Professor of Law, University of Oregon.
Daniel E. Murray, Professor of Law, University of Miami.
George W. Pugh, Professor of Law, Louisiana State University.

CRIMINAL JUSTICE ADMINISTRATION, Second Edition (1982)

Frank W. Miller, Professor of Law, Washington University.
Robert O. Dawson, Professor of Law, University of Texas.
George E. Dix, Professor of Law, University of Texas.
Raymond I. Parnas, Professor of Law, University of California, Davis.

CRIMINAL LAW, Second Edition (1979)

Fred E. Inbau, Professor of Law Emeritus, Northwestern University.
James R. Thompson, Professor of Law Emeritus, Northwestern University.
Andre A. Moenssens, Professor of Law, University of Richmond.

CRIMINAL LAW (1982)

Peter W. Low, Professor of Law, University of Virginia.
John C. Jeffries, Jr., Professor of Law, University of Virginia.
Richard C. Bonnie, Professor of Law, University of Virginia.

CRIMINAL LAW, Third Edition (1980)

Lloyd L. Weinreb, Professor of Law, Harvard University.

CRIMINAL LAW AND PROCEDURE, Fifth Edition (1977)

Rollin M. Perkins, Professor of Law Emeritus, University of California, Hastings College of the Law.
Ronald N. Boyce, Professor of Law, University of Utah.

CRIMINAL PROCEDURE, Second Edition (1980), with 1982 Supplement

Fred E. Inbau, Professor of Law Emeritus, Northwestern University.
James R. Thompson, Professor of Law Emeritus, Northwestern University.
James B. Haddad, Professor of Law, Northwestern University.
James B. Zagel, Chief, Criminal Justice Division, Office of Attorney General of Illinois.
Gary L. Starkman, Assistant U. S. Attorney, Northern District of Illinois.

UNIVERSITY CASEBOOK SERIES—Continued

CRIMINAL PROCEDURE, CONSTITUTIONAL (1977), with 1980 Supplement

James E. Scarboro, Professor of Law, University of Colorado.
James B. White, Professor of Law, University of Chicago.

CRIMINAL PROCESS, Third Edition (1978), with 1982 Supplement

Lloyd L. Weinreb, Professor of Law, Harvard University.

DAMAGES, Second Edition (1952)

Charles T. McCormick, late Professor of Law, University of Texas.
William F. Fritz, late Professor of Law, University of Texas.

DEBTOR–CREDITOR LAW, Second Edition (1981), with Statutory Supplement

William D. Warren, Dean of the School of Law, University of California, Los Angeles.
William E. Hogan, Professor of Law, New York University.

DECEDENTS' ESTATES (1971)

Max Rheinstein, late Professor of Law Emeritus, University of Chicago.
Mary Ann Glendon, Professor of Law, Boston College.

DECEDENTS' ESTATES AND TRUSTS, Sixth Edition (1982)

John Ritchie, Emeritus Dean and Wigmore Professor of Law, Northwestern University.
Neill H. Alford, Jr., Professor of Law, University of Virginia.
Richard W. Effland, Professor of Law, Arizona State University.

DECEDENTS' ESTATES AND TRUSTS (1968)

Howard R. Williams, Professor of Law, Stanford University.

DOMESTIC RELATIONS, see also Family Law

DOMESTIC RELATIONS, Third Edition (1978), with 1980 Supplement

Walter Wadlington, Professor of Law, University of Virginia.
Monrad G. Paulsen, Dean of the Law School, Yeshiva University.

ELECTRONIC MASS MEDIA, Second Edition (1979)

William K. Jones, Professor of Law, Columbia University.

EMPLOYMENT DISCRIMINATION (1983)

Joel W. Friedman, Professor of Law, Tulane University.
George M. Strickler, Professor of Law, Tulane University.

ENERGY LAW (1983)

Donald N. Zillman, Professor of Law, University of Utah.
Laurence Lattman, Dean of Mines and Engineering, University of Utah.

ENTERPRISE ORGANIZATION, Third Edition (1982), with 1982 Corporation and Partnership Statutes, Rules and Forms Supplement

Alfred F. Conard, Professor of Law, University of Michigan.
Robert L. Knauss, Dean of the Law School, University of Houston.
Stanley Siegel, Professor of Law, University of California, Los Angeles.

ENVIRONMENTAL POLICY LAW (1982)

Thomas J. Schoenbaum, Professor of Law, Tulane University.

EQUITY, see also Remedies

EQUITY, RESTITUTION AND DAMAGES, Second Edition (1974)

Robert Childres, late Professor of Law, Northwestern University.
William F. Johnson, Jr., Professor of Law, New York University.

ESTATE PLANNING, Second Edition (1982), with Documentary Supplement

David Westfall, Professor of Law, Harvard University.

ETHICS, see Legal Profession, and Professional Responsibility

ETHICS AND PROFESSIONAL RESPONSIBILITY (1981) (Reprinted from THE LAWYERING PROCESS)

Gary Bellow, Professor of Law, Harvard University.
Bea Moulton, Legal Services Corporation.

EVIDENCE, Fourth Edition (1981)

David W. Louisell, late Professor of Law, University of California, Berkeley.
John Kaplan, Professor of Law, Stanford University.
Jon R. Waltz, Professor of Law, Northwestern University.

EVIDENCE (1968)

Francis C. Sullivan, Professor of Law, Louisiana State University.
Paul Hardin, III, Professor of Law, Duke University.

EVIDENCE, Seventh Edition (1983) with Rules and Statute Supplement (1981)

Jack B. Weinstein, Chief Judge, United States District Court.
John H. Mansfield, Professor of Law, Harvard University.
Norman Abrams, Professor of Law, University of California, Los Angeles.
Margaret Berger, Professor of Law, Brooklyn Law School.

FAMILY LAW, see also Domestic Relations

FAMILY LAW (1978), with 1983 Supplement

Judith C. Areen, Professor of Law, Georgetown University.

FAMILY LAW AND CHILDREN IN THE LEGAL SYSTEM, STATUTORY MATERIALS (1981)

Walter Wadlington, Professor of Law, University of Virginia.

FEDERAL COURTS, Seventh Edition (1982)

Charles T. McCormick, late Professor of Law, University of Texas.
James H. Chadbourn, Professor of Law, Harvard University.
Charles Alan Wright, Professor of Law, University of Texas.

FEDERAL COURTS AND THE FEDERAL SYSTEM, Hart and Wechsler's Second Edition (1973), with 1981 Supplement

Paul M. Bator, Professor of Law, Harvard University.
Paul J. Mishkin, Professor of Law, University of California, Berkeley.
David L. Shapiro, Professor of Law, Harvard University.
Herbert Wechsler, Professor of Law, Columbia University.

FEDERAL PUBLIC LAND AND RESOURCES LAW (1981)

George C. Coggins, Professor of Law, University of Kansas.
Charles F. Wilkinson, Professor of Law, University of Oregon.

FEDERAL RULES OF CIVIL PROCEDURE, 1982 Edition

FEDERAL TAXATION, see Taxation

FOOD AND DRUG LAW (1980), with Statutory Supplement

Richard A. Merrill, Dean of the School of Law, University of Virginia.
Peter Barton Hutt, Esq.

FUTURE INTERESTS (1958)

Philip Mechem, late Professor of Law Emeritus, University of Pennsylvania.

FUTURE INTERESTS (1970)

Howard R. Williams, Professor of Law, Stanford University.

FUTURE INTERESTS AND ESTATE PLANNING (1961), with 1962 Supplement

W. Barton Leach, late Professor of Law, Harvard University.
James K. Logan, formerly Dean of the Law School, University of Kansas.

GOVERNMENT CONTRACTS, FEDERAL (1975), with 1980 Supplement

John W. Whelan, Professor of Law, Hastings College of the Law.
Robert S. Pasley, Professor of Law Emeritus, Cornell University.

INJUNCTIONS (1972)

Owen M. Fiss, Professor of Law, Yale University.

INSTITUTIONAL INVESTORS, 1978

David L. Ratner, Professor of Law, Cornell University.

INSURANCE (1971)

William F. Young, Professor of Law, Columbia University.

INTERNATIONAL LAW, see also Transnational Legal Problems and United Nations Law

INTERNATIONAL LAW IN CONTEMPORARY PERSPECTIVE (1981), with Essay Supplement

Myres S. McDougal, Professor of Law, Yale University.
W. Michael Reisman, Professor of Law, Yale University.

INTERNATIONAL LEGAL SYSTEM, Second Edition (1981), with Documentary Supplement

Joseph Modeste Sweeney, Professor of Law, Tulane University.
Covey T. Oliver, Professor of Law, University of Pennsylvania.
Noyes E. Leech, Professor of Law, University of Pennsylvania.

INTERNATIONAL TRADE AND INVESTMENT, REGULATION OF (1970)

Carl H. Fulda, late Professor of Law, University of Texas.
Warren F. Schwartz, Professor of Law, University of Virginia.

INTRODUCTION TO LAW, see also Legal Method, On Law in Courts, and Dynamics of American Law

INTRODUCTION TO THE STUDY OF LAW (1970)

E. Wayne Thode, late Professor of Law, University of Utah.
Leon Lebowitz, Professor of Law, University of Texas.
Lester J. Mazor, Professor of Law, University of Utah.

JUDICIAL CODE and Rules of Procedure in the Federal Courts with Excerpts from the Criminal Code, 1981 Edition

Henry M. Hart, Jr., late Professor of Law, Harvard University.
Herbert Wechsler, Professor of Law, Columbia University.

UNIVERSITY CASEBOOK SERIES—Continued

JURISPRUDENCE (Temporary Edition Hardbound) (1949)

Lon L. Fuller, Professor of Law Emeritus, Harvard University.

JUVENILE, see also Children

JUVENILE JUSTICE PROCESS, Second Edition (1976), with 1980 Supplement

Frank W. Miller, Professor of Law, Washington University.
Robert O. Dawson, Professor of Law, University of Texas.
George E. Dix, Professor of Law, University of Texas.
Raymond I. Parnas, Professor of Law, University of California, Davis.

LABOR LAW, Ninth Edition (1981), with Statutory Supplement

Archibald Cox, Professor of Law, Harvard University.
Derek C. Bok, President, Harvard University.
Robert A. Gorman, Professor of Law, University of Pennsylvania.

LABOR LAW, Second Edition (1982), with Statutory Supplement

Clyde W. Summers, Professor of Law, University of Pennsylvania.
Harry H. Wellington, Dean of the Law School, Yale University.
Alan Hyde, Professor of Law, Rutgers University.

LAND FINANCING, Second Edition (1977)

Norman Penney, Professor of Law, Cornell University.
Richard F. Broude, Member of the California Bar.

LAW AND MEDICINE (1980)

Walter Wadlington, Professor of Law and Professor of Legal Medicine, University
of Virginia.
Jon R. Waltz, Professor of Law, Northwestern University.
Roger B. Dworkin, Professor of Law, Indiana University, and Professor of Bio-
medical History, University of Washington.

LAW, LANGUAGE AND ETHICS (1972)

William R. Bishin, Professor of Law, University of Southern California.
Christopher D. Stone, Professor of Law, University of Southern California.

**LAWYERING PROCESS (1978), with Civil Problem Supplement and Criminal
Problem Supplement**

Gary Bellow, Professor of Law, Harvard University.
Bea Moulton, Professor of Law, Arizona State University.

LEGAL METHOD (1980)

Harry W. Jones, Professor of Law Emeritus, Columbia University.
John M. Kernochan, Professor of Law, Columbia University.
Arthur W. Murphy, Professor of Law, Columbia University.

LEGAL METHODS (1969)

Robert N. Covington, Professor of Law, Vanderbilt University.
E. Blythe Stason, late Professor of Law, Vanderbilt University.
John W. Wade, Professor of Law, Vanderbilt University.
Elliott E. Cheatham, late Professor of Law, Vanderbilt University.
Theodore A. Smedley, Professor of Law, Vanderbilt University.

LEGAL PROFESSION (1970)

Samuel D. Thurman, Dean of the College of Law, University of Utah.
Ellis L. Phillips, Jr., Professor of Law, Columbia University.
Elliott E. Cheatham, late Professor of Law, Vanderbilt University.

LEGISLATION, Fourth Edition (1982) (by Fordham)

Horace E. Read, late Vice President, Dalhousie University.
John W. MacDonald, Professor of Law Emeritus, Cornell Law School.
Jefferson B. Fordham, Professor of Law, University of Utah.
William J. Pierce, Professor of Law, University of Michigan.

LEGISLATIVE AND ADMINISTRATIVE PROCESSES, Second Edition (1981)

Hans A. Linde, Judge, Supreme Court of Oregon.
George Bunn, Professor of Law, University of Wisconsin.
Fredericka Paff, Professor of Law, University of Wisconsin.
W. Lawrence Church, Professor of Law, University of Wisconsin.

LOCAL GOVERNMENT LAW, Revised Edition (1975)

Jefferson B. Fordham, Professor of Law, University of Utah.

MASS MEDIA LAW, Second Edition (1982)

Marc A. Franklin, Professor of Law, Stanford University.

MENTAL HEALTH PROCESS, Second Edition (1976), with 1981 Supplement

Frank W. Miller, Professor of Law, Washington University.
Robert O. Dawson, Professor of Law, University of Texas.
George E. Dix, Professor of Law, University of Texas.
Raymond I. Parnas, Professor of Law, University of California, Davis.

MUNICIPAL CORPORATIONS, see Local Government Law

NEGOTIABLE INSTRUMENTS, see Commercial Paper

NEGOTIATION (1981) (Reprinted from THE LAWYERING PROCESS)

Gary Bellow, Professor of Law, Harvard Law School.
Bea Moulton, Legal Services Corporation.

NEW YORK PRACTICE, Fourth Edition (1978)

Herbert Peterfreund, Professor of Law, New York University.
Joseph M. McLaughlin, Dean of the Law School, Fordham University.

OIL AND GAS, Fourth Edition (1979)

Howard R. Williams, Professor of Law, Stanford University.
Richard C. Maxwell, Professor of Law, University of California, Los Angeles.
Charles J. Meyers, Dean of the Law School, Stanford University.

ON LAW IN COURTS (1965)

Paul J. Mishkin, Professor of Law, University of California, Berkeley.
Clarence Morris, Professor of Law Emeritus, University of Pennsylvania.

PERSPECTIVES ON THE LAWYER AS PLANNER (Reprint of Chapters One through Five of Planning by Lawyers) (1978)

Louis M. Brown, Professor of Law, University of Southern California.
Edward A. Dauer, Professor of Law, Yale University.

PLANNING BY LAWYERS, MATERIALS ON A NONADVERSARIAL LEGAL PROCESS (1978)

Louis M. Brown, Professor of Law, University of Southern California.
Edward A. Dauer, Professor of Law, Yale University.

PLEADING AND PROCEDURE, see Procedure, Civil

POLICE FUNCTION, Third Edition (1982)

Reprint of Chapters 1–10 of Miller, Dawson, Dix and Parnas' Criminal Justice Administration, Second Edition.

PREPARING AND PRESENTING THE CASE (1981) (Reprinted from THE LAWYERING PROCESS)

Gary Bellow, Professor of Law, Harvard Law School.
Bea Moulton, Legal Services Corporation.

PREVENTIVE LAW, see also Planning by Lawyers

PROCEDURE—CIVIL PROCEDURE, Second Edition (1974), with 1979 Supplement

James H. Chadbourn, Professor of Law, Harvard University.
A. Leo Levin, Professor of Law, University of Pennsylvania.
Philip Shuchman, Professor of Law, University of Connecticut.

PROCEDURE—CIVIL PROCEDURE, Fourth Edition (1978), with 1982 Supplement

Richard H. Field, late Professor of Law, Harvard University.
Benjamin Kaplan, Professor of Law Emeritus, Harvard University.
Kevin M. Clermont, Professor of Law, Cornell University.

PROCEDURE—CIVIL PROCEDURE, Third Edition (1976), with 1982 Supplement

Maurice Rosenberg, Professor of Law, Columbia University.
Jack B. Weinstein, Professor of Law, Columbia University.
Hans Smit, Professor of Law, Columbia University.
Harold L. Korn, Professor of Law, Columbia University.

PROCEDURE—PLEADING AND PROCEDURE: State and Federal, Fourth Edition (1979), with 1982 Supplement

David W. Louisell, late Professor of Law, University of California, Berkeley.
Geoffrey C. Hazard, Jr., Professor of Law, Yale University.

PROCEDURE—FEDERAL RULES OF CIVIL PROCEDURE, 1982 Edition

PRODUCTS LIABILITY (1980)

Marshall S. Shapo, Professor of Law, Northwestern University.

PRODUCTS LIABILITY AND SAFETY (1980), with Statutory Supplement

W. Page Keeton, Professor of Law, University of Texas.
David G. Owen, Professor of Law, University of South Carolina.
John E. Montgomery, Professor of Law, University of South Carolina.

PROFESSIONAL RESPONSIBILITY, Second Edition (1981), with Selected National Standards Supplement

Thomas D. Morgan, Dean of the Law School, Emory University.
Ronald D. Rotunda, Professor of Law, University of Illinois.

PROPERTY, Fourth Edition (1978)

John E. Cribbet, Dean of the Law School, University of Illinois.
Corwin W. Johnson, Professor of Law, University of Texas.

PROPERTY—PERSONAL (1953)

S. Kenneth Skolfield, late Professor of Law Emeritus, Boston University.

UNIVERSITY CASEBOOK SERIES—Continued

PROPERTY—PERSONAL, Third Edition (1954)

Everett Fraser, late Dean of the Law School Emeritus, University of Minnesota. Third Edition by Charles W. Taintor, late Professor of Law, University of Pittsburgh.

PROPERTY—INTRODUCTION, TO REAL PROPERTY, Third Edition (1954)

Everett Fraser, late Dean of the Law School Emeritus, University of Minnesota.

PROPERTY—REAL AND PERSONAL, Combined Edition (1954)

Everett Fraser, late Dean of the Law School Emeritus, University of Minnesota. Third Edition of Personal Property by Charles W. Taintor, late Professor of Law, University of Pittsburgh.

PROPERTY—REAL PROPERTY AND CONVEYANCING (1954)

Edward E. Bade, late Professor of Law, University of Minnesota.

PROPERTY—FUNDAMENTALS OF MODERN REAL PROPERTY, Second Edition (1982)

Edward H. Rabin, Professor of Law, University of California, Davis.

PROPERTY—PROBLEMS IN REAL PROPERTY (Pamphlet) (1969)

Edward H. Rabin, Professor of Law, University of California, Davis.

PROSECUTION AND ADJUDICATION, Second Edition (1982)

Reprint of Chapters 11–26 of Miller, Dawson, Dix and Parnas' Criminal Justice Administration, Second Edition.

PUBLIC REGULATION OF DANGEROUS PRODUCTS (paperback) (1980)

Marshall S. Shapo, Professor of Law, Northwestern University.

PUBLIC UTILITY LAW, see Free Enterprise, also Regulated Industries

REAL ESTATE PLANNING (1980), with 1980 Problems, Statutes and New Materials Supplement

Norton L. Steuben, Professor of Law, University of Colorado.

REAL ESTATE TRANSACTIONS (1980), with Statute, Form and Problem Supplement

Paul Goldstein, Professor of Law, Stanford University.

RECEIVERSHIP AND CORPORATE REORGANIZATION, see Creditors' Rights

REGULATED INDUSTRIES, Second Edition, 1976

William K. Jones, Professor of Law, Columbia University.

REMEDIES (1982)

Edward D. Re, Chief Judge, U. S. Court of International Trade.

RESTITUTION, Second Edition (1966)

John W. Wade, Professor of Law, Vanderbilt University.

SALES (1980)

Marion W. Benfield, Jr., Professor of Law, University of Illinois. William D. Hawkland, Chancellor, Louisiana State University Law Center.

SALES AND SALES FINANCING, Fourth Edition (1976), with 1982 Supplement

John Honnold, Professor of Law, University of Pennsylvania.

UNIVERSITY CASEBOOK SERIES—Continued

SALES LAW AND THE CONTRACTING PROCESS (1982)

Reprint of Chapters 1–10 of Schwartz and Scott's Commercial Transactions.

SECURITIES REGULATION, Fifth Edition (1982), with 1982 Selected Statutes, Rules and Forms Supplement

Richard W. Jennings, Professor of Law, University of California, Berkeley.
Harold Marsh, Jr., Member of the California Bar.

SECURITIES REGULATION (1982), with 1983 Supplement

Larry D. Soderquist, Professor of Law, Vanderbilt University.

SENTENCING AND THE CORRECTIONAL PROCESS, Second Edition (1976)

Frank W. Miller, Professor of Law, Washington University.
Robert O. Dawson, Professor of Law, University of Texas.
George E. Dix, Professor of Law, University of Texas.
Raymond I. Parnas, Professor of Law, University of California, Davis.

SOCIAL WELFARE AND THE INDIVIDUAL (1971)

Robert J. Levy, Professor of Law, University of Minnesota.
Thomas P. Lewis, Dean of the College of Law, University of Kentucky.
Peter W. Martin, Professor of Law, Cornell University.

TAX, POLICY ANALYSIS OF THE FEDERAL INCOME (1976)

William A. Klein, Professor of Law, University of California, Los Angeles.

TAXATION, FEDERAL INCOME (1976), with 1982 Supplement

Erwin N. Griswold, Dean Emeritus, Harvard Law School.
Michael J. Graetz, Professor of Law, University of Virginia.

TAXATION, FEDERAL INCOME, Fourth Edition (1982)

James J. Freeland, Professor of Law, University of Florida.
Stephen A. Lind, Professor of Law, University of Florida.
Richard B. Stephens, Professor of Law Emeritus, University of Florida.

TAXATION, FEDERAL INCOME, Volume I, Personal Income Taxation (1972), with 1982 Supplement; Volume II, Taxation of Partnerships and Corporations, Second Edition (1980)

Stanley S. Surrey, Professor of Law, Harvard University.
William C. Warren, Professor of Law Emeritus, Columbia University.
Paul R. McDaniel, Professor of Law, Boston College Law School.
Hugh J. Ault, Professor of Law, Boston College Law School.

TAXATION, FEDERAL WEALTH TRANSFER, Second Edition (1982)

Stanley S. Surrey, Professor of Law, Harvard University.
William C. Warren, Professor of Law Emeritus, Columbia University.
Paul R. McDaniel, Professor of Law, Boston College Law School.
Harry L. Gutman, Instructor, Harvard Law School and Boston College Law School.

TAXATION OF INDIVIDUALS, PARTNERSHIPS AND CORPORATIONS, PROBLEMS in the (1978)

Norton L. Steuben, Professor of Law, University of Colorado.
William J. Turnier, Professor of Law, University of North Carolina.

TAXES AND FINANCE—STATE AND LOCAL (1974)

Oliver Oldman, Professor of Law, Harvard University.
Ferdinand P. Schoettle, Professor of Law, University of Minnesota.

TORT LAW AND ALTERNATIVES: INJURIES AND REMEDIES, Second Edition (1979)

Marc A. Franklin, Professor of Law, Stanford University.

UNIVERSITY CASEBOOK SERIES—Continued

TORTS, Seventh Edition (1982)

William L. Prosser, late Professor of Law, University of California, Hastings College.
John W. Wade, Professor of Law, Vanderbilt University.
Victor E. Schwartz, Professor of Law, American University.

TORTS, Third Edition (1976)

Harry Shulman, late Dean of the Law School, Yale University.
Fleming James, Jr., Professor of Law Emeritus, Yale University.
Oscar S. Gray, Professor of Law, University of Maryland.

TRADE REGULATION (1975), with 1979 Supplement

Milton Handler, Professor of Law Emeritus, Columbia University.
Harlan M. Blake, Professor of Law, Columbia University.
Robert Pitofsky, Professor of Law, Georgetown University.
Harvey J. Goldschmid, Professor of Law, Columbia University.

TRADE REGULATION, see Antitrust

TRANSNATIONAL LEGAL PROBLEMS, Second Edition (1976) with 1982 Case and Documentary Supplement

Henry J. Steiner, Professor of Law, Harvard University.
Detlev F. Vagts, Professor of Law, Harvard University.

TRIAL, see also Evidence, Making the Record, Lawyering Process and Preparing and Presenting the Case

TRIAL ADVOCACY (1968)

A. Leo Levin, Professor of Law, University of Pennsylvania.
Harold Cramer, of the Pennsylvania Bar.
Maurice Rosenberg, Professor of Law, Columbia University, Consultant.

TRUSTS, Fifth Edition (1978)

George G. Bogert, late Professor of Law Emeritus, University of Chicago.
Dallin H. Oaks, President, Brigham Young University.

TRUSTS AND SUCCESSION (Palmer's), Third Edition (1978)

Richard V. Wellman, Professor of Law, University of Georgia.
Lawrence W. Waggoner, Professor of Law, University of Michigan.
Olin L. Browder, Jr., Professor of Law, University of Michigan.

UNFAIR COMPETITION, see Competitive Process and Business Torts

UNITED NATIONS IN ACTION (1968)

Louis B. Sohn, Professor of Law, Harvard University.

UNITED NATIONS LAW, Second Edition (1967), with Documentary Supplement (1968)

Louis B. Sohn, Professor of Law, Harvard University.

WATER RESOURCE MANAGEMENT, Second Edition (1980), with 1983 Supplement

Charles J. Meyers, Dean of the Law School, Stanford University.
A. Dan Tarlock, Professor of Law, Indiana Unversity.

WILLS AND ADMINISTRATION, Fifth Edition (1961)

Philip Mechem, late Professor of Law, University of Pennsylvania.
Thomas E. Atkinson, late Professor of Law, New York University.

WORLD LAW, see United Nations Law

University Casebook Series

EDITORIAL BOARD

SECURED TRANSACTIONS

IN

PERSONAL PROPERTY

By

ROBERT L. JORDAN
Professor of Law
University of California, Los Angeles

and

WILLIAM D. WARREN
Professor of Law
University of California, Los Angeles

Mineola, New York
THE FOUNDATION PRESS, INC.
1983

Library of Congress Catalog Card Number: 83–80833

ISBN   0–88277–135–3

J. & W. Secured Trans. UCB

PREFACE

We offer this book for use in courses on secured transactions in personal property of from 30 to 45 class hours. We cover in depth Article 9 of the Uniform Commercial Code. We supplement this material with a chapter on the impact of the new Bankruptcy Code on secured transactions. The importance of personal and bank guarantees in commercial transactions has led us to include a chapter on accommodation parties and letters of credit. Finally we have included a brief treatment of security interests and related rights arising under Article 2 of the UCC.

In selecting cases, we have favored recent cases that discuss trends in secured transactions decisions. The large number included that are less than five years old demonstrates the vitality of this field of law. Alas, clients stubbornly persist in their refusal to litigate some of the most interesting issues of the UCC. We make up for their lack of cooperation in this regard by including a large number of problems throughout the book that are analytical excursions into areas of the UCC as yet unexplored by the courts. Other problems are closely based on the facts of actual cases; their inclusion serves to give breadth to the course without undue length.

Our thrust is rigorous statutory analysis. We have designed the book to serve the needs of differing pedagogical styles. In using these materials we expect to discuss in class most of the principal cases and many of the problems. Other teachers may wish to spend virtually all of their class time either on the cases or on the numerous problems.

We find that students more easily learn a technical course like secured transactions if they are given some background in the field by way of text discussion. Hence, one of our major efforts has been to include text notes throughout the book designed to prepare students for coming to grips with the cases and problems.

We are particularly indebted to Marilyn Schroeter who bore the major burden of typing and preparing the manuscript for publication. Her unerring efficiency and attentiveness to detail greatly eased our task. We also want to thank Mary Portanova who aided in the typing of the manuscript.

ROBERT L. JORDAN
WILLIAM D. WARREN

April, 1983

*

SUMMARY OF CONTENTS

*

TABLE OF CONTENTS

TABLE OF CASES

The principal cases are in italic type. Cases cited or discussed are in roman. References are to Pages.

*

SECURED TRANSACTIONS

IN

PERSONAL PROPERTY

*

PREFATORY NOTE

Credit is the lifeblood of today's business world and the commercial lawyer must know how to deal with it. Manufacturers borrow to buy the materials needed for processing; wholesale and retail merchants need credit to allow them to acquire the inventory they sell; and end-use buyers often pay for the products they buy on installment credit. The remarkably broad distribution of goods and services in this country has been made possible largely through a plentiful supply of secured credit made available by financial institutions. When this supply of credit contracts, the impact on the economy is marked.

It is fair to conclude that if secured credit had not developed, mass distribution of goods and services might never have occurred. This is true because the position of the unsecured creditor is so weak. If the debtor fails to pay, the unsecured creditor's legal remedies are restricted to bringing a law suit against the debtor, obtaining a judgment, and collecting the judgment by seizing the debtor's property and having it sold—a tedious and expensive process. On the other hand, a secured creditor contracts for an interest in the debtor's property and can often realize on this collateral without the delay and expense of a law suit. Moreover, although bankruptcy may wipe out an unsecured debt entirely, a secured claim usually survives bankruptcy.

In this Part we introduce you to secured credit transactions law through the study of Article 9, the most innovative part of the Uniform Commercial Code. This Article is best understood against a brief historical background. Professor Grant Gilmore observes: "Until early in the nineteenth century the only security devices which were known in our legal system were the mortgage of real property and the pledge of chattels. Security interests in personal property which remained in the borrower's possession during the loan period were unknown. A transfer of an interest in personal property without delivery of possession was looked on as being in essence a fraudulent conveyance, invalid against creditors and purchasers." [1]

1. Gilmore, Secured Transactions in Personal Property 24 (1965). Reprinted with permission of the publisher, Little, Brown & Company. This introductory statement is largely based on Gilmore's extensive treatment of the history of chattel security devices in volume 1 of his treatise.

1

Not until a way could be found to allow the debtor to retain the possession and enjoyment of personal property collateral while paying off the debt would secured financing in personal property become economically significant. Two nineteenth century developments, one statutory and the other common law, legitimized nonpossessory personal property financing. Statutes allowed the creation of a mortgage in chattels in the possession of the mortgagor which was valid as against his creditors and purchasers so long as the chattel mortgagee spread the mortgage document on the public records. Meanwhile the courts were using the complex law of conditions to hold that a seller could sell a chattel to a buyer on condition that the buyer pay the price, and retake the property on the buyer's default. In contrast to the statutory chattel mortgage, the common law conditional sale was valid against third parties even though no public filing occurred.

Though the advent of the chattel mortgage and the conditional sale removed the traditional requirement that possession was required for the validity of secured transactions involving personal property, both these security devices were effective only when the collateral was static and the transaction was terminal. Neither device was sufficient when the collateral, as in the case of inventory or accounts receivable, would in the ordinary course of business be converted into cash or other proceeds in the hands of the debtor. In these cases the creditor required a security device that would attach automatically to the proceeds resulting from the sale of inventory or the collection of accounts, or would attach to the inventory or accounts acquired by the debtor as replacements for the original collateral.

The first half of the twentieth century saw the invention of a series of security devices—trust receipts, factors' liens, and assignments of accounts receivable—that gave secured creditors more or less effective security interests in shifting stocks of collateral like inventory and accounts. By the time drafting began on Article 9 in the late 40s, the leading commercial states had separate and wholly disparate laws on chattel mortgages, conditional sales, trust receipts, factors' liens, and assignments of accounts receivable. The law of chattel security was as provincial and nonuniform then as the law of real estate mortgages is today. Gilmore describes this body of law as one of "extraordinary complexity." [2]

2. Id. at 288.

The primary draftsmen of Article 9, Professors Grant Gilmore and Allison Dunham, went into the project resolved to junk the historical and conceptual categories that had characterized chattel security law and to strive for a functional approach to the area. Accordingly, instead of drafting revised and updated chattel mortgage or conditional sales acts, they set out to do a series of separate statutes on each major type of financing: business equipment, consumer goods, agricultural products, inventory and accounts, and intangibles. As their work went forward they found that there were more similarities than differences among the various kinds of financing transactions. Hence, they decided to draft a unified statute, covering all secured transactions in personal property, that contained within it different rules for what were functionally different transactions.[3]

Article 9 does not abolish the pre-Code security devices, but it renders the formal distinctions among them irrelevant. UCC § 9–102(2) specifically states that Article 9 applies to security interests created by any of the traditional security devices. Lawyers and judges can and do continue to talk about chattel mortgages and conditional sales, but the old categories have no meaning except as a shorthand way of describing familiar transactions. The overriding statement is found in UCC § 9–102(1) "* * * This Article applies (a) to any transaction (regardless of its form) which is intended to create a security interest in personal property. * * *" Comment 1 to UCC § 9–102 states "* * * the principal test whether a transaction comes under this Article is: is the transaction intended to have effect as security?" The old labels no longer matter.

The terminology is simple. The person granting the credit may become a "secured party" (UCC § 9–105(1)(m)) by contracting for a "security interest" (UCC § 1–201(37)) in property called "collateral" (UCC § 9–105(1)(c)), to secure the "debtor's" (UCC § 9–105(1)(d)) obligation. The contract is a "security agreement" (UCC § 9–105(1)(l)). In order to assure the validity of his security interest against third parties, the secured party must "perfect" the interest pursuant to Part 3. In certain instances this may be done by the secured party's filing a "financing statement" (UCC § 9–402) or by taking possession of the collateral. Different rules for perfection, priorities, and default apply depending on the kinds of transactions, e.g., whether "purchase money" (UCC § 9–107) or not, and the kinds of collateral,

3. Id. at § 9.2.

e.g., whether consumer goods, equipment, farm products, inventory (all defined in UCC § 9–109) or fixtures (UCC § 9–313), or accounts or general intangibles (UCC § 9–106), or chattel paper, documents, or instruments (all defined in UCC § 9–105).

Chapter 1

CREATION AND PERFECTION OF THE
SECURITY INTEREST

In this chapter we discuss the method by which the parties to a secured transaction may create and perfect a security interest. The issue is rarely the enforceability as between the debtor and the secured party. More commonly it is the validity of the security interest as against a third party with a claim to the collateral. The competing third party will be either a person who has bought the collateral, a person who has obtained a security interest in the collateral, or a person who has acquired a lien in the collateral as stated in UCC § 9–301(3). The last category is particularly important because the definition of "lien creditor" includes the trustee in bankruptcy of the debtor. The effect of § 9–301 is that an unperfected security interest, although enforceable against the debtor under the UCC, is not enforceable in bankruptcy. See Bankruptcy Code § 544(a)[1]. The bulk of litigation concerning UCC security interests takes place in the federal bankruptcy courts. The adversaries are the secured party claiming his right under the Bankruptcy Code to remove his collateral from the debtor's estate and the debtor's trustee in

---

1. § 544. **Trustee as lien creditor and as successor to certain creditors and purchasers**

(a) The trustee shall have, as of the commencement of the case, and without regard to any knowledge of the trustee or of any creditor, the rights and powers of, or may avoid any transfer of property of the debtor or any obligation incurred by the debtor that is voidable by—

(1) a creditor that extends credit to the debtor at the time of the commencement of the case, and that obtains, at such time and with respect to such credit, a judicial lien on all property on which a creditor on a simple contract could have obtained a judicial lien, whether or not such a creditor exists;

(2) a creditor that extends credit to the debtor at the time of the commencement of the case, and obtains, at such time and with respect to such credit, an execution against the debtor that is returned unsatisfied at such time, whether or not such a creditor exists; and

(3) a bona fide purchaser of real property from the debtor, against whom applicable law permits such transfer to be perfected, that obtains the status of a bona fide purchaser at the time of the commencement of the case, whether or not such a purchaser exists.

5

bankruptcy seeking to avoid the security interest and to relegate the secured party to the status of an unsecured creditor.

The trustee in bankruptcy represents the debtor's unsecured creditors and the issue of the validity in bankruptcy of the security interest may have great impact on how the bankrupt debtor's assets are distributed, for a valid security interest has absolute priority in bankruptcy. It is not uncommon for secured creditors to claim all the assets in the debtor's bankruptcy estate, leaving nothing for unsecured creditors who may have extended vitally needed credit to the debtor.

Bankruptcy law has as one of its goals the equitable distribution of the debtor's estate. The Article 9 draftsmen had as one of their goals that it should be easy for the parties to create valid security interests in any of the debtor's personal property. In the following cases we see what happens when these goals collide.

A. THE SECURITY AGREEMENT

The Code draftsmen selected the term "attachment" to denote when a security interest becomes enforceable between the debtor and the secured party. UCC § 9–203(1)(a) provides that a security interest cannot attach until either the "debtor has signed a security agreement which contains a description of the collateral" or the secured party has taken possession of the collateral as in a pledge. UCC § 9–105(1)(l) defines "security agreement" as "an agreement which creates or provides for a security interest." Since the debtor cannot sign an agreement unless it is in writing, UCC § 9–203(1)(a) is described in Comment 5 as "in the nature of a Statute of Frauds." This Comment notes that "this Article reduces formal requisites to a minimum" and refers to the requirement of a signed writing as a "simple formality." Nevertheless, the written security agreement requirement has generated much litigation. *Bollinger*, below, discusses the various views taken by the courts on this issue.

IN RE BOLLINGER CORP.

United States Court of Appeals, Third Circuit, 1980.
614 F.2d 924.

ROSENN, CIRCUIT JUDGE. This appeal from a district court review of an order in bankruptcy presents a question that has troubled courts since the enactment of Article Nine of the Uniform Commercial Code (U.C.C.) governing secured transactions. Can a creditor assert a secured claim against the debtor when no formal security agreement was ever signed, but where various documents executed in connection with a loan evince an intent to create a security interest? The district court answered this question in the affirmative and permitted the creditor, Zimmerman & Jansen, to assert a secured claim against the debtor, bankrupt Bollinger Corporation in the amount of $150,000. We affirm.

I.

The facts of this case are not in dispute. Industrial Credit Company (ICC) made a loan to Bollinger Corporation (Bollinger) on January 13, 1972, in the amount of $150,000. As evidence of the loan, Bollinger executed a promissory note in the sum of $150,000 and signed a security agreement with ICC giving it a security interest in certain machinery and equipment. ICC in due course perfected its security interest in the collateral by filing a financing statement in accordance with Pennsylvania's enactment of Article Nine of the U.C.C.

Bollinger faithfully met its obligations under the note and by December 4, 1974, had repaid $85,000 of the loan leaving $65,000 in unpaid principal. Bollinger, however, required additional capital and on December 5, 1974, entered into a loan agreement with Zimmerman & Jansen, Inc. (Z & J), by which Z & J agreed to lend Bollinger $150,000. Z & J undertook as part of this transaction to pay off the $65,000 still owed to ICC in return for an assignment by ICC to Z & J of the original note and security agreement between Bollinger and ICC. Bollinger executed a promissory note to Z & J, evidencing the agreement containing the following provision:

> *Security.* This Promissory Note is secured by security interests in a certain Security Agreement between Bollinger and Industrial Credit Company   *   *   *   and in a Financing Statement filed by [ICC]   *   *   *, and is further secured by security interests in a certain security agreement to be delivered by Bollinger to Z and J with this Promissory Note covering the identical machinery and equipment as identified in the ICC Agreement and with identical schedule attached in the principal amount of Eighty-Five Thousand Dollars. ($85,000).

No formal security agreement was ever executed between Bollinger and Z & J. Z & J did, however, in connection with the promissory note, record a new financing statement signed by Bollinger containing a detailed list of the machinery and equipment originally taken as collateral by ICC for its loan to Bollinger.

Bollinger filed a petition for an arrangement under Chapter XI of the Bankruptcy Act in March, 1975 and was adjudicated bankrupt one year later. In administrating the bankrupt's estate, the receiver sold some of Bollinger's equipment but agreed that Z & J would receive a $10,000 credit on its secured claim.

Z & J asserted a secured claim against the bankrupt in the amount of $150,000, arguing that although it never signed a security agreement with Bollinger, the parties had intended that a security interest in the sum of $150,000 be created to protect the loan. The trustee in bankruptcy conceded that the assignment to Z & J of ICC's original security agreement with Bollinger gave Z & J a secured claim in the amount of $65,000, the balance owed by Bollinger to ICC at the time of the assignment. The trustee, however, refused to recognize Z & J's asserted claim of an additional secured claim of $85,000 because of the absence of a security agreement between Bollinger and Z & J. The bankruptcy court agreed and entered judgment for Z & J in the amount of $55,000, representing a secured claim in the amount of $65,000 less $10,000 credit received by Z & J.

Z & J appealed to the United States District Court for the Western District of Pennsylvania, which reversed the bankruptcy court and entered judgment for Z & J in the full amount of the asserted $150,000 secured claim. The trustee in bankruptcy appeals.

II.

Under Article Nine of the U.C.C., two documents are generally required to create a perfected security interest in a debtor's collateral. First, there must be a "security agreement" giving the creditor an interest in the collateral. Section 9–203(1)(b) contains minimal requirements for the creation of a security agreement. In order to create a security agreement, there must be: (1) a writing (2) signed by the debtor (3) containing a description of the collateral or the types of collateral. Section 9–203, Comment 1. The requirements of section 9–203(1)(b) further two basic policies. First, an evidentiary function is served by requiring a signed security agreement and second, a written agreement also obviates any Statute of Frauds problems with the debtor-creditor relationship. Id. Comments 3, 5. The second document generally required is a "financing statement," which is a document signed by both parties and filed for public record. The financing statement serves the purpose of giving public notice to other creditors that a security interest is claimed in the debtor's collateral.

Despite the minimal formal requirements set forth in section 9–203 for the creation of a security agreement, the commercial world has frequently neglected to comply with this simple Code provision. Soon after Article Nine's enactment, creditors who had failed to obtain formal security agreements, but who nevertheless had obtained and filed financing statements, sought to enforce secured claims. Under section 9–402, a security agreement may serve as a financing statement if it is signed by both parties. The question arises whether the converse is true: Can a signed financing statement operate as a security agreement? The earliest case to consider this question was American Card Co. v. H.M.H. Co., 97 R.I. 59, 196 A.2d 150, 152 (1963) which held that a financing statement could/*not*/operate as a security agreement because there was no language *granting* a security interest to a creditor. Although section 9–203(1)(b) makes no mention of such a grant language requirement, the court in *American Card* thought that implicit in the definition of "security agreement" under section 9–105(1)(h) was such a requirement; some grant language was necessary to "create or provide security." This view also was adopted by the Tenth Circuit in Shelton v. Erwin, 472 F.2d 1118, 1120 (10th Cir. 1973). Thus, under the holdings of these cases, the creditor's assertion of a secured claim must fall in the absence of language connoting a grant of a security interest.

The Ninth Circuit in In re Amex-Protein Development Corp., 504 F.2d 1056 (9th Cir. 1974), echoed criticism by commentators of the *American Card* rule. The court wrote: "There is no support in legislative history or grammatical logic for the substitution of the word 'grant' for the phrase 'creates or provides for'." Id. at 1059–60. It concluded that as long as the financing statement contains a description of the collateral signed by the debtor, the financing statement may serve as the security agreement and the formal requirements of section 9–203(1)(b) are met. The tack pursued by the Ninth Circuit is supported by legal commentary on the issue. See G. Gilmore, Security Interests in Personal Property, § 11.4 at 347–48 (1965).

Some courts have declined to follow the Ninth Circuit's liberal rule allowing the financing statement alone to stand as the security agreement, but have permitted the financing statement, when read in conjunction with other documents executed by the parties, to satisfy the requirements of section 9–203(1)(b). The court in In re Numeric Corp., 485 F.2d 1328 (1st Cir. 1973) held that a financing statement coupled with a board of directors' resolution revealing an intent to create a security interest were sufficient to act as a security agreement. The court concluded from its reading of the Code that there appears no need to insist upon a separate document entitled "security agreement" as a prerequisite for an otherwise valid security interest.

> A writing or writings, regardless of label, which adequately describes the collateral, carries the signature of the debtor, and establishes that in fact a security interest was agreed upon, would satisfy both the formal requirements of the statute and the policies behind it.

Id. at 1331. The court went on to hold that "although a standard form financing statement by itself cannot be considered a security agreement, an adequate agreement can be found when a financing statement is considered together with other documents." Id. at 1332. See In re Penn Housing Corp., 367 F.Supp. 661 (W.D.Pa.1973); but see Union National Bank of Pittsburgh v. Providence Washington Insurance Co., 21 U.C.C. Rep.Serv. 1463 (W.D.Pa.1977).

More recently, the Supreme Court of Maine in Casco Bank & Trust Co. v. Cloutier, 398 A.2d 1224, 1231–32 (Me.1979) considered the question of whether composite documents were sufficient to create a security interest within the terms of the Code. Writing for the court, Justice Wernick allowed a financing statement to be joined with a promissory note for purposes of determining whether the note contained an adequate description of the collateral to create a security agreement. The court indicated that the evidentiary and Statute of Frauds policies behind section 9–203(1)(b) were satisfied by reading the note and financing statement together as the security agreement.

In the case before us, the district court went a step further and held that the promissory note executed by Bollinger in favor of Z & J, standing alone, was sufficient to act as the security agreement between the parties. In so doing, the court implicitly rejected the *American Card* rule requiring grant language before a security agreement arises under section 9–203(1)(b). The parties have not referred to any Pennsylvania state cases on the question and our independent research has failed to uncover any. But although we agree that no formal grant of a security interest need exist before a security agreement arises, we do not think that the promissory note standing alone would be sufficient under Pennsylvania law to act as the security agreement. We believe, however, that the promissory note, read in conjunction with the financing statement duly filed and supported, as it is here, by correspondence during the course of the transaction between the parties, would be sufficient under Pennsylvania law to establish a valid security agreement.

III.

We think Pennsylvania courts would accept the logic behind the First and Ninth Circuit rule and reject the *American Card* rule imposing the requirement of a formal grant of a security interest before a security agreement may exist. When the parties have neglected to sign a separate security agreement, it would appear that the better and more practical view is to look at the transaction as a whole in order to determine if there is a writing, or writings, signed by the debtor describing the collateral which demonstrates an intent to create a security interest in the collateral.[4] In connection with Z & J's loan of $150,000 to Bollinger, the relevant writings to be considered are: (1) the promissory note; (2) the financing statement; (3) a group of letters constituting the course of dealing between the parties. The district court focused solely on the promissory note finding it sufficient to constitute the security agreement. Reference, however, to the language in the note reveals that the note standing alone cannot serve as the security agreement. The note recites that along with the assigned 1972 security agreement between Bollinger and ICC, the Z & J loan is "further secured by security interests in a certain Security Agreement *to be delivered* by Bollinger to Z & J with this Promissory Note, * * *. (Emphasis added.) The bankruptcy judge correctly reasoned that "[t]he intention to create a separate security agreement negates any in-

---

4. We do not intend in any way to encourage the commercial community to dispense with signing security agreements as a normal part of establishing a secured transaction. Lawsuits over the existence of a security agreement may be avoided by executing a separate security agreement conforming to the minimal require-ments of section 9–203(1)(b). Our decision today only predicts, after our examination of the relevant case law, that Pennsylvania courts would adopt a pragmatic view of the issue raised here and recognize the intention of the parties expressed in the composite documents and not exalt form over substance.

ference that the debtor intended that the promissory note constitute the security agreement." At best, the note is some evidence that a security agreement was contemplated by the parties, but by its own terms, plainly indicates that it is not the security agreement.

Looking beyond the promissory note, Z & J did file a financing statement signed by Bollinger containing a detailed list of all the collateral intended to secure the $150,000 loan to Bollinger. The financing statement alone meets the basic section 9–203(1) (b) requirements of a writing, signed by the debtor, describing the collateral. However, the financing statement provides only an inferential basis for concluding that the parties intended a security agreement. There would be little reason to file such a detailed financing statement unless the parties intended to create a security interest.[5] The intention of the parties to create a security interest may be gleaned from the expression of future intent to create one in the promissory note and the intention of the parties as expressed in letters constituting their course of dealing.

The promissory note was executed by Bollinger in favor of Z & J in December 1974. Prior to the consummation of the loan, Z & J sent a letter to Bollinger on May 30, 1974, indicating that the loan would be made "provided" Bollinger secured the loan by a mortgage on its machinery and equipment. Bollinger sent a letter to Z & J on September 19, 1974, indicating:

> With your [Z & J's] stated desire to obtain security for material and funds advanced, it would appear that the use of the note would answer both our problems. Since the draft forwarded to you offers full collateralization for the funds to be advanced under it and bears normal interest during its term, it should offer you maximum security.

Subsequent to the execution of the promissory note, Bollinger sent to Z & J a list of the equipment and machinery intended as collateral under the security agreement which was to be, but never was, delivered to Z & J. In November 1975, the parties exchanged letters clarifying whether Bollinger could substitute or replace equipment in the ordinary course of business without Z & J's consent. Such a clarification would not have been necessary had a security interest not been intended by the parties.

---

5. Z & J would not have had to file a financing statement for the $65,000 covered by the 1972 security agreement between ICC and Bollinger, inas- much as the assignee of a security interest is protected by the assignor's filing. Section 9–302(2).

Finally, a letter of November 18, 1975, from Bollinger to Z & J indicated that "any attempted impairment of the collateral would constitute an event of default."

From the course of dealing between Z & J and Bollinger, we conclude there is sufficient evidence that the parties intended a security agreement to be created separate from the assigned ICC agreement with Bollinger. All the evidence points towards the intended creation of such an agreement and since the financing statement contains a detailed list of the collateral, signed by Bollinger, we hold that a valid Article Nine security agreement existed under Pennsylvania law between the parties which secured Z & J in the full amount of the loan to Bollinger.

Holding

IV.

The minimal formal requirements of section 9–203(1)(b) were met by the financing statement and the promissory note, and the course of dealing between the parties indicated the intent to create a security interest. The judgment of the district court recognizing Z & J's secured claim in the amount of $150,000 will be affirmed.

NOTE

A gross characterization of the conflict in the decisions regarding the existence of a valid security agreement follows:

The pro-secured-creditor view: The requirement of a written security agreement is merely evidentiary. If the creditor advances money to a debtor and the debtor signs a promissory note and a financing statement describing the collateral, this is enough to show intent to create a security interest; no additional formal security agreement is needed. Why else would the parties have done this unless they were entering into a secured transaction? *American Card* and its ilk are throwbacks to rigid, formalistic pre-Code thinking. *Bollinger* recognizes the clear intent of the parties even though the creditor was a little careless.

The pro-trustee-in-bankruptcy view: The secured creditor has a very strong position against other creditors in bankruptcy. Recognition of his security interest may clean out the bankrupt's estate, leaving nothing for others. Article 9 has made the formal requirements for creating a security so simple that Comment 5 to UCC § 9–203 tells us that creditors no longer need the assistance that courts traditionally gave under the doctrine of equitable mortgages by which they upheld the validity of security interests even though the parties had failed to meet some formal requirement to validity. Since the Article 9 requirements for creating an enforceable security agreement are so minimal and the benefits conferred by secured-creditor status are so conspicuous, we should demand the creditor who seeks these benefits to comply clearly with these requirements. *American Card* merely requires that the writing contain some words unequivocally granting a security interest to the creditor. *Bollinger* is wrong in protecting the negligent creditor by finding a security agreement when the promissory note stated that a security agreement would subsequently be delivered to the debtor and none was. This is latter-day equitable mortgage thinking.

Most courts have adopted the pro-secured-creditor view as indicated in the authorities cited in *Bollinger*. See White & Summers, Uniform Commercial Code § 23–3 (2d ed. 1980).

B. DESCRIPTION OF THE COLLATERAL

Before the UCC the secured party filed the security contract itself, e.g., the chattel mortgage agreement, to perfect a security interest, just as we record the real estate mortgage document today. The normal UCC case is one in which there are two documents, the security agreement and the financing statement. But there may be only one document, for the secured party may choose to file the security agreement as the financing statement. UCC § 9–402(1) provides that a copy of the security agreement is sufficient as a financing statement if it is signed by the debtor and contains the information a financing statement is required to contain.

A great deal of litigation under the UCC has concerned the description of the collateral. UCC § 9–203(1)(a) provides that the security agreement must contain a "description of the collateral." UCC § 9–402(1) provides that the financing statement must contain "a statement indicating the types, or describing the items, of collateral." UCC § 9–110 states that "any description of personal property or real estate is sufficient whether or not it is specific if it reasonably identifies what is described." Finally, UCC § 9–402(8) says "A financing statement substantially complying with the requirements of this section is effective even though it contains minor errors which are not seriously misleading."

In the following case we see that descriptions of collateral in the security agreement and the financing statement serve different purposes and may be judged by different standards.

THORP COMMERCIAL CORP. v. NORTHGATE INDUSTRIES, INC.

United States Court of Appeals, Eighth Circuit, 1981.
654 F.2d 1245.

McMILLIAN, CIRCUIT JUDGE.   Franklin National Bank (the Bank) appeals from an order of the District Court for the District of Minnesota granting summary judgment to Thorp Commercial Corp. (Thorp) dismissing the Bank's counterclaim against Thorp for conversion.   The conversion counterclaim arose out of Thorp's collection of proceeds from accounts receivable of a third party (the debtor, Northgate Industries, Inc.) who was indebted to both the Bank and Thorp.   The Bank argues that the district court erred in holding that the Bank's claim to a security interest in certain of the debtor's accounts receivable failed as against Thorp because the Bank had not filed an adequate financing statement before Thorp perfected its own security interest in the accounts receivable.   For the reasons discussed below, we reverse the district court's judgment and remand for further proceedings consistent with this opinion.

At issue in this appeal are security interests taken by both the Bank and Thorp in accounts receivable of a debtor, Northgate Industries, Inc., a firm engaged in repair of structures damaged by fires or other casualties.   On May 13, 1971, the Bank lent the debtor $6,500 and under a security agreement took a security interest in collateral including all of the debtor's accounts receivable and proceeds.   The security agreement indicated that ongoing financing arrangements were contemplated, because the security agreement purported to secure payment of all indebtedness existing or to be created afterward.   The Bank duly filed with the Minnesota Secretary of State on May 21, 1971, a financing statement describing the collateral as "assignment accounts receivable" and "proceeds."   On July 21, 1971, the Bank lent the debtor an additional sum of over $8,000; by May 4, 1972, the debtor had fully repaid both loans to the Bank, but the financing statement was not modified or withdrawn.

Meanwhile, on April 2, 1972, Thorp set up its financing arrangement with the debtor by entering into a security agreement covering certain collateral, including the debtor's accounts receivable and specifying coverage of both existing accounts and accounts which would be subsequently acquired. Thorp filed a financing statement identical to its security agreement two days later.

Subsequently, both the Bank and Thorp made further loans to the debtor. Prior to the business failure of the debtor, Thorp collected about $685,000 in repayment of its advances and apparently was owed as much as $100,000 more by the debtor; the Bank seems to have advanced a smaller amount, but as much as $60,000 of the debtor's indebtedness to the Bank appears to remain unpaid. On two occasions the Bank filed additional financing statements, one in July, 1972, describing the collateral in relevant part as "Assignment A/C Rec," and one in February, 1973, describing the collateral in relevant part as "All accounts receivable now or hereinafter acquired." The Bank, however, never withdrew or modified its 1971 financing statement.

The present case is part of litigation that arose out of the failure of the debtor's business. At the time of the failure the debtor owed substantial sums to both the Bank and Thorp. Thorp commenced a lawsuit against the Bank and others alleging common law fraud and violations of federal securities laws arising in part out of alleged improper relationships between officers of the Bank and the debtor. The Bank filed a counterclaim against Thorp for conversion. The counterclaim is based on a theory that Thorp had converted funds it received from the debtor, because the funds belonged to the Bank, which claimed a prior perfected security interest in the proceeds of the debtor's accounts receivable by virtue of its 1971 agreement and financing statement.

The district court dismissed the Bank's counterclaim because in its view the 1971 financing statement covered only accounts receivable in existence at the time and not accounts receivable subsequently created. The Bank has not disputed that Thorp also had a perfected security interest in the debtor's accounts receivable on the basis of Thorp's April, 1972, security agreement and financing statement securing collateral including the debtor's accounts. Under Article 9 of the Uniform Commercial Code (UCC) * * * where two creditors hold security interests in the same collateral of the kind involved in this case (a significant portion of the debtor's accounts receivable), the creditor which first perfects its security interest by filing a financing statement has the prior interest, regardless of the time of the creation of the security agreement. § 9–312(5). Thorp contended, and the district court agreed, that the 1971 financing statement filed by the Bank did not cover any accounts receivable coming into existence subsequent to the date the statement was filed. Thorp's April, 1972, financing statement would then be the earliest one covering the debtor's accounts receivable; therefore, Thorp would have the prior interest in the accounts and the Bank's conversion claim would fail. The district court certified its decision as a final order under Fed.R.Civ.P. 54(b), and this appeal followed.

The UCC provisions governing secured transactions in the financing of accounts receivable set up a system designed to facilitate arrangements by which a debtor may obtain ongoing financing by using a significant portion of its accounts receivable as collateral. The creditor's security interest in the accounts receivable "attaches" when the debtor signs a valid security agreement covering the collateral, § 9–203(1); the security interest is "perfected" when the creditor files a financing statement giving notice of the security interest, § 9–302. Cf. § 9–302(1)(e) (no financing statement required to perfect a security interest in an assignment of less than a significant portion of the debtor's outstanding accounts). Both the security agreement and financing statement may cover ongoing financing arrangements; once such an ongoing security arrangement attaches and is perfected, the creditor's interest in the accounts may be secured as collateral for future as well as past advances, see Thorp Finance Corp. v. Ken Hodgins & Sons, 73 Mich.App. 428, 251 N.W.2d 614 (1977), despite the rollover process of closing of the debtor's existing accounts and opening of new accounts that were not in existence at the time the arrangement was set up.[5] § 9–204; see Valley National Bank v. Flagstaff Dairy, 116 Ariz. 513, 570 P.2d 200 (Ct.App.1977).

---

5. Thorp does not claim that the Bank's filing of subsequent financing statements after 1971 directly affected the validity of the 1971 financing statement to perfect a security interest in accounts receivable. See § 9–303(2). Thorp argues, however, that the Bank did not intend to perfect a security interest in future accounts receivable in 1971, because the explicit coverage of future accounts in the Bank's 1973 financing statement shows that the Bank would have explicitly listed future accounts in 1971 if the Bank meant to take a security interest in future accounts. The standard for evaluating a financing statement is the notice given to subsequent creditors, however, and a financing statement need not describe the collateral, § 9–402(1), discussed infra. The mere fact that the Bank failed to describe the collateral in the 1971 financing statement is not determinative of the notice that statement gives to a future creditor to inquire as to the extent of collateral covered.

The security agreement and financing statement have different functions under the UCC. The security agreement defines what the collateral is so that, if necessary, the creditor can identify and claim it, and the debtor or other interested parties can limit the creditor's rights in the collateral given as security. The security agreement must therefore describe the collateral. § 9–203(1). The financing statement, on the other hand, serves the purpose of putting subsequent creditors on notice that the debtor's property is encumbered. The description of collateral in the financing statement does not function to identify the collateral and define property which the creditor may claim, but rather to warn other subsequent creditors of the prior interest. The financing statement, which limits the prior creditor's rights vis-a-vis subsequent creditors, must therefore contain a description only of the type of collateral. § 9–402(1). See James Talcott, Inc. v. Franklin National Bank, 292 Minn. 277, 194 N.W.2d 775, 782 & n.3 (1972). One corollary to this principle is that, as between two creditors with security interests in the accounts receivable of the same debtor, the first to provide notice by filing a financing statement has priority. §§ 9–302(1), 9–303, 9–312(5); James Talcott, Inc. v. Franklin National Bank, supra, 194 N.W.2d at 785–86. See also Allis-Chalmers Credit Corp. v. Cheney Investment, Inc., 227 Kan. 4, 605 P.2d 525 (1980). Moreover, the financing statement may be filed before the security agreement is made without affecting the first to file rule of priority. § 9–312(5). See James Talcott, Inc. v. Franklin National Bank, supra, 194 N.W.2d at 784–85.

Because the purpose of the financing statement is to warn subsequent creditors rather than to identify the collateral, the UCC makes clear that the collateral need not be specified in the financing statement but may be described by "type."[6] § 9–402(1). See generally Scult, Accounts Receivable Financing: Operational Patterns under the Uniform Commercial Code, 11 Ariz.L.Rev. 1, 12–13 (1969). The UCC commentary makes clear that it is ordinarily not expected that the financing statement itself will tell a subsequent creditor what collateral is already

---

6. The creditor does have the option of describing the collateral by item in the financing statement, § 9–402(1), and therefore perfecting a security interest only in the specific items described. The apparent purpose would be to allow creditors the option to avoid filing a broad financing statement, covering collateral in which no security interest was actually claimed or contemplated as part of ongoing financing arrangements. See 1 G. Gilmore, Security Interests in Personal Property § 15.3, at 479–80 (1965). The financing statement in this case did not list specific accounts, however, but rather a type of collateral, "assignment accounts."

covered by a prior security interest. "The notice itself indicates merely that the secured party who has filed may have a security interest in the collateral described. Further inquiry will be necessary to disclose the complete state of affairs." § 9–402, official comment 2; see James Talcott, Inc. v. Franklin National Bank, supra, 194 N.W.2d at 783. See also First National Bank & Trust Co. v. Atlas Credit Corp., 417 F.2d 1081 (10th Cir. 1969); Bramble Transportation, Inc. v. Sam Senter Sales, Inc., 294 A.2d 97 (Del.Super.Ct.1971), aff'd, 294 A.2d 104 (Del.1972). See generally J. White & R. Summers, Uniform Commercial Code § 23–16, at 961–64 (2d ed. 1980); Annot., 100 A.L.R.3d 10, § 13 (1980) (collecting cases).

The district court failed to focus upon whether the financing statement contained an adequate description of the type of collateral so that a subsequent creditor would reasonably make further inquiry; instead, the district court considered whether the financing statement adequately described the collateral itself. 490 F.Supp. at 201–03. The district court found great significance in the word "assignment" and reasoned that "assignment accounts" could only refer to specific accounts listed in the security agreement or actually transferred in some other way prior to the filing of the financing statement. Id. at 202. In the district court's view, the words "assignment accounts receivable" would not be adequate to cover future accounts receivable under § 9–110, which provides, "[A]ny description of personal property * * * is sufficient whether or not it is specific if it reasonably identifies what is described."

But, as noted above, the UCC requires a description of only the type of collateral, not the collateral itself, in the financing statement to perfect a security interest. Under § 9–110, a description of the collateral in a financing statement "is sufficient whether or not it is specific if it reasonably identifies" the type of collateral. The drafters of the UCC contemplated that the financing statement would need to give only enough description of the collateral to induce a subsequent creditor to make further inquiries. § 9–402, official comment 2. The description "reasonably identifies" the type of collateral, therefore, if it would reasonably induce further inquiry.[7]

7. One exception to this principle appears to arise in some cases where the financing statement fails to describe the collateral even by type, but instead simply designates all of the debtor's property or uses some other vague or all-encompassing term. Some courts have held such a financing statement inadequate, because Article 9, § 402(1) of the UCC specifically requires that the financing statement describe the collateral either by type or item. Other courts have, however, held such descriptions

The district court's approach, however, has support under a line of cases in which courts have largely ignored the function of a financing statement to suggest further inquiry about the collateral. A split in authority exists in this area. For example, one court has held that a financing statement describing the collateral as "accounts receivable" did not cover accounts created after the financing statement was filed, reasoning that some subsequent creditors may have been misled by the failure to specify subsequently created accounts and that the prior creditor could easily have made the financing statement clearer. In re Middle Atlantic Stud Welding Co., 503 F.2d 1133 (3d Cir. 1974). Other courts have, however, considered financing statements describing the collateral as "accounts receivable" or "accounts" as adequate to cover accounts created subsequent to the filing of the financing statement. Continental Oil Co. v. Citizens Trust & Savings Bank, 57 Mich.App. 1, 225 N.W.2d 209 (1974), aff'd, 397 Mich. 203, 244 N.W.2d 243 (1976); Heights v. Citizens National Bank, 463 Pa. 48, 342 A.2d 738 (1975) ("accounts"); South County Sand & Gravel Co. v. Bituminous Pavers Co., 106 R.I. 178, 256 A.2d 514 (1969) ("accounts receivable").[8] See generally Annot., 100 A.L.R.3d 10, supra, §§ 21, 23. Cf. In re Laminated Veneers Co., 471 F.2d 1124 (2d Cir. 1973) (court divided over whether description of collateral in financing statement as "equipment" is adequate to cover automobile).

A substantial theoretical difference seems to underlie these inconsistent results. Under one view a financing statement adequately covers collateral if it reasonably puts a subsequent cred-

adequate to perfect a security interest in all of the debtor's property. Compare In re JCM Coop., Inc., 8 U.C.C. Rep. 247 (W.D.Mich.Bankr.1970) (Michigan law; financing statement covering "all * * * personal property * * *" sufficient to perfect security interest in inventory and proceeds), with In re Fuqua, 461 F.2d 1186 (10th Cir.1972) (Kansas law; financing statement covering "all personal property" insufficient to perfect security interest in livestock and equipment). See generally B. Clark, The Law of Secured Transactions Under the Uniform Commercial Code ¶ 2.9[5][c], at 2–44 & nn.169 & 170 (1980). See also note 10 infra.

8. In Heights v. Citizens Nat'l Bank, 463 Pa. 48, 342 A.2d 738, 743 (1975), the financing statement covered "All accounts receivable * * * including proceeds both present and future but not limited to proceeds from inventory and receivables both present and future." The court could have read the financing statement to cover explicitly future receivables, but it correctly refrained from doing so, holding instead that the collateral description simply was sufficient to put subsequent creditors on notice that further inquiries should be made concerning the debtor's accounts. The court did not need to decide what was explicitly covered by the financing statement.

itor on notice of a need for further inquiry about the possibility that the collateral is subject to a prior security interest. The reasonableness of the notice would depend on balancing such factors as the difficulty of making further inquiry against factors such as the likelihood the type of collateral described in the financing statement might include the collateral which interests the subsequent creditor.

Under the second view of Article 9, a financing statement suffices to perfect a security interest in collateral if the financing statement itself contains a reasonable description of the collateral. The determination of reasonableness involves balancing such factors as the ease with which the prior creditor could make the description of the collateral more precise or clearer against factors like the danger that a subsequent creditor might fail to recognize that the collateral is covered. E. g., In re Middle Atlantic Stud Welding Co., supra, 503 F.2d 1133 (explicitly weighing these factors).

The district court in deciding the instant case relied upon an Oklahoma case involving similar facts which adopted this second view of financing statements. In Georgia-Pacific Corp. v. Lumber Products Corp., 590 P.2d 661 (Okla.1979), a financing statement covering "assignment accounts receivable" was held inadequate to perfect a security interest in accounts receivable other than those specifically assigned by the debtor to the secured party.[9] The court in *Georgia-Pacific* found that the words "assignment accounts receivable" were reasonably descriptive of only an assignment of specific listed accounts receivable and held that the words did not "reasonably identify the collateral as *all* accounts receivable." Id. at 664. Although the opinion does not elaborate on the factors which determine whether the description reasonably identifies the collateral, the Oklahoma court did not consider whether it would have been reasonable for subsequent creditors to make further inquiries about what the financ-

9. The Oklahoma court apparently did view the words "assignment accounts receivable" adequate to cover assignments of specific accounts receivable made subsequent to the date of filing of the financing statement. *Georgia-Pacific* is therefore not technically authority for the proposition that the words "assignment accounts receivable" fail to cover after acquired accounts. Nevertheless, the approach of the Oklahoma court in limiting the coverage of the financing statement to collateral described technically by the financing statement, like the approach of the district court in the present case, does not focus on the notice of need for further inquiry given by the financing statement. In that regard, the Oklahoma court's opinion is consistent with and supports the decision reached by the district court in this case.

ing statement covered, but rather considered what was described in the financing statement itself.

The approach of the Oklahoma court in the *Georgia-Pacific* case and other courts which requires that the financing statement by its own terms describe the collateral cannot be supported under Article 9. Article 9 simply does not require that the financing statement describe anything more than the type of collateral and leaves to interested parties the burden of seeking more information. Ultimately, such a requirement for a description of the collateral itself in a financing statement would eliminate the distinction between the financing statement and the security agreement, because the only way for a creditor to make sure that the financing statement describes the collateral would be to use the same description which identified the collateral in the security agreement setting up the security interest. Indeed, the district court suggested in the instant case that the "optimum practice" is for the creditor "to describe the collateral in the financing statement exactly as it appears in the security agreement." 490 F.Supp. at 203 n.5. Such a requirement was rejected by the drafters of the UCC who specifically commented,

> the financing statement is effective to encompass transactions under a security agreement not in existence and not contemplated at the time the notice was filed, if the description of collateral in the financing statement is broad enough to encompass them. Similarly, the financing statement is valid to cover after-acquired property * * * whether or not mentioned in the financing statement.

U.C.C. § 9–402, official comment 2 (Official Draft 1972). One central purpose of allowing a broad financing statement is to allow a creditor that envisions an ongoing financing arrangement to protect the priority of its interest by filing at an early date a notice to third parties which will cover the existing arrangement and broad range of potential future modifications. By requiring a description of the collateral in the financing statement itself, courts would destroy this flexibility.[10]

*   *   *

---

10. Another problem with requiring a description of the collateral in the financing statement is the possibility that a debtor might want to enter into a security agreement including information the debtor might not want

to put on the public record for competitors to see. Cf. § 9–208 & official comment 2 (list of collateral available only to debtor so that casual inquirers and competitors cannot obtain it). A vague financing statement referring

* * * If the financing statement covers not only existing security interests in the type of collateral described but also security interests which may arise in the future, then a financing statement covering "assignment accounts receivable" would cover any assignment of the debtor's accounts receivable that might exist or be made in the future. The word "assignment" might mean a specific assignment of named accounts receivable but is broad enough to refer to a general assignment of all the debtor's accounts receivable, including those acquired in the future. A subsequent creditor, faced with notice that a security interest may exist or be created in any or all of the debtor's accounts, would certainly have reasonable grounds for inquiring further before relying on any of the debtor's accounts for collateral. We conclude that under Minnesota law applying the UCC the financing statement covering "assignment accounts receivable" was adequate to perfect the Bank's security interest in accounts acquired subsequent to the filing of the financing statement, whether or not there was a specific assignment of particular accounts.

In reaching this conclusion we do not overlook the district court's concern that a creditor should not benefit from use of a misleading or overreaching financing statement. 490 F.Supp. at 203. The notice filing concept has a primary purpose of facilitating ongoing financing arrangements not merely by the first creditor on the scene but also subsequent creditors. The requirement for filing a financing statement provides notice, at least theoretically, to subsequent creditors of what assets may already be encumbered by prior creditors. The financing statement would not provide notice where the description of collateral is misleading, for example, if the description were simply wrong or if the description seemingly would not cover the collateral but contained coverage under some hidden ambiguity that could not be considered reasonable notice. See, e.g., In re California Pump & Manufacturing Co., 588 F.2d 717 (9th Cir. 1978). Cf. § 336.9–402(8) (financing statement is adequate despite minor errors which are not seriously misleading). Even assuming the words "assignment accounts receivable" could be interpreted narrowly to refer to a single assignment of specific accounts re-

generally to the type of collateral can obviate this problem. The interest of a subsequent creditor can be protected in such a case from the danger that the prior financing statement will enable the prior creditor to obtain a superior security interest by a subordination agreement from the prior creditor. See 1 G. Gilmore, Security Interests in Personal Property, supra, § 15.3, at 479–80 & nn.10 & 12.

ceivable, the words also have an obvious alternative broad meaning; in the present case notice filing has served its purpose of alerting subsequent creditors to the need for further inquiry. The UCC puts the burden on the subsequent creditor to seek clarification.

Accordingly, the judgment of the district court is reversed and the case is remanded for further proceedings consistent with this opinion.

NOTE: DESCRIPTION OF THE COLLATERAL IN THE SECURITY AGREEMENT

1. The requirement in UCC § 9–203(1)(a) that the security agreement must contain a description of the collateral amounts to a statute of frauds, and the issue to be decided is merely one of construction of the contract: What did the parties intend the collateral to be? The bias of the Code toward a liberal interpretation of descriptions of collateral is set out in UCC § 9–110 and in the Comment to that section which assures us that the Code rejects the view "that descriptions are insufficient unless they are of the most exact and detailed nature, the so-called 'serial number' test." By and large the courts have gone along with this bias toward upholding descriptions of collateral.

2. *Thorp* discusses whether the financing statement is adequate to cover after-acquired accounts, but this question is moot unless the security agreement reasonably identifies after-acquired accounts as part of the intended collateral. The bank's security agreement apparently described the collateral as "all of the debtor's accounts receivable and proceeds." How does the court conclude that this description covers after-acquired accounts? The court refers to In re Middle Atlantic Stud Welding Co., where the security agreement and the financing statement both described the collateral as "all of the debtor's accounts receivable" and contained a clause like that in *Thorp* stating that this collateral was security for "any and all indebtedness of debtor to secured party of every kind and description, now existing or hereafter arising." The court held that the security agreement did not cover after-acquired accounts receivable and said that it would have been so easy for the secured party to refer explicitly to after-acquired property that the courts should require him to do so. There was a strong dissent. Presumably *Thorp* would disagree with *Middle Atlantic Stud Welding* on

collateral that the parties contemplated would constantly be turning over like accounts receivable or inventory, but would it reach a different result if the security agreement described the collateral as "all of the debtor's equipment" and no reference was made to after-acquired property? See the definition of "equipment" in UCC § 9–109(2).

PROBLEMS

The following fact situations are based on two cases that were decided by the same court with opinions by the same judge. He upheld the validity of the collateral description in one case and rejected it in the other. In your view which is the more vulnerable description? Can you distinguish the cases?

1. The security agreement granted a security interest in certain specifically described items, including an International truck, and contained the following omnibus clause:

> In addition to all the above enumerated items, it is the intention that this mortgage shall cover all chattels, machinery, equipment, tables, chairs, work benches, factory chairs, stools, shelving, cabinets, power lines, switch boxes, control panels, machine parts, motors, pumps, electrical equipment, measuring and calibrating instruments, office supplies, sundries, office furniture, fixtures, and all other items of equipment and fixtures belonging to the mortgagor, whether herein enumerated or not, now at the plant of [Debtor] located at 115–02 15th Ave. College Point, New York, and all chattels, machinery, fixtures, or equipment that may hereafter be brought in or installed in said premises or any new premises of the mortgagor, to replace, substitute for, or in addition to the above mentioned chattels and equipment with the exception of stock in trade.

The issue was whether the omnibus clause covered two Oldsmobile automobiles used in Debtor's business. The clause covered "equipment," a term defined in UCC § 9–109(2). The two automobiles clearly are within the UCC definition. See In re Laminated Veneers Co., Inc., 471 F.2d 1124 (2d Cir. 1973).

2. The security agreement described the collateral as the following:

Items	Location, etc.
Machinery, equipment and fixtures; Molds, tools, dies, component parts including specifically the:	To be located either at the Debtor's plant in North Bergen, New Jersey; and in the case of the molds also at the plants of contractors who may be using said molds in the manufacture of products for the Debtor
1 x 1 two cavity cassette cover and base mold	
2 x 2 four cavity cassette cover and base mold	
One twenty-four cavity roller mold	
One sixteen cavity hub mold	

The issue was whether the security agreement covered only the specifically described molds or whether it also covered other machinery and tools of the Debtor. If it were held to apply to other machinery and tools, could one identify which articles of machinery and tools were covered? See In re Sarex, 509 F.2d 689 (2d Cir. 1975).

NOTE: DESCRIPTION OF THE COLLATERAL IN THE FINANCING STATEMENT

1. In order to understand the function of the description of collateral in a financing statement one must grasp the concept of notice filing. The authoritative statement on the subject is found in Comment 2 to UCC § 9–402:

> This section adopts the system of "notice filing" which proved successful under the Uniform Trust Receipts Act. What is required to be filed is not, as under chattel mortgage and conditional sales acts, the security agreement itself, but only a simple notice which may be filed before the security interest attaches or thereafter. The notice itself indicates merely that the secured party who has filed may have a security interest in the collateral described. Further inquiry from the parties concerned will be necessary to disclose the complete state of affairs. Section 9–208 provides a statutory procedure under which the secured party, at the debtor's re-

quest, may be required to make disclosure. Notice filing has proved to be of great use in financing transactions involving inventory, accounts and chattel paper, since it obviates the necessity of refiling on each of a series of transactions in a continuing arrangement where the collateral changes from day to day. Where other types of collateral are involved, the alternative procedure of filing a signed copy of the security agreement may prove to be the simplest solution. Sometimes more than one copy of a financing statement or of a security agreement used as a financing statement is needed for filing. In such a case the section permits use of a carbon copy or photographic copy of the paper, including signatures.

However, even in the case of filings that do not necessarily involve a series of transactions the financing statement is effective to encompass transactions under a security agreement not in existence and not contemplated at the time the notice was filed, if the description of collateral in the financing statement is broad enough to encompass them. Similarly, the financing statement is valid to cover after-acquired property and future advances under security agreements whether or not mentioned in the financing statement.

What is remarkable about the Code's notice filing system is how little information a financing statement—the only public document—need impart to third parties. It need only state the "types" of property covered; it need not tell where the property is kept or the amount of the indebtedness; and it may cover after-acquired property and future advances even though the financing statement never mentions these terms (Comment 2 to UCC § 9–402), and proceeds even though the financing statement is silent on this subject as well (UCC § 9–306(3)(a)).

2. As *Thorp* points out, the courts have usually tested the adequacy of financing statement descriptions of collateral in the light of the purpose of notice filing. Thus, generic descriptions—"inventory," "accounts receivable," and "equipment"—have been generally approved by the cases. Given the paucity of information discoverable from the financing statement about the relationship of Debtor and Secured Party with respect to the type of collateral involved, how does one who wants to deal with Debtor gain the information he must have to make an informed decision?

It is clear that a potential Subsequent Creditor must learn from Debtor and Secured Party themselves what collateral is covered by the security agreement and how much debt is owing. If Debtor is seeking a loan from Subsequent Creditor, Debtor must cooperate with Subsequent Creditor who should demand to see the security agreement and note. But desperate debtors lie and Subsequent Creditor cannot be safe without checking this information with Secured Party. However, Secured Party may have no incentive beyond business comity to make any disclosure to Subsequent Creditor.

UCC § 9–208 is designed to induce Secured Party to give information about his credit transaction with Debtor. Debtor may request that Secured Party approve Debtor's statement about the amount of the indebtedness and the extent of the collateral. The section imposes sanctions on Secured Party if he ignores the request. Note that this provision gives Subsequent Creditor no right to compel Secured Party to give him information directly. Only Debtor can activate the UCC § 9–208 mechanism. Thus UCC § 9–208 is of no use to a judgment creditor of Debtor looking for assets to seize; Debtor would normally have no interest in giving such a creditor information about his financial condition, let alone in helping him gain information from Secured Creditor. Later we shall point out how limited UCC § 9–208 is in assisting Subsequent Creditor in making his credit decisions.

3. The court in *Thorp* mentions two cases in note 7 as examples of extremely broad financing statements. In re JCM Cooperative, Inc. involved a security agreement granting "a security interest * * * in the following collateral including the proceeds and products thereof: all other equipment now owned or hereafter acquired by Debtor * * * including but not limited to * * * all tangible, personal property now owned by the Debtor * * * including * * * the assets described on Schedule A attached hereto * * *." Schedule A listed items of equipment only. The financing statement described the collateral as "all tangible, personal property" of the debtor and also covered proceeds of collateral. The court held that the secured party had a perfected security interest in accounts receivable which were proceeds resulting from the sale of inventory.

In re Fuqua, on the other hand, concerned a security agreement covering "All livestock, feed, and machinery to include but not limited to the following: [a specific enumeration of certain livestock]." The financing statement said: "This financing statement covers the following types (or items) of property: All Personal Property." The court held that the financing statement was invalid, saying "the phrase 'all personal property' does not even approach a description of property by type or description."

Can you reconcile the cases on the basis of the differences in the security agreements?

4. The issue before the class for debate is: Resolved: UCC § 9–402(1) should be amended to delete any requirement of a description of collateral in a financing statement. Arguments pro: The requirement of a description of collateral in the financing statement is a useless vestige from the pre-Code days when the security agreement itself had to be filed. Since the financing statement need do nothing more than describe in general terms the types of collateral in which the secured party may have an interest, the inquiring party cannot deal intelligently with the debtor until he obtains precise information from the debtor and prior secured parties on record concerning the amount of the debt and the items of collateral in which security interests are claimed. Hence, the description of collateral in the financing statement is irrelevant to the inquiring party's search for information. All a notice filing system need disclose to an inquiring party is the name and address of the debtor and secured party. What are the arguments, if any, contra?

C. THE FILING SYSTEM

UCC § 9–303(1) provides: "A security interest is perfected when it has attached and when all of the applicable steps required for perfection have been taken. Such steps are specified in Sections 9–302, 9–304, 9–305 and 9–306. If such steps are taken before the security interest attaches, it is perfected at the time when it attaches." Thus when the secured party has created a security interest good as between him and the debtor, he must in some instances take further steps to make his interest good as against third parties. With respect to transactions in which the debtor is to have possession of the collateral (nonpossessory security interests), the common method of perfection is by filing a financing statement. UCC §§ 9–302, 9–304. For transactions in which the secured party is to keep possession of the collateral—the traditional pledge transaction—the creditor's possession is sufficient public notice to perfect the security interest. UCC § 9–305.

The kind of collateral is another variable in determining the appropriate act of perfection. In most instances a security interest in investment securities and negotiable instruments can only be perfected by possession because of their negotiable nature. UCC § 9–304(1). At the other extreme, intangibles like accounts and general intangibles (UCC § 9–106) can only be perfected by filing because there is no physical embodiment of the property that can be pledged. Security interests in goods (UCC § 9–105(1)(h)), chattel paper (UCC § 9–105(1)(b)), and documents of title such as warehouse receipts and bills of lading (UCC § 9–105(1)(f)) may be perfected either by filing or by pledge. UCC §§ 9–302(1), 9–304(1) and 9–305.

Still another variable is the purpose of the secured transaction. A purchase money security interest in consumer goods (with some exceptions) is perfected at the moment it attaches with no further act of filing or possession required. UCC § 9–302(1)(d). Other secured transactions are outside the Code filing system because either the state or federal government maintains a separate registry for the transactions in question— state motor vehicle registration acts and the federal aircraft registration law are examples. UCC § 9–302(3).

1. NAME OF DEBTOR

IN RE GLASCO, INC.

United States Court of Appeals, Fifth Circuit, 1981.
642 F.2d 793.

RONEY, CIRCUIT JUDGE: The sole issue on appeal is whether a financing statement, filed with the Florida Secretary of State by a creditor, perfected a security interest in certain property of the bankrupt debtor. The bankruptcy court held the financing statement to be inadequate because it listed the debtor by the name in which it did business rather than its legal corporate name. The district court affirmed. Holding the debtor's name used in the financing statement was not seriously misleading, we reverse.

The facts are not disputed. Prior to its bankruptcy, the debtor engaged in the manufacture and sale of boats in Florida. Although its legal corporate name was "Glasco, Inc.," the debtor operated its business solely under the name, "Elite Boats, Division of Glasco, Inc."

Appellant, the Citizens Bank of Perry ("the bank"), was "floor planning" marine engines for the debtor. In 1977, in connection with this financing, the debtor executed promissory notes and a security agreement in the name of "Elite Boats, Division of Glasco, Inc." The bank, to perfect its security interest in the marine engines, timely filed a standard form UCC–1 financing statement with the Florida Secretary of State, as required by Florida law. The bank listed the debtor on the form as "Elite Boats, Division of Glasco, Inc." The form was signed at the bottom by an officer of the debtor, without any designation as to office, capacity or affiliation. A filing clerk in the Secretary of State's office indexed this financing statement under the name listed, but did not cross-index it under "Glasco, Inc."

Later in 1977, the debtor filed for bankruptcy. The trustee in bankruptcy, appellee here, inquired of the Secretary of State whether any financing statements had been filed under "Glasco, Inc." Since the trustee did not request a search under "Elite Boats" or "Elite Boats, Division of Glasco, Inc." as well, the bank's financing statement was not disclosed. With permission of the bankruptcy court and without notice to the bank, the trustee then sold the marine engines. The bank commenced this action against the trustee for the sale proceeds.

In granting the trustee's motion for summary judgment, the bankruptcy court held the financing statement to be improper because it did not list the debtor by its legal name, "Glasco, Inc." The court further held the Secretary of State had no duty to cross-index the financing statement under the debtor's legal name, and the trustee was not bound by its actual knowledge that the debtor did business as "Elite Boats, Division of Glasco, Inc." The district court affirmed. On appeal, the bank contends that (1) listing the debtor as "Elite Boats, Division of Glasco, Inc." was sufficient because it was not seriously misleading to future creditors; and (2) in any event, the Secretary of State should have cross-indexed under "Glasco, Inc."

To perfect a security interest in collateral, a creditor must file a financing statement which complies with the filing requirements of the Uniform Commercial Code. The purpose of the filing system is to give notice to creditors and other interested parties that a security interest exists in property of the debtor. Owen v. McKesson & Robbins Drug Co., 349 F.Supp. 1327, 1334 (N.D.Fla.1972). Perfect accuracy, however, is not required as long as the financing statement contains sufficient information to "put any searcher on inquiry." In re Excel Stores, Inc., 341

F.2d 961, 963 (2d Cir. 1965). See also In re Fowler, 407 F.Supp. 799, 802 (W.D.Okla.1975). The emphasis of the Uniform Commercial Code is thus on commercial realities rather than on corporate technicalities. Siljeg v. National Bank of Commerce, 509 F.2d 1009, 1012 (9th Cir. 1975). Section 9–402(5) [1972 Code § 9–402(8)] reflects this emphasis by providing: "A financing statement substantially complying with the requirements of this section is effective even though it contains minor errors which are not seriously misleading." See generally In re Hammons, 614 F.2d 399, 405–06 (5th Cir. 1980).

The effect of errors in the listing of the debtor's name has been the subject of extensive litigation. See generally Annotation, Sufficiency of Designation of Debtor or Secured Party in Security Agreement or Financing Statement Under UCC § 9–402, 99 A.L.R.3d 478–565 (1980). The decisions appear generally to turn on the particular factual circumstances involved. The case here, then, must be judged on its own facts, with the focus on whether potential creditors would have been misled as a result of the name the debtor was listed by in the bank's financing statement.

It is undisputed the debtor held itself out to the community and to creditors as "Elite Boats, Division of Glasco, Inc." Its checks, stationery, and bank account all bore the latter name. Apparently the same name was used in its bills, contracts and telephone listing, because there is no indication in the record the debtor ever used the name of just "Glasco, Inc.," or any other name. Thus, listing the debtor by the sole name in which it did business was not misleading, because any reasonably prudent creditor would have requested the Secretary of State to search under "Elite Boats" in addition to "Glasco, Inc." Of course, the trustee in bankruptcy is considered to be in the position of a hypothetical but prudent creditor. See, e.g., In re Federal's, Inc., 553 F.2d 509 (6th Cir. 1977); In re Leichter, 471 F.2d 785 (2d Cir. 1972).

Siljeg v. National Bank of Commerce, 509 F.2d 1009 (9th Cir. 1975), is analogous. *Siljeg* involved a security interest in property of a corporate debtor which later merged into another company. The parties disputed whether the "true name" of the debtor was the pre-merger or post-merger name, for the purpose of determining the accuracy of the financing statement. In rejecting this focus of inquiry, the court held:

> The issue to be determined is not the true name of the entity, but whether the filing was misleading. Filing under an as-

sumed trade name is effective unless it is misleading * * *. It is likely that the * * * corporation did business under only one name and it may well be that a filing under that name was not seriously misleading. 509 F.2d at 1012-13.

The court then remanded the case for consideration under this standard.

The trustee relies on several cases each involving an individual who is engaged in business under an assumed trade name. These cases generally hold that a financing statement listing only the trade name as the debtor will be insufficient to perfect a security interest effective against the individual. See, e.g., In re Leichter, 471 F.2d 785 (2d Cir. 1972); Citizens Bank v. Ansley, 467 F.Supp. 51 (M.D.Ga.1979), affirmed without opinion, 604 F.2d 669 (5th Cir. 1980). But see In re Platt, 257 F.Supp. 478 (E.D.Pa.1966). There is a crucial distinction, however, between these cases and the case here. In the former, a single debtor is necessarily held out to the credit community under two names, that of the individual and of the business. The individual's credit for personal needs is unrelated to the business. A personal creditor would not necessarily be aware of the business or trade name, and thus may not discover security interests filed solely under the business name. In the present case, where the company does business only under one name, the opportunity for creditors to be misled is substantially reduced, even though that name is not the company's ["true name."] See *Siljeg*, supra, 509 F.2d at 1012.

We hold the listing of the debtor as "Elite Boats, Division of Glasco, Inc." rather than as "Glasco, Inc." was not seriously misleading. The financing statement was therefore in substantial compliance with the filing requirements under Florida law and was sufficient to perfect the bank's security interest.

Holding

Because of our holding on the first issue presented by the bank, we need not decide whether the Secretary of State had a duty to cross-index the financing statement under "Glasco, Inc." A creditor who has complied with the filing requirements does not bear the risk of improper indexing by the Secretary of State. Official Comment to Section 9–407. See also In re Royal Electrotype Corp., 485 F.2d 394 (3d Cir. 1973); In re Fowler, 407 F.Supp. 799 (W.D.Okla.1975). Thus, the bank would have a perfected security interest whether or not the Secretary of State had breached a duty to cross-index.

Reversed.

TUTTLE, CIRCUIT JUDGE, dissenting: With deference, I dissent. The majority opinion treats this case as presenting a group of narrow issues arising under the filing provisions for perfection of security interest under the Uniform Commercial Code. The majority eschews technicality to reach what might be considered to be a common sense solution in finding a perfected security interest despite an irregularity in the filing. Because this superficially appealing result contains the seeds for future mischief I cannot concur.

The filing system under the Code revolves around the concept of "notice filing," where a filing is to " 'give the minimum information necessary to put any searcher on inquiry.' " In re Excel Stores, 341 F.2d 961, 963 (2d Cir. 1965); see UCC 9–402, comment 2. To effectuate the Code's spirit of liberality and disdain for rigid technicality the drafters included the provision, now relied upon by the majority, that a financing statement is effective even if "it contains minor errors which are not seriously misleading." § 9–402(5). [1972 Code § 9–402(8)]. This provision clearly was designed to accomplish substantial justice and "to discourage the fanatical and impossibly refined reading of such statutory requirements in which courts have occasionally indulged themselves." UCC § 9–402, comment 9. [1972 Code].

This provision of liberality, however, was never intended to vitiate the beneficial effects of having a simple filing system for the benefit of both existing creditors and searchers of the files. In its decision which protects the rights of the bank-appellant, the majority has unfairly burdened the other persons who must rely upon the filing system. A variety of different types of errors may cause the name on the financing statement to be erroneous and result in an incorrect filing of the statement. In deciding whether an error is "seriously misleading" a court must apply an "appropriate sensitivity to the relevant factors." J. White & R. Summers, Handbook of the Law Under the Uniform Commercial Code § 23–16, 958 (2d ed. 1980). In this regard the Court of Appeals for the Second Circuit has held that a subsequent creditor might never search the filings under the trade name of "Landman Dry Cleaners" where the debtor's name was "Leichter." In re Leichter, 471 F.2d 785, 787 (2d Cir. 1972). On the other hand, a filing under a trade name may be so similar to the debtor's real name that a searcher would be put on notice despite the technical error.

The Referee found that a search of the public records under the name of Henry Platt would not have disclosed

F.C.A.'s interest.   Platt Fur Co. was an unregistered fictitious name for the business of Henry Platt.   he also used
Kenwell Fur Novelty Co. as a fictitious name.

The use of Kenwell as the debtor would clearly have left
F.C.A. without a perfected security interest.   However, the
name Platt Fur Co. is sufficiently related to the name of the
debtor, Henry Platt, to require those who search the records
to make further investigation.   Furthermore, the Referee
found that the name was "not seriously misleading," the cri-
terion for effectiveness under § 9–402(5).

In re Platt, 257 F.Supp. 478, 482 (E.D.Pa.1966).[1]   The majority
distinguishes cases such as *Leichter* as cases where the credit
records of an individual's business should be distinguished from
the credit records of the individual.   The majority reasons that:
"A personal creditor would not necessarily be aware of the business or trade name, and thus may not discover security interests
filed solely under the business name.   In the present case,
where the company does business only under one name, the opportunity for creditors to be misled is substantially reduced,
even though that name is not the company's 'true name.'"   At
796.[2]   This distinction will not support the majority's result.

---

1. The Florida law, amended subsequent to the beginning of this case,
provides that: "A financing statement
sufficiently shows the name of the
debtor if it gives the individual partnership, or corporate names of the
debtor, whether or not it adds other
trade names or names of partners."
Fla.Stat.Ann. § 679.9–402(6) (West
Supp.1980).   Leading commentators
have inferred that this provision
would alter the result of *Platt*: "With
this provision on the books, the wise
lawyer would advise Henry Platt and
his creditors to use 'Henry Platt' as
the name on the financing statement."
White & Summers, supra, at 958.   Although not the law in any state, the
official comment to the revision behind this new Florida provision provides some insight on this situation:
"Trade names are deemed to be too
uncertain and likely not to be known
to be the basis for a filing system."
UCC § 9–402, comment 7.

2. The majority relies heavily on
Siljeg v. National Bank of Commerce,
509 F.2d 1009 (9th Cir. 1975), as a case
where a filing under a name that is
not the true name was potentially sufficient.   That case, however, presented a closer question than the issue in
this case.   In *Siljeg*, the debtor had
upon a merger taken the name of the
firm with which it merged.   Although
the debtor wanted to take back its former name and the legally proper steps
to change the name were not followed, the Secretary of State issued a
certificate erroneously certifying that
the former name survived the merger
and the records of the Secretary of
State were altered to reflect the former name as the legal name.   Thus, it
was possible that the debtor in *Siljeg*
always used as its corporate name
an ostensibly correct yet legally
flawed name.   In the present case, no
one has ever contended that "Elite
Boats, Division of Glasco, Inc." was a
legal name as opposed to a trade
name.   And in any event, *Siljeg* remanded for consideration of the fact
question of whether this situation was
"seriously misleading," a procedure
the present majority finds unnecessary in its reversal of the district court's
judgment.

The majority points to indications that the debtor always did business under the name "Elite Boats, Division of Glasco, Inc." and concludes that therefore any potential creditor would know to check under that non-legal name. But we are reviewing a case that was disposed of on a motion for summary judgment. Given this state of the record there may have existed creditors who would have perceived the debtor as simply "Glasco, Inc.," the legally proper title which, of course, it was. Surely the trustee could be taken to stand in the shoes of such an ideal creditor who had no notice. And in searching for "Glasco, Inc." one would not normally come across an item filed under the title of "Elite Boats." This is simply not a case where a searcher looking for the actual name would be put on notice by a filing under a similar trade name. A filing under the trade name in this case would not be filed near the actual name. Moreover, even if such creditors knew the trade name, they would still be justified to search only under the debtor's *legal* name. The terms of UCC § 9–402 require no more.[3] Searching under a trade name would be completely unnecessary but for the majority's opinion. From now on in this Circuit, potential creditors must undertake to discover trade names and to conduct additional searches in order to avoid a judicial determination that they lacked diligence. And even if they follow such precautions they might yet overlook one trade name and face potentially expensive litigation over whether they should have known about that trade name.

Of course, the majority's conclusion may yet be saved if the Secretary of State wrongly failed to carry out a duty to cross index the financing statement. A creditor who complies with the filing requirements may not bear the risk of errors by the filing officer. See UCC § 9–407, comment 1. This rule holds true because under the Code "Presentation for filing of a financing statement * * * constitutes filing under this chapter."

3. This is particularly true with regards to the trustee.

In this regard, the trustee in bankruptcy must be deemed to stand in the shoes of the most favored creditor, not simply one who could—by virtue of his dealings with the debtor acting under his trade name—be held to a semblance of knowledge of the true facts; even such a creditor, knowing how UCC § 9–402 reads, might never search the filings under the trade name. That is to say, the trustee is more than a subsequent creditor seeking to build up his own equities at the expense of good faith creditors. Here the assignee of the filing creditor seeking to be secured over others, engaged in the financing business so that it should surely be familiar with the requirements of the Code, must be held to substantial compliance with the notice statute. Filing under the trade name only, we hold, was insufficient.

In re Leichter, 471 F.2d at 787–88 (footnote omitted).

§ 9–403(1).   See In re Royal Electrotype Corp., 485 F.2d 394, 395–96 (3d Cir. 1973); In re Fowler, 407 F.Supp. 799 (W.D.Okla. 1975).   But those authorities do not aid the bank in the present case.   The error lay in the bank's submission of the debtor's name as "Elite Boats, Division of Glasco, Inc."   The filing officer dutifully filed the statement under precisely this name. The bank may argue that the filing officers usually cross index under all names given.   For example, a financing statement using a "doing business as" listing of a debtor would be indexed under the legal name and the trade name.   This argument by the bank differs from the position that the bank will not bear the risks of the filing officer's mistakes; rather this argument holds that the filing officer must correct the bank's errors.   If the bank had clearly indicated two names separated by a notation such as "d.b.a.", its position would be stronger.   But the fact remains that the bank's submission could very easily be taken to be *one* name especially by a clerk untrained in legal subtleties.[4] "A secured party does not bear the risk of improper filing or indexing *as long as his conduct does not lead to the error on the part of the filing officer.*"   In re Fowler, 407 F.Supp. at 803 (emphasis added.)

Courts may have the opportunity to view a situation with perfect hindsight which is unavailable to participants in daily activities.   The bank had the opportunity to submit the correct name of the debtor and failed to do so.   A searcher versed in the operation of the UCC would know that the filing should be under the debtor's legal name.   He would have no reason to look under a trade name, even if he is aware of the trade name's existence, because he should be able to rely on the bank to submit the legal name and not a trade name.   Future creditors must now anticipate mistakes by would-be secured creditors in order not to be ensnared in the hindsight of courts.   The trustee should prevail against the bank which is responsible for any confusion in this case.

I would affirm the district court's judgment.

NOTES

1.   Having the correct name of the debtor on the financing statement is crucial to the Code's notice filing system because

---

4.   The bank's argument that the filing officer should have recognized that there were two names on the form actually cuts against the bank. If it is so easy to see that "Elite Boats" is not a legal name then there is no reason or excuse for the bank's failure to submit the debtor's name as simply "Glasco, Inc."

financing statements are indexed under the debtor's name. In one line of cases the courts have upheld financing statements even though the secured party erred somewhat in giving the debtor's correct name. In re Excel Stores, Inc., referred to in the principal case, is prototypic. The court upheld a description of the debtor as "Excel Department Stores" instead of "Excel Stores, Inc." finding the mistake to be in the category of "minor errors which are not seriously misleading." UCC § 9–402(8). These cases seem to carry out the intent of the draftsmen expressed in Comment 9 to UCC § 9–402 to reject "the fanatical and impossibly refined reading" of statutes like that typified by the *Haley* case cited in the Comment. In *Haley* the court held defective a notice describing the debtor, "E. R. Millen Co., Inc.," as "E. R. Millen Company" and signed "E. R. Millen, Trustee." The test worked out was the sensible one of whether it is likely that one searching the records for the debtor's name would have found the financing statement in question.

In a second line of cases the difficulty arose when the secured party identified the debtor by his trade name. In re Leichter, referred to in the principal case, is an example. There the debtor, Leichter, had registered to do business as "Landman Dry Cleaners," and that apparently was the name used in the body of the financing statement. The financing statement was signed:

"Landman Dry Cleaners
by Matthew R. Leichter"

The financing statement was indexed only under the trade name "Landman Dry Cleaners." The court distinguished this case from *Excel Stores* on the ground that a searcher looking for financing statements in Leichter's name would not find the financing statement in question; hence, the error was seriously misleading and not saved by UCC § 9–402(8).

2. In the 1972 amendments to Article 9, subsection (7) was added to UCC § 9–402. The first sentence reads: "A financing statement sufficiently shows the name of the debtor if it gives the individual, partnership or corporate name of the debtor, whether or not it adds other trade names or names of partners." Suppose Elite Boats Company had been in business for fifty years before being sold to Glasco, Inc., whose sole business activity is Elite Boats. Assume that other than complying with the trade name registration statute, Glasco in no way informed the public that it owned Elite Boats. A secured party described the debtor on the financing statement as "Elite Boats Compa-

ny." Comment 7 to UCC § 9–402 indicates that subsection (7) contemplates filing only in the corporation's true name "and not in a trade name." It says: "Trade names are deemed to be too uncertain and too likely not to be known to the secured party or person searching the record, to form the basis for a filing system." Does subsection (7) actually say, as Comment 7 does, that a filing in a trade name is ineffective? See White & Summers, Uniform Commercial Code 959 (2d ed. 1980).

3. Is the dissenting opinion in *Glasco* persuasive? The financing statement contained both the debtor's name "Glasco, Inc." and its trade name "Elite Boats." Doesn't the financing statement comply literally with the first sentence of UCC § 9–402(7)? Does the order of the names make any difference? Is it reasonable to hold that the name "Glasco, Inc., Elite Boats Division" complies but "Elite Boats, Division of Glasco, Inc." does not? The lack of notice to subsequent creditors does not arise because of the name stated in the financing statement but rather by the way the financing statement was indexed. Is the secured party responsible for faulty indexing? UCC § 9–403(1) states: "Presentation for filing of a financing statement and tender of the filing fee or acceptance of the statement by the filing officer constitutes filing under this article." In In re Royal Electrotype Corp., cited in the principal case, the filing officer erred by listing the secured party as the debtor and the debtor as the secured party. The court held that under UCC § 9–403(1) the secured party who submits a correct financing statement does not bear the risk of the filing officer's error. The fact that the secured party was given a receipt at the time of filing showing the error did not change the court's view. In re Flagstaff Foodservice Corp., 16 B.R. 132 (Bkrtcy.N.Y.1981), involved the failure of the filing officer to file a financing statement. The fact that the secured party had not received a copy of a properly stamped financing statement and that its check for the filing fee had not been canceled by the time of the debtor's bankruptcy three years later did not impose a duty of investigation on the secured party. A subsequent creditor who is injured by a filing officer's error may seek recourse against the state, see, e.g., Hudleasco, Inc. v. State, 90 Misc.2d 1057, 396 N.Y.S.2d 1002 (Ct. of Cl. 1977), or the filing officer, see, e.g., Mobile Enterprises, Inc. v. Conrad, 177 Ind.App. 475, 380 N.E.2d 100 (1978), depending on the laws of the relevant state.

IN RE TAYLORVILLE EISNER AGENCY, INC.

United States District Court, S.D. Illinois, 1977.
445 F.Supp. 665.

J. WALDO ACKERMAN, DISTRICT JUDGE. This is an appeal
from an order of the Bankruptcy Judge disallowing a claim of
the First National Bank of Pana (First National Bank) as to proceeds of the sale of inventory and merchandise of a bankrupt
grocery store. It is necessary to consider, in a case of first impression in this State, the construction to be given Section
9–402(7) of the Illinois Uniform Commercial Code.

FACTS

On or about March 14, 1973, Charles E. Hebert and William
D. Cooper (buyers) entered into an agreement with Robert Al-
dridge (seller) to purchase certain fixtures, equipment and inventory of a premises in Taylorville, Illinois, being operated as
"Bob's Eisner Agency." The buyers made application to First
National Bank to borrow the necessary money and thereafter
executed a note to First National Bank dated April 1, 1973. A
security agreement bearing the same date covering fixtures,
equipment, inventory, and after-acquired property was also executed. Both the note and security agreement were signed by
William Cooper and his wife, Gloria, and Charles Hebert and his
wife Carolyn. The First National Bank filed a proper financing
statement with the Secretary of State on April 4, 1973, listing
William Cooper and Charles Hebert as debtors and the address
of the store in Taylorville.

Sometime prior to April 1, 1973, a corporate entity, Taylorville Eisner Agency, Inc., was formed. At 10:00 a.m., on the
same day as the note and security agreement were signed, the
Coopers and Heberts met as a board of directors of Taylorville
Eisner Agency, Inc. At this initial meeting of the corporation
the following officers were chosen: William Cooper, President;
Gloria Cooper, Vice President; Carolyn Hebert, Secretary; and
Charles Hebert, Treasurer. Among the business matters handled at this meeting, it was resolved that the corporation agreed
to assume and pay the indebtedness of William Cooper, Gloria
Cooper, Charles Hebert, and Carolyn Hebert, to the First National Bank in return for a transfer of the fixtures, equipment,
and store inventory.

After April 1, 1973, Taylorville Eisner Agency, Inc., owned and operated the business. All payments made to the First National Bank on the note were by checks drawn on a Taylorville bank from the account of Taylorville Eisner Agency, Inc., and all of the checks were properly credited on the account due the First National from the Coopers and Heberts. There was a continual change of merchandise and inventory held for resale in the store so that on October 1, 1975, the date on which the voluntary petition for bankruptcy was filed on behalf of Taylorville Eisner Agency, Inc., none of the original merchandise and inventory held for resale was the same as that owned on July 1, 1973. The fixtures and equipment of the bankrupt had remained the same following the transfer of ownership from the Coopers and Heberts to the corporation.

The First National Bank filed their proof of claim in bankruptcy as a secured creditor. A claimant, Jewel Companies, Inc., and the trustee in bankruptcy objected to the First National Bank claim insofar as it included merchandise and inventory acquired after four months from the filing of the April 4, 1973, financing statement. Their objection was based on UCC § 9–402(7).

The Bankruptcy Judge held that First National Bank was aware of the change in ownership and change in the name of this business entity; and that under Section 9–402(7) it was necessary for First National Bank to file a new appropriate financing statement before the expiration of four months from the date of the change in ownership. This was due to the finding that the filed financing statement became seriously misleading after the changes in ownership and name of the business entity. Based on these factual findings and his interpretation of the statute, the Bankruptcy Judge allowed First National Bank's secured claim as to the fixtures and equipment acquired within four months of the date on which the financing statement became misleading, but held First National Bank had only a general unsecured claim as to the proceeds of the sale of inventory and merchandise acquired after the four month period.

STATUTE

Article IX of the Illinois Commercial Code is a comprehensive system designed to cover chattel security law. Basically it provides a way in which a secured party and debtor may enter into a security agreement which gives the secured party certain rights in specified collateral. As one means of giving notice of that interest to third parties, the code adopts the concept of notice filing. Notice filing involves the preparation of a financing statement and filing of it as required by the code. When required (UCC § 9–302), proper filing makes the security interest "perfected" (UCC § 9–303) and this may provide the secured party protection under the priorities provision (UCC § 9–312) as against conflicting interests in the same collateral. The portion of this statutory scheme with which we are concerned here is UCC § 9–402 which covers the formal requisites of the initial filing and later amendment of a financing statement. Subsection 7 provides:

> A financing statement sufficiently shows the name of the debtor if it gives the individual, partnership or corporate name of the debtor, whether or not it adds other trade names or names of partners. Where the debtor so changes his name or in the case of an organization its name, identity, or corporate structure that a filed financing statement becomes seriously misleading, the filing is not effective to perfect a security interest in collateral acquired by the debtor more than four months after the change unless a new appropriate financing statement is filed before the expiration of that time. A filed financing statement remains effective with respect to collateral transferred by the debtor even though the secured party knows of or consents to the transfer.

No cases have been found interpreting this provision of the Illinois statute. Subsection 7 was a new provision added to the code effective July 1, 1973. While there is no legislative history for the amendment, it is noted that the Illinois code changes were exactly the same as the 1972 changes in the Uniform Commercial Code as promulgated by the American Law Institute, and National Conference of Commissioner's on Uniform State Laws. Thus, the Official Comments to the UCC may be of some help in interpretation.

ANALYSIS

Since we have a naked statute, unclothed with either legislative intent or judicial construction, the parties have striven mightily to dissect and give meaning to the words and sentences of the crucial subsection. The parties have endeavored to robe the statute according to their individual tastes. Under these circumstances it is necessary for me to lend a judicial imprimatur to one of the suggested interpretations.

The first question is what problem or problems did the legislature intend to address in UCC § 9–402(7) and the effect on the present facts. The subsection deals with several different problems. The first sentence speaks to the sufficiency of the debtor's name which must appear on a financing statement under UCC § 9–402(1). Since the statement is indexed according to the name of the debtor (UCC § 9–403(4)), it is essential that the proper debtor's name appear on the financing statement else one searching the index will be unable to detect the security interest. In this case there was no objection to the sufficiency of the financing statement as originally filed on April 4, 1973.

The second sentence appears to be related to the first in that they both are intended to insure indexing according to the current name of the debtor. While the first sentence deals with how the debtor is to be identified at the time of the original filing, the second sentence deals with the situation where there is a subsequent change: in the case of an individual, where there is a change of name, or in the case of an organization, where there is a change in its name, identity, or corporate structure. Where such a change occurs the secured party must determine whether the filed financing statement has become seriously misleading. If so, the filing is not effective to perfect a security interest in collateral acquired by the debtor more than four months after the change unless a new appropriate financing statement is filed before the expiration of that time. There is no knowledge requirement included in the sentence. That means that from the time a change occurs which makes the financing statement misleading there must be a refiling within four months. The burden of realizing a change has occurred, checking the effect the change has on the financing statement, and filing a new financing statement within four months if necessary, is upon the secured party.[1]

The third and final sentence of the subsection deals with a different problem, namely where the debtor transfers the secured collateral and what effect this has on the secured parties' interest. Prior to this provision it was debated as to whether the security interest would continue in the collateral even after it entered the possession of the transferee, whether any after-acquired property of the transferee could be included under the

1. It is possible, by reviewing filing required under Illinois law, to be advised of changes of names of individuals, Ill.Rev.Stat. ch. 96; partnerships, Ill.Rev.Stat. ch. 96 (as to whether a partnership exists see Ill.Rev. Stat. ch. 106½ §§ 6–7); and corporations, Ill.Rev.Stat. ch. 32 §§ 157.9, 157.10, 157.47, 157.52, 157.55, and 157.55a and 157.56.

original debtor's security interest, and whether a new filing was necessary. This question arose frequently because under UCC § 9–311 the secured party cannot prevent the debtor from transferring rights in collateral. The final sentence of this amendment to UCC § 9–402(7) settles the question by saying that no new financing statement must be filed.

As the Official Comments to the Uniform Commercial Code indicate:

> Any person searching the condition of the ownership of a debtor must make inquiry as to the debtor's source of title and must search in the name of a former owner if circumstances seem to require it.

The comments to the Illinois code which appear in Smith Hurd Illinois Statutes Annotated say in part:

> The proper interpretation (of the third sentence) it is believed, therefore limits the "transfer" in question to one by a debtor—e.g., an individual or a partnership—to a successor enterprise—e.g., a corporation whose stock is owned by the individual or the partners of the debtor transferor.

The secured party in this case, First National Bank, has taken the position that the individual debtors transferred the equipment and inventory subject to the security interest to the corporation. First National Bank contends that this transfer situation is governed by the third sentence and there was no need for a refiling regardless of whether they knew or consented to the transfer. It is the bank's position that the second sentence has no application to situations governed by the third sentence.

The claimant and trustee in bankruptcy argue, and the Bankruptcy Judge agrees, that while the final sentence may protect the secured party in a transfer situation as to collateral already transferred by the debtor, that the provisions of the second sentence may still apply to after-acquired property. Their interpretation would require the following actions on the part of a secured party: find out that the collateral has been transferred by the debtor, determine whether the possession of the collateral by the transferee has made the filed financing statement seriously misleading and if so file a new financing statement with the name of the transferee within four months after the transfer. Failure to do so would result in a loss of the perfected security interest in collateral acquired by the transferee after the four month period.

This attempt to reconcile the second and third sentences does not appear to me to be a correct interpretation. In practically all cases of transfer of secured collateral the transferee would have a different name, identity, or corporate organization. That would mean the secured party would have to refile in practically all instances within four months or lose all of its interest in after-acquired property. "Collateral" as used in the final sentence is not limited as it is in the second sentence where it is defined as that collateral acquired by the debtor more than four months after the change. Rather, the final sentence speaks of collateral transferred by the debtor, which must mean the property subject to the security interest as defined in UCC § 9–105(1)(c). In this case the security interest covered existing fixtures and equipment as well as acquired inventory and merchandise.

This opinion also appears to be consistent with the code's goal of promoting commercial reasonableness (UCC § 1–102). The secured party apparently has the duty under the second sentence of subsection 7 to monitor the identity of the debtor. A secured party must take steps to insure that it will become aware of any name, identity, or corporate changes of its debtors within four months or risk losing their perfected security interest in collateral acquired after that time should the financing statement be found seriously misleading at the time of the change.

The third sentence transfer situation is somewhat different. In the present case the transferee corporation clearly knew from the note and security agreement of the transferor debtor that the collateral, including after-acquired inventory and merchandise, was subject to a perfected security interest. The third sentence of subsection 7 is clear that the filed statement remains effective with respect to collateral transferred by the debtor regardless of the knowledge or consent of the secured party. This also means collateral which is after-acquired property. Prospective creditors of the transferee have a duty to inquire as to the source of title if circumstances dictate. For a discussion of this rule and some of the mitigating factors against its apparent harshness, see Coogan, The New UCC Article 9, 86 Harv.L.Rev. 477, 526–27 (1973).

In the instant case had any creditors checked the corporation's source of title they could have easily discovered the assumption of the notes which were in the individuals' names and by running a check on those names found the filed financing statements. This information appears to be more easily accessible to prospective creditors of the transferee than the secured party of the transferor debtor. The transferee or prospective creditor could expect to receive only what the transferor debtor had, that is, the right to the equipment, fixtures, inventory and future inventory subject to the security interest of the secured party.

It is thus my opinion that First National Bank did not have to file a new financing statement within four months after the transfer in order to retain its perfected security interest in after-acquired property. The decision of the Bankruptcy Judge is reversed.

NOTES

1. The collateral in *Taylorville* involved equipment and inventory owned by the corporation at the time of bankruptcy. Consider how each type of collateral is treated by UCC § 9–402(7) in light of the transaction between Hebert and Cooper and the corporation.

All of the equipment was owned by Hebert and Cooper when the security agreement with the bank was signed. When the equipment was subsequently transferred by Hebert and Cooper to the corporation what happened to the bank's security interest? UCC § 9–306(2) states that the security interest "continues in collateral notwithstanding sale, exchange or other disposition thereof unless the disposition was authorized by the secured party in the security agreement or otherwise." Thus, if the transfer to the corporation was not authorized by the bank, the bank can continue to claim the collateral. By the last sentence of § 9–402(7) the financing statement filed by the bank is effective to maintain perfection of the security interest notwithstanding the transfer. This means that the bank need not police the debtor to make sure that the collateral has not been disposed of. What is the policy basis for this rule? But the bank is protected even in cases in which it knows that the collateral has been disposed of. What is the policy basis for this rule? § 9–402(7) also covers the case in which the bank consents to the transfer. If the bank consents to the transfer hasn't it "authorized" the disposition and thus lost the security interest under UCC § 9–306(2)? Is there a distinction between cases in which the secured party consents to a transfer of the collateral that purports to be unrestricted and a transfer such as that in *Taylorville* in which the transferee specifically takes the collateral subject to the security interest? Does the second sentence of UCC

§ 9–402(7) have any relevance to the transfer of the equipment in *Taylorville*?

None of the inventory owned by the corporation on the date of bankruptcy was in existence when the corporation assumed the loan of Hebert and Cooper. Did the bank have a security interest in this inventory? Did the assumption of the loan by the corporation mean also that the corporation agreed to give to the bank a security interest in inventory that it might thereafter acquire? If it did was the requirement in UCC § 9–203(1)(a) that "the debtor has signed a security agreement" satisfied? "Debtor" is defined in UCC § 9–105(1)(d). If the bank can clear the hurdle of § 9–203(1)(a) is the security interest in inventory perfected? Does the last sentence of UCC § 9–402(7) apply? Does the second sentence apply? See Burke, Uniform Commercial Code Annual Survey: Secured Transactions, 34 Bus.Law. 1547, 1574–1576 (1979); Burke, The Duty to Refile Under Section 9–402(7) of the Revised Article 9, 35 Bus.Law. 1083 (1980).

2. The analysis of the court in *Taylorville* regarding after-acquired inventory should be compared to that of In re Centennial Industries, Inc., 3 B.R. 416 (Bkrtcy.N.Y.1980). Maremont had a security interest in inventory of Jabro, Inc. which it perfected in 1973 by a financing statement identifying Jabro, Inc. as the debtor. The next year Jabro, Inc. was merged into Centennial. By virtue of the merger Jabro ceased to exist and Centennial succeeded to all its assets and liabilities. Centennial continued Jabro's operations under the name Jabro as a division of Centennial. In 1978 Maremont filed a continuation statement (see UCC § 9–403(3)) naming Jabro, Inc. as debtor. A month later Centennial went into bankruptcy. The court held that Maremont's security interest was invalid in bankruptcy because unperfected. After the merger the debtor was Centennial and Jabro was simply a trade name. Thus, a financing statement naming Jabro as the debtor was seriously misleading. A creditor of Centennial searching the records under that name would not find the Jabro financing statement. Maremont had a duty either to name Centennial as the debtor or to utilize the available cross-indexing procedure so that a search under the name Centennial would reveal the Jabro filing. All of the inventory held by Centennial at the time of bankruptcy was acquired after the four-month period provided for by § 9–403(7). Would the result have been the same if the collateral had been equipment in existence at the time of Maremont's original filing in 1973?

3. The discussion in Note 1 treats the original transaction in *Taylorville* as one between the bank and the two individuals who subsequently transferred the collateral to a third party, a corporation controlled by the individuals. But the transaction can be analyzed in a different way. The corporation was already in existence on April 1, the date on which the security agreement and note were apparently executed. The corporation formally assumed the loan immediately following the transaction between the individuals and the bank. This strongly suggests that the individuals when they acquired the collateral and when they made the transaction with the bank were not acting for themselves but rather for the corporation which was formed for the purpose of carrying out the underlying business enterprise. Thus, the individuals were agents acting for an undisclosed principal, the corporation, if it is assumed that at the time of the loan transaction the bank did not know about the corporation. § 9–402(7) does not deal with the problem of undisclosed principals. Suppose SP and A sign a security agreement under which SP loans money to A and is granted a security interest in collateral of which SP believed A to be the owner. In fact A was acting for an undisclosed principal, P, who owned the collateral and who authorized A to make the transaction for P's benefit. Under agency law both A and P are bound under the security agreement. If SP filed a financing statement naming A as the debtor, did SP get a perfected security interest? "Debtor" is defined in UCC § 9–105(1)(d). Another aspect of this problem is dealt with in Note 2, infra p. 64. Suppose SP found out shortly after it filed the financing statement that the real party in interest was P. Would SP be required to file an amended financing statement identifying P as debtor? Is *Taylorville* like this case?

PROBLEM

The secured party, Kalamazoo Steel Process, Inc., sold equipment to the debtor, Roman Industrial Corporation, and was granted a security interest in the equipment by the debtor. The security agreement stated "it is anticipated that the debtor will change its name to that of the secured party and it is further anticipated that the secured party will change its name to H.C.H. Corp." The financing statement listed the debtor as Roman Industrial Corporation. About one year later Roman Industrial Corporation changed its name to Kalamazoo Steel Process, Inc. The secured party had some months before changed its name to H.O.U. Corporation. Three years after the debtor changed its name the debtor defaulted and the secured party seized the equipment. Shortly thereafter the debtor went into bankruptcy. The validity of the security interest of the secured party in bankruptcy depended upon whether it was perfected. Was it? See In re Kalamazoo Steel Process, Inc., 503 F.2d 1218 (6th Cir. 1974).

2. PLACE OF FILING

Before the Code chattel mortgages and conditional sales contracts were, like real estate mortgages, filed locally. Central filing on a state-wide basis was used only for trust receipts in those states having the Uniform Trust Receipts Act and for accounts receivable and factor's liens in some states. Article 9 was a major breakthrough in the movement toward state-wide central filing, but disagreement on how far to go with central filing produced three alternatives to UCC § 9–401(1).

The first alternative requires central filing in all cases except transactions involving timber, minerals, and fixtures.[1] Even security interests in crops are filed centrally.

The second alternative requires central filing in all cases except transactions involving timber, minerals, and fixtures (subsection (1)(b)) as well as consumer goods and agricultural collateral (crops, farm accounts, farm equipment, and farm products) (subsection (1)(a)).[2]

The third alternative provides that for those transactions that would be filed centrally under the second alternative there must be an additional local filing in the county where the debtor has an office or, if he has none, where he resides.[3]

---

1. This alternative was adopted by Connecticut, Delaware, Georgia, Iowa, Maine, Oregon, Utah, and Washington. 3A Uniform Laws Annotated, Uniform Commercial Code 14, 20 (1981).

2. This alternative was adopted by Alabama, Alaska, Arizona, California, Colorado, Florida, Idaho, Illinois, Indiana, Kansas, Michigan, Minnesota, Montana, New Hampshire, New Jersey, New Mexico, North Dakota, Oklahoma, Rhode Island, South Caro-

lina, South Dakota, Tennessee, Texas, and Wisconsin. 3A Uniform Laws Annotated, Uniform Commercial Code 14, 20 (1981) and 3 (1982 Supp.)

3. This alternative was adopted by Arkansas, Kentucky, Maryland, Massachusetts, Mississippi, Missouri, Nevada, New York, North Carolina, Ohio, Pennsylvania, Vermont, Virginia, West Virginia, and Wyoming. 3A Uniform Laws Annotated, Uniform Commercial Code 14, 20 (1981).

SEQUOIA MACHINERY, INC. v. JARRETT

United States Court of Appeals, Ninth Circuit, 1969.
410 F.2d 1116.

DUNIWAY, CIRCUIT JUDGE. This bankruptcy case involves the interpretation of § 9401(1) of the California Uniform Commercial Code.[9] Appellants sold combines to James C. Clark by conditional sales contracts which were filed in the office of the California Secretary of State, but not in the office of the County Recorder. The combines are specialized equipment usable only for harvesting grain. Clark was not a farmer. He owned no land. Instead, he was a "custom harvester" who used the combines in harvesting the crops of various farmers in Tulare and King Counties on a contract basis.

After Clark filed a voluntary petition in bankruptcy, appellants repossessed and sold the combines for $30,200, which has been stipulated to be their present fair value. Appellee trustee in bankruptcy then petitioned for an order that the moneys received from the sale be turned over to him. The referee held that the harvesting combines were "equipment used in farming operations," and that the trustee was therefore entitled to the moneys, because the appellants' failure to record their security interests in the office of the County Recorder rendered them invalid as against the trustee. The District Court affirmed. So do we.

Appellants contend that the phrase "equipment used in farming operations" should be interpreted in light of the occupational status or contractual arrangements of the debtor-purchaser, rather than as referring to the actual intended use of the equipment itself. They claim that the grain harvesting combines, even though only usable for harvesting grain, were not "equipment used in farming operations" in *this* case, because Clark was not a farmer.[10]

9. "The proper place to file in order to perfect a security interest is as follows:

(a) When the collateral is equipment used in farming operations, or farm products other than crops, or accounts or contract rights arising from or relating to the sale of farm products by a farmer, or consumer goods, then in the office of the county recorder in the county of the debtor's residence * * *.

(b) [crops or timber] * * *.

(c) In all other cases, in the office of the Secretary of State."

10. According to appellee, of the 49 states which have adopted the Uniform Commercial Code, 39 have adopted filing requirements under which this question could arise. However, this is evidently a case of first impression.

Appellants' argument is based on the language of various provisions of the Code. They point out that § 9109 classifies goods as "equipment" if, *inter alia*, they are not included in the definition of "farm products," and defines "farm products" as including supplies only "if they are in the possession of a debtor engaged in raising, fattening, grazing, or other farming operations." Appellants conclude that the term "farming operations" is therefore to be restricted to activities in the nature of "raising, fattening, or grazing," under the maxim "expressio unius est exclusio alterius" and the concept "ejusdem generis." Appellants also argue that Clark's operations were not "essentially local," since he worked in two different counties, and point out that, according to a Uniform Commercial Code comment,

> "It is thought that sound policy requires a state-wide filing system for all transactions except the essentially local ones covered in subsection (1)(a) * * *." [11]

They point out that another Code section indicates that the drafters of the Code did not regard commercial harvesting equipment as of an "essentially local" type.[12] Consequently, they conclude that the Clark financing statements were properly filed in the office of the Secretary of State.

We are not persuaded. If the drafters of the Code had intended such a result, they could merely have written § 9401(1) to refer to "equipment of a farmer used in his farming operations." We doubt that they expected anyone to divine such a result from the references to which appellants refer. And even if the overall rationale for the local filing of financing statements covering equipment used in farming operations is that such transactions are "essentially local," it would be unworkable to tell secured sellers to file all financing statements centrally unless the transaction is "essentially local." How does one determine what is or is not "essentially local"?

We think that the drafters of the Code carefully avoided defining "equipment used in farm operations" in terms of the occupational status or contractual arrangements of the debtor-use. In many cases it would be difficult to determine whether or not the debtor was a "farmer." One who owns or leases agricultural land, who raises crops thereon, and who purchases harvesting

11. 23 West's Ann.Cal.Codes, p. 547 (comment to Cal.Comm.C. § 9401).

12. West's Calif.Com.Code, § 9103, which deals with conflict of law rules, speaks of "goods of a type which are normally used in more than one jurisdiction (such as automotive equipment, rolling stock, airplanes, road building equipment, commercial harvesting equipment, construction machinery and the like)."

equipment solely for his own use on his own land, would clearly be a farmer within appellants' construction. But what of a person who owns or leases agricultural land, and farms it, but purchases harvesting equipment with the intention of using it on his own land some of the time, and using it at other times to harvest the crops of his neighbors on a contract basis? Under appellants' rationale he would be using the equipment *as a farmer* only when he was using it on his own land. In such a situation, would the equipment dealer have to determine what its "primary" intended use would be? Or would the intended use on a particular day or hour control? According to § 9401(3), a filing made in the proper place continues effective even though the use of the collateral should later change. But the Code does not say at what point one determines what the use is. Should it be when the security interest attaches, when the financing statement is filed, or when? Cf. In re Pelletier, D.Maine, 1968, 5 U.C.C.Rep. 327, 330.

The phrase "equipment used in farming operations" is clear and unambiguous. That was the only use to which this equipment could be or was put. We decline to resort to a construction that would raise more problems than it would solve.

Finally, the California Equipment Dealers Association as amicus curiae suggests that § 9401(1) is ambiguous, and that we should therefore hold that any good faith attempt by a conditional seller to file a financing statement in the proper place should be sufficient to protect the security interest against a trustee in bankruptcy. But the Code does not allow this result. Section 9401(2) provides:

> "A filing which is made in good faith in an improper place * * * is nevertheless effective * * * against any person who has knowledge of the contents of such financing statement."

Section 9301(1) provides, *inter alia*, that

> " * * * [A]n unperfected security interest is subordinate to the rights of * * * (b) A person who becomes a lien creditor * * *."

Under section 70c of the Bankruptcy Act, 11 U.S.C.A. § 110(c), the trustee in bankruptcy has the status of an ideal hypothetical lien creditor, similar to a creditor without notice—even if the trustee has actual notice. Collier, Bankruptcy, 14th ed., § 70.53. And even apart from the Bankruptcy Act provision, the secured party would, under § 9401(2), have to prove that either the trustee in bankruptcy or perhaps all the unsecured creditors had actual knowledge of the contents of the financing statement. See In re Lux's Superette, Inc., E.D.Pa., 1962, 206 F.Supp. 368, 371; In re Smith, E.D.Pa., 1962, 205 F.Supp. 27; In re Luckenbill, E.D.Pa., 1957, 156 F.Supp. 129. Appellants have not done so.

Affirmed.

NOTES

1. The Code's theory of place of filing is expounded in Comment 4 to UCC § 9–401:

> It is thought that sound policy requires a state-wide filing system for all transactions except the essentially local ones covered in paragraph (1)(a) of the Second and Third Alternatives and land-related transactions covered in paragraph (1)(b) of the Second and Third Alternatives. Paragraph (1)(c) so provides in both alternatives, as does paragraph (1)(b) in the First Alternative. In a state which has adopted either the Second or Third Alternative, central filing would be required when the collateral was goods except consumer goods, farm equipment or farm products (including crops), or was documents or chattel paper or was accounts or general intangibles, unless related to a farm. Note that the filing provisions of this Article do not apply to instruments (see Section 9–304).

Thus in those states adopting the Second Alternative, one inquiring about filings with respect to a business debtor looks to a central filing system while one inquiring about filings with respect to a consumer or a farmer looks to a local filing system. Is *Sequoia* consistent with the Code's place-of-filing policies as enunciated in Comment 4 quoted above? In In re Butler, 3 B.R. 182 (Bkrtcy.Tenn.1980), a "John Deere Dozer" used by Debtor for excavating purposes was not "equipment used in farming operations" even though half of Debtor's customers were farmers. The court said in criticism of *Sequoia*: "Local filing was intended for a farm operation in one locality. Central filing is more desirable for a commercial harvesting operation. It is not essentially local in nature. The operation is mobile and goes from one jurisdiction to another. A national filing system should require central filing for a commercial harvesting operation. That is where a creditor would look for information on a debtor who operates equipment in various jurisdictions." 3 B.R. at 185. How does a secured creditor avoid difficulties in applying the Code's place of filing rules?

2.   A good filing system should provide a reliable, cheap, and fast system that allows: (1) secured creditors to enter information required to perfect, amend, assign, continue, or terminate their security interests, and (2) searchers to learn of the potential existence of security interests affecting a debtor's property. An elementary model, given the present state of the art, might be a central electronic on-line data bank in each state with connecting terminals in local filing places throughout the state where input of information by secured parties and retrieval of information by searchers may be instantaneous.   Such a system would combine the convenience of local access with the reliability of central filing and, in doing so, would render the distinctions made between local and central filing in UCC § 9–402(1) irrelevant.

It is astonishing how far we are from this simple model today.   As best we can tell most states have an entirely manual UCC filing system.   Texas is the only state we know about that has an on-line computerized system.   A look at California's filing system is instructive.   That state has maintained a computerized central filing system since the Code became effective in 1965, but the system is not on-line and there is no local access in any form.   Currently there is a seven-day backlog in processing requests.   The Secretary of State requires a written request before instituting a record search; no telephone calls or verbal requests are honored.   Hence, the chain of events in the typical record search would resemble the following: (1) A written request for a record search is sent to Sacramento by mail.   (2) Two to three days later the request arrives at the filing office. (3) About seven business days later the filing officer issues his certificate regarding the search, encloses copies of any requested financing or other statements, and mails the material to the searcher.   (4) Two to three days later the material arrives by mail at the searcher's address.   Two weeks have probably gone by from initiation to conclusion of the record search.   For many years the technology has been available to reduce this two-week period to a very short time.   The costs of maintaining our present archaic filing systems seem high in terms of delay and inflexibility.

PROBLEMS

1.   Debtor granted a security interest in business equipment to First Bank which erroneously filed a financing statement locally.   The filing should have been made centrally.   Later Debt-

or granted a security interest in the same collateral to Second Bank which properly filed a financing statement centrally. At the time it filed, Second Bank knew about First Bank's filing. Who has priority to the collateral? See UCC § 9–312(5) and § 9–401(2). What is the policy basis for this result? Suppose First Bank had made no filing but Second Bank knew about the security interest of First Bank. Who has priority? See UCC § 9–301(1)(a) and § 9–312(5) which state priority rules that do not depend upon knowledge. What is the policy basis for this result?

2. Debtor granted a security interest in business equipment to First Bank which neglected to file a financing statement. Debtor then granted a security interest in the same collateral to Second Bank which erroneously filed a financing statement locally. The filing should have been made centrally. Then First Bank and Second Bank each found out about the transaction of the other and the filing by Second Bank. First Bank then filed centrally before Second Bank filed centrally. Who has priority? See UCC § 9–401(2). According to First National Bank and Trust v. First National Bank, 582 F.2d 524, 526–527 (10th Cir. 1978), First Bank should have priority. Is there any basis for distinguishing this case from Problem 1?

NOTE: SOME MECHANICS OF FILING

In order to perfect a security interest by filing the secured party must send the requisite number of copies of the financing statement to the filing officer with the filing fee. Commonly either Form UCC–1 (central filing) or Form UCC–2 (local filing) is utilized. The filing officer must give each statement a file number, mark it with the date and hour of filing, and index the form in the name of the debtor. UCC § 9–403(4). The filing officer then returns a copy of the financing statement to the secured party as an acknowledgement of receipt. If the secured party employs a nonuniform form, as he would if he files the security agreement, the filing officer is authorized by UCC § 9–403(5) to charge a higher fee.

The secured party may amend the financing statement pursuant to UCC § 9–402(4) by use of Form UCC–3. Both debtor and secured party must sign the amending form "to preclude either from adversely affecting the interests of the other." Comment 4 to UCC § 9–402. The secured party may also release all or part of the collateral covered by a filed financing statement under UCC § 9–406 by use of Form UCC–3.

STATE OF ILLINOIS

UNIFORM COMMERCIAL CODE — FINANCING STATEMENT — FORM UCC-1

INSTRUCTIONS:
1. PLEASE TYPE this form. Fold only along perforation for mailing.
2. Remove Secured Party and Debtor copies and send other 3 copies with interleaved carbon paper to the filing officer. Enclose filing fee.
3. If the space provided for any item(s) on the form is inadequate the item(s) should be continued on additional sheets, preferably 5'' x 8'' or 8'' x 10''. Only one copy of such additional sheets need be presented to the filing officer with a set of three copies of the financing statement. Long schedules of collateral, indentures, etc., may be on any size paper that is convenient for the secured party.

This STATEMENT is presented to a filing officer for filing pursuant to the Uniform Commercial Code.

Debtor(s) (Last Name First) and address(es)	Secured Party(ies) and address(es)	For Filing Officer (Date, Time, Number, and Filing Office)

1. This financing statement covers the following types (or items) of property:

ASSIGNEE OF SECURED PARTY

2. ☐ Products of Collateral are also covered.

_____ Additional sheets presented.
_____ Filed with Office of Secretary of State of Illinois.
_____ Debtor is a transmitting utility as defined in UCC §9-105.

By: _____
Signature of (Debtor)
(Secured Party)*

*Signature of Debtor Required in Most Cases.
Signature of Secured Party in Cases Covered By UCC §9-402 (2)

(1) Filing Officer Copy - Alphabetical   This form of financing statement is approved by the Secretary of State.

STANDARD FORM — UNIFORM COMMERCIAL CODE — FORM UCC-1 — REV. 2-74

[B1132]

---

* 5 Uniform Laws Annotated, Uniform Commercial Code Forms and Materials, Form 9:3200 (1982 Supp.). Reproduced by permission of the West Publishing Company.

UCC § 9–302(2) provides: "If a secured party assigns a perfected security interest, no filing under this Article is required in order to continue the perfected status of the security interest against creditors of and transferees from the original debtor." Hence, the filing of a statement of assignment (Form UCC–3) is permissive in terms of continuing the perfected security interest of the assignee against claimants from the debtor but is required before the assignee can become the secured party of record and entitled to file continuation, termination, or release statements. Comment to UCC § 9–405.

UCC § 9–403(2) provides that a filed financing statement is effective for five years. It lapses at the end of five years unless under UCC § 9–403(3) a continuation statement (Form UCC–3) is filed by the secured party within six months prior to the expiration of the five-year period. The 1972 amendment to UCC

STATE OF ILLINOIS

UNIFORM COMMERCIAL CODE — FINANCING STATEMENT — FORM UCC-2

INSTRUCTIONS:
1. PLEASE TYPE this form. Fold only along perforation for mailing.
2. Remove Secured Party and Debtor copies and send other 3 copies with interleaved carbon paper to the filing officer. Enclose filing fee.
3. If the space provided for any item(s) on the form is inadequate the item(s) should be continued on additional sheets, preferably 5'' x 8'' or 8'' x 10''. Only one copy of such additional sheets need be presented to the filing officer with a set of three copies of the financing statement. Long schedules of collateral, indentures, etc., may be on any size paper that is convenient for the secured party.

This STATEMENT is presented to a filing officer for filing pursuant to the Uniform Commercial Code.		For Filing Officer (Date, Time, Number, and Filing Office)
Debtor(s) (Last Name First) and address(es)	Secured Party(ies) and address(es)	

1. This financing statement covers the following types (or items) of property:

    ASSIGNEE OF SECURED PARTY

2. (If collateral is crops) The above described crops are growing or are to be grown on: (Describe Real Estate)

3. (If applicable) The above goods are to become fixtures on (The above timber is standing on...) (The above minerals or the like (including oil and gas) or accounts will be financed at the wellhead or minehead of the well or mine located on...) (Strike what is inapplicable) (Describe Real Estate)

and this financing statement is to be filed in the real estate records. (If the debtor does not have an interest of record) The name of a record owner is

4. ☐ Products of Collateral are also covered.

_____ Additional sheets presented.

_____ Filed with Recorder's Office of _____ County, Illinois.

By _____
    Signature of (Debtor)
                (Secured Party)*

*Signature of Debtor Required in Most Cases
Signature of Secured Party in Cases Covered By UCC §9-402 (2)

(1) Filing Officer Copy - Alphabetical   This form of financing statement is approved by the Secretary of State.

STANDARD FORM — UNIFORM COMMERCIAL CODE — FORM UCC-2 — REV. 4-73   [B1137]

* 5 Uniform Laws Annotated, Uniform Commercial Code Forms and Materials, Form 9:3201 (1982 Supp.). Reproduced by permission of the West Publishing Company.

§ 9–403(2) cleared up the effect of lapse on junior secured parties and lien creditors of the debtor who acquired their interests before the lapse. This subsection now provides: "If the security interest becomes unperfected upon lapse, it is deemed to have been unperfected as against a person who became a purchaser or lien creditor before lapse." Hence, the junior interests are given priority over the lapsed security interests.

Since the effectiveness of a financing statement ends automatically after five years unless a continuation statement is filed, UCC § 9–404(1) provides that, except in the case of consumer goods, the secured party has no duty to send the debtor a termination statement (Form UCC–3) after the debt is paid unless the debtor demands one. The debtor may do so if there is no further outstanding debt and no commitment on the part of the secured party to make advances or incur obligations. The debtor bears the burden of filing the termination statement.

STATE OF ILLINOIS
UNIFORM COMMERCIAL CODE
STATEMENTS OF CONTINUATION, PARTIAL RELEASE, ASSIGNMENT, ETC. — FORM UCC-3

INSTRUCTIONS:
1. PLEASE TYPE this form. Fold only along perforation for mailing.
2. Remove Secured Party and Debtor copies and send other 3 copies with interleaved carbon paper to the filing officer.
3. Enclose filing fee.
4. If the space provided for any item(s) on the form is inadequate the item(s) should be continued on additional sheets, preferably 5″ x 8″ or 8″ x 10″. Only one copy of such additional sheets need be presented to the filing officer with a set of three copies of Form UCC-3. Long schedules of collateral, etc., may be on any size paper that is convenient for the secured party.
5. At the time of filing, filing officer will return third copy as an acknowledgement.

This STATEMENT is presented to THE FILING OFFICER for filing pursuant to the Uniform Commercial Code:

Debtor(s) (Last Name First) and address(es)	Secured Party(ies) and address(es)	For Filing Officer (Date, Time, Number, and Filing Office)

This Statement refers to original Financing Statement No. _____
Date filed: _____, 19_____ Filed with _____

A. ☐ CONTINUATION..... The original financing statement between the foregoing Debtor and Secured Party, bearing the file number shown above, is still effective.
B. ☐ PARTIAL RELEASE.. From the collateral described in the financing statement bearing the file number shown above, the Secured Party releases the property indicated below.
C. ☐ ASSIGNMENT......... The Secured Party certifies that the Secured Party has assigned to the Assignee whose name and address is shown below, Secured Party's rights under the financing statement bearing the file number shown above in the property indicated below.
D. ☐ TERMINATION....... The Secured Party certifies that the Secured Party no longer claims a security interest under the financing statement bearing the file number shown above.
E. ☐ AMENDMENT......... The financing statement bearing the above file number is amended.
  ☐ To show the Secured Party's new address as indicated below;
  ☐ To show the Debtor's new address as indicated below;
  ☐ As set forth below:

_____ (Debtor)   _____ (Secured Party)
(Signature of Debtor, if required)
Dated: _____, 19_____   By: _____
(Signature of Secured Party)

(1) Filing Officer Copy - Alphabetical   This form of Financing Statement is approved by the Secretary of State.
STANDARD FORM — UNIFORM COMMERCIAL CODE — FORM UCC-3 REV. 4-73   [B1142]

* 5 Uniform Laws Annotated, Uniform Commercial Code Forms and Materials, Form 9:3202 (1982 Supp.). Reproduced by permission of the West Publishing Company.

However in cases concerning consumer goods the secured party must himself file a termination statement either within a month after the debt is paid or within ten days after a written demand by the debtor.

D. RIGHTS IN THE COLLATERAL

In providing that a security interest does not attach unless the debtor has "rights in the collateral," UCC § 9–203(1)(c) may be stating only the obvious. The phrase is not defined, and it is doubtful if any precise definition is possible. An owner of goods can create a security interest in the goods; a thief in possession cannot. Clearly the debtor must have some relationship to the collateral that empowers him to create a valid security interest, but the rights-in-collateral rubric of UCC § 9–203(1)(c) tells us nothing about the quantum of that relationship. We must look elsewhere for an answer.

Maxims like "no one can give what he has not" or "a creditor takes no greater rights than his debtor has" have been with us for a long time, and yet the books are full of cases in which transferors are found to have the power to pass on greater rights to their transferees than they had. Courts may find this power in the law of agency, fraud, estoppel, and other traditional bodies of law that UCC § 1–103 explicitly, if somewhat gratuitously, states shall be used to supplement the UCC. They may also find that the transferor is given this power by specific Code provisions, e.g., UCC § 2–403. One bit of guidance we find in the Code is that under UCC § 1–201(32) and (33) a secured party enjoys the status of a "purchaser"; hence, provisions like UCC § 2–403 that grant purchasers greater rights than their transferors apply to benefit secured parties.

The rights-in-collateral issue is significantly involved in the priority matters treated in the next chapter, and we will have more to say about it in that context. For now we briefly introduce you to the subject through the following case that presents a common fact situation. As you read this case and the cases in point in the next chapter, ask yourself whether the courts would have reached any different results in these cases had Article 9 said nothing at all about rights in collateral.

SWETS MOTOR SALES, INC. v. PRUISNER

Supreme Court of Iowa, 1975.
236 N.W.2d 299.

REES, JUSTICE. Plaintiff Swets Motor Sales, Inc., appeals from an order of trial court sustaining motion for summary judgment of defendant Chrysler Credit Corporation and therein adjudicating the latter's interest in certain automobiles to be superior to the interest of plaintiff. We affirm in part, reverse in part, and remand for appropriate proceedings in conformity with this opinion.

Plaintiff Swets Motor Sales, Inc., (hereinafter Swets), an Illinois automobile "wholesaler," sold used cars and trucks to defendant Pruisner, a retail automobile dealer at Waverly. Pursuant to an oral arrangement, plaintiff delivered vehicles to defendant Pruisner with unencumbered certificates of title and was paid by Pruisner at the time of delivery of the cars. Chrysler Credit Corporation, joined as a defendant in this action, financed defendant Pruisner's inventory under a floor planning arrangement which the parties have stipulated was a valid security agreement with filed financing statements covering new and used vehicles in Pruisner's possession.

From July 1973 until the end of September of the same year, Swets sold to Pruisner approximately 60 vehicles which were resold by Pruisner under the foregoing arrangement. In September 1973 four of Pruisner's checks written to plaintiff Swets, totalling approximately $31,000, were dishonored. Swets filed his petition at law and obtained a writ of attachment for the seizure of the vehicles then in Pruisner's possession, then amended his petition to an action sounding in equity, seeking a declaration that his interest in the automobiles was superior to that of Chrysler Credit Corporation. Chrysler Credit answered and counterclaimed against Swets, asserting therein that its interest in the vehicles was superior to that of plaintiff. It was stipulated that at the time of the issuance of the writ of attachment Chrysler Credit had in its possession the unencumbered titles to the vehicles in question.

Trial of the action commenced January 18, 1974, and on January 21, apparently after a substantial portion of the evidence had been presented, defendant Chrysler Credit moved for a summary judgment on the issue of priority of its security interest. Swets thereafter filed a resistance to such motion, alleging the existence of genuine issues of material fact regarding the possibility that, through fraud or mutual mistake, Swets' contract with Pruisner might be determined to be void. Swets also alleged the existence of genuine issues of material fact with respect to the proper valuation of the vehicles in question and Chrysler Credit's failure to minimize or mitigate damages.

On January 24 trial court sustained Chrysler Credit's motion for summary judgment and made various findings of fact and reached conclusions of law. In its findings of fact pertinent to this appeal was the trial court's determination the value of the attached vehicles was $9,300 at the date of the attachment and $5,100 on the date of the hearing. Trial court concluded as a matter of law that defendant Chrysler Credit Corporation had a right to assume defendant Pruisner's ownership of the vehicles in question from the latter's possession of unencumbered certificates of title. Trial court also concluded UCC § 2–403 precluded Swets from prevailing.

Accordingly, trial court decreed Chrysler Credit was entitled to possession of the vehicles under attachment and held valid title to them [with the exception of a certain Ford Torino automobile with which we are not concerned]. Trial court further found and adjudged the difference between the sum of $9,300 [which the court had determined to be the value of the vehicles at the time of attachment] and the subsequent sales price of the vehicles should be assessed against plaintiff Swets and paid out of its attachment bond.

* * *

It was stipulated by the parties to this action that defendant Chrysler Credit Corporation had a valid outstanding security agreement with defendant Pruisner covering new and used vehicles in the latter's possession at all times pertinent to the action. The Uniform Commercial Code provides the resolution of the priority problem in this case. Section 2–403 provides in pertinent part:

"1. A purchaser of goods acquires all title which his transferor had or had power to transfer except that a purchaser of a limited interest acquires rights only to the extent of the interest purchased. A person with voidable title has power to transfer a good title to a good faith purchaser for value. When goods have been delivered under a transaction of purchase the purchaser has such power even though

" * * *

"b. the delivery was in exchange for a check which is later dishonored, * * *."

The above section of the Uniform Commercial Code indicates that despite the fact Pruisner tendered, for the purchase of the vehicles, a check which was subsequently dishonored, he could, nonetheless, transfer good title to a "good faith purchaser for value."

"Good faith" is defined in the Uniform Commercial Code as "honesty in fact in the conduct or transaction concerned." Section 1–201(19). Plaintiff did not, and does not now, present any factual question as to the good faith of defendant Chrysler Credit, whose security interest under the floor planning scheme predated the execution and delivery to plaintiff of the dishonored checks.

A purchaser is defined by section 1–201(33) as "a person who takes by purchase." Section 1–201(32) defines "purchase" as including "taking by sale, discount, negotiation, mortgage, pledge, lien, issue or reissue, gift or any other voluntary transaction creating an interest in property."

Section 1–201(44)(b) provides that a person gives "value" for rights if he acquires them "as security for or in total or partial satisfaction of a pre-existing claim." From the above definitions it is abidingly clear that we must conclude defendant Chrysler Credit acted in good faith and "gave value." It is equally clear that a secured party under Article 9 of the Uniform Commercial Code (§ 9–105(1)(i)) is a "purchaser" within the meaning of § 1–201(33) above. The central contention of Swets, however, is that if his contract with Pruisner were affected by fraud or mutual mistake, defendant Chrysler Credit would not be a secured party with respect to the vehicles in question in this case.

In support of this contention Swets directs our attention to § 9–204(1) which provides that a security interest cannot attach until there is agreement that it attach and value is given and the debtor has rights in the collateral. Swets argues that if the purchase by Pruisner was accomplished as a result of fraud or mutual mistake, Pruisner would have no "rights" in the collateral and, consequently, defendant Chrysler Corporation would be neither a secured party nor a purchaser. We find this contention to be without merit.

Particularly pertinent to our conclusion in this regard is our decision in Herington Livestock Auction Company v. Verschoor, 179 N.W.2d 491 (Iowa 1970). In *Herington* plaintiff had sold 84 head of cattle to a speculator, using an invoice which provided on its face: "The purchaser agrees that title of stock listed above shall be retained by us until check or draft in payment of same is paid." The speculator, in turn, delivered the cattle to defendant who, acting on the speculator's directions, sold them and tendered a check to the latter. Subsequently plaintiff was not paid for the cattle by the speculator, and brought an action against defendant for conversion. After a motion for judgment notwithstanding verdict had been resolved adversely to plaintiff, he appealed, claiming title to the cattle had not passed to the speculator, due to the reservation in the invoice.

We affirmed in *Herington*, holding that plaintiff seller could at most have reserved only a security interest in the cattle. Pertinent to our disposition of the appeal was Code section 2–401(2) which provides in material part:

> "Unless otherwise explicitly agreed title passes to the buyer at the time and place at which the seller completes his performance with reference to the physical delivery of the goods, despite any reservation of a security interest
> *   *   * ."

In the matter before us here plaintiff did not even reserve a security interest in the vehicles in question. At the time of the delivery of the vehicles, Pruisner acquired sufficient rights in the same to permit Chrysler Credit Corporation's security interest to attach.

An almost identical analysis was employed by the Supreme Court of Nebraska under identical Uniform Commercial Code provisions in Jordan v. Butler, 182 Neb. 626, 156 N.W.2d 778, a case involving the respective rights of a defrauded initial seller and a subsequent good faith purchaser for value.

We also note that when goods have been delivered under a transaction of purchase the purchaser has power to transfer good title to a subsequent good faith purchaser for value even though the original delivery was procured through fraud punishable as larcenous under the criminal law. Section 2–403(1)(d).

We further observe § 2–702(2) provides that on a credit sale to an insolvent buyer, the seller has ten days to make reclamation, unless the buyer has misrepresented in writing his solvency within three months prior, in which case the time limit does not apply. That section further provides: "Except as provided in this subsection the seller may not base a right to reclaim goods on the buyer's fraudulent or innocent misrepresentation of solvency or of intent to pay." There is no indication by plaintiff here that he pursued this remedy against Pruisner. For the implication drawn by the Tenth Circuit Court of Appeals from a plaintiff's failure to comply with an identical statute in a case quite similar to the one at bar, see United States v. Wyoming National Bank of Casper, 505 F.2d 1064 (10 Cir. 1974).

In summary, we conclude and hold:

(1) Trial court was correct in sustaining motion for summary judgment of defendant Chrysler Credit Corporation insofar as it sought an adjudication that its interest in the automobiles in question was senior and superior to plaintiff's claim of ownership thereto.

(2) Trial court erred in failing to find there was a genuine issue of material fact regarding the value of the automobiles at time of attachment of same, and accordingly erred in fixing the value of the cars at $9,300.

We therefore affirm trial court in its findings, conclusions and decree adjudicating the rights of plaintiff Swets in the automobiles in question to be junior and inferior to the claim of ownership of defendant Chrysler Credit Corporation. We reverse the judgment of trial court relative to the value of the vehicles and remand for further hearing and determination of the value of the same. See rule 237(d) and rule 342(e), R.C.P. See also Bauer v. Stern Finance Co., 169 N.W.2d 850 (Iowa 1969) and Heins v. City of Cedar Rapids, 231 N.W.2d 16 (Iowa 1975).

Affirmed in part, reversed in part and remanded for further proceedings.

NOTES

1. In one line of cases courts rely on Article 2 provisions to find that debtors have the requisite rights in collateral to create a valid security interest. *Swets* is an example, along with In re Samuels & Co., Inc., infra p. 465. See Hogan, Future Goods, Floating Liens and Foolish Creditors, 17 Stan.L.Rev. 822 (1965).

2. In another line of cases courts find the debtor's rights in collateral by reference to law outside the Code. In Avco Delta Corp. Canada Limited v. United States, 459 F.2d 436 (7th Cir. 1972), the court was faced with this puzzle: Canadian Parkhill Pipe Stringing Ltd. owned both Canadian Parkhill Pipe Stringing, Inc. ("Taxpayer") and Canadian Parkhill Construction Equipment, Ltd. ("Construction"). Secured Party (SP) loaned Construction $600,000 and Construction granted a security interest in 29 pieces of heavy construction equipment. SP believed that Construction owned the equipment but it was actually owned by Taxpayer. Subsequently a federal tax lien was filed against the equipment based on a claim against Taxpayer. The court found that SP had a valid security interest in the equipment. Construction had sufficient rights in the collateral to support the security interest of SP because of representations made by all three Parkhill companies that Construction owned the equipment. The court concluded "Because the estoppel created an interest or rights in Construction, binding on taxpayer and its creditors, that interest or rights were sufficient under section 9–204 [1972 Code § 9–203] of the Code to permit [SP's] security interest to attach to the collateral." 459 F.2d at 442. For another estoppel case see In re Pubs, Inc. of Champaign, 618 F.2d 432 (7th Cir. 1980).

E. PERFECTION BY POSSESSION

IN RE COPELAND

United States Court of Appeals, Third Circuit, 1976.
531 F.2d 1195.

SEITZ, CHIEF JUDGE. This is a consolidated appeal from two separate orders of the district court in a Chapter XI bankruptcy proceeding instituted by Lammot duPont Copeland, Jr. (hereinafter "Copeland" or "debtor"). The appeals are united by a common factual basis. In July of 1967, Copeland personally guaranteed payment on a $2,700,000 loan by Pension Benefit Fund, Inc. ("Pension Benefit") to two corporations and entered into an agreement which required him to pledge as collateral security 18,187 shares of Christiana Securities Co. stock. An "escrow agreement" was simultaneously executed between Copeland, Pension Benefit and Wilmington Trust Company ("Wilmington Trust") which designated Wilmington Trust as escrow holder of the pledged stock.

Nearly three years later, in April, 1970, there was a default on the loan. Following written demand upon the principal corporations for payment, Pension Benefit notified Copeland and Wilmington Trust by letter of September 11, 1970 of the uncured default and of its intention to demand the surrender of the escrowed stock in accordance with the pledge agreement. Copeland did not respond to this letter, but on October 20, 1970, filed a petition for an arrangement under Chapter XI of the Bankruptcy Act, 11 U.S.C. § 701 et seq., and an application to stay enforcement of Pension Benefit's lien on the Christiana stock. Thereafter, Copeland withdrew his objection to the delivery of the stock to Pension Benefit, and the stock was turned over by Wilmington Trust on December 1, 1970. The market value of the stock on this date was less than the unpaid balance due on the loan. Subsequently, Pension Benefit filed an amended proof of claim to recover the difference.

It was not until July 27, 1972, nearly a year and a half later, that the debtor first objected to Pension Benefit's proof of claim and filed a counterclaim seeking, *inter alia*, an accounting for any surplus which might exist in the appreciated value of the stock over the amount due on the loan. Pension Benefit moved to dismiss the counterclaim for failure to state a claim upon which relief could be granted, and the debtor moved for summary judgment. By order of April 3, 1973, Pension Benefit's motion to dismiss was denied, and the debtor's motion for summary judgment was granted insofar as it requested an evaluation proceeding to ascertain the value of the stock. The order additionally required Pension Benefit to make application to the court before selling or encumbering the stock. Following the district court's affirmance of the referee's order, Pension Benefit appealed.

In addition to counterclaiming for recovery of the surplus value of the stock after payment of the debt, on October 19, 1973, debtor filed an independent application for an order requiring Pension Benefit to surrender the stock itself and dividends received with respect thereto. Debtor's application was denied by the district court, sitting as a bankruptcy court, by order dated February 3, 1975. Debtor and the Statutory Creditors' Committee appealed.

I. DEBTOR'S APPEAL

We shall consider first the issues raised in debtor's appeal since, if he is successful in recovering the stock, Pension Benefit's appeal will be rendered moot.

Copeland asserts a superior right to possession of the stock by virtue of his status as debtor-in-possession which enables him to exercise all the powers of a trustee in bankruptcy, Bankruptcy Act § 342, and specifically, to avail himself of all rights and remedies of any creditor—real or hypothetical—who had or could have obtained a lien on the debtor's property on the date of bankruptcy. Bankruptcy Act § 70c. The rights of a lien creditor must be determined by reference to state law. Pertinent here is § 9–301(1)(b) of the Uniform Commercial Code [1962 Official Text] which provides:

"(1) Except as otherwise provided in subsection (2), an unperfected security interest is subordinate to the rights of

* * *

"(b) a person who becomes a lien creditor without knowledge of the security interest and before it is perfected."

Since under § 70c of the Bankruptcy Act the trustee has all rights of an ideal lien creditor under § 9–301(1)(b) of the Code, his rights in the stock are superior to Article 9 claimants whose interests were unperfected as of the date of bankruptcy.

Copeland contends that Pension Benefit's security interest in the Christiana stock was unperfected on the date of bankruptcy. He asserts that the district court therefore erred in denying his application for an order requiring Pension Benefit to surrender the stock and dividends received with respect thereto.

*   *   *

B. PERFECTION

Relying on § 9–304(1) and § 9–305, Copeland next argues that even assuming the security interest had attached, it was not properly perfected on the date of bankruptcy. Section 9–304 provides that a security interest in instruments, defined in § 9–105(1)(g) and § 8–102 to include corporate securities such as the Christiana stock, can only be perfected by the secured party's taking possession. Section 9–305 modifies this rule by permitting a secured party to perfect his security interest through the possession of his bailee. Section 9–305 states in pertinent part:

> "A security interest in letters of credit and advices of credit (subsection (2)(a) of Section 5–116), goods, instruments, negotiable documents or chattel paper may be perfected by the secured party's taking possession of the collateral. If such collateral other than goods covered by a negotiable document is held by a bailee, the secured party is deemed to have possession from the time the bailee receives notification of the secured party's interest. *   *   * "

Debtor maintains that Pension Benefit's security interest was not perfected by Wilmington Trust's possession of the stock because Wilmington Trust was the agent of both parties. He asserts that this position is inconsistent with the degree of possession needed to perfect under the "bailee with notice" provision of § 9–305. To satisfy the requirement of this section, he urges, possession must be maintained by an agent under the sole control of the secured party.

In support of this contention, debtor places considerable emphasis upon what would have been the nature of the relationship between the parties at common law. Since the stock was held by Wilmington Trust as agent for both parties, he argues that the arrangement must be characterized as an escrow, rather than a perfected pledge which requires possession by the pledgee or an agent under his absolute dominion and control. Citing

In re Dolly Madison Industries, Inc.,* he further stresses that the simultaneous existence of an escrow and a pledge is a legal impossibility. Since the transaction fails as a common law pledge for lack of possession by the pledgee or his agent, and since the Code, he asserts, has incorporated the requirement of the common law pledge that the pledgee or an agent under his absolute control maintain possession of the collateral, Pension Benefit's security interest was unperfected under § 9–304 and § 9–305 on the date of bankruptcy.

Although concluding that Wilmington Trust was an escrow agent at common law and hence incapable of becoming Pension Benefit's agent for the purpose of perfecting the pledge, the district court held that the provision of § 9–305 permitting perfection by a "bailee with notice" had been satisfied, and that the security interest was consequently perfected under the Code. The court rejected debtor's argument that § 9–305 had incorporated the restrictive possession requirement of the common law pledge, finding that an acceptance of this proposition would frustrate the parties' intent to collateralize the loan as against third party creditors, would be in disregard of the policy considerations underlying both the law of pledge and the Code, and would unduly restrict the use of the escrow device.

We find it unnecessary to consider the parties' rights at common law because we believe that the language and policy underlying § 9–305 support the district court's conclusion that Pension Benefit's security interest was perfected upon delivery of the stock to Wilmington Trust in July, 1967. While it is true that the Code does not wholly displace the common law, § 1–103, nor abolish existing security devices, Official Comment 2, § 9–102, Article 9 simplifies pre-Code secured financing by providing for the unitary treatment of all security arrangements. It eliminates many of the antiquated distinctions between various security devices in favor of a single "security interest", §§ 9–102, 1–201(37), and a single set of rules regarding creation and perfection, designed to govern "any transaction (regardless of its form) which is intended to create a security interest in personal property or fixtures including goods, documents, instruments * * *." § 9–102. Since neither party denies that the pledge and escrow agreements were intended to create a security interest in the stock within the meaning of the Uniform Commercial Code, we attach no particular significance to the com-

---

* 351 F.Supp. 1038 (E.D.Pa.1972), aff'd mem., 480 F.2d 917 (3d Cir. 1973).

mon law distinctions between the pledge and the escrow which debtor stresses, except insofar as they bear on the question of whether Pension Benefit's security interest was properly perfected under § 9–305 of the Code through Wilmington Trust's possession of the stock.

It is to that question which we now turn. Historically and prior to the Code, possession of collateral by a creditor or third party has served to impart notice to prospective creditors of the possessor's possible interest therein. The Code carries forward the notice function which the creditor's possession formerly provided. Notice to future lenders is furnished under the Code by a filed financing statement, § 9–302, or by the possession of the property subject to the security interest by a secured party or his agent, §§ 9–304, 9–305, depending upon the nature of the collateral.

Where the Code requires perfection by possession of the secured party or his bailee, it is clear that possession by the debtor or an individual closely associated with the debtor is not sufficient to alert prospective creditors of the possibility that the debtor's property is encumbered. See, In re Black Watch Farms, Inc., 9 UCC Rep.Serv. 151 (Ref.Dec. S.D.N.Y.1971). Thus, Official Comment 2 to § 9–305 states:

"Possession may be by the secured party himself or by an agent on his behalf: it is of course clear, however, that the debtor or a person controlled by him cannot qualify as such an agent for the secured party.   *   *   *"

It does not follow from this statement or from the policy underlying § 9–305, however, that possession of the collateral must be by an individual under the sole dominion and control of the secured party, as debtor urges us to hold. Rather, we believe that possession by a third party bailee, who is not controlled by the debtor, which adequately informs potential lenders of the possible existence of a perfected security interest satisfies the notice function underlying the "bailee with notice" provision of § 9–305.

In the case presently before us, the collateral was held by Wilmington Trust pursuant to the terms of both the pledge and escrow agreements. Regardless of whether Wilmington Trust retained the stock as an escrow agent or as a pledge holder, its possession and the debtor's lack of possession clearly signaled future creditors that debtor's ownership of and interest in the stock were not unrestricted. As an independent, institutional entity, Wilmington Trust could not be regarded automatically as an instrumentality or agent of the debtor alone. There was consequently no danger that creditors would be misled by its possession.

The fact that debtor remained owner of record and was empowered to vote the shares and receive current income does not compel a different finding. The location of title to collateral is immaterial with respect to the rights and obligations of the parties to a security transaction. § 9–202; Barney v. Rigby Loan & Investment Co., 344 F.Supp. 694 (D.Idaho 1972).

Nor do we believe our summary affirmance of the district court's decision in In re Dolly Madison Industries, Inc., supra, dictates a contrary conclusion. In reversing a decision by the referee denying the trustee's application for a turnover order, the district court in *Dolly Madison* rested its decision on a finding that the security agreement, supra pp. 1201, 1202, postponed the attachment of the security interest asserted by a creditor of the bankrupt until after bankruptcy. In support of this decision, the court noted that the parties had evidenced their intent to delay attachment by placing the collateral in the neutral custody of an escrow agent pending payment or default. Statements by the court indicating that the simultaneous existence of an escrow and a pledge is a legal impossibility were merely intended to underscore the parties' deliberate choice of the escrow device rather than a pledge in order to assure that attachment would be postponed.[5] Since the district court found that attachment had been delayed by specific agreement of the parties, it was not called upon to determine whether an attached security interest had been perfected. Hence, any statements suggesting that the placement of collateral in escrow precludes a creditor from perfecting his security interest for lack of sufficient possession under § 9–305 are mere uncontrolling dicta.

Having found that Wilmington Trust's possession of the stock afforded the requisite notice to prospective creditors, we conclude that it was a "bailee with notice" within the meaning of § 9–305 and that its possession therefore perfected Pension Benefit's security interest. Hence, perfection occurred in July, 1967, more than three years in advance of bankruptcy, on the date the stock was delivered to Wilmington Trust with notification of Pension Benefit's interest therein. For this reason, the district court correctly concluded that debtor's interest in the

5. In the instant case, of course, both a pledge and an escrow agreement were executed, thereby negating a similar finding with respect to the parties' intent here.

stock as debtor-in-possession was subordinate to that of Pension Benefit and properly denied debtor's application for a turnover order.

*   *   *

NOTES

1. There is additional judicial precedent agreeing with the holding in *Copeland* that a secured party can possess collateral through the possession of an escrow agent. See Kruse, Kruse & Miklosko, Inc. v. Beedy, 353 N.E.2d 514 (Ind.App.1976); In re Barney, 344 F.Supp. 694 (D. Idaho 1972); and Estate of Hinds, 10 Cal.App.3d 1021, 89 Cal.Rptr. 341 (1970). In re Milam, 4 B.R. 621 (Bkrtcy.Ga.1980), may be contrary. In that case the secured party was granted a security interest in corporate stock. The certificates which represented the stock were at the time in the possession of the issuing corporation. The reason for the corporation's possession of the stock certificates was not stated by the court. The secured party gave oral notification to the corporation of its security interest. The court held, without further explanation, that the corporation was holding the stock as agent for the debtor and that the corporation could not serve as bailee of both the debtor and the secured party. The court went on to state that even if the corporation could be the bailee for both parties notification under UCC § 9–305 required written notice.

2. In re Mathews, 29 U.C.C. Rep. 684 (U.S. Ct. of App. 4th Cir. 1980), involved a stock split. The secured party took possession of stock certificates representing 114 shares of stock owned by the debtor. Later, without the knowledge of the secured party, the issuing corporation split the stock 2 for 1 and issued and delivered certificates for the additional 114 shares to the debtor. Because the secured party never received possession of the new certificates it was held that it did not have a perfected security interest in the new shares. What should secured party have done to prevent this result?

3. Suppose that C is willing to lend money to D if D can provide sufficient security for the loan. D owns investment securities that he has pledged as collateral for a previous loan made by SP. The investment securities, which are in the possession of SP, have a value greater than the combined amount of the loan from SP and the proposed loan from C. SP is unwilling to give up possession of any of the investment securities. Can C obtain a perfected security interest in the investment securities notwithstanding SP's unwillingness to cooperate?

It is clear that C can obtain a valid security interest in the investment securities by making the loan to D and obtaining D's signed agreement granting the security interest. UCC § 9–203(1). This security interest is a perfected security interest for 21 days after it attaches even though C has not taken possession. See UCC § 9–304(4) which states: "A security interest in instruments * * * is perfected without * * * the taking of possession for a period of 21 days from the time it attaches to the extent that it arises for new value given under a written security agreement." "Instrument" is defined in UCC § 9–105 to include investment securities. See UCC § 8–102. Except for this 21-day perfection a security interest in investment securities "can be perfected only by the secured party's taking possession." See UCC § 9–304(1).

Can C use the second sentence of UCC § 9–305 to perfect his security interest in the investment securities held by SP by simply notifying SP of that interest? The Code does not tell us whether SP in this case is a "bailee" within the meaning of this provision. The second sentence of UCC § 9–305 was taken from Section 8 of the Restatement of Security which provides as follows: "Where the chattel is in the possession of a third party a pledge may be created by assent of the pledgor and notification by either pledgor or pledgee, to the third person, that the chattel has been pledged to the pledgee."

The Restatement refers to creation of the pledge rather than perfection which is the subject of UCC § 9–305. But under pre-Code law which is reflected in the Restatement there was no distinction between creation and perfection. Possession was necessary for creation and that same possession gave to the pledgee "perfected" rights. A contract for the immediate creation of a pledge unaccompanied by delivery of the chattel or its control to the intended pledgee did not create a pledge unless the intended pledgee was already in possession or unless he complied with Restatement § 8. If the pledge was not created the intended pledgee obtained only an equitable interest in the chattel enforceable against the intended pledgor or third parties who obtained interests in the chattel with notice, (see Restatement of Agency § 9) but not against bona fide purchasers or lien creditors without notice. Restatement of Security § 10. This "equitable pledge" bears some resemblance to the unperfected security interest under the UCC although there are major differences between them. Thus, the use of the word "created" in Section 8 does not suggest any limitation to the effect of that section which applied equally to attachment and perfection in the UCC sense.

The second sentence of UCC § 9–305 and Restatement § 8 are directed at the same problem. The former uses the word "bailee" while the latter uses the term "third person." The issue is whether a secured party in possession comes within either term. The Reporter's Comments to § 8 do not refer to the problem. Case law which antedates § 8 supports the conclusion that possession by an existing pledgee can be used as the basis of possession to create a pledge to a subsequent pledgee. See Schram v. Sage, 46 F.Supp. 381 (E.D.Mich.1942); Robinson v. Exchange National Bank of Tulsa, 31 F.Supp. 350 (N.D.Okla. 1940); and Pierce v. National Bank of Commerce, 268 Fed. 487 (8th Cir. 1920). Gilmore, one of the principal draftsmen of Article 9, states his interpretation of § 9–305: "The collateral may be in the possession of the pledgee at the time value is given under the security agreement; in such a case the pledge is automatically perfected. Or the collateral may be in the possession of a third person who holds merely as a bailee or who may himself claim a pledge or other interest. If the collateral is goods which are not covered by a document of title, perfection occurs when the third party receives notification, from either pledgor or pledgee, of the pledgee's interest; some of the older cases suggest that there must also be an acknowledgment or attornment by the third person to the pledgee, but modern authority holds that the notification is all that is required." He cited the three cases referred to above and Section 8 of the Restatement of Security. Gilmore, Security Interests in Personal Property 440–441 (1965).*

A recent case, In re Kontaratos, 10 B.R. 956 (Bkrtcy.Me. 1981), comes to a different conclusion. There, the debtor granted a security interest in stock to First SP which took possession. The terms of the security agreement prohibited creation of any other encumbrances in the stock. The debtor also granted a security interest in the same stock to Second SP. The debtor subsequently defaulted in its obligation to Second SP. Second SP then notified First SP of its security interest in the stock. The question before the court was whether the security interest of Second SP was perfected by its notification to First SP. The court concluded that the second sentence of UCC § 9–305 did

---

* Reprinted with permission of the publisher, Little, Brown & Company.

not contemplate a "pledgee-bailee" and held that notification did not result in perfection.

Is it reasonable to impose on an unwilling pledgee the obligation of holding the collateral for the benefit of a second pledgee? What obligations would the first pledgee have to the second pledgee? How can the first pledgee protect himself against a second pledge of the same collateral?

F.   MULTIPLE STATE TRANSACTIONS

We have examined the procedures for perfection of a security interest. This examination assumed that the transaction was governed by the law of a single jurisdiction. It is sometimes the case, however, that the law of more than one jurisdiction will apply to a secured transaction. There are two principal groups of cases. In one group the collateral subject to the security agreement may be located in more than one jurisdiction or it may have no fixed location, or the collateral may be an intangible and the debtor may operate in more than one jurisdiction. The problem is to determine in what jurisdiction a financing statement must be filed in order to perfect the security interest. A second group deals with the effect of the unauthorized removal by the debtor of collateral from the jurisdiction in which perfection of the security interest was made to another jurisdiction. The problem is to determine to what extent the perfected security interest will continue to be recognized as such after removal of the collateral to the second jurisdiction. Because the most common cases in the second group involve automobiles the problem is complicated by the fact of differences in the automobile registration laws of the various states. UCC § 9–103 deals with these matters. For an analysis of this section see Kripke, The "Last Event" Test for Perfection of Security Interests under Article 9 of the Uniform Commercial Code, 50 N.Y.U.L.Rev. 47 (1975).

1.   ORDINARY GOODS

PROBLEM 1

In State A Bank and Retailer executed a loan and security agreement under which Bank agreed to lend money to Retailer and Retailer agreed to give to Bank a security interest in all existing and after-acquired inventory of Retailer. In State A Bank filed a financing statement covering inventory. Retailer's principal executive office is in State A but it has retail stores in State A and State B. After filing Bank loaned money to Retailer under the agreement. At that time Retailer had inventory on hand in all of its stores. Is the security interest in Retailer's inventory perfected? Perfection is defined in UCC § 9–303.

This case is governed by UCC § 9–103(1)(b). In this case what is the "last event" referred to in that provision? Is the last event the same in the case of existing inventory and after-acquired inventory?

PROBLEM 2

Retailer in Problem 1 bought, for cash, goods for its inventory from Seller located in State C. The contract of sale provided for rail shipment of the goods F.O.B. Seller's plant in State C. The goods were shipped pursuant to the contract from Seller's plant in State C to one of Retailer's stores in State A. Must Bank make any further filing of a financing statement to perfect its security interest in this inventory?

Under UCC § 2–401(2)(a) title to the goods passed from Seller to Retailer when the goods were delivered by Seller to the rail carrier in State C. What is the last event referred to in UCC § 9–103(1)(b)?

Suppose in this case a creditor of Retailer attached the goods while they were still in State C in the possession of the rail carrier. Would the security interest of Bank in the goods prevail over the attachment lien of the creditor in State C? In this case what is the last event referred to in UCC § 9–103(1)(b)?

PROBLEM 3

Seller sold industrial machinery to Buyer and delivery was made to Buyer at Seller's plant in State A. Buyer granted a security interest in the machinery to Seller as security for the price. Buyer had plants in State B and State C. The purchase agreement provided that the machinery was to be kept in Buyer's plant in State B until the price was fully paid. When Buyer took delivery of the machinery it immediately transported it to its plant in State C in violation of the agreement. The following day Seller filed in State B a financing statement covering the machinery. No financing statement was filed in either State A or State C. Later Buyer filed a petition in bankruptcy.

Read UCC § 9–103(1)(c). Assume the machinery was never present in State B. Was the security interest of Seller perfected at the time of bankruptcy if bankruptcy occurred within 30 days of the time Debtor took delivery? Was it perfected if bankruptcy occurred 60 days after delivery? How does UCC § 9–103(1)(b) bear on this question?

PROBLEM 4

Assume the same facts as Problem 3 except that the machinery was taken from State A to Buyer's plant in State B. Sometime later Buyer moved the machinery to Buyer's plant in State C. Seller filed its financing statement in State B before the machinery was moved from State B to State C. Buyer went into bankruptcy two months after the machinery entered State C. Was Seller's security interest perfected at the time of bankruptcy? UCC § 9–103(1)(c) and § 9–103(1)(d)(i). If bankruptcy occurred six months after the machinery entered State C was the security interest perfected at the time of bankruptcy? Would your conclusions be different if the machinery had not been used by Buyer in State B but had simply been stored there for a few days prior to removal to State C?

The present UCC § 9–103 resulted from the 1972 amendments to the Code. The case that follows, John Deere Co. v. Sanders, which was decided under the pre-1972 version of UCC § 9–103, deals with the problem with which UCC § 9–103(1)(d)(i) is concerned. In considering how Problem 4 and *John Deere* would be decided under UCC § 9–103(1)(d)(i) note that that section gives a rule for deciding the question of when a perfected security interest becomes unperfected and a rule for deciding the rights of a third party who was a "purchaser" before the security interest became unperfected.

JOHN DEERE CO. v. SANDERS

Missouri Court of Appeals, Southern District, Division Three, 1981.
617 S.W.2d 606.

PER CURIAM. On September 18, 1979, plaintiff, John Deere Company, filed a petition in the Circuit Court of Pemiscot County, Missouri, for replevin of a John Deere combine. Defendant filed a motion to dismiss the petition on the grounds that it did not state facts to show plaintiff was entitled to relief. The trial court, on February 11, 1980, entered an order sustaining the motion, and dismissed plaintiff's petition with prejudice. This appeal followed.

The basic factual allegations of the petition are as follows. On August 28, 1976, Danny Joe Grissom and Joe Grissom, who were residents of the state of Mississippi, purchased a John Deere combine from Rice's Equipment Company (Rice). The transaction occurred in Starkville, Oktibbeha County, Mississippi. The Grissoms executed a purchase money retail installment contract and security agreement for the balance of the purchase price, which amount, including finance charges, was $26,049.24. Rice, on the same day, for value received, assigned the contract and security agreement to plaintiff. On September 3, 1976, the security interest of plaintiff was perfected in Mississippi, by the filing of a financing statement in proper form, with the Clerk of the Chancery Court of Oktibbeha County, Mississippi.

The contract and security agreement, a copy of which was attached to the petition, provided that the Grissoms agreed to keep the combine in Oktibbeha County, Mississippi; would be in default if the Grissoms attempted to sell the combine; and, that in the event of default, the holder of the contract and agreement was authorized to take possession of the combine, and exercise other remedies provided by law. The Grissoms, in violation of the contract and security agreement and without the knowledge or consent of plaintiff, removed the combine from Oktibbeha County, Mississippi to the state of Missouri, where, on January 13, 1977, it was sold to Don Medlin in Pemiscot County, and was resold by Medlin to defendant J.W. Sanders on March 7, 1977. The petition does not state on what date the combine was removed from the state of Mississippi, but does state that the sales to Medlin and to Sanders both occurred within four months of the time that the combine was removed from the state of Mississippi.

The petition alleged that the sale of the combine from Medlin to defendant, within four months after the combine had been removed to Missouri, was subject to the security interest plaintiff had perfected in Mississippi; that defendant was in possession of the combine and refused to surrender possession of it to plaintiff; that plaintiff was legally entitled to immediate possession of the combine; that the combine had not been seized under any legal process; and, that plaintiff was in danger of losing its security interest unless it was given immediate possession of the combine or the property was otherwise secured. The petition also alleged that the present value of the combine was $24,000. The alleged facts in the petition were verified by plaintiff's affidavit.

The petition's prayer requested a prejudgment seizure of the combine, a judgment for its possession, and, in the event possession could not be obtained, that plaintiff be awarded a judgment of $24,000 against defendant.

* * *

The problem is whether the petition meets the requirement of Rule 99.03(b) by stating facts showing that the plaintiff is entitled to possession of the combine. The petition pleads that plaintiff has a properly perfected security interest in the state of Mississippi, that the Grissoms defaulted on their contract and removed the combine to Missouri, without the knowledge or consent of plaintiff, and that the combine was sold to Medlin and resold to defendant within four months after its removal from Mississippi to Missouri. Plaintiff's position is that the perfecting of its security interest in the state of Mississippi constituted constructive notice to Medlin and defendant in Missouri, and that defendant purchased the combine subject to the security interest of plaintiff. Defendant contends that plaintiff, by failing to reperfect its security interest by filing in Missouri, lost its preferential status, making its claim to the combine subordinate to that of defendant, who was an innocent purchaser. This is the issue on which battle was joined in the trial court, and is the only issue here.

There is no question that plaintiff's view was correct before Missouri adopted the Uniform Commercial Code. See Memphis Bank & Trust Co. v. West, 260 S.W.2d 866, 875 (Mo.App.1953); Finance Service Corporation v. Kelly, 235 S.W. 146, 147–148 (Mo. App.1921); and National Bank of Commerce v. Morris, 114 Mo. 255, 21 S.W. 511, 513 (1893). In these cases, the appellate court held, that based on the principles of comity, a chattel mortgage properly filed in the originating state gave constructive notice to innocent purchasers in Missouri, where the article was removed to Missouri without the knowledge or consent of the mortgagee, and where the mortgage had not been filed in Missouri prior to the time of its sale.

The only question remaining is whether Missouri's adoption of the Uniform Commercial Code (UCC) changed this rule of law. This question is one of first impression in Missouri. The pertinent portion of § 400.9–103(3), patterned after § 9–103 Uniform Laws Annotated—Uniform Commercial Code, reads as follows:

"If the security interest was already perfected under the law of the jurisdiction where the property was when the security interest attached and before being brought into this state, the security interest continues perfected in this state for four months and also thereafter if within the four-month period it is perfected in this state. The security interest may also be perfected in this state after the expiration of the four-month period; in such case perfection dates from the time of perfection in this state. If the security interest was not perfected under the law of the jurisdiction where the property was when the security interest attached and before being brought into this state, it may be perfected in this state; in such case perfection dates from the time of perfection in this state."

This section was adopted by the Missouri Legislature in 1963, and has not been amended since.

The four-month protection period proviso set out in the statute has been interpreted two different ways. The first view gives the secured party four months of absolute protection in the removal state, and the second gives him four months of conditional protection, the condition being refiling in the removal state within that four-month period. The absolute protection version is favored by the overwhelming weight of authority in both cases [2] and commentary.[3] The absolute protection version

2. The following cases follow the absolute protection version: American State Bank v. White, 217 Kan. 78, 535 P.2d 424 (1975); City Bank & Trust Co. v. Warthen Service Co., 91 Nev. 293, 535 P.2d 162 (1975); Community Credit Co. v. Gillham, 191 Neb. 198, 214 N.W.2d 384 (1974); General Motors Acceptance Corp. v. Long-Lewis Hardware Co., 54 Ala.App. 188, 306 So.2d 277 (1974); Morris v. Seattle-First National Bank, 10 Wash. App. 129, 516 P.2d 1055 (1973); First Bristol County National Bank v. Shirley, 11 U.C.C.Rep. 378 (Tenn.App. 1972); Newton-Waltham Bank & Trust Co. v. Bergen Motors, Inc., 68 Misc.2d 228, 327 N.Y.S.2d 77 (1971), aff'd without opinion 75 Misc.2d 103, 347 N.Y.S.2d 568 (1972); Phil Phillips Ford, Inc. v. St. Paul Fire & Marine Ins. Co., 454 S.W.2d 465 (Tex.Civ.App. 1970), aff'd on other grounds 465 S.W.2d 933 (Tex.1971); Pascack Val-

ley Bank & Trust Co. v. Ritar Ford, Inc., 6 Conn.Cir. 489, 276 A.2d 800 (1970); Utah Farm Production Credit Association v. Dinner, 302 F.Supp. 897 (D.Colo.1969); First National Bank v. Stamper, 93 N.J.Super. 150, 225 A.2d 162 (1966); Al Maroone Ford, Inc. v. Manheim Auto Auction, Inc., 205 Pa. Super. 154, 208 A.2d 290 (1965); Churchill Motors, Inc. v. A.C. Lohman, Inc., 16 A.D.2d 560, 229 N.Y.S.2d 570 (1962).

The following cases have preferred the conditional protection version: Arrow Ford, Inc. v. Western Landscape Construction Co., 23 Ariz.App. 281, 532 P.2d 553 (1975); United States v. Squires, 378 F.Supp. 798 (S.D.Iowa 1974).

3. The following commentators assert that § 9–103(3) gives four months of absolute protection, although not all agree that that is the better rule:

is compatible with substantive law in Missouri that predated the enactment of § 400.9–103(3). The statute merely modified Missouri substantive law by limiting the period during which an out-of-state lienholder would have absolute priority over a Missouri purchaser to a period of four months, without reperfecting the security interest by filing in Missouri. See Community Credit Co. v. Gillham, 191 Neb. 198, 214 N.W.2d 384, 388 (1974) for a similar view.

On appeal, defendant agrees that the absolute protection rule is the majority view, but argues that Missouri should apply the minority view, i.e., the conditional protection approach, for the reason that the Uniform Commercial Code has been amended to make the conditional protection view the prevailing one. In 1972, the following code revision was made in Uniform Commercial Code Section 9–103(1)(d)(i):

"(d) When collateral is brought into and kept in this state while subject to a security interest perfected under the law of the jurisdiction from which the collateral was removed, the security interest remains perfected, but if action is required by Part 3 of this Article to perfect the security interest,

(i) if the action is not taken before the expiration of the period of perfection in the other jurisdiction or the end of four months after the collateral is brought into this state, whichever period first expires, the security interest becomes unperfected at the end of that period and is thereafter deemed to have been unperfected as against a person who became a purchaser after removal; *   *   *."

Defendant urges that to insure uniformity under the code we should adopt this interpretation as the correct one. The argument is ingenuous but not persuasive. What we are dealing

---

Gilmore, Security Interests in Personal Property, § 22.8, pp. 626–27 (1965); 4 Anderson, Uniform Commercial Code (2d ed.) § 9–103:16; Note, Resolving Conflicts Arising From The Interstate Movement of Motor Vehicles: The Original UCC § 9–103 And Its Successor, 35 Ohio St.L.J. 990, 992 n.8 & 996 n.27 (1974); Coogan, The New UCC Article 9, 86 Harv.L.Rev. 477, 535 (1973); Headrick, The New Article Nine of the Uniform Commercial Code: An Introduction and Critique, 34 Mont.L.Rev. 218, 240 (1973); Hawkland, The Proposed Amendments to Article 9 of the UCC-Part 6: Conflict of Laws and Multistate Transactions, 77 Com.L.J. 145, 150–51 (1972); Weintraub, Choice of Law In Secured Personal Property Transactions: The Impact of Article 9 of The Uniform Commercial Code, 68 Mich.L. Rev. 684, 713 (1970).

The following commentators support the conditional protection version of § 9–103(3): White and Summers, Uniform Commercial Code, pp. 848–49 (1972); Vernon, Recorded Chattel Security Interests in the Conflict of Laws, 47 Iowa L.Rev. 346, 377–78 (1962). See also UCC § 9–103, Comment 7 (1962 Official Text).

with here is the interpretation of a state statute, which is § 400.9–103(3). We believe that a fair reading of this section mandates absolute protection of plaintiff's security interest that it had perfected in Mississippi for a period of four months from the time of the removal of the combine to Missouri, regardless of whether plaintiff had reperfected such interest by filing in Missouri. Defendant is asking us to judicially amend the statute to conform with the intent and meaning of the 1972 Uniform Commercial Code Revision. We decline to do so. The business of legislating should be left to the General Assembly. They have had eight years to adopt the proposed statutory revision, but have chosen not to do so. This being so, we do not believe that we should read into our present statute something that is not there.

The petition states the facts as required by Rule 99.03 and, therefore, states a claim for relief under present Missouri law. The trial court erred in sustaining the motion to dismiss plaintiff's petition.

The judgment of the trial court is reversed, and the cause is remanded to the trial court with directions to set aside its order of February 11, 1980, which order dismissed plaintiff's petition with prejudice, and to grant defendant sufficient time to file responsive pleadings to plaintiff's petition.

2. GOODS COVERED BY CERTIFICATES OF TITLE

Many states have certificate of title statutes covering automobiles, trailers, mobile homes, boats, tractors and the like, under which security interests in the goods are indicated on the certificate of title. In these states a security interest in the goods is perfected by complying with the certificate of title statute rather than by filing a financing statement under the UCC. See UCC § 9–302(3)(b). Collateral of this kind is covered by UCC § 9–103(2).

Automobiles are registered in all states. In some states registration is accompanied by a certificate of title on which any security interest in the automobile is indicated. In others the registration of the automobile does not indicate property interests in the automobile. Cases under UCC § 9–103(2) may arise when an automobile registered and subject to a perfected security interest in one state is taken to a second state where a new registration is obtained. The cases fall into three categories: 1. those in which the first state does not have a certificate of title statute but the second state does; 2. those in which the first state is a certificate of title state and the second is not; and 3. those in which both states have certificate of title statutes. Read Comment 4(a) and (b) to UCC § 9–103.

The following case arose under the pre-1972 version of UCC § 9–103 which is still in effect in some states. It discusses that statute as well as the changes made in the 1972 version. Consider how the case would have been decided under the 1972 Code. See UCC § 9–103(2)(c) and § 9–103(1)(d). The latter section refers to "action * * * required by Part 3 of this Article to perfect the security interest" that must be taken by the secured party prior to the expiration of the four months period. In the case of an automobile registered under a certificate of title statute, what is that action? See Comment 4(d) and (e) to UCC § 9–103.

IAC, LTD. v. PRINCETON PORSCHE–AUDI

Supreme Court of New Jersey, 1978.
75 N.J. 379, 382 A.2d 1125.

PASHMAN, J. The only question before the Court is whether the interest of a holder of a valid foreign lien remains superior to that of an innocent purchaser of the encumbered goods where the buyer is a dealer with respect to the goods and the purchase takes place within four months of the transfer of the property to New Jersey. Simply put, the issue is one of straightforward statutory construction involving [1962 UCC §] 9–103(3) and (4).

On August 2, 1976 Charles Ryan applied to IAC, Ltd., a Canadian corporation, to finance his purchase of a new Porsche automobile from Auto Hamer, Inc., a registered Porsche dealer located in Quebec, Canada. Ryan made a down payment of $5,700 and received financing for the purchase from IAC in the amount of $10,000. Later that day Auto Hamer was tendered the full purchase price and Ryan received his car.

Ryan had executed a conditional sales agreement with Auto Hamer in which title of the vehicle remained in the vendor until payment of the $10,000 loan principal and a $2,470.26 finance charge. The agreement further provided for an immediate assignment of the contract, title and all rights of the vendor to IAC. This contract fully complied with the applicable requirements of the Canadian Consumer Protection Act. According to the Appellate Division, "it is not disputed that * * * the security interest of plaintiff was perfected in Canada and that plaintiff thereby obtained a valid lien on the automobile under the law of Canada." 147 N.J.Super. 212, 215, 371 A.2d 84, 85 (App.Div.1977).

At some point between August 2 and August 6, 1976, Ryan acquired a certificate of registration in Quebec. This document did not require disclosure of the IAC security interest and no notation of the existence of the lien appeared on its face. Ryan then drove the vehicle to Trenton, New Jersey, where he changed the Canadian registration to one in New Jersey and acquired a certificate of title from the Division of Motor Vehicles. The New Jersey certificate of title requires disclosure of any encumbrances on the vehicle. Nevertheless, as a result of Ryan's false representation that there were no such liens, he was issued a "clean" certificate of title.

On August 6, 1976 Ryan sold the car to defendant Princeton Porsche-Audi, a good faith purchaser without knowledge of the security interest, for $9,000. The vehicle had some 610 total miles on its odometer. Princeton Porsche-Audi would normally have paid $10,500 for a comparable vehicle in the wholesale market.

It is undisputed that at some point thereafter Princeton Porsche-Audi became aware of the lien. The exact time is contested, as is an alleged promise by defendant not to resell the auto. However, these factual disputes and the good faith of Princeton Porsche-Audi were disposed of by stipulation of the parties in order to permit summary disposition of the case. At any rate, an attempted sale to a Pennsylvania dealer fell through when the buyer received notice of the lien. Defendant then sold the automobile to a customer of its own.

Plaintiff abandoned any effort to regain possession of the automobile through replevin, and sought damages for conversion. IAC's motion for summary judgment on the issue of defendant's liability was granted. The Appellate Division reversed the grant of summary judgment. 147 N.J.Super. 212, 371 A.2d 84. We granted certification to consider this troublesome issue under the Uniform Commercial Code (U.C.C.) which had spawned inconsistent results across the country. 74 N.J. 277, 377 A.2d 681 (1977).

Resolution of this dispute turns on our interpretation of the applicable conflict of laws rule of the U.C.C., codified in N.J.S.A. 12A:9-103(3), and the scope of the section which serves as an exception to that rule, N.J.S.A. 12A:9–103(4). These statutes provide, in pertinent part, as follows:

N.J.S.A. 12A:9–103:

(3) If personal property * * * is already subject to a security interest when it is brought into this state, the validity of the security interest in this state is to be determined by the law (including the conflict of laws rules) of the jurisdiction where the property was when the security interest attached. * * * If the security interest was already perfected under the law of the jurisdiction where the property was when the seurity interest attached and before being brought into this state, the security interest continues perfected in this state for four months and also thereafter if within the four month period it is perfected in this state.

*   *   *

(4) * * * [I]f personal property is covered by a certificate of title issued under a statute of this state or any other jurisdiction which requires indication on a certificate of title of any security interest in the property as a condition of perfection, then the perfection is governed by the law of the jurisdiction which issued the certificate.

The first section represents a compromise between the harsh common law rule under which a good faith purchaser would always lose against the claim of the secured party, and the equally undesirable rule which would permit such a purchaser to always prevail, with the consequent encouragement of fraud and theft. The four month period was deemed to be a reasonable time in which a vigilant creditor could locate the vehicle and register his lien in the new jurisdiction. The real issue is the meaning of the second section, 9–103(4), and the type of situation in which it applies. A commentator has noted the difficulties in interpreting this statutory provision.

Subsection (4) suffers from an inherent ambiguity in that it is textually susceptible to two interpretations as to what point in time the property must be 'covered by a certificate of title' for the subsection to apply. Although not articulated in the decision, *Stamper* construes the statute to mean that subsection (4) applies only if the property is covered by a certificate of title (indicating the existence of a security interest) at the time it is brought into the enacting state (New Jersey). However, another possible interpretation is that subsection (4) applies if the property is covered by a certificate of title (indicating the existence of a security interest) at the time of the transaction under scrutiny * * * even though this may be subsequent to entry. [Comment, 47 Boston Univ.L. Rev. 430, 433 (1966)]

The case referred to in the note, The First Nat'l Bank of Bay Shore v. Stamper, 93 N.J.Super. 150, 225 A.2d 162 (Law.Div. 1966), is still considered to be the leading case on the issue at bar. In *Stamper*, the court held that the conditional seller's assignee could recover from the defendant who had bought a used automobile from the conditional buyer. The conditional seller's security interest had been validly perfected in New York, and the conditional buyer had sold the car within four months of moving to New Jersey, under a "clean" certificate of ownership issued by the Division of Motor Vehicles. The conditional seller did not file his security interest within four months of the transfer of the vehicle to New Jersey. Nevertheless, the court found 9–103(3) applicable and the innocent purchaser from the conditional buyer was held liable.

Stamper relied heavily on Casterline v. General Motors Acceptance Corp., 195 Pa.Super. 344, 171 A.2d 813 (Super.Ct.1961); Churchill Motors, Inc. v. A. C. Lohman, Inc., 16 A.D.2d 560, 229 N.Y.S.2d 570 (App.Div.1962), and Al Maroone Ford Inc. v. Manheim.Auto Assoc., Inc., 205 Pa.Super. 154, 208 A.2d 290 (Super. Ct.1965). *Stamper* was in turn relied on by the trial court in the instant case. The Appellate Division herein questioned the validity of this authority. It noted that *Casterline* was concerned with transactions which took place before the enactment of U.C.C. 9–103(4) in Pennsylvania and had not even discussed the effect of that subsection. As recognized by the Appellate Division, *Churchill Motors* and *Al Maroone,* supra, erroneously relied on *Casterline.* The Appellate Division also rejected the comment of the Editorial Board of the Uniform Commercial Code with respect to subsection (4).

Subsection 4 is new to avoid the possible necessity of duplicating perfection in the case of a vehicle subject to a certificate of title law requiring compliance therewith to perfect security interest. The certificate of title law requirements are adopted as the test for perfection.

This comment was also relied on by the *Stamper* court, but the Appellate Division refused to consider it because our legislature did not include it in the Code comments which follow N.J.S.A. 12A:9–103.

To compound our difficulties, the explanatory comment 7 to N.J. S.A. 12A:9–103 is not free of ambiguity.

(7) Collateral other than accounts, contract rights, general intangibles and mobile equipment may be brought into this State subject to a security interest which has attached and may have been perfected under the laws of another jurisdiction. If the property is covered by a certificate of title, subsection (4) applies. In other cases, under subsection (3) this Article applies from the time the collateral comes into this state, except that (1) validity of the security interest is determined by the law of the jurisdiction where it attached (unless pursuant to an understanding of the parties the collateral is brought here within 30 days thereafter) and (2) if the security interest was perfected in the jurisdiction where the collateral was kept before being brought here, it continues perfected in this state for four months after the collateral is brought in, although the filing requirements of this Article have not been complied with here. After the four month period the secured party must comply with the perfection requirements of this Article (i.e., must file if filing is required).

The comment does not address the significance of the timing of the procurement of the certificate of title. Thus, neither the statute nor the commentary thereto clearly indicates whether N.J.S.A. 12A:9–103(3) or (4) applies under the facts at bar.

Insofar as the case law is concerned, the majority view is that if a security interest is perfected under the law of the jurisdiction in which it attaches, its priority cannot be defeated by the unauthorized securing of a "clean" certificate of title in another jurisdiction. Associates Realty Credit Ltd. v. Brune, 89 Wash.2d 6, 568 P.2d 787 (1977); Community Credit Co. v. Gillham, 191 Neb. 198, 214 N.W.2d 384 (1974); General Motors Acceptance Corp. v. Long-Lewis Hardware Co., 54 Ala.App. 188, 306 So.2d 277 (Cir.Ct.App.1974) cert. denied, 293 Ala. 752, 306 So.2d 282 (1974); First Nat'l Bank v. Stamper, supra. The Supreme Court of Texas held to the contrary in Phil Phillips Ford, Inc. v. St. Paul Fire & Mar. Ins. Co., 465 S.W.2d 933 (Tex.1971), ruling that once a Texas certificate of title issued, the applicable law was that of Texas and under its statutes only a lien actually noted on the certificate could be asserted against an innocent purchaser. As with the New Jersey statutes, the Texas statutory codification of the U.C.C. had omitted the comment to subsection (4) relied on in *Stamper*.

The 1972 amendments to Article 9 of the U.C.C. changed section 9–103. Some of the revisions were substantive, but the major purpose of the new section was one of clarification.

OFFICIAL REASONS FOR 1972 CHANGE

The section has been completely rewritten to clarify the relationship of its several provisions to each other and to other sections defining the applicable law. [Uniform Commercial Code (U.L.A.) § 9–103. (1977 pamphlet)]

Although our legislature has not yet enacted the 1972 amendments to Article 9, we believe it is appropriate to accord some deference to the views of the Code drafters where they might shed light on the instant problem. Under the reversed section 9–103, a professional buyer in the business of selling goods of the particular type involved, such as Princeton Porsche-Audi, would be defeated by the claim of the secured party, but a nonprofessional (consumer) buyer in such a position would prevail.

U.C.C. 9–103(2)(d), the amended code section provides:

If goods are brought into this state while a security interest therein is perfected in any manner under the law of the jurisdiction from which the goods are removed and a certificate of title is issued by this state and the certificate does not show that the goods are subject to the security interest or that they may be subject to security interests not shown on the certificate, the security interest is subordinate to the rights of a buyer of the goods who is not in the business of selling goods of that kind to the extent that he gives value and receives delivery of the goods after issuance of the certificate and without knowledge of the security interest.

The commentary to revised section 9–103, applicable to 9–103(2)(d), states:

(d) If a vehicle not described in the preceding paragraph (i.e., not covered by a certificate of title) is removed to a certificate state and a certificate is issued therefor, the holder of a security interest has the same 4-month protection, subject to the provision discussed in the next paragraph of Comment. (e) Where 'this state' issues a certificate of title on collateral that has come from another state subject to a security interest perfected in any manner, problems will arise if this state, from whatever cause, fails to show on its certificate the security interest perfected in the other jurisdiction. This state will have every reason, nevertheless, to make its certificate of title reliable to the type of person who most needs to rely on it. Paragraph (2)(d) of the section therefore provides that the security interest perfected in the other jurisdiction is subordinate to the rights of a limited class of persons buying the goods while there is a clean certificate of title issued by this state, without knowledge of the security interest perfected in the other jurisdiction. The limited class are buyers who are non-professionals, i.e., not dealers and not secured parties, because these are ordinarily professionals.

Turning to our statute in its present form, we feel constrained to differ with the Appellate Division's conclusion that under N.J.S.A. 12A:9–103(4) a professional buyer who purchases a vehicle with a clean certificate of title must prevail over the holder of a valid, but undisclosed, foreign lien. While we recognize that there is authority for this view, Phil Phillips Ford, Inc., supra, nevertheless we favor an interpretation of N.J.S.A. 12A:9–103(3) and (4) which protects the interest of the foreign lienholder. This position not only promotes interests of comity but also discourages the fraudulent conduct indirectly sanctioned by the Appellate Division's construction.

We agree with the observation of the Supreme Court of Washington with respect to the narrow scope of subsection (4).

Does the subsection apply to all security interests, or only to those which attach after the certificate is issued? If it was meant to apply to all such interests, there is no way in which a person in the appellant's [a foreign lienholder from a non-title jurisdiction] position can protect himself. It would seem that if the draftsmen and the legislature had intended such a harsh result, the intent would have been more clearly expressed. [Associates Realty Credit Ltd. v. Brune, supra, 568 P.2d at 790]

Also pertinent is the succinct observation about subsection (4) in Judge Wright's special concurrence in General Motors Acceptance Corp. v. Long-Lewis Hardware Co., supra, 306 So.2d at 281, that "[i]t certainly was not intended to provide a loophole through which swindlers could pass and defeat a security interest legally perfected where it attached." Thus, we hold that N.J.S.A. 12A:9–103(4) should only be applied to goods which at the time of entry into this state are covered by a certificate of title. N.J.S.A. 12A:9–103(3) should apply to all goods which are moved into New Jersey from non-certificate of title jurisdictions. If a certificate of title is subsequently acquired, N.J.S.A. 12A:9–103(3) remains applicable according to its terms.

With respect to professional buyers such as Princeton Porsche-Audi the four month grace period is absolute, and bonafide status is no protection. Such buyers need look no further than the upper right hand corner of a Certificate of Ownership issued by New Jersey to know that a vehicle was once registered in another jurisdiction. Where such is the case, the alphabetic notation "Z" is prominently printed. Such a notation should put the buyer on notice that some investigation may be in order. To be completely safe without the necessity of further inquiries, the buyer should purchase such a vehicle only after four months have elapsed since the New Jersey registration date.

Since this case involves a professional buyer, it is not necessary for us to consider whether the same result would occur if an innocent consumer had purchased the automobile directly from Ryan. The 1972 amendments were primarily concerned with clarification of the meaning of 9–103, which was inartfully drafted in the 1962 version, and our holding is supportive of the purposes sought to be served by those amendments and in no sense constitutes a usurpation of the legislative function. However, since resolution of the issue is unnecessary to our disposition of this case, we reserve consideration thereof for an appropriate future case. Thus, our holding is limited to professional buyers in the application of the statute.

The judgment of the Appellate Division is reversed and the judgment of the trial court is reinstated.

PROBLEMS

1. Secured Party had a perfected security interest in Debtor's personal automobile under a certificate of title of State A. Secured Party retained possession of the certificate. Debtor took the automobile to State B and immediately registered it there. State B does not have a certificate of title statute. Assume that two months later Debtor a. sold the automobile to a car dealer; or b. sold the automobile to a non-dealer; or c. granted a security interest in the automobile. What are the rights of Secured Party? See UCC § 9–103(2)(b) and Comment 4(c) to UCC § 9–103. How would your answer change if the rights of the third parties arose six months after the automobile entered State B?

2.   Assume the same facts as in Problem 1 except that State B has a certificate of title statute and that Debtor obtained in that state a clean certificate of title.   What are the rights of Secured Party?   See UCC § 9–103(2)(b) and (d).

Chapter 2

PRIORITIES

One of the most ambitious reforms accomplished by Article 9 was the creation of a comprehensive structure for determining priorities as between UCC secured parties and such competing claimants as other secured parties, buyers, lien creditors (including trustees in bankruptcy), real property mortgagees, statutory lienors, and others. Although the priority rules had to be revised somewhat in the 1972 amendments, they have yielded a degree of predictability never before experienced in the chattel security area. However, some problems remain and doubtless others will emerge in time.

Article 9 works, but whether its priority rules operate fairly raises policy questions that will be addressed throughout this chapter. In greatly strengthening the position of the first party to file, has the Code been overly protective of banks and other institutional creditors at the expense of other meritorious claimants, or has the Code in fact succeeded in constructing the most economically efficient system of priority allocation? The classic tension between efficiency and fairness is evident in this area.

A. THE FIRST–TO–FILE RULE. EQUIPMENT FINANCING

ALLIS-CHALMERS CREDIT CORP. v. CHENEY INVESTMENT, INC.

Supreme Court of Kansas, 1980.
227 Kan. 4, 605 P.2d 525.

PRAGER, JUSTICE. This is a dispute between two secured creditors over the priority of their security interests in an Allis-Chalmers combine. The facts in the case are undisputed and are covered generally by a stipulation of facts filed by the parties in district court. The factual circumstances giving rise to the controversy are set out in chronological order as follows: On November 16, 1970, Lloyd Catlin executed a retail installment contract to Ochs, Inc., a dealer for Allis-Chalmers Corporation, to cover the purchase price of an Allis-Chalmers combine identified

91

as G–7754. This contract was in a total amount of $10,149.44 including the financing charge. There was no provision in the contract for future advances. In the course of the opinion, this will be referred to as contract # 1. This contract was assigned to plaintiff-appellant, Allis-Chalmers Credit Corporation, who financed the transaction. On November 27, 1970, a financing statement covering combine G–7754 was filed by Allis-Chalmers with the register of deeds of Barber County, Kansas.

On December 19, 1970, Cheney Investment Company, Inc., the defendant-appellee, made a cash advance to Lloyd Catlin, taking a security interest (chattel mortgage) in combine G–7754. On December 24, 1970, Cheney Investment filed a financing statement covering combine G–7754 with the Barber County register of deeds. In the course of the opinion, we will refer to the security interest of Cheney Investment as the chattel mortgage. On September 17, 1971, Catlin purchased a new Allis-Chalmers combine G–17992 from Highway Garage and Implement Company, another dealer of Allis-Chalmers. The retail installment contract which created the security interest included both the new combine, G–17992, and the used combined, G–7754. This contract will be referred to in the opinion as contract # 2. Contract # 2 provided that contract # 1 was cancelled and the notation "Payoff ACCC-Wichita $4,542.00" was written on its first page. The balance owing under contract # 1 was included in the purchase price stated in contract # 2. There was no other reference to the prior security agreement or financing statement. On September 29, 1971, Allis-Chalmers Credit Corporation, as assignee of contract # 2 from Highway Garage and Implement Company, filed a financing statement covering both the new combine G–17992 and the used combine G–7754. On February 16, 1972, Allis-Chalmers notified Cheney Investment of its claim to a senior security interest on combine G–7754, as Cheney had taken possession of that combine when Catlin defaulted on his loan payments to Cheney Investment.

On May 30, 1972, Allis-Chalmers and Cheney Investment executed a letter agreement to allow combine G–7754 to be returned to Catlin, the debtor, with each party to notify the other if Catlin defaulted on either financing agreement. On September 11, 1973, after several revisions and amendments to contract # 2, Catlin sold combine G–17992 and paid Allis-Chalmers $11,641.12, leaving an unpaid balance of $8,300. A new payment schedule was prepared for the balance owing plus a new finance charge. Thereafter, Catlin defaulted on his payments, both to Allis-Chalmers and to Cheney Investment. On March 1, 1974, Cheney Investment sold combine G–7754 at a chattel mortgage sale, having taken possession shortly after Catlin defaulted on the Allis-Chalmers obligation. Allis-Chalmers participated in the sale but was not the purchaser. The sale proceeds totaled $8,560. Subtracting the amount then owing to Cheney Investment and costs, there remained $2,111.80 to satisfy the security interest of Allis-Chalmers.

Following the above events, the plaintiff, Allis-Chalmers, brought this action against Cheney Investment for conversion of combine G–7754, claiming a senior and prior security interest. At that time, Catlin's indebtedness to Allis-Chalmers was in the amount of $8,650 plus interest. In its answer, Cheney Investment claimed a first and prior lien against the combine in the amount of $6,093.79 plus interest. All of the above facts were stipulated by the parties. In addition to the stipulation, the case was submitted on the deposition of Richard F. Ellis, vice-president of Allis-Chalmers. In his deposition, Ellis testified that contract # 1 between Ochs, Inc., and Lloyd Catlin was paid off and canceled at the time contract # 2 was executed and the balance owing on contract # 1 was carried forward and became a part of the consideration for contract # 2. He agreed that contract # 2 was a new and separate contract.

The district court held in favor of defendant Cheney Investment, reasoning that contract # 2 cancelled the prior contract # 1 and was thus an entirely new and separate agreement which created an entirely new and distinct security interest. In its memorandum decision, the trial court emphasized that contract # 1 was one involving only the sale of combine G–7754 and, since it contained no provision covering future advances or sales, it was a distinct and separate transaction from contract # 2. The trial court then concluded that the advances made under contract # 2, dated September 17, 1971, did not relate back and were not covered by the financing statement filed by Allis-Chalmers on November 27, 1970. Thus, it concluded that the intervening security interest of Cheney Investment, created by its chattel mortgage on December 19, 1970, and perfected by the filing of its financing statement on December 24, 1970, was a security interest, senior and prior to the security interest of Allis-Chalmers created by contract # 2 in September of 1971. The trial court entered judgment in favor of defendant Cheney Investment, and Allis-Chalmers has appealed to this court.

The question of priority presented in this case is one of first impression in this state under the Kansas Uniform Commercial

Code. * * * The question of priorities between conflicting security interests is controlled by 9–312(5)(a). However, that section interrelates with and must be read with other sections of Article 9 in order to be properly understood. At the outset, we should consider some of these provisions of the code before turning to a resolution of the issue presented. 9–303 requires both "attachment" and "perfection" for a security interest to come into existence. Attachment occurs when a creditor extends value and enters into an agreement for the debtor to give a security interest to the creditor in some property of the debtor (9–204[1]). Perfection is accomplished (with exceptions not here pertinent) upon the filing of a financing statement (9–302). It is immaterial which of these steps occurs first. It is provided in 9–402 that a "financing statement may be filed before a security agreement is made or a security interest otherwise attaches." The UCC comment to 9–303 states:

> "If the steps for perfection have been taken in advance (as when the secured party files a financing statement before giving value or before the debtor acquires rights in the collateral), then the interest is perfected automatically when it attaches."

In this case, both of the parties have perfected their respective security interests. Simply stated, the issue to be determined is which of their security interests is entitled to priority over the other. Section 9–312(5)(a) governs the priority as between conflicting security interests. Prior to 1975, 9–312 provided in part as follows:

> "Priorities among conflicting security interests in the same collateral. (1) The rules of priority stated in the following sections shall govern where applicable:

> * * *

> "(5) In all cases not governed by other rules stated in this section * * * priority between conflicting security interests in the same collateral shall be determined as follows:

> "(a) *In the order of filing if both are perfected by filing, regardless of which security interest attached first under section 9–204(1) and whether it attached before or after filing;*" (Emphasis supplied.)

At this point, we should examine 9–402. Subsection (1) sets out the simple formal requisites of a financing statement under this article:

(1) Signatures of the debtor and secured party;

(2) addresses of both parties; and

(3) a description of the collateral by type or item.

It is important to note that the security agreement itself is not filed of record. As pointed out in the official UCC comment to 9–402, this section adopts a system of "notice filing." The notice itself indicates merely that the secured party may have a security interest in the collateral described. The burden is placed upon other persons to make further inquiry from the parties concerned in order to obtain a disclosure of the complete state of affairs. The code philosophy is that a simple, filed notice that the secured party and debtor *may* be financing with respect to collateral described in the financing statement should be a "red flag" warning to third parties not to proceed with any financing on the same collateral of the debtor until investigation is made to see that the road ahead has been cleared. See In Re Rivet, 299 F.Supp. 374, 379 (E.D.Mich.1969), citing Professor Roy L. Steinheimer, Jr., of the University of Michigan Law School, in a commentary on 9–402 in 23 M.C.L.A. 467. In his article, Professor Steinheimer suggests that if there is a prior filing, the second lender should do one of the following things:

(1) Insist that the record be cleared by the filing of a termination statement under 9–404, or

(2) Enter into a subordination agreement with the first lender which appropriately apportions priorities in the collateral under 9–316.

The controversy arose in this case, as it has in other cases, because 9–312(5)(*a*), as originally adopted, did not have clear and specific language governing the right of a lender to include later advances made in subsequent transactions under the financing statement filed at the time of the original transaction. It should be noted that 9–204(5) provided that "[o]bligations covered by a security agreement may include future advances or other value whether or not the advances or value are given pursuant to commitment."

The issue as to the priority of the security interest of a lender, who made advances after the filing of the original financing statement, over the security interest of an intervening creditor came before a Rhode Island superior court in Coin-O-Matic Service Co. v. Rhode Island Hospital Trust Co., 3 U.C.C.Rptr.Serv. 1112 (R.I.Super.Ct.1966). The district court in the present case relied upon *Coin-O-Matic* in holding that the security interest of Cheney Investment was prior to the security interest of Allis-Chalmers. In *Coin-O-Matic*, the debtor gave a security interest in an automobile to the seller, who assigned the debt to Rhode Island Hospital Trust Company which filed a financing statement. One year later, the debtor gave Coin-O-Matic a security interest. It filed a financing statement. The following month, Rhode Island Hospital Trust Company loaned the debtor an additional sum of money, one-third of which was used to pay off the first note to Rhode Island Hospital Trust Company. The first note was cancelled, a new security agreement executed, and a new financing statement filed. When the debtor went into bankruptcy, both Coin-O-Matic Service Company and Rhode Island Hospital Trust Company claimed a prior security interest in the automobile. Rhode Island Hospital Trust Company argued that the first financing statement was sufficient to protect the second contract, as it effectively put the whole world on notice that the collateral was subject to present and future security interests in favor of the filing party. This argument was rejected by the Rhode Island superior court. The *Coin-O-Matic* court first recognized that giving the first-to-file priority in all subsequent transactions placed the lender in an unusually strong position. The court reasoned that, under such a holding, the debtor would be precluded from obtaining a second loan, even to pay off the first, because subsequent lenders would be reluctant to lend money based on the collateral already mortgaged, as their security interest would always be subject to preemption by a subsequent security agreement in favor of the first creditor. The court stated that to construe the UCC to give the first lender an interest in collateral for future advances, absent future advance provisions in the security agreement, would render information obtained under 9–204 irrelevant. The court noted that the first creditor could easily protect future advances by including a future advance provision as authorized by 9–204(5).

The ultimate conclusion in *Coin-O-Matic* was that a reasonable interpretation of 9–312(5)(*a*) should be that a "single financing statement in connection with a security agreement, when no provision is made for future advances, is not an umbrella for future advances based upon new security agreements, notwithstanding the fact that involved is the same collateral." (3 U.C.C. Rptr.Serv. at 1120.) This portion of the decision in *Coin-O-Matic* caused controversy and widespread criticism of the rule announced therein.

The holding in *Coin-O-Matic*, requiring a future advance clause in the original security instrument in order for future advances to have 9–312 priority, has been rejected by the vast majority of the jurisdictions in subsequent cases. In rejecting

Coin-O-Matic, those courts generally stress the "notice" or "red flag" function of the code and hold that a financing statement on file is notice to the entire world of present or *future* security interests in the collateral. Cases taking this approach which are contrary to the rule of *Coin-O-Matic* are the following: In Re Rivet, 299 F.Supp. 374; First Nat. Bank & T. Co. of Vinita, Okl. v. Atlas Credit Corp., 417 F.2d 1081 (10th Cir. 1969); James Talcott, Inc. v. Franklin National Bank, 292 Minn. 277, 194 N.W.2d 775 (1972); In re Wilson, 13 U.C.C.Rptr.Serv. 1195 (E.D. Tenn.1973); In Re Gilchrist Company, 403 F.Supp. 197 (E.D.Pa. 1975); Index Store Fixture Co. v. Farmers' Trust Co., 536 S.W. 2d 902 (Mo.App.1976); Thorp Finance v. Ken Hodgins, 73 Mich. App. 428, 251 N.W.2d 614 (1977); Matter of Gruder, 89 Misc.2d 477, 392 N.Y.S.2d 203 (1977); Genn v. CIT Corp., 40 Md.App. 516, 392 A.2d 1135 (1978); Chrysler Credit Corp. v. Community Banking Co., 35 Conn.Sup. 73, 395 A.2d 727 (1978).

The rationale found in James Talcott, Inc. v. Franklin National Bank, 292 Minn. at 290–292, 194 N.W.2d at 784, well illustrates the approach taken by those courts which have rejected the rule adopted in *Coin-O-Matic:*

"Even where the parties originally contemplate a single debt, secured by a single item of property or a single group of items, the secured party and the debtor may enter into further transactions whereby the debtor obtains additional credit and the secured party is granted more security. The validity of such arrangements as against creditors, trustees in bankruptcy, and other secured parties has been widely recognized by many courts. See, DuBay v. Williams, 417 F.2d 1277 (9 Cir. 1969); Grain Merchants of Indiana, Inc. v. Union Bank & Sav. Co., 408 F.2d 209 (7 Cir.), certiorari denied sub nom. France v. Union Bank & Sav. Co., 396 U.S. 827, 90 S.Ct. 75, 24 L.Ed.2d 78 (1969); Rosenberg v. Rudnick, 262 F.Supp. 635 (D.Mass.1967).

"Using future-advance clauses and using after-acquired property clauses in the original security agreement are not the only means by which perfected security interests can be obtained in subsequently contracted obligations or in goods the debtor may later come to own. There is nothing exclusive about § 9–204(3, 5). Parties may use future-advance and after-acquired clauses, and they are a great convenience. But, if they are not used, there is nothing in the code which prevents the parties from accomplishing the same result by entering into one or more additional security agreements.

"* * * The better view holds that, where originally a security agreement is executed, an indebtedness created, and a financing statement describing the collateral filed, followed at a later date by another advance made pursuant to a subsequent security agreement covering the same collateral, the lender has a perfected security interest in the collateral not only for the original debt but also for the later advance."

Matter of Gruder, 89 Misc.2d at 481, 392 N.Y.S.2d at 206, reached the same result, quoting White & Summers, U.C.C. HB, § 25–4, at p. 908, as follows:

"We reject the *Coin-O-Matic* holding for three reasons. First, it provides little protection against overreaching, for a creditor can avoid the holding simply by including a future advance clause in his security agreement. Second, we suspect that the *Coin-O-Matic* court misunderstands commercial practice. We suspect that it is a rare banker who will lend against the same collateral which secures a prior loan; in our experience the commercial practice is for the second lender to pay off the first and so take a first priority as to all of the collateral. Finally, *Coin-O-Matic* conflicts with the most obvious and we think intended meaning of 9–312(5)(a); if the draftsmen had wished to qualify the rule as the *Coin-O-Matic* court did, they could have done so."

The only case supporting *Coin-O-Matic* called to our attention is Texas Kenworth v. First Nat. Bank of Bethany, 564 P.2d 222 (Okl.1977). We have concluded that the district court in this case was not justified in relying upon the decision in *Coin-O-Matic*. The rule of *Coin-O-Matic* was immediately rejected by the UCC permanent editorial board. It conceded that under the 1962 code, as originally adopted, the position of an intervening creditor in reference to a subsequent advance by an earlier secured party was debatable. In order to clarify the matter, the editorial board suggested an amendment to 9–312 by the addition of a new subsection (7) which was subsequently adopted in various states. Subsection (7) was adopted by the Kansas legislature by amendment of K.S.A. 84–9–312 in 1975, effective January 1, 1976. The new subsection (7) is as follows:

"(7) If future advances are made while a security interest is perfected by filing or the taking of possession, the security interest has the same priority for the purposes of subsection (5) with respect to the future advances as it does with respect to the first advance. If a commitment is made before or while the security interest is so perfected, the security interest has the same priority with respect to advances made pursuant thereto. In other cases a perfected security interest has priority from the date the advance is made."

The issue has clearly been laid to rest in Kansas by the adoption of the new subsection (7) of 9–312 by the Kansas legislature in 1975. We note the official UCC comment to that section which states as follows:

"7. The application of the priority rules to future advances is complicated. In general, since any secured party must operate in reference to the Code's system of notice, he takes subject to future advances under a priority security interest while it is perfected through filing or possession, whether the advances are committed or non-committed, and to any advances subsequently made 'pursuant to commitment' (Section 9–105) during that period."

Comment (7) is followed by example 5, which sets forth a hypothetical factual situation involving a question of priority which essentially presents the same issue to be decided in this case. It states:

"Example 5. On February 1 A makes an advance against machinery in the debtor's possession and files his financing statement. On March 1 B makes an advance against the same machinery and files his financing statement. On April 1 A makes a further advance, under the original security agreement, against the same machinery (which is covered by the original financing statement and thus perfected when made). A has priority over B both as to the February 1 and as to the April 1 advance and it makes no difference whether or not A knows of B's intervening advance when he makes his second advance.

"A wins, as to the April 1 advance, because he first filed even though B's interest attached, and indeed was perfected, before the April 1 advance. The same rule would apply if either A or B had perfected through possession. Section 9–204(3) and the Comment thereto should be consulted for the validation of future advances.

"The same result would be reached even though A's April 1 advance was not under the original security agreement, but was under a new security agreement under A's same financing statement or during the continuation of A's possession."

Also note should be taken of the official UCC comment to 9–402, which states as follows:

"However, even in the case of filings that do not necessarily involve a series of transactions the financing statement is effective to encompass transactions under a security agreement not in existence and not contemplated at the time the notice was filed, if the description of collateral in the financing statement is broad enough to encompass them. Similarly, the financing statement is valid to cover after-acquired property and future advances under security agreements whether or not mentioned in the financing statement."

It is clear that subsection (7) was adopted by the Kansas legislature to make it clear that 9–312(5)(a) should be applied to future advances made by the first creditor, whether such advances are "committed" or "noncommitted" thus making it immaterial whether or not there was a future advance provision in the original security agreement. We regard this amendment as a clarification of the original intent of the legislature when it adopted the Uniform Commercial Code in 1965.

On the basis of the reasoning set forth above, we hold that the security interest of Allis-Chalmers in combine G–7754 is prior and superior to the security interest of the defendant, Cheney Investment, Inc. Under the undisputed facts, the proceeds from the sale of the Allis-Chalmers combine G–7754 totaled $8,650. At the time the suit was filed, Catlin's indebtedness to Allis-Chalmers was in the total amount of $8,650 plus interest. Since the security interest of Allis-Chalmers equals or exceeds the amount of the net proceeds received from the sale of the combine, after expenses of sale, Allis-Chalmers is entitled to apply the net proceeds to its debt.

The judgment of the district court is reversed and the case is remanded to the district court with directions to enter judgment in favor of the plaintiff Allis-Chalmers, awarding it the net proceeds from the sale of combine G–7754, after deducting the expenses of sale, together with interest as allowed by law and for the costs of the action.

HOLMES, JUSTICE, dissenting.

I must respectfully dissent. In my opinion the trial court reached the right conclusion in this case and I would adopt the rule and reasoning set forth by the Rhode Island Superior Court in Coin-O-Matic Service Co. v. Rhode Island Hospital Trust Co., 3 U.C.C.Rptr.Serv. 1112 (R.I.Super.Ct.1966), cited and discussed in the majority opinion. The facts are adequately set forth by the majority and need not be repeated.

As noted by the majority, a basic theory behind the UCC is one of notice filing and that a notice when filed becomes a red flag to be heeded by all. However, the same applies to the filing made by defendant Cheney Investment, Inc. Their filing is also a red flag to all who might thereafter undertake dealings with the original debtor, Catlin. In the instant case it appears clear that the initial contract and obligation underlying the first filing by Allis-Chalmers was paid and satisfied at the time the second contract was entered into and a second financing statement filed. To say that, lacking a future advance clause as contemplated by the code, life could be breathed back into the first filing when the underlying obligation upon which it was based has been satisfied is difficult to accept.

The majority chooses to follow the majority rule that no future advance clause was necessary in the initial security instrument but concedes that the meaning of the statute (9–312[5]), upon which this conclusion rests, was debatable. The UCC permanent editorial board recognized the deficiency and recommended the addition of 9–312(7) to the code. Kansas adopted this new provision, to cover situations like the one before this court, in 1975. However, this case must be determined under the "debatable" meaning of the code prior to that amendment.

Plaintiff could have protected its future advances and its second contract by the notice filed under the first contract, if it had desired to do so, by complying with former 9–204(5) and including an after-acquired property and future advance clause in the original security agreement. The official UCC comment to 9–204(5) states in part:

"8. Under subsection (5) collateral may secure future as well as present advances when the security agreement so provides. * * * In line with the policy of this Article toward after-acquired property interests this subsection validates the future advance interest, provided only that the obligation be covered by the security agreement."

* * *

In *Coin-O-Matic*, the court, after quoting section 9–312(5)(a), states at 1115–1120:

"The defendant relies wholly upon what it considers the compelling literal meaning of the language of the section. That is to say, that having entered into a security transaction which covered the 1963 Chevrolet Greenbrier Station Wagon and having filed a financing statement it comes ahead of the plaintiff who had a security interest in the same collateral but whose filing of a financing statement was subsequent in time to the original filing and ahead of defendant's second filing. Obviously with respect to the original transaction there is no dispute that the prior filing of the financial statement would govern. But the defendant carries its argument a step further and contends that the original financing statement is an umbrella which gives the defendant a priority with respect to its second security transaction notwithstanding that the plaintiff's security interest was established in point of time prior to defendant's second security transaction.

"The defendant contends that as long as there is a financing statement on file the whole world is given notice that the debtor is obligated; that there is a security interest in the particular collateral and that the debtor may at any time after the original transaction become further indebted and enter into an additional security agreement with respect to the collateral.   *   *   *

*   *   *

"It will be observed as already noted that the original conditional sales agreement   *   *   *   has no provision for future advances.

"Section 9–204, subsection (5) provides:

'Obligations covered by a security agreement may include future advances or other value whether or not the advances or value are given pursuant to commitment.'

Defendant contends that this provision merely permits a lender to include a provision for future advances in the original security agreement and that when this is so provided it obviates the necessity of executing subsequent security agreements with respect to the collateral in question but that it does not in any way affect the priority with respect to future advances as long as the financing statement covering the collateral in question is prior in time and additional security agreements are obtained with each new loan.   *   *   *   If this is so, it places a lender in an unusually strong position, vis-a-vis, the debtor and any subsequent lenders. In fact, it gives the lender a throttle hold on the debtor. For example, a debtor borrows $25,000.00 from a lender to be paid over a three-year period without any right of anticipation. The security is the equipment of the debtor. No provision is made for future advances. The financing statement is filed.

The debtor reduces the obligation to $12,500.00 and now seeks to borrow an additional $5,000.00   The original lender is not interested in making a second loan.   The debtor is in no position to pay off the loan without borrowing from another lender.   The original lender does not desire to liquidate the obligation except in strict accordance with the agreement.   Under the theory advanced by the defendant the original debtor cannot borrow from the second lender because no second lender can safely advance the money as long as there is a possibility that a future advance by the original lender would have priority in the collateral over the second lender.   *   *   *

*   *   *

"Section 9–312(5) deals with priority between conflicting security interests in the same collateral and gives a priority in the order of the filing but that obviously does not relate to separate and distinct security transactions.   Moreover, a careful examination of 9–312 and the other applicable provisions of the Code lead to the conclusion that the reasonable interpretation of 9–312 is that a security agreement which does not provide for future advances is a single transaction and in the case of subsequent security agreements there is required a new financing statement.   That is to say, a single financing statement in connection with a security agreement when no provision is made for future advances is not an umbrella for future advances based upon new security agreements, notwithstanding the fact that involved is the same collateral."

In the instant case the parties appear to have considered the original transaction as a single transaction.   No provision was made in the security agreement for future advances or after-acquired collateral.   At the time of the second transaction a new combine was purchased, a new contract prepared, the old contract was paid off and cancelled.   The case falls squarely within the rationale and holding of *Coin-O-Matic* and the opinion in that case is, in my opinion, a correct application of the UCC provisions as they existed prior to the 1975 amendment to the statute.

I would affirm the trial court with the proviso that any funds collected by Cheney Investments, Inc., in excess of the indebtedness due it together with appropriate costs, storage and other items properly included, be paid to plaintiff to apply on its claim against Catlin and the security.

SCHROEDER, C. J., and HERD, J., join the foregoing dissenting opinion.

PROBLEMS

1.   On February 1 A advanced $30,000 on the security of D's equipment and filed an appropriate financing statement covering the equipment.   When A refused to grant more credit, D induced B to advance $40,000 on the security of D's equipment.   B filed an appropriate financing statement on June 15.   Before making the loan to D, B had noted A's financing statement on the records and had requested that D submit to A under UCC § 9–208 a statement requesting A's approval of the fact that only $30,000 had been loaned by A.   A promptly approved the statement.   B examined D's security agreement in favor of A and found that it did not contain a future advance clause.   B assumed from the § 9–208 statement and the fact that neither A's financing statement nor security agreement mentioned future advances that A would not be loaning D more money on the security of D's equipment.   But he was wrong, for in July A advanced another $60,000 to D pursuant to a new security agreement granting A a security interest in D's equipment.   A did not file another financing statement.   D's equipment is worth $100,000.   What are the priorities between A and B? Would it matter if A had known about B's interest before making the second advance?   See Comment 7 to UCC § 9–312. Does B have rights against A based on UCC § 9–208(2)?

2.   Debtor granted Secured Party a security interest in certain equipment worth $100,000 to secure a loan of $30,000.   The security agreement contained an after-acquired property clause and stated that the collateral would secure any future advances made but that secured party had no commitment to make future advances.   Secured Party filed a financing statement on January 2.   On July 1, Secured Party advanced an additional $40,000 to Debtor, pursuant to the original security agreement.   What are the priorities of Secured Party with respect to the following persons?

a.   Creditor of Debtor who obtained a lien on the equipment by judicial process on June 1.   See UCC § 9–301(4).

b.   Purchaser who bought the equipment from Debtor (who was not a dealer) on May 1.   See UCC § 9–307(3).

c.   Lender who advanced $6,000 to Debtor and took possession of $10,000 worth of the equipment on April 1 as collateral for the loan.   Lender had no knowledge of Secured Party's interest. See UCC § 9–312(7). Compare the present version of UCC § 9–312(5) with the 1962 version which said: "In all cases not governed by other rules stated in this section * * * priority between conflicting security interests in the same collateral shall be determined as follows: * * * (b) in the order of perfection unless both are perfected by filing, regardless of which security interest attached first. * * * ''

IN RE PRIOR BROTHERS, INC.

Court of Appeals of Washington, 1981.
29 Wn.App. 905, 632 P.2d 522.

ROE, JUDGE. In 1974, Prior Brothers, Inc. (PBI) began financing its farming operations through the Bank of California, N. A. (Bank). The Bank's loans were secured by PBI's equipment and included any after-acquired property. On March 22, 1974, the Bank filed a financing statement perfecting its security interest. In April 1976, PBI needed a new tractor to use in its potato farming operation, as its tractor had broken down. A. Fred Prior, the president of PBI, contacted Jim Castle, a salesman at the International Harvester (IH) dealership in Sunnyside. On April 8, 1976, after considering various tractors, Prior signed a retail installment sales contract for a model 1066 IH tractor. In an affidavit Castle explained that Prior signed the contract "[i]n accordance with our customary practices," but that Prior took delivery of the tractor on approval and if PBI decided to purchase the tractor, it could do so by informing IH of its intention and sending a $6,000 down payment. Castle's recital of the arrangement is confirmed by Prior. The tractor was physically delivered to PBI sometime after April 8. On April 22, 1976, IH received a check for $6,000 from PBI. On April 27, 1976, IH filed a financing statement on the tractor. (purchase money security interest)

Later, PBI went into voluntary receivership and its assets were ordered liquidated. On January 11, 1979, IH filed a complaint asking the court to declare its purchase money security interest [1] in the tractor had priority over the Bank's security interest. On December 13, 1979, IH moved for a summary judgment on its complaint. The trial court denied the motion and held the Bank's security interest had priority, as it was filed before IH's security interest,[2] and that IH had failed to perfect its security interest within the time period allowed by statute.[3]

1. [UCC § 9–107].   3. [UCC § 9–312(4)].
2. [UCC § 9–312(5)].

IH appeals. It argues this was a sale on approval, [UCC §] 2–326(1)(a), PBI did not become a debtor [5] under the code until it had signaled its acceptance of the contract and made the down payment, and that it did not possess the tractor as a debtor until that time. Thus, it claims it had 10 days from April 22, 1976, the date it received PBI's down payment, to perfect its purchase money security interest. Since its financing statement was filed on April 27, 1976, 5 days after receipt of the down payment, it urges it did file within the 10 days allowed under section 9–312(4) and its security interest is thus prior to that of the Bank's.

Conversely, the Bank argues the sales contract signed by Prior on April 8, 1976, was the complete agreement between the parties and that the financing statement should have been filed within 10 days of April 8 in order to enjoy the protection of section 9–312(4).

This case was decided on a motion for summary judgment. Thus, our review is limited to deciding whether there are issues of material fact and whether judgment should have been entered as a matter of law. CR 56(c). Because the contract includes an entire agreement clause, the Bank argues parol evidence was inadmissible to show the contract was one on approval. However, the trial court must hear all extrinsic evidence to determine whether the parties intended the agreement to be a final integration before it can apply the parol evidence rule. Barovic v. Cochran Elec. Co., 11 Wash.App. 563, 565, 524 P.2d 261 (1974); Diel v. Beekman, 1 Wash.App. 874, 880, 465 P.2d 212 (1970); cf. Nashem v. Jacobson, 6 Wash.App. 363, 492 P.2d 1043 (1972) (no contention collateral agreement existed).

* * *

[The court's discussion of the parol evidence rule is omitted.]

Thus, we hold parol evidence is admissible to show a condition precedent to the contract between IH and PBI and remand for a determination whether the sale of the tractor was absolute or on approval. If the trial court finds the sale was absolute, i.e., took effect on April 8, 1976, it was correct in granting judgment to the Bank, as IH filed its security interest more than 10 days after PBI executed the contract. If, however, the trial court finds there was a sale on approval, with acceptance of the contract not occurring until April 22, 1976, it must then decide when PBI became a debtor in possession of collateral in order to

---

5. [UCC § 9–105(1)(d)].

determine when the 10-day grace period of section 9–312(4) had run. For the remainder of this opinion, we assume the sale between PBI and IH was a sale on approval accepted on April 22, 1976.

A purchase money security interest in collateral other than inventory has priority over other security interests in the same collateral if it is perfected within 10 days of when the "debtor receives possession of the collateral." [UCC §] 9–312(4). We do not believe PBI became a debtor in possession of the tractor collateral until it accepted the conditional contract of sale on April 22, 1976.[9] Thus, IH's financing statement was timely filed on April 27, 1976.

A security interest is an interest in personal property or fixtures which secures payment or performance of an obligation. The retention or reservation of title by a seller of goods notwithstanding shipment or delivery to the buyer (§ 2–401) is limited in effect to a reservation of a "security interest."[10]

[UCC §] 1–201(37). A sale on approval, which gives the purchaser the right to use and the option to purchase after a reasonable period of time, is a bailment. McGinness v. Gossman, 64 Wash. 2d 363, 391 P.2d 967 (1964); W. Raushenbush, Brown on Personal Property § 10.5 at 234 (3d ed. 1975). In a bailment, title to the goods delivered remains in the bailor, while the bailee has possession only. W. Raushenbush, Brown on Personal Property § 10.5 at 228 (3d ed. 1975); see Yokohama Specie Bank, Ltd. v. Geo. S. Bush & Co., 121 Wash. 272, 209 P. 676, 212 p. 583 (1922).

Thus, a vendee on approval (such as PBI) owes an obligation to either buy the property subject to the sale or to reject it within a reasonable time. A sale on approval may appear to be a security interest under article 9. However, article 9 applies only to "any transaction * * * which is *intended* to create a security interest * * *" (Italics ours.) 9–102(1)(a). Attachment, which is evidenced by intent and which occurs (1) when

9. Because he may never approve the sale, a conservative and cautious prospective purchaser of goods taken on approval might not wish a financing statement filed upon delivery in which he is listed as a debtor and which could conceivably cover all after-acquired property. [UCC §] 9–404, which allows the debtor to demand a termination statement, is hardly an adequate answer.

10. [UCC §] 2–401(1) provides that when a seller retains title, the interest of the seller is limited to retention of a security interest. However, this article 2 security interest terminates when the debtor is in possession of the goods. [UCC §] 9–113; J. White & R. Summers, Uniform Commercial Code 898 (2d ed. 1980).

the parties agree that it attaches, (2) when value is given, and (3) when the debtor has rights in the collateral, is necessary. 9–204(1); Kreiger v. Hartig, 11 Wash.App. 898, 900, 527 P.2d 483 (1974). Here, PBI purported to grant IH a security interest in the tractor under the terms of the contract; thus, there was agreement subject to the condition precedent of approval. Value [12] was given by PBI when it sent IH the down payment of $6,000.

The third element necessary to show attachment is that the debtor have rights in the collateral. Collateral is "property subject to a security interest * * *" 9–105(1)(c). Here, until PBI accepted the contract by approving the sale, the tractor was not subject to a security interest and thus was not "collateral" until that time.

The final consideration in determining whether IH may rely on the priority of section 9–312(4) is when did PBI become a "debtor in possession" of the tractor. There are two lines of cases which consider this question in applying section 9–312(4). We believe that Brodie Hotel Supply, Inc. v. United States, 431 F.2d 1316 (9th Cir. 1970), and its progeny, which focus on the time the debtor/creditor relationship arose, is the better statement of the law.

In *Brodie*, Lyon took possession of restaurant equipment belonging to Brodie in June 1964, but did not execute a chattel mortgage to secure its unpaid purchase price until November 12, 1964. Brodie gave Lyon a bill of sale on that day but did not file a financing statement covering the equipment until November 23, 1964. Meanwhile, on November 2, 1964, Lyon borrowed money from the National Bank of Alaska, using the equipment as security for the loan. The bank filed a financing statement on November 4, 1964, and assigned its interest to the Small Business Administration (SBA). In a priority dispute between Brodie and the SBA, the question was when did Lyon become a debtor in possession of the equipment. The court held Lyon became a debtor on November 12, 1964 when he became obligated to pay the purchase price. "Until that obligation came into being, Lyon was not Brodie's debtor with power to mortgage the restaurant equipment as collateral for the unpaid purchase price." Brodie Hotel Supply, Inc. v. United States, supra at 1318. The court noted Lyon might have been liable for reasonable rental of the equipment or its return, but he did not owe performance of any obligation until November 12, the date on

12. [UCC § 1–201(44)].

which he executed the chattel mortgage in Brodie's favor and Brodie gave him a bill of sale. Thus, Lyon was not a "person who owes payment or other performance of the obligation secured," 9–105(1)(d), until the sales transaction was completed.

The Ninth Circuit refined the *Brodie* holding in In re Ultra precision Indus., Inc., 503 F.2d 414 (9th Cir. 1974). On March 3, 1967, Ultra executed a chattel mortgage on its after-acquired property in favor of National Acceptance Corporation. On April 30, June 30, and August 7, 1968, Ultra accepted delivery of three machines from Wolf Machinery Co. The agreement between Wolf and Ultra allowed Ultra to test the machines for a reasonable period. Ultra accepted two of the machines and executed a security agreement covering them on July 31, 1968; this security agreement was assigned and a financing statement filed on August 5, 1968. The third machine was accepted and a security agreement executed on October 23, 1968; the financing statement was filed on October 30, 1968. Ultra later declared bankruptcy. National asserted its priority in the three machines under the security agreements executed in 1967. Wolf argued it had perfected its purchase money security interests in the machines by filing within the 10 days allowed by section 9–312(4).

The issue again was when did Ultra become a debtor in possession of the collateral. National contended Ultra became a debtor when it received physical delivery of the machines. Wolf claimed Ultra was not a debtor until the terms of the proposed sale had been met and a security agreement executed and delivered. The court agreed with Wolf's position. Ultra did not become a debtor until it executed and delivered the security agreements, which occurred after it had tested the machines and accepted them. Before that time,

> Wolf held no definitive security interest in the machines which could be perfected by the filing of a Financing Statement, and * * * Ultra held no assignable legal interest in the machines which could fall into the grasp of National's after-acquired property security clause.

In re Ultra Precision Indus., Inc., supra at 417. In both *Brodie* and *Ultra*, the debtor had possession of the collateral before the sale of the goods was complete, i.e., before there was acceptance of the contract of sale. In both cases, the court looked to the time at which the relationship between the parties became that of debtor/creditor to trigger the grace period of section 9–312(4). In the case at bench, the relationship between PBI and IH was in the first instance bailor/bailee; it did not become debtor/creditor until PBI accepted the tractor and tendered the down payment. Had PBI never approved the contract, it would never have become a debtor. See also Commerce Union Bank v. John Deere Indus. Equip. Co., 387 So.2d 787 (Ala.1980).

Some courts have held the critical inquiry under section 9–312(4) is when the debtor received *possession* of the collateral. In James Talcott, Inc. v. Associates Capital Co., 491 F.2d 879 (6th Cir. 1974), Getz gave Talcott a security interest in after-acquired property which was filed on December 12, 1968. On February 17, 1969, Getz took delivery of a tractor from Highway Equipment Co. On February 25, 1969, Getz signed a lease agreement with an option to purchase on the tractor. A financing statement covering this tractor was filed on March 3, 1969. The lease/option agreement provided the lease dated back to the date of first possession. A second tractor was leased under similar terms; the lease was signed on April 22, 1969, and the financing statement filed on April 28, 1969. On October 27, 1969, Getz exercised the options and signed security agreements on both tractors. In a subsequent dispute between Talcott and Associates, the assignee of Highway, the court held Talcott's security interest had priority. Under the lease agreements, Getz owed an obligation to Highway on the date he received possession under the lease, not the date on which he signed the leases. In distinguishing *Brodie*, the *Talcott* court found this difference "critical."

In In re Automated Bookbinding Servs., Inc., 471 F.2d 546 (4th Cir. 1972), Automated had signed a chattel mortgage in favor of Finance Company of America (FCA), which included an after-acquired property clause, on November 20, 1968. FCA filed a financing statement on November 21, 1968. On January 30, 1970, Automated contracted to buy equipment from Hans Mueller Corp. (HMC), which retained a purchase money security interest in the equipment. The equipment was shipped in crates, which arrived at Automated between May 26 and June 2, 1970. Installation was completed sometime between June 13 and June 19; Automated acknowledged delivery and satisfaction on June 18, 1970. HMC filed a financing statement on June 15, 1970. In the dispute between HMC and FCA, the district court held HMC had timely perfected its interest, finding the critical time to be the time of the installation (June 13–19), rather than the time of delivery (June 2); Automated did not receive possession until the tender of delivery terms were completed. In re Automated Bookbinding Servs., Inc., supra at 550. The Court of Appeals reversed, holding possession occurs when the debtor receives physical control of the collateral. In re Automated Bookbinding Servs., Inc., supra at 552. The court noted that tender of delivery under section 2–503 affects only the rights of the seller and buyer against each other.[13] Thus, "possession   *   *   *   is not dependent upon completion of tender of delivery terms which affect only the buyer and seller of the goods." In re Automated Bookbinding Servs., Inc. supra at 553. To hold otherwise would allow sellers to postpone indefinitely the filing requirement by failing to comply with a tender of delivery term and still take advantage of the grace period of section 9–312(4).

Such a concern is not present when the triggering event is acceptance of a sale on approval. The buyer must give seasonable notice of acceptance. 2–327(1)(b); 1–204(3). He may not postpone acceptance indefinitely. The seller, extending the privilege, has no authority to rescind once he has granted it; he has no security interest to protect until there has been acceptance. The *Automated* court recognized that a situation in which the debtor receives possession before the goods are sold to him and the security agreement is entered into might produce a different result. See In re Automated Bookbinding Servs., Inc., supra at 553, n. 14 (distinguishing *Brodie*). We agree, as possession alone, without a concomitant obligation to perform, is not sufficient to call into play the provisions of article 9. Thus, it is when the purchaser of goods becomes a debtor, i.e., owes an obligation secured by the collateral, that the time period allowed under section 9–312(4) begins to run. When the sale is one on approval, that event takes place at the approval of the contract. For other transactions, different events will trigger the running of the 10-day period. See Rainier Nat'l Bank v. Inland Machinery Co., 29 Wash.App. 725, 739, 631 P.2d 389 (1981). (Execution of purchase agreement.)

Thus, if the trial court finds this was a sale on approval, until PBI approved purchase of the tractor, it was not a debtor under section 9–105(1)(d), nor was the tractor collateral under section 9–105(1)(c). Therefore, the 10-day period granted to purchase money secured creditors to file by section 9–312(4) did not commence to run until that time.

---

13. This is an added distinction between *Automated* and the case at bench. Although sales on approval are also covered by article 2, there is a specific provision in [UCC §] 2–326 which relates to the rights of the creditors of those who buy on approval.

Except as provided in subsection (3), goods held on approval are not subject to the claims of the buyer's creditors until acceptance; goods held on sale or return are subject to such claims while in the buyer's possession.

[UCC §] 2–326(2).

Judgment of the trial court is reversed and remanded for proceedings consistent with this opinion.

MUNSON, J., concurs.

MCINTURFF, CHIEF JUDGE (dissenting).

I respectfully dissent from the views expressed by the majority. Although there is no language in the contract to support Harvester's "on approval" argument, I will, for the sake of argument, assume that parol evidence plus the foregoing facts of this case describe a sale on approval. Thus, two questions are presented: (a) When did PBI become a "debtor", and (b) as a "debtor", when did PBI possess the "collateral"? The answer to these questions determines whether Harvester can take advantage of the PMSI priority outlined in 9–312(4).

In answer to the first question, the majority maintains PBI became a debtor only after making the first down payment. The parol evidence relative to a sale on approval does not purport to establish the date upon which PBI became obligated to perform under the written contract.[2] Rather, it merely establishes the condition which must be set aside before the written contract legally obligates PBI to perform. Harvester admits the conditions were satisfied and that the contract became legally binding. The determination of the date PBI became obligated to perform, once the contract became legally binding, should be made by reference to the written contract.

The April 8, 1976, contract provides in pertinent part:

7. UNPAID BALANCE (Amount Financed)
    (Total of 5 and 6)   21,151.76

8. FINANCE CHARGE   5,708.68

ANNUAL PERCENTAGE RATE 12%

2. The contract contained the following provisions:

"*Purchaser hereby purchases*, and seller hereby sells, subject to all terms, conditions and agreements contained herein, * * * the following described property, delivery, inspection and acceptance of which are hereby acknowledged by purchaser:

" * * *

"13. SECURITY INTEREST: In order to secure payment of the indebtedness contained herein, seller hereby retains, and purchaser hereby grants, a purchase money security interest under the Uniform Commercial Code in and to the above described property sold hereunder, * * *

"14. ENTIRE AGREEMENT: Purchaser agrees that this contract * * * which he has read and to which he agrees, *contains the entire agreement* relating to the instalment sale of said property * * *" (Italics mine.)

9. TOTAL OF PAYMENTS
(Total of 7 and 8)   26,860.44

10. DEFERRED PAYMENT PRICE
(Total of 3, 6 and 8)

DATE   FINANCE   CHARGE   BEGINS   TO
ACCRUE
(*If different than contract date*)   /   /

(Italics mine). From the foregoing, the date the finance charge began to accrue was the date of the contract, not acceptance. Hence, I would recognize PBI as the "debtor" within the purview of 9–105(1)(d), as of April 8, 1976, the date the contract was signed.

With regard to the second question, the majority maintains the tractor could not become "collateral" until PBI indicated its approval by making the down payment. I differ from this reasoning and conclude Harvester failed to come within the requirements of 9–312(4), by not filing within 10 days of the date PBI received possession.

When goods are sold "on approval", the seller retains title. 2–327(1)(a). The retention or reservation of title to goods by the seller, notwithstanding delivery of goods to the buyer, constitutes the reservation of the security interest. 1–201(37). From a commercial viewpoint, it seems clear that Harvester retained an interest in the tractor to secure PBI's performance of an obligation which existed legally on the date PBI took possession of the tractor. 1–201(37). When the parties agreed to a "sale on approval", PBI was then legally obligated to: (1) use the tractor only in a manner consistent with the utilization thereof; (2) approve or disapprove of the tractor within a reasonable period of time; and (3) either (a) approve the tractor and perform the terms of written contract, or (b) disapprove the tractor and return it to Harvester. 2–327(1)(a)–(c). Hence, Harvester's reservation of title was a device to secure PBI's obligation to return the tractor should the tractor not be approved. While it is true that 2–326(2) provides that goods held on approval are not subject to the claims of the buyer's creditors, this only assures the creditor if there is *no* sale, (which is not the case here) but has no applicability to extend the time period of 9–312(4).[6] Thus, the

---

6. This approach is also consistent with the fact that the risk of loss remains with the seller until acceptance.

tractor was "collateral" within the meaning of 9–105(1)(c) from the date of its delivery.

The majority relies upon Brodie Hotel Supply, Inc. v. United States, 431 F.2d 1316 (9th Cir. 1970), as favorable to its position. However, the Ninth Circuit held that *Brodie* had fulfilled the demands of the exception provided in section 9–312(4) because "Although Lyon might have been liable for the reasonable rental of the equipment   *   *   *   he did not owe performance of an 'obligation secured' by the collateral in question until" the agreemeent had been executed. *Brodie,* supra at 1319. But *Brodie* is inapposite on the facts. Here, the executed agreement called for the obligation of interest on the contract to begin to accrue from the date of the contract. Thus, PBI is considered a debtor as of April 8, 1976.

In James Talcott, Inc. v. Associates Capital Co., 491 F.2d 879 (6th Cir. 1974), the court decided a similar issue. There, Getz, a heavy construction contractor, executed a promissory note to Talcott giving a security interest in all after-acquired property. Subsequently, Getz negotiated with Highway Equipment Co. (Highway) for the sale of two Caterpillar tractors. One tractor was delivered to Getz on February 17, 1969; an agreement was signed on February 25, 1969, and Highway filed on March 3, 1969. Getz failed to make payments and a priority dispute arose. The court resolved the issue in favor of Talcott by stating:

> The only question that remains is when did Getz receive possession of the collateral as a "debtor"   *   *   *
>
> The District Court answered this   *   *   *   by noting that "Getz's obligation was owed   *   *   *   on the date that he received possession   *   *   *   Perhaps the most telling exposure of the flaw in Highway's analysis was delivered by the District Court.
>
>> *"It would be a frustration of this purpose* [certainty in commercial transactions under the U.C.C.] *to hold that a purchase money secured party can deliver goods to his debtor, delay indefinitely before entering into a security agreement which binds the debtor retroactively as of the delivery date, and still obtain a perfected security interest by filing within ten days of the agreement."*

(Italics mine.) *James Talcott, Inc.,* supra at 882–83. The court reasoned that regardless of when the agreement was entered into, Getz possessed the equipment as a debtor for more than 10 days prior to the filing of the statement. See also Sunshine v. Sanray Floor Covering Corp., 64 Misc.2d 780, 315 N.Y.S.2d 937, 941 (1970).

A similar result was reached in North Platte State Bank v. Production Credit Ass'n, 189 Neb. 44, 200 N.W.2d 1 (1972). There Gerald Tucker received an operating loan from Production Credit Association (PCA) and granted a security interest in all after-acquired livestock. He took delivery of some cattle from a third party with an agreement that payment and transfer of a bill of sale were to take place after the date of possession. He later borrowed funds from North Platte State Bank (to make payment). The bank took a security interest in the cattle. A priority dispute arose when Tucker defaulted on his payments to PCA. The Nebraska Supreme Court held that PCA had priority since the bank had failed to satisfy the requirements of section 9–312(4) by not filing within 10 days after Tucker took possession. *North Platte State Bank*, supra 200 N.W.2d at 6. The court noted: "[A]lthough [the bank] filed its statement within 10 days after it made its loan, the filing occurred almost 2 months after the cows had been delivered * * *" Id. Although the code does not define the term "possession" priority rules turn on the time of receipt of possession and not upon the time the debtor obtained rights in the collateral. See 2 P. Coogan, Secured Transactions Under the Uniform Commercial Code, § 19.02(3)(a) (1979). The rationale behind this approach was eloquently stated as follows:

> We observe that the 10-day grace period in itself allows for a permissible flexibility in the practical aspects of consummating a purchase money transaction. By their nature grace periods must have a fixed time limit, or they become meaningless. We cannot extend judicially another grace period over the Code grace period. We cannot pile flexibility upon flexibility. The purchase money priority is an exception to the first to file rule, and it should be applied only in accordance with the limitations established by the Code. To interpret section 9–312(4), U.C.C., in the manner the Bank urges would not only be contrary to the plain meaning of the language used in the statute but would expose an original lender to such serious practical risks that the whole structure of the Code would be impaired or endangered, because the original lender could never feel sure that he could rely on his collateral in his future dealings with the debtor.

North Platte State Bank, supra 200 N.W.2d at 7.   Moreover, the court in distinguishing *Brodie,* supra, stated:

> The language and the reasoning of the *Brodie* case * * * have been seriously criticized. * * * see 27 the Business Lawyer, Kennedy, Secured Transactions, 755 at p. 768 (1972); and Comment, 49 N.C.L.Rev. 849 (1971).

Id.

The code's general purpose is to create a precise guide for commercial transactions under which businessmen can confidently predict the results of their dealings. Harvester merely had to file the agreement within 10 days of the tractor's delivery into possession of PBI for the protection of its interest pursuant to RCW 62A.9–312(4).   Its failure to take this simple, reasonable step should have resulted in the loss of its PMSI priority to the Bank of California.

For these reasons and for the rationale expressed in Rainier Nat'l Bank v. Inland Mach. Co., 29 Wash.App. 725, 631 P.2d 389 (filed June 30, 1981) (McInturff, C. J. dissenting) I would affirm the judgment of the superior court.

NOTES

1.   What is the policy basis for the purchase money exception of UCC § 9–312(4) to the first-to-file rule of UCC § 9–312(5)?   See Comment 3 to UCC § 9–312.

2.   Why does UCC § 9–312(4) use the time at which the debtor "receives possession" to start the running of the 10-day grace period?   Two other events could have been used: 1) the attachment of the security interest, or 2) the debtor's acquiring rights in collateral.   The commentators explain why the possession test was adopted.

Professor Gilmore states: " 'Receives possession' is evidently meant to refer to the moment when the goods are physically delivered at the debtor's place of business—not to the possibility of the debtor's acquiring rights in the goods at an earlier point by identification or appropriation to the contract or by shipment under a term under which the debtor bears the risk."   Gilmore, Security Interests in Personal Property 787 (1965).*

Messrs. Coogan, Hogan & Vagts state: "The time at which the debtor receives possession starts the running of the ten-day grace period for perfection.   Problems will undoubtedly arise as

* Reprinted with permission of the publisher, Little, Brown & Company.

to when the debtor 'receives possession' of the collateral. The Code does not offer a specific definition of the term, but there are indications that actual delivery to the buyer or to a third party is crucial. It is important to realize that this priority rule turns on the more easily ascertainable time of receipt of possession and not upon the time the debtor obtains 'rights' in the collateral." Coogan, Hogan & Vagts, Secured Transactions under the UCC § 19.02(3)(a).**

Apparently, the commentators believe the possession test is better than a rights-in-collateral test because of the possibility that a debtor might acquire rights in collateral before taking possession of the collateral. In such a case it is easier to ascertain when possession is taken than it is to discover when rights in the collateral are acquired. What the commentators didn't discuss is the fact situation that has actually been happening, i.e., the debtor takes possession before he acquires rights in collateral. Does the possession test make sense in this kind of case? We have used *Prior Bros.* as the principal case not only because it poses a nice question but also because it sets out the other cases in point. The majority in *Prior* followed *Brodie* and *Ultra Precision* in giving priority to the purchase money interest. The dissenting opinion relied on *James Talcott, North Platte* and *Automated Bookbinding.* Can you reconcile these two lines of authority by a requirement that the financing statement be filed within 10 days after the time that the debtor acquired both possession and rights in the collateral?

   3. A *seller* purchase money secured creditor (UCC § 9–107(a)) should be able to comply with the 10-day rule of UCC § 9–312(4) because it controls when the debtor receives possession of the collateral sold. On the other hand, the possession test can cause operational difficulties for a *lender* purchase money secured creditor (UCC § 9–107(b)) because its loan officers may have no reliable way of determining when the debtor actually received possession short of communicating directly with the seller. What procedure would you advise loan officers to follow to be sure that the lender's purchase money priority is established?

PROBLEMS

1. On July 1 Seller sold goods to Debtor on unsecured credit. On July 7 Debtor borrowed $50,000 from Bank to pay Seller. Bank wrote the check to Seller and Debtor as joint payees and Debtor indorsed the check to Seller. Does Bank have a purchase money security interest when Debtor granted Bank a security interest in the goods to secure the debt? See UCC § 9–107(b).

2. Debtor borrowed $10,000 from Bank on July 1 for the purpose of buying a machine. Bank advanced the money by crediting Debtor's deposit account. Bank filed a financing statement on July 1. Debtor located the machine he wanted on July 3 and paid Seller by a check for $10,000 drawn on his deposit account in Bank. Does Bank have a purchase money security interest in the machine? The balance in Debtor's account just before Bank credited the account was $15,000. When Debtor's check to Seller was paid the balance was $22,000. See UCC § 9–107(b).

3. At the beginning of the year, Bank held a security interest perfected by filing in all Debtor's equipment, inventory, and accounts. In March Seller agreed to sell Debtor a machine for a price of $100,000, on terms calling for 20% down. Bank agreed to advance $20,000 to enable Debtor to buy the machine. Bank wrote a check for $20,000 to Debtor and Seller as joint payees and Debtor indorsed it to Seller. Seller retained a security interest in the machine which it perfected by filing upon delivery of the machine to Debtor. What are the priorities as to the machine between Bank and Seller and which UCC provision controls, § 9–312(4) or (5)? See Gilmore, Security Interests in Personal Property 784 (1965); Henson, Secured Transactions under the UCC 128 (1979).

B. INVENTORY

1. PURCHASE MONEY PRIORITY

KING'S APPLIANCE & ELECTRONICS, INC.
v. CITIZENS & SOUTHERN BANK

Court of Appeals of Georgia, 1981.
157 Ga.App. 857, 278 S.E.2d 733.

CARLEY, JUDGE. The instant appeal involves priority between conflicting security interests in the same collateral and interpretation of [UCC §] 9–312. The relevant facts are as follows: On August 3, 1978, The Citizens and Southern Bank (C & S) filed a financing statement listing itself as the secured party and Randall B. Helton, d/b/a United TV (Helton) as the debtor. The financing statement covered the following types of property: "All equipment of the Debtor of every description used or useful in the conduct of the Debtor's business, now or hereafter existing or acquired, and all accessories, parts and equipment now or hereafter affixed thereto or used in connection therewith. All inventory, accounts receivable and contract rights of borrower whether now or hereafter existing or acquired; all chattel paper and instruments, whether now or hereafter existing or acquired, evidencing any obligation to borrower for payment for goods sold or leased or services rendered; and all products and proceeds of any of the foregoing."

On November 27, 1978, Helton entered into an "Inventory Financing Agreement" with Appliance Buyers Credit Corporation (ABCC) "to finance the acquisition by [Helton] of certain merchandise of inventory from time to time from" King's Appliance & Electronics, Inc. (King's Appliance). On November 29, 1978, ABCC filed a financing statement listing itself as the secured party and Helton as the debtor. The financing statement covered the following property: "Television sets, phonographs, stereos, radios and combinations, tape recorders, organs, pianos and other musical instruments, refrigerators, freezers, ice makers, dish and clothes washers and dryers, ranges, food waste disposers, trash compactors, dehumidifiers, humidifiers, room air conditioners, heating and air conditioning equipment, vacuum cleaners, and other types of mechanical or electrical, commercial, household or industrial equipment and accessories or replacement parts for any of such merchandise." On December 1, 1978, pursuant to [UCC §] 9–312(3)(d), ABCC sent notification to C & S that it "has or expects to acquire a purchase money security interest in the inventory of [Helton]" and described the inventory by item or type.

Thereafter, King's Appliance apparently began to ship to Helton merchandise which had been financed by ABCC as well as certain merchandise on consignment. The security interest held by ABCC in that part of Helton's inventory financed under the agreement with ABCC was eventually assigned to King's Appliance. When Helton subsequently defaulted on his obligations to both C & S and King's Appliance, C & S took possession of all of Helton's inventory and gave notice of its intent to sell the inventory and apply the amount realized to Helton's indebtedness to it. King's Appliance, contending that as ABCC's assignee it held a perfected security interest in part of the inventory under [UCC §] 9–302(2), filed a complaint seeking, in effect, a determination that its security interest in the inventory had priority over that of C & S under [UCC §] 9–312(3). C & S answered and, after discovery, both parties moved for summary judgment. The trial court entered its order granting summary judgment to C & S and denying summary judgment to King's Appliance. The order was based upon the trial court's following interpretation of [UCC §] 9–312: "Subpart (3)(b)(i) absolutely requires the purchase money secured party to give notification in writing to the holder of the conflicting security interest *before* the date of the filing [of the financing statement] by the purchase money secured party   *   *   *   The notice given C & S [dated December 1, 1978] was *after* the filing of the security interest of [ABCC on November 29, 1978]   *   *   *   Failure to give a timely notice prevents priority from being accorded the purchase money security interest   *   *   * " King's Appliance appeals, urging that the trial court misconstrued [UCC §] 9–312(3)(b) and that summary judgment was erroneously granted to C & S and denied to it.

1. [UCC §] 9–312(3)(b) provides: "A perfected purchase money security interest in inventory has priority over a conflicting security interest in the same inventory and also has priority in identifiable cash proceeds received on or before the delivery of the inventory to a buyer if   *   *   *   the purchase money secured party gives notification in writing to the holder of the conflicting security interest if the holder had filed a financing statement covering the same types of inventory, (i) *before the date of the filing made by the purchase money secured party*, or (ii)

before the beginning of the 21-day period where the purchase money security interest is temporarily perfected without filing or possession * * * " (Emphasis supplied.) The trial court interpreted the emphasized language of this statute as requiring that in order for the purchase money security interest to be afforded priority the notification must be given to the holder of the conflicting security interest *before* the purchase money secured party files (perfects) his interest. While the 1978 amendments to [UCC §] 9–312(3) are less than a model of clarity, we conclude that the trial court erred in [its construction.]

Under the former § 9–312(3)(b), in order for a purchase money security interest in inventory to gain priority over a conflicting prior security interest in the same collateral it was necessary that the purchase money secured party notify any other secured party whose security interest was either *known* to him *or* had been *perfected* by a previously filed financing statement covering the debtor's inventory. With reference to timing, under the former law, this notification had to be received by the secured party holding the prior security interest in the inventory *before the debtor received possession of the collateral covered by the purchase money security interest.* The purpose behind this notification system was clear. "The reason for the additional requirement of notification is that typically the arrangement between an inventory secured party and his debtor will require the secured party to make periodic advances against incoming inventory or periodic releases of old inventory as new inventory is received. A fraudulent debtor may apply to the secured party for advances even though he has already given a security interest in the inventory to another secured party. The notification requirement protects the inventory financer in such a situation: if he has received notification, he will presumably not make an advance; if he has not received notification (or if the other interest does not qualify as a purchase money interest), any advance he may make will have priority." Anderson, U.C.C. Vol. 4, § 9–312:1, p. 355 (2d Ed. 1977). Thus, because the timing of the notification of a purchase money security interest was tied to the date the debtor received the possession of the purchase money financed inventory the previously secured party was afforded adequate protection and the debtor was allowed to secure additional inventory from other sources. See White & Summers, U.C.C., § 25–5, p. 913 (1972).

Current § 9–312(3)(b), which the trial court interpreted as requiring the purchase money secured party to give notification *before* he files his financing statement, is not subject to that interpretation. While the 1978 "amendments" to § 9–312(3) made changes in the notification procedure they did *not* effectuate a change in the timing of the notification. That the notification need not *precede* the filing is clear, if for no other reason than that 9–312(3)(d) contemplates that the notification may state that a purchase money security interest "has" been acquired in the debtor's inventory. Surely then filing may precede the notification envisioned under the statute. In our opinion the 1978 amendment to § 9–312(3)(b) merely redefines *which holders* of conflicting security interests are entitled to receive notification: those who had filed a financing statement covering the inventory of the debtor prior to the date the purchase money secured party filed his statement and those who had filed statements prior to the beginning of the 21-day period contemplated by § 9–304(5). Thus [the 1978 amendment] amended the former law only so as *to redefine and limit the class* of secured parties entitled to receive notification of the purchase money security interest to those who had previously *filed* a financing statement covering the same types of inventory. Subsections (i) and (ii) of existing § 9–312(3)(b) are descriptive of the secured parties who must be notified of the subsequent purchase money secured interest; those subsections do not establish that the purchase money secured party must give notification of his interest before he files his financing statement. No other change in the previous law was contemplated or effectuated by the 1978 amendment to § 9–312(3)(b) other than this change in the class of those previously secured parties entitled to receive notification. The timeliness of the notification continues to be determined by the date the debtor *receives possession* of the inventory secured by a purchase money security interest. Under current § 9–312(3)(c) notification is timely if the holder of the conflicting prior security interest receives it no more than five years before the date "the debtor receives possession of the inventory."

In summary, § 9–312(3) provides that a perfected purchase money security interest in inventory has priority over a conflicting prior security interest in the same property if:

(a) The purchase money security is perfected at the time the debtor receives possession of the inventory; and

(b) The purchase money secured party gives written notice to those holders of conflicting prior security interests who have perfected their interest in the same types of inventory before the purchase money secured party perfects his; and

(c) The holder of the previously perfected security interest receives the notification no more than five years before the date the debtor receives possession of the inventory secured by the purchase money interest; and

(d) The notification states that a purchase money security interest in the debtor's inventory, described by item or type, has been or is expected to be acquired.

Insofar as the trial court in the instant case misconstrued § 9–312(3) and granted summary judgment to C & S on the basis of this misconstruction, the judgment must be reversed.

We conclude, however, that summary judgment for King's Appliance was not authorized under the evidence. Under the proper construction of § 9–312(3), even if C & S has been given proper notification in compliance with subsections (b) and (d), the record before us shows neither the date upon which Helton, the debtor, received possession of the inventory in which King's Appliance holds the assigned purchase money security interest nor the date that C & S received notification of that security interest. Under subsections (a) and (c) of the current § 9–312(3) the security interest of King's Appliance is entitled to priority only to that part of the inventory received by and in the possession of Helton 1) after the purchase money security interest therein was first perfected *and* 2) after C & S received notification. If Helton received possession of any items of inventory before a purchase money security interest therein was perfected *or* before C & S received notification of the conflicting purchase money security interest in Helton's inventory the purchase money security interest of King's Appliance in those items is not entitled to priority over the prior security interest of C & S in Helton's inventory. We conclude, therefore, that there remain genuine issues of material fact for jury resolution and it was not error to deny the motion of King's Appliance for summary judgment.

* * *

NOTE

The following is a covenant of the debtor taken from a standard loan and security agreement used in inventory financing by a leading financial institution:

The Borrower is, and as to inventory to be acquired after the date hereof, shall be, the owner of all inventory and shall neither create nor suffer to exist any lien or encumbrance thereon or security interest therein * * * in favor of any person other than the Lender.

Assume that breach of this covenant constitutes an event of default which results in the debt secured by the inventory becoming immediately due and payable. In the light of this covenant, what is the commercial significance of the priority created by UCC § 9–312(3)?

2. CONSIGNMENT AND SALE OR RETURN

The classic sale "on consignment" refers to a transaction in the following form: The owner of goods—the consignor—gives possession of the goods to the consignee who acts as the consignor's agent in selling the goods. Sometimes the consignee is authorized to sell the goods and in other cases the consignee is authorized only to solicit offers to buy the goods and to convey the offer to the consignor who can accept or reject. In either case title to the goods remains with the consignor until effectiveness of the sale, and at that time title passes from the consignor directly to the purchaser. The consignee, who acts solely as an agent, may or may not be a dealer in goods like those consigned. Sometimes retention of title in what in form is a consignment sale is in fact a security interest. In that case the transaction is treated under Article 9 in the same way as other security-interest transactions. If the retention of title is not a security interest the agency relationship and the title of the consignor are recognized as such, subject to any rights that third parties dealing with the goods might have as a result of the giving up of possession to the consignee. These rights are found in Article 2.

UCC § 1–201(37) defines "security interest" as "an interest in personal property * * * which secures payment or performance of an obligation. * * * Unless a * * * consignment is intended as security, reservation of title thereunder is not a 'security interest' * * * *" This definition is meant to distinguish between "true consignments" and security interests that are consignments only in form. The key to the distinction can be found in the first part of the definition. A security interest can exist only if there is some obligation to be secured. If the consignee is obligated to purchase or to sell the goods—i.e., is liable for the price payable to the consignor—the transaction is treated as a credit sale of the goods by the consignor to the consignee and the retention of title is simply a security interest. Article 9 applies to the transaction as in other cases of purchase money security interests.

On the other hand, if the consignee is not liable for the price there can be no security interest because there is no obligation to secure. In this case the transaction is governed by Article 2 but by different terminology. The consignment sale transaction is treated as a "sale or return" the incidents of which are spelled out in UCC § 2–326 and § 2–327. The first of these provisions states the conditions under which creditors of the consignee may in effect treat the consigned goods as the property of the consignee. If the consignee is a merchant UCC § 2–403(2) and (3) also apply. UCC § 9–114, which was added to the Code in 1972, applies only to true consignments and deals with conflicting claims to the goods between the consignor and a creditor of the consignee who has a security interest in inventory of the consignee.

Some transactions that are also covered by § 2–326 as sales or return do not take the agency or consignment form. For example, a manufacturer of a new product may have difficulty in finding dealers who will buy his product for their inventory because they don't know whether it will be readily salable. The manufacturer offers to supply the dealer with a quantity of the product which the dealer can sell for the dealer's account. The dealer can return any unsold products at any time and without obligation. He pays only for products not returned. The transaction can be set up as a present sale to the dealer with an option in the dealer to sell back to the manufacturer, or it may be provided that the goods remain the property of the manufacturer with the dealer holding the goods as bailee with the right to buy when he chooses. In the latter case no sale by the manufacturer to the dealer occurs until the dealer resells to his customer. The dealer does not act as agent for the manufacturer in the sale to the customer. Rather, the dealer buys from the manufacturer and immediately resells to the customer.

In the case of a true consignment or other sale or return that falls within subsection (3) of UCC § 2–326, if the consignor or seller does not comply with (a), (b) or (c) the consequence under subsection (2) is that the goods in the possession of the consignee are "subject" to the claims of the consignee's creditors. This produces three results: 1. Creditors of the consignee can levy on the goods held by the consignee as though they were the property of the consignee; 2. If the consignee goes into bankruptcy the goods held by him become part of the estate in bankruptcy by virtue of Bankruptcy Code § 544(a) which gives to the trustee in bankruptcy the rights of a creditor of the consignee who levied on the goods at the time of bankruptcy. See, e.g., In re KLP,

Inc., 7 B.R. 256 (Bkrtcy.Ga.1980); and 3. the consignee when he gets possession of the goods has sufficient "rights" in the goods to allow a security interest in his inventory to attach under UCC § 9–203(1)(c). See In re Bildisco which follows. The consignor or seller normally gets protection from the claims of the creditors of the consignee or buyer by filing a financing statement pursuant to UCC § 9–408.

There are a few cases that have attempted to restrict "sales or return" transactions under UCC § 2–326 to consignments by commercial sellers. An example is Founders Investment Corp. v. Fegett, 23 U.C.C.Rep. 903 (Ky.App.1978). In that case a noncommercial owner of a mobile home delivered it to a dealer for the purpose of having the dealer secure offers for its purchase and to submit them to the owner for approval. The dealer was to get a commission in the event of a sale. A creditor of the dealer levied on the mobile home and sold it. The court held that the owner simply made a bailment to the dealer not a sale or return under UCC § 2–326. The court stated "We believe it would be an unjust and unwise policy to impose upon an *individual* owner, as distinguished from a *commercial* one, the deemed sale or return provision of [UCC 2–326(3)] unless the underlying facts indicate that a sale or return was intended or did, in fact, occur. Our decision does no disservice to the utilization of the Uniform Commercial Code between commercial dealers. It does reserve protection to the private individual owner vis-à-vis the commercial financier when such owner merely attempts, as in this case, to utilize the marketing or sales services of a commercial dealer with no intention of transferring any ownership interest to such dealer. Because transactions of the type in question are relatively few we do not think that commercial dealers or financiers will suffer unduly, but we do believe that the individual owner, to whom the loss in a given situation would be relatively more severe, will be afforded fair and reasonable protection." The court in Bischoff v. Thomasson, 400 So.2d 359 (Ala.1981), refused to follow *Founders* and referred to it and another case reaching a similar result as "maverick cases." Is the statement by the court in *Founders* persuasive? Is there any basis for it in UCC § 2–326?

IN RE BILDISCO

United States District Court, D.New Jersey, 1981.
11 B.R. 1019.

DEBEVOISE, DISTRICT JUDGE. Gerber Industries, Inc.
[Gerber] appeals from an order of the Bankruptcy Court for the
District of New Jersey holding that goods consigned by Gerber
to the debtor Bildisco, a general partnership in the State of New
Jersey [Bildisco], were subject to the claims of Bildisco's credi-
tors. Matter of Bildisco, 7 B.R. 225 (U.S.Bkrtcy.Ct.N.J.1980).
For the reasons that follow, the Bankruptcy Court's order is af-
firmed.

I.

In October, 1979, Bildisco and Gerber entered into a written
"Consignment Sale Agreement" which covered: "Consignment
inventories of goods manufactured and shipped by Gerber Industries Secured Party to Bildisco * * *". On December 31,
1979, Gerber filed a financing statement giving notice of that
agreement; however, Gerber gave no actual notice of the consignment agreement to Bildisco's secured creditors, nor did
Gerber post a sign at Bildisco's place of business declaring its
ownership of the goods. Moreover, Bildisco was not generally
known to its creditors to be a seller of goods on consignment.

Less than four months later, on April 14, 1980, Bildisco filed
a Voluntary Petition for Reorganization under Chapter 11 of the
Bankruptcy Code, 11 U.S.C. § 1101, et seq. On April 17, 1980,
the Bankruptcy Court entered a judgment establishing that by
virtue of two financing statements filed by appellee Congress
Financial Corporation [Congress] with the Secretary of State on
December 14, 1976 and on December 10, 1979, Congress held a
valid and duly perfected security interest in various assets of the
debtor. Included in these assets were the consigned Gerber
products. Gerber, however, was not a party to that proceeding.

On April 28, 1980, Gerber instituted an adversary proceeding
in the Bankruptcy Court against Bildisco and Congress, seeking
possession of the goods delivered to Bildisco pursuant to the
"Consignment Sale Agreement" and a determination that its interest in the goods was paramount to that of Congress.

After a trial, the Bankruptcy Court, in a written opinion, concluded that Gerber's failure to give written notice to Congress

of its intention to deliver goods on consignment to Bildisco rendered the goods subject to the rights of Bildisco's creditors.

* * *

III.

As its second ground for reversal, Gerber submits that the Bankruptcy Court erred when it treated the consignment as a security interest and applied the provisions of [UCC §] 9–312 which require that written notice be given by the holders of a purchase money security interest to parties claiming under an after-acquired property clause. Gerber argues that the consignment between itself and Bildisco was a "true" consignment and that, as such, the proper procedure under New Jersey's Uniform Commercial Code was to comply with § 2–326 and require a consignor to follow the "filing" provisions of Article 9 and not any other action for perfection. Since Gerber filed a financing statement on December 31, 1979 for its consignment inventory, Gerber concludes that its interests in the consigned goods are superior to that of Congress.

In its decision, the Bankruptcy Court, with little discussion, found the Gerber-Bildisco consignment agreement, like all consignments, to give a "kind of security interest" in the consignor. Matter of Bildisco, supra, at 227. Assuming the validity of that determination, section 9–312 of the Code would be applicable for it expressly assigns priorities among conflicting security claimants to the same collateral.

* * *

By virtue of Section 9–107, a security interest in the consigned goods would be a purchase money security interest since the rights in consigned goods are reserved "to secure all or part of its price". The consigned goods are "inventory" as defined by Section 9–109(4), which includes goods held "for sale or lease". Congress has a conflicting security interest in those goods. Thus, if Gerber's consignment to Bildisco creates a security interest, under Section 9–312(3) Gerber would be required, in addition to perfecting its security interest before the collateral reached the hands of the consignee, to notify Congress, as a known secured party, of its consignment. See Manufacturers Accept. Corp. v. Penning's Sales, Inc., 5 Wash.App. 501, 487 P.2d 1053 (1971).

Gerber challenges the Bankruptcy Court's characterization of the consignment agreement as a security interest on the basis that the terms of the agreement, as well as the parties' conduct with respect to the agreement, evidence no intent to create security interests in the consigned goods. Gerber views the consignment as a "true consignment" by stressing that the agreement provides:

for title to remain in Gerber;

for the inventory to be clearly marked as Gerber's;

for the inventory to be segregated from all other goods of the debtor;

for periodic inspections of the inventory to be made by Gerber;

for monthly reports to be made by Bildisco;

for concurrent payments to be made by Bildisco to Gerber "for the merchandise sold from each such inventory sixty (60) days from the invoice date";

for the balance of inventory to be made by exchanging merchandise with inventory already delivered.

Characterization of the Gerber-Bildisco consignment, however, does not require resolution as it is not determinative of the outcome of this appeal. Even if the consignment at issue was intended to create a true consignment without any security interest in the consignor, the same policy considerations which require that a holder of a purchase money security interest give the secured creditors written notice of that interest are applicable to a true consignment and suggest that the same procedures be followed in order to prevent the consignee's creditors from establishing greater rights in the consigned goods.

Article 2 governs the relative rights of the parties in a true consignment situation. The relevant section [is] 2–326.

* * *

That section recognizes the ability of consignments to hide the consignor's interests to the detriment of creditors—even where the transaction is not intended to create a security interest—and thus requires the consignor to take one of three steps to perfect his rights. Failure to perform one of these steps makes the consignor's interest inferior to the claims of the consignee's creditors, while perfecting the interests renders the section inapplicable. This negative statement does not clarify the relationship between the prior-in-time secured creditor and the consignor. It may mean that perfection immunizes the consigned goods from all attacks made by creditors (including those prior in time) or only from those attacks by creditors whose claims were made after perfection (thus recognizing the basic law that prior in time is prior in right). It may also mean that an exception is recognized by giving the consignor, like the purchase money security interest holder, priority over an earlier created and perfected interest in after-acquired property, provided that actual notice of the consignment is given to prior in time secured parties. Thus, there was a gap in Section 2–326 at the time pertinent to this case.

Section 2–326 does not suggest how this matter of priority is to be handled, and no cases dealing directly with this point have been found. To fill the gap we should look to an analogous situation in the Code and the policy considerations underlying it—purchase money security interests and Section 9–312.

In considering the relationship of a secured party vis-a-vis a holder of a purchase money security interest, the drafters of the Code recognized that purchase money security interests may put secured parties with an after-acquired property clause in inventory to a serious disadvantage. These secured parties are quite susceptible to the loss of their collateral through the replacement of inventory on a purchase money security basis and, unless notified of this change, may be lulled into a false sense of security. If notified, however, the secured parties can protect their rights by acting quickly to correct or salvage the situation. To protect against an unfair dissipation of a creditor's collateral in inventory, the Code requires that actual notification be given. These considerations are equally applicable to all kinds of consignments.

Consignors, like holders of a purchase money security interest, enable a consignee secretly to replace inventory with goods on consignment and thereby undermine the secured party's position of priority in the inventory. Requiring that consignors, in addition to filing, check for and notify secured parties with conflicting interests of the consignment is a reasonable and workable answer for the problem at hand. Moreover, this resolution permits all consignments—those creating security interests and those which do not—to be treated in the same manner. See, Hawkland, Uniform Commercial "Code" Methodology, Univ. of Ill.Law Forum, vol. 1962, pp. 314–320 (1962).

Further support for the conclusion that the gap which existed in Section 2–326 should be filled by analogizing the situation to that covered in Section 9–312(3) is found in UCC 9–114, which was adopted by the New Jersey Legislature after the events in the instant case took place. Laws 1981, c. 138, § 11. That section of the Code treats goods on consignment like purchase money security interests and requires both filing and actual notice to the prior in time secured party. While this legislation does not directly control the requirements for perfection applicable in the present case, it may be considered in seeking to determine how the New Jersey courts would have construed Section 2–326, cf., Shell Oil Co. v. Marinello, 63 N.J. 402, 409, 307 A.2d 598 (1973).

As the Bankruptcy Court pointed out, the authors of the amendment recognized that uncertainty existed under the Code as originally drafted whether the filing rule in Section 2–326(3) applicable to true consignments required only filing under Part 4 of Article 9 or also required notice to prior inventory secured parties of the debtor under Section 9–312(3). It could be argued, as Gerber does, that the amendment requiring notice demonstrates that prior to the amendment no notice was required. I think the better view is that prior to the amendment there was a gap in the law, and the manner in which that gap should be filled is suggested not only by the policy considerations referred to above but also by the statutory amendment which ultimately clarified the statute.

For these reasons, whether the consignment agreement between Bildisco and Gerber is viewed as a purchase money security interest or a true consignment, notice was required to give Gerber priority over Congress.

The order of the Bankruptcy Court will be affirmed.

NOTE

In the light of UCC § 9–114 and the decision in *Bildisco* does it make any difference whether a consignment transaction is treated as a true consignment or a credit sale secured by a security interest? Consider the following facts taken from GBS Meat Industry Pty. Limited v. Kress-Dobkin Co., Inc., 474 F.Supp. 1357 (W.D.Pa.1979). Finance Co. had a security interest in "all existing and hereinafter [sic] acquired inventory and all proceeds of * * * the foregoing" of the debtor, Kress-Dobkin. Finance Co. perfected the security interest by filing a financing statement. Later Kress-Dobkin agreed to act as consignee of meat owned by GBS and to sell it in accordance with instructions by GBS. GBS agreed to pay Kress-Dobkin a commission on the sales. After receipt of the consigned meat Kress-Dobkin sold it pursuant to instructions of GBS but did not remit the proceeds. Instead, Kress-Dobkin paid the proceeds to

Finance Co. GBS brought an action against Finance Co. for conversion of the proceeds of the sale of the consigned meat. GBS had not complied with any of the conditions set forth in UCC § 2–326(3)(a), (b) and (c). Finance Co. conceded that the sale by GBS was a true consignment and that UCC § 2–326 applied. The jury found that Finance Co. had actual knowledge that the meat was received by Kress-Dobkin on consignment. Finance Co. argued that since GBS had not complied with UCC § 2–326(3)(a), (b) or (c), its security interest defeated the title of GBS and it was entitled to the proceeds of sale because its knowledge of the consignment was immaterial under UCC § 2–326. The court, relying on Comment 2 to UCC § 2–326, held in favor of GBS. The court stated " * * * where a secured creditor knows that the proceeds rightfully belong to a consignor, the consignor must have priority. Any other construction of § 2–326 would contravene the intent of that section and would sanction intentional conversion of goods or proceeds." Suppose the court had found that the transaction was not a true consignment, i.e., that the reservation of title by GBS had been a security interest. Since GBS did not file a financing statement its security interest would have been unperfected. Would knowledge by Finance Co. of the unperfected security interest of GBS have affected the right of Finance Co. to the meat? See UCC § 9–301(1)(a) and § 9–312(3) and (5). Does the quoted language of the court apply to this situation as well?

3. PROCEEDS. CHATTEL PAPER

REX FINANCIAL CORP. v. GREAT WESTERN BANK AND TRUST

Court of Appeals of Arizona, Division 1, Department A, 1975.
23 Ariz.App. 286, 532 P.2d 558.

DONOFRIO, JUDGE. This is an appeal from a judgment in favor of the appellee, Great Western Bank & Trust, on a motion to dismiss which was treated by the trial court as a motion for summary judgment under Rule 56 of the Arizona Rules of Civil Procedure, 16 A.R.S. The trial court considered all of the pleadings, affidavits, other matters of record, and the oral arguments of counsel and determined that there was no genuine issue of material fact, in reaching its judgment. For the reasons given below we affirm the judgment of the trial court.

The relevant facts are undisputed. In December of 1971 appellant entered into an agreement with Liberty Mobile Home Centers, Inc., a dealer in mobile homes, under which appellant agreed to finance this dealer's inventory of mobile homes. The dealer delivered to appellant certain manufacturer's certificates of origin on mobile homes to secure repayment of the loans, and gave appellant a security interest in the vehicles by way of a security agreement between the parties. This appeal concerns four of those mobile homes. The four mobile homes were sold by the dealer in the regular course of his business to certain individuals on security agreement contracts. These four security agreement contracts were then sold and assigned to the appellee, Great Western, in the ordinary course of its business for a certain sum which was paid to the dealer. Unfortunately, the dealer did not use these funds to pay off its outstanding loans owed to the appellant.

The basis for attacking a Rule 56 summary judgment ruling is that there were material factual issues disputed by the parties. All facts considered by the trial court appear in the pleadings, affidavits, depositions, and of course, oral arguments of the parties. On reviewing the record we are compelled to agree with the trial court that there were no material issues of fact, and that this was a question of law concerning the construction and application of U.C.C. § 9–308 concerning the priority between certain secured creditors and purchasers of chattel paper.

[UCC § 9–308] states:

"A purchaser of chattel paper or a nonnegotiable instrument who gives new value and takes possession of it in the ordinary course of his business and without knowledge that the specific paper or instrument is subject to a security interest has priority over a security interest which is perfected under § [9–304] (permissive filing and temporary perfection). *A purchaser of chattel paper who gives new value and takes possession of it in the ordinary course of his business has priority over a security interest in chattel paper which is claimed merely as proceeds of inventory subject to a security interest (§ [9–306]), even though he knows that the specific paper is subject to the security interest.* Added Laws 1967, Ch. 3, § 5." (Emphasis added.)

Since it was established that Great Western Bank had knowledge of the security interest claimed by Rex Financial Corporation in the four mobile homes, the second sentence of the foregoing section is the critical one for our purposes.

Appellant's first argument concerns the definition of "chattel paper" used in the above-mentioned sentence of [UCC § 9–308]. Appellant argues that the manufacturer's certificates of origin, which remained in its possession, were a part of the chattel paper and were necessary ingredients along with the security agreements purchased by Great Western to make up the "chattel paper" which must be possessed by the purchaser. We do not agree. [UCC § 9–105(1)(b)] defines "chattel paper" as:

> " 'Chattel paper' means a writing or writings which evidence both a monetary obligation and a security interest in or a lease of specific goods. When a transaction is evidenced both by such a security agreement or a lease and by an instrument or a series of instruments, the group of writings taken together constitutes chattel paper."

Appellant asserts that A.R.S. § 42–643 and § 28–325 of the Motor Vehicle Code contemplate that a manufacturer's certificate of origin is a part of the "transaction" where chattel paper is purchased as in [UCC § 9–105(1)(b)] above. We do not think that such comparison is relevant here. "Chattel paper" clearly must evidence "both a monetary obligation and a security interest in or a lease of specific goods." The manufacturer's certificates of origin do not meet this definition, and the trial court's construction of [UCC § 9–105(1)(b)] was correct in the application to this factual situation. It was undisputed that Great Western gave "new value" for the four security agreements it purchased from the dealer, all in accordance with [UCC § 9–308].

The next requirement of [UCC § 9–308] which is attacked by appellant is the requirement that the purchase of the chattel paper be "in the ordinary course of *his business*." (emphasis added) Appellant maintains that this refers to a practice which "should have been followed" and not to the practice of this particular purchaser of chattel paper. Again we do not agree. The plain language of the statute refers to *"his business"* (meaning the purchaser of the chattel paper). It is undisputed that this purchase was the normal means used at Great Western to obtain this type of chattel paper. As was stated in the deposition of Mr. McFadden, a representative of Great Western, he expected the *dealer* to disburse funds to appellant to pay off the loans for the "floor plan" financing that the dealer had obtained from appellant. The term "buyer in the ordinary course of business" with its requirements of good faith, as used elsewhere in the Uniform Commercial Code, is to be distinguished from the use here of "[buyer] in the ordinary course of *his* business." In fact, [UCC § 9–308] (second sentence) allows the purchaser of the chattel paper to have priority even if he has knowledge of a prior security interest in the collateral. As noted by White and Summers in their Treatise on the Uniform Commercial Code, " * * * the later party is favored on the assumption that chattel paper is his main course but merely the frosting on the cake for the mere proceeds claimant." White and Summers, Uniform Commercial Code, Sec. 25–17, p. 951 (1972 Edition).

This brings us to the final issue raised by appellant: the fourth requirement of the second sentence of [UCC § 9–308], that the security interest claimed by appellant is claimed "merely as proceeds of inventory subject to a security interest." We find Comment 2 to this section of the U.C.C. (as found in the Final Report of the Permanent Editorial Board for the Uniform Commercial Code, Review Committee for Article 9, April 25, 1971) instructive on this issue. There it is stated:

> "Clause (b) of the section deals with the case where the security interest in the chattel paper is claimed merely as proceeds—i.e., on behalf of an inventory financer who has not by some new transaction with the debtor acquired a specific interest in the chattel paper. In that case a purchaser, even though he knows of the inventory financer's proceeds interest, takes priority provided he gives new value and takes possession of the paper in the ordinary course of his business."

We take this language to mean that the drafters of the Code contemplated a situation such as the instant one where the inventory financer, Rex Financial Corp., had a security interest in the collateral (mobile homes) and the proceeds upon sale. The record before us does *not* indicate that Rex entered into any new transaction with the debtor/dealer. The trial court had before it the security agreement between Rex and the dealer as well as the affidavit of Rex's president, and found that Rex's claim was merely to the proceeds of the inventory when sold. We do not find error in this construction and application of the term "mere proceeds of inventory" by the trial court. We think it is a reasonable interpretation of the record that the appellant, Rex, did *not* place a substantial reliance on the chattel paper in making the loan, but rather relied on the collateral (mobile homes) and the proceeds when the collateral was sold. The proceeds of the sale of these four mobile homes included the chattel paper sold by the dealer to Great Western. Rex could have protected itself by requiring all security agreements executed on sale of the mobile homes to be turned over immediately to Rex, or if sold, that all payments for the security agreements (chattel paper) be made to itself.

A case that aptly illustrates the operation of U.C.C. § 9–308 is Associates Discount Corporation v. Old Freeport Bank, 421 Pa. 609, 220 A.2d 621 (1966). In that case a finance company which purchased chattel paper from an auto dealer (in a factual situation somewhat similar to ours) prevailed over a bank which had "floor planned" the inventory of the dealer. The court found that the bank's claim was a mere proceeds claim to the chattel paper and that U.C.C. § 9–308 (second sentence) would operate to give priority to the purchaser of the chattel paper. The inventory financer's interest in the "proceeds" of the sale of the inventory had been shifted to the money paid by the purchaser of the chattel paper to the dealer. Another case in which the same result was obtained was Chrysler Credit Corporation v. Sharp, 56 Misc.2d 261, 288 N.Y.S.2d 525 (1968), a New York case, which again applied U.C.C. § 9–308 and held that the purchaser of an installment contract from an automobile dealer would prevail over a secured inventory financer.

The case of Price v. Universal C.I.T. Credit Corporation, 102 Ariz. 227, 427 P.2d 919 (1967), although decided before our state's adoption of the Uniform Commercial Code, is still instructive in the instant case. The court there held that an inventory financer who brought an action against, among others, the purchase money lender on the sale of an automobile should not have priority over the purchase money lender. The inventory financer sought to recover money loaned to the dealer on a "flooring loan" when the automobiles were sold out of trust. We realize that the Price case did not involve application of U.C.C. § 9–308, but it is indicative of the general feelings of our courts in the area of priorities between secured creditors and purchasers of chattel paper as proceeds of the sale of inventory collateral.

In any case, the construction and application of U.C.C. § 9–308 to undisputed facts is a question of law for the trial court which was reasonably determined in the instant case.

Affirmed.

PROBLEMS

1. Bank was granted a security interest in all inventory and chattel paper (whether then owned or after-acquired) of Debtor, a dealer in appliances. Bank filed a financing statement covering inventory and chattel paper. Debtor sold a refrigerator to a

buyer in ordinary course under an installment sale contract under which Debtor was granted a security interest in the refrigerator. Debtor sold the installment sale contract to Bank which paid Debtor new value. Bank did not take possession of the installment contract. It left it with Debtor with instructions to collect the installments and to remit to the Bank. Debtor then sold the installment contract to Finance Co. which paid new value and took possession of the paper. Finance Co. had actual knowledge of Bank's financing statement. It did not know, however, that Debtor had sold the installment contract to Bank. What are the priorities of Bank and Finance Co. to the installment contract?

2. Debtor is an appliance dealer. Bank advanced $100,000 operating capital to Debtor and took a perfected interest in all Debtor's inventory then owned or thereafter acquired including all proceeds from the disposition of that collateral. Debtor sold a refrigerator to A for $1,000 and reserved a security interest in the refrigerator for the unpaid price plus the finance charge pursuant to an installment sale contract. Debtor sold a washing machine and dryer unit to B for $1,000 and accepted B's unsecured negotiable promissory note for the balance of the price. Debtor leased a large screen television set to C for one year at $100 per month rental. Debtor sold the installment contract, the promissory note, and the lease to Finance Co. which paid cash to the Debtor less a 10% discount. Finance Co. knew Bank was financing Debtor's inventory.

a. What are the priorities between Bank and Finance Co. with respect to the contract, note, and lease? See UCC § 9–308 and § 9–309. Would your answer change if Bank's security agreement and financing statement specifically mentioned chattel paper and instruments as primary collateral?

b. What are the priorities between Bank and Finance Co. with respect to Debtor's residual right to the television set? See In re Leasing Consultants, 486 F.2d 367 (2d Cir. 1973); In re Watertown Tractor & Equipment Co., Inc., 94 Wis.2d 622, 289 N.W.2d 288 (1980).

4. BUYERS

Inventories are meant to be sold, and the law has traditionally protected the inventory buyer against the inventory financer. See generally Skilton, Buyer in the Ordinary Course of Business under Article 9 of the Uniform Commercial Code (and Related

Matters), 1974 Wis.L.Rev. 1. If the secured party authorizes the debtor to dispose of the inventory, UCC § 9–306(2) provides that the security interest continues in the proceeds of the sale and not in the goods in the hands of the buyer. Even if the secured party does not authorize the debtor to dispose of the goods, UCC § 9–307(1) provides that the goods pass free of the security interest so long as the buyer qualifies as a "buyer in ordinary course of business" (UCC § 1–201(9)). Such a buyer must buy from a person in the business of selling goods of that kind, that is, he must buy inventory, and he must do so in ordinary course.

All in all the Code goes far in protecting the inventory buyer. He may take free of a security interest of which he has knowledge; he need not take possession of the goods; and he may buy either for cash or on secured or unsecured credit. We will learn more about the rights of buyers when we consider farm products and consumer goods covered later in this chapter. But first we consider a controversial case on inventory buyers.

TANBRO FABRICS CORP. v. DEERING MILLIKEN, INC.

New York Court of Appeals, 1976.
39 N.Y.2d 632, 385 N.Y.S.2d 260, 350 N.E.2d 590.

BREITEL, CHIEF JUDGE. In an action for the tortious conversion of unfinished textile fabrics (greige goods), plaintiff Tanbro sought damages from Deering Milliken, a textile manufacturer. Tanbro, known in the trade as a "converter", finishes textile into dyed and patterned fabrics. The goods in question had been manufactured by Deering, and sold on a "bill and hold" basis to Mill Fabrics, also a converter, now insolvent. Mill Fabrics resold the goods, while still in Deering's warehouse, also on a bill and hold basis, to Tanbro.

Deering refused to deliver the goods to Tanbro on Tanbro's instruction because, although these goods had been paid for, there was an open account balance due Deering from Mill Fabrics. Deering under its sales agreements with Mill Fabrics claimed a perfected security interest in the goods.

At Supreme Court, Tanbro recovered a verdict and judgment of $87,451.68 for compensatory and $25,000 for punitive damages. The Appellate Division, by a divided court, modified to strike the recovery for punitive damages, and otherwise affirmed. Both parties appeal.

The issue is whether Tanbro's purchase of the goods was in the ordinary course of Mill Fabrics' business, and hence free of Deering's perfected security interest.

There should be an affirmance. Mill Fabrics' sale to Tanbro was in the ordinary course of business, even though its predominant business purpose was, like Tanbro's, the converting of greige goods into finished fabrics. All the Uniform Commercial Code requires is that the sale be in ordinary course associated with the seller's business (§ 9–307, subd. [1]). The record established that converters buy greige goods in propitious markets and often in excess of their requirements as they eventuate. On the occasion of excess purchases, converters at times enter the market to sell the excess through brokers to other converters, and converters buy such goods if the price is satisfactory or the particular goods are not available from manufacturers. Both conditions obtained here.

Tanbro and Mill Fabrics were customers of Deering for many years. Goods would be purchased in scale on a "bill and hold" basis, that is, the goods would be paid for and delivered as the buyers instructed. When the goods were needed, they were delivered directly where they were to be converted, at the buyers' plants or the plants of others if that would be appropriate. Pending instructions, the sold and paid for goods were stored in the warehouses of the manufacturer, both because the buyers lacked warehousing space and retransportation of the goods to be processed would be minimized.

Mill Fabrics, like many converters, purchased greige goods from Deering on credit as well as on short-term payment. Under the sales notes or agreements, all the goods on hand in the seller's warehouse stood as security for the balance owed on the account. Tanbro was familiar with this practice. It was immaterial whether or not particular goods had been paid for. If the goods were resold by Deering's customers, Deering obtained for a period a perfected security interest in the proceeds of resale for the indebtedness on the open account (Uniform Commercial Code, § 9–306, subds. [2], [3]).

Deering's sales executives advised Tanbro that it had discontinued production of a certain blended fabric. Upon Tanbro's inquiry, the Deering sales executives recommended to Tanbro that it try purchasing the blended fabric from Mill Fabrics, which Deering knew had an excess supply. Ultimately, Tanbro purchased from Mill Fabrics through a broker 267,000 yards at 26 cents per yard. Tanbro paid Mill Fabrics in full.

During October and November of 1969, approximately 57,000 yards of the blended fabric was released by Deering on Mill Fabrics' instructions and delivered to a Tanbro affiliate. There remained some 203,376 yards at the Deering warehouse.

In early January of 1970, Tanbro ordered the remaining fabric delivered to meet its own contractual obligation to deliver the blended fabric in finished state at 60 cents per yard. Deering refused.

By this time Mill Fabrics was in financial trouble and its account debit balance with Deering at an unprecedented high. In mid-January of 1970, a meeting of its creditors was called and its insolvency confirmed.

As noted earlier, under the terms of the Deering sales agreements with Mill Fabrics, Deering retained a security interest in Mill Fabrics' "property" on a bill and hold basis, whether paid for or not. This security interest was perfected by Deering's continued possession of the goods (Uniform Commercial Code, § 1–201, subd. [37]; § 9–305). Tanbro argued that if it had title by purchase its goods were excluded from the security arrangement which was literally restricted to the "property of the buyer", that is, Mill Fabrics. In any event, unless prevented by other provisions of the code, or the sale was not unauthorized, Tanbro took title subject to Deering's security interest.

Under the code (§ 9–307, subd. [1]) a buyer in the ordinary course of the seller's business takes goods free of even a known security interest so long as the buyer does not know that the purchase violates the terms of the security agreement. As defined in the code (§ 1–201, subd. [9]) "a buyer in ordinary course" is "a person who in good faith and without knowledge that the sale to him is in violation of the ownership rights or security interest of a third party in the goods buys in ordinary course from a person in the business of selling goods of that kind but does not include a pawnbroker. 'Buying' may be for cash or by exchange of other property or on secured or unsecured credit and includes receiving goods or documents of title under a preexisting contract for sale but does not include a transfer in bulk or as security for or in total or partial satisfaction of a money debt." Critical to Tanbro's claim is that it purchased the goods in the ordinary course of Mill Fabrics' business and that it did not purchase the goods in knowing violation of Deering's security interest.

Under the code whether a purchase was made from a person in the business of selling goods of that kind turns primarily on whether that person holds the goods for sale. Such goods are a person's selling inventory. (Uniform Commercial Code, § 1–201, subd. [9]; § 9–307, subd. [1]; Official Comment, at par. 2.) Note, however, that not all purchases of goods held as inventory qualify as purchases from a person in the business of selling goods of that kind. The purpose of section 9–307 is more limited. As indicated in the Practice Commentary to that section, the purpose is to permit buyers "to buy goods from a dealer in such goods without having to protect himself against a possible security interest on the inventory" (Kripke, Practice Commentary, McKinney's Cons.Laws of N.Y., Book 62½, Uniform Commercial Code, § 9–307, p. 491, par. 1). Hence, a qualifying purchase is one made from a seller who is a dealer in such goods.

A former Mill Fabrics' employee testified that there were times when Mill Fabrics, like all converters, found itself with excess goods. When it was to their business advantage, they sold the excess fabrics to other converters. Although these sales were relatively infrequent they were nevertheless part of and in the ordinary course of Mill Fabrics' business, even if only incidental to the predominant business purpose. Examples of a nonqualifying sale might be a bulk sale, a sale in distress at an obvious loss price, a sale in liquidation, a sale of a commodity never dealt with before by the seller and wholly unlike its usual inventory, or the like (see National Bank of Commerce v. First Nat. Bank & Trust Co. [Tulsa], 446 P.2d 277, 282 [Okl.]; cf. Sternberg v. Rubenstein, 305 N.Y. 235, 239, 112 N.E.2d 210, 211; Whitmire v. Keylon, 12 U.C.C.Rept.Serv. 1203, 1206–1207 [Tenn.]).

The combination of stored, paid for goods, on a hold basis, and the retention of a security interest by Deering makes commercial sense. Mill Fabrics' capacity to discharge its obligation to Deering was in part made possible because it sold off or converted the goods held at the Deering warehouse. Mill Fabrics, as an honest customer, was supposed to remit the proceeds from resale or conversion to Deering and thus reduce, and eventually discharge its responsibility to Deering. Thus, so long as it was customary for Mill Fabrics, and in the trade for converters, to sell off excess goods, the sale was in the ordinary course of business. Moreover, on an alternative analysis, such a sale by Mill Fabrics was therefore impliedly authorized under the code if its indebtedness to Deering was to be liquidated (see Official Comment to § 9–307, par. 2; Draper v. Minneapolis-Moline, 100 Ill. App.2d 324, 329, 241 N.E.2d 342).

All subdivision (1) of section 9–307 requires is that the sale be of the variety reasonably to be expected in the regular course of an on-going business (see Newton-Waltham Bank & Trust Co. v. Bergen Motors, 68 Misc.2d 228, 230, 327 N.Y.S.2d 77, 81, affd., 75 Misc.2d 103, 347 N.Y.S.2d 568; cf. First Nat. Bank, Martinsville v. Crone, 301 N.E.2d 378, 381 [Ind.App.]). This was such a case.

Hempstead Bank v. Andy's Car Rental System, 35 A.D.2d 35, 312 N.Y.S.2d 317, stands for no contrary principle. Rightly or wrongly, it was there held as a matter of law, unlike the situation here, that the selling of used rental cars was not in the ordinary course of business for an auto rental company (compare Bank of Utica v. Castle Ford, 36 A.D.2d 6, 9, 317 N.Y.S.2d 542, 544). It may be significant that the used cars were in no sense an "inventory" of a sales business, but the capital inventory of a leasing company, usually subject to extended term financing.

With respect to Tanbro's claim for punitive damages, the evidence was not clear that Deering was guilty of a wanton or willful obstruction to Tanbro's rights as a secondary buyer, let alone of fraud or a high degree of moral turpitude (cf. Walker v. Sheldon, 10 N.Y.2d 401, 404–405, 223 N.Y.S.2d 488, 490–491, 179 N.E.2d 497, 498–499). Deering could have believed in good faith that its security interest survived the sale by Mill Fabrics to Tanbro. Hence, the Appellate Division properly struck the award for punitive damages.

Accordingly, the order of the Appellate Division should be affirmed, with costs to plaintiff Tanbro.

NOTES

1. Case 1. Debtor sold expensive watches and jewelry. Business was bad and in order to meet his payroll Debtor induced Bank to make an emergency loan to him by pledging to Bank some slow-selling watches that Debtor thought he could get along without for a few weeks. Ironically, a few days later Buyer came to Debtor's store stating that he wanted to buy a watch that he had seen in Debtor's store a few days earlier. It was one of the watches that Debtor had just pledged. Debtor accepted. He took Buyer's payment and told him that he had the watch at another retail outlet and would have it for him at the store the next day. At the time of the sale, Debtor had intended to take the money to Bank and have the watch released from the pledge. However, by the close of business on the day

of the sale, Debtor realized his situation was hopeless and absconded with all of the cash and much of the inventory.

Case 2. Debtor sold expensive watches and jewelry. For several years Hamilton had financed Debtor's inventory of Hamilton watches on a purchase-money basis. You may assume that Hamilton's security interest was perfected by filing and that it had complied with the notice requirements of UCC § 9–312(3) with respect to Debtor's other inventory financers. Debtor fell so far behind in his account that Hamilton repossessed all Debtor's inventory of Hamilton watches and held the watches preparatory to resale under UCC § 9–504. The day after the repossession Buyer stated to Debtor that he wanted to buy a certain model of Hamilton that he had seen in Debtor's store a few days before. Debtor accepted. He took Buyer's payment and told him that he had the watch at another retail outlet and would have it for him at the store in a few days. When Buyer returned he found Debtor's store closed and learned that Debtor had absconded with everything.

Does *Tanbro* compel a decision for Buyer against Bank in Case 1 or against Hamilton in Case 2? Can you distinguish *Tanbro* from either case? See Kripke, Should Section 9–307(1) of the Uniform Commercial Code Apply Against a Secured Party in Possession? 33 Bus.Law. 153 (1977). Professor Kripke, who participated in *Tanbro* on the side of the secured party, contends that the *Tanbro* court's literal reading of UCC § 9–307(1) yields bad policy results and recommends that the section be amended to protect inventory financers in possession of the property sold. Harold Birnbaum, like Professor Kripke, an Article 9 pioneer, disagrees with Kripke's recommendation in his article, Section 9–307(1) of the Uniform Commercial Code Versus Possessory Security Interest—A Reply to Professor Homer Kripke, 33 Bus. Law. 2607 (1978). The lawyer for *Tanbro*, Samuel Gottlieb, weighed in with his own reply to Professor Kripke in Section 9–307(1) and *Tanbro Fabrics:* A Further Response, 33 Bus. Law. 2611 (1978), in which he contends that on its facts *Tanbro* makes good commercial sense.

2. UCC § 1–201(9) defines "buyer in ordinary course of business" as one who buys "in good faith and without knowledge that the sale to him is in violation of the ownership rights or security interest of a third party." UCC § 9–307(1) provides that a buyer in ordinary course of business can take free of an inventory lien "even though the buyer knows of its existence." How can the buyer be in good faith under UCC § 1–201(9) if he

knows of the security interest in the inventory? An ordinary
course buyer of inventory which is subject to a security interest
can assume that his purchase does not violate the rights of the
secured party because it will invariably be the case that the secured party has authorized the debtor to sell. Thus, in most
cases UCC § 9–306(2) can be used as the basis for protecting the
buyer. UCC § 9–307(1) is important only in those cases in which
the authorization to sell may be subject to certain conditions that
were not met in the particular case. See *First National Bank*,
the case that follows these notes. The effect of UCC § 9–307(1)
is to free the buyer of the burden of determining the actual authority of the seller. The good faith of the buyer should come
into play only in those cases in which the buyer not only knows
that there is a security interest but also that the sale to him
violates the rights of the secured party. See Comment 2 to UCC
§ 9–307(1). Should *Tanbro* have been decided solely on the basis of UCC § 9–306(2)? Didn't Deering Milliken in fact authorize the sale?

3. Was Mill Fabrics "in the business of selling goods" of the
kind that Tanbro bought? UCC § 1–201(9). Mill Fabrics' primary business was converting and selling fabrics in a finished state
and it sold the unconverted greige goods to other converters in
what the court describes as the "relatively infrequent" cases
when it had ordered more than it could process. The court concedes that such sales were "only incidental to the predominant
business purpose" of Mill Fabrics, supra p. 141. In Hempstead
Bank v. Andy's Car Rental System, Inc., 35 A.D.2d 35, 312
N.Y.2d 317 (2d Dep't 1970), the debtor was in the business of
leasing and renting cars. Periodically the debtor sold some of
its used cars and replaced them with new ones. Buyer was a
wholesale auto dealer who bought used cars from auto dealers
and rental companies and resold them to used car dealers. In
violation of its security agreement with the bank, the debtor sold
13 used cars to buyer over a period of some six months. The
court held for the bank as against the buyer on the ground that
debtor was in the business of leasing or renting cars and that
sales of its leasing inventory were merely incidental to its leasing and rental. See O'Neill v. Barnett Bank, 360 So.2d 150 (Fla.
App.1978). See White and Summers, Uniform Commercial Code
§ 25–13 (2d ed. 1980), for a discussion of *Tanbro* and *Hempstead Bank* on this point.

5.　FARM PRODUCTS

FIRST NATIONAL BANK & TRUST CO. OF OKLAHOMA CITY v. IOWA BEEF PROCESSORS, INC.

United States Court of Appeals, Tenth Circuit, 1980.
626 F.2d 764.

LOGAN, CIRCUIT JUDGE.　First National Bank & Trust Company of Oklahoma City (the bank) brought suit against Iowa Beef Processors, Inc. (IBP), asserting claims under the Oklahoma version of the Uniform Commercial Code.

* * *

The facts are undisputed. Wheatheart, Inc. (Wheatheart) owned and operated feedlots. Under its auspices investor limited partnerships were formed to acquire cattle to be fattened in the lots. Wheatheart Cattle Company (Cattle Company), a wholly owned subsidiary of Wheatheart, was a managing partner in these partnerships. Four of these partnerships—Wheatheart Cattle Feeding Funds 4, 11, 12 and 13 (Funds)—borrowed money from the bank to purchase cattle. The bank took a perfected security interest in the cattle. These cattle were fed out in the Wheatheart lots until they reached the desired weights and were sold by Wheatheart.

Under the financing arrangement with the bank, Wheatheart would receive payment for the cattle in its own name directly from the purchaser. Wheatheart would then deposit this check or draft in its account and write its own check for that amount, payable jointly to the Funds and the bank. A bonded warehouseman, Lawrence Systems, Inc., was used to control the delivery of the cattle to the purchasers and to monitor the transfer of the payment check to the bank.

In 1974 Wheatheart began experiencing severe financial trouble. During December 1974 and January 1975, Wheatheart sold almost all the cattle in its feedlots without notifying the bank of the sales or remitting any of the proceeds to the bank or the Funds. On January 22 Wheatheart filed for bankruptcy, leaving the bank with a large outstanding loan balance and no collateral in the hands of the debtor or its agents. Consequently, the bank sought to recover some of its loss from IBP which had bought Wheatheart cattle in two transactions during this period. There is no contention that IBP was not a good faith purchaser.

The circumstances surrounding the sales are these: IBP had made the first purchase in December. * * * The next day the cattle were slaughtered and a final price of $183,676 was set.[2] IBP paid this amount by check on January 13. Wheatheart deposited this check.

* * *

The district court granted summary judgment on the first sale in favor of IBP. It ruled the bank had given express consent to the sale, which cut off any continuing security interest in the collateral pursuant to [UCC] § 9–306(2). The bank attacks this decision, arguing that whether consent was given is in issue and therefore not properly a matter for summary judgment.

Section 9–306(2) authorization can be given "in the security agreement or otherwise." The security agreement here contained no reference to sales and therefore, of course, gave no authorization for sales. Thus, we must look elsewhere for authorization. Under Oklahoma law, authorization to sell collateral can be both express and implied. See Poteau State Bank v. Denwalt, 597 P.2d 756, 760 (Okl.1979). Here the revolving credit agreement between the Funds and the bank provides only that "all proceeds of the sale of cattle" are to be applied to reduce the loan balances, and that the Funds "will not dispose of any of its assets except for full, fair and reasonable compensation." Also, the bank made the following statement in response to an interrogatory: "[T]he borrowers had standing consent to sell cattle. However, such consent was conditioned upon prompt remission of the proceeds of such sale to plaintiff." Further, depositions in the record contain the following responses by bank officers to questions concerning the authority to sell:

> A. [Bank Vice President for agricultural loans Samuel Gilmore] I guess he has, I guess Lawrence has the implied consent from the bank to release those cattle, so long as they get me the money for the cattle.
>
> Q. Where is that implied consent?
>
> A. In the delivery instructions.

---

2. The cattle were sold on a grade and yield basis; thus, the exact price could not be determined until the packer had slaughtered the cattle. Because of the time lag, the purchaser would often advance a part of the purchase price to the feedlot.

Q. Did the Lawrence people have the authority from the bank to open the gate and let the cattle out into the chute to be loaded onto the truck without checking with the bank?

A. So long as they got me the check for the proceeds within seven days.

and

Q. Now, that security agreement, and I'm talking about the standard printed agreement,[4] did provide that the collateral could not be sold without the consent of the bank, did it not?

A. [Bank Senior Vice President Ronald Bradshaw] I believe that's right.

Q. But in fact that was not required of your borrowers?

A. In the trade itself, I've never seen—I haven't seen it done that way. I mean in the trade, I don't—I haven't seen it a requirement that the bank give permission that the cattle be sold.

Q. Prior to the time of sale you mean?

A. Right.

Q. That is not customary in the cattle business, is it?

A. Not to my knowledge, no.

Q. And you, in making your cattle loans, did not require that, did you?

A. We didn't, no.

Plaintiffs point to no contrary evidence in the record. Based on the documents and admissions by the bank officers that consent to sell was given, we conclude there is no disputed issue of fact.

The bank contends, however, that even if consent was given, it was conditioned on the bank receiving the proceeds from the sale—a condition not performed here. Assuming the authorization was so qualified, we must decide whether the bank could condition its consent in this way.

The normal rule is that a buyer in ordinary course of business cuts off the security interest in collateral sold. [UCC] § 9–307. Cattle feeding arrangements are unusual in at least two respects, however. First, they may be sales of "farm prod-

4. Apparently the reference here is to a standard security contract used by the bank in other circumstances; no printed agreement was utilized in the transactions at issue in this case, nor was there any reference in the forms used here to the effect collateral could not be sold without consent of the bank.

ucts from a person engaged in farming operations," which are excepted from the usual rule of section 9–307. This exception permits the secured party to reach the collateral in the hands of a good faith purchaser unless consent to the sale has been given pursuant to section 9–306(2). Second, because a feeding operation entails the continuing process of acquisition and, after only a short feeding period, sale, the cattle are more like inventory than farm crops, which might be harvested only once each year. The reality of cattle financing arrangements is that the secured party expects and wants the collateral to be sold continually in order for it to receive payment on the line of credit it has extended. At the same time, however, the secured party is reluctant to give blanket consent to the sales because it would lose its right to go against the purchaser should the debtor default. Consequently, secured parties in this area have tried to protect themselves by placing conditions on sales authorizations.

Courts have recognized the validity of certain of these conditions. See, e.g., North Central Kan. Prod. Credit Ass'n v. Washington Sales Co., 223 Kan. 689, 577 P.2d 35, 38 (1978) (authorization to sell if payment made jointly to seller and bank); Baker Prod. Credit Ass'n v. Long Creek Meat Co., 266 Or. 643, 513 P.2d 1129, 1134 (1973) (authorization to sell on condition buyer's drafts drawn on defendant bank were honored and paid); Farmers State Bank v. Edison Non-Stock Coop. Ass'n, 190 Neb. 789, 212 N.W.2d 625, 628 (1973) (consent to sell so long as no prior default has occurred). In all these cases the condition was either a condition precedent ascertainable by the purchaser prior to the sale or a matter within the control of the buyer.

There are a few cases involving conditions like the one imposed here. In Southwest Washington Prod. Credit Ass'n, 92 Wash.2d 30, 593 P.2d 167, 169 (1979), the court, after concluding consent was conditioned on the secured party receiving the proceeds, found that violation of the condition left the secured party with a right to reach the collateral that was sold. Unlike the instant case, however, the security agreement expressly prohibited sale of the collateral without the written consent of the lender.[5] Also, the buyer had failed to pay the debtor for the

5. The buyer had argued that the bank, by its action of permitting sales by the debtor, had waived its right to insist upon written consent. Cases involving a course of dealing as a waiver of a requirement in a written contract involve the policy of U.C.C. § 1–205(4) that express terms control over course of dealing and trade usage. Compare Clovis Nat'l Bank v. Thomas, 77 N.M. 554, 425 P.2d 726 (1967) with Garden City Prod. Credit Ass'n v. Lannan, 186 Neb. 668, 186 N.W.2d 99 (1971).

encumbered goods and consequently the seller was unable to pay the secured party.

Other courts have held that when consent is conditioned on the debtor's agreement to remit the proceeds, the consent is effective to release the lien on the collateral sold even though the secured party never received the proceeds. In these cases the buyer had paid the debtor, yet the debtor failed to remit the proceeds to the secured party.

> In the present case there is substantial evidence from which the trier of fact could find the bank gave general authority to Glenn Meier [the debtor] to sell collateral subject to his duty to account for the proceeds. The bank acknowledges no complaint would have been made here had the proceeds been applied against the note. The bank lost because it trusted Glenn Meier to do what he had done before when he sold collateral. Murray [the buyer] trusted his assurance the sale was free of lien. As between the bank and Murray, the law imposes the risk of loss in these circumstances on the bank.

Lisbon Bank & Trust Co. v. Murray, 206 N.W.2d 96, 99 (Iowa 1973). See also United States v. Hansen, 311 F.2d 477, 480 (8th Cir. 1963) (applying Iowa law); North Central Kan. Prod. Credit Ass'n v. Washington Sales Co., 223 Kan. 689, 577 P.2d 35, 41 (1978).

The Code puts a greater burden on the buyer of farm products to check for liens on the collateral because a good faith purchase of those products does not automatically cut off the security interest. [UCC] § 9–307. IBP did not check to determine whether a security interest was involved and, if so, what the terms of the agreement were. We hold this failure is irrelevant here because the bank gave the debtors actual authority to sell; it was not necessary that this authority be communicated to the purchaser. See Lisbon Bank & Trust Co. v. Murray, 206 N.W.2d at 99. See also First Nat'l Bank & Trust Co. v. Stock Yards Loan Co., 65 F.2d 226, 229–30 (8th Cir. 1933) (pre-UCC chattel mortgage case). Even if IBP had checked, the bank presumably would have informed IBP that it had agreed to allow buyers to pay Wheatheart directly. Moreover, IBP could not have known at the time of the sale that Wheatheart would not remit the proceeds to the bank.

Consent to sell in the debtor's own name "provided" the seller remits by its own check to the bank is not a true conditional sales authorization. In essence, such a condition makes the buyer an insurer of acts beyond its control. The bank has made performance of the debtor's duty to remit proceeds to the bank a condition of releasing from liability a third party acting in good faith. IBP could not ascertain in advance whether this condition would be met, as it could if a condition precedent was involved; nor did IBP have any control over the performance of the condition, as long as it paid Wheatheart. A secured party has an interest in protecting its security by conditioning its consent, but it can place conditions that would afford it protection without great unfairness to the good faith purchaser.

We conclude that the policy of the Uniform Commercial Code to promote ready exchange in the marketplace, see Riverside Nat'l Bank v. Law, 564 P.2d 240, 243 (Okl.1977), outweighs the secured party's interest in the collateral under these circumstances. Therefore, we hold that even though the secured party conditions consent on receipt of the proceeds, failure of this condition will not prevent that consent from cutting off the security interest under section 9–306(2).

* * *

NOTES

1. Why are buyers in ordinary course of farm products not given the same protection as buyers in ordinary course of inventory? Pre-Code law usually protected the chattel mortgagee of crops or livestock against the grain merchant or meatpacker who purchased from the mortgagor. Professor Gilmore states that the exclusion from UCC § 9–307(1) of "a person buying farm products from a person engaged in farming operations" was the result of "bowing before the weight of case law authority." Gilmore, Security Interests in Personal Property 714 (1965).

2. Would the result in the principal case have been different if plaintiff had proved that the security agreement had specifically provided that the collateral could not be sold without consent of the bank? *Clovis*, cited in footnote 5, involved such a security agreement. Because of a course of dealing between the bank and the debtor of accepting proceeds from the sale of livestock sold without the bank's consent, it was held that the bank could not assert the consent requirement in a subsequent transaction in which the debtor sold collateral and did not remit the proceeds. In effect the bank "authorized" the sale under UCC § 9–306(2). Most cases have not followed *Clovis* and the result of that case was promptly reversed by an amendment to

UCC § 9–306(2) in the state in which it was decided. As a matter of policy should the financer or the buyer bear the burden of assuring that proceeds of collateral are remitted to the secured party?

PROBLEM

Debtor is a dairy farmer. He sells milk produced by his herd of cows to Local Dairy that buys all of his production. Male offspring of the herd are usually sold, as are older cows when their milk production declines below minimum levels. Female calves are normally retained to replenish and augment the herd. Debtor is heavily indebted to State Bank and has granted State Bank a security interest in all of Debtor's "present and after-acquired livestock, equipment, farm products and accounts receivable." State Bank perfected the security interest by filing.

In order to expand his production Debtor purchased 100 cows (the "new herd") which are housed in a separate barn. Funds to enable Debtor to acquire the new herd were obtained from National Bank. Under the loan agreement National Bank was granted a security interest in the new herd and in "all offspring and milk produced by them" and Debtor is obligated to pay over to National Bank 80% of all cash proceeds of collateral to reduce the loan. Prior to delivery of the cows to Debtor, National Bank filed a financing statement and informed State Bank of the terms of the loan.

Debtor has fallen behind in his payments to State Bank. To prevent State Bank from declaring a default he has begun to sell substantial number of cows and calves and has paid the proceeds to State Bank. Sales included animals from the new herd. Debtor has also diverted more than half of payments for milk produced by the new herd to State Bank.

National Bank has declared Debtor in default because of breach of the loan agreement. It has also brought an action against State Bank to recover all payments made to it by Debtor from proceeds of sale of animals from the new herd and milk produced by the new herd. What are the rights of State Bank and National Bank? State Bank will rely on UCC § 9–312(5). National Bank will rely on UCC § 9–312(4). Are offspring of the new herd and milk produced by them proceeds under UCC § 9–306(1)?

C. ACCOUNTS RECEIVABLE

GREENBERG, INVENTORY AND ACCOUNTS RECEIVABLE FINANCING*

1956 U. of Ill.L.Forum 601, 612–618.

ACCOUNTS RECEIVABLE FINANCING

Accounts receivable financing consists of arrangements whereby a financing agency either purchases accounts receivable from a business concern or makes loans or advances to it secured by an assignment of its accounts receivable. In the first type of financing, commonly called "factoring," the purchaser of the accounts normally assumes the credit risks, without recourse against the seller, and the seller's customers are notified to make payment directly to the factor. In the second type, the financing agency makes loans or advances against assigned accounts receivable, without assuming the credit risk and generally without notifying the assignor's customers. The absence of notification has led such financing to be called "non-notification financing." While there may be some variations, which will be referred to later, factoring and non-notification financing are the two principal methods of accounts receivable financing.

Like most forms of inventory financing, accounts receivable financing is based upon a continuing series of short-term transactions. The factor or lender makes periodic purchases of or loans against assigned accounts as often as the business concern which it is financing requires funds. Thus a business in need of working funds has available a revolving line of credit which fluctuates with its sales. Unlike a straight loan, which must be negotiated as to amount and which becomes due in a lump sum at maturity, or in fixed installments, accounts receivable financing supplies funds in proportion to the volume of accounts assigned. This ordinarily coincides with the needs of the business, since more funds become available as sales increase, permitting the replacement or increase of inventories needed to fill sales orders.

In addition to being geared to fluctuating requirements for working funds, accounts receivable financing has other attractions for many businesses. In factoring, the function of the factor in passing credits and assuming the credit risk on approved sales, as well as collecting the resulting accounts, is a valuable service to many concerns. No sizable staff is required to handle credits and collections, and the principals of small businesses are freed to concentrate on production and sales. In non-notification financing, these considerations are absent, the furnishing of working funds being the only significant function. Some businesses may be unable to obtain any open-line credit, but nevertheless their accounts receivable, because of their high degree of liquidity, may constitute acceptable security for loans, the lender looking to the responsibility of the borrower's customers, rather than to the borrower's own financial position. Other businesses may have some lines of credit, but may require funds greatly in excess of any unsecured lines obtainable. This type of need is typical of seasonal businesses, and is well served by the fluctuating nature of accounts receivable financing. Many under-capitalized businesses have found that the sale or pledge of their accounts will furnish necessary working funds without the dilution of ownership which would result from seeking equity capital. In some cases, an accounts receivable accommodation may even permit a savings in cost as compared with a straight bank loan. Interest is charged only on the funds actually in use, by netting advances and collections, which may result in a lower cost than paying interest at a lower rate on the entire amount of a straight loan, taking into consideration balances which the borrower may be required to maintain at the lending bank.

For all of these reasons, accounts receivable financing has come to be recognized as an important part of our modern credit structure. Its growth has been largely due to its own merits, since its development was accomplished without organized support, and in the face of some resistance. The simplicity and convenience of the technique make it a matter of wonder that its extensive use is of such recent development. Commercial finance companies have grown to important size only in the past three decades or so. * * * The entry of commercial banks into the accounts receivable financing field in significant volume is even more recent, dating from the depression days of 1933 when unused lending capacity caused them to turn in this direction. Now a large number of commercial banks are in the field.

It was not too long ago, and remnants of the attitude still persist, that financing of accounts receivable was stigmatized as "hocking" accounts, and raised the suspicion that bankruptcy was just around the corner. Today, however, especially with the tight money problem aggravating working capital needs, accounts receivable financing is recognized as a legitimate and useful means of financing. Many businesses owe their increased volumes, and some their very existence, to working funds obtained through financing their accounts.

Development of Accounts Receivable Financing

Although the widespread commercial acceptance and employment of accounts receivable financing is of rather recent development, its history is not. A brief reference to the origins of factoring, the first form of accounts receivable financing, gives some insight into the parallel development of the law.

Factoring is said to have originated as early as the fourteenth century, when commission merchants became active in financing foreign trade. The tremendous expansion of commerce and industry following the industrial revolution in England gave new importance and scope to these functions. By the eighteenth century, the commission merchant or factor was a well-accepted part of English commerce, although his functions did not yet include financing. The factor was then primarily engaged in selling goods which had been shipped to him on consignment. The limited methods of transportation and communication then existing made it impractical for a manufacturer to sell his products directly in distant or foreign markets. Rather the practice was developed of shipping the goods on consignment to a factor doing business in the potential market area. The factor would make sales and collections and remit to the manufacturer. For his services he would receive an agreed commission, which he was entitled to deduct from the proceeds of sales before remitting to the manufacturer. It was only natural that the manufacturer relied heavily on the factor for advice, not only on style and selling, but also on approving credits.

The next step was for the factor to guarantee sales to his customers in cases where there was doubt as to their ability to pay. The factor, having first-hand credit information and wishing to earn a commission, was often in a position to guarantee payment to the manufacturer where the manufacturer would otherwise hesitate to approve the sale. As factors prospered and accumulated capital, it was also natural that manufacturers whom they represented should look to them for financial assistance. It followed that factors began not only to guarantee credits, but also to make advance payment to the manufacturer for an additional commission, thus assisting the manufacturer in financing his operations.   *   *   *

Non-notification accounts receivable financing has developed more recently, being little used until the present century. Before that time credit sales were usually evidenced by a note or a trade acceptance, with longer terms than are usually granted today. Expanding markets and more impersonal customer relationships led to a shortening of credit terms, and the open account largely supplanted notes and trade acceptances. Sellers came to rely more and more upon open lines of bank credit, although some banks which had discounted customers' notes and trade acceptances began making loans secured by the assignment of accounts receivable, but without assuming the credit risk or notifying the account-debtors of the assignment.

Today factoring and non-notification financing serve the same basic need for working funds. Yet their divergent origins continue to find expression in the common law relating to their conduct. Perhaps, however, a closer look at the respective mechanics of these devices should precede an examination of the applicable law.

Factoring

Factoring, as we have seen, is characterized by assumption of the credit risk by the factor and by notification to the account-debtor of the assignment of the account to the factor. It follows that the factor collects the account directly. Sometimes the factor will accept an account which has not been approved as to credit, at the client's risk. Occasionally, too, the factor will make arrangements to factor accounts without notification. In such cases the client will be permitted to collect the accounts in trust for the factor. Such variations are not common. They arise either from a desire to utilize the factor's credit guaranty without the client's customers knowing that he is financing his accounts, or in order to avoid framing the transaction as a loan secured by the pledge of accounts in states where the legal rate of interest is too low to cover the normal charge.

Aside from such infrequent variations, the typical factoring agreement is not complex. It provides that all sales accounts will be assigned to the factor; sales will be made only with written credit approval by the factor; the factor assumes any loss by reason of the insolvency of the customer; the factor does not assume any loss arising from merchandise or delivery disputes;

the factor will pay for each invoice its face amount, less any discount or allowance which the customer may take (thus any discounts not taken by the customer belong to the factor as compensation for the time the account remains unpaid after the expiration of the discount period); the factor will make advance payment of the purchase price upon assignment of the accounts, but frequently it is specified that a portion of the purchase price, usually ten per cent or fifteen per cent, may be withheld to cover possible merchandise or delivery disputes; usually interest is charged for advance payments from the time of the payment until the average due date of the accounts purchased (plus a short period, such as ten days, to allow for collection), ordinarily at the rate of six per cent per annum, but no interest is charged thereafter, as the factor has assumed the credit risk, and interest is sometimes waived altogether; the factoring commission is specified as a percentage, usually less than two per cent, of sales as compensation for the services of the factor in making credit investigations, supervising the ledgering and collection of the accounts, and assuming the credit risk; and it is agreed that the factor will be furnished with invoices bearing an endorsement that they are payable to the factor and with evidence of shipment of the merchandise.

The factor usually sets up lines of credit for all of his client's regular customers. Upon receipt of the invoices, shipping evidences, and a formal assignment schedule, the factor makes advance payment. In the event of any customer disputes concerning the merchandise or its delivery, the factor may charge the account back to the client who must assume the collection of the account.

Non-Notification Financing

Non-notification financing in its usual form differs from factoring in several ways. First, the lender, as we shall call him, does not assume the credit risk. The borrower-assignor is required to guarantee prompt payment of the accounts at maturity. If an account is not paid at maturity for any reason, it is charged back to the borrower, although some period of grace is often permitted. Secondly, the accounts are assigned without notice to the customer, who makes payment directly to the assignor. * * * Lastly, this type of transaction is, in substance, a loan of money, rather than a purchase of accounts. This conclusion follows from the fact that the financing agency is primarily engaged in furnishing funds, since it performs no other material service, as is the case in factoring, and charges for the use of its money. For a variety of reasons, such as custom, sales appeal, or a desire to avoid usury problems, many concerns in this field frame their contracts as a purchase of the accounts receivable. * * *

One other difference from factoring is the practical application of non-notification financing to the special, but not infrequent, situation of a company which has large numbers of accounts, each for a relatively small amount, and often coming from several different branch offices. The separate scheduling and handling of such accounts, both from the point of view of the assignor and the assignee, may involve prohibitive expenditure of time and expense. But it is often practical to finance such accounts on a non-notification "bulk" basis, since there is no need for an individual credit analysis of each account. The accounts can be assigned by reference to all sales accounts generated in a day, or some other specified period, bearing consecutive invoice numbers, and duplicate invoices can be given to the lender in groups, without individual treatment. A specified percentage can be advanced against the total value of assigned accounts.

The usual forms of non-notification agreement are framed either as loans against collateral, or as purchases of the accounts. As noted above, both arrangements are in essence loans of money. Most commercial banks use the collateral loan form of agreement, since they lack express statutory authority to purchase accounts receivable. Many commercial finance companies use the purchase form of agreement. Where a collateral loan agreement is used, each advance is evidenced by a promissory note, usually payable on demand since the collections on the accounts will ordinarily liquidate the obligation in a short, but indefinite period. Both forms of agreement contain full warranties by the assignor that there are no defenses or rights of setoff and that the assignor has full right to assign the accounts and has made no previous assignment. These forms also contain warranties concerning the genuineness of the accounts, the correctness of the amounts shown as owing, the capacity of the account-debtor, and other matters required for the protection of the assignee. The assignor is required to guarantee the prompt payment of the accounts at maturity. Under a collateral loan agreement, the assignor is required to pledge accounts of a value in excess of the amount loaned, such as 125 per cent. Under a purchase form of agreement, the accounts are purchased for 100 per cent of their value, but the assignee retains a reserve, such as 20 per cent of the purchase price, to secure the collection of the accounts. The effect of both procedures is the same. In addition, the agreements will specify the charges and the procedure for assigning the accounts, marking the assignor's books, keeping of records, collecting the accounts, holding returned merchandise for the benefit of the assignee, endorsing the assignor's name on checks representing collections, and other protection for the assignee.

PROBLEM

Debtor is a dry goods wholesaler which sells on open account to retailers. Bank has a security interest in all present and future accounts receivable of Debtor. After Bank filed a financing statement covering Debtor's accounts, Seller sold dry goods to Debtor on credit and was granted a security interest in the goods to secure payment of the price. Before making any deliveries to Debtor Seller filed a financing statement covering inventory.

If Debtor sells to a retailer, on open account and in ordinary course, all of the dry goods it had purchased from Seller, does Seller have a security interest in the resulting account receivable? UCC § 9–306(2). Is it perfected? UCC § 9–306(3), § 9–302 and § 9–103(3). If we assume that it is perfected does it have priority over the security interest of Bank? Does UCC § 9–312(3) apply? Does UCC § 9–312(5) apply? As a matter of policy who should have priority?

Under the 1962 Code § 9–312(3) stated that "a purchase money security interest in inventory collateral has priority over a conflicting security interest in the same collateral" if the purchase money party met the conditions stated. It was not clear under this language whether the special priority applied not only to inventory but also to the proceeds of the inventory, and particularly to resulting accounts receivable financed by a secured party who filed before the inventory financer. The question under the 1962 Code has never been settled, but the conflict has been resolved in states that have adopted the 1972 amendments to the Code. Professor Gilmore summarized his views on the problem under the 1962 Code as follows:

> * * * A persuasive case can be made that the receivables financer should take priority over the inventory financer with respect to the proceeds, whether the proceeds are in the form of chattel paper or in the form of accounts. Over the past thirty or forty years receivable financing has gradually dis-

placed inventory financing which, outside the area of the pre-Code trust receipt transaction, has come to be looked on as an unsatisfactory or second-best arrangement. Resolving the priority issue in favor of the accounts receivable financers would merely reinforce this long-established trend. This is a reasonable argument, at all events, so long as the receivables financer follows the pre-Code pattern of making new advances against new accounts. The inventory financer's purchase-money interest by definition reflects a new value advance: he should not be subordinated to the competing interests of a secured party who, taking advantage of the Code's floating lien provision, claims all the debtor's receivables under an all-embracing after-acquired property clause. The condition for priority of the accounts receivable interest should be, following the explicit provisions of § 9–308, that it, like the inventory interest, arose for new value.

Gilmore, Security Interests in Personal Property 797 (1965).* See the discussion of purchase money security interests by the Reporters for the 1972 amendments to Article 9 in Reasons for 1972 Change, § 9–312, Paragraphs (2)(c) and (4).

CITIZENS AND SOUTHERN FACTORS, INC. v. SMALL BUSINESS ADMINISTRATION

Supreme Court of Alabama, 1979.
375 So.2d 251.

BEATTY, JUSTICE. The United States Court of Appeals for the Fifth Circuit has requested this Court, under ARAP 18, to answer certain questions involving Alabama law deemed by that Court to be determinative of an action pending before it and on which there is no clear controlling precedent in the decisions of the Supreme Court of Alabama. The certification opinion follows:

* * *

PER CURIAM. The Court has determined that this case presents questions of Alabama law appropriate for resolution by the courts of that state.

Following our practice, we requested that the parties submit a proposed statement of facts and proposed agreed certificate of the questions for decision, which they have done.

* Reprinted with permission of the publisher, Little, Brown & Company.

CERTIFICATION FROM THE UNITED STATES COURT OF APPEALS FOR THE FIFTH CIRCUIT TO THE SUPREME COURT OF ALABAMA PURSUANT TO ARTICLE 6, § 140(b) (3) OF THE ALABAMA STATE CONSTITUTION AS AMENDED 1973

TO THE SUPREME COURT OF ALABAMA AND THE HONORABLE JUSTICES THEREOF:

It appears to the United States Court of Appeals for the Fifth Circuit that this case involves questions or propositions of the law of the State of Alabama that are determinative of the cause, and there appear to be no clear controlling precedents in the decisions of the Supreme Court of Alabama. This Court certifies the following question of law to the Supreme Court of Alabama for instructions concerning said question of law, based on the facts recited herein, such case being an appeal from the United States District Court for the Northern District of Georgia.

* * *

II. *Statement Of Facts*

On April 18, 1972, Vernon Carpet Mills, Inc., an Alabama corporation ("Vernon"), entered into a factoring agreement with The Citizens and Southern National Bank ("Bank"). Pursuant to the factoring agreement, the Bank purchased all the accounts, instruments, contract rights, chattel paper, documents and general intangibles of Vernon and the proceeds thereof ("Receivables").

Also, Paragraph 6 of the factoring agreement provided:

> We [Vernon] further sell and assign to you all our title and/or interest in the goods (unless released by you) represented by receivables as well as goods returned by customers. You have the right to stop goods in transit or to replevy or to reclaim such goods for your protection. All returned, replevied, and reclaimed goods coming into our possession shall be held in trust by us for you.

On April 20, 1972, the Bank filed a Uniform Commercial Code financing statement with the office of the Secretary of State, Montgomery, Alabama, describing, in relevant part, the property as:

> All present and future accounts, instruments, contract rights, chattel paper, documents and general intangibles, including those arising from the sale of raw materials, goods in pro-

cess, and finished goods, together with the debtor's rights in returned and reclaimed or repossessed goods.

The Bank subsequently assigned its right in and under the factoring agreement and all things collateral thereto to Citizens and Southern Factors, Inc. ("C & S").

Approximately two years later, Vernon obtain an SBA guaranteed loan in the amount of $438,000 from the Bank of Wedowee, Wedowee, Alabama, as evidenced by the execution of Note and Security Agreement in favor of the latter dated February 28, 1974. As collateral securing the loan, Vernon granted the Bank of Wedowee a security interest in its inventory and proceeds therefrom which is further reflected in a financing statement filed appropriately in the office of the Secretary of State of Alabama on March 11, 1974. The financing statement covered "all inventory now owned and hereafter acquired" as well as proceeds. On September 30, 1975, the Bank of Wedowee assigned its interest in the security agreement to SBA.

Certain of the account debtors on the Receivables which had been purchased by C & S returned to Vernon the goods which they had purchased ("Returned Goods"). Vernon failed and each of C & S and the SBA claimed prior rights to the Returned Goods. Vernon was indebted to each of C & S and the SBA in amounts in excess of $5,000. By agreement of the parties, the Returned Goods were sold for $15,000 and such sum was paid into the registry of the United States District Court for the Northern District of Georgia.

C & S filed suit in the United States District Court for the Northern District of Georgia against the SBA for a declaratory judgment that it had the superior interest in the fund representing the Returned Goods. The District Court ruled that the SBA was entitled to priority to the fund, and C & S appealed that judgment to the United States Court of Appeals for the Fifth Circuit.

III. *Issues Certified*

(1) Whether under the Uniform Commercial Code the conveyance of title to returned goods to an accounts receivable purchaser in a factoring agreement prevents the attachment of the security interest of an inventory financer in the returned goods or results in simply a retention of a security interest in the returned goods in favor of the accounts receivable purchaser.

(2) If it is determined that the conveyance of title to returned goods results simply in a retention of a security interest in favor

of the accounts receivable purchaser, whether § 9–306(5) or § 9–312(5) of the Uniform Commercial Code governs the priority in returned goods where the accounts receivable purchaser by contract has taken an express security interest in the returned goods and been the first to file with respect thereto.

The entire record in this case, together with copies of the briefs of the parties, the proposed questions of fact and law, and memoranda thereon, are transmitted herewith.

CERTIFIED.

Our answer to the first question must be that the arrangement under consideration resulted merely in the retention of a security interest in the returned goods in favor of the accounts receivable purchaser. Although plaintiff-appellant C & S, the assignee of the accounts purchaser, had previously argued in the federal courts that the conveyance of title to the returned goods operated to prevent the attachment of the subsequent security interest of the inventory financer, it now concedes in brief that the provisions of Article 9 of the Alabama UCC control in this situation.

We must therefore consider the second certified question. At issue is whether § 9–306(5) or § 9–312(5) of the Code governs the priority of security interests in returned goods when the accounts purchaser *expressly* took a security interest in returned goods and was the first to file a financing statement with respect to goods of that nature. It is our opinion that § 9–312(5) is controlling.

Section 9–312(5) is the general rule that governs priority between secured creditors under Article 9, while § 9–306(5) is a special rule which was drafted to provide a means for determining priorities among secured creditors when collateral, after its sales, has been returned to, or repossessed by, the debtor. Section 9–306(5) provides:

> (5) If a sale of goods results in an account or chattel paper which is transferred by the seller to a secured party, and if the goods are returned to or are repossessed by the seller or the secured party, the following rules determine priorities:

> > (a) If the goods were collateral at the time of sale for an indebtedness of the seller which is still unpaid, the original security interest attaches again to the goods and continues as a perfected security interest if it was perfected at the time when the goods were sold. If the security interest was originally perfected by a filing which is still

effective, nothing further is required to continue the perfected status; in any other case, the secured party must take possession of the returned or repossessed goods or must file.

(b) An unpaid transferee of the chattel paper has a security interest in the goods against the transferor. Such security interest is prior to a security interest asserted under paragraph (a) to the extent that the transferee of the chattel paper was entitled to priority under section 9–308.

(c) An unpaid transferee of the account has a security interest in the goods against the transferor. Such security interest is subordinate to a security interest asserted under paragraph (a).

(d) A security interest of an unpaid transferee asserted under paragraph (b) or (c) must be perfected for protection against creditors of the transferor and purchasers of the returned or repossessed goods.

A surface level reading of this section could lead one to conclude that subsection 5(a) in conjunction with subsection 5(c) controls the situation at hand: that is, it could be argued that the inventory financer's security interest in inventory follows the goods upon their return or repossession [*see* § 9–306(5)(a)] and defeats the security interest which the transferee of the accounts took in the goods when they were returned [*see* § 9–306(5)(c)]. Such a construction of the provision, however, ignores the fact that the accounts receivable transferee in this case *explicitly reserved* a security interest in "returned goods," both in the factoring agreement and in the financing statement, which was on file *before* SBA's statement covering inventory and proceeds was filed. The language of § 9–306(5) does not contemplate such a situation. The section would apply if C & S had filed with respect to the accounts merely, but the accounts transferee is not, under these facts, forced to rely on § 9–306(5)(c) to give it a *previously non-existent* security interest in returned goods, for C & S had *already expressly reserved* a security interest in such returned goods. The inclusion of the reference to "returned goods" in C & S's filed financing statement effectively rendered § 9–306(5) inoperative under the facts of this case. We must therefore look elsewhere in order to determine which security interest has priority.

Code § 9–312(5) is the controlling provision.   *   *   *

Under the undisputed facts, both security interests were perfected by filing; because the accounts purchaser filed first, its security interest prevails over the interest of the inventory financer under § 9–312(5).

Our holding is in accord with the principle of "first in time, first in right," which underlies most priority provisions of Article 9. The application of § 9–312(5) in this case should also serve to further creditor confidence in the integrity of the filing system. If § 9–306(5) were deemed to govern in this situation, the incongruous result would be that an accounts receivable creditor—who had done everything possible under Article 9 to assure the priority of his interest in returned goods over secured creditors who filed later—would lose his rights in adequately described collateral simply because the subsequent creditor filed with respect to the collateral as it existed at an earlier point in the *production process.* See A Look at the Work of the Article 9 Review Committee, 26 Bus.Law. 307, 321–23 (1970) (remarks of Professor Kripke). Such a result is clearly undesirable in that it could portend the demise of accounts receivable financing. See Kripke, Suggestions for Clarifying Article 9: Intangibles, Proceeds, and Priorities, 41 N.Y.U.L.Rev. 687, 716–19 (1966).

In accord with the foregoing discussion it is this Court's conclusion that § 9–312(5) governs the priority in returned goods between these creditors.

PROBLEM

Suppose in Problem, supra p. 158, that the retailer returns all of the dry goods that it had bought from Debtor and that Debtor rescinds the sale. Under UCC § 9–306(5)(c) Bank gets a security interest in the returned goods. Why? Are the returned goods proceeds of the account? UCC § 9–306(2). Is the security interest in the returned goods already perfected or must Bank file a financing statement covering the goods? Must the financing statement be signed by debtor? UCC § 9–402(2). By § 9–306(5)(c) the security interest of Bank in the returned goods is subordinate to that of Seller. Why? Chattel paper and an account are both proceeds of the sale of inventory. Under the 1972 Code, the transferee of either can get priority over the inventory financer if it qualifies under UCC § 9–308 or § 9–312(5) as the case may be. In the case of returned goods § 9–306(5)(b) also gives the transferee of the chattel paper priority in the returned goods, but § 9–306(5)(c) denies this priority to the transferee of the account. Why are the two transferees treated differently? Is it as important for the accounts financer to have a security interest in the returned goods as it is for the purchaser of chattel paper?

In *Citizens and Southern* the accounts financer was given priority in returned goods over the inventory financer because the security agreement and financing statement of the accounts financer specifically covered returned goods. The accounts financer was treated as a financer of both accounts and inventory to the extent of returned goods. It can be expected that accounts financers as a matter of course will cover returned goods in these documents. Thus, under the holding of the principal case the second sentence of UCC § 9–306(5)(c) would appear to be a dead letter. What can a purchase money supplier of inventory do to assure its priority in returned goods inventory? See UCC § 9–312(3).

IN RE B. HOLLIS KNIGHT CO.

United States Court of Appeals, Eighth Circuit, 1979.
605 F.2d 397.

HEANEY, CIRCUIT JUDGE. The trustee in bankruptcy appeals from a decision of the District Court directing him to pay Union National Bank of Little Rock $8,444.69, the amount owed to Union National by the debtor, B. Hollis Knight Company, Inc. (BHK), on the date BHK filed its petition in bankruptcy. The sole issue on appeal is whether Union National has a security interest in an account receivable of BHK that was perfected prior to the lien of the trustee. We conclude that the District Court applied an incorrect legal standard and, therefore, reverse and remand for further proceedings.

BHK, a mechanical contractor, received a $12,000 loan from Union National on November 26, 1976. The loan was evidenced by a promissory note and secured by various accounts receivable and other collateral. The security interest was supposedly perfected by means of financing statements that Union National had filed on all accounts receivable and contract rights owned or thereafter acquired by BHK. These financing statements had been prepared in connection with another loan to BHK and were filed on August 29, 1974, at the Pulaski County Circuit Clerk's office and at the office of the Arkansas Secretary of State. The filing in the office of the Secretary of State designated Ben H.

Knight [1] and BHK as debtors. The filing in the Circuit Clerk's office, however, designated only Ben H. Knight as the debtor. Thus, as of November 26, 1976, Union National did not have a perfected security interest in BHK's accounts receivable since it failed to list BHK as a debtor on the filing in the Circuit Clerk's office as required by Arkansas law. See [Arkansas UCC] §§ 9–401, 9–402.

On January 11, 1977, BHK received another loan from Union National in the amount of $6,800. The loan was evidenced by a promissory note and secured by an assignment of an account receivable from a general contractor who owed $9,720 to BHK for work on a construction job completed on January 3, 1977. The assignment stated that it was intended

> as security for the repayment of indebtedness owing by the undersigned [BHK] to the said Union National Bank of Little Rock now in the sum of Six Thousand Eight Hundred & No/100—($6,800.00) and of any other indebtedness that may become due to the said Bank by the undersigned so long as any of the debt mentioned herein remains unpaid[.]

The assignment was signed by the president of BHK and a notice of the assignment was acknowledged by an authorized representative of the general contractor on January 11, 1977. This assignment was the only assignment to Union National from BHK. No financing statements were filed in connection with the transaction. On January 11, 1977, BHK's accounts receivable totaled $68,374.58.

On January 19, 1977, BHK filed a voluntary petition in bankruptcy. On that date, it owed Union National $6,814.90 on the January 11, 1977, note and $1,629.79 on the November 26, 1976, note for a total indebtedness of $8,444.69. The schedules filed with the petition listed accounts receivable of $68,364.68. The trustee, however, was unable to collect any accounts receivable other than the account which had been assigned to Union National. The trustee collected $8,919.72 of this account and placed this sum in a special bank account by agreement of the parties pending the outcome of this action.

In his complaint, the trustee alleged that Union National's security interest in the account receivable was unperfected and subordinate to the trustee's lien which came into existence on the date of bankruptcy. The Bankruptcy Court disagreed. It determined that Union National's security interest in the ac-

1. Ben H. Knight was the owner of BHK prior to July 1, 1976.

count receivable was perfected on January 11, 1977, prior to the trustee's lien. The court reasoned that the assignment of the account receivable was not a "significant part" of BHK's outstanding accounts receivable within the meaning of § 9–302(1)(e) and, thus, Union National was not required to file a financing statement. Consequently, Union National's security interest was perfected without filing under § 9–303(1). The court directed the trustee to pay Union National $8,444.69. The District Court affirmed the Bankruptcy Court.

The parties agree that for Union National to prevail, it must show that it has a perfected security interest in the account receivable under Arkansas law. The answer to this question turns on an interpretation of § 9–302(1)(e) which provides:

(1) A financing statement must be filed to perfect all security interests except the following:

* * *

(e) an assignment of accounts which does not alone or in conjunction with other assignments to the same assignee transfer a significant part of the outstanding accounts of the assignor[.]

The parties have not cited to, nor has our research disclosed any Arkansas state court cases that discuss subsection (e). The only case that has interpreted it appears to be Standard Lumber Company v. Chamber Frames, Inc., 317 F.Supp. 837 (E.D.Ark. 1970). In *Standard*, Chamber Frames, Inc., the debtor, a manufacturer of picture frames, sold K–Mart picture frames valued at $2,212.20. Standard Lumber Company, the secured party and a seller of building materials and millwork, was Chamber Frames' supplier. In order to secure its debt for supplies, Chamber Frames assigned Standard Lumber the $2,212.20 account receivable from K–Mart. Standard Lumber did not file a financing statement. In an action to recover on the debt, the United States was permitted to intervene and assert a claim under liens arising from unpaid taxes. The District Court determined that Standard Lumber had a perfected security interest in the account receivable notwithstanding its failure to file a financing statement which was perfected prior to the government's lien. The court reasoned that since the total of accounts receivable assigned amounted to only sixteen percent of Chamber Frames' outstanding accounts receivable, the assignment was not a significant part of the total accounts. Consequently, Standard Lumber was not required to file a financing statement under § 9–302(1)(e) to perfect its security interest.

The District Court relied on *Standard* in reaching its decision. It reasoned that the account receivable assigned to Union National represented roughly fourteen percent of the outstanding accounts and, thus, was not a "significant part" within the meaning of § 9–302(1)(e).

The trustee argues, initially, that the District Court erred in considering the bulk of BHK's accounts receivable as outstanding accounts, since most of the accounts were unearned by performance at the time of the assignment and, thus, were uncollectible by the trustee after bankruptcy intervened. The evidence established that out of the $68,374.58 listed by BHK as accounts receivable, approximately fifty percent of this amount constituted retainage on construction contracts. The retained amounts were listed on BHK's balance sheet as accounts receivable, although successful completion of the job was a condition precedent to receiving payment. Since BHK did not complete its work on any projects after it filed bankruptcy, the retainage proved to be uncollectible due to various counterclaims and set-offs.

In our view, the District Court correctly included the retainage in the total outstanding accounts of BHK. § 9–106 defines "account" as "any right to payment for goods sold or leased or for services rendered * * * whether or not it has been earned by performance." Since an account need not be earned by performance, the retainage was properly classified as part of BHK's outstanding accounts although it would not be paid until the job was satisfactorily completed. Moreover, the mere fact that the trustee was unable to collect certain accounts after bankruptcy would not remove these accounts from inclusion as BHK's outstanding accounts. The determination of whether an assignment constitutes a significant part of the assignor's outstanding accounts must be made on the basis of the facts available at the time of the assignment.

The trustee also argues that the District Court's interpretation of *Standard* was unduly restrictive. He contends that the court should have examined all of the circumstances surrounding the transaction in deciding whether the assignment was a significant part of the outstanding accounts.

The term "significant part" is not defined in the U.C.C. Although most courts have not undertaken a careful analysis of this term, see In re Munro Builders, Inc., 20 U.C.C.Rep. 739 (W.D.Mich.1976), two tests appear to have emerged as aids in its interpretation, the "casual or isolated" test and the "percentage" test. See generally J. White and R. Summers, Uniform Commercial Code § 23–8 at 807–809 (1972).

The casual or isolated test is suggested by the language of Comment 5 to U.C.C. § 9–302 which provides that

> [t]he purpose of the subsection (1)(e) exemptions is to save from *ex post facto* invalidation casual or isolated assignments: some accounts receivable statutes have been so broadly drafted that all assignments, whatever their character or purpose, fall within their filing provisions. Under such statutes many assignments which no one would think of filing may be subject to invalidation. The subsection (1)(e) exemptions go to that type of assignment. Any person who regularly takes assignments of any debtor's accounts should file.

The test requires a court to examine the circumstances surrounding the transaction, including the status of the assignee, to determine whether the assignment was casual or isolated. See, e.g., Abramson v. Printer's Bindery, Inc., 440 S.W.2d 326 (Tex. Civ.App.1969). If a court finds that the transaction was not part of a regular course of commercial financing, it will not require filing. The underlying rationale behind the test appears to be the conclusion that it would not be unreasonable to require a secured creditor to file if he regularly takes assignments of a debtor's accounts, but it would be unreasonable if this was not a usual practice.

The percentage test, in contrast, focuses on the size of the assignment in relation to the size of the outstanding accounts. Standard Lumber Company v. Chamber Frames, Inc., supra, is generally cited as a case applying this test. J. White and R. Summers, Uniform Commercial Code § 23–8 at 808. See also In re Boughner, 8 U.C.C.Rep. 144, 149–153 (W.D.Mich.1970). The test attempts to define the term "significant part" in a manner that is consistent with the statute and that promotes certainty in application. J. White and R. Summers, Uniform Commercial Code § 23–8 at 808–809.

Some courts have taken the approach that a proper interpretation of the section requires application of both tests. See, e.g., City of Vermillion, S. D. v. Stan Houston Equipment Co., 341 F.Supp. 707, 712 (D.S.D.1972). We are in substantial agreement with the courts that take this eclectic approach.

Both of the policies underlying the two tests appear to be valid limitations on the scope of U.C.C. § 9–302(1)(e). The language of the section would not permit an assignee to escape the filing requirement if he received a large proportion of an assignor's accounts whether or not the transaction was an isolated one. See In re Boughner, supra. On the other hand, it is not unfair to require a secured party who regularly takes such assignments to file, since the comments to U.C.C. § 9–302(1)(e) indicate that the section was designed as a narrow exception to the filing requirement—not applicable if the transaction was in the general course of commercial financing.

We note, moreover, that Standard Lumber Company v. Chamber Frames, Inc., supra, is not inconsistent with this position. In *Standard*, the secured party, Standard Lumber Company, did not regularly take assignments from its suppliers. There was no question that the assignment was an isolated one and, thus, there was no reason for the District Court to consider the issue.

Thus, in the absence of any Arkansas law to the contrary, we hold that in determining what is a significant part of the outstanding accounts of the assignor, a court must examine all of the facts and circumstances surrounding the transaction, including the relative size of the assignment and whether it was casual or isolated.

The trustee contends that we should not consider the assignment an isolated or casual one simply because Union National is a national banking institution that regularly lends money and has, on previous occasions, made loans to BHK. We disagree with the trustee's analysis. The relevant question is whether Union National regularly took assignments of accounts receivable. There is no evidence in the record that they did. The Bankruptcy Court found that BHK had not assigned any other account receivable to Union National and the trustee does not dispute this finding. The record does not indicate that Union National ever received another assignment of accounts receivable from any other person. While Union National may do so as a matter of fact, the assignment of accounts receivable is a specialized method of securing loans, and we are not willing to assume that it was a regular practice.

The trustee also contends that, under the circumstances of this case, it was inappropriate for the District Court to have applied an arbitrary percentage. We agree. The District Court improperly limited its inquiry since its analysis ignores the qualitative differences in accounts receivable.

The ultimate uncollectibility of an account receivable standing by itself would not remove the account from consideration as one of the assignee's outstanding accounts. If, however, the assignee knew when an assignment was made that certain accounts were uncollectible, he would also recognize that their value as outstanding accounts is minute. The reasoning is similar when there are significant limitations on the collectibility of some accounts.

An assignee would have to discount their value as outstanding accounts to determine whether his assigned account constituted a significant part of the total.

This analysis merely recognizes that the liquidity of an account receivable is one of the primary considerations of a lender who is secured by a lien on the account. An assignee who receives accounts that are not subject to any limitations is usually in a better position than one who receives accounts that are subject to some limitations, although each may hold the same dollar amount of accounts. Thus, the account assigned to Union National may be a significant part of BHK's outstanding accounts although it represented only fourteen percent of the total amount since it was the only account that was not subject to significant limitations on collectibility.

Although the District Court did not make a specific factual finding in this regard, there is sufficient evidence in the record to support a finding that Union National knew there were significant limitations on the collectibility of BHK's accounts receivable. The president of BHK testified that he knew the only account he could collect within thirty days was the account assigned to Union National. It is reasonable to infer that he communicated this knowledge to Union National when he applied for the $6,800 loan, since Union National specifically requested the assignment of that particular account. Moreover, Union National had some familiarity with BHK's business practices and its assets insofar as it had loaned money to BHK on prior occasions. We infer from this that Union National may have known of BHK's precarious financial position and that there was a substantial risk that the remaining accounts would not be collected because the jobs would not be completed.

Since additional factual findings must be made prior to a determination of whether the account assigned to Union National constituted a significant part of BHK's outstanding accounts, we remand the cause to the District Court. On remand, the District Court shall examine the extent of Union National's knowledge of BHK's accounts receivable and determine how Union National's knowledge affected, or should have affected, its valuation of BHK's accounts. The court must then decide whether the account assigned to Union National was a significant part of the outstanding accounts in light of this valuation. The District Court should look at all of the facts and circumstances surrounding the transaction in making its decision.

The decision of the District Court is reversed and remanded for further proceedings consistent with this opinion.

MICHELIN TIRES (CANADA) LTD. v. FIRST NATIONAL BANK OF BOSTON

United States Court of Appeals, First Circuit, 1981.
666 F.2d 673.

MAZZONE, DISTRICT JUDGE. This appeal is from a district court's denial of restitution to the plaintiff, a contractual obligor, of monies mistakenly paid to the defendant, an assignee of contract rights. We begin with a summary of the record.

Michelin Tires (Canada) Ltd. ("Michelin"), a Canadian corporation based in New Glasgow, Nova Scotia, and J. C. Corrigan, Inc. ("JCC"), a building contractor, entered into an agreement on June 19, 1970 for the design and installation of a carbon black handling and storage system, which was to form part of a Michelin tire factory under construction in Pictou County, Nova Scotia. Michelin entered into the agreement through its agent, Surveyor, Nenniger & Chenevert ("SNC"), an engineering firm retained by Michelin to procure and supervise the building of the factory.

The construction contract provided that Michelin would make periodic progress payments to JCC in the amount of 90% of each invoice submitted by JCC for work completed. The amounts due were based on a schedule of values of the various parts of the entire project. JCC's invoices were to be submitted first to SNC for its review and certification that the work had been performed and the amount was correct. That certification was contained in an Engineers Progress Certificate ("EPC") and was completed by the SNC project manager. With each invoice, Michelin had the right to require JCC to submit a "Statutory Declaration," or sworn statement, stating the amount JCC owed to subcontractors, supplier, and others in connection with the work and listing any claims that could result in liens on Michelin's property. If JCC failed to make prompt payments to subcontractors and suppliers, SNC could withhold or nullify its certification and Michelin could deduct from its progress payments to JCC the amount necessary to protect its property from liens.

Prior to signing the construction contract with JCC, neither SNC nor Michelin made inquiries concerning JCC's financial situation. Initially, SNC had requested that JCC provide a performance bond to cover its work, and JCC had requested that Michelin provide a letter of credit to cover the payments due for work performed. Michelin, or SNC, dropped its proposal that JCC be required to provide a performance bond in return for JCC's withdrawal of its request for a letter of credit for Michelin.

The First National Bank of Boston ("FNB"), a commercial bank in Boston, Massachusetts, provided financing to JCC under a longstanding agreement dating from 1960. Under that agreement, FNB agreed to loan JCC an amount not greater than 80% of JCC's outstanding invoices. In return, FNB took a security interest in all JCC's accounts receivable and contract rights— including, of course, JCC's right to receive payments under its contract with Michelin.

On August 14, 1970, two months after the construction contract was executed, JCC assigned its rights under the contract to FNB. The bank notified SNC of the assignment and requested that future JCC invoices be paid directly to FNB. This assignment was acknowledged by SNC on September 3, 1970.

Shortly after JCC's assignment of its contract rights to FNB, Michelin sent FNB the payments it seeks to recover in the instant suit. The first payment was in response to JCC's invoice of August 24, 1970 in the amount of $118,000. JCC presented no EPC and no Statutory Declaration in support of this invoice. SNC prepared an EPC for the invoice and asked JCC to submit a Statutory Declaration with future invoices. Michelin paid 90% of the invoice, to FNB, as provided by the construction contract.

JCC submitted its next invoice on September 23, 1970 in the amount of $187,000. As with the previous invoice, no Statutory Declaration was presented. Michelin withheld payment and asked JCC to submit the Statutory Declaration. JCC did so on October 16, 1970.

JCC then sent Michelin an invoice dated October 22, 1970 in the amount of $313,000, accompanied by a Statutory Declaration and an EPC. Michelin paid 90% of the amounts of the latter two invoices on December 15, 1970, deducting amounts for uncompleted work and for a change order.

Michelin's last payment to FNB was in response to JCC's invoice for $200,000, dated December 21, 1970. JCC sent the corresponding Statutory Declaration to Michelin on January 18, 1971, and Michelin sent its progress payment to FNB on January 20, 1971, including the amount previously withheld for uncompleted work.

It was not until March of 1971 that Michelin learned that JCC had not been paying its subcontractors. Accordingly, the above progress payments were not due under the construction contract, and JCC's Statutory Declarations of October 12, 1970 and January 18, 1971 were fraudulent, JCC made an assignment for the benefit of creditors on April 6, 1971 and was subsequently adjudicated a bankrupt.

The carbon black system was substantially completed by May 1, 1971, and the district court found that JCC performed all the work it could have done prior to May 1, 1971. JCC left, however, a total indebtedness of over. $500,000 (Canadian) after its adjudication in bankruptcy.

Throughout this time, FNB maintained its lending relationship with JCC. FNB knew of JCC's financial difficulties. By early 1970, before JCC contracted with Michelin, FNB regarded its loan to JCC as a problem and was concerned about repayment. The bank knew from examining JCC's books that the company's earnings were declining, its trade debt was rising, and its customers were slow to pay. It was further evident from JCC's books that JCC was overstating its income in its reports to the bank. By late August of 1970, the bank was aware that JCC's outstanding indebtedness was greater than the agreed-upon loan ceiling of 80% of JCC's accounts receivable, and a bank officer reminded JCC that loan funds received while JCC was "over-advanced" were to be used only to meet payroll and pay taxes. FNB used the payments it received from Michelin after the assignment to reduce the outstanding amount on its loan to JCC. In October of 1970, FNB sent an inquiry to SNC to verify the accuracy of copies of invoices the bank had received from JCC, used by the bank to calculate the 80% loan ceiling. SNC replied that the invoices were "OK."

The district court specifically found that FNB knew of JCC's contractual obligations to Michelin. Those obligations included prompt payment of subcontractors. FNB, however, did not know that JCC was sending false Statutory Declarations to Michelin, stating under oath that the subcontractors had been paid.

On December 22, 1970, FNB notified JCC that it would extend no further loans to JCC after March 31, 1971 and that JCC should seek financing elsewhere. It was after JCC failed to find a new lender that the company made its assignment for the benefit of creditors on April 6, 1971 and filed a petition in bankruptcy.

After discovering JCC's fraud, Michelin brought this suit to recover the payments it made to FNB, a total of $724,197.60. Michelin asserted it was entitled to restitution under two theories. First, it claimed that since its right to restitution arose from its contract with JCC, the claim could be successfully asserted against FNB, the assigneee of contract rights to payment, pursuant to § 9–318(1)(a) of the Uniform Commercial Code (UCC), Mass.Gen.Laws Ann. ch. 106, § 9–318(1)(a).[1] Second, Michelin asserted that FNB was liable because it has been unjustly enriched under traditional restitutionary principles.

The district court tried the case without a jury and upon a stipulated record. In a detailed memorandum, the court found that JCC had breached its contract with Michelin by submitting fictitious invoices and fraudulent Statutory Declarations and by failing to pay its subcontractors when payment was due. It further found that Michelin's payments to FNB had been made in reliance on the fraudulent Statutory Declarations. The district court then ruled, first, that § 9–318(1)(a) does not create a new affirmative cause of action by an account debtor as against an assignee and, second, that since FNB did not know of the fraudulent Statutory Declarations or of JCC's indebtedness to subcontractors, FNB had not been unjustly enriched at the expense of Michelin. This appeal followed.

We affirm because we believe that (1) § 9–318(1)(a) of the UCC was not intended to create a new cause of action by an account debtor against an assignee and (2) the facts the district

---

1. Michelin's complaint framed this claim as one in breach of contract. On appeal, however, Michelin characterizes the claim as purely restitutionary, although "arising from" its contract with JCC. Apparently, then, Michelin is not attempting to assert that it is entitled to restitution as an alternative remedy for breach of contract. If it were, Michelin would have to show the breach was total, warranting rescission of the contract. See 5 A. Corbin, Corbin on Contracts § 1104 (1964). On the other hand, restitution of property transferred in the course of performance of a contract can be had under equitable principles without regard to the totality of the breach. See Restatement of Restitution § 28, Comment a (1937).

Given our interpretation of § 9–318(1)(a) of the UCC, we need not reach the next question—whether this claim, essentially one in equity, can nevertheless be said to "arise from" the contract.

court found were available to FNB did not put it on notice of JCC's fraud and Michelin's mistake.

I.

Michelin's first argument is that it has an independent cause of action against FNB under § 9–318 of the UCC. * * *

In essence, Michelin contends that its restitution claim arises from its contract with JCC, and that § 9–318(1)(a) accordingly permits Michelin to recover from FNB as JCC's assignee. Although Michelin emphasizes the narrow application of this theory to the instant case, the theory rests upon a construction of § 9–318 that would impose full contract liability on assignees of contract rights. Under this view, a bank taking an assignment of contract rights as security for a loan would also receive as "security" a delegation of duties under the contract and the risk of being held liable on the contract in place of its borrower. We do not believe it was the intent of § 9–318(1)(a) to create such a result.

The key statutory language is ambiguous. That "the rights of an assignee are *subject to* * * * (a) all the terms of the contract" connotes only that the assignee's rights to recover are limited by the obligor's rights to assert contractual defenses as a set-off, implying that affirmative recovery against the assignee is not intended. See Englestein v. Mintz, 345 Ill. 48, 61, 177 N.E. 746, 752 (1931), *quoted in* Anderson v. Southwest Savings & Loan Association, 117 Ariz. 246, 248, 571 P.2d 1042, 1044 (1977):

> The words "subject to," used in their ordinary sense, mean "subordinate to," "subservient to," or "limited by." There is nothing in the use of the words "subject to," in their ordinary use, which would even hint at the creation of affirmative rights.

On the other hand, the use of the word "claim" raises the possibility that affirmative recovery was indeed contemplated. However, the section's title and the official Comment support the view that the section does not create affirmative rights. The title reads, "Defenses Against Assignee." Official Comment 1 states in pertinent part:

> Subsection (1) makes no substantial change in prior law. An assignee has traditionally been subject to defenses or set-offs existing before an account debtor is notified of the assignment.

Under prior law, an assignee of contract rights was not liable on the contract in the place of his assignor. Wright v. Graustein, 248 Mass. 205, 142 N.E. 797 (1924). Common sense requires that we not twist the "precarious security" [2] of an assignee into potential liability for his assignor's breach.

It is evident that § 9–318 has become a red herring in suits against an assignee. We note two cases that have denied account debtors the right to sue. James Talcott, Inc. v. Brewster Sales Corp., 16 UCC Rep.Serv. 1165 (N.Y.Sup.Ct.1975); Meyers v. Postal Finance Co., 287 N.W.2d 614 (Minn.1979). There are also cases that have allowed affirmative claims, at least in limited circumstances. Benton State Bank v. Warren, 263 Ark. 1, 562 S.W.2d 74 (1978); Farmers Acceptance Corp. v. DeLozier, 178 Colo. 291, 496 P.2d 1016 (1972); K Mart Corp. v. First Penn. Bank, 29 UCC Rep.Serv. 70 (Pa.1980).

The decisions permitting an affirmative suit all rely on the pre-UCC case of Firestone Tire and Rubber Co. v. Central Nat. Bank, 159 Ohio St. 423, 112 N.E.2d 636 (1953). There the court required the bank to return payments to an account debtor because, although the bank was innocent of the assignor's fraud, the bank had unwittingly assisted that fraud by independently requesting periodic payment from the account debtor. The bank attached invoices from the assignor to each request thereby impliedly representing that the underlying obligation was valid. The court found that the account debtor relied on the genuineness of the invoices forwarded by the bank. Id., 112 N.E.2d at 639. In the case at hand there was no such reliance. Rather, Michelin established its own system of assuring compliance, including approval of an intermediary, SNC. In addition, they required a Statutory Declaration under oath from JCC. The stipulated record indicates that FNB had no involvement in verifying

---

2. This phrase was coined by Professor Gilmore in his article, The Assignee of Contract Rights and His Precarious Security, 74 Yale L.J. 217 (1964). This article has been the source of some of the confusion regarding section 9–318. In it, Professor Gilmore analyzes the early case of Firestone Tire and Rubber Co. v. Central National Bank, 159 Ohio St. 423, 112 N.E.2d 636 (1953), and concludes that account debtors should be entitled to sue for repayment of funds mistakenly transferred to assignees even if the transfer was negligent, so long as the assignee has not changed its position. With all due respect to Professor Gilmore, we disagree with this conclusion for the reasons stated in this opinion. We further note, however, that even under Gilmore's analysis, Michelin's suit would fail here since Massachusetts law suggests that a bank's crediting of a debtor's account involves a change of position. Merchants' Insurance Co. v. Abbott, 131 Mass. 397 (1881).

JCC's performance and was completely unaware of the Statutory Declaration.

Benton State Bank, supra, represented a situation similar to *Firestone*. In *Benton State Bank* the bank advanced progress payments to the assignor. Each request for a progress payment was then forwarded by the bank to the general contractor accompanied by the assignor's certification, a representation similar to the Statutory Declaration submitted by JCC in this case. The court permitted the contractor to recover against the bank because the bank "had solid reasons for suspecting the truth of Harp's [the assignors] assertions, which the bank forwarded to the Warrens [the account debtors], that all past-due bills for labor and materials had been paid." Id., 562 S.W.2d at 76. FNB did not assume an active role in sending JCC's statements to Michelin, nor were they even aware of JCC's misrepresentation to Michelin in any way.

The bank in *K Mart Corp.*, supra, was also actively involved in the relationship between the account debtor and the assignor. In *K Mart Corp.*, the court permitted the account debtor, K Mart, to recover from the assignee certain payments made for goods that were later found to be defective. Id. at 707. However, the recovery permitted in *K Mart Corp.* is best viewed as merely anticipated repayment. For nearly 8 years the bank accepted payment from K Mart equal to the value of the assignor's, PSM, invoices *minus* an allowance for defective goods received and paid for in the prior month. The assignor's bankruptcy prevented such an adjustment on the final payment so the court allowed recovery. The court noted "that merely because PSM is bankrupt and can no longer be expected to repay K Mart, the bank may not now *unilaterally ignore its prior understanding, which was clearly in the contemplation of the parties*, and retain funds which should not have been paid to it initially." Id. at 706 (emphasis added). There is no indication that Michelin and FNB agreed to make periodic adjustments depending upon the quality of JCC's performance.

Finally, the Colorado Supreme Court permitted recovery by the account debtor against the assignee in *DeLozier*, supra. The extent of the involvement by the assignee, Farmers Acceptance Corp. ("FAC"), in the underlying contract is ambiguous in that case. The brief opinion indicates that FAC, first used the payment it received from the account debtor to satisfy the personal indebtedness of the assignor and then applied the remainder to the assignor's unpaid account with a materialman. Id.,

496 P.2d at 1017. This latter payment to the subcontractor's creditor suggests knowledge and involvement by the assignee that exceeds that of FNB. In the case before us, the stipulated facts indicate that FNB had no involvement in the payments by JCC to its subcontractors. In any event, to the extent that *DeLozier* can be read to permit an affirmative suit against a lender who is completely unrelated to the underlying contract, we decline to follow this departure from traditional common law principles of restitution. See Massey-Ferguson Credit Corp. v. Brown, 173 Mont. 253, 567 P.2d 440, 443 (1977).

In each of the cases permitting an affirmative suit, with the possible exception of *DeLozier*, the assignee actively participated in the transactions to a degree not approached here. We are aware of no case that has gone beyond those we have cited and actually permitted an affirmative suit against a nonparticipating assignee like FNB. We do not anticipate that the Supreme Judicial Court would extend the law in this way and we are unwilling to do so ourselves. Given the factual distinctions between the cases discussed above and the transactions at issue here, we do not need to reach the issue of whether Massachusetts law would permit suit against an assignee who became more involved in the course of dealings.

While it is our judgment that analysis of the statutory language, taken in context, indicates that no affirmative right was contemplated and further that those cases that have permitted such a right are factually inapposite, we also believe it would be unwise to permit such suits as a matter of policy. As the dissenting justice in *Benton State Bank*, 562 S.W.2d 74, noted, allowing affirmative suits would "make every Banker, who has taken an assignment of accounts for security purposes, a deep pocket surety for every bankrupt contractor in the state to whom it had loaned money." Id. at 77 (Byrd, J., dissenting).

We are unwilling to impose such an obligation on the banks of the Commonwealth without some indication that this represents a considered policy choice. By making the bank a surety, not only will accounts receivable financing be discouraged, but transaction costs will undoubtedly increase for everyone. The case at hand provides a good example. In order to protect themselves, FNB would essentially be forced to undertake the precautionary measures that Michelin attempted to use, independent observation by an intermediary and sworn certifications by the assignor. FNB would have to supervise every construction site where its funds were involved to ensure performance and payment. We simply do not believe that the banks are best suited to monitor contract compliance. The party most interested in adequate performance would be the other contracting party, not the financier. Given this natural interest, it seems likely to us that while the banks will be given additional burdens of supervision, there would be no corresponding reduction in vigilance by the contracting parties, thus creating two inspections where there was formerly one. Costs for everyone thus increase, without any discernible benefit. It is also difficult to predict the full impact a contrary decision would have on the availability of accounts receivable financing in general.

Our holding, of course, is not that § 9–318 *prohibits* claims against the assignee. We hold merely that § 9–318 concerns only the preservation of defenses to the assignee's claims and, as such, is wholly inapposite in an affirmative suit against an assignee.

II.

The Restatement of Restitution, § 28(d) (1937), states:

§ 28.   Mistake Due to Fraud or Misrepresentation.

A person who has paid money to another because of a mistake of fact and who does not obtain what he expected in return is entitled to restitution from the other if the mistake was induced:

*   *   *

(d) By the fraud or material misrepresentation of a third person, provided that the payee has notice of the fraud or representation before he has given or promised something of value.

For cases where the mistake was not due to fraud, substantially the same rule is stated in § 14 of the Restatement: [3]

§ 14.   Discharge for Value.

(1) A creditor of another or one having a lien on another's property who has received from a third person any benefit in discharge of the debt or lien, is under no duty to make resti-

---

3. The Restatement gives the following illustration:

A falsely represents to B that he has done work for him to the value of $100 and B gives to A a non-negotiable note for that amount. A assigns this note to C who pays value therefor and has no reason to know of A's fraud. B pays the amount of the note to C. B is not entitled to restitution from C. Restatement of Restitution, § 14 (1937).

tution therefor, although the discharge was given by mistake of the transferor as to his interests or duties, if the transferee made no misrepresentation and did not have notice of the transferor's mistake.

(2) An assignee of a non-negotiable chose in action who, having paid value therefor, has received payment from the obligor is under no duty to make restitution although the obligor had a defense thereto, if the transferee made no misrepresentation and did not have notice of the defense.

The Supreme Judicial Court of Massachusetts has followed the Restatement in denying restitution against an assignee for value who is without notice of the assignor's fraud. The threshold question, therefore, is whether FNB, by reducing JCC's indebtedness on its outstanding loan, gave value for the funds it received from Michelin. We agree with the district court that value was given. In Merchants' Insurance Co. v. Abbott, 131 Mass. 397 (1881), the plaintiff insurance company paid a claim for fire loss to the insured's assignee. A year later, the plaintiff discovered the fire was the result of the insured's arson and sought restitution from the assignee. Restitution was denied because the assignment was for value—the discharge of a debt—and because the assignee was "wholly innocent" of the insured's fraud. Id. at 400. Cf. National Shawmut Bank v. Fidelity Mutual Life Insurance Co., 318 Mass. 142, 61 N.E.2d 18 (1945) (applying §§ 1 and 14 of the Restatement); Old Colony Trust Co. v. Wood, 321 Mass. 519, 527, 74 N.E.2d 141, 146 (1947) (consistent with, § 14 of the Restatement); Rockland Trust Co. v. South Shore National Bank, 366 Mass. 74, 79, 314 N.E.2d 438 (1974) (comparing contract law principle of voiding contract for fraud of third party with the similar rule if § 28(d) of the Restatement).

Having decided that FNB gave value, the crucial question becomes whether the defendant, assignee FNB, had notice of the fraudulent conduct of assignor JCC. We have found no Massachusetts cases directly addressing the standard to be applied in determining whether a party has notice of fraud under the law of restitution. Under the analogous rule for voiding of a contract because of fraud, the Supreme Judicial Court held in *Rockland Trust* that a contract is voidable where a party has "reason to know" of the fraud before giving value or materially changing its position. 366 Mass. at 79, 314 N.E.2d at 441.

The "reason to know" standard has been incorporated into the general definition of notice as it is used in the UCC. Mass.

Gen.Laws Ann. ch. 106, § 1–201(25) (West 1958) states in pertinent part:

> A person has "notice" of a fact when (a) he has actual knowledge of it; or (b) he has received a notice or notification of it; or (c) from all the facts and circumstances known to him at the time in question he has reason to know that it exists. A person "knows" or has "knowledge" of a fact when he has actual knowledge of it.

*   *   *

Although, as we discuss below, the present issue does not involve the UCC, we look to the statutory definition of notice under the UCC as adopted by the Massachusetts legislature, as well as to analogous case law, for guidance in determining the standard that would be applied by the Supreme Judicial Court in Massachusetts. In the absence of a definitive ruling by the highest state court, a federal court may consider "analogous decisions, considered dicta, scholarly works, and any other reliable data tending convincingly to show how the highest court in the state would decide the issue at hand," taking into account the broad policies and trends so evinced. McKenna v. Ortho Pharmaceutical Corp., 622 F.2d 657, 663 (3d Cir. 1980). We believe that, under Massachusetts law, a person has notice of a fact when, from all the information at his disposal, he has reason to know of it. Organizations are chargeable with knowledge of information in their possession when reasonable communications routines would disseminate that information to the appropriate individuals.

*   *   *

Since FNB, the district court found, was unaware of the fraudulent Statutory Declarations that caused Michelin to make the disputed payments, FNB cannot be held to have had notice of JCC's fraud merely from its knowledge of JCC's finances. *   *   * Recovery under § 28 of the Restatement of Restitution is accordingly foreclosed.

Under § 14 of the Restatement, FNB would be liable to make restitution if it had notice of Michelin's defense or mistake before giving value for the payments—*i.e.*, if it had notice that the subcontractors had not been paid. While Michelin does not assert that any of FNB's officers actually knew, or that the bank had actually been informed that JCC was not paying its subcontractors, Michelin argues that FNB had constructive notice of this fact. In support of its argument, Michelin directs us to portions of the Stipulation of Facts purporting to establish that FNB was JCC's only source of funds at the time of the payments and that FNB knew JCC could not have paid its subcontractors because its loan funds had been restricted to use for payroll and taxes. The district court, however, did not find that JCC had no other sources of income, and it specifically found that the bank did nothing to enforce the restrictions on use of loan funds. The record supports these findings and the implication to be drawn from them that FNB did not have reason to know of JCC's failure to pay subcontractors.

If we were to hold FNB chargeable with notice of JCC's nonpayment of subcontractors on this record, we would be imposing an affirmative duty on lenders to look out for the interests of account debtors such as Michelin. In order for FNB to have discovered JCC's failure to pay its subcontractors, FNB would have had to initiate an investigation of JCC's business practices under the Michelin contract, not aimed at determining the company's financial health for purposes of the bank's continued financing, but aimed at verifying JCC's compliance with the Michelin contract. That JCC was in monetary straits could not have indicated that subcontractors had gone unpaid without such an investigation. We are unwilling to impose such a responsibility on lenders.

Here, FNB did attempt to verify the accuracy of the copies of invoices it was receiving from JCC by contacting Michelin. Michelin's agent, SNC, responded that the invoices were "OK." Michelin's losses might have been avoided if it had required JCC to provide a performance bond or if it had availed itself of its right to visit the offices of subcontractors and investigate the progress of the work. It might have demanded more vigilance from its agent, SNC. SNC was on the site and was charged with supervising the job and certifying its progress. The one area where Michelin was most vulnerable to fraud—the Statutory Declarations—was the area that it could have checked very easily and where, unfortunately, it failed to check at all. It cannot shift its loss to the bank by arguing now that the bank should have monitored JCC's compliance when it failed to do so.

Affirmed.

BOWNES, CIRCUIT JUDGE (dissenting).

I dissent from the majority's holding that Michelin does not have an independent cause of action against First National Bank of Boston (FNB). The pertinent portion of the Uniform Commercial Code as enacted in Massachusetts reads as follows:

Defenses Against Assignee; Modification of Contract After Notification of Assignment; Term Prohibiting Assignment Ineffective; Identification and Proof of Assignment. (1) Unless an account debtor has made an enforceable agreement not to assert defenses or claims arising out of a sale as provided in section 9–206 the rights of an assignee are subject to

(a) all the terms of the contract between the account debtor and assignor and any defense or claim arising therefrom[.]

Mass.Gen.Laws Ann. ch. 106, § 9–318(1)(a).

Although the words "subject to" suggest that the limitations that follow are merely restrictions on the assignee's affirmative rights and are not affirmative rights themselves, the word "claim" suggests that the account debtor may assert affirmative rights of action against the assignee.

No Massachusetts court has ruled directly on this question. In Fall River Trust Co. v. B. G. Browdy, Inc., 346 Mass. 614, 195 N.E.2d 63, 2 U.C.C.Rep.Serv. 1 (1964), however, the Massachusetts Supreme Judicial Court indicated that an account debtor could assert as a setoff the type of claim Michelin is seeking to assert affirmatively here. That case involved an attempt by the account debtor of a bankrupt business, in an action by the bankrupt's creditor and assignee of accounts against the account debtor for amounts due, to set off the amount of value of the account debtor's goods that the bankrupt had lost. The bankrupt was engaged in the finishing and dyeing business, and the account debtor had earlier delivered certain goods to him to be finished and dyed. Because of ambiguities in the record, the court remanded the case for further fact finding. The court said, however, that if the goods lost had been delivered pursuant to the accounts that the assignee was now suing on, the account debtor could, under section 9–318(1)(a), set off the value of the goods lost. The question in this case, then, is whether an account debtor's claims against the assignee for payments mistakenly made due to fraud are restricted to situations where they may be asserted in setoff or whether they may be asserted originally.

I believe that the sounder view is that an account debtor may sue the assignee directly under section 9–318(1)(a) for payments received under the assigned contract. This section provides than an assignee's rights are subject to claims and defenses that the account debtor had against the assignor. The Uniform Commercial Code, as enacted in Massachusetts does not define "claim," but the word "claim" is commonly understood to include original cause action. For example, when "claim" is used in the Massachusetts Rules of Civil Procedure (admittedly the rules quoted were effective only as of 1974), it includes original claims. See Mass.R.Civ.P. 8(a) ("[a] pleading which sets forth a claim for relief, whether an original claim, counterclaim, cross-claim, or third-party claim shall contain   *   *   *   a short and plain statement of the claim showing that the pleader is entitled to relief[.]"); Mass.R.Civ.P. 18(a) ("[a] party asserting a claim to relief as an original claim, counterclaim, cross-claim, or third party claim, may join, either as independent or as alternate claims, as many claims, legal or equitable, or both, as he has against an opposing party.")

It is, in my opinion, incorrect to conclude that the words of limitation, "subject to," foreclose original claims. A party's rights can be subject to whatever affirmative claims or defenses another party might assert. Under section 9–318(1)(a), an assignee's rights to retain payments made to it under an assignment are subject to, or are exposed to, affirmative actions brought by the account debtor to recover payments mistakenly made. The definition of "subject to" taken by the court from Englestein v. Mintz, 345 Ill. 48, 61, 177 N.E. 746, 752 (1931), and Anderson v. Southwest Savings & Loan Association, 117 Ariz. 246, 248, 571 P.2d 1042, 1044 (1977), is too broad. The "affirmative rights" denied to the plaintiffs in those cases were open-ended rights, that is, the plaintiffs were seeking amounts in excess of and unrelated to amounts provided for under the original contracts. In *Englestein,* plaintiff asserted that because his partnership agreement with defendant to purchase part of a parcel of real estate was "subject to" the terms of an earlier contract defendant had with the vendor of the real estate, he was entitled to share as a partner in other purchase transactions defendant had with respect to the parcel. The court rejected the claim, in part on the basis of its definition of "subject to." In *Anderson,* plaintiff sued for breach of implied warranties in the sale of a mobile home, naming as defendants the vendor, the manufacturer, and the vendor's secured creditor. The Arizona court affirmed dismissal of the suit against the secured creditor, reasoning that "subject to" in section 9–318(1)(a) did not expose a secured creditor to such claims against the creditor's assignor. These cases do not reject the result I support, that payments received by an assignee of accounts (FNB) are subject to a claim by an account debtor (Michelin) that payments were mistakenly made because of fraud by the assignor (JCC).

This interpretation of section 9–318(1)(a), that the account debtor has rights of action against the assignee, is the fairest way to reconcile the rights of account debtors and secured creditors, particularly where, as here, credit is advanced through a line of credit. This case boils down to the question of whether the secured creditor or the account debtor should bear the cost of not finding out that JCC falsely claimed that it had paid its subcontractors. The secured creditor is in a better position than the account debtor to determine whether the assignor/borrower is complying with the terms of the contract in which the creditor has an interest. The reason is that the secured creditor can employ an effective sanction without having to initiate litigation and without risking any loss itself to ensure compliance; it can threaten to cut off credit unless it is satisfied with the borrower's performance. The other party, the account debtor, has no similar sanction. If he is not satisfied, he must litigate and bear the expense of litigation and the sure delay in completion of the contract. The creditor/assignee is not deterred from enforcing compliance by such costs. Obviously, either the secured creditor or the account debtor can make inquiries regarding compliance with the contract, but at some point both will have to rely on the representations of others, which creates opportunities for fraud, as occurred here. The secured creditor is accustomed to looking over the borrower's shoulder on an ongoing basis and can check compliance. By virtue of his control over credit, the creditor can ensure compliance with the contract. The account debtor can only investigate and if it holds up payments, it puts the contract in jeopardy.

The majority contends that holding for appellants will disrupt the free flow of credit because creditors will have additional duties. This argument goes too far because it counsels against any imposition on creditors. Besides, whatever increased credit costs arise will fall on the class truly at fault in these cases—the borrower/assignors.

The majority also stresses the concern that actions under section 9–318(1)(a) will make creditors fully liable for the contracts of their borrowers, which would contravene section 9–317. This case does not present this problem, and this result need not occur. I do not argue that the creditor should be the surety for the assignor. The creditor should be exposed only to the extent that he benefits from the assigned contract rights. Tracking the language of section 9–318(1)(a), whatever rights of payment a secured creditor has are subject to the terms of the contract between the account debtor and the borrower/assignor. The account debtor cannot go beyond the benefits the creditor/assignee obtains under the assignment in an action against the creditor. Whether the account debtor asserts the claim as a counterclaim or as an original claim should be irrelevant.

In reaching a contrary conclusion, the court has relied on the Official Comment to section 9–318 to clarify the supposed conflict between "claim" and "subject to." This reliance is misplaced because the Comment is at least as ambiguous as the language of section 9–318(1)(a) itself.[2] The relevant portion of the Comment reads, "[s]ubsection (1) makes no substantial change in prior law." The argument that the provision for an original right of action in section 9–318(1)(a) would not change prior law substantially is at least as plausible as the majority's argument that it would make a substantial change.

The prior law in Massachusetts was that an account debtor could assert "all defences and rights of counter-claim, recoupment or set-off" against the creditor/assignee when the creditor/assignee sued him on the account. Mass.Gen.Laws Ann. ch. 231, § 5 (repealed 1975). This statute had primarily a procedural purpose: an assignee was enabled for the first time to sue in his own name rather than in the assignor's, and, accordingly, an account debtor was permitted to assert defensive rights directly against the assignee when he sued. Quality Finance Co. v. Hurley, 337 Mass. 150, 155, 148 N.E.2d 385, 389 (1958). It seems reasonable to suppose that the question of affirmative rights for account debtors was simply not contemplated. Section 9–318(1)(a) now speaks more broadly than did ch. 231, § 5: the account debtor's rights against the assignee are not restricted explicitly to defensive claims. Thus, the Massachusetts legislature quite conceivably could have decided to give account debtors an affirmative right, and this would not have represented a substantial change in the law. Putting the point more strongly, given the plainly broader language of section 9–318(1)(a), it seems curious to turn to what is effectively the legislative history of the

---

2. I would also point out that the Official Comments have not been enacted as part of the UCC in Massachusetts. Furthermore, in some states the comments were not placed before the legislatures when they considered the UCC, and the comments occasionally expand on or retract from enacted sections of the Code. J. White & R. Summers, Handbook of the Law Under the Uniform Commercial Code § 4, at 12–13 (1972).

section in order to give it the same apparent meaning as the old statute.

I agree with the majority that the decisions from other jurisdictions are not illuminating. I cannot agree, however, with its suggestion that the decisions allowing the account debtor to sue originally are founded on an exception to section 9–318(1)(a) that is based on the common law of restitution. These decisions mark a hazy line if one is seeking to identify an exception to the rule that original rights of action by account debtors are not allowed. The element these cases do share is emphasis on some degree of participation by the assignee in the contract between the assignor and the account debtor. See Benton State Bank v. Warren, 263 Ark. 1, 562 S.W.2d 74 (1978); Farmers Acceptance Corp. v. DeLozier, 178 Colo. 291, 496 P.2d 1016 (1972); Massey-Ferguson Credit Corp. v. Brown, 173 Mont. 253, 567 P.2d 440 (1977). The function of the "participation" requirement is unclear. In *Benton State Bank*, the participation seems most clearly to mean that the assignee had notice of the terms of the contract between the assignor and the account debtor and so received payments subject to any actions for breach of contract.[4] The court in *Benton State Bank* also balanced the negligence of both the account debtor and the assignee in not enforcing compliance with the contract to determine whether the assignee should be held liable. The *Massey-Ferguson* court emphasized participation by the assignee much more strongly, apparently on the unarticulated theory that the assignee could be sued as a sort of cocontractor or surety. The critical point for the court was that the assignee had orally affirmed the assignor's promises. *DeLozier* falls somewhere in the middle: the assignee's participation was greater than the assignee's in *Benton State Bank* and less than the assignee's in *Massey-Ferguson*. The *DeLozier* court seemed to follow the *Benton State Bank* notice theory.

As to contrary cases, Minnesota has held that an account debtor does not have a right of action under section 9–318(1)(a) a decision with which, of course, I do not agree. Meyers v. Postal Finance Co., 287 N.W.2d 614 (Minn.1979). A lower New York court has also appeared to hold similarly, James Talcott, Inc. v.

---

4. This characterization of *Benton State Bank* is different than the majority's in that I do not believe that the fact that the bank passed along the assignor's assertions of compliance to the account debtor is particularly significant. The crucial aspect of *Benton State Bank* was the existence of "solid reasons" for doubting that the assignor was fulfilling its contractual obligations. Thus *Benton State Bank* is not so much different than this case, where FNB also had solid reasons for doubting JCC's performance.

Brewster Sales Corp., 16 U.C.C.Rep.Serv. 1165 (N.Y.Sup.Ct. 1975), but in that case the court emphasized that the assignor was still solvent and could be sued and that because the account debtor's guarantor had paid an earlier judgment to the assignee in an action arising out of the same accounts, the account debtor was trying to get a refund of money it had not paid.

When these cases are applied to the instant case, FNB seems to be exposed to liability as an assignee with notice. The notice required in *Benton State Bank* and *DeLozier* is only notice of the terms of the contract, not notice of the breach. As in *Benton State Bank*, FNB was in a better position to detect or prevent breaches than Michelin. I do not rest my dissent, however, on an assignee-with-notice rule. An account debtor should be able to sue without proving notice; it is only realistic to assume that a creditor taking a security interest in accounts will acquaint himself with their terms.

For the foregoing reasons, I would hold that Michelin has a direct cause of action against FNB for the monies it received from Michelin under its assignment from JCC.

NOTE

Comment 1 to UCC § 9–318 states that subsection (1) of that provision "makes no substantial change in prior law." Restatement of Restitution § 14, quoted by the court in *Michelin*, reflects the pre-UCC law. A person receiving a benefit by mistake is not required to give it back if he made no misrepresentation, and if he received the benefit in good faith and for value and without notice of the mistake. The rule is based on the principle of bona fide purchase and the absence of unjust enrichment.

In Gaffner v. American Finance Co., 120 Wash. 76, 206 P. 916 (1922), a person who had stolen an automobile used it as collateral for a loan obtained from Finance Co. The thief then sold the automobile to Plaintiff who paid part of the price by paying the thief's debt to Finance Co. After the fraud came to light Plaintiff sued to recover the money paid to Finance Co. on the theory that the payment was made under the mistaken belief that Finance Co. had a valid security interest in the automobile. Plaintiff was denied recovery. Finance Co. made no misrepresentations. It received the payment in good faith and without notice of the mistake. It gave value because it discharged a valid debt owed by the thief. Thus there was no unjust enrichment. This case is an example of the rule of § 14(1) of the Restatement.

Michelin falls within the rule of § 14(2) of the Restatement. That rule is an extension of the rule of § 14(1). An illustration is Daniels v. Parker, 209 Or. 419, 306 P.2d 735 (1957). Plaintiff bought an automobile from Seller on an installment contract under which Seller was granted a security interest in the automobile. Seller assigned the installment contract to Finance Co. Plaintiff then made all payments under the installment contract to Finance Co. It turned out that the automobile was stolen and Plaintiff lost it to the owner. Plaintiff sued to recover the payments made to Finance Co. on the theory of payment by mistake. Recovery was denied. Finance Co. was not unjustly enriched. If the transaction between Seller and Finance Co. is analyzed as a loan to Seller secured by an assignment of Seller's secured claim against Plaintiff, there is no unjust enrichment because Finance Co. received Plaintiff's payments for value in that it discharged Seller's debt to Finance Co. If the transaction between Seller and Finance Co. is considered a sale of Seller's secured claim against Plaintiff, there is no unjust enrichment because Finance Co. had previously paid value to Seller for the claim against Plaintiff.

The Reporter's comment to Restatement § 14(2) is directly relevant to a case such as *Michelin* and to UCC § 9–318(1). The comment is in part as follows: *

> The rule stated in this Subsection presupposes that, had there been no payment, the assignee would have no rights against the payor. * * * The rule is based upon the principle that in determining whether or not one gives value it is immaterial whether he pays value at the time he acquires the title or has paid value at some prior time in order that he might acquire the title * * *. It is consistent with the rule that one who pays value for a transfer of property to be made in the future is a purchaser for value thereof if the property is subsequently transferred to him and that he is a bona fide purchaser if, when he receives title, he has no notice of adverse interests.

> The rule stated in this Subsection applies, and applies only, to those cases where there was a transaction between the payor and the assignor or some prior assignor from which a cause of action would have arisen but for failure of consideration, fraud, mistake, duress, the failure of a condition, or a similar defense. Thus the rule applies where a promise has

been obtained by fraud or without consideration, or where the promise was conditional and the condition has not been performed. It also applies where there was a mistake common to both of the original parties to the transaction, a mistake for which there might have been rescission or reformation. * * *

The rationale for the rule of Restatement § 14(2) would seem to be that if the account debtor and the assignee are both innocent parties and if there has been no unjust enrichment the court will leave the loss where it falls. If the assignor is insolvent and the account debtor has not yet paid, the loss falls on the assignee; if the account debtor has already paid the loss falls on him.

For a thorough discussion of Restatement § 14 see Palmer, The Law of Restitution, Vol. III 480–510 (1978).

Skip to 220

D. CONSUMER GOODS

Article 9 was drafted at the dawn of the movement for reform of consumer credit law. By the end of the 40s a few states had retail installment sales acts and most had personal loan laws. Professor Gilmore recalls that at an early drafting stage it was contemplated that a number of the provisions found in retail installment sales acts would be incorporated into Article 9. Disclosure requirements and abolition of holding in due course with respect to consumer paper were examples of these provisions. It soon became apparent that no agreement could be reached on the desirability of these consumer protection provisions, and the final draft contained only a few remnants of the original grand scheme to protect the consumer debtor. The story is told in Gilmore, Security Interests in Personal Property § 9.2 (1965). The fall-back position taken was to provide in UCC § 9–203(4) that Article 9 should be subordinate to those consumer protection laws passed in states that enacted the Code. This handed back to state legislatures the bone of contention concerning consumer credit protection on which they were to gnaw for the next 30 years. UCC § 9–206 also relinquished to the enacting states the determination of the validity of waiver of defenses clauses in consumer credit transactions.

Special protection for defaulting consumer debtors is found in UCC §§ 9–505(1) and 9–507(1). The most interesting vestige of the consumer protection phase of Article 9 is UCC § 9–204(2) which greatly limits the effect of an after-acquired property clause in secured transactions involving consumer goods. The purpose of this section was to prevent a seller from adding on new sales to the balances of old ones merely by use of an after-acquired property clause in the original security agreement. But all a seller had to do to avoid this provision was to require the buyer to sign new security agreements at the time of subsequent sales. Nothing in Article 9 then prevented the seller from consolidating the sales and subjecting all the goods sold to the buyer to a security interest securing the combined balances of all the sales. This left the unfortunate buyer in the position described in Williams v. Walker-Thomas Furniture Co., 350 F.2d 445 (D.C.Cir. 1965), of being subjected to a lien on all property purchased until the last dollar of the consolidated balance was paid off. The solution to this abuse is found in Uniform Consumer Credit Code § 3.303 (1974) and other state statutes which allocate the debtor's payments entirely to discharging the debts first incurred, thus releasing from the seller's security interest each item sold as soon as the debtor's payments equal the debt arising from that sale. In short, there is no evidence that UCC § 9–204(2) has been of any significance in protecting consumers. A business debtor is able to obtain loan credit by giving a floating lien on his assets. Why is this denied to an affluent consumer?

The major difference in the Code's treatment of consumer goods is that a purchase money security interest in consumer goods is automatically perfected at the time of attachment with no requirement of filing. UCC § 9–302(1)(d). The reasons for this exception are: (1) consumer transactions are frequently small so the expense of filing can significantly add to the price that the consumer will have to pay; (2) consumer transactions are very numerous and they would unduly burden the filing system; (3) the pre-Code rule in most states did not require filing in conditional sale transactions; and (4) parties to consumer transactions are less likely to search the records. See Gilmore, Security Interests in Personal Property § 19.4 (1965).

However, the most important kind of consumer goods, motor vehicles, fall outside the Code's filing system because of the requirement in most states that security interests in motor vehicles be perfected by listing the interest on the certificate of title. UCC § 9–302(3)(b). See White & Summers, Uniform Commercial Code § 23–19 (2d ed. 1980). Some states have similar requirements for boats. Security interests in airplanes must be recorded in the federal registry. See Sigman, The Wild Blue Yonder: Interests in Aircraft Under Our Federal System, 46 So.

Cal.L.Rev. 316 (1973). A few states have set dollar limits above which filing is required for consumer goods, e.g., Colorado, $250, Maine, $1,000, Maryland, $500, and Wisconsin, $500. See Editor's Note, 27 U.C.C. Rep. 564 (1979).

PROBLEMS

1. Your client, Music Center, sells musical instruments of all kinds: strings (electric guitars are its best seller), pianos, brasses, and woodwinds. Music Center reserves a security interest in goods sold on credit. Some items run in excess of $1,000 in price, but most sales are between $50 and $200. Among his customers are amateur musicians: high school band and orchestra members and adults who play instruments for their own pleasure. Perhaps a fourth of Music Center's credit sales are made to professional musicians: members of professional performing groups and teachers who use their instruments in giving lessons. Advise your client how to set up workable operating procedures which will protect his security interest in goods sold. See UCC § 9–109(1) "consumer goods" and (2) "equipment" and § 9–302(1)(d). See UCC § 9–307(2). See also Strevell-Paterson Finance Co. v. May, 77 N.M. 331, 422 P.2d 366 (1967).

2. Manufacturer sold furniture to Retailer on credit, reserving a security interest in the furniture and its proceeds after it had been sold. Retailer sold furniture to numerous consumers, reserving a security interest in the furniture. Neither Manufacturer nor Retailer filed financing statements covering the furniture they sold. Does Manufacturer have a perfected security interest in the furniture that it sold to Retailer which is still in Retailer's possession? Does Retailer have a perfected security interest in furniture sold to consumers? See UCC § 9–109(1) "consumer goods" and (4) "inventory."

NATIONAL SHAWMUT BANK OF BOSTON v. JONES

Supreme Court of New Hampshire, 1967.
108 N.H. 386, 236 A.2d 484.

Action of replevin to recover possession of a 1964 Dodge Dart "270" station wagon. Defendant's motion for custody under RSA 536:5 was granted upon his filing a bond in the amount of $2,000.00 to secure payment of any judgment which might be rendered against him. According to an agreed statement of facts, Robert D. Wever of Hampton, New Hampshire, purchased

the Dart from Wentworth Motor Company Inc. of Exeter on
February 15, 1965 under a conditional sale contract for personal,
family or household purposes. He executed a "Retail Installment Contract" which was assigned by Wentworth to the plaintiff. This contract was filed with the Town Clerk of Hampton
pursuant to [UCC §] 9–401 on February 24, 1965. Sometime
thereafter, without the consent of the plaintiff, Wever traded or
sold the Dart to Hanson-Rock Inc. of Hampton, an automobile
dealer in the business of selling new and used cars to the public.
[UCC §] 1–201(9). Defendant, a resident of Hampton, purchased
the Dart from Hanson-Rock on April 8, 1966 for good and sufficient consideration in good faith and without any actual knowledge of any security interest of the plaintiff or anyone else.
Neither the defendant nor the Hampton National Bank from
which he borrowed the purchase price examined or searched for
any filing in the office of the town clerk. (It was agreed at argument that unless a search was made under the name Wever,
the Retail Installment Contract could have been found only by
examining all such contracts for the serial number of the vehicle.) An unpaid balance of $1,490.17 is still due under the in-
stallment contract.

The following questions were transferred without ruling by
Leahy, C. J.:

1. Whether the defendant is liable to the plaintiff in the
amount of $1,490.17, the amount outstanding under the Retail
Installment Contract executed by Robert Wever in favor of
Wentworth Motors, Inc., and subsequently assigned to the plaintiff.

2. Whether under the provisions of the Uniform Commercial
Code in New Hampshire a buyer in ordinary course of business
takes free of a perfected security interest created by a person
other than the seller from whom the buyer purchased the goods.

GRIMES, JUSTICE. Since Wever purchased for personal, family or household purposes, the Dart is classified as consumer
goods. § 9–109. The plaintiff's security interest was perfected
by filing the financing statement with the Town Clerk of Hampton where Wever resided, (§ 9–401(1)(a)), and continues when
the collateral is sold without its consent as was the case here
unless Article 9 provides otherwise. § 9–306(2). In the case of
buyers of goods, § 9–307(1) does provide otherwise in certain instances, as follows:

"A buyer in ordinary course of business (subsection (9) of
Section 1–201) other than a person buying farm products from a

person engaged in farming operations takes free of a security interest created by his seller even though the security interest is perfected and even though the buyer knows of its existence."

Since defendant purchased in good faith without knowledge that the sale to him was in violation of the security interest of another and bought in the ordinary course from a person in the business of selling automobiles, he was a "buyer in the ordinary course of business." § 1–201(9). However, § 9–307(1) permits him to take free only of "a security interest created by his seller." The security interest of the plaintiff was not created by Hanson-Rock, Inc., the defendant's seller, but by Wentworth Motor Co., Inc. Defendant, therefore, does not take free of the plaintiff's security interest under this section. Neither does he take free of the security interest by reason of the provisions of § 9–307(2) relating to consumer goods even if he purchased for his own personal, family or household purposes (a fact not agreed upon) because "prior to the purchase, the secured party * * * filed a financing statement * * *." These are the only two provisions of Article 9 under which a buyer of goods can claim to take free of a security interest where a sale, exchange or other disposition of the collateral was without the consent of the secured party. The defendant does not benefit from either one. Section 9–306(2) gives the court no leeway to create any other exceptions to its dictates and no custom, usage or agreement has been brought to our attention which would permit us to do so. § 1–102(2). See Lincoln Bank & Trust Co. v. Queenan, 344 S.W.2d 383 (Ky.).

Defendant contends that § 2–403(1) provides an escape from plaintiff's security interest when it provides " * * * a person with a voidable title has power to transfer a good title to a good faith purchaser for value. * * * "

The contention has two answers. § 9–306(2) provides for the continuance of the security interest "except when this Article provides otherwise," thereby limiting any exceptions to those contained in Article 9; and § 2–403 itself provides that the rights of "lien creditors are governed by the Articles on Secured Transactions (Article 9) * * *." See also, § 2–402 which provides "(3) Nothing in this article shall be deemed to impair the rights of creditors of the seller (a) under the provisions of the Article on Secured Transactions (Article 9) * * *." It is clear, therefore, that a security interest in the case of a sale without consent was to be impaired only as provided in Article 9 and is unaffected by Article 2.

Our answer to question 1 is in the affirmative and to question 2 is in the negative.

Remanded.

NOTES

1. In Exchange Bank of Osceola v. Jarrett, 180 Mont. 33, 588 P.2d 1006 (1979), the Court upheld the view of the principal case but said: "This Court recognizes that this is a harsh result, since the purchaser * * * had no means to learn * * * that the property he purchased was subject to a security interest. It may be that legislative action is necessary to prevent such results in the future." 588 P.2d at 1009. Do you agree?

2. Assume that the goods in the principal case had been a refrigerator and assume further than Wentworth had perfected a security interest without filing a financing statement pursuant to UCC § 9–302(1)(d). Could Jones now prevail as against Wentworth's assignee under UCC § 9–307(2)? New England Merchants National Bank of Boston v. Auto Owners Finance Co., 355 Mass. 487, 245 N.E.2d 437 (1969), answers in the negative. The court said:

> The crucial point is whether under § 9–307(2) the seller as well as the buyer must be a consumer. This subsection, as far as material, reads: "In the case of consumer goods * * * a buyer takes free of a security interest even though perfected if he buys without knowledge of the security interest, for value and for his own personal, family or household purposes * * * unless prior to the purchase the secured party has filed a financing statement covering such goods." Careful reading of the entire subsection leads to the conclusion that the opening phrase, "In the case of consumer goods," must require that the seller as well as the buyer be a consumer. If the buyer alone has to be a consumer, the opening phrase would be surplusage because of the subsequent provision that the buyer purchase "for his own personal, family or household purposes," which is nothing more than a repetition of the definition of consumer goods in § 9–109(1).
>
> We hold that under § 9–307(2) both the buyer and seller must be consumers. The view has unanimous support in the authorities so far as they have come to our attention. In Everett Natl. Bank v. DeSchuiteneer, 109 N.H. 112, 244 A.2d 196, the same conclusion was squarely reached. See National Shawmut Bank of Boston v. Vera, 352 Mass. 11, 17, 223

N.E.2d 515. This is conceded by the defendant, which disputes its soundness. See Coogan, Article 9 of the Uniform Commercial Code: Priorities among Secured Creditors and the "Floating Lien," 72 Harv.L.Rev. 838, 848; Vernon, Priorities, The Uniform Commercial Code and Consumer Financing, 4 B.C.Ind. & Comm.L.Rev. 531; Protection of a Buyer at an Execution Sale under UCC Section 9–307, 9 B.C.Ind. & Comm.L.Rev. 97, 193–205; Coogan, Hogan and Vagts, Secured Transactions under the UCC §§ 7.02(4) and 19.02(3)(c); Gilmore, Security Interests in Personal Property, § 26.12, p. 716.

3. Although a seller need not file to perfect his security interest in consumer goods under UCC § 9–302(1)(d), his security interest is cut off when his buyer sells the goods to another consumer buyer unless the seller had filed a financing statement. UCC § 9–307(2). Thus filing as to consumer goods is irrelevant as to the rights of relatively sophisticated parties like creditors who are used to using a filing system but is determinative as to the rights of a buyer of a used refrigerator at a garage sale who would never dream of examining the records. How can this be? When California adopted the UCC it omitted entirely subsection (2) to UCC § 9–307. Under the California Code a purchase money security interest in consumer goods is perfected for all purposes without filing.

PROBLEM

In State A, pursuant to an installment sale contract, Seller sold a piano to Buyer for his personal use. Buyer granted Seller a security interest in the piano to secure payment of the price. Shortly thereafter Buyer moved to State B and took the piano with him. Two months after moving to State B Buyer sold the piano to T, who had no knowledge that it was subject to a security interest. Buyer then defaulted on the installment sale contract with Seller.

(a) What are the rights of Seller and T to the piano if (1) T is a dealer in musical instruments who bought the piano as a trade-in, and (2) Seller never filed a financing statement in either State A or State B.

(b) What are the rights of Seller and T to the piano if (1) T is an individual who bought it for his personal use and (2) Seller filed a financing statement in State A prior to the time the piano was removed from that state but did not file a financing statement within four months of the time that the piano entered State B.

See UCC § 9–103(1)(d)(i) and (iii).

FARMERS AND MERCHANTS BANK
AND TRUST v. KSENYCH

Supreme Court of South Dakota, 1977.
252 N.W.2d 220.

MORGAN, JUSTICE (on reassignment).   Plaintiff-appellant, Farmers and Merchants Bank and Trust of Watertown, South Dakota (Bank), filed an action on October 24, 1974 against defendant-respondent, Nick Ksenych (Ksenych), seeking to recover a new 1974 Dodge pickup or its value.   Ksenych counterclaimed for title to the vehicle.   The case was submitted to the court on a Stipulation of Fact, the court's memorandum decision was delivered on June 19, 1975, and judgment entered July 11, 1975, finding against the Bank and declaring that title to the Dodge pickup belonged to Ksenych.   The Bank appeals from the judgment.   We affirm as to the result.

According to the stipulation of facts which has the status of special findings for the purpose of review, Williamson Dodge, a dealer in Dodge vehicles, entered into a "floor-plan" arrangement with the Bank.   Under this arrangement Chrysler Motors Corporation would mail a draft drawn on the Bank covering Williamson Dodge's cost of a specific vehicle and would also mail the manufacturer's statement of origin for that vehicle to the Bank.   Once the draft was drawn on the Bank, Williamson Dodge would then execute a note with the Bank.   After Williamson Dodge sold the vehicle and deposited the proceeds of the sale with the Bank, the Bank would give Williamson Dodge the manufacturer's statement of origin for the vehicle.   Through this arrangement Chrysler Motors agreed to transport a 1974 Dodge pickup to Williamson Dodge November 12, 1973.   The manufacturer's statement of origin to the vehicle was retained by the Bank, and the vehicle was placed on Williamson Dodge's lot.   On December 26, 1973 the Bank filed a financing statement with the Secretary of State, State of South Dakota, showing the debtor as Williamson Dodge and T. V. Williamson, Watertown, South Dakota and covering all "1974 Dodge vehicles."

On December 28, 1973 Williamson Dodge sold a new 1974 Dodge pickup to Ksenych for $5,000 cash, plus a trade-in.   Williamson Dodge was to make an application for a certificate of title in Ksenych's name, which is allowable under SDCL 32–3–25. However, the certificate of title was never given to Ksenych since Williamson Dodge did not gain possession of the manufacturer's statement of origin when it failed to remit the proceeds of the Ksenych sale to the Bank. On January 5, 1974 Williamson Dodge closed its business with its remaining assets taken over by Williamson Dodge's secured creditors.

On October 24, 1974 the Bank, while asserting their superior interest in the collateral upon Williamson Dodge's default, filed this action to recover the 1974 Dodge pickup from Ksenych. Ksenych counterclaimed for clear title to the vehicle and responded by alleging that the purchase out of Williamson Dodge's inventory conveyed clear title to him according to the provisions of the Uniform Commercial Code.

The court ruled by its memo decision of June 19, 1975 that the Certificate of Title Act, SDCL 32–3–1, et seq. controlled the outcome, not the Uniform Commercial Code, and that the Bank legally held title to the vehicle under SDCL 32–3–1. He further held however that the Bank, by its conduct in clothing Williamson Dodge with the apparent authority to sell the vehicle, was estopped from asserting such title.

The first question on appeal as stated by the appellant is "Do the general provisions of the Uniform Commercial Code which protects buyers of encumbered consumer goods revoke sections 32–3–10 and 32–3–37 of the South Dakota Compiled Laws of 1967 which protect the lien of the holder of a security interest in a motor vehicle when the title documents are in his possession?" Respondent paraphrases this question to be whether or not the plaintiff's claim to the vehicle under SDCL 32–3–10 and 32–3–37 is paramount and superior to the claim of defendant in said vehicle under the Uniform Commercial Code.

In certain particulars including those which relate to this action, [Article 9] relating to secured transactions under the Uniform Commercial Code and Chapter 32–3 relating to registrations, liens and transfers under the motor vehicle code deal with the same subject matter and when statutes are in pari materia they should be considered concurrently whenever possible. If they can be made to stand together, effect should be given to both as far as possible.

In reviewing the legislative history of the statutes in question, we find no conflict that cannot be resolved while giving full force and effect to each. The sections in question which are part of SDCL Chapter 32–3 titled "Registration, liens and transfers" will be referred to collectively as the Title Statutes. These statutes appear to have their inception in Chapter 229 of the Session Laws of 1951. Section 2 of that enactment at (4) provides that "no person, *except as provided in this chapter* (emphasis added) obtaining or getting possession of a motor vehicle shall acquire any right, title, claim, or interest in or to such motor vehicle, until he shall have had issued to him a certificate of title to such motor vehicle, or delivered to him a manufacturer's or importer's certificate for the same;" and goes on to provide "nor shall any waiver or estoppel operate in favor of such person against a person having possession of such certificate of title * * * for a valuable consideration." This provision is now codified as SDCL 32–3–10. Section 3(1) of the same Chapter 229, Session Laws of 1951, goes on to provide in substance that any secured transaction, if accompanied by delivery of a manufacturer's certificate, shall be valid against the creditors of the mortgagor and subsequent purchasers. This portion of the section as later crucially amended is now codified as SDCL 32–3–41. The entire section goes on to include all the materials contained in the present codification as SDCL 32–3–35 to 41, inclusive, SDCL 32–3–43 and 32–3–44, thus encompassing all of the title sections which appear to be in controversy.

Chapter 186 of the Session Laws of 1965 amended Chapter 229 by adding trailers and semitrailers to the provision of the statute and amended, most importantly, the provisions of section 3(1) to specifically except trust receipts from the enumerated security documents contained in the statute and added a provision: Provided, however, that "this Section shall not apply to any security interest in a motor vehicle in stock or acquired for stock purposes if such security interest was created in a trust receipt transaction governed by the uniform trust receipts act, 39.18 SDC 1960 Supp." In 1967 by enactment of Chapter 188 the legislature again amended the provision by substituting "financing statement" for "trust receipt" and changing the reference to the Trust Receipts Act to the Uniform Commercial Code. This crucial enactment is now codified as SDCL 32–3–41 and 32–3–42.

Thus, reviewing the history of the enactments, it is not difficult to give reasonable interpretation to all of the provisions in accordance with the rule of pari materia, the object of which is to carry into effect the intention of the legislature and which proceeds upon the supposition that several statutes were governed by one spirit and policy and were intended to be consistent and harmonious in their several parts and provisions.

First of all, the provisions of SDCL 32–3–10, including the reference to "waiver or estoppel", are subject to any exceptions provided elsewhere in the chapter. We then find that the provisions regarding the secured transactions were amended in 1965 to except "trust receipt transactions." The trust receipt was the principal device used in "floor-planning" arrangements. The Trust Receipts Act was repealed by enactment of Chapter 150 of the 1966 Session Laws which was the enactment of the Uniform Commercial Code effective July 1, 1967. The 1967 Legislature by enactment of Chapter 188 amended the financing portion of the Title statutes to substitute financing statement, the appropriate Uniform Commercial Code document, for trust receipt and substitute the provisions of the Uniform Commercial Code for the then repealed Trust Receipts Act. The intent of the legislature to except floor-planning arrangements from the provisions of the Title statutes in question is thus clearly documented.

The floor-planning arrangement between the Bank and Williamson as described in the stipulation of facts is clearly under the provisions of the Uniform Commercial Code, and the defendant who, the stipulation further discloses was a buyer in the ordinary course of business, is entitled to the protection afforded by the Uniform Commercial Code.

*   *   *

The respondent   *   *   *   contends that he is entitled to the benefit of [§ 9–307(1)], sale of goods in ordinary course of business, which provides that a buyer in the ordinary course of business other than a person buying farm products or a person engaged in farming operations takes free of a security interest created by his seller even though the security interest is perfected and even though the buyer knows of its existence. The section which the bank contends for is, as far as pertinent to this transaction, confined to consumer goods which are defined as "used or bought for use primarily for personal, family or household purposes." The section the defendant relies on is restricted to "buyers in the ordinary course of business" which under the provisions of [§ 1–201(9)] restricts the application to buyers (except pawnbrokers) "from a person in the business of selling goods of that kind", thus, in the terminology of the article is primarily restricted to inventory. It is obvious to us that the motor vehicle purchased constituted inventory as opposed to consumer goods and thus the provisions of [§ 9–307(1)] are applicable. It would seem that the bank was originally of a similar view inasmuch as under the provisions of [§ 9–401] the proper place to file a financing statement to perfect a security interest in consumer goods is in the office of the register of deeds in the county of the debtor's residence and the proper place to file in order to perfect a security interest in inventory is in the office of the secretary of state, which as previously noted is where the bank did indeed file its financing statement.

Having considered all of the applicable statutes together, we are of the opinion that upon the sale of a new automobile from inventory by a dealer in the ordinary course of business, the buyer takes free of any security interest under a floor-planning arrangement, even though perfected, and even though the buyer knows of the terms of the security agreement.

We therefore hold that the defendant was entitled to a judgment in his favor and against the bank under the provisions of the applicable Motor Vehicle Title Statutes and the Uniform Commercial Code. Having thus decided, we have no need to consider the second question presented in the appeal as to whether or not the plaintiff is estopped from asserting a superior claim upon which basis the trial court did enter judgment.

The trial court having reached the right result, regardless of the reasoning or theories on which it is predicated, its judgment will be affirmed.

NOTES

1. In Finance America Commercial Corp. v. Econo Coach, Inc., 95 Ill.App.3d 185, 50 Ill.Dec. 667, 419 N.E.2d 935 (1981), the new car buyer prevailed over the secured party when the sale occurred before the security interest was created.

2. What result in the principal case if Dealer had been a used-car dealer? When an owner traded in a car he would sign the transfer form on the back of the certificate of title. Dealer would leave blank the name of the transferee until the vehicle was sold when he would fill in the name of the new buyer and send the old certificate of title to the state department of motor vehicles with an application signed by the new owner for issuance of a new certificate of title in the buyer's name. Suppose Bank had a blanket security agreement with Dealer covering used cars as well as new cars and a financing statement on file with the same description of collateral. However, before Bank

would loan money on Dealer's used-car inventory it required Dealer to turn over possession of the certificate of title to it containing the indorsement of the previous owner. Dealer sold and delivered to Buyer a used car for $5,000 in cash, had Buyer sign an application for a new title, and promised Buyer that the new certificate of title would be mailed to him within three weeks. Actually Bank held the old certificate of title pursuant to a loan it had made to Dealer. When Dealer failed, Bank claimed the car in Buyer's possession. Compare Stroman v. Orlando Bank & Trust, 239 So.2d 621 (Fla.App.1970), and Correria v. Orlando Bank & Trust Co., 235 So.2d 20 (Fla.App.1970), holding in favor of the buyer, with Sterling Acceptance Co. v. Grimes, 194 Pa. Super. 503, 168 A.2d 600 (1961) ("The purchaser of a used automobile knows that a certificate of title has been issued for the automobile and expects to have it produced at the time of sale, but the purchaser of a new vehicle expects no such certificate to exist.") and United Carolina Bank v. Sistrunk, 158 Ga.App. 107, 279 S.E.2d 272 (1981), holding against the buyer.

3. Would the results in the principal case and in the case posed in Note 2 change if the buyers were automobile dealers? See Weidinger Chevrolet, Inc. v. Universal C.I.T. Credit Corp., 501 F.2d 459 (8th Cir. 1974) (Secured party's security agreement allowed dealer "to exhibit and to sell each chattel only to buyers in the ordinary course of business." Held, sale of 22 cars to another dealer was a sale to a buyer in the ordinary course of business.); Sherrock v. Commercial Credit Corp., 290 A.2d 648 (Del.1972) (UCC § 2–103(1)(b) standard of good faith in "observance of reasonable commercial standards of fair dealing in the trade" does not apply to Article 9.); Cessna Finance Corp. v. Skyways Enterprises, Inc., 580 S.W.2d 491 (Ky.1979) (A dealer which buys an airplane with respect to which creditor had recorded a mortgage with the FAA takes free of that interest if it otherwise qualifies as a buyer in ordinary course of business under UCC § 1–201(9)); Associates Discount Corp. v. Rattan Chevrolet, Inc., 462 S.W.2d 546 (Tex.1970) (Dealer can be buyer in ordinary course of a new car subject to an inventory lien.)

E. ACCESSIONS

1. PRE–CODE LAW

The rights of a secured party can be affected by the law of accession, a venerable but imprecise doctrine of the law of property. The following is taken from Brown, The Law of Personal Property 49–53 (3d ed. W. Raushenbush 1975) *

An accession is literally something added. In law the addition of new value to a chattel may raise some interesting and difficult questions, whether the addition of value is by labor or the addition of new materials or both combined. In general it may be postulated that the accession follows the title of the principal thing to which it is annexed. To put it another way, an owner of a chattel has title to lesser things united to that chattel either artificially or naturally. For example, in the case of domestic animals it is well settled that in the absence of an express or implied agreement to the contrary the owner of the mother acquires the ownership of the offspring.

The difficulty arises, however, when an accession is made by one person to the property of another. * * *

When the goods of two different owners are incorporated together, the title to the resulting product goes to the owner of the principal goods. Thus, if the owner of materials employs a mechanic or other artisan to make for him a garment, a wagon, or a boat, fabricating into the product the materials of both the employer and the employee, the title thereto before the final sale belongs to the owner of the principal goods. Such a result seems to accord both with reason and the intent of the parties. But even if a wrongdoer takes another's goods and attaches them to his principal materials he acquires title to the accession, and the mala fides of the converter seems immaterial. Thus, it may be supposed that if A steals B's paint, and with it paints A's automobile, both the automobile and the paint will belong to A. * * *

It has been stated by the courts that the principle of accession does not apply when the attached articles can be sep-

* Published by Callaghan & Co., 3201 Old Glenview, Wilmette, IL 60091. Reprinted with permission.

arated and removed from the principal thing without damage to the latter. This principle is, however, frequently ignored, and the decisions of individual cases are found to turn on the presumed intention of the annexor and the equities of the particular situation. * * *

The way this doctrine was applied to security interests in personal property under the pre-Code law is illustrated by the case that follows.

SASIA & WALLACE, INC. v. SCARBOROUGH IMPLEMENT CO.

District Court of Appeal, Third District, California, 1957.
154 Cal.App.2d 308, 316 P.2d 39.

SCHOTTKY, JUSTICE. Sometime prior to August, 1953, at Merced, California, defendant, Scarborough Implement Company, a copartnership (sued herein as a corporation), sold, under a conditional sales contract, 6 tractors, equipped as complete unit cotton pickers, with gasoline carburetion equipment, to one William Goforth. These tractors, so equipped, were taken to Kern County by Goforth. Thereafter, in August, 1953, while the tractors were in Goforth's possession, plaintiff sold to Goforth, under a title retaining contract, 6 butane tanks with butane carburetion equipment, and removed the gasoline tanks and equipment from the tractors and installed the butane tanks and carburetion equipment on them. In July, 1954, defendant repossessed said tractors because of the failure of Goforth to make the payments under the contract. Plaintiff learned that the tractors had been repossessed, and about six weeks after such repossession, and after the tractors with the butane equipment thereon had been sold by defendant, telephoned to defendant at Merced demanding that defendant return to them the butane tanks and carburetion equipment that plaintiff had installed thereon. The defendant refused to return the butane equipment or pay plaintiff therefor, and plaintiff commenced an action in claim and delivery against defendant to recover said butane equipment or the value thereof. Defendant filed an answer denying plaintiff's right to recover, and alleging that plaintiff, without defendant's consent, removed the gasoline carburetion equipment from said tractors and replaced same with butane carburetion equipment and that thereupon said butane carburetion equipment became an integral part of said cotton picking machines so as to be incapable of severance without injury to the whole of said machines.

*   *   *

The court concluded that the defendant was the legal owner of said equipment at the time plaintiff installed the butane equipment; that the carburetion equipment was an integral part of the cotton picking machines so as to be incapable of severance without injury to the whole of said machines; that plaintiff was negligent in ascertaining the true title to the machines, and that defendant was entitled to judgment. Plaintiff has appealed from the judgment.

Appellant's first contention is that an agreement for a conditional sale, reserving title in the vendor, is good against third parties as well as against parties to the transaction and that the butane tanks and carburetion equipment having been sold by it under a conditional sales contract, it was entitled to recover them from respondent. Appellant argues that respondent cannot justify the taking of appellant's said equipment by virtue of the doctrine of accession, which doctrine is set out in section 1025 of the Civil Code as follows:

"When things belonging to different owners have been united so as to form a single thing, and cannot be separated without injury, the whole belongs to the owner of the thing which forms the principal part; who must, however, reimburse the value of the residue to the other owner, or surrender the whole to him."

Appellant quotes from 68 A.L.R. page 1243, as follows:

"The general rule with respect to accession to property which is the subject of a conditional sale or chattel mortgage may be stated to be that property incorporated with, or labor expended upon, property which is the object of a chattel mortgage or a conditional sale, will pass by accession with the principal article upon foreclosure of the mortgage, or upon the vendor reclaiming it under a conditional sale, where the articles attached become so closely incorporated with the principal article that they cannot be readily identified and detached without injury to the latter, but that when it is possible readily to identify and detach them without injury to the principal article they will not pass, by accession, to the chattel mortgagee or conditional vendor of the principal article."

Appellant cites the case of A. Meister & Sons Co. v. Harrison, 56 Cal.App. 679, 206 P. 106. In that case there were also two conditional sellers involved. The defendant sold motor trucks to buyer and plaintiff sold or leased passenger bus bodies to be attached to the trucks. The defendant repossessed the trucks from the buyer and plaintiff gave notice to the defendant that he wanted the passenger bus bodies. The defendant ignored plaintiff and sold the trucks with the passenger bus bodies. Plaintiff then filed suit and was awarded judgment for the reasonable value of the passenger bus bodies. In affirming the judgment the court said in 56 Cal.App. at page 682, 206 P. at page 108:

> " * * * The bodies were attached to the trucks in a manner which permitted an easy separation, without damage to the trucks. Plaintiff was entitled to the possession of its property upon Hark's default, and the defendants were without right in their entire dealings with the plaintiff's property."

Respondent argues that appellant was not justified in removing from the machines the gasoline carburetion equipment and replacing it with butane carburetion equipment, and that to permit appellant to recover its carburetion equipment and leave the machines without any carburetion equipment would be neither equitable nor in accordance with the authorities. As pointed out by respondent, the *Meister* case is clearly distinguishable from the instant case. For it is to be noted that in the *Meister* case the bus bodies were added to the trucks and when they were removed from the trucks the trucks were the same as when they were purchased under contract from defendant. As stated by the court, the bus bodies could be removed without damage to the trucks. However, in the instant case, appellant removed the gasoline carburetion equipment from the machines and installed the butane carburetion equipment in its place. The removal of the butane carburetion equipment from the machines would leave the machines without any carburetion equipment, and, as found by the trial court, "the carburetion equipment was an integral part of the cotton picking machines so as to be incapable of severance without injury to the whole of said machines." Respondent cites Dersch v. Thomas, 138 Cal.App.Supp. 785, at page 789, 30 P.2d 630, 631, in which the court said:

> "Alterations in or additions to articles of personal property belonging to another do not constitute transfers of title within the meaning of the section. If the addition is of such a nature that the thing added cannot be removed without in-

jury, title passes by accession and not by transfer. Civ.Code, § 1025."

The case of D. Q. Service Corporation v. Securities Loan & Discount Co., 210 Cal. 327, 292 P. 497, is cited by appellant in his reply brief. Appellant states that in that case the conditional vendor of truck tires who added tires on a truck had knowledge that the lessee of the truck did not have title to said truck and the court found that the conditional vendor of the truck tires was entitled to have his tires back. Appellant quotes from page 329 of 210 Cal., at page 498 of 292 P. as follows:

" *   *   * If the appellant had placed the tires on the truck in ignorance of the provisions of the auto lease contract, there would be no doubt as to its immediate right to recover in this action."

However, in that case the court also said, 210 Cal. at page 330, 292 P. at page 498:

" *   *   * There is uncontroverted evidence to the effect that, at the time the appellant attached its tires to the truck wheels the vehicle was in need of new tires, the old ones having 'worn out.' Therefore the removal of the tires furnished by the appellant will leave the truck in substantially the same condition that it was prior to their attachment, and the respondent will not suffer any injury."

It is therefore apparent that the foregoing case is clearly distinguishable from the instant case for in the instant case respondent would suffer substantial injury by the removal of the butane carburetion equipment.

Appellant seeks to justify its removal of the gasoline carburetion equipment from the machines upon the ground that it was ignorant of the conditional sale by respondent of the machines in question. However, it should be noted that appellant's asserted lack of knowledge of the conditional sale of the machines is based upon only the testimony of one of the appellant's officers which the court was under no duty to believe and apparently did not believe, because it found: "That plaintiff knew that the machines were encumbered at that time [when installing the butane equipment] but did not make sufficient inquiry to learn as to who actually held title to the machines." This finding is supported by the record and we are satisfied that the court was justified in concluding, as it did conclude, that if appellant did not actually know of the conditional sale of the machines, appellant should have known and appellant was possessed of sufficient knowledge to put it on inquiry. Appellant's witness Wallace testified that he knew the machines were encumbered although he stated that he was informed that the San Joaquin Cotton Oil Company was financing Mr. Goforth. This should have put him upon inquiry to learn the truth.

Appellant's final contention is that if the doctrine of accession is applicable, the court erred in not awarding appellant the value of the butane carburetion equipment in accordance with section 1025 of the Civil Code which provides that the owner of the principal part under the doctrine of accession "must, however, reimburse the value of the residue to the other owner, or surrender the whole to him."

We think that the most reasonable construction of the term "value of the residue" is that it is intended to mean the value that has been added to the principal part, in the instant case the whole machine, by the accession. The implied finding of the trial court is that the machines were not enhanced in value by the addition of the butane equipment, and the testimony of one of the respondents, Mr. Scarborough, that "I would rather have the gas. We don't use butane," is sufficient to support a finding that when appellant removed the gasoline carburetion equipment and substituted the butane equipment nothing of value was added to the machines. Testimony by the president of appellant corporation as to the value of the butane carburetion equipment merely created a conflict in the evidence. We are therefore unable to agree with appellant's contention that the court erred in not reimbursing appellant for the value of the butane carburetion equipment.

No other points require discussion.

The judgment is affirmed.

NOTE

Most of the more recent pre-Code cases regarding accessions to personal property involved automobiles. In the typical case the automobile was sold under a conditional sale to a buyer who after the sale added or replaced a part of the car. When the buyer subsequently defaulted on the conditional sale contract and the conditional vendor repossessed, the question presented was the right of the conditional vendor to the new part. Sometimes the conditional sale contract specifically provided that the vendor retained title to, or the benefit of, all repairs to the car, replacements of parts and accessions to the car. In other cases the contract was silent concerning accessions. The cases were usually determined by deciding whether the property involved was or was not an accession. An affirmative answer meant victory for the conditional vendor of the car and a negative answer meant defeat. But the courts did not use any consistent definition of "accession" in deciding the cases. Two situations can be contrasted:

Group #1. The conditional vendee of the car replaced the original tires or the original motor in the car with a new replacement which he owned outright. When the conditional vendor repossessed the car the usual result was that with respect to the vendee the vendor was entitled to the new replacement parts whether or not there was a clause in the conditional sale contract specifically giving the vendor a right to accessions. The theory apparently was that replacement parts were similar to repairs in that they maintained the value of the car. Each benefits both the vendor and the vendee because the resulting enhancement of value of the car will tend to increase the proceeds when the car is resold after repossession. Thus more of the vendee's debt is paid and he has less liability for a deficiency judgment. See, e.g., Blackwood Tire & Vulcanizing Co. v. Auto Storage Co., 133 Tenn. 515, 182 S.W. 576 (1916); Purnell v. Fooks, 32 Del. 336, 122 A. 901 (1923).

Group #2. The conditional vendee replaced the original tires or motor with a new replacement purchased from a third party who sold the replacement part on conditional sale. *Sasia & Wallace* falls within this category. In these cases the courts distinguished between parts that were readily detachable and those that were so incorporated into the car that they could not readily be detached without injury to the car. Tires and motors that were held to be accessions in Group #1 were almost always held not to be accessions in Group #2. See, e.g., Mossler Acceptance Co. v. Norton Tire Co., 70 So.2d 360 (Fla.1954); Passieu v. B.F. Goodrich Co., 58 Ga.App. 691, 199 S.E. 775 (1938). Thus, the question of what constituted an accession was determined not so much by the nature of the property involved or its removability, but by the equities in the conflicting claims. This is evident in the discussion in *Sasia & Wallace*. The pre-Code cases are thoroughly discussed in Nickles, Accessions and Accessories under Pre-Code Law and UCC Article 9, 35 Ark.L.Rev. 111 (1981).

2. ACCESSIONS UNDER THE UCC

Rights concerning accessions are set forth in UCC § 9–314. That section relates only to the rights of a person having a security interest in the accession vis-à-vis other persons having claims to the host goods to which the accession is made. Thus, cases falling in Group #1 in the preceding note are not affected by UCC § 9–314. The term "accession" is neutral; it does not have the meaning that it was given in the pre-Code cases. It refers to "goods installed in or affixed to other goods." UCC § 9–314(1). It applies equally to goods that are readily removable without damage to the host goods and to goods that cannot be removed without causing such damage. Whether or not the accession can be removed without damage to the host goods is still relevant (see UCC § 9–314(4)) but this factor plays a significantly different role than it did in the pre-Code cases.

PROBLEMS

1. Consider the facts of *Sasia & Wallace* under the UCC. Assume that Scarborough obtained a perfected security interest in the cotton pickers at the time they were sold to Goforth. Assume also that Goforth signed a contract giving to Sasia & Wallace a security interest in the butane equipment that Sasia & Wallace installed in the cotton pickers and that this security interest was promptly perfected by filing. At the time Scarborough repossessed the cotton pickers who had priority in the butane equipment? Would it make any difference if Goforth signed the security agreement relating to the butane equipment before or after they were installed in the cotton pickers? Would the rights of Sasia & Wallace be any different if its security interest had not been perfected? Would the rights of Scarborough be any different if its security interest in the cotton pickers had not been perfected at the time the butane equipment was installed? Is the knowledge or lack of knowledge by Sasia & Wallace of Scarborough's security interest relevant? Did Sasia & Wallace incur any liability to Scarborough when it removed the gasoline equipment from the cotton pickers? If Sasia & Wallace have a right under UCC § 9–314 to remove the butane equipment does it have to reimburse Scarborough in any way?

2. A state statute provides as follows: "Every person who makes, alters or repairs any article of personal property at the request of the owner or legal possessor of the property has a lien on the same for his reasonable charges for the balance due for such work done and materials furnished, and may retain possession of the same until the charges are paid." Owner owns an automobile on which there is a perfected security interest in

favor of Finance Co. Owner takes the car to Garageman and requests him to replace the motor. Nothing was said at the time about payment. Garageman did the work requested and presented to Owner a bill for $1,200 consisting of $900 for the new motor and $300 for labor charges. Owner told Garageman that he was temporarily short of funds and behind in his payments to Finance Co. He told Garageman that he could pay $300 cash and would pay the rest of the bill within 60 days if Garageman released the car. Advise Garageman concerning how he can best protect himself against the possibility of nonpayment by Owner or repossession of the car by Finance Co. UCC § 9–310 and § 9–314.

F. COMMINGLED AND PROCESSED GOODS

The doctrine of accession is also applicable to cases in which goods in which one person has a property interest are transformed by a second person into different goods. For example, suppose that A owns grapes which B, either innocently or knowingly, converts by taking them without A's consent. B then makes wine from the grapes. A, of course, has a cause of action to recover the value of the converted grapes. But, under the doctrine of accession, A probably has a valid claim to the wine as well, although the result is not certain. If B acted innocently and if his labor accounted for a very large part of the value of the wine A's claim might be defeated to avoid an unconscionable windfall. See Brown, The Law of Personal Property 51 (3d ed. W. Raushenbush 1975).

This doctrine can also be applied to secured transactions. Suppose A sells grapes to B and retains a purchase money security interest in the grapes. B then makes wine from the grapes. UCC § 9–315(1) applies to this case and it states the conditions under which A's security interest in the grapes is transformed into a security interest in the wine. Compare how the Code deals with this case and how it deals with an analogous case: the shifting of a security interest from the collateral disposed of by the debtor to the proceeds of the disposition. UCC § 9–306(2).

The pre-Code case that follows is one of the very few cases dealing with the rights of a person having a security interest in raw materials to the product into which the raw materials were processed.

BANCROFT STEEL CO., INC. v. KUNIHOLM MANUFACTURING CO.

Supreme Judicial Court of Massachusetts, 1938.
301 Mass. 91, 16 N.E.2d 78.

DONAHUE, JUSTICE. The plaintiff, a corporation engaged in the selling of steel, on December 6, 1934, entered into a written agreement of conditional sale with the Industrial Hardware Corporation, hereinafter referred to as the industrial company, which manufactured a product called "baby-walkers," whose basic material was steel. Among other things the agreement provided that "title to all merchandise delivered" to the industrial company, "whether in the original, manufactured or completed state, shall at all times remain in" the plaintiff "until payment therefor in cash is made" to the plaintiff, that the industrial company "shall have the right to sell the merchandise in the completed state for the benefit" of the plaintiff, that "the monies owing as the result of the sale of said completed merchandise shall be the property of" the plaintiff, that the industrial company should act as the agent of the plaintiff in collecting the accounts receivable and that in the event of default the plaintiff should have "all rights to repossess all the property in whatever form the same may be."

Prior to the time of the execution of the conditional sale agreement, the industrial company for good consideration on June 25, 1932, gave to the defendant a chattel mortgage which included "All of the goods, wares and merchandise either in process of manufacture or completed and including such completed and incompleted stock as may be stored in warehouses. Also all of the raw materials used by us in our manufacturing business including steel * * * and any and all other raw materials used by the said * * * [mortgagor] in the manufacture of its goods." The mortgagor reserved the right to sell and ship its finished product free of the mortgage. The mortgage further provided that "in consideration of the above reservation the * * * [mortgagor] agrees that this instrument shall cover all property acquired after this date and used in the conduct of its business, whether the said property shall be in a raw state, in process or completed."

The defendant on May 2, 1936, took possession under its mortgage of all the personal property then in the plant of the industrial company. Twelve days later at a foreclosure sale the defendant purchased all such personal property in bulk after making the statement through the auctioneer that title to a portion of the personal property was in dispute between the plaintiff and the defendant.

On May 6, prior to the foreclosure sale, the plaintiff sent to the defendant a copy of its contract of conditional sale and a demand for all merchandise "belonging to it" on the premises of the industrial company, specifying particularly "all sheet metal whether in the original, manufactured or completed state, delivered" by the plaintiff to the industrial company "under the terms of the conditional sales contract dated December 6, 1934."

On the day before the foreclosure sale, authorized representatives of the plaintiff and of the defendant met on the premises of the industrial company and discussed the matter of the title to the personal property demanded by the plaintiff. An agreement was then and there reached to the effect that the defendant would pay to the plaintiff the fair value of any personal property on the premises belonging to the plaintiff. The representative of the defendant stated that he would "check up on the property and straighten things out later." The plaintiff brings this action to recover the value of such property.

The case was heard by a judge of the Superior Court on the report of an auditor whose findings, by the terms of the order appointing him, were to be final. The case comes to this court on the defendant's exceptions to the denial of its motion for judgment and to the granting of the plaintiff's motion for judgment in its favor on the auditor's report.

In addition to the facts hereinbefore related the auditor found that the defendant took and retained possession of the following property which consisted of or included steel which had been sold to the industrial company by the plaintiff under the conditional sale agreement, and the value of such property; (a) five tons of unfabricated steel, $322.50; (b) parts consisting entirely of fabricated steel, not painted, $600; (c) parts, which consisted entirely of fabricated steel, painted, $146; (d) parts, made of fabricated steel attached to other materials, $397.78; (e) completed products of the industrial company including steel, $465.27.

The auditor also found that the plaintiff was entitled to recover from the defendant the five amounts above stated aggregating $1,931.55, with interest thereon from the date of the writ, unless the defendant by reason of its mortgage, and its taking possession thereunder, acquired rights superior to the rights of the plaintiff under its conditional sale agreement to the property decribed in the preceding paragraph.

All the steel here in question was delivered to the industrial company after the defendant's mortgage was given. Under the settled law of this Commonwealth the mortgage did not attach to the steel as it came into the hands of the industrial company (Massachusetts Gasoline & Oil Co. v. Go-Gas Co., 259 Mass. 585, 593, 156 N.E. 871) and the defendant could acquire no interest in it until possession was taken under the mortgage. Davis v. Smith-Springfield Body Corp., 250 Mass. 278, 283, 145 N.E. 434, and cases cited.

No other material was added to certain portions of the steel taken by the defendant, namely the five tons which remained in the same state as when delivered by the plaintiff, and the steel in such fabricated parts as were unpainted. By the terms of the conditional sale contract the plaintiff did not part with the title to the steel delivered. The vendee under the contract of sale could not give title thereto, good as against the plaintiff, either to a bona fide purchaser for value without notice of the plaintiff's title (Bousquet v. Mack Motor Truck Co., 269 Mass. 200, 201, 202, 168 N.E. 800) or to a mortgagee. C. B. Cottrell & Sons Co. v. Carter, Rice & Co., 173 Mass. 155, 53 N.E. 375; Hough v. Omansky, 263 Mass. 112, 160 N.E. 330. Although the vendee named in the conditional sale contract had a special interest in the steel which it could mortgage or sell (Rowe Vending Machine Co., Inc., v. Morris, 276 Mass. 274, 280, 177 N.E. 112), a vendee or mortgagee under such a transfer would thus acquire no greater or other interest than the original vendee had, that is, the right to acquire the full title to the property by performing the conditions of the conditional sale contract. Colella v. Essex County Acceptance Corp., 288 Mass. 221, 228, 192 N.E. 622; Hyland v. Hyland, 278 Mass. 112, 117, 179 N.E. 612. Those conditions have not been fulfilled and the title to the five tons of steel and the steel in the unpainted parts remained in the plaintiff unaffected by the defendant's mortgage or the possession taken under it.

The same thing is true of the remainder of the steel, possession of which was taken by the defendant, including the steel in the fabricated parts which were painted and in the parts to which other material had been added and the steel which was in the finished product of the industrial company, unless, as the defendant contends, through the operation of the doctrine of accession the plaintiff's title to the steel had become lost.

The parties to the contract of conditional sale contemplated that some materials should be added to the steel in the manufacture of the vendee's product, but the basic material in the finished product was to be the steel sold by the plaintiff. The auditor has described the processes of manufacture and has enumerated and described the various parts of fabricated steel which when assembled constituted the finished product. It is manifest from his findings that by far the greater part of such finished product consisted of steel sold by the plaintiff under the conditional sale contract. The industrial company by furnishing labor in the fabricating and assembling of the parts, and by the annexation of some other material, added to the value of the steel in the parts and in the finished product. This was done before the defendant, by taking possession, had acquired an interest in any material or merchandise bought by the industrial company after the mortgage was given. In the circumstances appearing the plaintiff, which had furnished and retained title to the principal materials in the parts and in the finished product, did not lose the title to such materials. It acquired title to the lesser materials added as against the vendee and the defendant. Glover v. Austin, 6 Pick. 209, 220; Sumner v. Hamlet, 12 Pick. 76, 83; Mitchell v. Stetson, 7 Cush. 435, 439; Harding v. Coburn, 12 Metc. 333, 340, 46 Am.Dec. 680; Putnam v. Cushing, 10 Gray 334, 336; Atchison, Topeka & Santa Fe Railway Co. v. Schriver, 72 Kan. 550, 84 P. 119, 4 L.R.A.,N.S., 1056; Mack v. Snell, 140 N.Y. 193, 35 N.E. 493, 37 Am.St.Rep. 534; Pulcifer v. Page, 32 Me. 404, 54 Am.Dec. 582.

All the steel here in question belonged to the plaintiff at the time the agreement with the defendant was made on the date before the foreclosure sale. In that agreement the defendant agreed to pay to the plaintiff "the fair value of any property on the premises" of the industrial company "belonging to" the plaintiff. This provision was not too indefinite to be enforced because the amount to be paid for the property was its "fair value" (Noble v. Joseph Burnett Co., 208 Mass. 75, 82, 94 N.E. 289; Silver v. Graves, 210 Mass. 26, 29, 95 N.E. 948), nor because the subject matter was described as "any property on the premises belonging to" the plaintiff. Ramey Lumber Co., Ltd., v. John Schroeder Lumber Co., 7 Cir., 237 F. 39, 44. The word "belonging" adequately describes legal ownership. Spear v. Hooper, 22 Pick. 144; Commonwealth v. Hamilton, 15 Gray 480, 483; Maddocks v. Gushee, 120 Me. 247, 250, 113 A. 300. It does not import only an absolute, unqualified title. The Isabela, D.C.,

258 F. 934, 935; Baltimore Dry Docks & Ship Building Co. v. New York & Porto Rico Steamship Co., 4 Cir., 262 F. 485, 488.

Since the defendant by its mortgage and by taking possession thereunder did not acquire rights superior to the rights of the plaintiff under the conditional sale contract the plaintiff is entitled to recover the sum of $1,931.55 with interest thereon from July 31, 1935, the date of the writ.

Exceptions overruled.

NOTE

How would *Bancroft* be decided under the UCC? Assume that the security interests of both the plaintiff and the defendant had been perfected at the time the plaintiff delivered the steel to the industrial company, that the financing statements of each covered inventory, and that the defendant had filed its financing statement first. When the defendant repossessed the collateral after default it found unfabricated steel as well as partially completed and finished baby walkers. Consider the priorities of the parties to each class of inventory.

With respect to the unfabricated steel UCC § 9–315 would not apply because the unfinished steel had not yet "become part of a product." Thus, the case would be decided under UCC § 9–312(3) since each party had a security interest in inventory. If the plaintiff had complied with the requirements of UCC § 9–312(3) its purchase money security interest would prevail. Otherwise the security interest of the defendant would have priority under UCC § 9–312(5) because it filed first.

Does the same rule of priority apply with respect to the partially completed and completed baby walkers? If the steel supplied by the plaintiff had become part of the product—the baby walkers—and its identity had become lost, UCC § 9–315 applies. If UCC § 9–315 applies UCC § 9–312 does not apply. See UCC § 9–312(1). At least with respect to finished baby walkers it would seem that the conditions of UCC § 9–315(1)(a) have been met. But even if it can be argued that the steel maintained its identity in the partially completed and completed baby walkers, UCC § 9–315(1)(b) should apply. The plaintiff had a perfected security interest in the baby walkers. The security agreement granted to the plaintiff a security interest in the steel "whether in the original, manufactured or completed state" and the plaintiff's financing statement covering inventory covered both the unfinished steel and the resulting product. If UCC § 9–315 applies the security interests of the plaintiff and the defendant "rank equally according to the ratio of the cost of the goods to which each interest originally attached bears to the cost of the total product * * *" UCC § 9–315(2). There are two difficulties in applying UCC § 9–315. If the policy underlying UCC § 9–312(3) is sound with respect to unfinished steel why should its priority rule be changed once the steel entered the manufacturing process? Even if the policy conflict between UCC § 9–312(3) and § 9–315 can be resolved, is it possible to apply UCC § 9–315(2)? That subsection contemplates a case in which a product is made up of several ingredients or components and in which security interests had attached to each of the ingredients or components prior to the time that they were welded into the product or mass. See Comment 3 to UCC § 9–315. An examination of the reported cases discloses no case of that kind arising under the UCC. But in the case at hand both the plaintiff and the defendant had security interests in the same ingredient—the steel—and their security interests attached in perfected form at the same instant. How then can UCC § 9–315(2) be applied? There is no hint of an answer in the Official Comments. Professor Gilmore, one of the principal draftsmen of Article 9, acknowledges the difficulty in applying that section to a case such as *Bancroft*, and he makes a valiant effort to make it make sense, largely by ignoring its language. See Gilmore, Security Interests in Personal Property 851–856 (1965).

NOTE: RELATIONSHIP BETWEEN UCC § 9–314 and § 9–315

Suppose X, a manufacturer of bicycles, purchases components from various suppliers: seats from A, pedals from B and handlebars from C. Suppose X has outstanding loans from Bank secured by a perfected security interest in X's inventory of bicycles. Under UCC § 9–314, if A, B and C sell components to X on credit they can obtain prior security interests in the components that they sell to X. If their security interests attach prior to the time that the components are affixed to the bicycles they will have priority over Bank. If their security interests are perfected they will also have priority over the subsequent parties listed in UCC § 9–314(3). In the event of default the remedy of each is repossession of the collateral. Any components affixed to bicycles can be removed and returned to the original suppliers. See UCC § 9–314(4). Thus, there is no difficulty in resolving any conflicts between A, B or C and Bank and there are no conflicts among A, B and C. But because UCC § 9–314 is subject to UCC § 9–315(1), these results might be modified in some cases.

In cases in which UCC § 9–315(1)(a) applies the remedy provided by UCC § 9–314(4) is not feasible. If D supplies paint to X and the paint is applied to the bicycles D must as a practical matter lose any security interest that it may have had in the paint. The paint has effectively lost its identity as paint and has become an integral part of the bicycle. Removal of the paint obviously will produce no economic benefit. D's remedy must be found in a security interest in the bicycles under § 9–315(1) (a). Under that provision if D had a perfected security interest in the paint when it was applied to the bicycles D's interest continues in the bicycles, and although § 9–315 is not specific on the point, it would seem that the security interest should continue in perfected form. D in effect is given a modified right of accession even though its goods are not dominant. D's resulting security interest is then subject to the Delphian formula of § 9–315(2). D's problem is like that of the supplier of steel discussed in the previous note.

But can A, B and C also fall into the morass of UCC § 9–315? If A filed a financing statement covering "bicycle seats," neither subsections (a) nor (b) of UCC § 9–315(1) applies so A is left to its satisfactory remedy under UCC § 9–314. But suppose A's financing statement covered "inventory," a term that covers both the bicycle seats and the bicycles. Does subsection (b) now apply? Comment 3 to UCC § 9–315 states that A "is put to an election at the time of filing, by the last sentence of subsection (1), whether to claim under this section or to claim a security interest in one component under Section 9–314." But the comment does not say how the election is made. To talk of an election by A in this case is somewhat misleading. A cannot get a security interest in the bicycles unless X has agreed to grant it. A and X might have agreed in the security agreement that A's security interest applied both to the bicycle seats and the bicycles. In that event, if the financing statement covered inventory A would have a perfected security interest in the bicycles, and under the last sentence of UCC § 9–315(1), it would have lost its security interest in the bicycle seats. But if the security agreement covered only the bicycle seats, the fact that the financing statement covered inventory should not result in A's getting a security interest in the bicycles. Thus, UCC § 9–314 and not § 9–315 should apply.

Financing statements usually are made on Form UCC–1 which follows the information set forth in UCC § 9–402(3). This form allows the person making the statement to indicate that "Products of Collateral Are Also Covered" by checking a box printed on the form. Comment 3 to UCC § 9–315 apparently is referring to covering products in this manner when it refers to making an election at the time of filing. The financing statement is a document signed by the debtor, and by the checking of the products box the intent of the debtor to give a security interest in the bicycle is manifested. Thus, even if the security agreement relates only to bicycle seats, the financing statement might provide the basis for giving A a security interest in the bicycles. A, by filing the financing statement, is bound by the election. In the case of easily removable components it would seem a rare case in which it would be to the interest of the secured party to elect UCC § 9–315 rather than § 9–314.

There are no reported cases that shed much light on the proper interpretation of UCC § 9–315.

pick up

G. FIXTURES

The following is taken from Brown, The Law of Personal Property 514–515 (3d ed. W. Raushenbush 1975) *:

A fixture can best be defined as a thing which, although originally a movable chattel, is by reason of its annexation to, or association in use with land, regarded as a part of the land. The law of fixtures concerns those situations where the chattel annexed still retains a separate identity in spite of annexation, for example a furnace or a light fixture. Where the chattel annexed loses such identity, as in the case of nails, boards, etc., the problem becomes one of accession, * * *. The question whether a particular article, formerly a chattel, has become part of the realty may arise in several different ways. (I) The owner of land and building may buy and install therein a new improvement—a furnace, a water heater, a gas range. He later sells or mortgages the real estate. Does the purchaser of the land, in absence of specific exclusions, obtain the above articles or any of them, or do they remain the personal property of the grantor? A similar problem arises when the landowner dies. Do the above articles pass to his heirs as part of the real estate, or are they

* Published by Callaghan & Co.,
3201 Old Glenview, Wilmette, IL
60091. Reprinted with permission.

personal property passing to the administrator? A related question is whether the article is subject to levy of execution or attachment, or to replevin, as personalty, or has become part of the real estate. Also, can the unpaid vendor of an article annexed to the realty claim a statutory mechanic's or construction lien for an improvement to the realty? (II) The owner of a chattel may annex it to the land of another, or to land in which another has an interest. The most common example of this is where a tenant for years attaches to the land of his landlord articles necessary or convenient for the tenant's trade or his domestic enjoyment. In this situation the question arises whether the tenant on the termination of his lease can remove from the premises those articles which he has attached, or whether they remain the property of the landlord. (III) Lastly the annexor of the chattel may not own the same, or his ownership may be encumbered by the security interest of another. When such a chattel is placed on the annexor's land or on land in which others have an interest, question inevitably arises as to the respective rights of the chattel owner and the landowner. * * * Much of the confusion in the law of fixtures is due, it is believed, to the attempt to consider together as analogous these three different fact situations, when in fact they are quite dissimilar. To attempt to discover an all-inclusive definition for a "fixture" or to posit tests for fixtures in all circumstances is not a profitable undertaking. The important quest is the determination of the rights of the parties in the different type situations above outlined. Whether the particular article involved be denominated a fixture or not is of little importance.

Article 9 of the UCC is concerned with the conflict between holders of security interests in the chattel that becomes the fixture and a person with a property interest in the land. The 1962 Official Text of the UCC dealt with this problem in UCC § 9–313 which we reproduce below.

Section 9–313. Priority of Security Interests in Fixtures.

(1) The rules of this section do not apply to goods incorporated into a structure in the manner of lumber, bricks, tile, cement, glass, metal work and the like and no security interest in them exists under this Article unless the structure remains personal property under applicable law. The law of this state other than this Act determines whether and when other goods become fixtures. This Act does not prevent cre-

ation of an encumbrance upon fixtures or real estate pursuant to the law applicable to real estate.

(2) A security interest which attaches to goods before they become fixtures takes priority as to the goods over the claims of all persons who have an interest in the real estate except as stated in subsection (4).

(3) A security interest which attaches to goods after they become fixtures is valid against all persons subsequently acquiring interests in the real estate except as stated in subsection (4) but is invalid against any person with an interest in the real estate at the time the security interest attaches to the goods who has not in writing consented to the security interest or disclaimed an interest in the goods as fixtures.

(4) The security interests described in subsections (2) and (3) do not take priority over

(a) a subsequent purchaser for value of any interest in the real estate; or

(b) a creditor with a lien on the real estate subsequently obtained by judicial proceedings; or

(c) a creditor with a prior encumbrance of record on the real estate to the extent that he makes subsequent advances

if the subsequent purchase is made, the lien by judicial proceedings is obtained, or the subsequent advance under the prior encumbrance is made or contracted for without knowledge of the security interest and before it is perfected. A purchaser of the real estate at a foreclosure sale other than an encumbrancer purchasing at his own foreclosure sale is a subsequent purchaser within this section.

(5) When under subsections (2) or (3) and (4) a secured party has priority over the claims of all persons who have interests in the real estate, he may, on default, subject to the provisions of Part 5, remove his collateral from the real estate but he must reimburse any encumbrancer or owner of the real estate who is not the debtor and who has not otherwise agreed for the cost of repair of any physical injury, but not for any diminution in value of the real estate caused by the absence of the goods removed or by any necessity for replacing them. A person entitled to reimbursement may refuse permission to remove until the secured party gives adequate security for the performance of this obligation.

You can see that subsections (2) through (5) of that section are almost identical to UCC § 9–314, relating to accessions, which we have just examined. The belief of the draftsmen of Article 9 that the problem of resolving conflicts with respect to security interests in tires, batteries and other accessories in automobiles (UCC § 9–314) could be equated successfully to the problem of resolving conflicts regarding fixtures (UCC § 9–313) proved erroneous. In 1972 UCC § 9–313 was drastically revised to its present form. The reasons for the changes are set forth by the Reporters for the 1972 Official Text as follows:

As the Code came to be widely enacted, the real estate bar came to realize the impact of the fixture provisions on real estate financing and real estate titles. They apparently had not fully appreciated the impact of these provisions of Article 9 on real estate matters during the enactment of the Code, because of the commonly-held assumption that Article 9 was concerned only with chattel security matters.

The treatment of fixtures in pre-Code law had varied widely from state to state. The treatment in Article 9 was based generally on prior treatment in the Uniform Conditional Sales Act, which, however, had been enacted in only a dozen states. In other states the word "fixture" had come to mean that a former chattel had become real estate for all purposes and that any chattel rights therein were lost. For lawyers trained in such states the Code provisions seemed to be extreme. Some sections of the real estate bar began attempting with some success to have Section 9–313 amended to bring it closer to the pre-Code law in their states. In some states, such as California and Iowa, Section 9–313 simply was not enacted.

Even supporters of Article 9 and of its fixture provisions came to recognize that there were some ambiguities in Section 9–313, particularly in its application to construction mortgages, and also in its failure to make it clear that filing of fixture security interests was to be in real estate records where they could be found by a standard real estate search.

Section 9–313 and related provisions of Part 4 have been redrafted to meet the legitimate criticisms and to make a substantial shift in the law in favor of construction mortgages. The specific changes are described in the 1972 Comments to Section 9–313, and the Comments to the several sections of Part 4.

The cases set forth below involved the 1962 version of UCC § 9–313. Consider how each case would have been decided if the 1972 version of UCC § 9–313 had been in effect.

The 1962 version did not define "fixture" a term which has never had a commonly-accepted definition and a term which, within a single jurisdiction, is often variously interpreted depending upon the nature of the dispute before the court. The application of the 1962 provision was thus uncertain because in different states it might or might not apply depending upon the local definition of fixture. The present version maintains this difficulty in that the "definition" of the term in subsection (1)(a) also depends on how the local real estate law treats the particular property involved. But most of the problems under the 1962 provision related to readily-removable factory and office machines and household appliances, and the 1972 provision deals specifically with these goods in subsection (4)(c).

IN RE PARK CORRUGATED BOX CORP.

United States District Court, D. New Jersey, 1966.
249 F.Supp. 56.

AUGELLI, DISTRICT JUDGE. This matter is before the Court on petition of Manufacturers Leasing Corporation (Manufacturers) for review of an order of the Referee in Bankruptcy (Referee), made on March 25, 1965, which denied Manufacturers' petition for reclamation of a certain machine from the Bankrupt herein, Park Corrugated Box Corp. (Park).

On February 8, 1965 Park filed a petition for an arrangement under Chapter XI of the Bankruptcy Act. Manufacturers was listed in Park's schedules as a security-holding creditor in the amount of $34,952.60. On March 8, Manufacturers filed its petition to reclaim from Park the machine above mentioned, which was used in the manufacture of corrugated boxes, and known as a "Hooper Combined Printer Slotter, Model WSG2P–200–E, size $50 \times 103\frac{1}{2}$ inches". On that date the Referee signed an order directed to James J. Murner, Jr., Receiver for Park, to show cause why that relief should not be granted.

On March 18, the Referee held a hearing on said order to show cause, and denied the petition for reclamation on the ground that the security agreement covering the machine was not properly filed with the Secretary of State, and that therefore Manufacturers was not a secured creditor entitled to reclamation. An order to this effect was entered on March 25, 1965. In the meantime, also on March 18, Park was adjudicated a bankrupt, and the Receiver, Murner, was thereafter appointed Trustee.

The Referee filed his opinion in this matter on June 14, 1965, and Manufacturers' petition for review was filed on June 28. The following are the facts disclosed by the record in this case.

On September 4, 1963, Manufacturers and Park entered into a "Conditional Sale and Security Agreement", whereby Park purchased the subject machine from Manufacturers for the sum of $47,405.00. The agreement stated that Manufacturers was to have a purchase money security interest in the collateral to secure the balance due, that Manufacturers was to have all the rights of a secured party under applicable state law, and that Manufacturers was to retain title to the collateral until the balance was paid in full.

The agreement between Manufacturers and Park was filed twice with the Register of Deeds of Passaic County, on September 10, 1963 and again on October 10, 1963. It had not been filed with the Secretary of State in Trenton, New Jersey.

Under the Uniform Commercial Code as adopted in New Jersey, § 9–401(1) provides that:

"The proper place to file in order to perfect a security interest is as follows:

(a) * * * (not applicable);

(b) when the collateral is goods which at the time the security interest attaches are or are to become fixtures, then in the office where a mortgage on the real estate concerned would be filed or recorded;

(c) in all other cases, in the office of the Secretary of State."

Manufacturers contends that the machine was a fixture, that under § 9–401(1)(b), the agreement was properly filed in the County Register's Office, and that therefore Manufacturers has a perfected security interest in the machine prior to the rights of the Trustee. The Trustee argues, as the Referee has found, that the machine was not a fixture, that under § 9–401(1)(c), the agreement should have been filed in the office of the Secretary of State, and that therefore Manufacturers' security interest was not perfected. The issue in this case is thus simply whether the machine in question is or is not a fixture within the meaning of § 9–401(1)(b).

§ 9–313(1) provides that the law of New Jersey determines whether and when goods become fixtures. The law in New Jersey concerning fixtures has most recently been reviewed in the case of Fahmie v. Nyman, 70 N.J.Super. 313, 175 A.2d 438 (App.Div.1961). In that case, the court discussed the two tests used in New Jersey to determine whether and when a chattel becomes a fixture. They are known as the "traditional test" and the "institutional doctrine."

Under the "traditional test", intention is the dominant factor. A chattel becomes a fixture when the party making the annexation intends a permanent accession to the freehold. This intention may be "inferred from the nature of the article affixed, the relation and situation of the party making the annexation, the structure and mode of annexation, and the purpose or use for which the annexation was made." 70 N.J.Super. at 317, 175 A.2d at 441.

The testimony before the Referee at the reclamation proceeding shows that there was no intention to annex the machine permanently to the freehold. A witness for Manufacturers testified that although the machine was annexed to the building, it could easily be removed in one hour without material physical damage to the building. He described the machine as being about 125 inches wide by 8 feet long, weighing 45,000 pounds, anchored by two or three leg screws on each side and connected to a 220 volt electric line. This same witness testified that a rigger could remove the machine quite easily by merely unbolting the screws, disconnecting the 220 volt line, jacking it up, putting it on rollers and taking it out. Park's president testified that the machine had been moved two or three times to other sections of the plant by employees of Park during the time it was located in the plant.

Under the "institutional doctrine", the test is whether the chattel is permanently essential to the completeness of the structure or its use. A chattel is a fixture if its severance from the structure would cause material damage to the structure or "prevent the structure from being used for the purposes for which it was erected or for which it has been adapted." Smyth Sales Corp. v. Norfolk B. & L. Ass'n, 116 N.J.L. 293, 298, 184 A. 204, 206, 111 A.L.R. 357 (E. & A. 1935). Thus, in Temple Co. v. Penn Mutual Life Ins. Co., 69 N.J.L. 36, 38, 54 A. 295 (Sup.Ct.1903), the Court stated, in holding lighting equipment and seats to be fixtures under the "institutional doctrine", that "[t]he building was erected and used as a theatre, and whatever was incorporated with the building to fit it for use as a theatre became part of the realty."

Again, the testimony before the Referee shows that the machine in question was not essential to the structure or its use, and that the severance of the machine would not prevent the structure from being used for the purposes for which it was erected or could be adapted. There was testimony that after the machine was removed from the building, the structure could be used for industrial uses generally; also testimony that different prior uses had been made of the structure. Thus, both before the machine was installed and after it was removed, the structure was and could be used for any number of different purposes. Cf. Fahmie v. Nyman, supra. Finally, there was attached to the agreement between the parties a statement by Manufacturers that the machine is "to be affixed to real property * * * by removable screw joints or otherwise, so as to be severable from the realty without material injury to the freehold."

While the machine in question does not appear to be a fixture under either the "traditional test" or the "institutional doctrine", Manufacturers makes the further contention that the machine is a "trade fixture" under New Jersey law, and therefore a "fixture" pursuant to § 9–401(1)(b). However, the term "trade fixture" is generally applied only in landlord and tenant cases to describe a chattel which the tenant has installed on the landlord's premises for trade purposes and which the tenant is allowed to remove if it can be severed without material injury to the freehold. Otherwise, the chattel would be a fixture and belong to the landlord. Crane v. Brigham, 11 N.J.Eq. 29 (Ch.1855); Handler v. Horns, 2 N.J. 18, 65 A.2d 523 (1949). Thus, a "fixture" is just the opposite of a "trade fixture" under landlord and tenant law; the latter can be removed by the tenant without material injury to the freehold. A "trade fixture" is not a fixture within the meaning of § 9–401(1)(b).

Since the machine here involved was not a fixture under § 9–401(1)(b), and the agreement between Manufacturers and Park was not filed in the office of the Secretary of State pursuant to § 9–401(1)(c), Manufacturers' security interest was not perfected prior to the filing of the Chapter XI petition. Therefore the Trustee's rights to the machine take priority over the rights of Manufacturers.

Under the circumstances, and for the reasons so well stated in the Referee's opinion, the order denying reclamation in this case will be affirmed. Counsel for the Trustee, on notice to counsel for Manufacturers, will please submit an appropriate order.

NOTES

1. Under the 1972 Code would the machine involved in *Park* fall within the definition of fixture in § 9–313(1)(a)? The court indicated that the machine was a "trade fixture" and used that term as an opposite of fixture; the first term referring to removable property and the second referring to nonremovable property. 1972 § 9–313(4)(c) covers readily removable factory machines like the machine in *Park*. Does this indicate an intention to treat such machines as fixtures for filing purposes? If a machine like that in *Park* is held not to be a fixture, a filing in the land records will not perfect the seller's security interest. See UCC § 9–401.

2. 1972 § 9–313 can be compared to UCC § 9–312. § 9–313(4)(b) states a residual first-to-file rule based on filings in the land records. Compare § 9–312(5). § 9–313(4)(a) is an exception to the residual rule in favor of purchase money security interests in property that feed existing interests. Compare § 9–312(4). § 9–313(6) states a special rule for conflicts between financers under construction mortgages who provide the funds for the construction of a building (a purchase-money type interest) and purchase money security interests in property which become fixtures of the building. Compare § 9–312(3).

PROBLEMS

Answer the following problems on the basis of 1972 UCC § 9–313.

1. Debtor owned a house that was unencumbered. He replaced the furnace with a new one purchased from Vendor. The purchase was made by an installment-sale contract in which Vendor was granted a security interest in the furnace. Vendor filed a financing statement covering the furnace with the Secretary of State. Thereafter Debtor sold the house to Owner. Shortly after the sale Debtor left the jurisdiction and defaulted on his payments to Vendor. Vendor seeks to remove the furnace. Owner opposes removal. How is the conflict decided? See § 9–313(4)(b).

2. Suppose in Problem 1 that Debtor had purchased a kitchen range from Vendor instead of a furnace and that Vendor had made no filing of any kind. How would the conflict between Vendor and Owner be decided? See § 9–313(4)(c).

3. Debtor owned and lived in a house on which there is a recorded mortgage in favor of Bank. Debtor bought a furnace

from Vendor by an installment-sale contract in which Vendor was granted a security interest in the furnace. Five days after installing the furnace in the house Vendor made a fixture filing covering the furnace. Debtor then defaulted on his payments to Vendor. Vendor seeks to remove the furnace. Bank opposes removal. How is the conflict decided? See § 9–313(4)(a).

4. Lessee rented a house from Owner. When the central hot water heater irreparably broke down and Owner refused to replace it, Lessee bought a new one from Vendor and immediately installed it in the house. The purchase was made by an installment-sale contract in which Vendor was granted a security interest in the heater. Vendor initially made no filing with respect to the heater but a month after the sale, on the advice of his lawyer, he made a fixture filing. Two months later Owner borrowed money from Bank and as security for the loan gave to Bank a mortgage on the house which was promptly recorded. Shortly thereafter Lessee defaulted on his payments to Vendor. Owner is also in default on his loan to Bank. Vendor seeks to remove the heater and Bank opposes removal. Assume that the heater can be removed without physical damage to the house by disconnecting it from the hot-water-pipe system that leads to hot-water outlets throughout the house. How is the conflict resolved applying § 9–313(4)(a) and (b)? See Comment 4(b) to UCC § 9–313.

5. Consider how the conflict in Problem 4 is resolved if § 9–313(5) is applied and the following statute, which codifies common law rights, is in effect.

> "A tenant may remove from the demised premises, any time during the continuance of his term, anything affixed thereto for purposes of trade, manufacture, ornament, or domestic use, if the removal can be effected without injury to the premises, unless the thing has, by the manner in which it is affixed, become an integral part of the premises." See Calif.Civ.Code § 1019.

KARP BROTHERS, INC. v. WEST WARD SAVINGS AND LOAN ASSOCIATION OF SHAMOKIN

Supreme Court of Pennsylvania, 1970.
440 Pa. 583, 271 A.2d 493.

EAGEN, JUSTICE. This is a replevin action instituted by Karp Brothers, Inc. (Karp) against West Ward Savings & Loan Association of Shamokin (West Ward) for the return of fifty items of property or their value in damages. The case was tried nonjury below, after which a money award for the value of the goods was entered in favor of the plaintiff by the trial court. Exceptions to the adjudication were dismissed, and a final judgment entered. West Ward appeals.

The record discloses the following pertinent facts:

On April 29, 1964, J. N. McCown and Florence W. McCown, his wife, the owners of land in State College, Pennsylvania, upon which the Ranch Court Motel is constructed, obtained a loan in the amount of $240,000 from West Ward. Payment of the loan was secured by a mortgage on the motel real estate executed by the McCowns in favor of West Ward as mortgagee. The mortgage was duly recorded. Subsequent thereto or on January 8, 1965, the McCowns entered into an agreement with Joseph S. Karp & Bros., now Karp Bros., Inc., a wholesale distributor of restaurant equipment, utensils and supplies. Under the terms of the agreement, Karp agreed to provide the McCowns with an assortment of fifty items of restaurant equipment to be used in furnishing a proposed restaurant which was to become part of the motel complex. These items are the subject of this replevin action.

On February 10, 1965, Karp filed a financing statement in the office of the Prothonotary of Centre County and the office of the Secretary of the Commonwealth. Attached to the financing statement filed in the prothonotary's office was a copy of the agreement of January 8, 1965.

On March 8, 1965, Karp, as lessor, and the McCowns, as lessees, executed a "Bailment Lease" covering the pieces of equipment mentioned previously. On the same day, this lease was negotiated to the Hollidaysburg Trust Company (Hollidaysburg) with all of Karp's interest and title in and to the restaurant equipment. The McCowns made ten payments totaling $5,107.97 towards the total time balance owing of $17,120.41. On January 11, 1966, a second "Bailment Lease" was entered into by the McCowns and Karp for a total time balance of $14,907.82, representing the balance still outstanding under the first "Bailment Lease," together with carrying charges. This lease was set over to Hollidaysburg in the same manner as the former.

On November 25, 1966, West Ward caused a writ of execution to issue on the bond accompanying its mortgage. A sheriff's sale followed on January 31, 1967, at which West Ward purchased the interest of the McCowns in the motel property. Prior to the sale, Karp notified the sheriff of the "Bailment Lease" and its interest in the restaurant equipment. Following the sale, when West Ward refused to permit Karp to remove the restaurant equipment, this action was instituted. Hollidaysburg was granted permission by the court to intervene as a party plaintiff.

West Ward's primary contention is that Karp failed to establish any replevin rights. With this we do not agree.

We first note that Karp assigned its "Bailment Lease" to Hollidaysburg, together with all its right, title, and interest in and to the subject goods. However, before trial, Hollidaysburg assigned back to Karp any rights it may thereby have received. Thus, for the purposes of this case, it is as if no assignment ever took place.

The most important remedy available to a secured party is the right to take possession of the collateral following a debtor's default. Uniform Commercial Code, Act of April 6, 1953, P.L. 3, as amended by the Act of October 2, 1959, P.L. 1023, 12A P.S. § 9–503(1) (Supp.1970) [hereafter UCC 9–503]. In order to clarify any doubt as to what judicial process is available to a secured party in the event he is unable to obtain possession without breaching the peace, the Pennsylvania legislature added a proviso augmenting the official text of the Code which specifically provided that a secured party "may proceed by writ of replevin or otherwise." UCC § 9–503(2).

Thus, Karp, having established the default, thereby established its right to immediate possession of any collateral covered by its secured agreement with the debtor.

The only interest, which West Ward had, is a real property interest. Therefore, if the property in question remained personal property and never became a part of the realty, West Ward would have gained no interest therein as purchaser at the sheriff's sale. The lower court did not see fit to make any finding as to whether the goods ever became part of the realty, but for the reasons that follow, we deem such a determination is unnecessary to a disposition of the case.

Even if we assume that the goods did, in fact, become affixed to the realty, nevertheless, Karp does have a priority interest in the goods under the Act of April 6, 1953, as amended by the Act of October 2, 1959, § 9–313.

Under UCC § 9–313(2): "A security interest which attaches to goods before they become fixtures takes priority as to the goods over the claims of all persons who have an interest in the

232 PRIORITIES Ch. 2

real estate except as stated in subsection (4)." The only category listed in subsection (4) in which West Ward could hope to be included is that of a "subsequent purchaser for value of any interest in the real estate", UCC § 9–313(4). However, subsection (4) makes clear that "an encumbrancer purchasing at his own foreclosure sale" [such as West Ward herein] is not deemed to be a "subsequent purchaser" within the meaning of Section 9–313. UCC § 9–313(4).

Thus, if Karp had a "security interest" and that interest "attached" before the goods became fixtures, its interest takes priority.

A "security interest" is defined as "an interest in personal property or fixtures which secures payment or performance of an obligation. * * * Whether a lease is intended as security is to be determined by the facts of each case; however, * * * (b) an agreement that upon compliance with the terms of the lease the lessee shall become or has the option to become the owner of the property for no additional consideration or for a nominal consideration does make the lease one intended for security." UCC § 1–201(37). The "Bailment Lease" in the instant case does so provide. Thus the execution of the "Bailment Lease" did create a "security interest" in Karp.

The question of when a "security interest" "attaches" is dealt with in UCC § 9–204(1), which provides: "A security interest cannot attach until there is agreement (subsection (3) of Section 1–201) that it attach and value is given and the debtor has rights in the collateral. It attaches as soon as all of the events in the preceding sentence have taken place unless explicit agreement postpones the time of attaching." When the first "Bailment Lease" was executed on March 8, 1965, there was a manifest agreement that the security interest attach, and value given, in that credit was thereby extended to the bailment lessees. UCC § 1–201(44)(a). Moreover, the lessee-debtors had rights in the collateral in that the lease gave them a right to possession of the goods. All this occurred before the goods could possibly have become affixed to the realty, since there was testimony found to be true by the court below that none of the goods referred to in the lease were delivered prior to the execution of the first bailment contract.

Thus, if the goods became fixtures, this occurred at a time after Karp's "security interest" "attached" under the first "Bailment Lease", and Karp's interest, based on the first security agreement, was superior to that of West Ward, the prior real estate encumbrancer.

As previously noted, the parties executed a second "Bailment Lease" dated January 6, 1966. West Ward contends that this new lease in effect paid off the original indebtedness and completely extinguished the first "Bailment Lease," and, as a consequence, any secured interest arising therefrom. In other words, it is maintained that Karp's present security interest, if such exists, must be viewed as "attaching" as of the date the second "Bailment Lease" was executed, and since this was subsequent in time to the date the goods became fixtures, Karp's interest is subordinate to that of West Ward's. A post-affixation security interest is invalid against prior real estate claims unless such real estate interest holder consents in writing to the security interest, or disclaims in writing any interest in the goods. UCC § 9–313(3).

It would appear that the Code itself and prior court decisions are not helpful in resolving this issue of the significance of the second lease. However, we conclude that under the present record West Ward's position cannot prevail.

It is clear from the record that the second "Bailment Lease" was merely a refinancing of the indebtedness covered by the first "Bailment Lease", and it was the intent of the parties that the original indebtedness was to continue. This being so, we are of the view that Karp's security interest under the first "Bailment Lease" and his priority rights flowing therefrom continued and were not affected by the execution of the second "Bailment Lease."

Judgment affirmed.

PROBLEM

How would *Karp* be decided under the 1972 § 9–313? Assume the following: a. the loan from West Ward was made to finance the land purchase and construction of the Ranch Court Motel; b. the restaurant equipment was installed during the construction of the motel; c. prior to making the bailment lease Karp filed a financing statement covering the equipment with the Secretary of State as well as making a fixture filing regarding the equipment; d. the equipment would be classified under local law as a fixture under the "institutional doctrine" discussed in *Park*, supra. See § 9–313(4)(a) and § 9–313(6).

H. LEASES

Another title-retention device that may or may not fall within the definition of security interest is the lease. Under pre-Code law the lease was sometimes used as a device for avoiding statutory filing requirements or default provisions applicable to conditional sales or chattel mortgages. It was normally used in transactions in consumer goods or industrial or business equipment. Any secured installment credit sale can be recast into the form of a lease. The buyer is given possession of the goods as lessee. The payments over the term of the lease which the lessee is required to pay are about equal to the installment purchase price of the goods. At the end of the term the lessee who has made all the rental payments is either entitled to keep the goods or he may be given an option to purchase them at a price which is either nominal or far below the value of the goods. In the event of default the lessor as owner of the goods can simply reclaim them from the lessee. If the transaction is recognized as a lease the lessor not only avoids statutory filing and default requirements applicable to credit sales, but is protected against any sale of the goods by the lessee, any levy on the goods by creditors of the lessee and the bankruptcy of the lessee.

In cases in which the lease was economically indistinguishable from a conditional sale the courts routinely treated them as conditional sales. Section 1 of the Uniform Conditional Sales Act treated as a conditional sale any lease or bailment under which "the bailee or lessee contracts to pay as compensation a sum substantially equivalent to the value of the goods, and by which it is agreed that the bailee or lessee is bound to become, or has the option of becoming the owner of such goods upon full compliance with the terms of the contract." Compare UCC § 1–201(37).

Sometimes transactions were cast in lease terms in order to avoid other statutory restraints applicable to sales, most notably usury or sales-finance statutes that put a limit on the amount of finance charges that could be imposed on the buyer. Today, the equipment-lease transaction is most likely to be designed to obtain a tax advantage which would not be available if the transaction were cast as a sale. In such cases the lessor of the goods might well comply with Article 9 requirements regarding filing or default while asserting that the transaction is nevertheless a lease for tax purposes. See UCC § 9–408. Whether a lease is intended as security or is a "true lease" is often a difficult question to answer. Consider the two leases analyzed in the following case:

IN RE PEACOCK

United States Bankruptcy Court, N.D. Texas, 1980.
6 B.R. 922.

JOHN FLOWERS, BANKRUPTCY JUDGE. The issue in this case arises from a novel application of the "cram down" provisions of Chapter 13 to lease agreements which the debtor asserts are intended as security devices. Chapter 13 authorizes the Court to confirm a plan in which the present value of any deferred payments to a secured creditor equals the value of the collateral, 11 U.S.C. §§ 1325(a)(5), 506(a). The issue here is whether claims arising under the debtor's lease agreements may be treated as secured claims for purposes of the § 1325(a)(5) "cram down."

FINDINGS OF FACT

The business relationship between the debtors and Borg-Warner Leasing, Inc. began in August, 1979, when the debtor and representatives of Borg-Warner traveled to Ohio for the purpose of purchasing dairy cows which Borg-Warner then leased to the debtors. The parties entered into three agreements under which the debtors received 68 Holstein cows and various items of farm equipment.

The agreement labeled Equipment Lease reflects that Borg-Warner paid $20,884.50 for certain farm equipment. It then delivered the equipment to the debtor under a lease that obligated the debtors to pay a total of $33,672.00 over a 60 month term. In the event of default, the lessor is entitled to repossess the equipment, and may recover from the lessee a sum equal to the total unpaid rental which would have accrued for the balance of the rental term less only the net proceeds of any reletting or sale. No option to purchase is granted the lessee in the equipment lease.

The parties also executed two documents entitled Cow Lease Agreement. These documents contain in essence identical terms, one pertains to a transfer of 35 cows in August, 1979, and the other to a transfer of 33 cows in November, 1979. Borg-Warner paid the third party Ohio seller $124,495.00 for the 68 cows which it then transferred to the debtors pursuant to the leases. In turn under the cow leases the debtors became unconditionally obligated to pay $223,848.00 over the 60 month term.

Unlike the equipment lease, the cow leases grant the lessee an option to purchase the cows at the end of the lease term at a combined option price of $24,899 which amounts to approximately $366 per cow. In the event of default, the lessee is obligated to deliver the cows to the lessor and is liable for the option price of any cow not delivered. If the lessor then sells the repossessed cows, and a deficiency results, the lessee is liable for such deficiency.

Under all the leases involved, the lessee is obligated to obtain insurance and bears the entire risk of loss to the property. Financing statements regarding all three leases were properly filed in the public records.

The debtors filed their joint petition for relief under Chapter 13 of the Bankruptcy Code on May 16, 1980. On July 9, 1980 the debtors filed their Chapter 13 plan which provided that "Debtor elects to treat Borg-Warner as a secured creditor and will pay to Borg-Warner the fair market value of the 60 dairy cows ($60,000) and the dairy equipment ($18,000) as of the date of this plan, in sixty monthly installments of $1820 each * * * " The debtors have not asserted a claim of usury. Borg-Warner filed an application under § 365 of the Bankruptcy Code requesting the Court to order the debtor to accept or reject the leases according to the terms originally agreed upon.

At trial, the debtor testified that but for the option to purchase he would not have signed the cow lease agreements. The Debtors and Borg-Warner introduced conflicting testimony regarding the value of the cows. I find that the fair market value of the cows to be $875.00 per cow, as of the date the purchase option could be exercised by the debtor.

CONCLUSIONS OF LAW

The issue squarely presented is whether any or all of the leases are actually intended as security devices. An examination of the case law reveals a lack of uniformity in the methods used to analyze leases alleged to be security devices. The problem of determining an appropriate legal standard for the issue is further complicated by the almost infinite variety of leases found in contemporary leasing arrangements which are being utilized in an ever growing number of consumer and commercial transactions.

The Bankruptcy Code does not define "lease." It does define "security interest" to be a lien created by agreement, 11 U.S.C. § 101(37). The legislative history states, "Whether a consignment or a lease constitutes a security interest under the bankruptcy code will depend on whether it constitutes a security interest under applicable state or local law." House Report No. 95–595, 95th Cong. 1st Sess. (1977) 313–314, U.S.Code Cong. & Admin.News 1978, p. 5787.

The principal state law authority on this question is the definition of a "security interest" found in the Uniform Commercial Code [Texas Business & Commercial Code § 1.201(37)] which provides in pertinent part:

"Security interest" means an interest in personal property or fixtures which secures payment or performance of an obligation. Unless a lease or consignment is intended as security, reservation of title thereunder is not a "security interest * * *" Whether a lease is intended as security is to be determined by the facts of each case; however, (a) the inclusion of an option to purchase does not of itself make the lease one intended for security, and (b) an agreement that upon compliance with the terms of the lease the lessee shall become or has the option to become the owner of the property for no additional consideration or for a nominal consideration does make the lease one intended for security.

Professor Gilmore has pointed out that the word "intended" as used in the § 1.201(37) definition has nothing to do with the subjective intention of the parties. GILMORE, SECURITY INTERESTS IN PERSONAL PROPERTY § 11.2, at 338. The question then becomes by what objective criteria are lease agreements to be adjudged security devices. An examination of the authorities reveals that the following three-tier analysis is an appropriate, though not exclusive, procedure to review lease agreements which are alleged to be security devices.

The first tier of analysis is mandated by the opening sentence of § 1.201(37): "Security interest means an interest in personal property or fixtures which secures payment or performance of an obligation." In order to find that a lease is intended as security, it is necessary to find an obligation on the part of the lessee that is to be secured. A definite obligation to pay rentals during the lease term totaling an amount substantially equivalent to the fair market value of the leased property plus a financing factor as viewed at the time the property is transferred to the lessee, is a precondition to finding that the lease is intended as security. Conversely an agreement that gives the lessee the right to terminate the lease at any time during the lease term, without any obligation for rents accruing during the remainder of the lease term, should undoubtedly be viewed as a true lease.

Upon finding a sufficient obligation on the part of the lessee, it is necessary to proceed to a second tier of analysis. If the agreement provides that upon compliance with the terms of the lease the lessee shall become or has the option to become the owner of the property for no additional consideration or for a nominal consideration, the court is compelled as a matter of law to find that the lease is intended as security, § 1.207(37), In re Vaillancourt, 7 U.C.C.Rep. 748, 759 (U.S.Dist.Ct., D.Maine, 1970). Tackett v. Mid-Continent Refrigeration Co., 579 S.W.2d 545 (Tex. Civ.App.–Ft. Worth, 1979, writ ref'd n.r.e.).

The Uniform Commercial Code does not define "nominal". Common usage of the word as indicated in Webster's Third New International Dictionary (1976), defines nominal as one "being so small, slight, or negligible as scarcely to be entitled to the name". In re Vaillancourt, supra, is a decision involving a negligible consideration; the lessee was given an option to purchase at the end of the lease term for a consideration of $1.00. In *Tackett*, supra, no additional consideration was required at the end of the term for the lessee to become owner.

Other cases have found substantial dollar amounts to be nominal consideration after comparing the option price to the fair market value of the leased property at the termination of the lease; $1,350 option price described as "nominal" in In re Washington Processing Co., Inc., 3 U.C.C.Rep. 475 (U.S.Dist.Ct. S.D.Cal., 1966); $1,000 option price described a "nominal" in Peco, Inc. v. Hartbauer Tool and Die Co., 262 Or. 573, 500 P.2d 708 (1972). By characterizing significant dollar amounts as nominal, those courts have implicitly adopted a relative rather than absolute definition of nominal. Invariably the large dollar "nominal price" cases also cite other factors in finding that the lease is intended as a security device. In view of the mandate of § 1.201(37) which compels a court to hold a nominal option price lease is intended as security regardless of other lease terms, the adopted approach is to construe "nominal consideration" in a narrow and absolute fashion to mean a few dollars.

A finding that the lease agreement contains an option to purchase for a consideration that is more than nominal or that the agreement contains no option requires the court to proceed to a third tier of analysis to determine by the facts of each case whether the lease is intended as security, Davis Brothers v. Misco Leasing, Inc., 508 S.W.2d 908 (Tex.Civ.App.–Amarillo, 1974, no writ); see also *Peco, Inc.* supra. In other words a finding of more than nominal consideration does not compel a conclusion that a true lease is intended.

The third tier of analysis is an inquiry into whether the lessor has effectively bargained away the absolute right to retake control and use the leased property. That absolute right to retake control and use the leased property is a significant characteristic of a true lease, Transamerica Leasing Corp. v. Bureau of Revenue, 80 N.M. 48, 450 P.2d 934 (1969); see also Gershwin v. U. S., 153 F.Supp. 477 (U.S.Ct.Cl.1957).

A review of the authorities reveals at least three types of agreements in which the lessor has effectively bargained away the right of absolute control.

(a) OBLIGATION TO DISPOSE

The lease provides that at the termination of the lease, the lessor is obligated to dispose of the property, and the lessee is entitled to any profit and bears any loss resulting from such disposition, Matter of Tillery, 571 F.2d 1361 (5th Cir., 1978); In re Tulsa Post Warehouse Co., Inc., 4 B.R. 801, (U.S.Dist.Ct.N.D. Okla.1980). In these decisions the Court found that the lessee had an equity in the property and that the lessee had the real interest in the final disposition of the property.

(b) REASONABLY ANTICIPATED OPTION

The lease agreement grants the lessee an option to purchase which the parties at the inception of the lease could have reasonably anticipated that the lessee would exercise. Several courts have contemplated the significance of an option to purchase at a price that is more than nominal, *Davis Brothers*, supra; All-States Leasing Co. v. Ochs, 27 U.C.C.Rep. 808, 42 Or.App. 319, 600 P.2d 899 (Or.App.1979); In re Joe Necessary and Son, Inc., 27 U.C.C.Rep. 551, 475 F.Supp. 610 (U.S.Dist.Ct.W.D.Va., 1979).

As indicated in the discussion of the second tier analysis, some cases deal with the problem of a high dollar purchase option by characterizing an option price to be nominal when the option price is smaller than the fair market value of the leased property. An example of such price balancing is reflected by the evolution of the "only sensible alternative" test. Under this test options have been deemed nominal and consequently leases treated as security when the lessee has no sensible alternative except to exercise the option, *Davis Brothers*, supra; *All-States*, supra. The "only sensible alternative" test unfortunately may result in substantial dollar sums being described as nominal, including some amounts which unduly extend the common meaning of a nominal amount.

The above cited cases recognize that in certain instances a lease agreement containing an option price of a substantial dollar amount may be intended as a security device. The Uniform Commercial Code § 1.201(37) is silent as to the significance of a more than nominal option price. The Code of course states that the inclusion of an option to purchase does not of itself make the lease one intended for security. However a finding that the parties could reasonably anticipate the lessee would exercise the option, when coupled with an obligation to pay the capitalized cost of the leased property, is persuasive evidence that the lease is intended as security. Some pre-Code law, including the Uniform Conditional Sales Act, (U.S.C.A.) declared leases to be intended as security where (1) the lessee-debtor is obligated to pay an amount substantially equal to the purchase price; and (2) the lessee-debtor thereby acquires, or has the option to acquire the status of "owner" of the item conditionally sold. See Coogan, Leases of Equipment and Some Other Unconventional Security Devices: An Analysis of U.C.C. § 1–201(37) *and Art. 9,* 1973 Duke L.J. 909 (1973). The "reasonably anticipated" option test is a narrower analysis than that of the U.S.C.A. The lease will be deemed a security device only in those cases where the lessor could reasonably anticipate that his absolute right to retake control would be divested by the lessee's exercise of the option.

A "reasonably anticipated" option is indicated where the option price is less than the fair market value. Such an option may also be found where the evidence establishes that the lessee would not have entered into the lease but for the purchase option, or where the lessee expresses an intent to exercise the option in unequivocal language or conduct.

(c) THE USEFUL LIFE LEASE

The lessee is entitled to possess the leased property for a primary term and applicable renewal terms substantially corresponding to the estimated useful life of the property. Leasing Service Corp. v. American National Bank & Trust Co., 19 U.C.C. Rep. 252 (U.S.Dist.Ct., D.N.J.1976); O. P. M. Leasing Services, Inc. v. Homestead Fabrics, Inc., 18 U.C.C.Rep. 1342 (N.Y.S.Ct., 1976); In re Pomona Valley Inn, 4 U.C.C.Rep. 893 (U.S.Dist.Ct. C.D.Calif., 1967); In re Transcontinental Industries, Inc., 3 U.C.C.Rep. 235 (U.S.Dist.Ct.N.D.Ga.1965). By definition, where the lessee retains the property for its entire useful life the lessor can have no significant residual proprietary rights in the property. In effect the lessor has bargained away the absolute right to retake control and use the property.

In summary the first tier obligation requirement is a precondition to all findings that a lease is intended as security. The second tier nominal option test in an appropriate case compels a finding that the lease is intended as security. The third tier of inquiry into whether the lessor bargained away the absolute right to retake control may provide persuasive evidence that the lease functions as a security device. Other factors may be relevant to the ultimate determination, such as a duty on the lessee to insure, risk of loss and liability for taxes on lessee, and lessor's status as a "financing lessor", however such factors are less persuasive as they are essentially matters of contract negotiation.

Borg-Warner cites a line of cases suggesting that an obligation on the lessee to purchase the leased property is a necessary prerequisite to finding that the purported lease is intended as a security device; Security Life Insurance Co. v. Executive Car Leasing Co., 433 S.W.2d 915 (Tex.Civ.App.-Texarkana, 1968, writ ref. n.r.e.); Southwest Park Outpatient Surgery, Ltd. v. Chandler Leasing Divisions, 572 S.W.2d 53 (Tex.Civ.App.-Houston, [1st Dist.] 1978); Brokers Leasing Corp. v. Standard Pipeline, 602 S.W.2d 278 (Tex.Civ.App.-Dallas, 1980).

In the line of cases cited by Borg-Warner, the question presented is whether the purported lease is actually a sales agreement which is subject to the usury law. The Broker's Leasing opinion recognizes that the *Davis Brothers* decision noted supra, and Tom Benson Chevway Rental & Leasing v. Allen, 571 S.W.2d 346 (Tex.Civ.App.-El Paso, 1978, writ ref'd n.r.e.), cert. denied, 442 U.S. 930, 99 S.Ct. 2861, 61 L.Ed.2d 298 (1979), were concerned with whether a purported lease was intended as security. However the Court concludes, "These two cases are not controlling here because they do not concern the question of whether a contract which purports to be a lease is actually a conditional sale subject to the usury laws", *Brokers Leasing* at 280.

The opinion in *Brokers Leasing* is limited to those cases in which a usury claim is asserted. Consequently I find the obligation to purchase test is not controlling in the instant case where the debtor has not asserted a usury claim. Although an express obligation on the part of the lessee to purchase the leased property may be very clear evidence that the parties intend the lease as security, to hold that it is a prerequisite to such a finding would create a narrow, inflexible rule inconsistent with the broad factual inquiry anticipated by the definition of "security interest" in the Uniform Commercial Code.

Applying the three tier analysis to the lease agreements between the debtors and Borg-Warner the following results are reached. Regarding the equipment lease, the first tier of analysis reflects that the lessee is unconditionally obligated to pay an amount ($33,672) substantially equivalent to the initial value of the equipment ($20,884.50) plus a financing factor. The equipment lease contains no purchase option, therefore, it does not fall within the second tier nominal option analysis. Finally the evidence does not affirmatively show that the lessor has bargained away the right to retake control and use the equipment. No evidence was presented as to whether the 60 month lease term was substantially equivalent to the useful life of the equipment. It would be improper to speculate as to its useful life, consequently I hold that the equipment lease is a true lease. It should be noted that an affirmative first tier finding is of itself insufficient evidence that the lease is intended as security. Lessor is entitled to set rentals in an amount sufficient to cover anticipated depreciation of the asset.

Regarding the cow leases, the first tier of analysis reflects that the lessee is unconditionally obligated to pay an amount ($223,848) substantially equal to the capitalized cost ($124,495) of the cows. The cow lease contains a purchase option at a price that is 41% of the disposition value of the cows. The option price is more than nominal. I find however that the option was of a nature that the parties at the inception of the lease reasonably anticipated that the lessee would exercise it. The option price is significantly less than the fair market value of the cows. Furthermore, the debtor testified that he would not have entered into the lease agreement if no purchase option was contained in the agreement. Borg-Warner could reasonably anticipate that effectively it had bargained away the right to retake control and use the cows. In view of this persuasive evidence, and recognizing the agreement contains other terms consistent with a sales transaction, I hold that the cow leases are intended as a security device.

PROBLEMS

1. Lessor leased a compressor with a cash price of $14,500 and a useful life in excess of 5 years to lessee for $800 on a month to month basis with the right on the part of the lessee to

renew each month. The lessee was allowed to apply 85% of the rentals to the $14,500 price and take title when that amount had been paid. Thus were the lessee to keep the property for 21 months he would become the owner. The lessor failed to file a financing statement and a creditor of the lessee attached the compressor during the 8th month of the lease. What result? See United Rental Equipment Co. v. Potts & Callahan Contracting Co., 231 Md. 552, 191 A.2d 570 (1963); Stanley v. Fabricators, Inc., 459 P.2d 467 (Alaska 1969); Note, 49 Cornell L.Q. 672 (1964).

2. Lessor leased machinery with a cash price of $12,348 and a useful life of ten years to lessee for three years for a total rental of $14,358 and an option to renew at the expiration of the 3-year term for as long as lessee wished at $185 per year. There was no option on the part of the lessee to take title. Was a security interest created? See Matter of Wright Homes, Inc., 279 F.Supp. 598 (M.D.N.C.1968).

NOTE

Each year a spate of new cases on whether a lease creates a security interest appears. The simple admonition "when in doubt, file" has not solved the problem as yet. Has the Code taken the correct approach in making filing depend on the sometimes difficult decision of when a lease creates a security interest under UCC § 1–201(37)? With respect to consignments the Code requires filing to protect the consignor's interest against third parties even though no security interest is created. UCC § 2–326(3). The same is true of sales of accounts and chattel paper. UCC § 9–102(1)(b). Should the same approach be taken in the leasing area with filing required for all leases of personal property in which the term of the lease exceeds, say, four months? See the UCCC definition of "Consumer lease" as a "lease of goods * * * which is for a term exceeding four months." UCCC § 1.301(14) (1974).

I. REAL PROPERTY INTERESTS

IN RE BRISTOL ASSOCIATES, INC.

United States Court of Appeals, Third Circuit, 1974.
505 F.2d 1056.

ADAMS, CIRCUIT JUDGE. The Court is here asked to determine whether a Pennsylvania lender, who takes as collateral for a loan a security interest in a lessor-borrower's lease and in the rents thereunder, must comply with the filing provisions of Article 9 of the Uniform Commercial Code to perfect its interest against attack by a Receiver in bankruptcy.

In 1969, Bristol Associates, Inc. as lessor, entered into an Agreement of Lease, letting certain store premises for a period of 10 years to the Commonwealth of Pennsylvania, agent for the Pennsylvania Liquor Control Board. Two years later, in 1971, in consideration for a loan, Bristol gave Girard Trust Bank a promissory note and, as security, assigned to Girard its interest in the lease. Girard did not record its security interest in the real estate lease by filing a financing statement under Article 9 or make any other public record of the assignment of the lease.

The following year, in 1972, Bristol filed a petition under Chapter XI of the Bankruptcy Act, 11 U.S.C. § 701 et seq. (1966), and a Receiver was appointed. Apart from the first month's rent from the Commonwealth inadvertently paid to Girard, the Receiver retained all rentals and applied them to Bristol's business operations. Girard thereupon filed a reclamation petition with the Bankruptcy Court to recover the rentals paid to the Receiver under the lease that had been assigned. The Bankruptcy Court denied the petition, and the denial was affirmed by the district court. 369 F.Supp. 1 (E.D.Pa.1973).

Under section 70(c) of the Bankruptcy Act, 11 U.S.C. § 110, and section 9–301(3) of the Code, the Receiver assumes the rights of a lien creditor. In this status, the Receiver takes priority over those other creditors of the insolvent debtor who hold unperfected security interests. Unperfected secured parties are relegated to the pool of general creditors.

If the assignment of the lease to Girard is a transaction within the scope of Article 9 and if Girard's interest has not been perfected, then Girard cannot successfully assert its security interest against the Receiver. If, however, the assignment of a lease is excluded from Article 9, the filing and perfection provisions of that Article are not applicable, and Girard's security interest in the lease and in the rents from the lease would not be subordinated to the Receiver.

The apposite statutory provisions and official Comment provide:

§ 9–102.   Policy and Scope of Article.

(1) Except as otherwise provided   *   *   *   in Section 9–104 on excluded transactions, this Article applies so far as concerns any personal property and fixtures within the jurisdiction of this State

(a) to any transaction (regardless of its form) which is intended to create a security interest in personal property   *   *   *

(3) The application of this Article to a security interest in a secured obligation is not affected by the fact that the obligation is itself secured by a transaction or interest to which this Article does not apply.

Comment 4.   An illustration of subsection (3) is as follows:

The owner of Blackacre borrows $10,000 from his neighbor, and secures his note by a mortgage on Blackacre. This Article is not applicable to the creation of the real estate mortgage. Nor is it applicable to a sale of the note by the mortgagee, even though the mortgage continues to secure the note. However, when the mortgagee pledges the note to secure his own obligation to X, this Article applies to the security interest thus created, which is a security interest in an instrument even though the instrument is secured by a real estate mortgage. This Article leaves to other law the question of the effect on rights under the mortgage of delivery or non-delivery of the mortgage or of recording or non-recording of an assignment of the mortgagee's interest. See Section 9–104(j).

§ 9–104.   Transactions Excluded from Article.   This Article does not apply   *   *   *

(j)   *   *   *   to the creation or transfer of an interest in or lien on real estate, including a lease or rents thereunder.

Comment 2.   The exclusion   *   *   *   of leases and other interests in or liens on real estate by paragraph (j) merely reiterates the limitations on coverage already made explicit in Section 9–102(3). See Comment 4 to that section.

We are required to apply the law of Pennsylvania to issues such as the one before us. In Re Royal Electrotype Corp., 485 F.2d 394 (3d Cir. 1973). However, the Pennsylvania courts have made no ruling on the interplay of sections 9–102 and 9–104 to resolve the question whether a real estate lease used as collateral falls within the ambit of Article 9. Therefore, it is incumbent on the federal court not only to apply the relevant state law, but to ascertain what that law, in fact, is.

Our analysis proceeds from the statute. We must give effect insofar as possible to the language and intent of the legislators, giving each section a meaningful interpretation while not eclipsing any other portion of the statute.[3]

The question confronting us here thus becomes whether "an interest in real estate" subsequently employed in a "transaction which is intended to create a security interest" is covered by section 9–102, placing the transaction under the Code, or by section 9–104(j), placing the transaction outside the Code.

The Receiver contends that, when the borrower assigned the lease to the lender, the transaction came within the ambit of Article 9 and its provisions for perfecting security interests. In support of this position, the Receiver advances as a syllogism that Article 9 expressly covers security interests in all personal property; that a lease in Pennsylvania is personal property;[4] and that the transaction in question here therefore falls within Article 9 coverage. Section 9–104(j) would, under this analysis,

---

3. Two situations relating to the present case are specifically addressed by Article 9: In one case the provisions of Article 9 control, in the other case the transaction is excluded from coverage. First, had a borrower, such as Bristol, mortgaged its real property to a bank as collateral for a loan, rather than assigning a lease it held as landlord, the Code, under section 9–104(j), explicitly excludes such transaction from its provisions.

On the other hand, where a borrower holds a promissory note in conjunction with a mortgage of real property and then assigns the note as collateral for a loan by a bank, the provisions of Article 9 govern the transaction. The latter situation is the case which the Code includes in section 9–102, Comment 4. Appellant Girard appears to question even this latter application of the Code. But see P. Coogan, W. Ho-

gan & D. Vagts, 1A Secured Transactions Under the Uniform Commercial Code § 23.11 (1973); Warren, Coverage of the Secured Transactions Division of the California Commercial Code, 13 U.C.L.A.L.Rev. 250 (1966).

4. We assume, arguendo, that a lease in Pennsylvania is personalty. M. Stern, Trickett on The Law of Landlord and Tenant in Pennsylvania 2 (rev. 3d ed. 1972). Case law support for this proposition is scant. See Wilford v. Dickey, 196 Pa.Super. 468, 174 A.2d 98 (1961). The characterization of mortgages has been more fully developed; mortgages generally have been held to be personalty in Pennsylvania. Gallagher v. Rogan, 322 Pa. 315, 185 A. 707 (1936); McGlathery's Estate, 311 Pa. 351, 166 A. 886 (1933); Equitable Trust Co. v. Schwebel, 40 F.Supp. 112 (E.D.Pa.1941).

be read narrowly, exempting from Article 9 only those transactions touching on the real estate itself, such as the creation of a lease or mortgage; subsequent uses of the lease or mortgage, "intended to create a security interest," would not be excluded. Under the Receiver's approach the "transfers" excluded from Article 9 by section 9–104(j) would be only those where no intent to create a security interest was present, for example, transfers of blocks of mortgages and the sale of real estate on which outstanding leases were transferred as part of the sale.

The Receiver would place the lease within the scope of section 9–102, Comment 4, supra, asserting that, analogous to the promissory note, the lease evidences an obligation to pay. Although the Receiver concedes that the underlying lessor-lessee contract is excluded from the Code by section 9–104(j), he nevertheless maintains that its use as security could, under a reasonable interpretation of the language, fall within section 9–102(3). If section 9–104(j) is construed narrowly, claims the Receiver, so that the "transfers" it excludes do not cover transfers as security pledges, a consistent reading of the two sections emerges.

Girard argues in opposition that section 9–104(j) explicitly exempts from compliance with the provisions of Article 9 any transfer of an interest in realty, no matter what the purpose. Under this reading of the statute, it becomes irrelevant whether a lease is considered realty or personalty under the state law for other purposes. Even if the lease is deemed personalty, its transfer is claimed by Girard to be the subject of express exclusion from the provisions of Article 9.

Responding to the Receiver's reading of section 9–104(j), Girard suggests that the Receiver would nullify the effect of that section by interpreting it to exclude from Article 9 only transactions which that Article does not purport to cover, namely, real property transactions and transfers where there is no intent to create a security interest. Girard contends that a proper reconciliation of the two sections results only from interpreting section 9–104(j) to exclude from Article 9 transactions that would otherwise fall within it, such as the transactions involved in the present litigation.

The evolution of the Code since its original enactment, the views of authorities and the realities of the pertinent business practices have persuaded us that the intent of the Legislature was to exclude from the filing and perfection provisions of Article 9 the use of a lease as collateral for a loan.

Sections 9–102 and 9–104 have both been amended since their original enactment. Together, the amendments limit the application of section 9–102 where transactions touch realty and, simultaneously, provide greater explicitness in section 9–104(j), exempting both the creation and transfer of interests in realty. The amendments were proposed in order to clarify the Code as ambiguities in language became evident, rather than to alter the direction or scope of the Code.

As originally enacted in Pennsylvania, section 9–102 did not contain subsection (3). In 1959 subsection (3) was added, accompanied by the explanatory Comment 4. Since the effect produced by Comment 4 was not clear, the Conference of Commissioners on Uniform State Laws and the American Law Institute recommended, in 1962, that the Comment be modified. Before and after the amendment, the relevant portion of Comment 4 read:

> However, when the mortgagee in turn pledges this note *and mortgage* to secure his own obligation to X, this Article is applicable to the security interest thus created in the note *and the mortgage* [which is a security interest in an instrument even though the instrument is secured by a real estate mortgage]. (Emphasis indicates the relevant 1962 deletions; brackets indicate the relevant 1962 addition.)

The changes in wording produced two effects. First, deletion of the references to mortgages distinguishes between the pledge of a note, a separate and distinct contract, and the underlying real estate mortgage. Where a promissory note and mortgage together become the subject of a security interest, only that portion of the package unrelated to the real property is now covered by section 9–102. Second, the added language makes explicit that the promissory note itself falls within the scope of Article 9 by virtue of its status as an instrument.[8] Since a lease of real property is clearly not an instrument, inclusion of its assignment in Article 9 by reason of analogy to the promissory note would be strained. The amendments clarify the rationale of applying Article 9 to the promissory note. They refute the possibility that Article 9 reaches out to encompass every transaction colorably included under section 9–102.

---

8. "Instrument" is defined for purposes of Article 9 as "a negotiable instrument, or a security or any other writing which evidences a right to the payment of money and is not itself a security agreement or lease. * * * " 12A Pa.Stat.Ann. § 9–105(g) (1970) (cross references deleted).

The amendments made to section 9–104 lend further support to the position that the legislators did not intend to include in Article 9 the assignment of a real estate lease. As originally enacted, the Code did not contain section 9–104(j); rather, section 9–104(b) excluded from Article 9 coverage "a landlord's lien or a lien on real estate." Act of April 6, 1953, P.L. 3, § 9–104. Following the recommendation of the Permanent Editorial Board of the Uniform Commercial Code, the Legislature in 1959 adopted the language presently set forth in section 9–104(j). Act of October 2, 1959, P.L. 1023, § 9. The change was promoted by the Board in the interest of "greater clarification and precision as to the types of transactions entirely excluded from the operation of Article 9." 1956 Recommendations of the Editorial Board for the Uniform Commercial Code, 257–58. The language of section 9–104(j) substantially broadens the earlier exclusion by providing that Article 9 does not apply to "the creation or transfer of an interest in or lien on real estate, including a lease or rents thereunder."

Our conclusion, that lenders need not conform to the requirements of Article 9 in order to retain their security interest in a real estate lease assigned to them as collateral, is supported, apparently unanimously, by authorities who have considered this problem. Included are many of the persons responsible for the drafting of the Code and its subsequent revisions. Carl Funk, a leading expert on the Code and its application in Pennsylvania, stated that "a bank lending on the security of an assignment of a lease or of the rentals payable by the tenant need not comply with the Code in any way." [10]

In their treatise, Coogan, Hogan & Vagts first aver that a promissory note when used as collateral is covered by the Code even if secured by a mortgage, citing section 9–102(3) and Comment 4. However, they continue by asserting that, "[t]hough estates for years are for some purposes considered personal property, the Code would not seem to cover the mortgage of a lease on realty." 1A Secured Transactions under the Uniform Commercial Code § 16.04[1] at 1698 (1973). The authors cite section 9–104(j) for this proposition. The notion that the assignment of a lease or of rents thereunder as collateral might be considered a security interest in personal property controlled by Article 9 is dismissed as "unduly fearful." The authors state

---

10. This statement is found under the subsection "Loans Secured by Other Types of Personal Property." Banks & the Uniform Commercial Code, 60, 61 (2d Ed. 1964).

that "[t]he clear intent of section 9–104(j) * * * would be completely nullified" by such an interpretation.[11]

These views of the authorities in no way bind this Court nor are they determinative of the intent of the legislators who enacted Article 9 into law. Nonetheless, the composite picture is suggestive of what the experts expected to be the effect of section 9–104(j). The legislators could not have been wholly unmindful of the views of authorities in the areas affected by the Code. Had the legislators intended a different effect for the language, they might well have given some indication of this. That they did not is surely some evidence that the intended scope of section 9–104(j) was not in sharp contrast to what was generally believed to be its ambit by the leaders in the field. Therefore, a broad reading of section 9–104(j) which would exclude the present transaction from Article 9 is consistent with the views of the authorities and is not controverted by an indication from the legislators that these views are mistakenly held.

One final consideration buttresses the conclusion that the lease when used as collateral should be exempted from Article 9. The universal practice of Pennsylvania lenders in these circumstances is to ignore any application of the Code to leases received as collateral. A bank often takes an assignment of a lease or the rents due under a lease as security for a loan. C. Funk, Banks and the Uniform Commercial Code 61 (2d ed. 1964). Collateral of very substantial value is involved in such loans, which are granted regularly and repeatedly in the world of finance. Parties to these loans "are apt to think for good reasons that they are outside the scope of Article 9." Hawkland, 77 Com.L.J. 79, 84 (1972).[12]

---

11. However, out of an abundance of caution, the authors recommend clarification of the language by revision. Section 23.11[6] at 2401. Accord, Coogan, Kripke & Weiss, The Outer Fringes of Article 9: Subordination Agreements, Security Interests in Money and Deposits, Negative Pledge Clauses and Participation Agreements, 79 Harv.L.Rev. 229, 268 (1965).

See also Warren, Coverage of the Secured Transactions Division of the California Commercial Code, 13 U.C. L.A.L.Rev. 250 (1966). Professor Hawkland also has noted the confusion inadvertently generated by the language of §§ 9–102 and 9–104. The Proposed Amendments to Article 9 of the U.C.C.—Part IV: The Scope of Article 9, 77 Com.L.J. 79 (1972). Convinced that no one in the lending field intended the pledge of a realty lease to fall within Article 9, Professor Hawkland proposes further amendments to the Code to clarify the matter.

12. It was suggested at oral argument without contradiction that lenders believe they are excluded because "literally hundreds of opinion letters" from attorneys have so informed the banking community.

While a uniform trade practice does not constitute proof that the legal consequences of the practice are what those in the field take them to be, neither can it be assumed that a legislature which passed the Code and which has considered and passed amendments to it on several occasions would let stand practices or beliefs which it disapproved. In fact, the amendments passed by the Legislature have tended in the other direction, restricting the application of Article 9 when transactions touch real property. (See discussion supra.)

Where language is susceptible of two reasonable meanings, a court, in the commercial field, should choose that interpretation which comports with current universal practice in the business world.

* * *

The decision of the district court will be reversed, and the case will be remanded for entry of an order consistent with this opinion.

NOTES

1. Accord: Citizens Bank and Trust Co. v. Wy-Tex Livestock Co., Inc., 611 S.W.2d 168 (Tex.Civ.App.1981) (assignment of rents under real estate lease falls within UCC § 9–104(j) exclusion). In Ingram v. Ingram, 214 Kan. 415, 521 P.2d 254 (1974), the court held that the assignment of an oil and gas lease for security purposes is not controlled by the provisions of the UCC.

2. Debtor was payee of a note secured by a mortgage on real property. He borrowed money from Lender and entered into an agreement assigning the note and mortgage to Lender as security for his loan. Debtor recorded the assignment of the mortgage on Lender's behalf in the real property records but retained possession of the note in order to make collections on behalf of Lender. When Debtor went into bankruptcy Lender was held to have no interest in the note and mortgage because it did not perfect its security interest by taking possession of the note (an "instrument" under UCC § 9–105(1)(i)) pursuant to UCC § 9–304(1). Huffman v. Wikle, 550 F.2d 1228 (9th Cir. 1977); and Greiner v. Wikle, 625 F.2d 281 (9th Cir. 1980). See also First Valley Bank v. First Savings and Loan Association, 412 N.E.2d 1237 (Ind.App.1980). A contrary holding is Rucker v. State Exchange Bank, 355 So.2d 171 (Fla.App.1978), in which the court relied on the recording of the assignment of the mortgage

as sufficient perfection of the secured party's interest. See UCC § 9–102(3) and Comment 4.

3. In In re Freeborn, 94 Wn.2d 336, 617 P.2d 424 (1980), the court held that a land sale contract vendor's interest is personal property; hence, a lender taking this interest as security must perfect under Article 9. How would you classify a land sale contract vendor's interest under the UCC? In re Cowsert, 14 B.R. 340 (Bkrtcy.Fla.1981), holds that the beneficial interest under a land trust is personal property and is a general intangible. See UCC § 9–106. How do you perfect with respect to a general intangible? See UCC § 9–302(1) and § 9–103(3).

PROBLEM

Lessor leased a motel to lessee and took as security for the rental payments an assignment of "rents, issues, income and profits due and to become due from any sublease, subletting or other use of any room or space in the demised premises or from any concession therein, or arising out of the operation of the demised premises or the hotel business conducted therein or any part thereof." The lease document assigning these rights was recorded in the land records but no UCC filing was made. When Lessee went into bankruptcy a sum of money was identified as coming from charges paid by guests for rooms. Lessor claimed the money under the above-quoted clause. He contended that no UCC filing was required because the collateral was real estate rentals, falling within the UCC § 9–104(j) exclusion. A competing secured party argued that Lessor had no perfected security interest in the money because it was not from the rental of real estate but was from charges the lessee made for services it provided its patrons, including the furnishing of rooms; these charges were accounts (UCC § 9–106) and the lessor should have filed with respect to them. Who wins? See United States v. P.S. Hotel Corp., 404 F.Supp. 1188 (E.D.Mo.1975), aff'd per curiam, 527 F.2d 500 (8th Cir.).

J. CONFLICTING INTERESTS NOT GOVERNED BY ARTICLE NINE. SUBROGATION, SUBORDINATION AND SET–OFF

CANTER v. SCHLAGER

Supreme Judicial Court of Massachusetts, 1971.
358 Mass. 789, 267 N.E.2d 492.

BRAUCHER, JUSTICE. This is an action of contract brought by the trustee in bankruptcy of Zef Parabicoli & Sons, Inc. (the contractor) against S. Lawrence Schlager, Judith R. Schlager, Alba A. Jameson and Arlene T. Vecchi (the owners) for money owed under a written construction contract. In May, 1963, the contractor agreed with the owners to build a post office on their property in Wellesley for a price later amended to $109,000. By the amendment the work was to be substantially completed by July 1, 1964, and time was to be of the essence. In accordance with the contract, the contractor provided performance and payment bonds, and in its application for the bonds assigned to the surety, Maryland Casualty Company, all payments due or to become due under the contract. No financing statement with respect to the assignment was filed under the Uniform Commercial Code. The surety appears to be the real defendant in this action, under an agreement to indemnify the owners.

Work began in January, 1964, and by June 26, 1964, the owners had paid the contractor $66,650. On June 26, 1964, an involuntary petition in bankruptcy was filed against the contractor, but by order of the referee in bankruptcy the contractor continued to operate under the supervision of a receiver. On August 1, 1964, the Post Office Department accepted the building and began to pay rent under a lease from the owners. On October 27, 1964, the contractor was adjudicated a bankrupt and the plaintiff, who had been the receiver, was appointed trustee.

The owners refused to pay a requisition in the amount of $27,990 submitted by the contractor on July 1, 1964, for work completed up to that date. On July 21, there was a conference of representatives of the Post Office Department, the surety, the contractor, its receiver and the owners; the attorney for the surety, at the request of the owners and with the approval of the contractor, agreed that the surety would assume responsibility for completion. Late in September, the contractor submitted a final requisition in the amount of $42,850, which the owners refused to pay. In October, 1964, the surety paid more than $60,000 to subcontractors who had furnished labor and materials for the building. On August 30, 1965, the owners paid the balance of the contract price, less more than $5,000 in disputed "back charges," to the surety in the net amount of $36,630.11. The owners now contend that payment to the surety discharged any obligation to the plaintiff.

The judge, sitting without a jury, held that the surety's claim to the contract balance was not subject to the Uniform Commercial Code and found for the owners. We agree.

1. If the surety were claiming the balance due under the contract by virtue of the assignment to it in the contractor's bond application, it would be fairly arguable that it was claiming a "security interest" in a "contract right." UCC §§ 1–201(37), 9–102, 9–106. If there were such a security interest, it would be subordinate to the rights of a person who became a lien creditor without knowledge of the security interest and before it was perfected, and a trustee in bankruptcy would ordinarily have the rights of such a lien creditor. UCC §§ 9–301(1)(b), 9–301(3). Bankruptcy Act, § 70, sub. c., 11 U.S.C.A. § 110(c) (1964). To perfect a security interest, a financing statement must be filed unless the case is within one of several exceptions. UCC § 9–302(1). We do not pass on the question whether the assignment to the surety in this case was excepted as "a transfer of a contract right to an assignee who is also to do the performance under the contract," UCC § 9–104(f), or "an assignment of accounts or contract rights which does not alone or in conjunction with other assignments to the same assignee transfer a significant part of the outstanding accounts or contract rights of the assignor * * *." UCC § 9–302(1)(e). See Gilmore, Security Interests in Personal Property, §§ 10.5, 19.6.

2. The surety makes an alternative claim, not resting on the assignment to it by the contractor, that it is subrogated to the rights of the contractor to the contract balance, to the rights of the owners, and to the rights of the subcontractors it paid. Such claims are not superseded by the Uniform Commercial Code. Section 1–103 of the Code provides in part, "Unless displaced by the particular provisions of this chapter, the principles of law and equity * * * shall supplement its provisions." "No provision of the Code purports to affect the fundamental equitable doctrine of subrogation." French Lumber Co. Inc. v. Commercial Realty & Finance Co. Inc., 346 Mass. 716, 719, 195 N.E.2d 507, 510. "Of basic importance is the general rule of

Section 9–102(2) that Article 9 'applies to security interests *created by contract.*' (Emphasis supplied.) Rights of subrogation, although growing out of a contractual setting and ofttimes articulated by the contract, do not depend for their existence on a grant in the contract, but are created by law to avoid injustice. Therefore, subrogation rights are not 'security interests' within the meaning of Article 9." Jacobs v. Northeastern Corp., 416 Pa. 417, 429, 206 A.2d 49, 55.

Our conclusion that filing under the Code is unnecessary to preserve the priority of a surety's right of subrogation over the rights of a construction contractor's trustee in bankruptcy is reinforced by decisions of other courts. Jacobs v. Northeastern Corp., supra (receiver against surety, Pennsylvania law). National Shawmut Bank v. New Amsterdam Cas. Co. Inc., 411 F.2d 843 (1st Cir.) (assignee bank against surety on Federal contract, Massachusetts law). Framingham Trust Co. v. Gould-Natl. Batteries, Inc., 427 F.2d 856 (1st Cir.) (assignee bank against surety, Massachusetts law). Home Indem. Co. v. United States, 433 F.2d 764 (Ct.Cl.) (surety on Federal contract against trustee in bankruptcy of assignee finance company, Illinois law). National Sur. Corp. v. State Natl. Bank, 454 S.W.2d 354, 356 (Ky.) (surety against assignee bank, Kentucky law). Aetna Cas. & Sur. Co. v. Perrotta, 62 Misc.2d 252, 308 N.Y.S.2d 613 (surety against assignee finance company, New York law). Contrary decisions in United States v. G. P. Fleetwood & Co. Inc., 165 F.Supp. 723 (W.D.Pa.) (surety on subcontract against trustee in bankruptcy of subcontractor), and Hartford Acc. & Indem. Co. v. State Pub. Sch. Bldg. Authy., 26 D. & C.2d (Pa.) 717 (surety against assignee bank), are not authoritative with respect to Pennsylvania law after the decision in Jacobs v. Northeastern Corp., supra. So far as Maryland Cas. Co. v. Mullett, 295 F.Supp. 875 (W.D.Pa.), is contrary, it also departs from Pennsylvania law. The Uniform Commercial Code is to be "liberally construed and applied to promote its underlying purposes and policies," which include a purpose and policy "to make uniform the law among the various jurisdictions." § 1–102.

3. The plaintiff here argues that we should "establish a degree of certainty (indeed, even a degree of sanity) to the determination of priorities among claimants to construction contract proceeds" by enunciating "an absolute requirement that sureties engaged in bonding construction projects perfect security interests in their assignment by filing." See Notes, 4 B.C.Ind. & Commercial L.Rev. 748, 755; 65 Col.L.Rev. 927, 933. We find that the draftsmen and sponsors of the Uniform Commercial

Code did not overlook the problems of construction contract sureties. The 1952 Official Draft included § 9–312(7), subordinating the surety's interest to a later interest taken by a party who gave new value to enable the debtor to perform his obligation; that provision was deleted in 1953, with an explanation by the editorial board that representatives of the surety companies had complained that it changed settled law and that the problem should be left to agreements for subordination.[27] See National Shawmut Bank v. New Amsterdam Cas. Co. Inc., 411 F.2d 843, 846, c. 4 (1st Cir.). The 1952 proposal did not include a requirement of filing to perfect rights of subrogation, and we do not believe we should insert a requirement omitted by legislative draftsmen who considered the problem. It is possible for parties dealing with a construction contractor to be ignorant of the existence of a surety bond. See, e.g., Aetna Cas. & Sur. Co. v. Harvard Trust Co., 344 Mass. 160, 164, 181 N.E.2d 673. But it could well be a rational legislative judgment that the practice of furnishing performance and payment bonds in connection with construction contracts is so common and so well known that a

27. "The Surety Companies' representatives convincingly took the position that subsection (7) as it stands is a complete reversal of the case law not only of the Supreme Court of the United States but also of the highest courts of most of the states. They cited Prairie State [National] Bank [of Chicago] v. United States, 164 U.S. 227 [17 S.Ct. 142, 41 L.Ed. 412] (1896); Henningsen v. United States F. & G. [Co.], 208 U.S. 404 [28 S.Ct. 389, 52 L.Ed. 547] (1908); United States v. Munsey Trust [Co.], 332 U.S. 234 [67 S.Ct. 1599, 91 L.Ed. 2022] (1947), at 240; 9 Am.Jur. 72, §§ 114, 115; 43 Am.Jur. 939, § 197 et seq.; 60 C.J. Subrogation § 87; Stearns Law of Suretyship, 5th Ed. (1951), Page 472; Appeal of Lancaster County Natl. Bk., 304 Pa. 437 [155 A. 859] (1931); and 127 A.L.R. 974, 976.

"The typical case involved is a case in which a surety company, as a prerequisite to the execution of a performance bond, requires a contractor to make an assignment of all moneys coming to the contractor from the owner. Later, the contractor goes to a bank and obtains a loan presumably or actually for the purpose of enabling him to perform his contract.

"Under the cited case law, the surety's rights come first as to the funds owing by the owner unless the surety has subordinated its right to the bank. Subsection (7) of the Code as written would reverse the situation and give the bank priority in all cases.

"Under existing case law, both the contractor and the bank are in a position to bargain with the surety which may or may not be willing to subordinate its claim. Under subsection (7), as written in the Code the surety company would have nothing to bargain about." Recommendations of the Editorial Board for Changes in the Text and Comments of the Uniform Commercial Code, Official Draft, Text and Comments Edition, pp. 24–25, April 30, 1953. See Uniform Commercial Code § 9–312(7), Official Draft, Text and Comments Edition, 1952; Cramer, Uniform Commercial Code: Surety v. Lender, 3 Forum 295, 300–302. In Gilmore, Security Interests in Personal Property § 36.7, it is erroneously stated that the offending provision "disappeared, without official explanation."

requirement of public filing is unnecessary. Compare Aetna Cas. & Sur. Co. v. Harvard Trust Co., supra, at 173, 181 N.E.2d 673.

4. The plaintiff argues that, even if "the anachronistic doctrine of equitable subrogation still has vitality," the surety has only the rights of those to whose rights it would be subrogated, and that they had none. Under Pearlman v. Reliance Ins. Co., 371 U.S. 132, 141, 83 S.Ct. 232, 9 L.Ed.2d 190, and similar cases, the surety may stand in the shoes of either (1) the contractor whose obligations are discharged, (2) the owners to whom it was bound, or (3) the subcontractors whom it paid. So far as the trustee in bankruptcy asserts the rights of the contractor, any one of these three bases of subrogation should be sufficient. Regardless of whether the contractor was aggrieved by the delay in payment of his requisition of $27,990 submitted July 1, 1964, or his final requisition of $42,850 submitted late in September, 1964, he could not avoid the surety's right to reimbursement for more than $60,000 paid by the surety to discharge his obligations in October, 1964. Nor could he avoid recoupment by the owners for amounts properly paid by them to the subcontractors. See American Bridge Co. of N. Y. v. Boston, 202 Mass. 374, 377, 88 N.E. 1089; Berkal v. M. De Matteo Constr. Co., 327 Mass. 329, 334, 98 N.E.2d 617. A different case might be presented if it were found that the owners or the surety, to induce the contractor to continue, promised after trouble arose to make payments regardless of offsets. Compare National Sur. Corp. v. State Natl. Bank, 454 S.W.2d 354, 357 (Ky.). There is no such showing here.

* * *

The plaintiff is not helped by Bankruptcy Act § 70, sub. c, 11 U.S.C.A. § 110(c) (1964), giving him the rights of a judgment creditor of the bankrupt with a lien by legal proceedings. Such rights date from June 26, 1964, when the petition in bankruptcy was filed; the surety's right dates back to the date of its bond. Aetna Cas. & Sur. Co. v. Harvard Trust Co., 344 Mass. 160, 166–168, 181 N.E.2d 673. Prairie State Bank v. United States, 164 U.S. 227, 240, 17 S.Ct. 142, 41 L.Ed. 412, relied on in Labbe v. Bernard, 196 Mass. 551, 553, 82 N.E. 688. Henningsen v. United States Fid. & Guar. Co., 208 U.S. 404, 411, 28 S.Ct. 389, 52 L.Ed. 547. United States v. Munsey Trust Co., 332 U.S. 234, 240, 67 S.Ct. 1599, 91 L.Ed. 2022. Hence the right of subrogation prevails over the rights of a lien creditor such as the trustee in bankruptcy. Pearlman v. Reliance Ins. Co., 371 U.S. 132, 136,

83 S.Ct. 232, 9 L.Ed.2d 190.   See Commercial Cas. Ins. Co. of
Newark, N.J. v. Murphy, 282 Mass. 100, 104, 184 N.E. 434;
Duteau v. Salvucci, 330 Mass. 531, 536, 115 N.E.2d 726.

5.   The plaintiff complains that the surety improperly yielded to the owners' claims of more than $5,000 of "back charges."
The surety paid more than $60,000 of debts owed by the contrac-
tor, and was reimbursed $36,630.11.   In these circumstances, if
$5,000 more was owed, it should have been paid to the surety
rather than to the plaintiff.

There was no error.

Exceptions overruled.

NOTE

It is not uncommon for a debtor, which is usually a corporation, to have classes of unsecured debt, i.e., an unsecured creditor has agreed that his debt shall be subordinated to the debt of
another unsecured creditor.   The purpose of the subordination
agreement is usually to allow the debtor to obtain credit which
might otherwise not be available.   The effect of subordination is
to transfer to the favored creditor the amount that would otherwise have gone to the subordinated creditor in any insolvency
distribution.   Subordination agreements are enforceable in bankruptcy.   See Bankruptcy Code § 510(a).   To the extent that the
favored creditor enjoys a priority with respect to the assets of
the debtor it can be argued that he has an interest in personal
property of the debtor which secures payment of his obligation
and thus has a security interest as defined by UCC § 1–201(37).
But this "security interest" is different from conventional security interests in that it does not affect any creditor except those
who have subordinated their claims.   Thus, it would serve little
purpose to make enforceability of subordination agreements depend upon perfection under Article 9.   Because the status of
subordination agreements under Article 9 was not clear, the
UCC was amended in 1966 to add § 1–209 as an optional provision to make it clear that subordination agreements do not come
within UCC § 1–201(37).   The comment to UCC § 1–209 discusses the problem in detail.   See also UCC § 9–316.

NATIONAL ACCEPTANCE CO. OF AMERICA v. VIRGINIA CAPITAL BANK

United States District Court, E.D.Virginia, 1980.
498 F.Supp. 1078.

CLARKE, DISTRICT JUDGE. This diversity action was brought pursuant to 28 U.S.C. § 1332 by two creditors of Concrete Structures, Inc., a Virginia corporation recently the subject of bankruptcy proceedings under Chapter XI of the Bankruptcy Act. Claiming a prior, perfected security interest in certain funds deposited in several deposit accounts maintained by Concrete Structures in the Virginia Capital Bank, the plaintiffs allege that the Bank unlawfully appropriated these funds to set-off certain debts owed to the Bank by Structures. Evidence was submitted by the parties in support of their various positions at a hearing held before this Court on June 19, 1980, and the matter is ripe for a determination on the merits. The following opinion represents the Court's findings of fact and conclusions of law under Fed.R.Civ.P. 52(a).

Although certain facts relating to this controversy were recited by the Court in a previous Order denying the Bank's motion for summary judgment, 491 F.Supp. 1269 (1980), a more complete picture of the circumstances surrounding this case can now be drawn. Concrete Structures, Inc. was at all relevant times engaged in the business of manufacturing and distributing concrete blocks and prestressed concrete building materials. Beginning in 1964, National Acceptance Company of America (NAC), a Delaware corporation, lent Structures various amounts of money pursuant to certain loan and security agreements and other financing documents. A significant portion of these loans were made as part of an accounts receivable financing arrangement whereby NAC agreed to lend Structures a certain percentage of the face amount of Structures' accounts receivable. NAC reserved the right reasonably to reject unsound accounts which might be tendered by Structures for financing, and took a security interest in the financed accounts and in other collateral. For its part, Structures was obligated to submit all payments received from customers in payment of any account financed under this arrangement directly to NAC.

During the period January 1, 1978, to June 30, 1978, NAC continued to lend money pursuant to these financing arrangements. These transactions were governed by a Loan and Security Agreement dated January 5, 1973; an Extension Agreement dated October 1, 1976, which extended payments on certain outstanding loans; an Accounts Rider dated November 18, 1977; and an Inventory Rider dated November 18, 1977. Under the Loan and Security Agreement, Structures granted NAC a security interest in the following collateral to secure loans made under these agreements:

(a) existing and future accounts, chattel paper, contract rights and instruments (sometimes hereinafter individually and collectively referred to as "Accounts"), whether Accounts are acceptable or unacceptable to Lender and whether Accounts are scheduled to Lender on Schedules of Accounts or not, and all goods whose sale, lease or other disposition by Borrower has given rise to any Accounts and which goods have been returned to or repossessed or stopped in transit by Borrower;

(b) presently owned and hereafter acquired inventory ("Inventory");

(c) presently owned and hereafter acquired general intangibles, goods (other than Inventory), equipment, vehicles and fixtures, together with all accessions, parts and appurtenances thereto appertaining or attached or kept or used or intended for use in connection therewith and all substitutions, renewals, improvements and replacements of and additions thereto (sometimes hereinafter individually and collectively referred to as "Equipment") and all Equipment described in Equipment Rider attached hereto;

(d) presently owned and hereafter acquired Inventory evidenced by warehouse receipts (whether negotiable or non-negotiable) now or at any time or times hereafter issued by any bailee in Lender's name or negotiated to Lender evidencing such bailee's possession of any Inventory now or at any time or times hereafter deposited with such bailee;

and all proceeds and products of and accessions to all of the foregoing described properties and interests in properties.
*   *   *

It is agreed that this security interest was duly perfected and remained so throughout all relevant times. As of June 1978, when Structures instituted bankruptcy proceedings, Structures was indebted to NAC in an amount exceeding the funds in dispute in this action, under the various financing arrangements governed by the Loan and Security Agreement and related documents.

At the time it instituted bankruptcy proceedings, Structures also was indebted to the other plaintiff in this action, Mitsubishi International Corporation. For some period prior to April 1976, Mitsubishi had been selling steel products to Concrete Structures on open account. Concrete Structures fell behind in its payments on this account and in April 1976, it issued a note promising to pay Mitsubishi the sum of $210,415.20 by July 23, 1976, according to a schedule of payments established in the note. However, Concrete Structures soon failed to meet this schedule of payments and on June 1, 1976, Concrete Structures and Mitsubishi entered into a security agreement to secure "payment and performance of all liabilities and obligations of [Concrete Structures] to [Mitsubishi] of any kind and description, direct or indirect, absolute or contingent, due or to become due, now existing or hereafter arising and howsoever evidenced or acquired and whether joint, several or joint and several. * * * " Under this security agreement, which was duly perfected by the recording of a financing statement, Mitsubishi acquired a security interest in:

(a) Debtor's inventory including all goods and merchandise, raw materials, goods in process, finished goods, goods in transit now owned or hereafter acquired and the proceeds thereof.

(b) Debtor's accounts receivable and notes receivable and contract rights including all sais [sic] accounts [sic] receivable and notes receivable and contract rights outstanding as of this date and all future accounts receivable and notes receivable, and contract rights and proceeds thereof.[1]

As of June 30, 1978, Structures remained indebted to Mitsubishi in the amount of $278,298.65, exclusive of interest.

In December 1977, Concrete Structures opened several deposit accounts with Virginia Capital Bank, including accounts 010–716–6 and 010–722–0, the two accounts at issue in this litigation. Thereafter, on March 21, 1978, the Bank loaned Concrete Structures $40,249.92, payable in installments over a two-year period. The Bank took as security nineteen vehicles listed in an accompanying security agreement. On April 4, 1978, the Bank

1. In a later subordination agreement between Mitsubishi and the other plaintiff, National Acceptance Company of America (NAC), Mitsubishi's security interest in inventory and in accounts and contract rights, both present and future, arising from the sale of concrete blocks manufactured by Concrete Structures was subordinated to NAC's security interest. This subordination agreement was entered into in October 1977 and was perfected on December 8, 1977.

made a demand loan of $12,000 to Concrete Structures. This loan was unsecured. A third loan, in the amount of $50,000, was made by the Bank on or about April 27, 1978,[2] to refinance an outstanding loan previously made to Concrete Erectors, Inc., a subsidiary of Structures. The Bank concedes that, although this April 27 loan ostensibly was secured by an interest in the accounts receivable of Concrete Erectors, this security interest was never perfected.

Almost immediately Structures encountered difficulty in meeting its obligations to the Bank under the terms of these loans. Beginning on June 1, 1978, Structures' impending insolvency became apparent, and without notice to or the authorization of the plaintiffs, the Bank made the following debits to Structures' deposit accounts to satisfy that company's remaining indebtedness under the loans:

Account No. 010–716–6

6/1/78	$10,000.00	
6/5/78	5,000.00	
6/6/78	5,000.00	
6/7/78	22,829.94	
6/16/78	6,151.67	
6/19/78	5,505.53	
	$54,487.14	$54,487.14

Account No. 010–722–0

6/12/78	$ 6,000.00	
6/19/78	18,840.62	
	$24,840.62	$24,840.62
Total		$79,327.76

There is no dispute that the entire balance of these accounts at the time of these set-offs was attributable to funds derived from cash sales of inventory, collections of accounts receivable, or funds wired by NAC to Structures pursuant to their loan agreements.

Actuated in part by this drain of its operating funds, Structures filed a petition for an arrangement under Chapter XI of

---

2. While the plaintiffs urge that this loan was made not to Concrete Structures, but to a sister corporation, Concrete Erectors, we need not decide this question in light of our holding which is dispositive of the issues presented even if it is assumed that this loan was attributable to Concrete Structures.

the Bankruptcy Act on or about June 29, 1978. The Bank received notice of these proceedings and was listed as a general creditor of Structures. In connection with these bankruptcy proceedings, the plaintiffs entered into an Inter-Creditor Agreement, approved by the Bankruptcy Court, in which the plaintiffs agreed upon a plan for sharing any proceeds of certain of Structures' pre-bankruptcy accounts which might be collected in this litigation.

On July 19, 1979, NAC brought the present action, contending that the funds in the accounts set-off by the Bank represented identifiable proceeds of collateral secured by its loan and security agreement with Structures, that its security interest expressly extended to these proceeds and was superior to any interest of the Bank, and that it was entitled to these funds by reason of Structures' default on its obligations to NAC evidenced by its petition in bankruptcy. Mitsubishi later intervened also alleging that it had a prior security interest in the proceeds deposited in the accounts set-off by the Bank, and that it was entitled to these funds by reason of Structures' default. The Complaints demanded return of the sums and that judgment be entered against the Bank for the amount of the funds appropriated from these accounts by the Bank, plus interest from the dates of the set-offs. The Complaints also seek punitive damages and an award of attorney's fees.

The first point we must consider is whether the plaintiffs had a security interest in the funds set-off by the Bank. There is not much question that the funds in the accounts did not fall within the first generation of collateral listed in the various security agreements. Therefore, these funds could be covered by these agreements only if found to be proceeds of the enumerated collateral. "Proceeds," as defined by section 9–306(1) of the Uniform Commercial Code includes "whatever is received upon the sale, exchange, collection or other disposition of collateral or proceeds." This definition is to be given a flexible and broad content.

[The court found the funds to be identifiable proceeds.]

We come now to the key issue in this action: whether the Bank's right of set-off was subordinate to the plaintiffs' security interest in the proceeds deposited in Structures' deposit accounts. In this diversity action, the answer to this issue is, of course, governed by the law of Virginia. Virginia law long ago recognized the common-law right of a bank, as a debtor of its depositors, to set-off a matured debt owed to the bank by a de-

positor against funds on deposit. See, e.g., Federal Reserve
Bank v. State & City Bank & Trust Co., 150 Va. 423, 143 S.E.
697 (1928); Nolting v. National Bank of Va., 99 Va. 54, 37 S.E.
804 (1901); Ford's Adm'r v. Thornton, 3 Leigh 695 (1832). Although often referred to as a "banker's lien," this right of set-
off is not properly a lien upon a depositor's account. Rather, it
is "a mere right of the bank to retain in its own possession property the title of which (absolute or special) is, or, in the case of
negotiable paper, purports to be, in one against whom the bank
has some demand until that demand is satisfied." Nolting v.
National Bank of Va., 99 Va. 54, 60–61, 37 S.E. 804, 806 (1901),
quoting, 1 Morse, Banks, § 323. This right, however, is not absolute. Virginia adheres to the majority rule that if the bank
can be charged with knowledge of the interest of a third party in
a deposit account, or notice of facts sufficient to put it on inquiry that such an interest exists, it may not apply the account
to satisfy a debt owed by the depositor. See Peoples Nat. Bank
v. Colemen, 175 Va. 483, 9 S.E.2d 333 (1940); Federal Reserve
Bank v. State & City Bank & Trust Co., supra. See also Skilton,
The Secured Party's Rights in a Debtor's Bank Account Under
Article 9 of the Uniform Commercial Code, 1977 So.Ill.U.L.J.
120, 190–96 (distinguishing this "legal" rule from the "equitable" rule giving precedence to the third-party over the bank even
if the bank lacked knowledge or notice). If called upon to evalu-
ate this case under the common-law doctrine of set-off in Virginia, therefore we would be put to the task of determining whether the Bank had either actual knowledge of the plaintiffs'
interests in Structures' deposit accounts, or notice of facts sufficient to put the Bank to a further inquiry as to the existence of
such interests.

It is not clear, however, whether this common-law approach
to the present priority issue has been altered by Virginia's adoption of Article 9 of the Uniform Commercial Code, which establishes a comprehensive scheme of rules governimg secured
transactions and the relative dignity of conflicting interests in
collateral. Section 9-104(i) of the Code states:

This title does not apply * * * to any right of set-off.
* * *

Two views of this language have been espoused. Several jurisdictions have held that this exclusion was intended to indicate
only that a right of set-off arises under state law as a result of
the parties' status, without regard to compliance with the Code,
and not that an otherwise extant right of set-off is exempt from

Article 9's rules concerning priority of interests in collateral. See Citizens Nat. Bank v. Mid-States Development Co., Ind.App., 380 N.E.2d 1243, 1247 (1978); Morrison Steel Co. v. Gurtman, 113 N.J.Super. 474, 274 A.2d 306, 310 (1971); Associates Discount Corp. v. Fidelity Union Trust Co., 111 N.J.Super. 353, 268 A.2d 330, 332 (1970). These courts find support for this conclusion in the remarks of a principal reporter of Article 9, Professor G. Gilmore, who has stated the following view of this exclusion:

> This exclusion is an apt example of the absurdities which result when draftsmen attempt to appease critics by putting into a statute something that is not in any sense wicked but is hopelessly irrelevant. Of course a right of set-off is not a security interest and has never been confused with one: the statute might as appropriately exclude fan dancing. A bank's right of set-off against a depositor's account is often loosely referred to as a "banker's lien," but the "lien" usage has never led anyone to think that the bank held a security interest in the bank account. Banking groups were, however, concerned lest someone, someday, might think that a bank's right of set-off, because it was called a lien, was a security interest. Hence the exclusion, which does no harm except to the dignity and self-respect of the draftsmen.

This position could also be supported by reference to section 9–306(4) of the Code which provides in pertinent part:

> (4) In the event of insolvency proceedings instituted by or against a debtor, a secured party with a perfected security interest in proceeds has a perfected security interest only in the following proceeds:
>
> *   *   *
>
> (d) in all cash and deposit accounts of the debtor, in which proceeds have been commingled with other funds, but the perfected security interest under this paragraph (d) is
>
> (i) subject to any right of setoff *   *   *.

Arguably, this provision would be unnecessary if the relative priority of any right of set-off was unaffected by Article 9 because all perfected security interests, and not merely those recognized under section 9–306(4)(d), would be equally "subject to any right of setoff." [5]

5. Section 9–306(4)(d)(i) does not create a right of set-off. Rather, it continues any right of set-off which might otherwise exist under prior state law. See, e.g., Middle Atlantic Credit Corp. v. First Pa. Banking & Trust Co., 199 Pa.Super. 456, 185 A.2d 818 (1962). This section, however, is not applicable in this case. That exception applies only "in the event of

Further support could be found in another exclusion under section 9–104(h) which provides:

> This title does not apply * * * to a right represented by a judgment (other than a judgment taken on a right to payment which was collateral. * * *

The priority of a judgment lien creditor's interest in secured property clearly is governed by the various priority rules of Article 9, notwithstanding this exclusion. See, e.g., U.S.C. § 9–301(1)(b) (stating that an unperfected security interest is subordinate to the rights of a lien creditor without knowledge of the security interest and before it is perfected).

Other jurisdictions and commentators have disagreed with this interpretation of section 9–104(i), declaring instead that this provision renders inapplicable not only those portions of Article 9 governing the creation of security interests, but also the various priority provisions of that Article. See, e.g., First National Bank v. Lone Star Life Ins. Co., 529 S.W.2d 67, 68 (Tex.1975) (disapproving a lower court's holding that § 9–104(i) did not preclude application of the Article 9 priority provisions). See also Skilton, The Secured Party's Right in a Debtor's Bank Account Under Article 9 of the Uniform Commercial Code, 1977 So.Ill. U.L.J. 120, 203–04; Note, Conflicts Between a Bank's Common Law Right of Setoff and a Secured Party's Interest in Identifiable Proceeds, 9 Loyola U. of Ch.L.J. 454, 462–65 (1978).

The last cited commentator makes several persuasive arguments regarding the construction of section 9–104(i) together with various other provisions of Article 9, indicating that the Code's drafters intended the exclusion of set-off rights to be absolute.[6]

---

insolvency proceedings." The present proceedings, while occasioned by Structures' insolvency, are not insolvency proceedings, defined at section 1–201(22) of the Code, Va.Code § 8.1–201(22), as "any assignment for the benefit of creditors or other proceedings intended to liquidate or rehabilitate the estate of the person involved." See Citizens Nat. Bank v. Mid-States Develop. Co., Ind.App., 380 N.E.2d 1243, 1246 (1978).

6. Controversy over whether the exclusions enumerated in section 9–104 of the Code should be given a broad or narrow construction has not been limited to the exclusion of set-offs under subsection (8). For exam-

ple, some courts have narrowly construed exclusion of "a landlord's lien" under section 9–104(b) to mean only that such liens may be asserted without complying with Article 9, though they remain subject to the priority rules of that Article. See Peterson v. Ziegler, 39 Ill.App.3d 379, 350 N.E.2d 356(1976). Other courts have broadly construed this provision to exclude any application of Article 9 to disputes involving the formation or priority of a landlord's lien. See Bates & Springer, Inc. v. Friermood, 109 Ariz. 203, 507 P.2d 668 (1973); Jenkins v. Archer-Daniels-Midland Co., 570 S.W.2d 823 (Mo.App.1978).

Other indications as to the scope of the exclusion of rights of setoff, may be gleaned from several sources in the commentary accompanying Article 9. The first such indication is found in the Official Comment to section 9–101, the first sentence of which states:

> This Article sets out a comprehensive scheme for the regulation of *security interests* in personal property and fixtures.

As noted above, a bank's right of set-off is not a "security interest" within the meaning of Article 9, leaving one to speculate that interests in property other than security interests are beyond the scope of all portions of Article 9. See also U.C.C. § 1–201(37) (defining "security interest" as "an interest in personal property or fixtures which secures payment or performance of an obligation"). That this distinction between security interests and the interest such as that represented by rights of set-off underlies the exclusion of set-off rights from Article 9 under section 9–104(i) is confirmed by paragraph 8 of the Official Comment to section 9–104, which states:

> The remaining exclusions go to other types of claims which do not customarily serve as commercial collateral: judgments under paragraph (h), *set-offs under paragraph (i)* and tort claims under paragraph (k).

No Virginia case has been uncovered aligning that jurisdiction with either of these two schools of thought concerning the scope of section 9–104(i). Nor is any decisive interpretive guidance provided by the Virginia Comments to that provision or other portions of Article 9. It is fortunate, therefore, that this Federal Court is not called upon to resolve this ambiguity of state law in this action, for the result we would reach under either interpretation is the same: The set-off accomplished by the Bank was improper and constituted a conversion of the property of at least one of the plaintiffs, NAC. We need not go further and decide whether it also constituted a conversion of property in which Mitsubishi had a superior interest. The security interest of each of the plaintiffs in the deposit accounts exceeded the amount set-off by the Bank. In view of their October 1978, Inter-Creditor Agreement as to the distribution of certain proceeds collected by NAC in this action, and the subordination agreement previously entered into by the plaintiffs, it is sufficient to determine that NAC's interest prevails, leaving it to the plaintiffs to distribute the proceeds in accordance with their agreement.

As stated previously, NAC possessed a perfected security interest in all of the funds set-off by the Bank, while the Bank's position was that of an unsecured general creditor. If we were to follow the lead of those jurisdictions which have narrowly construed section 9–104(i) of the Code, our decision in this case would be governed by the cornerstone principle underlying the Code's complex priority scheme, stated in section 9–201:

> Except as otherwise provided by this act a security agreement is effective according to its terms between the parties, against purchasers of the collateral and against creditors.

This section states the fundamental rule that "the secured creditor, even an unperfected secured creditor, has greater rights in his collateral than any other creditor unless Article Nine provides otherwise." White & Summers, Handbook of the Law Under the Uniform Commercial Code 901 (1972). There being nothing in Article 9 providing otherwise, the Bank's unsecured interest would be subordinate to the secured interest of NAC. See Citizens Nat. Bank v. Mid-States Develop. Co., Ind.App., 380 N.E.2d 1243 (1978); Associates Discount Corp. v. Fidelity Union Trust Co., 111 N.J.Super. 353, 268 A.2d 330 (1970). Cf. Middle Atlantic Credit Corp. v. First Pennsylvania Banking & Trust Co., 199 Pa.Super. 456, 185 A.2d 818 (1962).

Alternatively, were we to conclude that section 9–104(i) precludes application of any portion of Article 9 to this controversy, we are persuaded that the Bank was sufficiently aware of NAC's interest in the deposit accounts to prohibit it from appropriating the funds from those accounts to satisfy its own claims.

At the time the deposit accounts were opened at the Bank, principals of Structures disclosed to the Bank's President, Harry Grymes, that various amounts of money would be wired into these accounts by NAC, pursuant to an accounts receivable financing arrangement. At least some aspects of this financing arrangement were conveyed to Mr. Grymes at a later meeting between he, Jack Lacy, Chief Administrative Officer of Structures, and Hyman Kanes, a former executive officer of NAC. While NAC's security interests may not have been specifically mentioned at these meetings, Mr. Grymes clearly was acquainted with the relations between NAC and Structures and the source of at least some of the funds deposited in the accounts, wired by NAC. Mr. Grymes conceded that he knew of these arrangements in his testimony.

The Bank's Cashier, Richard Wyatt, who worked closely with Mr. Grymes on the Structures' accounts and loans, testified that he knew in the early part of 1978, prior to the dates of the set-offs, that funds were being wired to Structures' accounts, and that there was a strong likelihood that these funds arose from an accounts receivable financing arrangement. Mr. Wyatt explained that he understood the mechanics of accounts receivable financing, and that he suspected that there were security agreements supporting the financing arrangement between Structures and NAC.

Notwithstanding this knowledge, Bank officials made the various loans later satisfied by set-offs without any effort to search the appropriate records to determine whether any security agreements or financing statements had been filed covering Structures' assets by NAC or any other entity. Such a search would have uncovered the interests held by both plaintiffs. Nor did it take the logical step of inquiring of Structures' officers whether any such security agreement existed and whether any interest in funds in the accounts had been conveyed to Structures' other creditors. The Bank failed even to ascertain whether its own purported security interests taken to secure payment of these loans had been properly perfected.

In short, the Bank chose to ignore evidence which would have led a reasonable man to conclude that the funds deposited in the deposit accounts were encumbered by the liens of third parties, or at least to inquire whether such interests existed. This knowledge or notice was sufficient to preclude any right of set-off it might otherwise have had and rendered its actions unlawful under Virginia commonlaw. See Peoples Nat. Bank v. Coleman, supra; Federal Reserve Bank v. State & City Bank, supra.

For these reasons, we conclude that the Bank converted property belonging to NAC when it set-off $79,327.76 from Structures' deposit accounts numbered 010–716–6 and 010–722–0 in June 1978, and that these funds must be returned to NAC. For the reasons stated previously, we need not decide whether the Bank had knowledge or notice of Mitsubishi's interest in these accounts.

* * *

NOTE

The principal case was affirmed in part and reversed in part and remanded in 662 F.2d 353 (4th Cir. 1981). The Court of Appeals decided that certain of the funds in the bank account that the District Court had treated as proceeds were not proceeds.

Chapter 3

SECURITY INTERESTS IN BANKRUPTCY

A. INTRODUCTORY NOTE

All legal or equitable interests in property that a debtor has at the time of his bankruptcy become part of the bankruptcy estate, subject to exemption laws that may allow the debtor to keep certain property free of claims of his creditors. See Bankruptcy Code § 541 and § 522. Before bankruptcy a third party may have obtained property of the debtor by a transfer from the debtor. The transfer may have been a voluntary conveyance of all of the ownership interest of the debtor, or of part of that interest, as in the case of a security interest in the property. Or, the transfer may have been involuntary as in the case of a statutory lien or in the case of a judicial lien resulting from a levy on the property. To the extent that pre-bankruptcy transfers conflict with the overriding bankruptcy policy in favor of preservation of the debtor's estate for the benefit of creditors and in favor of equal treatment of creditors, they may be invalidated by the trustee in bankruptcy even though they may have been valid under state law. These avoiding powers are set forth in Bankruptcy Code § 544(a) (transfers invalid against lien creditors and certain bona fide purchasers); § 544(b) (transfers voidable by unsecured creditors); § 545 (statutory liens); § 547 (preferential transfers); § 548 (transfers in fraud of creditors); and § 553 (setoffs).

We have previously referred to the power of the trustee in bankruptcy to invalidate a security interest that was unperfected at the date of bankruptcy. If the security interest was subordinate to the rights of a lien creditor under UCC § 9–301(1)(b) it can be invalidated by the trustee under Bankruptcy Code § 544(a).

The other principal avoiding power applicable to security interests is that pertaining to preferential transfers. A debtor who is insolvent, and therefore unable to pay all of his creditors, may prefer some of his creditors by transferring property to them while leaving others unpaid. In most cases these preferen-

270

tial transfers cannot be invalidated by unpaid creditors under state law. This reflects the state system of debt collection under which the creditor who first reaches the debtor's property gets priority with respect to that property. To carry out the policy of the bankruptcy law in favor of equal treatment of creditors who have equal claims, Bankruptcy Code § 547 provides that some preferential transfers that frustrate this bankruptcy policy can be invalidated by the trustee in bankruptcy. The five elements of a voidable preference are set forth in subsection (b) of § 547. For example, if an insolvent debtor on the eve of bankruptcy grants a security interest in his property to secure the debt of a previously unsecured creditor who is demanding payment, the security interest may be invalidated by the trustee even though it was perfected and enforceable under state law. Matter of Christian, which follows this note, illustrates how other perfected security interests that are not preferential in the normal sense may nevertheless be invalidated under § 547.

A creditor holding a security interest that cannot be avoided by the trustee in bankruptcy is guaranteed in bankruptcy the full economic value of his security interest, but his specific rights under the UCC to possess and dispose of the collateral in the event of default may be curtailed. The secured creditor has a claim in bankruptcy measured by the amount of the debt owed by the debtor. To the extent of the value of the collateral the claim is a "secured claim." If the debt is more than the value of the collateral the secured creditor has, in addition, an "unsecured claim" for this excess amount. Bankruptcy Code § 506(a). Under the UCC in the event of default the secured party is entitled to possess the collateral and to dispose of it to pay the secured debt. UCC § 9–503 and § 9–504. Although bankruptcy of the debtor is normally made an event of default in the security agreement a secured party may not repossess the collateral after bankruptcy. By virtue of Bankruptcy Code § 362 the filing of the petition in bankruptcy operates as an automatic stay against any action by creditors to enforce claims against the debtor. The collateral becomes subject to the jurisdiction of the bankruptcy court and to the control of the trustee in bankruptcy (or the debtor in possession under some bankruptcy proceedings). If the debtor has no equity in the collateral, i.e., the collateral is worth less than the debt, the secured party may be entitled to relief from the stay. In that event the collateral will be released to him and he may proceed with his remedy under UCC § 9–504. But even if the debtor has no equity, in many cases relief from the stay will be denied if the bankruptcy proceeding is a reorganization under Chapter 11 or Chapter 13 of the Bankruptcy Code and the collateral is necessary to carry out the reorganization. If relief is denied the secured party files a secured claim in bankruptcy. But relief can be denied only if the secured party is "adequately protected" which means in most cases that payment to him on his secured claim will equal the present value of the claim and that this payment will be secured by preservation of the security interest. Bankruptcy Code § 361.

If the secured party has repossessed the collateral before bankruptcy but has not yet disposed of it under UCC § 9–504 he is subject to the automatic stay. In order to proceed with disposition of the collateral he must ask the bankruptcy court for relief from the stay as stated above. If it is not granted because the estate has equity in the collateral or if the collateral is necessary to a reorganization the secured party must deliver the collateral to the trustee and file a secured claim. Bankruptcy Code § 542.

Bankruptcy Code § 547 is as follows:

§ 547. Preferences.

(a) In this section—

(1) "inventory" means personal property leased or furnished, held for sale or lease, or to be furnished under a contract for service, raw materials, work in process, or materials used or consumed in a business, including farm products such as crops or livestock, held for sale or lease;

(2) "new value" means money or money's worth in goods, services, or new credit, or release by a transferee of property previously transferred to such transferee in a transaction that is neither void nor voidable by the debtor or the trustee including proceeds of such property, under any applicable law, but does not include an obligation substituted for an existing obligation;

(3) "receivable" means right to payment, whether or not such right has been earned by performance; and

(4) a debt for a tax is incurred on the day when such tax is last payable without penalty, including any extension, without penalty.

(b) Except as provided in subsection (c) of this section, the trustee may avoid any transfer of property of the debtor— an interest of the debtor in property

(1) to or for the benefit of a creditor;

(2) for or on account of an antecedent debt owed by the debtor before such transfer was made;

[handwritten margin note: liabilities exceed assets]

(3) made while the debtor was insolvent;

(4) made—

(A) on or within 90 days before the date of the filing of the petition; or

(B) between 90 *[handwritten: ninety]* days and one year before the date of the filing of the petition, if such creditor, at the time of such transfer— *[handwritten: was an insider;]*

(i) was an insider; and

(ii) had reasonable cause to believe the debtor was insolvent at the time of such transfer; and

(5) that enables such creditor to receive more than such creditor would receive if—

(A) the case were a case under chapter 7 of this title;

(B) the transfer had not been made; and

(C) such creditor received payment of such debt to the extent provided by the provisions of this title.

(c) The trustee may not avoid under this section a transfer—

(1) to the extent that such transfer was—

(A) intended by the debtor and the creditor to or for whose benefit such transfer was made to be a contemporaneous exchange for new value given to the debtor; and

(B) in fact a substantially contemporaneous exchange;

(2) to the extent that such transfer was— *[handwritten: by the debtor]*

(A) in payment of a debt incurred, in the ordinary course of business or financial affairs of the debtor and the transferee;

(B) made not later than 45 days after such debt was incurred;

[handwritten: (B)] (C) made in the ordinary course of business or financial affairs of the debtor and the transferee; and

[handwritten: (C)] (D) made according to ordinary business terms;

(3) *[handwritten: that creates]* of a security interest in property acquired by the debtor—

(A) to the extent such security interest secures new value that was—

(i) given at or after the signing of a security agreement that contains a description of such property as collateral;

(ii) given by or on behalf of the secured party under such agreement;

(iii) given to enable the debtor to acquire such property; and

(iv) in fact used by the debtor to acquire such property; and

(B) that is perfected ~~on or~~ before 10 days after *receives possession of such property* ~~such security interest attaches;~~ *the debtor*

(4) to or for the benefit of a creditor, to the extent that, after such transfer, such creditor gave new value to or for the benefit of the debtor—

(A) not secured by an otherwise unavoidable security interest; and

(B) on account of which new value the debtor did not make an otherwise unavoidable transfer to or for the benefit of such creditor;

(5) of *that creates* a perfected security interest in inventory or a receivable or the proceeds of either, except to the extent that the aggregate of all such transfers to the transferee caused a reduction, as of the date of the filing of the petition and to the prejudice of other creditors holding unsecured claims, of any amount by which the debt secured by such security interest exceeded the value of all security interests for such debt on the later of—

(A)(i) with respect to a transfer to which subsection (b)(4)(A) of this section applies, 90 days before the date of the filing of the petition; or

(ii) with respect to a transfer to which subsection (b)(4)(B) of this section applies, one year before the date of the filing of the petition; ~~and~~ or

(B) the date on which new value was first given under the security agreement creating such security interest; ~~or~~

(6) that is the fixing of a statutory lien that is not avoidable under section 545 of this title; or

¶(7)

(d) ~~A~~ *The* trustee may avoid a transfer of *an interest in* property of the debtor transferred to *or for the benefit of a surety to* secure reimbursement of ~~a~~ *such* surety that furnished a bond or other obligation to dissolve a judicial lien that would have been avoidable by the trustee under subsection (b) of this section. The liability of such surety under such bond or obligation shall be discharged to the extent of

if in a case filed by an individual debtor whose debts are primarily consumer debts, the aggregate value of all property that constitutes or is affected by such transfer is ~~less~~ less than $600

the value of such property recovered by the trustee or the amount paid to the trustee.

(e)(1) For the purposes of this section—

(A) a transfer of real property other than fixtures, but including the interest of a seller or purchaser under a contract for the sale of real property, is perfected when a bona fide purchaser of such property from the debtor against whom applicable law permits such transfer to be perfected cannot acquire an interest that is superior to the interest of the transferee; and

(B) a transfer of a fixture or property other than real property is perfected when a creditor on a simple contract cannot acquire a judicial lien that is superior to the interest of the transferee.

(2) For the purposes of this section, except as provided in paragraph (3) of this subsection, a transfer is made—

(A) at the time such transfer takes effect between the transferor and the transferee, if such transfer is perfected at, or within 10 days after, such time;

(B) at the time such transfer is perfected, if such transfer is perfected after such 10 days; or

(C) immediately before the date of the filing of the petition, if such transfer is not perfected at the later of—

(i) the commencement of the case; and or

(ii) 10 days after such transfer takes effect between the transferor and the transferee.

(3) For the purposes of this section, a transfer is not made until the debtor has acquired rights in the property transferred.

(f) For the purposes of this section, the debtor is presumed to have been insolvent on and during the 90 days immediately preceding the date of the filing of the petition.

(g) For the purposes of this section, the trustee has the burden of proving the avoidability of a transfer under subsection (b) of this section, and the creditor or party in interest against whom recovery or avoidance is sought has the burden of proving nonavoidability of a transfer under subsection (c) of this section.

B. DELAYED PERFECTION

MATTER OF CHRISTIAN

United States Bankruptcy Court, M.D.Florida, 1981.
8 B.R. 816.

ALEXANDER L. PASKAY, CHIEF BANKRUPTCY JUDGE. The matter under consideration involves the validity, vel non, of a lien claim by the Exchange Bank of Polk County (the Bank), a lien which encumbers a 1980 Ford 2 door Sedan. Exchange Bank instituted an adversary proceeding and sought a recovery of the vehicle in question in order to enforce its lien claim. The trustee in turn filed a counterclaim and sought to invalidate the lien on the ground that it was a voidable preference, and as such was invalid and not enforceable against the estate. By agreement of the parties, the vehicle was sold with the understanding that if the lien was found to be valid the same will be satisfied out of the proceeds of the sale. Both the plaintiff and defendant agree that there are no genuine issues of material facts and the court should determine the respective rights of the parties and resolve this controversy as a matter of law.

The undisputed facts germane to this controversy may be summarized as follows:

On February 18, 1980, Donald Gene Christian (Christian), the debtor involved in the above-captioned liquidating proceeding, purchased a 1980 Ford 2 door Sedan from Dexter Daniels Ford (Dealer). Christian applied for and obtained a loan to finance the purchase from Exchange Bank and executed a Security Agreement Retail Installment Contract which was assigned by the Dealer to the Bank. On February 19, 1980, the Dealer took the necessary documentation of this financed purchase to Frierson Nichols Post # 8 in Winter Haven Legion Tag Agency (the Tag Agency). The Tag Agency recorded the documentation on a form entitled "Department of Motor Vehicle Report Form 101–10SPT" and forwarded the same to the Polk County Tax Collector. The Tax Collector prepared an application for Certificate of Title and forwarded the same to the Department of Highway Safety and Motor Vehicle (the DMV) located in Tallahassee, Florida.

The application for title certificate together with the lien documents were received by the DMV on March 4, 1980, and the certificate of title on the subject vehicle, which was issued on

March 20, 1980, had a properly noted lien indicating the Bank to be the holder of the lien.

The DMV has its own offices which process both normal applications for certificates of title and lien recordation on title certificates and also an office which provides an expedited service for an extra charge. One can obtain a lien recordation and the issuance of a title certificate on motor vehicles within 72 hours from the time the request is made either in person or by mail. Fla.Stat. 319.27(2) and 319.323 (1979).

In Florida, security interests in automobiles are expressly excluded from the operation of the Uniform Commercial Code and liens on motor vehicles are perfected by a notation on the title certificate, F.S. § 319.27(2) (1979), which is issued by the DMV pursuant to Fla.Stat. Chap. 319 (1979). There is no doubt that by virtue of § 547(e)(2)(B) of the Bankruptcy Code, if perfection occurs more than ten days after the attachment of the security interest, the transfer is deemed to have occurred on the date of perfection, a point conceded by the Bank. It is the position of the Bank, however, that by taking the lien documentation to the Tag Agency, it followed the commercially accepted method to perfect its lien, a method expressly authorized by Statute. Thus, according to the Bank, the lien cannot possibly be a preference. In this connection the Bank points out that Fla.Stat. § 319.08 (1979) permits the DMV to employ all necessary personnel to enforce all provisions pertaining to the registration, certification, or sale and distribution of a motor vehicle in this State. Thus, according to the Bank, the Tag Agency to whom the Bank delivered the application for a title certificate together with the lien documentation, was an agent or sub-agent of the DMV, thus, filing the papers with the Tag Agency was tantamount to filing the same with the DMV in Tallahassee and it is immaterial when the application was filed or when the actual title certificate was issued by the DMV in Tallahassee.

Although there is evidence of a contractual relationship between the Tag Agency and the Tax Collector, there is no evidence in this record and this Court is satisfied that an agency relationship did not exist between the Tag Agency and DMV. The Tag Agency was an independent contractor charged with limited responsibilities such as processing applications for title certificates for motor vehicles, but these responsibilities did not include the power to record liens or issue title certificates.

It is conceded by the Bank that all of the operating elements of a voidable preference of § 547(b) of the Bankruptcy Code have been established, including the requirement that the lien was technically granted to secure an antecedent debt. Therefore, the Bank's lien cannot be saved as a non-voidable preference unless this transaction comes within any of the savings provisions of § 547(c).

This subsection of the Code, § 547(c), contains specific exceptions to the avoiding power granted to the trustee under § 547(b) and if a creditor can qualify under any one of the exceptions, the creditor is protected to that extent and if he can qualify under several, he is protected by each to the extent he can qualify under each. House Report No. 95–595, 95th Cong., 1st Sess. 373–374 (1977), U.S.Code Cong. & Admin.News 1978, 5787. The provisions dealing with the granting of security interests are set forth in § 547(c)(3).

* * *

This exception to the trustee's voiding power was designed to protect certain enabling loans that is, loans made to a debtor for a purpose of enabling the debtor to acquire property. There is no question that if the transaction under consideration qualified under this exception, it would be protected as an enabling loan. The difficulty is, however, that this Section gives a limited ten-day grace period to perfect a lien and the record reveals that Christian acquired the automobile on February 18, the lien was not perfected by filing the lien documentation with the Tag Agency, but was perfected at the earliest on March 4, thus, after the ten-day grace period had expired. See Bank of Hawthorne v. Shepherd, 330 So.2d 75 (Fla. 1st DCA 1976). Accordingly, this Sub-clause furnishes no solace to the Bank and the Bank's lien is not immunized from the Trustee's attack under § 547 as a preferential transfer.

The Bank also intimated a proposition, not very well articulated, that this was intended to be a contemporaneous transaction and was, in fact, a contemporaneous transaction. Thus, the transaction would appear to fall within the savings proviso of § 547(c)(1)(A), (B). Section 547(c)(3), however, contains the only specific provision, as noted above, dealing with a security interest granted in connection with an enabling loan. Thus, the first exception to the Trustee's voiding power set forth in § 547(c)(1)(A), (B) dealing with contemporaneous transactions is not applicable to situations involving security interests. If the provisions set forth in § 547(c)(1)(A), (B) were applicable to an enabling loan, the enabling loan provisions of § 547(c)(3)(A), (B) which specifically deal with security interests granted by the Debtor in exchange for new value would be obviously redundant and un-necessary. In fact, the legislative history indicates that the first exception set forth in § 547(c)(1)(A), (B) was designed to protect so-called cash transactions where a transfer involved a payment by check which is intended to be a transfer for a contemporane-ous transfer for value and not a credit transaction. Even as-suming, but not admitting, that the contemporaneous transac-tion exception is an additional exception to the Trustee's voiding power, this Court is satisfied that while the transaction was clearly intended to be contemporaneous, in fact, it was not. This is so especially in light of the fact that the Bank could have re-sorted to the expedited procedure, F.S. § 319.323 (1979), and ob-tained a recorded lien on the title certificate within 72 hours. See, In re Kelley, 3 B.R. 651, 2 C.B.C.2d 15 (Bkrtcy.E.D.Tenn. 1980).

Having concluded that all operating elements of a voidable preference transfer required by § 547(b) of the Code are pre-sent, and none of the savings provisos set forth in § 547(c) would immunize this transfer from attack as a preference, the Trustee is entitled to a final judgment invalidating the Bank lien provided, however, that the Bank is entitled to prove a general unsecured claim for the amount owed to it by the Debtor.

A separate final judgment will be entered in accordance with the foregoing.

NOTES

1. It is clear in *Christian* that, under the UCC and under bankruptcy law other than § 547, there was no transfer of prop-erty of the debtor on account of an antecedent debt. The prop-erty at issue was the security interest granted to the dealer and transferred to the bank. Under the UCC it attached, and under Bankruptcy Code § 101(40) it was transferred, at exactly the same time that the debt arose. § 547(e)(2)(B), which artificially defines transfer in terms of perfection rather than attachment, has the effect of turning what was in fact a contemporaneous exchange into a transfer for an antecedent debt. Thus, the evil addressed by that provision is not a problem of preferences but a problem of secret liens. There has long been a bankruptcy policy against secured creditors who may mislead unsecured creditors of the debtor by keeping their secured status secret by not making any public record of it until shortly before bankrupt-cy when the debtor's financial position has deteriorated. This

history is summarized in In re Burnette, 14 B.R. 795 (Bkrtcy. Tenn.1981), as follows:

> The predecessor to the present statute was § 60 of the Bankruptcy Act of 1898. The original § 60 did not make it clear whether a transfer that had to be recorded to be effective against some creditors was to be treated as made when made or when recorded. In 1903 Congress amended § 60 to make the date of recording the time of the transfer. Congress's effort was less than successful. It amended § 60 several more times before 1938. * * * Finally, in 1938 Congress found the right track.
>
>> The fumbling of previous legislative enactments proved that drastic and incisive action was needed. Moreover, it must be borne in mind at all times that throughout a period of thirty-five years, beginning in 1903, it was fairly evident that Congress intended to strike down secret transactions by establishing a test as to perfection of transfer that would fix the date of notoriety of the transfer as the time when its preferential character should be determined. It was only the expression of this intent that proved faulty.
>
> 3 Collier on Bankrupty ¶ 60.38 at 941–942 (14th ed. 1964).
>
> The 1938 amendment adopted a perfection test to determine the time of transfer. Perfection occurred when a bona fide purchaser from the debtor or a creditor could not acquire rights superior to the transferee. Unfortunately, the bona fide purchaser test was too stringent. Some transfers were avoided that should have been protected. 3 Collier on Bankruptcy ¶ 60.38 at 943–946 (14th ed. 1964). To cure the problem, Congress once again amended § 60.
>
> The amendment is the forerunner to the present definition of perfection.

Under this 1950 amendment a transfer of personal property was deemed to have been made when it became so far perfected that no subsequent judicial lien on that property could become superior to the rights of the transferee. § 60a(2). But there was an exception to this rule, § 60a(7). If the state law provided for prior perfection by filing or possession in order to defeat a judicial lien, § 60a(7) gave the transferee a grace period of not more than 21 days to perform the perfecting act. If action was taken within the grace period the transfer was deemed to have taken place not at the date of perfection but at the date of the actual transfer. If the state law also provided for a grace period that period controlled if it was less than 21 days. Thus, the length of the grace period varied according to state law.

The court in *Burnette* continues its summary of the legislative history of § 547 as follows:

> In 1966 the National Bankruptcy Conference established the "Committee on the Coordination of the Bankruptcy Act and the Uniform Commercial Code", more commonly known as the Gilmore Committee, after its chairman, Professor Grant Gilmore. In 1970 the committee recommended to Congress that § 60 be amended so that, without regard to grace periods under state law, § 60 would determine when late perfection made the transfer for an antecedent debt.

> > [P]resent § 60 was * * * written in [pre-UCC] terminology, which leads to difficult, indeed logically insoluble, problems of statutory construction in applying the § 60 rules to Article 9 security interests. For example, § 60a(7) deals with the problem of late filing of security interests subject to a filing perfection requirement. The Article 9 filing system is quite different from the filing systems set up under the [pre-UCC] security statutes. For one thing, there is no grace period for filing under Article 9, except for purchase money security interests which get a 10-day grace period. Present § 60a(7) clearly assumes that all filing statutes have grace periods for all required filings. Consequently no one really knows what § 60a(7) means when it is applied to Article 9 filings and, indeed, the commentators * * * have proposed divergent and contradictory solutions. * * *

> > > * * *

> The only change of substance from present § 60a(7) to Draft § 60a(2) is that the Draft allows a flat 21-day period for perfection, running from the time the "transfer" (security interest) "became effective between the parties," without any provision for cutting back the 21-day grace period if an applicable filing statute uses a shorter period.

> Under Article 9 no grace period for filing is provided except for filing with respect to purchase money security interests; under § 9–301(2) a purchase money secured party [who] files within 10 days after the collateral comes into the debtor's possession takes priority over intervening lien creditors * * *

The Committee concluded that the sanctions which Article 9 itself imposes on delayed perfection are such that no additional sanctions need be imposed through § 60. * * * While there may be no compelling reason in logic or policy for carrying forward the 21-day period * * * that period has become familiar to the bar and is retained.

* * * The Committee has seen no reason to complicate the statute by going into refined distinctions. Any kind of transferee gets 21 days * * * If he delays more than 21 days, the late perfection is treated as a transfer for an antecedent debt.

Reprinted in H.R.Rep.No.95–595, 95th Cong., 1st Sess. 209, 212–213 (1977); Collier on Bankruptcy, Appendix 2 (15th ed. 1979).

The committee's recommendation was adopted by the Commission on Bankruptcy Laws of the United States, except the grace period was changed from twenty-one days to ten days. The commission recommended statutory language essentially like the language of the present statute.

* * *

Report of the Commission on Bankruptcy Laws of the United States, H.R.Doc.No.93–137, 93d Cong., 1st Sess., Part II § 4–607 at 168–175 (1973); Collier on Bankruptcy, Appendix 2 (15th ed. 1979).

The court believes that Congress intended to follow the recommendations of the Gilmore Committee and the Bankruptcy Commission. One commentator has said:

The earlier ten-day reference period provides a specific grace period, unlike Bankruptcy Act § 60(a)(7)(I), which provides for a variable grace period of up to twenty-one days. Consequently, greater uniformity and less reliance on state laws are achieved under the Code * * *.

C. Young, Preferences under the Bankruptcy Reform Act of 1978, 54 Am.Bankr.L.J. 221, 231 (1980).

* * *

It is evident that Congress did not intend for state grace periods to be relevant under the preference statute. There was to be a uniform rule throughout the nation. In any jurisdiction, a transferee was to have only ten days to perfect a transfer and thereby avoid the antecedent debt problem. Ten days was picked apparently because it corresponded to state law, but Congress did not specifically refer to grace periods under state law. * * *

2. Professor Robert Morris made the following comment on § 60 of the Bankruptcy Act of 1898:

Students in my bankruptcy course do not readily understand the status of unperfected transfers in bankruptcy. Until it is spelled out for them, they do not understand that a mortgage given at the time of the secured debt and which would not be a preference if seasonably recorded becomes a preference if it is withheld from record or is recorded too late and less than four months before the mortgagor's petition in bankruptcy. I have always enjoyed teaching this subject because here was clearly a teaching task which I could accomplish. I could show them how, under section 60 of the Bankruptcy Act, such a transaction is voidable as a preference.

I have come to the conclusion, however, that my students' initial intuition is correct. The law is wrong. Such a transaction is not factually a preference and the law of preferences is not the appropriate vehicle for handling secret liens in bankruptcy. The fiction whereby section 60 transforms secret liens into preferences has long been a source of mischief. This mischief could be abated by a new provision directed at the avoidance of secret transfers and by the rewriting of section 60 so that it governs only preferences in fact.

Reprinted with permission from Morris, Bankruptcy Law Reform: Preferences, Secret Liens and Floating Liens, 54 Minn.L. Rev. 737 (1970).

3. In *Christian* the lawyer for the bank conceded that the factually contemporaneous exchange in the case was by virtue of § 547(e)(2)(B) a transfer for an antecedent debt. He then found himself in the rather bizarre position of having to argue that this artificially created preference was by virtue of § 547(c) (1) not voidable because in fact it was a contemporaneous exchange. The court allowed that "the transaction would appear to fall within [this] proviso" but then stated that it was not meant to apply to security interests. The same argument made by the bank has been made in other cases with Alice-in-Wonderland results. In In re Hall, 14 B.R. 186 (Bkrtcy.Fla.1981), the judge noted his agreement with In re Kelley, 3 B.R. 651 (Bkrtcy. Tenn.1980), in which it was held that perfection after 60 days was not a "substantially contemporaneous exchange" under § 547(c)(1), and he went on to state that he "would have difficulty with any interval over 45 days." In In re Arnett, 17 B.R. 912

(E.D.Tenn.1982), we find the following: "This Court is of the opinion that as a matter of law any security interest perfected in the ten day grace period will be treated as being 'in fact substantially contemporaneous' while it will be a question of fact as to whether any transaction extending beyond those limits is 'in fact substantially contemporaneous.'" The court then accepted a delay of 33 days in perfection because the secured party acted reasonably.

PROBLEMS

1. On April 1 Bank loaned $10,000 to D by crediting that amount to D's checking account. The loan agreement signed on that day provided that the loan was to be used to buy described equipment in which D granted a security interest to Bank. Bank filed a financing statement covering equipment of D on April 1. On April 7 D bought the equipment described in the loan agreement. On June 20 D filed a petition in bankruptcy. Under § 547(e)(2) and (3) when did the transfer occur? If D was insolvent on April 1 and at all times thereafter can Bank's security interest be avoided under § 547(b)? Can the security interest be saved by § 547(c)(1)? Can it be saved by § 547(c)(3)? Compare UCC § 9–107. Would your answers be different if D had acquired the equipment on April 12?

2. On April 1 D, while in New York, called Bank which is located in Los Angeles and requested an immediate emergency loan. On that day Bank wired $10,000 to D in New York on the understanding that D, on his return to Los Angeles, would sign a security agreement granting Bank a security interest in collateral owned by D and located in Los Angeles. On April 4, when D returned to Los Angeles, he signed a security agreement granting a security interest in the collateral to Bank. The same day Bank filed a financing statement covering the collateral. On June 20 D filed a petition in bankruptcy. If D was insolvent on April 1 and at all times thereafter can Bank's security interest be avoided under § 547(b)?

3. Bank made a one-year loan of $10,000 to Debtor on September 1, 1981 and to secure the loan Debtor granted Bank a security interest in equipment owned by Debtor. Bank promptly perfected by filing a financing statement. On September 1, 1982 Debtor paid Bank $10,000 plus interest in discharge of the debt. Bank filed a termination statement under UCC § 9–404. Debtor filed a petition in bankruptcy on November 1, 1982. Debtor was insolvent on September 1, 1982 and at all times

thereafter. Was the payment to Bank on September 1, 1982 a transfer on account of an antecedent debt? Can the transfer be avoided by the trustee in bankruptcy under § 547(b)? Assume that the value of the equipment was greater than the payment made to Bank and that there were no other security interests or liens in the equipment superior to the security interest of Bank. Would the outcome of the case be different if Bank had been undersecured at the time it received payment from Debtor?

4. Debtor bought and took possession of a truck on November 14, 1980. At the same time Debtor granted a security interest in the truck to the seller to secure payment of the price. The seller immediately assigned the security interest to Bank. On December 4, 1980, twenty days later, Bank perfected the security interest in the truck. The transaction occurred in Tennessee where UCC § 9–301(2) reads as follows: "If the secured party files with respect to a purchase money security interest before or within twenty (20) days after the collateral comes into the possession of the debtor, he takes priority over the rights of * * * a lien creditor which arise between the time the security interest attaches and the time of filing." On February 11, 1981 Debtor filed a petition in bankruptcy. Assume that on November 14 and at all times thereafter Debtor was insolvent. Can Bank's security interest be avoided under § 547(b)? When was the security interest perfected under the UCC? See UCC § 9–303. Bank argued that under § 547(e)(1)(B) its security interest was perfected on November 14. What is the basis of that argument? Should a court accept that argument? See In re Burnette, 14 B.R. 795 (Bkrtcy.Tenn.1981). Compare the interpretation of the phrase "so far perfected" in former § 60a(2) made by the court in *Grain Merchants*, the case that follows.

C. THE FLOATING LIEN

Grain Merchants, set forth below, was decided under § 60 of the Bankruptcy Act of 1898. The theories enunciated in this case played an important part in the drafting of § 547 of the Bankruptcy Code. Particular attention should be paid to § 547(e)(3) which reverses one conclusion of Judge Cummings' analysis and § 547(c)(5) which adopts another part of that analysis.

GRAIN MERCHANTS OF INDIANA, INC. v. UNION
BANK & SAVINGS CO.

United States Court of Appeals, Seventh Circuit, 1969.
408 F.2d 209.

CUMMINGS, CIRCUIT JUDGE. In September 1965, Grain Merchants of Indiana, Inc. commenced its business of buying and selling grain and feed ingredients. On the 17th of that month, Grain Merchants entered into a security agreement with Union Bank and Savings Company of Bellevue, Ohio. Pursuant to Section 9–302 of the Uniform Commercial Code appropriate financing statements were filed in the office of the Indiana Secretary of State and of the Allen County, Indiana, Recorder that same month. The security agreement granted the Bank a security interest in all of Grain Merchants' accounts receivable "now or hereafter received by or belonging to Borrower [Grain Merchants] for goods sold by it or for services rendered by it." This security interest was to secure loans to be made by the Bank to Grain Merchants, but the loans were not to exceed 60 per cent of the total of said accounts receivable which were not more than 60 days old.

During the October 1965—September 1966 period that the Bank was lending working capital to Grain Merchants, on or about the 20th day of each month Grain Merchants submitted to the Bank a financial statement as of the end of the previous month, a list of all accounts receivable, and a promissory note in the sum of 60 per cent of the outstanding accounts receivable as of the last day of the previous month. As the proceeds of accounts receivable were collected by Grain Merchants, they were deposited in an account with the Bank, and, prior to October 3, 1966, Grain Merchants was permitted to draw on this account in order to satisfy its day-to-day expenses of doing business.

For the purposes of this case, three promissory notes executed by Grain Merchants in the Bank's favor are pertinent. Two notes in the amounts of $30,000 and $20,000 were executed in December 1965, and a $100,000 note was executed on September 20, 1966. Upon receipt of this last note, the Bank cancelled a note for a like amount which had been executed by Grain Merchants the previous month. All parties concede that the cancellation of this August note on September 20 constituted the last formal extension of new value to Grain Merchants.

On September 30, 1966, Grain Merchants, which had become insolvent in June of that year, ceased doing business. On October 27, 1966, it filed its petition in bankruptcy.

On October 3, the Bank took various steps to apply assets in the hands of Grain Merchants toward payment of the $152,255.55 balance, including interest, owed on these three notes. Out of an October 3 deposit by Grain Merchants with the Bank, $13,575.53 appropriated by the Bank represented collections on accounts receivable which came into existence after September 20, 1966. On October 3, Grain Merchants turned over to the Bank its then outstanding uncollected accounts receivable. The Bank then proceeded to collect these accounts, and $38,865.96 of these collections were on accounts receivable which arose after September 20, 1966.

In Grain Merchants' bankruptcy proceedings, the referee ordered the Bank to turn over to the bankruptcy trustee the aforesaid amounts totaling $52,441.49, less $7,116.52, which represents an excess over the total indebtedness to the Bank and is in escrow. Therefore, the present proceeding involves $45,324.97.

The bankruptcy referee held that the transfer of accounts receivable to the Bank took place at the time that the individual accounts came into existence and that therefore the transfer of accounts receivable post September 20, 1966, were transfers on account of an antecedent debt. He concluded that the transfers of such accounts receivable constituted preferences within Section 60a of the Bankruptcy Act (11 U.S.C. § 96(a)). He also concluded that at the time of the transfers of such accounts the Bank had reasonable cause to believe that Grain Merchants was insolvent, so that the preferences were voidable under Section 60b of the Bankruptcy Act (11 U.S.C. § 96(b)). The district court set aside the referee's turnover order, holding that the transfers to the Bank of these accounts receivable did not constitute a preference. The facts are set out in more detail in Judge Eschbach's thorough opinion, reported at 286 F.Supp. 597 (N.D. Ind.1968).

The Transfer Occurred a Year Before Bankruptcy.

The Bankruptcy Act permits a bankruptcy trustee to avoid a "preference," as defined in the Act, if the creditor had reasonable cause to believe that the debtor was insolvent at the time of the transfer (Section 60b; 11 U.S.C. § 96(b)). The referee found that the Bank had such cause, and the district court did not dispute this finding. The bankruptcy referee held that there was a "preference" on the ground that there had been a transfer of property of Grain Merchants to the Bank within four months before the filing of the bankruptcy petition, on account of an antecedent debt (Section 60a(1); 11 U.S.C. § 96(a)(1)).[3] In its contrary holding that there had been no such transfer, the district court relied on Section 60a(2) of the Bankruptcy Act providing that a transfer of property is deemed to have been made "when it became *so far perfected* that no subsequent lien upon such property obtainable by legal or equitable proceedings on a simple contract could become superior to the rights of the transferee" (11 U.S.C. § 96(a)(2); emphasis supplied). This is, in the first instance, a question of priorities between creditors rather than a question of complete perfection in the abstract. The district court concluded that Grain Merchants' transfer to the Bank of the security interest in the post September 20, 1966, accounts receivable was "so far perfected" when the financing statements were filed in September 1965 that it must be deemed to have been made then by virtue of Section 60a(2). Therefore, there was no transfer within four months of filing the bankruptcy petition and consequently no preference within Section 60a(1) of the Act.

The agreement between Grain Merchants and the Bank was executed on September 17, 1965, and granted the Bank "a security interest" in all of Grain Merchants' accounts receivable "now or hereafter received." The parties thus intended to accomplish a transfer to the Bank of a security interest in Grain Merchants' present and future accounts receivable. In conformity with Section 9–302 of the Commercial Code, appropriate financing statements were duly filed later that month.

Reference to state law is necessary to determine whether a secured creditor has "so far perfected" his lien as to cut off the rights of a subsequent lien creditor under Section 60a(2) of the Bankruptcy Act. McKenzie v. Irving Trust Co., 323 U.S. 365, 370, 65 S.Ct. 405, 89 L.Ed. 305; Matthews v. James Talcott, Inc., 345 F.2d 374 (7th Cir. 1965), certiorari denied, 382 U.S. 837, 86 S.Ct. 84, 15 L.Ed.2d 79. Since the Uniform Commercial Code was in effect in Indiana at the time of this transaction, this ques-

---

3. Section 60a(1) defines a preference as follows:

"A preference is a transfer, as defined in this Act, of any of the property of a debtor to or for the benefit of a creditor for or on account of an antecedent debt, made or suffered by such debtor while insolvent and within four months before the filing by or against him of the petition initiating a proceeding under this Act, the effect of which transfer will be to enable such creditor to obtain a greater percentage of his debt than some other creditor of the same class."

tion must be answered by reference thereto. Section 9–204(3) of the Commercial Code validates a floating lien by providing that "a security agreement may [as here] provide that collateral, *whenever acquired,* shall secure all obligations covered by the security agreement" (emphasis supplied). This Section obviously permits a security agreement to create a lien in after-acquired accounts receivable.

Under Section 9–301(1)(d) of the Code, the Bank's unperfected security interest in the future accounts receivable would be subordinate to the rights of "a person [lien creditor] who is not a secured party and who is a transferee to the extent that he gives value without knowledge of the security interest and *before it is perfected*" (emphasis supplied). A lien creditor is defined in Section 9–301(3) as "a creditor [including a bankruptcy trustee] who has acquired a lien on the property involved by attachment, levy or the like * * * ." Thus we are presented with a situation where as soon as an account receivable comes into existence and is sought to be attached by a lien creditor, it has already become subject to a perfected security interest—here that of the Bank.[4] The very occurrence which gives rise to the full perfection of the security interest prevents the subsequent lien creditor from obtaining a priority as to the property. Although the Code does not explicitly resolve this problem, we are persuaded by virtue of Section 9–301(1)(d), taken in conjunction with Section 9–204(3), that a secured creditor who has duly filed a financing statement covering after-acquired collateral is entitled to priority over a subsequent lien creditor seeking to levy on the same property. Thus by promptly filing the financing statements required by the Code, the Bank's security interest in the future accounts receivable then became superior to subsequent liens obtainable by "proceedings on a simple contract" as prescribed in Section 60a(2) of the Bankruptcy Act.

Our conclusion that this transfer occurred in September 1965 is consistent with the purposes of the Bankruptcy Act. A bankruptcy trustee is meant to take the assets subject to all liens conferred by state law, except where necessary to avoid preferences or fraudulent transfers. 2 U.S.Code Cong. Service, 81st Cong., 2d Sess. p. 1986 (1950). To implement the first exception, Section 60 of the Bankruptcy Act permits a trustee in bankruptcy to treat "preferences" as voidable. However, under the pref-

---

4. The Bank's security interest in the accounts receivable was fully perfected when it attached, and it attached when the Bank had rights in the collateral, which was when the accounts receivable came into existence. See Sections 9–303(1), 9–204(1) and 9–204(2)(d) of the Commercial Code.

erence Section as it existed prior to 1938, a series of cases sustained transfers of security interests attacked as preferences so long as the agreement bound the debtor prior to the 4-month period, even though the interest was unrecorded or non-possessory until the creditor sought to perfect his right on the eve of bankruptcy. The tardy recordation or seizure of the collateral was said to "relate back" to the date of the original security agreement under state law as incorporated by reference in Section 60. See 286 F.Supp. at 603.

But the significance of these cases was not limited entirely to the evil of the secret lien. Even in cases where a security interest was duly recorded, if under state law taking possession of the collateral was required for perfection, as was the case for after-acquired accounts in so-called Massachusetts rule states, the courts relied on the doctrine of relation back to determine whether the trustee in bankruptcy could avoid security interests perfected just prior to bankruptcy. See Thompson v. Fairbanks, 196 U.S. 516, 25 S.Ct. 306, 49 L.Ed. 577. This suggests that the real basis for decision in these cases was not that state law provided no protection against secret liens but that even though creditors without knowledge could obtain a priority over the unperfected security interest by attaching the property prior to perfection, as a matter of federal law the trustee was not in the position of a prior attaching lien creditor. See, e.g., Sexton v. Kessler & Co., 225 U.S. 90, 97, 32 S.Ct. 657, 56 L.Ed. 995. The trustee's rights were said to attach as of the filing of the petition, and the doctrine of relation back was relied on for the proposition that as to one not standing in the position of an attaching lien creditor, the operative event was the creation of rights between the parties which took place before the 4-month period. See Bailey v. Baker Ice Mach. Co., 239 U.S. 268, 275–276, 36 S.Ct. 50, 60 L.Ed. 275. The Act was not interpreted to specify the moment of perfection as the point at which a transfer took place.

That this was the problem Congress intended to remedy is supported by the fact that the revision of Section 60 in 1938 did not take the form of withdrawal of the reference to state law or the super-imposition of federal standards as to recordation or perfection. Instead the revisers merely delayed the effectiveness of a transfer to the point at which it became effective against bona fide purchasers and creditors under state law and placed the trustee in the position to exercise the rights of those parties under state law as to transfers taking place within the 4-month pre-filing period. See H.R.Rep. No. 1409, 75th Cong., 1st

Sess. 30 (1937). There is nothing in the legislative history which suggests that Congress intended to cast doubt on the method of financing by means of a rotating stock of accounts receivable. Indeed, the 1950 legislative repeal of Corn Exchange Nat'l Bank & Trust Co. v. Klauder, 318 U.S. 434, 63 S.Ct. 679, 84 L.Ed. 884, suggests that Congress was aware of the importance of accounts receivable financing and approved its utility where the unsecured creditors of the bankrupt had record notice of the existence of such a financing agreement. In recommending the further amendment of Section 60 to restrict the bona fide purchaser test to real property transactions, the House Committee made the following observations:

> "The present language of the act tends to impede and choke the flow of credit, principally to small-business men, and the object of the bill is to free its channels.

*   *   *

> "In 1938 the Bankruptcy Act was amended to obviate the effect of these cases,[7] which were regarded with disfavor by the great majority. But, in so doing, the authors of the amendment went further than was necessary, and it brought about results which they did not anticipate. The amendment placed the trustee in the position of an artificial potential bona fide purchaser, and, by so doing, unintentionally invalidated many types of liens acquired in good faith and for value, in normal and accepted business and financial relationships." (2 U.S.Code Cong. Serv., 81st Cong., 2d Sess., pp. 1985, 1986–1987 (1950).)

Our upholding of the practice followed here by the Bank against attack as a preference does not depend on any relation back of actions taken on the eve of bankruptcy in order to save a theretofore defeasible security interest from attack by the trustee. Rather, it relies on the relation forward of record notice prior to the 4-month pre-bankruptcy period as being sufficient to give the secured party a priority over subsequently attaching lien or judgment creditors, including the trustee. As the district court stated, these were "assets which the general creditors never reasonably expected and could not expect to have available to satisfy their claims." 286 F.Supp. at p. 604. To hold otherwise would result in "a windfall to the general creditor who had long

---

7. Sexton v. Kessler & Co., 225 U.S. 90, 32 S.Ct. 657, 56 L.Ed. 995; Bailey v. Baker Ice Mach. Co., 239 U.S. 268, 36 S.Ct. 50, 60 L.Ed. 275; Carey v. Donohue, 240 U.S. 430, 36 S.Ct. 386, 60 L.Ed. 726; and Martin v. Commercial National Bank, 245 U.S. 513, 38 S.Ct. 176, 62 L.Ed. 441.

been on constructive notice that the debtors' future assets were to be made a part of the secured creditor's collateral"! Friedman, note 5 supra, at p. 221. Accordingly, it does not distort the Congressional purpose to conclude that the "so far perfected" language of Section 60a(2) of the Bankruptcy Act was satisfied at the time of the September 1965 filing of the financing statements.

The Transfer Was Not on Account of Antecedent Debt.

As an alternative holding, the district court reasoned that there was no voidable preference because there had been no transfer of Grain Merchants' property to the Bank "on account of an antecedent debt" within the meaning of Section 60a(1) of the Bankruptcy Act. The referee had reached the opposite conclusion by regarding the Bank's security interest in the accounts receivable as a separate interest in individual accounts. Under his reasoning, the transfers of this property of Grain Merchants to the Bank occurred at the moment the individual accounts receivable came into existence. Since the accounts receivable in question arose after September 20, 1966, the last date that the Bank extended credit to Grain Merchants, the referee held that those accounts receivable were transferred to secure antecedent debt of Grain Merchants to the Bank.

The district court considered the post September 20, 1966, accounts receivable as part of the entire stock of the accounts receivable transferred when the Bank filed its financing statements, stating that "From a business standpoint, the most accurate view of the transaction is to regard the stock of accounts receivable together as an entity which was given as security for a new loan" (286 F.Supp. at pp. 604–605). The entity theory was first advanced in Manchester National Bank v. Roche, 186 F.2d 827 (1st Cir. 1951), by Judge Magruder. As he stated (at p. 831):

> "By analogy it might be possible to treat a merchant's accounts receivable as a unit presently and continuously in existence, the component elements of which (the particular accounts) may be constantly changing, without affecting the identity of the *res;* so that a general assignment by way of security of accounts receivable present and future might be deemed to create *in praesenti* a lien upon this enduring unit, the accounts receivable, which lien would persist as a floating charge upon such *res,* however much its component elements might change from time to time by the payment of old accounts and the creation of new ones."

As has been observed elsewhere, "this is a simple, common-sense approach that has long been accepted, though not in name, by decisions and statutes." Henson, " 'Proceeds' Under the Uniform Commercial Code," 65 Colum.L.Rev. 232, 235–236 (1965). The concept has been depicted as a stream:

> "The secured creditor's interest is in the stream of accounts flowing through the debtor's business, not in any specific accounts. As with the Heraclitean river, although the accounts in the stream constantly change, we can say it is the same stream." (Footnote omitted.) Hogan, note 5 supra, at p. 560.

The entity theory is consistent with the approach to revolving loans adopted in Section 9–204(3) of the code permitting a security agreement to provide that collateral, whenever acquired, secure the obligations covered by the agreement. Under this approach, "Advances and collateral interact as a single organism," thus negating antecedent debt. Kohn, "Preferential Transfers on the Eve of the Bankruptcy Amendments," 2 Prospectus 259, 267 (1968).

We agree with the decisions below and in In the Matter of Portland Newspaper Publishing Co., Inc., 271 F.Supp. 395 (D.Ore.1967), pending on appeal, that the creditor's security interest was in the entity of the accounts receivable as a whole, and not in the individual components, so that the transfer of property occurred here when the interest in the accounts receivable as an entity was created and the financing statements were duly filed in September 1965. This recognizes business realities, for the business community has depended upon a revolving or flow type of accounts receivable financing for many years. As stated in the *Portland Newspaper* case, "Good business practice should be good business law" (271 F.Supp. at p. 400).

Accepting the entity theory here as to accounts receivable does not conflict with Section 60 of the Bankruptcy Act. Its purpose is to protect general creditors against those seeking unfair advantages during the four months before bankruptcy. The Bank is seeking merely to enforce a 1965 security agreement and not to press for any unfair advantage that occurred within four months of bankruptcy. As the court stated in Rosenberg v. Rudnick, 262 F.Supp. 635, 639 (D.Mass.1967), about a comparable after-acquired inventory problem:

> "The statutory provisions for notice filing were fully complied with. No supplier who sold merchandise on credit to Boyle can justifiably claim he relied on the appearance of

Boyle's inventory. He could easily have determined the extent of Rudnick's interest in it, and could have protected himself, if he so wished, either by perfecting a purchase money security interest under § 9–312(3), or, as some suppliers did, by getting Rudnick to guarantee payment."

As pointed out in the *amicus* brief of the National Commercial Finance Conference, many lenders making loans secured by a revolving pool of collateral have dispensed with the assignment of individual receivables and the use of special cash collateral accounts for receiving and disbursing the proceeds therefrom. This flexible method of financing, with its minimum cost, is authorized by Section 9–205 of the Code, which abrogates the state law "debtor dominion" rule of Benedict v. Ratner, 268 U.S. 353, 45 S.Ct. 566, 69 L.Ed. 991, and would be jeopardized if financing institutions had to insist on individual assignment of after-arising accounts receivable. The trustee conceded at oral argument that if these somewhat archaic pre-Code procedures had been followed, with a new loan advanced for each account receivable, no attack under the preference Section of the Bankruptcy Act would have been possible. An objection of this nature which can be satisfied by the mere multiplication of unnecessary paper work which in itself contributes nothing to the protection of unsecured creditors does not persuade us that the method of accounts receivable financing employed here conflicts with anything in the Bankruptcy Act.

In holding that the post September 20, 1966, accounts receivable were part of an entity, it follows that they were transferred when the financing statements were filed in September 1965. Since the Transfer preceded the extensions of credit with which we are concerned here, such transfer could not have been made "for or on account of antecedent debt" under Section 60a(1) of the Bankruptcy Act.

The Substitution of Collateral Doctrine Negates Any Preference Here.

Under the Bankruptcy Act, it is well settled that a transfer by an insolvent debtor within four months of bankruptcy is not a "preference" where the transfer to the creditor is "for a substantially contemporary advance." Dean v. Davis, 242 U.S. 438, 443, 37 S.Ct. 130, 61 L.Ed. 419. If such a transfer does not deplete the estate, it is not made "on account of an antecedent debt," nor does it have the effect of enabling the creditor "to obtain a greater percentage of his debt than some other creditor of the same class" (Section 60a(1) of the Bankruptcy Act, 11

U.S.C. § 96(a)(1). See 3 Collier on Bankruptcy ¶ 60.20 (14th ed. 1968).

Under the leading case of In re Pusey, Maynes, Breish Co., 122 F.2d 606 (3d Cir. 1941), through the substitution of collateral doctrine, a transfer of accounts receivable to the secured creditor made during the four months prior to bankruptcy is not considered preferential where the accounts transferred are substituted for prior released accounts. See In the Matter of Portland Newspaper Publishing Co., Inc., 271 F.Supp 395, 401 (D.Ore. 1967).

Here, as existing accounts receivable were collected by Grain Merchants and deposited to its accounts at the Bank, the funds from previously collected accounts were made available to the debtor, enabling it to continue in business and obtain new accounts receivable. During the critical period from September 20 when the Bank last extended value until September 30 when Grain Merchants ceased doing business, the debtor's withdrawals appear generally to have been in line with the deposits from new accounts receivable. See Appendix to this opinion. Our study of this record shows that at the end of each of the four months preceding bankruptcy, there was an excess of collateral over secured debt, indicating that collateral was regularly transferred in substitution for other collateral without diminishing the bankruptcy assets available for creditors. Here the newly arising accounts receivable may be considered as having been taken in exchange for the release of rights in earlier accounts and for a present consideration. Since the relative positions of the Bank and the debtor were unaltered by the exchanges, the debtor's other creditors cannot be considered harmed by the transactions with the Bank. See Hogan, note 5 supra, at pp. 561–565.

As previously observed under Section 9–205 of the Commercial Code, it was unnecessary for the Bank to assume dominion over individual accounts receivable. Therefore, it is no longer appropriate to apply strict timing or value rules [10] so long as at all relevant times the total pool of collateral, as here, exceeded the total debt. The trustee's purported distinction of In re Pusey, Maynes, Breish Co. on this ground is thus unpersuasive. In this connection, it is noteworthy that amendments to Section 60

10. The timing rule is that the new collateral must be transferred to the secured party either prior to or contemporaneously with the release of the old collateral. The value rule is that if the new collateral is of greater value than the collateral which is released, a voidable preference to the extent of the difference in value will result.

of the Bankruptcy Act have been submitted by a committee of the National Bankruptcy Conference so that transfers of receivables, pursuant to a security agreement, within four months of bankruptcy will not constitute preferences if they arose in the ordinary course of the debtor's business. But under a proposed two-point test, there will be a preference to the extent that the aggregate value of the receivables subject to the security agreement on the date of filing the bankruptcy petition exceeds the aggregate value subject to the security agreement four months earlier. The preference is measured by reference to these two points of time regardless of the fluctuations of the collateral that might occur in the 4-month period. See Kohn, "Preferential Transfers on the Eve of the Bankruptcy Amendments," 2 Prospectus 259, 261 (1968). This two-point test does not require a detailed tracing of individual accounts receivable. Here the pool of accounts receivable was remarkably steady in aggregate value through the entire period of the security agreement (see Appendix), justifying the applicability of the substitution of collateral principle to these facts. Hence for this additional reason we conclude that there was no forbidden preference.

The trustee strongly contends that the conclusion that the transfers of accounts receivable to the Bank were not on account of antecedent debt cannot be sustained without the aid of Section 9–108 of the Code. He reasons that Section 9–108 must fall before the superior command of federal law as contained in Section 60a of the Bankruptcy Act. We would be reluctant to hold that the Congressional reference to state law in Section 60a does not encompass the provisions of the Code, now adopted in 49 states and enacted by Congress for the District of Columbia and which has been recognized to be a valuable source for determining federal commercial law (United States v. Wegematic Corp., 360 F.2d 674, 676 (2d Cir. 1966); United States v. National Optical Stores, 407 F.2d 754 (7th Cir. 1969)). However, there is no need to resolve any asserted conflict, for Section 9–108 is unnecessary to the result reached here. That Section merely attempts to codify as state law the substitution of collateral doctrine, which is implicit in the provisions of the Bankruptcy Act, with the additional safeguard that such substitution arise in the ordinary course of business.

* * *

For the foregoing reasons, the judgment is affirmed.

APPENDIX

Grain Merchants' Deposits and the Balance of its Accounts at Union Bank at the End of Each Day Shown.

Date in 1966	Amount Deposited	Account Balance
September 20		$17,518.68
21	$ 4,691.88	17,685.72
22	8,702.65	22,006.80
23	9,548.49	29,145.64
26	7,530.01	23,127.26
27	4,270.77	20,770.01
28	3,486.75	16,304.58
29	6,247.63	16,806.03
30	3,564.80	18,985.45
	$48,042.98	

Total debt of Grain Merchants to Union Bank between January 1966 and September 1966, compared to accounts receivable of Grain Merchants.

1966	Total Debt	Accounts Receivable
January	$162,000.00	$176,483.21
February	162,000.00	191,439.52
March	162,000.00	177,343.26
April	160,000.00	183,021.65
May	160,000.00	172,192.84
June	156,850.00	172,816.20
July	155,000.00	169,629.81
August	150,000.00	185,292.43
September	150,000.00	176,841.77

PROBLEM 1

In exchange for new value Bank was granted a security interest in Debtor's existing equipment which it perfected by filing a financing statement covering equipment. Later, Debtor want-

ed to replace Old Machine which was part of the equipment subject to the security interest. Debtor purchased New Machine
and paid the purchase price of $15,000 by giving the seller
$8,000 cash and Old Machine which was taken by the seller at a
trade-in value of $7,000. Bank agreed to the transaction in re-
turn for Debtor's granting to Bank of a security interest in New
Machine. Bank made no additional advance to Debtor at the
time the security interest in New Machine attached. One month
later Debtor filed a petition in bankruptcy. At the time the security interest in New Machine attached and at all times thereafter Debtor was insolvent. Can Bank's security interest in New
Machine be avoided by Debtor's trustee in bankruptcy?

When the security interest in New Machine attached it was
perfected. UCC § 9–303. When it attached was there a transfer by Debtor to Bank on account of an antecedent debt? See
subsections (e)(1)(B), (e)(2)(A) and (e)(3) of § 547. Was the transfer preferential? See § 547(a)(2) and § 547(c)(1).

PROBLEM 2

Debtor was engaged in the business of repairing machines.
It carried an inventory of replacement parts in connection with
this business. On February 1 Bank loaned $50,000 to Debtor
and was granted a security interest in Debtor's existing and after-acquired inventory. Bank perfected by filing a financing
statement the same day. The security agreement required
Debtor to make daily deposits into a special checking account
controlled by Debtor of an amount equal to the previous day's
receipts from sales of inventory. Deposits in this account could
be used to buy replacement inventory and, to the extent not so
used, were to be applied to the loan. On February 1 Debtor's
inventory, consisting of 1000 units, was recorded on its books at
its cost of $30,000. Debtor's business was profitable; however,
on February 2 Debtor became insolvent as the result of a judgment in a personal injury action. On April 1 Debtor filed a petition in bankruptcy.

From February 2 to the date of bankruptcy Debtor sold 750
units of inventory for $37,500 cash, which it deposited in the spe-
cial account, and purchased 400 units of inventory for $12,000.
On the date of bankruptcy it had on hand 650 units which the
Trustee in bankruptcy sold for $18,200. At the date of bank-
ruptcy the amount owing on the loan was $24,500. All
purchases of inventory and payments on the loan were made

from cash proceeds deposited into the special account. On the date of bankruptcy the balance in this account was zero.

What are the rights of Bank and the trustee in bankruptcy to the $18,200 received for the inventory sold by the trustee? Can the trustee recover any of the $25,500 paid by Debtor to Bank to reduce the loan balance?

To answer these questions consider the following points. When a unit of inventory which cost Debtor $30 was sold to a customer for $50 Bank got a perfected security interest in the $50. See UCC § 9–306(2) and (3)(b). With respect to this $50 was there a transfer by Debtor to Bank on account of an antecedent debt? See subsections (e)(1)(B), (e)(2)(A) and (e)(3) of § 547. If Debtor deposited the $50 in a special bank account and $30 was applied to the purchase of replacement inventory and $20 was applied to the loan how do we know if either transfer was preferential? Does § 547(c)(5) help you solve this problem? The House and Senate Reports explaining this provision state the following:

> Paragraph (5) codifies the improvement in position test, and thereby overrules such cases as * * * Grain Merchants of Indiana, Inc. v. Union Bank and Savings Co. * * * A creditor with a security interest in a floating mass, such as inventory or accounts receivable, is subject to preference attack to the extent he improves his position during the 90-day period before bankruptcy. The test is a two-point test, and requires determination of the secured creditor's position 90 days before the petition and on the date of the petition. If new value was first given after 90 days before the case, the date on which it was first given substitutes for the 90-day point.

House Report No. 95–595, 95th Cong., 1st Sess. 373 (1977); Senate Report No. 95–989, 95th Cong., 2d Sess. 88 (1978).

Did Bank in this case improve its position during the 90-day period? What is the meaning of "value of all security interests" in § 547(c)(5)? Does the phrase "and to the prejudice of other creditors holding unsecured claims" bear on this question? Consider the following cases: Debtor files a petition in bankruptcy a few weeks before Christmas. His inventory of Christmas cards is subject to a security interest. The same cards were worth less at the beginning of the 90-day period before bankruptcy because of their seasonal nature. Did the secured party improve his position? Would the case be different if the cards had not been printed yet at the beginning of the 90-day period but were completed during that period? These cases are discussed in 4 Collier on Bankruptcy ¶ 547.41 (15th ed. 1982). Is the position of Bank in this Problem like that of the secured party in the Christmas card cases?

D. COMMINGLED CASH PROCEEDS

Under UCC § 9–306(2) if collateral is disposed of the secured party is given a security interest in identifiable proceeds resulting from the disposition. If the proceeds are "cash proceeds," defined in § 9–306(1) as "money, checks, deposit accounts and the like," the security interest is continuously perfected. § 9–306(3)(b). Although the Code does not state how the key word "identifiable" is to be defined, some cases do not cause difficulty. If an undeposited check was given by a buyer in payment for a purchase of collateral the check is identifiable as cash proceeds. Similarly, with respect to currency or deposit accounts (UCC § 9–105(1)(e)) there is no problem of identification if there is no commingling of proceeds and nonproceeds. The meaning of "identifiable" in the case of commingling, however, is not clearly indicated by UCC § 9–306.

PROBLEM

Secured Party has a perfected security interest in the inventory of Debtor. The security agreement requires that all cash proceeds resulting from sale of inventory be deposited into a special bank account controlled by Secured Party and representing only deposits of proceeds. Debtor sold a unit of inventory to a buyer in ordinary course and received a check for $1,000 in payment of the price. At the time of receipt of the buyer's check Debtor also had a general checking account in which there was a credit balance of $1,000. At the time of receipt of the check Debtor owed $1,000 to Third Party. Consider the rights of Secured Party to the $1,000 represented by the buyer's check in each of the following alternatives:

Case 1. Debtor is in possession of the buyer's check at the time Secured Party made its claim. Immediately after receiving the check Debtor paid the debt owing to Third Party by a check for $1,000 drawn on Debtor's general checking account. Secured Party claimed the buyer's check.

Case 2. Debtor, in violation of the security agreement, indorsed the buyer's check and delivered it to Third Party. Secured Party claimed the $1,000 in Debtor's general checking account.

Case 3. Debtor, in violation of the security agreement, deposited the buyer's check in Debtor's general checking account and then drew a check for $1,000 on that account to the order of Third Party. Secured Party claimed the $1,000 in Debtor's general checking account.

Assume in all cases that, because Third Party received payment of its debt in good faith and without knowledge of any violation by Debtor of the security agreement with Secured Party, it is entitled to keep the $1,000 received.

The three alternatives are essentially similar. In each Debtor in substantially contemporaneous transactions received $1,000 of proceeds and paid $1,000 to Third Party. After the transactions Debtor had $1,000 which Secured Party claimed. But in spite of the essential similarity of the alternatives the rights of Secured Party may differ in each. All courts would agree that Secured Party wins in Case 1 and loses in Case 2. They would say that in Case 1 Debtor paid Third Party with Debtor's money and in Case 2 Debtor used Secured Party's money to pay Third Party. But to the extent that money is fungible the result depends upon what is a fortuitous circumstance.

Whose money was used to pay Third Party in Case 3? Here, the answer is not clear. Secured Party's identifiable cash proceeds in the form of the check were lost when the check was deposited and collected. Whether Secured Party can claim the $1,000 in Debtor's general checking account depends upon whether that $1,000 can be identified as the cash proceeds of the sale of inventory. It is obvious that identification in this case is not like identification in the case of the check which was deposited. To say that Debtor had $1,000 in the account means simply that Debtor was creditor of the bank in that amount. One might therefore conclude that when identifiable cash proceeds are deposited into an account in which nonproceeds have also been deposited the cash proceeds are no longer identifiable to the extent that withdrawals were subsequently made from the account.

But all states have tracing rules that are designed to resolve disputes of this kind. These rules are based on arbitrary assumptions that may bear no relationship to reality. But their virtue is that they provide a basis for identifying what in fact is not identifiable. For example, in Case 3 if we assume that funds first deposited into a bank account are the first to be withdrawn (a first-in-first-out or FIFO rule) the result is victory for Secured Party because Third Party was paid with Debtor's money. If we assume that funds withdrawn from an account are the last funds deposited (a last-in-first-out or LIFO rule) Secured Party loses because its funds were used to pay Third Party. We might also apply the rule for tracing trust funds under which it is assumed that a fiduciary who pays a personal debt by drawing on a bank account containing trust funds and personal funds expends his own funds before encroaching on the trust fund. If the debtor is required to pay over to the secured party proceeds of the sale of collateral he can be considered a constructive trustee of these funds. If the trust fund tracing rule is applied to our example Secured Party wins.

The meaning of "identifiable" in UCC § 9–306(2) and (3)(b) is discussed in the case that follows.

ANDERSON, CLAYTON & CO. v. FIRST AMERICAN BANK OF ERICK

Supreme Court of Oklahoma, 1980.
614 P.2d 1091.

OPALA, JUSTICE. The issues on this appeal are: [1] Does a security interest attach to any part of the debtor's general bank account in which proceeds from sale of collateral have been deposited and commingled with other funds? [2] If so, did the security interest remain impressed upon those funds, under the circumstances of this case, after the debtor has transferred them by check to the depositary bank in payment of an obligation? and [3] Was the bank's subordination agreement to another creditor's security interest latently ambiguous so as to allow parol testimony to ascertain the intent of the parties?

We hold that in this case a perfected security interest in cash proceeds was not destroyed by their deposit in debtor's general as distinguished from special checking account. We further hold that the debtor's transfer of funds to depositary bank for payment of debt was not "in ordinary course of business" and thus did not impair seller's security interest therein. The subordination agreement between the depositary bank and another secured creditor is unambiguous on its face and cannot be explained or completed by parol evidence.

The First American Bank of Erick [Bank] agreed with Jerry Slatton [debtor] to lend him money for the purchase of hogs to be fed and sold. The hogs became Bank's collateral for the loan. Later debtor sought credit from Anderson, Clayton & Co. d/b/a Acco Feeds [Acco] to buy hog feed. In an effort to induce Acco's extension of credit to the debtor the Bank subordinated to Acco its superior security interest in all of debtor's hogs. Some six months later debtor sold part of the hogs which were subject to the Bank's and Acco's security interest. He then placed the proceeds in his general account at the Bank. His deposit raised the balance from $27.44 to $16,946.59. Debtor drew two checks against this account, one to the Bank for $11,100 (as partial repayment of the loan for hogs, although not yet due) and the other to Acco for $9,819.15. As Bank processed its check first, the debtor's account became depleted of funds sufficient to pay Acco's check.

Acco brought suit against Bank alleging that the refusal to honor its check from debtor was wrongful and that Bank had no right to any of the proceeds in debtor's account since it represented proceeds from the sale of the collateral in which Acco had a security interest superior to that of Bank.

The trial court found that the money in debtor's account was a fund handled in the ordinary course of banking business, and that the check made payable to Bank was received first, honored and paid in the ordinary course of business.

I

For many years, the requirement that proceeds must be "identifiable" in order for a security interest in them to continue caused courts to conclude that a security interest in proceeds deposited in a debtor's bank account terminated.[2] This viewpoint was based in part upon the belief that it was inconsistent for the secured party to assert a security interest in proceeds which he permitted the debtor to treat as his own.[3]

A recent trend in the other direction is reflected in a series of cases which hold that a security interest in cash proceeds deposited into the debtor's general banking account continues even

---

2. Skilton, The Secured Party's Rights in a Debtor's Bank Account Under Article 9 of the Uniform Commercial Code, 1 So.Ill.U.L.J. 120, 133 [1977]. This point of view was also expressed in Gilmore, Security Interests in Personal Property, v. II, p. 735 [1965]: "It should be noted that the interest in proceeds continues only so long as the proceeds (including collections received by the debtor) remain identifiable. The interest continues, therefore, identifiable (e.g. checks received by the debtor but not yet deposited in his bank account). *The cutoff point is when the collections cease to be identifiable * * * normally by deposit in a bank account."* (Emphasis added)

3. Gilmore, supra note 2, at p. 739.

when commingled with the debtor's other [non-proceeds] funds.[4] The reasons for the emergency of this trend are twofold. First, § 9–205 of the UCC, which provides that a security interest is not invalid or fraudulent because of liberty in the debtor to use, commingle or dispose of proceeds of collateral, negates the objection to the continuation of a proceeds security interest into a bank account. Second, the requirement of § 9–306(2) that proceeds be "identifiable"[7] can be satisfied by the use of common tracing principles.

We hold that whenever proceeds of the sale of collateral can be traced into a bank account, the proceeds remain identifiable and a security interest in them continues as provided by § 9–306(2). This pronouncement will not dispose of the instant case because the proceeds here were not only deposited into the debtor's bank account, they were also disbursed from the account by the drawing of two checks by the debtor. The effect of this disbursement upon the continuation of Acco's security interest turns upon whether the payment to Bank was in the "ordinary course" of business.[9] In short, a security interest in proceeds remaining in a bank account continues until the funds are actually transferred in the ordinary course of business.[10]

---

4. Brown & Williamson Tobacco Corp. v. First Nat'l Bank, 504 F.2d 998, 15 UCC Rep.Serv. 553 [7th Cir. 1974]; Universal CIT Credit Corp. v. Farmers Bank, 358 F.Supp. 317, 13 UCC Rep.Serv. 109 [E.D.Mo.1973]; Domain Indus., Inc. v. First Security Bank & Trust Co., 230 N.W.2d 165, 16 UCC Rep.Serv. 1417 [Iowa 1975]; Associates Discount Corp. v. Fidelity Union Trust Co., 111 N.J.Super. 353, 268 A.2d 330, 7 UCC Rep.Serv. 1350 [1970]; Michigan Nat'l Bank v. Flowers Mobile Homes Sales, Inc., 26 N.C. App. 690, 217 S.E.2d 108, 17 UCC Rep. Serv. 861 [1975]; Girard Trust Corn Exchange Bank v. Warren Lepley Ford, 25 Pa.D. & C.2d 395, 1 UCC Rep.Serv. 531 [Pa.Com.Pl.1958].

7. The UCC does not define the term "identifiable." Support for the proposition that commingling destroys identity can be found in the UCC. However, the comments to § 9–306 begin by reference to § 10 of the Uniform Trust Receipts Act which approves the tracing of commingled funds as a means of establishing iden-

tity. See also Skilton, supra note 2, at p. 127.

9. UCC Comment 2(c) to § 9–306 states in part:

"Where cash proceeds are covered into the debtor's checking account and paid out in the operation of the debtor's business, recipients of the funds of course take free of any claim which the secured party may have in them as proceeds. What has been said relates to payments and *transfers in ordinary course.* The law of fraudulent conveyances would no doubt in appropriate cases support recovery of proceeds by a secured party from a transferee out of ordinary course or otherwise in collusion with the debtor to defraud the secured party." (Emphasis added)

10. Citizens National Bank of Whitley County v. Mid-States Development Company, Inc., 380 N.E.2d 1243 [Ind.App.1978].

The Code contains no definition of transfer or transferee in ordinary course. Section 1–201(9) defines "buyer in ordinary course of business" as a "person who in good faith and without knowledge that the sale to him is in violation of the ownership rights or security interest of a third party in the goods * * * ". It is suggested in the UCC Comments to § 9–306 that the drafters intended for the same factors—good faith and lack of knowledge—to qualify a payment or transfer as one in ordinary course. Measuring the instant transaction by this test, if the Bank received payment from the debtor's bank account in good faith and without knowledge that the receipt was in violation of Acco's security interest [assuming that Acco in fact had a prior security interest], the transfer would be one in ordinary course and Bank would take free of Acco's claim to the funds as proceeds. The Code defines "good faith" as an "honesty in fact in the conduct or transaction concerned." [11] "Knowledge" is defined as "actual knowledge." [12]

The circumstances surrounding this transfer reveal that Bank demanded payment of a note not yet due out of an account known to it to contain the proceeds of the sale of collateral in which both it and Acco claimed a security interest. It also shows that Bank had reason to believe the debtor still owed money to Acco for feed. Moreover, the Bank had actual knowledge of Acco's potential claim based on the subordination agreement giving Acco a security interest in the proceeds superior to that held by the Bank. As a signatory to that agreement, the Bank must be held to actual knowledge of what it contained.

The last question to be resolved here is whether the subordination agreement gave Acco priority in the collateral and its proceeds, or whether, as Bank contends, the agreement had terminated, thereby restoring the Bank to its position of priority in the collateral and its proceeds.

On its face, the agreement subordinates Bank's security interest in *all of debtor's hogs* to Acco's security interest in the same collateral *for all indebtedness owed by debtor to Acco* for feed. Bank contends that the agreement is ambiguous and incomplete principally because it contains no terms indicating the limit to which Bank agreed to subordinate its lien. Bank contends that parol evidence is admissible to supplement this incomplete written instrument.

While an ambiguous instrument may be explained by parol, nothing inconsistent with it may be added or taken away. The

11. § 1–201(19).   12. § 1–201(25).

agreement involved here, although somewhat loosely drafted, does not appear ambiguous or incomplete. It gives Acco a prior security interest to the extent of all indebtedness owed by debtor to Acco. Hence, when Bank took the check drawn on the proceeds of the sale of the hogs, it was bound to actual knowledge that its receipt was in violation of Acco's security interest and therefore could not pass legally as transfer in ordinary course. Acco must be allowed to follow the proceeds of its collateral out of the debtor's bank account and into the hands of the Bank as payee of debtor's check.

NOTE

In C.O. Funk & Sons, Inc. v. Sullivan Equipment Co., Inc., 89 Ill. 2d 27, 59 Ill.Dec. 85, 431 N.E.2d 370 (1982), the Supreme Court of Illinois made the following statement:

Although the Code provides no guidance as to how proceeds might be identified, § 1–103 directs that the Code be supplemented by "principles of law and equity," and this provision has been construed to permit application of a tracing theory known in the law of trusts as the "lowest intermediate balance" rule. * * * see generally Skilton, The Secured Party's Rights In A Debtor's Bank Account Under Article 9 of the Uniform Commercial Code, 1977 So.Ill.U.L.J. 120, 140–43, 152–57). * * * As Professor Skilton notes (1977 So.Ill.U.L.J. 120, 133 n. 21), the argument that a proceeds security interest terminates when those proceeds are deposited in a bank account since they can no longer be identified has found little favor with the courts.

The rule, which operates on a common-sense view that dollars are fungible and cannot practically be earmarked in an account, provides a presumption that proceeds remain in the account as long as the account balance is equal to or greater than the amount of the proceeds deposited. The proceeds are "identified" by presuming that they remain in the account even if other funds are paid out of the account. If [the debtor] is likened to the trustee of a constructive trust imposed because he commingled funds, then the lowest-intermediate-balance rule directs that [the secured party's] proceeds in [the debtor's] account are preserved to the greatest extent possible as the account is depleted. * * * Under the rule, however, if the balance of the account dips below the amount of deposited proceeds, [the secured party's] security interest in the identifiable proceeds abates accordingly.

This lower balance is not increased if, later, other funds of the debtor are deposited in the account, i.e., the added amounts are not subject to an equitable lien, unless the latter deposits are made in restitution. (Restatement of Restitution sec. 212 (1937).) Thus the claimant has no priority over other creditors to any amount in excess of the lowest intermediate balance. (See Skilton, The Secured Party's Rights In A Debtor's Bank Account Under Article 9 of the Uniform Commercial Code, 1977 So.Ill.U.L.J. 120, 140.) In this case, [the secured party] cannot assert a security interest in proceeds superior to that asserted by the bank unless [the secured party] can show that those proceeds were preserved in [the debtor's] commingled account or that other inventory was purchased with those proceeds at a time, and to the extent, that those proceeds were identified in the account. The identification of the funds, as stated, is subject to the lowest intermediate balance of the account.

The problem of interpretation of "identifiable" in UCC § 9–306(2) is complicated by the fact that UCC § 9–306(4) contains a detailed statement of the secured party's rights to proceeds, and particularly rights in commingled deposit accounts, in the event debtor is in an insolvency proceeding, which in most cases means bankruptcy. Since the question of rights to cash proceeds will usually arise, if at all, in bankruptcy, subsection (4) is of paramount importance. The two cases that follow interpret this provision. Both cases were decided under the Bankruptcy Act of 1898 and *Gibson Products* assumes that the applicable preference rule regarding floating liens is that stated in *Grain Merchants*, supra p. 286.

MATTER OF GIBSON PRODUCTS OF ARIZONA

United States Court of Appeals, Ninth Circuit, 1976.
543 F.2d 652.

HUFSTEDLER, CIRCUIT JUDGE. On this appeal we must referee a collision between the "proceeds" provision of the Uniform Commercial Code (U.C.C. § 9–306(4), A.R.S. § 44–3127(d) [1]) and

---

1. For convenience, we refer hereafter solely to U.C.C. § 9–306, rather than to the Arizona statute adopting the U.C.C. We also use the text of U.C.C. § 9–306 prior to the 1972 amendments because Arizona did not adopt the 1972 amendments until 1975, effective January 1, 1976, a date long after this litigation began. (Arizona Laws of 1975, Ch. 65.) The 1972

the bankruptcy trustee's power to avoid preferences under Section 60 of the Bankruptcy Act.[2] The provisions collide under circumstances that place the creditor, asserting a perfected security interest in the debtor's bank account, in the dimmest equitable light: If the creditor prevails, it receives $19,505.27 from the debtor's account on proof that the debtor, within ten days of the insolvency, deposited $10 in the account from the sale of a hair dryer in which the creditor had a perfected security interest. The district court affirmed the bankruptcy judge's order awarding $19,505.27 to the secured creditor. We reverse because we conclude that the operation of U.C.C. Section 9–306(4)(d) created a voidable preference by the transfer to the creditor of a perfected security interest in the cash deposited in the debtor's account that exceeded the amount of the creditor's proceeds.

The creditor, Arizona Wholesale Supply Co. ("Wholesale") sold General Electric and Proctor-Silex appliances to the debtor, Gibson Products of Arizona ("Gibson"). Wholesale has a perfected security interest in the appliances. On January 13, 1972, Gibson initiated Chapter XI proceedings. During the ten-day pe-

amendments, even if applicable, do not affect the issues in this case.

2. The impending collision between U.C.C. § 9–306(4)(d) and Bankruptcy Act § 60, 11 U.S.C.A. § 96, has been the subject of much scholarly debate:

4A Collier on Bankruptcy, ¶ 70.62A[4.3] (14th ed. J. Moore & J. King 1976); 2 G. Gilmore, Secured Interests in Personal Property, § 45.9 (1965); Coogan & Vagts, "The Secured Creditor and the Bankruptcy Act: An Introduction," in 1 P. Coogan, W. Hogan & D. Vagts, Secured Transactions under the Uniform Commercial Code § 9.03[3][b][iii] (1968); Countryman, "Code Security Interests in Bankruptcy," 4 U.C.C.L.J. 35, 40–49 (1971); Duesenberg, "Lien or Priority under Section 10, Uniform Trust Receipts Act," 2 B.C.Ind. & Com.L.Rev. 73 (1960); Epstein, " 'Proceeding' Under the Uniform Commercial Code," 30 Ohio State L.J. 787, 796–808 (1969); Gillombardo, "The Treatment of Uniform Commercial Code Proceeds in Bankruptcy: A Proposed Redraft of Section 9–306," 38 U.Cinc.L.Rev. 1, 7–13, 22–30 (1969); Hawkland, "The Proposed Amendments to Article 9 of the U.C.C., Part II Proceeds," 77 Com. L.J. 12, 18–19 (1972); Henson, " 'Proceeds' Under the Uniform Commercial Code," 65 Colum.L.Rev. 232, 242–53 (1965); Kennedy, "The Impact of the Uniform Commercial Code on Insolvency: Article 9," 67 Com.L.J. 113, 116–17 (1962); Kennedy, "Trustee in Bankruptcy Under the Uniform Commercial Code: Some Problems Suggested by Articles 2 and 9," in 1 P. Coogan, W. Hogan & D. Vagts, supra, § 10.03[3] (1968); Levy, "Effect of the Uniform Commercial Code Upon Bankruptcy Law and Procedure," 60 Com.L.J. 9, 11–12 (1955); Marsh, "Triumph or Tragedy?: The Bankruptcy Act Amendments of 1966," 42 Wash. L.Rev. 681, 715–17 (1967); Comment, "The Commercial Code and the Bankruptcy Act: Potential Conflicts," 54 N.W.U.L.R. 411, 420–24 (1958); Comment, "Toward Commercial Reasonableness: An Examination of Some of the Conflicts Between Article 9 of the Uniform Commercial Code and the Bankruptcy Act," 19 Syr.L.Rev. 939, 954–55 (1968); Marsh, "Book Review," 13 U.C.L.A.L.Rev. 898, 907–09 (1966).

riod immediately preceding the institution of these proceedings, Gibson deposited $19,505.27 in its bank account. During the same period, Gibson deposited in the account $10 from the sale of a Proctor-Silex dryer.[3]   At the time insolvency proceedings were instituted, Gibson was indebted to Wholesale in the amount of $28,800 for the appliances it had sold to Gibson and for which it has perfected security interests.

* * *

The proceeds section of the Code generally follows the pre-Code law that a security interest continues in any identifiable proceeds received by the debtor from the sale or other disposition of the collateral.   The Code's new twist is extending the creditor's security interest to commingled funds without specifically tracing the creditor's proceeds into the fund, when the debtor has become insolvent.   (U.C.C. § 9–306(4)(d).)   No collision between the proceeds provision of the Code and the preference sections of the Bankruptcy Act occurs when the creditor's perfected security interest in his collateral is attached to the proceeds from the sale or other disposition of the collateral if (1) his interest was initially perfected in the collateral more than four months before bankruptcy, and (2) he can identify the proceeds to which his security interest has attached.   Under these circumstances, the creditor has priority over later creditors when he first perfected his security interest, and his priority relates back to his initial perfection.   (Cf. DuBay v. Williams (9th Cir. 1969) 417 F.2d 1277, 1286–87.)   The problem arises in the U.C.C. Section 9–306(4)(d) situation because that subsection gives the secured creditor a perfected security interest in the entire amount deposited by the debtor within ten days before bankruptcy without limiting the interest to the amount that can be identified as the proceeds from the sale of the creditor's collateral.   With respect to the funds that are not the creditor's proceeds, the creditor has no security interest except that conferred by U.C.C. Section 9–306(4)(d).   His interest in these nonproceeds arises upon the occurrence of two events: (1) insolvency proceedings instituted by or against a debtor, and (2) commingling of some of the proceeds from his collateral with the debtor's cash on hand or with other deposits in this debtor's bank account.   His security

---

3. No other sales during the 10-day period were proved, regardless of the disposition of the proceeds.   Under these circumstances, some alternative interpretations of U.C.C. § 9–306(4)(d) were not advanced and are not before us.   Wholesale tried, but failed to prove that the proceeds from the sale of some television sets were also deposited in the account during the ten-day period.

interest is limited to an "amount not greater than the amount of any cash proceeds received by the debtor within ten days before institution of the insolvency proceedings" and is subject to the additional set-offs in Section 9–306(4)(d).

The draftsmen's intent was not to deliver a security bonanza to any secured creditor. As Professor Gilmore observes: "It goes without saying that a provision of state law which purported to give a secured creditor greater rights in the event his debtor's estate was administered in bankruptcy than he would have apart from bankruptcy would be invalid. However, * * * § 9–306(4) does not in the least aim at such a result. Indeed, § 9–306(4) is the reverse of such a statute, since it sharply cuts back the secured party's rights when insolvency proceedings are initiated." (2 G. Gilmore, Security Interests in Personal Property ¶ 45.9, at 1337–38 (1965). The intent was to eliminate the expense and nuisance of tracing when funds are commingled and to limit the grasp of secured creditors to the amount received during the last ten days before insolvency proceedings, which, the draftsmen assumed, would usually be less than the same creditor could trace if he had a grip on the entire balance deposited over an unlimited time. (Id. at 1340.) On that assumption, awarding a perfected security interest to the secured creditor, good for a short time on the entire balance, gives the secured creditor no windfall to the detriment of general creditors. On our facts, the contrary is true.

When confronted with an analogous situation, the Seventh Circuit limited the secured creditor's interest to those proceeds in the bank account traceable to the sale of the creditor's collateral. The Seventh Circuit's theory was that the term "any cash proceeds" used in Section 9–306(4)(d) does not refer to all receipts from any source deposited in the bank account, but, instead, refers to "proceeds" as defined in Section 9–306(1), and thus the phrase means "cash proceeds from the sale of collateral in which the creditor had a security interest." (Fitzpatrick v. Philco Finance Corp. (7th Cir. 1974) 491 F.2d 1288, 1291–92.)

Although we reach a similar result, we reject the Seventh Circuit's reasoning because, in our view, that construction impermissibly bends the language and structure of Section 9–306. The general definition of "proceeds" in Section 9–306(1) cannot be transplanted into Section 9–306(4) shorn of its statutory freight. The statute divides "proceeds" into two categories, "identifiable" and "commingled," i.e., nonidentifiable proceeds, and alters the reach of a perfected security interest, depending upon whether the proceeds are identifiable or nonidentifiable. (Compare § 9–306(4)(a), (b), (c) with § 9–306(4)(d).) Section 9–306(4)(d) deals only with nonidentifiable cash proceeds. If the cash proceeds could be "identified," i.e., had not been commingled, the secured party would have a perfected security interest in the whole fund under Section 9–306(4)(b), just as he did in pre-Code days, without any of the limitations imposed by Section 9–306(4)(d). Under the Code scheme, the secured creditor also has a perfected security interest under subsection (d) when he cannot identify his proceeds in the commingled fund, as long as he can show that some of his proceeds were among those in the commingled fund. (See Section 9–306, Comment in U.C.C.Rep. Serv., Current Materials, ¶ 9306, at 60 (1968); Gilmore, supra, § 45.9, at 1336–37.)

We leave the language of Section 9–306(4) as it was drafted and apply Section 60 of the Bankruptcy Act to resolve the problem. As defined by Section 60a(1), a preference is "[1] a transfer * * * of the property of a debtor [2] to or for the benefit of a creditor [3] for or on account of an antecedent debt, [4] made or suffered by such debtor while insolvent and [5] within four months before the filing * * * [of bankruptcy], [6] the effect of which transfer will be to enable such creditor to obtain a greater percentage of his debt than some other creditor of the same class." Section 60a(2) of the Bankruptcy Act provides that "a transfer of property * * * shall be deemed to have been made or suffered at the time when it became so far perfected that no subsequent lien upon such property obtainable by legal or equitable proceedings on a simple contract could become superior to the rights of the transferee." As we held in DuBay v. Williams, supra, 417 F.2d at 1287:

> " 'Transfer' for the purpose of section 60a(2) is thus equated with the act by which priority over later creditors is achieved and not with the event which attaches the security interest to a specific account."

With respect to Wholesale's security interest in the proceeds from the sale of the collateral, no later creditor could obtain priority over Wholesale from the time its financing statement was filed and further perfected pursuant to Section 9–306(3), at least until Wholesale's proceeds were commingled with that of other secured creditors or with cash from other sources deposited in Gibson's bank account. Wholesale's security interest in those proceeds relates back to its initial financing statement. (Cf. DuBay v. Williams, supra, 417 F.2d at 1287–88.) However, Wholesale had no interest in cash other than its own proceeds, and hence no priority over later creditors in such cash, until (1) some part of Wholesale's proceeds were deposited with other cash in Gibson's bank account, (2) within ten days of Gibson's filing its Chapter XI petition. The effect of Section 9–306(4) is thus to transfer to Wholesale a security interest in the cash in Gibson's bank account which does not derive from the sale of its collateral. In this situation, the act that gives Wholesale priority and the events that attach the security interest to the question asset occur at the same time. The transfer cannot occur earlier than ten days before the institution of bankruptcy. The transfer of the excess, above the wholesaler's proceeds, is a preference unless we can say that the transfer was neither for nor on account of an antecedent debt. We cannot avoid the conclusion that the transfer was on account of an antecedent debt. Wholesale could not qualify for Section 9–306(4) treatment absent the antecedent debt; moreover, the transfer does not happen unless the debt owed exceeds the payments made to the creditor during the ten-day period before the bankruptcy petition has been filed.

The result is that Wholesale cannot successfully assert its claim under U.C.C. Section 9–306(4)(d) to thwart the trustee's power to set that interest aside as a preference. However, the conclusion does not necessarily also follow that the creditor loses his security interest both in the proceeds from the sale of his collateral and in the nonproceeds in the debtor's bank account. In his contest with the trustee, he only loses his claim to the amounts in excess of his proceeds because only that amount is a preference. His security interest in the whole account, subject to the limitations of U.C.C. Section 9–306(4), is valid except that the trustee can avoid it. To the extent that a creditor is able to identify his proceeds to trace their path into the commingled funds, he will be able to defeat *pro tanto* the trustee's assertion of a preference.

By this construction of Section 60 of the Bankruptcy Act and Section 9–306(4) of the U.C.C., we do violence neither to statute nor to substantial justice among the parties. The creditor's security interest in the whole account under Section 9–306(4) is *prima facie* valid, except as to the trustee, and, as to him, the creditor's security interest is presumptively preferential. The creditor can rebut the presumption by appropriately tracing his proceeds. We think that it is fair to place the burden on the creditor to identify his own proceeds and thus to defeat, in whole or in part, the trustee's claim of preference. The creditor is in a better position than the trustee to trace his proceeds; moreover, if the creditor wants to avoid both the limitations of U.C.C. Section 9–306(4)(d) and the burden of proof in a potential contest with the trustee, all he needs to do is to prevent commingling of his proceeds and thus to follow U.C.C. Section 9–306(4)(a)–(c).

Reversed and remanded for further proceedings consistent with the views herein expressed.

MATTER OF GUARANTEED MUFFLER SUPPLY CO., INC.

United States Bankruptcy Court, N.D. Georgia, 1980.
5 B.R. 236.

A. D. KAHN, BANKRUPTCY JUDGE. Before the court is Plaintiff/Trustee's motion for "judgment on the pleadings regarding the specific issue of law whether the application of [UCC §] 9–306(4)(d) (1962) shall be limited by National Bank of Georgia's having to trace the proceeds from the disposition of each piece of [property in which NBG holds a valid security interest]." The court will interpret the Trustee's motion to constitute a request for a ruling that would limit a secured party's proceeds claim under UCC § 9–306(4)(d) [1] to those proceeds which are appropriately identified as having been collected upon disposition of property which is validly encumbered by the secured party's lien. For the reasons outlined below, the court is inclined to grant the Trustee's request.

As explained more fully by court order entered November 27, 1979 (reported at 1 B.R. 324, 27 U.C.C.Rep. 1217), the relationship between the above-named parties was initiated in 1976 when Defendant National Bank of Georgia (NBG) took a security interest in all inventory and accounts owned by a predecessor

---

1. As pointed out by previous order, the 1962 version of the U.C.C. governs the instant case. See In Re Guaranteed Muffler Supply Co., Inc., 1 B.R. 324, 326 n. 1, 27 U.C.C.Rep. 1217, 1220 n. 1 (Bkrtcy.N.D.Ga.1979).

The applicable provision provides, in pertinent part, as follows:

(4) In the event of insolvency proceedings instituted by or against a debtor, a secured party with a perfected security interest in proceeds has a perfected security interest
* * *

(d) in all cash and bank accounts of the debtor, if other cash proceeds

have been commingled or deposited in a bank account, but the perfected security interest under this paragraph (d) is

(i) subject to any right of set-off; and (ii) limited to an amount not greater than the amount of any cash proceeds received by the debtor within 10 days before the institution of the insolvency proceedings and commingled or deposited in a bank account prior to the insolvency proceedings less the amount of cash proceeds received by the debtor and paid over to the secured party during the 10-day period.

partnership of the corporate Bankrupt. Some two years later, after the corporation was formed and the assets of the old partnership were transferred to the new entity, Defendant Hamilton took a security interest in all inventory and accounts of the newly formed corporation.

In March of 1979, the corporation filed a petition in bankruptcy, but the lien-holding Defendants and the Trustee could not resolve their conflicting claims to property of the estate. The Trustee, therefore, commenced the above-styled proceeding to resolve the conflict.

Although Defendant Hamilton's lien on property of the estate is subordinate to those claims which NBG validly asserts to the same property (see UCC § 9–312(5) and order entered February 6, 1980), the court made clear in its November 1979 order that NBG's lien on property of the estate is limited to the following: (1) partnership accounts and inventory which survived until the date of bankruptcy; (2) proceeds collected by the partnership upon sale of the accounts and inventory; and (3) proceeds collected by the now bankrupt corporation upon its sale of partnership property encumbered by NBG's lien. These limitations are imposed upon NBG's lien because NBG failed to obtain a security interest in property of the corporate entity and because no party has urged the court to pierce the corporate veil.

Of tremendous practical significance is the fact that NBG may assert a lien on property which is alleged to constitute proceeds only after it is shown that the property is indeed the fruit obtained upon disposition of NBG's collateral. This requirement is otherwise known as the requirement that proceeds be "identifiable." [UCC §] 9–306 (1962); In Re Guaranteed Muffler Supply Co., Inc., 1 B.R. 324, 328, 27 U.C.C.Rep. 1217, 1223 (Bkrtcy. N.D.Ga.1979); Howarth v. Universal C.I.T. Credit Corp., 203 F.Supp. 279, 1 U.C.C.Rep. 515 (W.D.Pa.1962). See especially In Re Guaranteed Muffler Supply Co., Inc., 27 U.C.C.Rep. 1228 (Bkrtcy.N.D.Ga.1980).

Since NBG's claim to property of the estate is largely rooted in U.C.C. article 9 proceeds theory, the court declared in its November order that the general U.C.C. restrictions placed upon proceeds rights should apply not only to NBG's claims to proceeds collected by the partnership, but also to NBG's claims to proceeds collected by the corporate Bankrupt, (otherwise known as the "transferee's proceeds"). One such restriction discussed in the order was the one found in U.C.C. § 9–306(4)(d) (1962) which "eliminates secured parties' rights in cash proceeds which are on hand as of the date of a bankruptcy unless a secured party can show that the cash was collected within ten days before bankruptcy or that the cash was not mingled with [non-proceeds] cash." In Re Guaranteed Muffler Supply Co., Inc., 1 B.R. 324, 329, 27 U.C.C.Rep. 1217, 1224 (Bkrtcy.N.D.Ga.1979).

That characterization of the nature of U.C.C. § 9–306(4)(d) implicitly answers the question posed by the Trustee's motion. The court's view of § 9–306(4)(d) as a provision which RESTRICTS secured parties' claims to proceeds is an implicit rejection of any interpretation of § 9–306(4)(d) through which secured parties obtain greater lien rights than they would in the absence of § 9–306(4)(d).

Admittedly, at least one court has taken the position that U.C.C. § 9–306(4)(d) "gives the secured creditor a perfected security interest in the entire amount [of cash proceeds] deposited [or received] by the debtor within ten days before bankruptcy without limiting the interest to the amount that can be identified as the proceeds from the sale of the creditor's collateral." In Re Gibson Products of Arizona, 543 F.2d 652, 655 (9th Cir.), cert. denied 430 U.S. 946, 97 S.Ct. 1586, 51 L.Ed.2d 794 (1976). The *Gibson Products* court elaborated on its position by stating that "with respect to the funds that are not the creditor's proceeds, the creditor has no security interest except that conferred by UCC Section 9–306(4)(d)." Id. at 655.

It is this court's position that the *Gibson Products* view misinterprets the language and logic of the UCC proceeds section.[3] Although the *Gibson Products* court ultimately relied upon bankruptcy preference law to invalidate that portion of the secured party's claim to proceeds conferred solely by § 9–306(4)(d), this court is of the opinion that there is absolutely no conflict between § 9–306(4)(d) and the Bankruptcy Act.[4] Accord Fitzpatrick v. Philco Finance Corp., 491 F.2d 1288 (7th Cir. 1974). To create a false conflict in this circumstance is not only to raise complicated questions involving the meaning of a preferential "transfer,"[5] but also to cause unnecessary argument about the extent to which portions of the UCC are to be invalidated as dis-

---

3. Leading commentators have referred to the *Gibson Products* view as "not defensible." J. White & R. Summers, Uniform Commercial Code 1016 (2d ed. 1980).

4. Although the instant case is governed by the old Bankruptcy Act, the proceeds analysis which appears herein is relevant in cases pending un-

der the new Bankruptcy Code. See especially 11 U.S.C. § 552.

5. The existence of a "transfer" is a prerequisite to the finding of a voidable preference. See, e.g., First Nat'l Bank of Clinton v. Julian, 383 F.2d 329, 334 (8th Cir. 1967) (proceeds claims which arose within four months of bankruptcy held not to con-

guised state priorities or voidable statutory liens. See In Re Dexter Buick—GMG Truck Co., 2 B.R. 242 (Bkrtcy. D.R.I.1980).

The point of departure between the position taken by this court and the Ninth Circuit *Gibson Products* panel is rooted in conflicting views about the very nature of secured parties' rights to proceeds. Such rights are obtained by authority of UCC § 9–306(2), which states that an article nine lien "continues in collateral notwithstanding [an unauthorized] sale, and also continues in any identifiable proceeds * * *." This important provision makes proceeds claims, by definition, depend upon a showing that the property claimed is identified as the fruit of a sale or other disposition of the original collateral. Thus, a right to proceeds of any kind, whether in bankruptcy or not, arises out of the language of § 9–306(2); the limitations upon "cash proceeds" listed in § 9–306(4)(d)(ii), therefore include, by definition, the identifiability limitations which apply to all claims made to all proceeds.[6] To require that proceeds claims be so limited is consistent with the fact that the exercise of lien rights is confined to specific property which the debtor has chosen to make available as a surrogate for his own performance.

Accordingly, the Trustee's motion is hereby GRANTED. No secured party in this proceeding may claim property of the estate on the basis of U.C.C. article nine proceeds theory unless the property is shown to have been collected upon the disposition of property in which the secured party held a valid lien.

PROBLEM

Secured Party has a perfected security interest in all of the inventory of Debtor. During the ten days preceding Debtor's filing of a petition in bankruptcy Debtor received $20,000 in proceeds of inventory all of which was deposited into Debtor's checking account. Assume that application of the lowest-intermediate-balance rule set forth in *Funk,* supra p. 306 will determine that at the beginning of the 10-day period the balance of $3,000 in Debtor's checking account was made up of $1,000 of proceeds deposited before the 10-day period and $2,000 of nonproceeds. During the 10-day period no payments were made by

stitute a transfer, since the proceeds claims which arose during the four-month period were a mere surrogate for the original collateral, in which the secured party had lost its lien).

6. As the Seventh Circuit has pointed out, state law which governs the creation of consensual liens on personalty "also limits the application [of such liens] to co-mingled proceeds in the event of insolvency * * *." Fitzpatrick v. Philco Finance Corp., 491 F.2d 1288, 1291 (7th Cir. 1974).

Debtor to Secured Party and Debtor made the following deposits to the account and payments to third parties from the account.

	Deposit Proceeds	Deposit Nonproceeds	Payment to Third Parties	Balance
Day 1				$ 3,000
3	$9,000			12,000
5	9,000			21,000
6			$20,000	1,000
7		$20,000		21,000
9	2,000			23,000

Secured Party and the trustee in bankruptcy both make claims to Debtor's checking account. How much goes to each by applying UCC § 9–306(4)(d)? Assuming that Debtor was insolvent at all times during the 10-day period, is any amount to which Secured Party is entitled under UCC § 9–306(4)(d) voidable as a preference? If a judgment creditor of Debtor had obtained a judicial lien on Debtor's checking account just prior to the filing of the petition in bankruptcy what would the priorities have been between him and Secured Party to the $23,000 balance? See UCC § 9–306(2) and *Anderson, Clayton,* supra. Is Secured Party's security interest in the deposit account subject to attack under Bankruptcy Code § 544(a)?

Chapter 4

DEFAULT

The law has long struggled with the problem of how to strike a fair balance between the interest of the foreclosing creditor in being able to realize on collateral quickly and cheaply and the interest of the defaulting debtor in having his rights safeguarded in any disposition of the property. The traditional view was to require a public sale to the highest cash bidder after public notice of the sale. As in the foreclosure of real estate mortgages, if the creditor complied with all of the procedural requirements, the sale was a valid termination of all the debtor's rights in the collateral even though the price obtained for the property might be only a fraction of what the debtor thought the property was worth. The Uniform Conditional Sales Act was an example of the assimilation of the procedures for disposition on default of personal property to the rigid procedures long used in the foreclosure of real property mortgages.

The Code draftsmen wanted something better than the "sale on the courthouse steps" held before a listless audience of courthouse loiterers or, still worse, before a conniving group of professional public sale bidders colluding to keep the bids down. In Part 5 of Article 9, they strove to loosen up the disposition process, make it more businesslike, and get a better return. They encouraged the creditor to resell in private sales at market prices. In balancing the freedom the creditor enjoyed, he was held to a post-audit standard of "commercial reasonableness" in all aspects of the realization process with strict accountability for failure to meet this flexible standard.

A difficulty faced by the Code draftsmen was in drawing provisions equally appropriate for both commercial and consumer default cases. Part 5 of Article 9 contains only two special provisions applying to consumer cases, UCC § 9–505(1) and § 9–507(1). However, a number of states have enacted consumer credit protection laws adding provisions designed to safeguard the defaulting consumer debtor. For instance the Uniform Consumer Credit Code (1974) limits creditors' rights to deficiency judgments (§ 5.103), narrows the definition of default (§ 5.109), affords debtors the right to cure (§ 5.110) before the creditor can repossess (§ 5.111), and bars the right of creditors

318

to repossess certain goods in nonpurchase money cases without judicial authorization (§ 5.116).

Another body of law that bears heavily on the rights of the parties in default cases is the Bankruptcy Code, because defaulting debtors often choose or are forced into bankruptcy. As indicated in Chapter 3, when the debtor goes into bankruptcy, the secured creditor's rights under Article 9 are subject to the automatic stay of Bankruptcy Code § 362. In brief, this means that unless the secured creditor is able to lift the stay and reclaim the collateral from the bankruptcy estate, the property is either sold or used pursuant to orders of the bankruptcy court, and Part 5 of Article 9 is inapplicable. The secured creditor is able to reach the collateral in liquidation cases (Chapter 7) if the bankrupt has no equity in the property and in reorganization cases (Chapters 11 and 13), if the bankrupt has no equity and the property isn't needed for the reorganization. When the secured creditor is able to wrest his property from the grasp of the bankruptcy court, the provisions of Part 5 govern once again.

A.　REPOSSESSION

PENNEY v. FIRST NATIONAL BANK OF BOSTON

Supreme Judicial Court of Massachusetts, 1982.
385 Mass. 715, 433 N.E.2d 901.

O'CONNOR, JUSTICE. Frederick Penney, a commercial fisherman who borrowed money from the defendant bank, appeals from a summary judgment for the bank on his complaint and from an award of attorney's fees in favor of the bank on its counterclaim. We affirm.

On March 28, 1975, Penney borrowed $32,802.39 from the bank, and executed a promissory note and a security agreement involving a lobster boat. The back of the note provided that upon default all obligations would become immediately due and payable without notice or demand and the holder would then have the rights and remedies of a secured party under the Uniform Commercial Code of Massachusetts (UCC).

The security agreement provided as follows: "Borrower may have possession and use of the Collateral until default. Upon the happening of any of the following events or conditions, namely: (a) default in the payment or performance of any of the obligations　*　*　*　contained or referred to herein or in any

note evidencing any of the obligations   *   *   * , thereupon, and
as long as such default continues Bank may declare all of the
Obligations to be immediately due and payable, and Bank shall
then have   *   *   * in addition to all other rights and remedies,
the rights and remedies of a secured party under the Uniform
Commercial Code of Massachusetts, including without limitation
thereto the right to take immediate possession of the Collateral
*   *   * . Bank will give Borrower at least five days' prior written notice of the time and place of any public sale of the Collateral or of the time after which any private sale thereof is to be
made." Penney's obligation was guaranteed by William Regan,
who agreed to pay in the event Penney defaulted.

On March 4, 1976, Penney executed another note, payable to
the bank on demand, in the amount of $4,244.40. This note also
expressly gave the bank the rights and remedies of a secured
party under the UCC.

Penney defaulted on both notes. On July 29, October 11,
November 4, and December 30, 1977, the bank wrote to Penney
demanding full payment of all sums due. Penney made some
further payments after each letter except the last, but he remained in default on both notes throughout that period. The
bank brought an action on Regan's guaranty and on August 25,
1977, attached Regan's real estate in the amount of $18,500.
The bank never exercised its remedies against Regan. The bank
seized the lobster boat without prior notice on January 19, 1978,
at which time Penney's total indebtedness to the bank was approximately $19,000. The bank notified Penney five days later
of the repossession, of its intention to sell the boat, and of his
right to redeem. Penney did not exercise his right to redeem,
and the boat was sold at public auction for $13,500. Penney as-
serts by affidavit that as a result of the repossession he lost
$34,000 worth of fishing equipment which was at sea.

Penney commenced this action to recover for the losses he
alleges resulted from a wrongful seizure and sale of the boat.
He claims that the seizure and sale violated G.L. c. 93A, § 2, and
his due process rights secured by the Fourteenth Amendment to
the Constitution of the United States. The bank answered and
counterclaimed for the balance due on the two notes together
with interest, costs and attorney's fees. The bank's motion for
summary judgment on the counterclaim was allowed by agreement, subject to later assessment of interest, costs, and attorney's fees, on the condition that no execution would issue until
Penney's action was decided. The bank then moved for summa-

ry judgment on Penney's action and the motion was allowed, based on pleadings, affidavits, a deposition, admissions, and answers to interrogatories. Thereafter, interest, costs, and attorney's fees were assessed in connection with the counterclaim. Penney appeals from the summary judgment on his complaint and from the assessment of attorney's fees on the counterclaim. Penney claims that the award of attorney's fees in connection with the bank's defense against his complaint was erroneous.

1. *Constitutionality of § 9–503.* We interpret the security agreement as neither adding to nor detracting from the bank's right to repossess without notice under UCC § 9–503. Penney attacks that section as violating the due process guarantees of the Fourteenth Amendment. Section 9–503 provides in pertinent part that "[u]nless otherwise agreed a secured party has on default the right to take possession of the collateral. In taking possession a secured party may proceed without judicial process if this can be done without breach of the peace or may proceed by action." The Fourteenth Amendment by its terms applies only to the States. In order for the Fourteenth Amendment to be invoked against a private actor, the government must not only act but must be "significantly involved" in the actor's underlying conduct. Moose Lodge No. 107 v. Irvis, 407 U.S. 163, 173, 92 S.Ct. 1965, 1971, 32 L.Ed.2d 627 (1972), quoting from Reitman v. Mulkey, 387 U.S. 369, 380, 87 S.Ct. 1627, 1633, 18 L.Ed.2d 830 (1967). Penney argues that the Legislature's enactment of § 9–503 was sufficient State action to render unconstitutional a private party's self-help repossession in reliance thereon.

Neither this court nor the United States Supreme Court has reached this precise question. The constitutionality of UCC § 9–503 has been considered in many other jurisdictions, however, and has been almost uniformly held to involve no State action. See, e.g., Gibbs v. Titelman, 502 F.2d 1107 (3rd Cir.), cert. denied, 419 U.S. 1039, 95 S.Ct. 526, 42 L.Ed.2d 316 (1974); Brantley v. Union Bank & Trust Co., 498 F.2d 365 (5th Cir.), cert. denied, 419 U.S. 1034, 95 S.Ct. 517, 42 L.Ed.2d 309 (1974); Gary v. Darnell, 505 F.2d 741 (6th Cir. 1974); Turner v. Impala Motors, Inc., 503 F.2d 607 (6th Cir. 1974); Nowlin v. Professional Auto Sales, 496 F.2d 16 (8th Cir.), cert. denied, 419 U.S. 1006, 95 S.Ct. 328, 42 L.Ed.2d 283 (1974); Bichel Optical Laboratories v. Marquette Nat'l Bank, 487 F.2d 906 (8th Cir. 1973); Adams v. Southern Cal. First Nat'l Bank, 492 F.2d 324 (9th Cir. 1973), cert. denied, 419 U.S. 1006, 95 S.Ct. 325, 42 L.Ed.2d 282 (1974); John Deere Co. of Kansas City v. Catalano, 186 Colo. 101, 525 P.2d 1153 (1974); King v. South Jersey Nat'l Bank, 66 N.J. 161, 330

A.2d 1 (1974); Colonial Swimming Pool Co. v. Camperama of Vt., Inc., 134 Vt. 463, 365 A.2d 262 (1976).

Flagg Bros. v. Brooks, 436 U.S. 149, 98 S.Ct. 1729, 56 L.Ed. 2d 185 (1978), is persuasive authority for the proposition that there is no State action in mere legislative authorization of creditors' self-help remedies that do not involve the participation of any governmental employees. In *Flagg Bros.*, the Court rejected a due process attack on a warehouseman's sale, pursuant to UCC § 7–210, of another's goods to satisfy overdue storage charges because the sale involved no State action. Section 9–503, like § 7–210, authorizes but does not compel private action and does not delegate a function traditionally reserved to the State. *Id.* at 161–162, 164–166, 98 S.Ct. at 1736, 1737–1738. See Annotation to G.L. c. 106, § 9–503, Mass.Ann.Laws, Uniform Commercial Code at 428 (Law. Co-op. 1976) (creditor's right to repossess on default predates enactment of § 9–503).

We hold that self-help repossession by a private party pursuant to § 9–503, does not involve State action and does not violate the Fourteenth Amendment. Our holding is consonant with our decision in Debral Realty, Inc. v. DiChiara, 383 Mass. 359, Mass. Adv.Sh. (1981) 1140, 420 N.E.2d 343, where we held that the lis pendens procedure under G.L. c. 184, § 15, does not violate due process.

2. *Consumer Protection Act violations.* Penney contends that summary judgment was improper even if § 9–503 is constitutional. He argues that the bank's repossession without prior notice in the circumstances presented here constituted an "unfair or deceptive" act entitling him to damages under G.L. c. 93A, §§ 2 & 11. Chapter 93A applies to the conduct of Banks. Raymer v. Bay State Nat'l Bank, ___ Mass. ___, ___, Mass.Adv. Sh. (1981) 1870, 1879, 424 N.E.2d 515. The precise question presented is whether there is any substantial question of fact material to whether the bank's conduct was unfair or deceptive. Mass.R.Civ.P. 56(c), 365 Mass. 730, 824 (1974).

Penney asserts that there are four facts, each of which is either established or subject to substantial dispute, that show a violation of c. 93A when taken together. These are (1) that the bank repossessed without notice (2) when it had previously attached real property with a value in excess of the attachment under the guaranty (3) leaving a balance owed of $600 over the attachment amount (4) when it knew or should have known Penney had equipment at sea that he would be unable to retrieve.

Chapter 93A, § 2, provides that unfair or deceptive acts or practices in the conduct of any trade or commerce are unlawful (§ 2[*a*]), and that in construing § 2(*a*) the courts will be guided by the interpretations given by the Federal Trade Commission and the Federal courts to § 5(a)(1) of the Federal Trade Commission Act (15 U.S.C. 45[a][1]), as from time to time amended. Section 2(*c*) authorizes the Attorney General to promulgate rules and regulations defining "unfair or deceptive." No case or Federal Trade Commission interpretation, or rule or regulation of the Attorney General, has been brought to our attention making repossession without prior notice in the circumstances of this case an unfair or deceptive act or practice.

Regulation XV of the regulations promulgated by the Attorney General pursuant to c. 93A, provides in pertinent part that an act or practice is a violation of c. 93A, § 2, if it is oppressive or otherwise unconscionable in any respect. 940 Code Mass. Regs. § 3.16(1) (1978). We therefore consider whether the bank's repossession without notice was in any way unconscionable or oppressive.

In Zapatha v. Dairy Mart, Inc., 381 Mass. 284, ___–___, Mass. Adv.Sh. (1980) 1837, 1845–1848, 408 N.E.2d 1370, we considered the meaning of "unconscionable" in UCC § 2–302, which authorizes a court to refuse to enforce any clause of a contract that the court finds "to have been unconscionable at the time it was made." Penney argues that under Regulation XV the security agreement was unconscionable at the time it was made and that its enforcement by repossession without notice was also unconscionable. Our consideration in *Zapatha* of unconscionability with respect to contract terms, within the meaning of UCC § 2–302, is helpful not only to our determination whether the provisions in the notes and security agreement here were unconscionable but also to our determination whether the repossession was unconscionable within the meaning of Regulation XV. In *Zapatha*, we said, "Because there is no clear, all-purpose definition of 'unconscionable,' nor could there be, unconscionability must be determined on a case by case basis (see Commonwealth v. Gustafsson, 370 Mass. 181, 187 [346 N.E.2d 706] [1976]), giving particular attention to whether, at the time of the execution of the agreement, the contract provision could result in unfair surprise and was oppressive to the allegedly disadvantaged party." *Zapatha*, supra 381 Mass. at ___, Mass.Adv.Sh. (1980) at 1845, 408 N.E.2d 1370. "The fact that particular conduct is permitted by statute or by common law principles should be considered, but it is not conclusive on the question of unfairness,"

Schubach v. Household Fin. Corp., 375 Mass. 133, 137, 376 N.E. 2d 140 (1978), nor is it conclusive as to fairness that conduct is expressly permitted by a contract between the parties, Fortune v. National Cash Register Co., 373 Mass. 96, 104–105, 364 N.E.2d 1251 (1977).

UCC § 9–503, permits self-help repossession independent of similar contractual permission. Accordingly, neither the act of repossession nor a contract permitting it is per se unconscionable. Furthermore, the security agreement specifically provides that Penney "may have possession and use of the Collateral *until default*" and that upon default the bank shall have "the rights and remedies of a secured party under the Uniform Commercial Code of Massachusetts, *including without limitation thereto the right to take immediate possession of the Collateral*" (emphasis added). Regardless of whether Penney was familiar with the provisions of § 9–503, he was fairly put on notice of the bank's unconditional right to take immediate possession upon default. In addition, the contract provision for notice before sale, together with the lack of provision for notice before repossession, fairly implied that notice was not a prerequisite to repossession. There was no potential for unfair surprise in the note and security agreement provisions allowing immediate repossession upon default. If Penney was surprised by the repossession, he was not surprised unfairly.

There was no oppression in including in the notes and security agreement a provision confirming the remedies available under § 9–503. We view the question of oppression as directed to the substantive fairness to the parties of permitting the repossession provisions as written. See *Zapatha*, supra 381 Mass. at ___, Mass.Adv.Sh. (1980) at 1847, 408 N.E.2d 1370. The right of repossession without notice was reasonably related to the bank's need for assurance that the collateral would be available to it in the event of default. The risk to the bank of having a right of repossession only after notice to Penney was not disproportionate to Penney's risk of loss upon repossession without notice. In light of the bank's commercial needs, it was not unfair to impose upon Penney the practical requirement that after default he limit the amount of his equipment at sea or that he make arrangements for retrieving it other than by means of the collateral.

Penney argues that it was unfair for the bank to repossess the boat when it knew or should have known that Penney might have fishing equipment at sea worth thousands of dollars, and when it had an attachment in the amount of $18,500 on land with an equity of $35,000 owned by Regan, the guarantor. What we have said in the preceding paragraph disposes of the contention that it was unfair to repossess without notice, apart from the attachment, and we know of no authority or sound reason for requiring that a creditor exhaust his rights against a guarantor before proceeding against the debtor's property. We hold that the facts established here require that neither the contractual provisions permitting self-help repossession, nor the implementation thereof, are "oppressive or otherwise unconscionable" within the meaning of the Attorney General's Regulation XV. The bank's motion for summary judgment on Penney's complaint was properly allowed.

3. *Attorney's fees.* Penney challenges the award of any attorney's fees incurred by the bank to defend the wrongful repossession and c. 93A claims, as well as the claims (presented below but not argued here) that the bank inadequately cared for the boat and failed to sell it in a commercially reasonable manner. He also appears to argue for the first time on appeal that the award was excessive because it reflected an unreasonable amount of attorney's time to defend against Penney's complaint, prosecute the bank's counterclaim, and enforce the guaranty. The latter contention is not properly before us. Paro v. Longwood Hosp., 373 Mass. 645, 652 n. 9, 269 N.E.2d 985 (1977).

Each note provided that Penney would pay all costs of collection and attorney's fees paid or incurred by the bank in enforcing the note on default. The order of the judge allowing the bank's motion for summary judgment on its counterclaim with the assent of both parties provided that no execution was to issue until resolution of Penney's claims or further order of the court. Defense of Penney's claims was therefore essential to collection on the notes, and the attorney's fees incurred for that defense were incurred by the bank in enforcing the notes. In addition, those fees were required to withstand attack upon the repossession and sale of the boat, which were an integral part of the collection process. They were expenses of the collection process and so were within the fee provisions of the notes.

Judgments affirmed.

NOTES

1. The right of self-help repossession, set out in UCC § 9–503, is the creditor's most cherished weapon. It is cheap, fast, and effective. On the other hand, in allowing creditors to

act extra-judicially, this remedy is particularly offensive to debtor groups which claim that it is subject to abuse. The revolution in creditors' remedies law occasioned by Sniadach v. Family Finance Corp., 395 U.S. 337, 89 S.Ct. 1820, 23 L.Ed.2d 349 (1969), threatened the legality of self-help repossession. Both creditor and debtor groups threw maximum resources into a series of test cases that raged across the country throughout the 70s. But, as *Penney* indicates, the creditors won all of the battles and the great debtor-creditor issue of the decade never reached the United States Supreme Court. See Burke & Reber, State Action, Congressional Power and Creditors' Rights: An Essay on the Fourteenth Amendment, 47 So.Cal.L.Rev. 1 (1973); McCall, The Past as Prologue: History of the Right to Repossess, 47 So. Cal.L.Rev. 58 (1973).

2. The secured party has the rights and remedies provided for in Part 5 of Article 9 even though the security agreement is silent on the subject. UCC § 9–501(1). Hence, it is possible that the secured party has the right of self-help repossession without knowledge of that fact by the debtor. But other law may apply. For example, Maryland has enacted a statute making self-help repossession a crime unless the security agreement specifically authorizes the remedy. Maryland Code, Art. 27, § 343. See Opinion of the Attorney General of Maryland, 32 U.C.C.Rep. 359 (1980).

3. The UCC does not define default. In the security agreement the parties may, and usually do, set out the circumstances constituting default. Sometimes the security agreement contains an "insecurity clause" which allows the creditor to accelerate the balance of the debt if it "deems itself insecure." UCC § 1–208 provides that such words "shall be construed to mean that he shall have power to do so only if he in good faith believes that the prospect of payment or performance is impaired." In Mechanics National Bank of Worcester v. Killeen, 377 Mass. 100, 384 N.E.2d 1231 (1979), the debt secured by shares of stock was evidenced by a note that provided that the debtor's obligation "shall, at the option of Bank, become immediately due and payable upon * * * Bank deeming itself insecure." The court held that Bank, although it had good reason to feel insecure, had no right to sell the collateral without notifying the debtor that the debt was due and that it demanded payment. The court pointed out that the security agreement did not state that a default existed when Bank deemed itself insecure, nor that Bank had an immediate right to foreclose on the stock. Compare the security agreement in Bankers Trust Co. v. J.V.

Dowler & Co., Inc., 47 N.Y.2d 128, 417 N.Y.S.2d 47, 390 N.E.2d 766 (1979), which provided that the collateral could be sold whenever the Bank deemed itself insecure.

4. Uniform Consumer Credit Code § 5.109 (1974) defines default as follows:

An agreement of the parties to a consumer credit transaction with respect to default on the part of the consumer is enforceable only to the extent that:

(1) the consumer fails to make a payment as required by agreement; or

(2) the prospect of payment, performance, or realization of collateral is significantly impaired; the burden of establishing the prospect of significant impairment is on the creditor.

PROBLEM

Cobb bought a truck from Mack for $28,886, of which $23,886 was to be paid pursuant to an installment contract calling for 48 monthly payments of $497.63 each. The installment contract provided that time was of the essence and that if Cobb failed to pay any installment when due the full balance would become due thereby giving Mack the right to repossess without notice or demand. It also stated "Any waiver of any breach or default shall not constitute a waiver of any other subsequent breach or default." Cobb's payment record was irregular almost from the start. For two years he was always at least two payments in default and there were times when he made no payments for three or more months. When Cobb was particularly delinquent Mack would send him form letters, couched in the stilted language of the bill collector, that if he didn't get current Mack would "terminate his financial agreement" or "pursue a course of action outlined in your contract." Mack never mentioned the crude word "repossession" and consistently accepted Cobb's late payments, assessing late charges respecting these payments. With Cobb still two payments behind and only $2,000 remaining unpaid, Mack had had enough and repossessed the truck. Cobb sued for conversion because Mack had failed to notify him that strict compliance would be required in the future after late payments had been accepted. Mack defended on the basis of the nonwaiver provisions of the contract. What result? See Cobb v. Midwest Recovery Bureau Co., 295 N.W.2d 232 (Minn.1980), and Nevada National Bank v. Huff, 94 Nev. 506, 582 P.2d 364 (1978).

CENSUS FEDERAL CREDIT UNION v. WANN

Court of Appeals of Indiana, First District, 1980.
403 N.E.2d 348.

NEAL, JUDGE.

STATEMENT OF THE CASE

This is an appeal by the defendant-appellant, The Census Federal Credit Union, from an adverse judgment for trespass to personal property, in favor of the plaintiff-appellee, Richard Henry Wann.

We reverse.

FACTS

The facts most favorable to support the judgment are as follows: Plaintiff borrowed money from defendant and executed a note and a security agreement on his automobile to defendant. The parties stipulated at the trial that the note was in default and that defendant had "every right under the security agreement to repossess the automobile." The security agreement contained a provision that in the event of default, defendant had all remedies of a secured creditor under the Uniform Commercial Code. Defendant made demand on plaintiff for possession of the automobile, but plaintiff refused to give possession of it to defendant. Defendant, through its agents, thereafter, without benefit of any judicial process, took possession of the automobile by taking it from the parking lot of the apartment building where plaintiff lived at approximately 12:30 a.m. During this second and successful attempt to repossess the automobile, no contact whatever was had by defendant's agents with plaintiff or other person in the immediate control of the automobile.

ISSUE

The sole issue in this case is whether defendant was subject to any civil liability under the facts herein stated for exercising self-help repossession of the automobile under the authority of [UCC §] 9–503. Defendant contends that under this statute it had every right to take possession of the automobile without judicial process so long as it committed no breach of the peace in doing so. Plaintiff concedes that this general statement of the law is correct, but argues that defendant committed a breach of the peace by its actions. Therefore the sole issue in this appeal is whether the acts of the defendant amounted to a breach of the peace. At the trial the plaintiff proceeded upon the theory that when the defendant repossessed the automobile without the consent of plaintiff, it violated Ind.Code 35–43–2–2(4) (Supp.1979) which is a criminal trespass statute, and thereby committed a technical breach of the peace.

* * *

DISCUSSION

[Section] 9–503 of the Uniform Commercial Code (U.C.C.) adopted by Indiana, provides, in part, as follows:

"Unless otherwise agreed a secured party has on default the right to take possession of the collateral. In taking possession a secured party may proceed without judicial process if this can be done without breach of the peace or may proceed by action."

* * *

A breach of the peace includes all violations of public peace, order, or decorum. A breach of the peace is a violation or disturbance of the public tranquility or order, and the offense includes breaking or disturbing the public peace by any riotous, forceful, or unlawful proceedings. In accordance with the above definition, a breach of the peace may be an element of, or involved in, other offenses. 4 I.L.E. Breach of Peace, § 1 (1958).

* * *

We have examined holdings in other jurisdictions addressed to this issue under the U.C.C.

In Morris v. First National Bank and Trust Co. of Ravenna, (1970) 21 Ohio St.2d 25, 254 N.E.2d 683, the court held that intimidation or putting a person in fear for his safety exceeded the secured party's rights under the self-help provisions of the U.C.C. The court said that a breach of the peace for these purposes may consist of an act of violence or an act likely to produce violence, and that it was a public policy to discourage extrajudicial acts by citizens where those acts are fraught with the likelihood of resulting violence.

In Deavers v. Standridge, (1978) 144 Ga.App. 673, 242 S.E.2d 331, the court held that blocking the movement of the defaulting debtor's automobile after his oral protest to the secured party's repossession attempt was a breach of the peace.

A definitive statement of this type of suit and the rights and limitations of a secured party and the defaulting debtor was expressed in Thompson v. Ford Motor Credit Company, (5th Cir. 1977) 550 F.2d 256. In that case the finance company under a similar self-help statute winkled the automobile of a defaulting party away from a garageman who had custody of it for repairs. There the court, in ruling for the finance company, said, in 550 F.2d at 258:

> "The gist of the action of trespass is an injury to the possession of personal property by use of unlawful force. Unlawful force is the essential element of the action. * * * Such force may be actual physical force or it may be constructive force. Constructive force in such cases has been defined in a general way as that sort, such as threats or intimidation, to compel the submission of plaintiff against his will to the appropriation of what he asserts to be his property. * * * The threats or intimidation referred to are those which if carried out would amount to a breach of peace or if resisted would tend to promote a breach of peace. We have found no case in which such threats and intimidation did not occur in the presence of the plaintiff and at the time of the taking." (Citations omitted.)

Cases in other jurisdictions have held that absence of consent of the defaulting party to repossession is immaterial to the right of a secured party to repossess without judicial process. *Thompson,* supra; Speigle v. Chrysler Credit Corporation, (1975) 56 Ala.App. 469, 323 So.2d 360; Ford Motor Credit Company v. Ditton, (1974) 52 Ala.App. 555, 295 So.2d 408; Hollembaek v. Alaska Rural Rehabilitation Corporation, (1968 Alaska) 447 P.2d 67; Ford Motor Credit Company v. Cole, (1973 Tex.Civ.App.) 503 S.W.2d 853. This, of course, is a necessary result, for contrary to the argument of plaintiff [UCC §] 9–503, by its very existence, presupposes that the defaulting party did not consent. Should the defaulting party consent, no statutory authority would be required for a secured party to repossess, with or without judicial process. To hold otherwise would emasculate that statute.

Analysis of the above authorities reveals no substantial conflict. They reveal to us, in regard to the right of a secured party to repossess a chattel upon default without resort to judicial process pursuant to [UCC §] 9–503, a proscription of a secured party's use of force, intimidation, or harassment in the repossession of a chattel. The secured party may not in the process of repossession break into or enter into homes or other buildings or enclosed spaces, or commit any crime against the defaulting party, or disturb the peace, or otherwise commit any breach of the peace. Repossession upon default is not, in and of itself, a criminal trespass under Ind.Code 35–43–2—2(4). Consent for the repossession of the chattel by the defaulting party is not necessary. The secured party may, in repossession without judicial process under [UCC §] 9–503, take a chattel off a street, parking lot or unenclosed space. However, even in the attempted repossession of a chattel off a street, parking lot or unenclosed space, if the repossession is verbally or otherwise contested at the actual time of and in the immediate vicinity of the attempted repossession by the defaulting party or other person in control of the chattel, the secured party must desist and pursue his remedy in court. We approve the reasoning contained in these authorities.

DECISION

Plaintiff has not cited any authority, nor have we found any, in Indiana or elsewhere, that holds that the secured party cannot, under the self-help provisions of the U.C.C., repossess an automobile off a street, parking lot, or unenclosed space in absence of the defaulting party or any person in control of the chattel, as was done here. The plain policy of the law, as stated in *Morris*, supra, is to forbid acts that tend to provoke violence or any breach of the peace. We are of the opinion that under the facts of this case the act of the defendant in repossessing the automobile by taking it off the parking lot late at night, in absence of plaintiff or other person in immediate control of the vehicle, did not constitute a breach of the peace for the purposes of [UCC §] 9–503.

For the above stated reasons we order this cause reversed and direct the trial court to enter a judgment for defendant.

Reversed.

NOTES

1. In Thompson v. Ford Motor Company, quoted in the principal case, the automobile sought by the seller was found in a repair garage. The garageman refused to allow the seller to take the vehicle unless he had obtained the debtor's consent. The seller lied in telling the garageman that he had the debtor's consent. The court said "Merely to connive to repossess does not make [the seller] liable *   *   *   * " In Reno v. General Motors Acceptance Corp., 378 So.2d 1103 (Ala.1979), the finance company repossessed an automobile from the parking lot of a

grocery supermarket where the debtor worked by use of a duplicate key obtained from the dealer who had sold the installment contract to the finance company. The court held that there was no breach of the peace because possession was obtained without fraud, artifice, stealth, or trickery. The same court found a breach of the peace when the "repo man" induced a debtor to drive his car to the dealer's office to discuss whether his payments were in arrears. While the debtor was inside discussing the account, his car was removed. Ford Motor Credit Co. v. Byrd, 351 So.2d 557 (Ala.1977).

2. If the collateral is in an enclosed area the creditor must either obtain the consent of the debtor to take the property or must resort to judicial process. Replevin statutes allow levying officers to use force to enter and seize the collateral. The following provisions are found in the California Code of Civil Procedure § 514.010:

> (c) If the specified property or any part of it is in a private place, the levying officer shall at the time he demands possession of the property announce his identity, purpose, and authority. If the property is not voluntarily delivered, the levying officer may cause any building or enclosure where the property may be located to be broken open in such a manner as he reasonably believes will cause the least damage and may call upon the power of the county to aid and protect him, but, if he reasonably believes that entry and seizure of the property will involve a substantial risk of death or serious bodily harm to any person, he shall refrain from seizing the property and shall promptly make a return to the court from which the writ issued setting forth the reasons for his belief that the risk exists. In such case, the court shall make such orders as may be appropriate.

> (d) Nothing in this section authorizes the levying officer to enter or search any private place not specified in the writ of possession or other order of the court.

PROBLEM

Seller sold Buyer a tractor and Buyer fell in default. When Seller demanded payment, Buyer was unable to pay and said that he would not give up possession of the tractor unless Seller established his right to repossess by judicial proceedings. He said that "someone would get hurt" if an attempt was made to repossess without "proper papers." Seller filed suit in Washington but was unable to locate the tractor. Later he located the tractor in Oregon and contacted the local sheriff, requesting him to accompany him in retaking the tractor. Proceeding to the site of the tractor was a convoy made up of Seller's car, his mechanic in a pickup, a lo-boy truck to transport the tractor, and the sheriff's official car. The sheriff was in uniform, wearing his badge and sidearms. The sheriff, who had seen the contract, informed Buyer that Seller had the right to repossess and said, "We come to pick up the tractor." Buyer asked whether the sheriff had the proper papers to take the tractor and the sheriff replied, "No." Buyer protested the repossession but offered no physical resistance because, as he later testified, he didn't think he could disregard the order of a sheriff. Seller testified that he had the sheriff present to prevent anticipated violence. Is Seller liable in conversion? See Stone Machinery Co. v. Kessler, 1 Wn. App. 750, 463 P.2d 651 (1970).

B. RESALE AND REALIZATION

HALL v. OWEN COUNTY STATE BANK

Court of Appeals of Indiana, First District, 1977.
175 Ind.App. 150, 370 N.E.2d 918.

ROBERTSON, CHIEF JUDGE. Defendant-appellant, Howard Hall (Hall) brings this appeal from an adverse judgment by the trial court, sitting without a jury, in an action by Owen County State Bank (Bank) for judgment on three promissory notes executed by Hall. The fifteen issues raised by Hall on appeal may be grouped and summarized as follows:

1. Is the decision of the trial court that Hall waived his right to notice under UCC § 9–504(3) not supported by sufficient evidence and contrary to law? (Hall's issues 9 & 10).

2. Is the decision of the trial court that Hall received sufficient notice of the sale of collateral under UCC § 9–504(3) not supported by sufficient evidence and contrary to law? (Hall's issues 1, 3, 4, 5 and 7).

3. Is the decision of the trial court that the fair value of the collateral did not exceed $25,000.00 not supported by sufficient evidence? (Hall's issue 6).

4. Is the trial court's decision that the sale of the collateral was commercially reasonable not supported by sufficient evidence and contrary to law? (Hall's issues 11 and 12).

5. Did the trial court err by not awarding certain attorney's fees to Hall? (Hall's issue 15).

6. Did the trial court err in not allowing Hall to testify as to certain elements of his claim for punitive damages? (Hall's issue 2).

7. Is the decision of the trial court that the bank did not act in a willful and malicious manner not supported by sufficient evidence and contrary to law? (Hall's issue 8).

8. Is the decision of the trial court on the complaint and on Hall's counterclaim not supported by sufficient evidence and contrary to law? (Hall's issues 13 and 14).

The relevant facts of this case show that sometime in late 1971, Hall and his son-in-law, Allan Reed, began a trucking business under the name of H & R Trucking Company. In order to finance the needed trucking equipment, it was necessary for Hall and Reed to apply for loans from the Bank. The Bank granted loans aggregating approximately $56,000.00 in return for promissory notes and a security interest in the equipment purchased with the loan proceeds.

All went well until late 1973 or early 1974 when the business began to fail and Hall and Reed became delinquent in their monthly installments on the notes. At one point in the spring of 1974, one Bank officer, Lewis Cline, testified he called on Hall at his home to discuss the delinquent loan payments and that Hall stated he could not afford to make any more payments, that he "washed his hands" of the entire matter and did not want to be bothered any more, and that the Bank should thereafter talk with Reed.

The Bank then contacted Reed on numerous occasions concerning the delinquent loans and an attempt was made to restructure the payment schedule. However, Reed was unable to make the payments required under the new schedule and the Bank, on June 8, 1974, sent a letter to Reed demanding possession of the collateral, which consisted of two tractor-trailer rigs. On Sunday, June 30, 1974, Reed delivered both tractors and both trailers to the Bank's parking lot without any prior notice to the Bank. He returned the next morning, Monday, July 1, to surrender to the Bank the keys to the trucks.

Robert Ingalls, a used car and truck dealer in the area, was in the Bank on Monday morning and noticed the trucks in the parking lot. He inquired as to whether the equipment was for sale, and upon receiving an affirmative response, began to negotiate with Bank officers for the purchase of the equipment. Later that day, the negotiations ended with a take-it or leave-it offer for that day only of $25,000 in cash for all four units.

After deciding to accept the offer, the Bank notified Reed, who was at Hall's residence in Gosport, by telephone and Reed returned to the Bank. Bank officers explained the terms of the sale to him and explained that the proceeds of the sale were less than the amount due on the notes. Reed agreed that Ingalls' offer was fair and endorsed the truck titles without objection. Ingalls then paid the $25,000.00 to the Bank and the Bank credited the entire amount, without any deductions for expenses, to the amount due on the notes.

On June 9, 1975, the Bank filed its action against Hall and Reed for the amount still due under the notes. Default judgment was rendered against Reed and he has not joined in this appeal. Hall filed his answer, certain affirmative defenses, and a counterclaim against the Bank for compensatory and punitive damages. The trial court found in favor of the Bank and against Hall and awarded judgment against Hall in the sum of $2,328.25 in principal and interest and $500.00 in attorneys' fees. Hall then timely perfected this appeal.

The trial court stated in its findings that Hall had waived his right to notice of sale and that he was therefore estopped to assert any lack of notice. This finding is based on the meeting between Hall and Lewis Cline in which Hall allegedly stated that he "washed his hands" of the whole matter and directed the Bank to deal exclusively with Reed. Hall argues that this finding is contrary to law and not supported by sufficient evidence. He argues that he was entitled to notice of sale under UCC § 9–504(3). He further cites UCC § 9–501(3) as being a statutory prohibition of a waiver of that notice and also cites a provision incorporated in each of the notes which states:

> "If any notification of intended disposition of any of the collateral is required by law, such notification shall be deemed reasonably and properly given if mailed at least ten (10) days before such disposition, postage pre-paid, addressed to the Borrower at the address shown on other side."

The Bank argues, on the other hand, that UCC § 9–501(3) does not apply in this situation, that notice of sale can be waived, and that Hall did in fact waive his right to any notice.

UCC § 9–501(3) reads in pertinent part as follows:

(3) To the extent that they give rights to the debtor and impose duties on the secured party, the rules stated in the subsections referred to below may not be waived or varied

. . . .

(b) subsection (3) of section 9–504 and subsection (1) of section 9–505 which deal with disposition of collateral;

While this section has not been the subject of interpretation by the Indiana appellate courts, it appears that a question has arisen in the cases from other jurisdictions dealing with UCC § 9–501(3) as to the extent of this non-waiver provision. The cases seem to be in agreement, and we would also agree, that under this section the secured party may not incorporate a waiver provision in the security agreement. However, there is a split of authority as to whether or not the debtor may waive notice of sale after default. In Nelson v. Monarch Investment Plan of Henderson, Inc. (1970), Ky., 452 S.W.2d 375, it was held that UCC § 9–501 applied only to the antecedent agreement between the debtor and secured party (the security agreement) and did not affect the right to invoke the principles of waiver and estoppel to transactions of the parties subsequent to default. In O'Neil v. Mack Trucks, Inc. (Tex.Civ.App.1975), 533 S.W.2d 832, 19 UCC Rep. 984, the court held that only a written waiver signed after default would be effective against the debtor. Finally, the court in Aimonetto v. Keepes (Wyo.1972), 501 P.2d 1017, 11 UCC Rep. 1081, ruled that UCC § 9–501(3) prevented any waiver of the debtor's right to notice under UCC § 9–504(3).

Although it has been argued that UCC § 1–103 brings in the common law of waiver and estoppel so as to allow a waiver by the debtor after default, we feel that the general provisions of UCC § 1–103 are supplanted by the specific language in section 9–501(3) prohibiting any waiver. Furthermore, Indiana has not adopted the 1972 amendments to the UCC proposed by the Commissioners on Uniform State Laws which would amend UCC § 9–504(3) to allow the debtor to sign after default a renunciation of his rights to notification. Finally, we find very persuasive as to the policy behind UCC § 9–501(3) the following portion of Official Comment 4 to UCC § 9–501:

The default situation offers great scope for overreaching; the suspicious attitude of the courts has been grounded in common sense.

Subsection (3) of this section contains a codification of this long standing and deeply rooted attitude: the specified rights of the debtor and duties of the secured party may not be waived or varied except as stated.

Although there are persuasive arguments in favor of allowing a waiver of rights by the debtor after default, we feel the better interpretation of UCC § 9–501(3), and that which is more in line with the policy of UCC § 9–504 to protect the rights of the debtor, is that the non-waiver provision of UCC § 9–501(3) applies both before and after default. We therefore hold that UCC § 9–501(3) does not allow a waiver by the debtor of his right to reasonable notification under UCC § 9–504(3) and that the trial court erred in finding that Hall waived notice of the sale and was estopped by this waiver to contest the sale because of insufficient notice.[3]

Hall further argues that the trial court erred in its findings of fact that sufficient notice was sent by the Bank to Hall. Although the trial court's findings do not specifically state that sufficient notification was sent by the Bank, its Finding Number 14 implies that the trial court felt the notice sent to Reed was sufficient to bind Hall due to their relationship as partners.

There seems to be no doubt that the sale of collateral in this case should be classified under the UCC as a private sale rather than a public sale. The only notice requirement for a private sale under UCC § 9–504(3) is that the secured party give "reasonable notification" to the debtor "of the time after which" the sale or disposition will be made. There is no formal step by step procedure which the secured party must follow, and there are no rigid time limits which must be obeyed. This type of procedure for sale of collateral after repossession is a rejection of the formal notice and sale requirements of the Uniform Conditional Sales Act which was the law in this state (and in many other states) prior to the enactment of the UCC in 1963. According to Official Comment 1 to UCC § 9–504, the intent of the drafters of the UCC in this section was to encourage private sales through normal commercial channels. The drafters recognized the tradi-

---

3. Because the trial court's finding that Hall was estopped to deny the validity of the notice was based upon Hall's purported waiver, we need not decide whether the doctrine of estoppel might be applicable under different facts or circumstances.

tionally dismal results of the sheriff's public auction at the courthouse door and hoped that informal private sales through the regular course of business would "result in higher realization on collateral for the benefit of all parties."

The term "reasonable notification" is not specifically defined in the UCC. In § 1–201(26), the following definition of "notifies" is given:

> A person "notifies" or "gives" a notice or notification to another by taking such steps as may be reasonably required to inform the other in ordinary course whether or not such other actually comes to know of it.

Under this definition, the test is not whether or not the debtor receives the notice, but only whether the secured party made a good faith effort and took such steps as a reasonable person would have taken to give notice. Accordingly, most courts have held that there is no absolute requirement under § 9–504 that the debtor actually received notice.

The word "send", which is found in § 1–201(38), is defined in such a manner as to imply that the notice must be in writing. While some courts have indeed held that only a written notice will suffice under § 9–504,[5] there is also authority to the contrary.[6] We feel that a rigid rule of law mandating a written notice in all cases conflicts with the general tenor of the UCC to reject strict procedural requirements and we would therefore read § 1–201(38) in conjunction with § 1–201(26) so as to impose upon the secured party the duty of taking reasonable steps to notify the debtor. The fact that the notice was oral instead of written should not invalidate that notice as a matter of law but should instead be one of the factors considered in deciding whether or not the notice was reasonable.

Although no definition of "reasonable notification" is contained in the UCC itself, Official Comment 5 to § 9–504 contains this definition:

> "Reasonable notification" is not defined in this Article; at a minimum it must be sent in such time that persons entitled to receive it will have sufficient time to take appropriate

---

5. DeLay First National Bank & Trust Co. v. Jacobson Appliance Co. (1976), 196 Neb. 398, 243 N.W.2d 745, 19 UCC Rep. 994; Foundation Discounts, Inc. v. Serna (1970), 81 N.M. 474, 468 P.2d 875, 7 UCC 854.

6. Fairchild v. Williams Feed, Inc. (Mont.1976), 544 P.2d 1216, 18 UCC Rep. 822; Crest Investment Trust, Inc. v. Alatzas (1972), 264 Md. 571, 287 A.2d 261.

steps to protect their interests by taking part in the sale or other disposition if they so desire."

At least one state has grafted onto this definition, as a matter of law, a minimum number of days' notice needed to make the notice reasonable. DeLay First National Bank & Trust Company v. Jacobson Appliance Co. (1976), 196 Neb. 398, 243 N.W.2d 745, 19 UCC Rep. 994 (three days). Again, however, we must reject that line of thinking as being contrary to the basic purposes of the UCC. Although we feel that any case involving a very brief notice to the debtor should be closely scrutinized by the trial court, we also feel that the length of time of the notice should be included as one component in the decision as to whether reasonable notification was given by the secured party.

On the facts of this case, we feel the conclusion is inescapable that the Bank was required to send reasonable notification of the sale to Hall and that the Bank failed to do so.

Although H & R Trucking Company was named on the note and security agreement as debtor, the complaint filed by the Bank named Hall and Reed individually as defendants and did not name the partnership. Furthermore, Hall apparently signed the note in his individual capacity thereby making himself personally liable. UCC § 3–403(2)(b). Therefore, he would fall within a definition of debtor under UCC § 9–105(1)(d) and would be entitled to reasonable notification under UCC § 9–504(3).

It is uncontested that no written notice of the sale was ever sent to Hall. The record shows that the bank official who telephoned Hall's house on the date of sale did not remember speaking to Hall or even if Hall was present at that time. More importantly, the notice was given only hours before the sale and Hall testified that he did not receive any notice until after the sale was completed. We feel that the notification sent by the Bank was insufficient to allow Hall to protect his interest in the collateral. We therefore hold that the Bank failed to send the reasonable notification required under UCC § 9–504(3).

The other errors raised by Hall concerning the admission of certain partnership evidence bear only on the sufficiency of the Bank's notice to Hall. As we have decided in favor of Hall on this issue, we need not discuss these other issues.

Having decided that the Bank failed to send reasonable notification to Hall under UCC § 9–504(3), the question arises as to the effect of such a failure. It appears that there are no Indiana cases dealing with this question.

The cases decided in other states are hopelessly divided on the question as to whether the secured party should be barred from recovering a deficiency judgment from the debtor when there has been insufficient notice of the disposition of collateral after repossession.[7] In addition to these courts, it seems that the commentators are also in disagreement on this question.[8] From the language of UCC § 9–504, it appears that the drafters of the UCC either did not consider this question or else decided to leave the question open. At least one notable authority has stated that the drafters indeed failed to consider this issue.[9]

It has been argued that because § 9–504(2) and § 9–502(2) specifically give the secured party a right to collect any deficiency and because there is no language in § 9–504 to indicate that a creditor should be barred from a deficiency, the courts should have no authority to supply such a sanction. In contrast, the language of § 2–706, which allows the seller of goods to resell those goods after breach by the buyer and collect damages from the buyer (much like a repossession sale and suit for deficiency

---

7. For decisions allowing a deficiency, see Grant County Tractor Co., Inc. v. Nuss (1972), 6 Wash.App. 866, 496 P.2d 966, 10 UCC Rep. 1104; Norton v. National Bank of Commerce of Pine Bluff (1966), 240 Ark. 143, 398 S.W.2d 538, 3 UCC Rep. 119; Alliance Discount Corp. v. Shaw (1961), 195 Pa. Super. 601, 171 A.2d 548, 1 UCC Rep 644; T & W Ice Cream, Inc. v. Carriage Barn, Inc. (1969), 107 N.J.Super. 328, 258 A.2d 162, 6 UCC Rep. 1230; Weaver v. O'Meara Motor Co. (Alaska 1969), 452 P.2d 87, 6 UCC Rep. 415; Mallicoat v. Volunteer Finance & Loan Corp. (1966), 57 Tenn.App. 106, 415 S.W.2d 347, 3 UCC 1035, 4 UCC Rep. 49; Leasing Associates, Inc. v. Slaughter & Son, Inc. (8th Cir. 1971), 450 F.2d 174, 9 UCC Rep. 1292; Universal C.I.T. Credit Co. v. Rone (1970), 248 Ark. 665, 453 S.W.2d 37, 7 UCC Rep. 847; Community Management Association of Colorado Springs, Inc. v. Tousley (1973), 32 Colo.App. 33, 505 P.2d 1314, 11 UCC Rep. 1101.

For decisions barring a deficiency judgment see Braswell v. American National Bank (1968), 117 Ga.App. 699, 161 S.E.2d 420, 5 UCC Rep. 420; Foundation Discounts, Inc. v. Serna (1970), 81 N.M. 474, 468 P.2d 875, 7 UCC Rep. 854; Washington v. First National Bank of Miami (Fla.App. 1976), 332 So.2d 644, 19 UCC Rep. 989; C.I.T. Corporation v. Haynes (1965), 161 Me. 353, 212 A.2d 436, 2 UCC Rep. 1000; Atlas Thrift Co. v. Horan (1972), 27 Cal.App.3d 999, 104 Cal.Rptr. 315, 11 UCC Rep. 417; Aimonetto v. Keepes (Wyo.1972), 501 P.2d 1017, 11 UCC Rep. 1081.

At least two states have reported conflicting decisions from the same court: Leasco Computer, Inc. v. Sheridan Industries, Inc. (1975), 82 Misc.2d 897, 371 N.Y.S.2d 531 (allowing deficiency), and Leasco Data Processing Equipment Corp. v. Atlas Shirt Co., Inc. (1971), 66 Misc.2d 1089, 323 N.Y.S.2d 13 (barring a deficiency); Abbott Motors, Inc. v. Ralston (1964), 28 Mass.App.Dec. 35, 5 UCC Rep. 788 (allowing a deficiency) and One Twenty Credit Union v. Darcy (Mass.App. Div. 1968), 5 UCC Rep. 792.

8. See Hogan, Pitfalls in Default Procedure, 86 Banking L.J. 965, 978 (1969); 2 G. Gilmore, Security Interests in Personal Property § 44.9.4 (1965).

9. 2 G. Gilmore, supra, note 6, at p. 1264.

judgment) strongly implies that notice to the buyer in that case is a condition precedent to the recovery of damages.

It can also be argued that the adoption of a rule which strictly bars a deficiency judgment in cases of faulty notice contravenes the intent and purpose of the UCC. First of all, as stated above, the drafters of the UCC intended to do away with rigid rules of law designed to govern in all situations in favor of more fluid guidelines which allow a case by case analysis. It was hoped that this procedure would allow parties to reach the merits of each case instead of becoming entangled in procedural technicalities:

> "Article 9 imposes few formal requirements and relies instead on the general obligation of commercial reasonableness. It was hoped that Article 9 default litigation would reach, and be decided on, the merits of the case, without being deflected either by the debtor's allegations of a technical defense or the secured parties' demonstration of equally technical compliance with formalities. 2 Gilmore, Security Interests and Personal Property, § 44.9.4 at p.1264 (1965)."

Furthermore, the policy of the UCC as expressed in § 1–106 is to allow full recompense to an aggrieved party by a liberal application of the remedies provided in the UCC and to avoid the assessment of penal damages, unless such damages are expressly allowed by the UCC or other law.[10] It would seem that an automatic denial of a judgment for the remaining portion of a debt would amount to a rejection of that policy. The Nebraska Supreme Court, in rejecting a strict rule barring deficiency judgments because of insufficient notice, also felt that such a rule would be unduly punitive: "No sound policy requires us to inject a drastic punitive element into a commercial context." Cornett v. White Motor Corp. (1973), 190 Neb. 496, 501, 209 N.W.2d 341, 344, 13 UCC 152.

---

10. By this, we do not mean to imply that punitive damages should never be allowed in this type of situation. We are merely stating that punitive damages have no place in the normal commercial transaction, including most repossessions, just as such punitive damages have no place in the normal breach of contract suit. However, as stated in UCC § 1–106 where the debtor can plead and prove the facts necessary to support some other theory, an award of punitive damages might be appropriate. Such circumstances might include a situation where the debtor can clearly show that the secured party is intentionally and maliciously violating the rights of the debtor. See Hibschman Pontiac, Inc. v. Batchelor (1977), Ind., 362 N.E.2d 845; Vernon Fire & Casualty Ins. Co. v. Sharp (1976), Ind., 349 N.E. 2d 173; Jones v. Abriani (1976), Ind. App., 350 N.E.2d 635.

Probably the most persuasive argument for allowing a secured party to proceed with an action for a deficiency judgment is the fact that the UCC has already provided the debtor with a remedy in § 9-507. Under the latter section, if a secured party is not proceeding properly, the debtor may either restrain the creditor from proceeding further, or may recover from him any loss that the debtor may have suffered due to the secured party's failure to comply with the provisions of Article 9. Further protection is afforded under § 9-507 to the debtor in a consumer transaction in that a minimum damage figure is set out, which roughly equals the interest charge plus 10% of the cash price of the goods. In addition, under the provision of § 5-103 of the Uniform Consumer Credit Code the debtor is not liable for any deficiency where the secured party elects to repossess goods which had a price of $1100.00 or less and which were a part of a consumer credit sale.

Some rather persuasive arguments have also been advanced in favor of barring deficiency judgments in all cases where the secured party does not proceed properly. Such a rule would seem to be easier to apply, might bring about more uniform results and could possibly force creditors to be more careful in giving notice to debtors. Furthermore, there is nothing in the language of the UCC to suggest that the remedy provided in § 9-507 was intended to be an exclusive remedy. Section 1-103 brings traditional common law into play, such as equitable principles and principles of justice and fair play, which should suggest that a creditor should not be allowed a deficiency judgment when he breaks the law:

> "The rule and requirements are simple. If the secured creditor wishes a deficiency judgment he must obey the law. If he does not obey the law, he may not have his deficiency judgment. Atlas Thrift Company v. Horan (1972), 27 Cal. App.3d 999, 104 Cal.Rptr. 315, 11 UCC Rep. 417, 426."

It must also be considered that by failing to take proper steps to notify the debtor, the secured creditor can effectively deprive the debtor of his right to redeem the collateral under § 9-506 and his right to protect his interest by procuring bids or buyers at any private or public sale that is held.

After considering both the cases and policy arguments on this issue, we feel that the better rule of law would allow the secured creditor a right to an action for a deficiency judgment notwithstanding a failure to send proper notice under § 9-504(3).

In addition to the reasons cited above, we feel that the UCC should function on the premise that the majority of commercial transactions are carried out in good faith. In those cases in which the secured creditor has not complied with the appropriate notice provisions, or has otherwise not proceeded in good faith, it is better to adopt a more flexible standard which will allow the secured party to recover the damages caused by the debtor's breach, but which will also allow protection to the debtor on a case-by-case basis. The debtor is provided a remedy in § 9–507 and we see no reason to attach a further penalty to the creditor by declaring an automatic forfeiture of his right of a deficiency judgment.

A majority of the cases allowing the creditor to proceed in an action for a deficiency under these circumstances have ruled that the creditor before recovering his judgment, must rebut the presumption that the collateral was at least equal in value to the amount of the debt. We think that this is a sound policy, for in cases where the debtor was not notified of an impending sale, the creditor should be in a much better position to prove the value of the collateral at the time of the disposition. See Universal C. I. T. Credit Co. v. Rone (1970), 248 Ark. 665, 453 S.W.2d 37, 7 UCC Rep. 847. Furthermore, it seems fundamentally unfair to put the burden of showing the value of collateral after it has been repossessed and sold upon a debtor who has received insufficient notice of the disposition. We hold, therefore, that when a secured creditor disposes of collateral without proper notice under § 9–504(3), he must then prove, in his action for a deficiency judgment, that the reasonable value of the collateral at the time of the sale was less than the amount of the debt.

In meeting the burden outlined above, the creditor may not merely rely on the value which he received from the repossession sale. We agree with the Arkansas Supreme Court that "it is only where the sale is conducted according to the requirements of the code that the amount received or bid at a sale of collateral is evidence of its true value in an action to recover a deficiency." Universal C. I. T. Credit Corp. v. Rone (1970), 248 Ark. 665, 669, 453 S.W.2d 37, 39–40.

Furthermore, the secured party may not rely solely on testimony of his credit manager or his other employees as to their opinions of the fair value of the collateral. Instead, the creditor must introduce other additional credible objective evidence of value. See Weaver v. O'Meara Motor Co. (Alaska 1969), 452 P.2d 87, 6 UCC Rep 415.

Hall also contends that the trial court's finding that the sale of collateral was conducted in a commercially reasonable manner is not supported by sufficient evidence and is contrary to law, and that its finding that the value of the collateral at the time of sale did not exceed $25,000 is also not supported by sufficient evidence. We shall consider these issues together.

The UCC does not give a specific definition of a commercially reasonable sale of collateral. § 9–504(3) states that the disposition, whether by sale or otherwise, "may be as a unit or in parcels and at any time and place and on any terms, but every aspect of the disposition including the method, manner, time, place and terms must be commercially reasonable." Some examples of a commercially reasonable sale are given in § 9–507(2). If the collateral is sold in the usual manner in a recognized market for those goods, or if the goods are sold for the price that is current in that market, then the sale is presumed to be proper. Also, if the sale is conducted in conformity with "the reasonable commercial practices among dealers in the type of property sold", or if the disposition is approved in a judicial proceeding, it will be presumed to be commercially reasonable. However, it is also specifically provided that this is not an exclusive list of commercially reasonable dispositions.

Because the statutory definition of a commercially reasonable sale is vague, and because a judgment as to whether or not a sale was reasonable will generally depend upon the circumstances of each particular case, many courts have held this to be a question of fact. Jones v. Morgan (1975), 58 Mich.App. 455, 228 N.W.2d 419, 16 UCC Rep. 1450. We also feel that whether a sale was held in a commercially reasonable manner is a question of fact. We further agree with the decisions holding that the secured creditor has the burden of showing, as a part of his burden of proof in an action for a deficiency judgment, that the sale or disposition was performed in a commercially reasonable manner. Beneficial Finance Company of Black Hawk County v. Reed (Iowa 1973), 212 N.W.2d 454, 13 UCC Rptr. 1974; Tauber v. Johnson (1972), 8 Ill.App.3d 789, 291 N.E.2d 180, 11 UCC Rptr. 1106.

Certainly one of the most important factors to be weighed in deciding whether or not a disposition or sale was commercially reasonable will be the price received by the secured party. In cases where a fair sale price was received, the debtor will have suffered no injury and normally will have no complaint (except, perhaps, in cases where the debtor would have been able to find alternate financing and redeem the collateral). In cases where a fair sale price was not received, the other items to be considered will generally be relevant to the extent that they may have prevented a fair price or contributed to an unfair price.

It is expressly provided in § 9–507, however, that the sale price is not the only item to be considered:

(2) The fact that a better price could have been obtained by a sale at a different time or in a different method from that selected by the secured party is not of itself sufficient to establish that the sale was not made in a commercially reasonable manner * * *

The above provision gives recognition to the fact that only on rare occasions will a repossession sale bring the highest bids or the highest value for the collateral and therefore such sales could always be vulnerable to attack by a showing that a higher price *might* have been obtained under different circumstances. This means that a secured creditor may not be held liable to the debtor or be deprived of a deficiency judgment when the secured party has, in good faith, conducted a commercially acceptable sale or disposition, even where a low sale price is received:

If the secured creditor makes certain that conditions of the sale, in terms of the aggregate effect of the manner, method, time, place and terms employed conform to commercially accepted standards, he should be shielded from the sanctions contained in Article 9 [of the UCC]. In Re Zsa Zsa Limited (S.D.N.Y.1972), 352 F.Supp. 665, 671, 11 UCC Rep. 1116.

However, even though a low sale price itself is insufficient to overturn a sale, closer scrutiny will generally be given sales in which there is a *substantial* difference between the sale price and the fair value to determine whether there were legitimate causes for the low price such as a depressed or non-existent market, or whether the low price was caused by the secured party's failure to proceed in a commercially reasonable manner.

One relevant factor to be considered in determining whether the sale price was reasonable may be the price received by the buyer of the collateral in a subsequent sale. A showing that the collateral was sold only a short time later, after little or no reconditioning or cleaning, at a substantially or disproportionately higher price may strongly imply that the secured party failed to receive a fair price for the collateral. See Mercantile Financial Corp. v. Miller (E.D.Pa.1968), 292 F.Supp. 797, 7 UCC Rep. 402.

Another factor which may be relevant is whether the collateral is sold on a retail or wholesale market. It is certainly true that a retail sale of goods will in most cases command a much higher price. However, a retail sale will usually generate considerably more expenses, such as reconditioning expenses, advertising expenses and sales commissions, insurance costs, etc., and usually will take much longer to consummate. This in turn may result in higher storage expenses and a higher interest accrual under the original obligation. Therefore, a sale to a dealer on the wholesale market will probably be the more reasonable approach in most cases. Sales to a dealer also seem to be suggested by UCC § 9–504 and the Official Comments to that section (which suggest that a private sale will be preferable in many cases) and also by Official Comment 2, to UCC § 9–507:

> One recognized method of disposing of repossessed collateral is for the secured party to sell the collateral to or through a dealer—a method which in the long run may realize better average returns since the secured party does not usually maintain his own facilities for making such sales."

While we feel that in most cases a sale or disposal of collateral to a dealer or on a wholesale market or auction will be commercially reasonable, the answer to this question will generally depend upon the circumstances of each particular case and will therefore be a question of fact for the factfinder in most cases.

Other factors to be considered in deciding whether a sale was commercially reasonable include the number of bids received or solicited, particularly in a private sale. While we would not hold sales invalid as a matter of law where only 1 or 2 bids were received, such sales must receive the closest scrutiny and should be declared invalid where there is evidence of collusion, self-dealing, or bad faith. In addition, the time and place of the sale must be such that they are reasonably calculated to bring a satisfactory turnout of bidders, particularly in the case of a public sale. In deciding whether or not the disposition of collateral was accomplished in a commercially reasonable manner all of the relevant factors should be considered together. This means that the sale or disposition should be considered to be one transaction, as stated by the court in In Re Zsa Zsa Limited, supra:

> "It is the aggregate of circumstances in each case—rather than specific details of the sale taken in isolation—that should be emphasized in a review of the sale. The facets of manner, methods, time, place and terms cited by the Code are

to be viewed as necessary and interrelated parts of the whole transaction. 352 F.Supp. at 670.''

In attacking the trial court's findings as not being supported by sufficient evidence and as being contrary to law, Hall carries a heavy burden on appeal. The decision of the trial court will be sustained on appeal, when being attacked as not being supported by sufficient evidence, when there is substantial evidence of probative value to support its findings. Furthermore, we will neither weigh the evidence, nor judge the credibility of witnesses and we cannot substitute our judgment for that of the trial court. Rieth-Riley Construction Co. Inc. v. McCarrell (1975), Ind.App., 325 N.E.2d 844. Finally, it is only where the evidence is without conflict and can lead to but one conclusion and the trial court has reached an opposite conclusion, that the decision of the trial court will be set aside on the grounds that it is contrary to law. Blankenship v. Huesman (1977), Ind.App., 362 N.E.2d 850.

Hall advances four arguments in support of his contention that the sale was not conducted in a commercially reasonable manner. First, the value of the collateral exceeded the sale price of $25,000.00. Next, the Bank as seller was unfamiliar with the equipment it was selling and with the value of the equipment. Third, the Bank failed to publish notice of the sale and failed to contact any purchasers other than the ultimate purchaser. Finally, there was no appraisal of the collateral before the sale.

We feel that the evidence produced by the Bank, although minimal, was sufficient to carry its burden of proof as to the value of the collateral so as to rebut the presumption that the collateral was at least equal in value to the outstanding debt and was sufficient to sustain the trial court's finding that the value of the collateral did not exceed $25,000.00.

One of the witnesses called by the Bank was Robert Ingalls, who was the original purchaser of the collateral and who was an experienced used car and truck dealer in Spencer. Ingalls testified that he had trouble selling the equipment and that Reed, Hall's partner, had been trying to sell the equipment for some weeks prior to the bank's repossession, but had been unsuccessful. He further testified that the trucks were not roadworthy when he bought them, that they would not have passed state inspection, and that $25,000.00 was the full value of the equipment.[11]

The Bank also called as a witness James Roemer who was General Manager of Indiana Truck Center, a large truck dealership in Indianapolis. Roemer testified that his dealership had purchased three pieces of the collateral (two tractors and one trailer) from another dealer that had purchased the equipment from Ingalls. Although Roemer had purchased these three pieces for $23,000.00, he testified that after spending over $5,400.00 to recondition the equipment, he sold them, at retail, for only $30,500.00.

The trial judge received testimony, from experienced truck dealers, that the equipment was not in good shape, that $25,000 was a fair price under the circumstances, and that the equipment was eventually sold at retail, after substantial reconditioning and after passing through three dealers, for a sum not substantially greater than the original sale price. While there was other credible evidence which tended to show a higher value of the collateral, we cannot say that the finding of the trial court was supported by insufficient evidence and we must therefore affirm that finding.

---

11. The following is a portion of Ingalls' testimony on direct examination:

Q. Now then, when you purchased these vehicles, Mr. Ingalls, from the bank lot there, did you look at them before you made an offer?

A. Yes, I did.

Q. Did you attempt to ascertain their physical and mechanical condition?

A. Yes, I did.

Q. How did they appear to you? What did you decide?

A. Well, my first thought when I looked at these vehicles, was they were worth $20,000 to me. This is strictly my own opinion, but I make my living doing this. After thinking about it for awhile, and so forth, I went back and raised my figure, but these vehicles, when I purchased them from the bank lot, were not capable of passing safety inspection to run on the state highways of the state of Indiana. I trade better trucks off in my business, in my trucking business, I trade better trucks off than I bought here, by far. I would call these trucks pretty common trucks, that needed a lot of money spent on them to make them roadworthy.

Q. In your opinion were they roadworthy at the time?

A. No way.

Q. Mr. Ingalls, do you feel that the $25,000 in cash that you paid for these four units was the full, fair market value of them at that time?

A. I most certainly do. I'd have been tickled to death the next day to have took $500 loss and send them down the road.

Q. You mean to give them back to the bank and give them $500 in addition, and say, "let me out of the deal"?

A. I'd have been tickled to death.

Q. You would?

A. Yes Sir.

(R. p. 452, 453).

Hall further contends that the sale of the collateral was not reasonable because no appraisal of the equipment was made and because the bank officials conducting the sale were unfamiliar with the equipment. However, Hall has failed to explain how an appraisal of the equipment could have been of any possible benefit in this case. We would agree that an appraisal might be a prerequisite to a commercially reasonable sale of some types of goods, but we do not feel that used trucks would necessarily fall into that category.

In his argument that the sale was unreasonable because the Bank employees were not familiar with the equipment Hall relies on the case of Liberty National Bank & Trust Co. of Oklahoma City v. Acme Tool Division of Rucker Company (10th Cir. 1976), 540 F.2d 1375, 19 UCC Rptr. 1288. The *Rucker* case, however, concerned the sale of an oil rig by the bank's attorney, who was totally unfamiliar with oil rigs and with auctions of such rigs and who had taken no steps to prepare the rig for auction. In addition, the purchasers at the auction, who paid $42,000.00 for the rig, sold the rig shortly thereafter for over $77,000, even though there had been no change in the market. Finally, the Circuit Court in that case was affirming the trial court's finding of fact that the sale was not commercially reasonable. We feel that the *Rucker* case is distinguishable on its facts in that the Bank employees conducting the sale in this case were experienced in selling repossessed cars and trucks, and one employee, Evans, testified he had previously worked for a used car and truck dealer for six years. Furthermore, the trial court in this case, unlike the trial court in *Rucker*, made a finding of fact that the sale was commercially reasonable.

Hall also argues that the sale was improper because the Bank failed to publish notice of the sale and because there was only one bid made. However, the sale in this case was a private sale to a dealer, not a public sale, and we see no reason to require public advertisement or publication in the case of a private sale.

The case of Atlas Construction Co. v. Dravo Doyle Corp. (Pa. C.P.1965), 3 UCC Rptr. 124, 114 Pitt.L.J. 34 is cited by Hall in support of his argument that the sale should be voided because the Bank failed to solicit more than one bid. Although the court in that case ruled that a repossession sale of a crane was not commercially reasonable because of the low sale price and because only one bid was made, this was a case in which the jury made the finding of fact that the sale was not commercially reasonable. Furthermore, the creditor in *Dravo Doyle* was a dealer in cranes and yet did not attempt to solicit any further bidding from any of its customers. The debtor in that case had also produced a witness who testified that he would willingly have paid between five and eight thousand dollars more for the crane had he been given the opportunity to bid.

We agree with Hall that any private sale of collateral in which only one bid is received or solicited is highly questionable and should be closely scrutinized by the trial court. However, under the rather distinctive facts of this case, we cannot hold that the trial court erred in finding the sale to be commercially reasonable and we cannot say that the sale was improper as a matter of law.

The Bank had no prior notice as to when the equipment would be returned or in what condition it might be, but instead found the equipment in its parking lot on a Monday morning. The Bank therefore had no opportunity to solicit any bids before the day of the sale. The equipment was in need of repairs, as it had been used for some time in a failing business. That same morning, a reputable used car and truck dealer approached the Bank's loan officers and made a bid for the trucks. After several hours of negotiations with those officers, he made a take-it or leave-it offer of $25,000.00, good only for that day. This offer was particularly attractive in that the Bank was able to apply the entire sale price against the outstanding debt, without deduction for any expenses, such as insurance, transportation and storage charges, clean-up and repair charges, advertising expense and sales expenses or commissions (Roemer of Indiana Truck Center testified that his salesmen received a 25% commission on their sales). Although the equipment was later resold by other dealers at a profit, none of the subsequent dealer-purchasers sold the equipment for a disproportionate profit. Furthermore, there was evidence that Reed had been unable to find a buyer for the equipment for several weeks prior to the repossession. He made no objection when the Bank informed him of Ingalls' bid and willingly returned to the Bank to endorse the titles.

Finally, we find most persuasive the fact that there is evidence of nothing but good faith conduct on the part of the Bank. There is no evidence in the record of any collusion or underhanded dealing by the Bank. Reed in his deposition stated that he had no criticism of the manner in which the Bank conducted the sale and Hall also stated that he did not feel that the Bank had cheated him in any way and that his only criticism was that the Bank had not given him sufficient time to sell the trucks himself.

* * *

Judgment affirmed.

NOTES

1. UCC § 9–504(3) provides that disposition may be made by public or private sale. Comment 1 to UCC § 9–504 says, "Although public sale is recognized, it is hoped that private sale will be encouraged where, as is frequently the case, private sale through commercial channels will result in higher realization on collateral for the benefit of all parties." Actually, in allowing the secured party to buy at a public sale UCC § 9–504(3) encourages creditors to opt for public sales. If there are no higher bids the secured creditor may acquire the property at a public sale without laying out any cash at all merely by bidding the amount of the debt. Then the creditor may dispose of the property in any manner he wishes.

The notice requirement of UCC § 9–504(3) varies depending upon whether the sale is public or private. If the sale is public the notice must give the time and place of the sale; if private, the notice need only state the time after which the private sale is to be held.

Article 9 offers only the barest hint about what is meant by a public or private sale. Comment 1 to UCC § 9–504 refers to UCC § 2–706, and Comment 4 to that section says, "By 'public' sale is meant a sale by auction. A 'private' sale may be effected by solicitation and negotiation conducted either directly or through a broker." In Morrell Employees Credit Union v. Uselton, 28 U.C.C. Rep. 269 (Tenn.App.1979), the court opined that since public and private sale are not defined by the UCC reference should be made to the Restatement of Security, § 48, Comment (c) (1944), where public sale is defined as "one to which the public is invited by advertisement to appear and bid at auction for the goods to be sold." In *Morrell* an auto was offered for sale only to members of a credit union; no other bid would have been accepted. The court held that the sale was private. In White & Summers, Uniform Commercial Code 1120 (2d ed. 1980) it is contended that public sale should be interpreted to include a regularly scheduled dealer's auction even though the general public is not admitted.

2. UCC § 9–504(3) says little about the "reasonable notification" the creditor must give of the disposition of the collateral. For a public sale the time and place of disposition must be given; for a private sale only the time after which the disposition will be made. In Wilmington Trust Co. v. Conner, 415 A.2d 773 (Del.1980), the court stated the purposes of the reasonable notification requirement: "(1) it gives the debtor the opportunity to exercise his redemption rights under § 9–506 *   *   * ; (2) it affords the debtor an opportunity to seek out buyers for the collateral *   *   * ; and (3) it allows the debtor to oversee every aspect of the disposition, thus maximizing the probability that a fair sale price will be obtained *   *   * " 415 A.2d at 776. Do you agree with the view of the court in the principal case that the notice can be oral in the face of use of the word "send" in UCC § 1–201(38) and "sent" in UCC § 9–504(3)?

3. If Article 9 allows, in fact encourages, the creditor to opt for a public sale aren't we back where we started before the Code: a funereal auction on the courthouse steps with the only people present being the local public-sale vultures and the secured creditor prepared to bid the amount of his claim? Not if the court takes to heart the admonition of UCC § 9–504(3) that "every aspect of the disposition including the method, manner, time, place and terms must be commercially reasonable."   In Farmers Bank v. Hubbard, 247 Ga. 431, 276 S.E.2d 622 (1981), the creditor sold a tractor and trailer at public sale after advertisement and notice. The creditor sued for a deficiency judgment. The court said, "In passing, however, we note that it was not shown that selling a tractor-trailer on the courthouse steps was commercially reasonable, where there was no evidence that tractor-trailers are customarily sold on the courthouse steps where the sale occurred. We note further that there was no evidence as to what a dealer in used tractor-trailers would have paid for the tractor-trailer or what an auctioneer would have been able to sell it for. That is to say, courthouse sales may not be commercially reasonable as to all types of collateral, especially where there are better recognized means of marketing the particular collateral involved." 276 S.E.2d at 627.

4. Article 9 is generally very favorable to secured creditors but, in applying the "commercially reasonable" test of UCC § 9–504(3), some courts have imposed standards of conduct on secured creditors that would have been unthinkable under pre-Code procedure-oriented foreclosure laws. An example is Liberty National Bank & Trust v. Acme Tool Division of the Rucker Co., 540 F.2d 1375 (10th Cir. 1976), referred to in the principal

case. The court described Liberty Bank's actions in selling an oil rig as follows:

> It had no previous experience in selling an oil rig and so the officers inquired or investigated as to the usual manner of such sales. Liberty was told that the ordinary method for selling a drilling rig was to employ an auctioneer to move the rig to a convenient location to clean and paint it and then notify interested persons and, in addition, advertise the sale in trade journals and newspapers. The bank followed none of these suggestions. Indeed, it sold the rig without any professional help. Notices were sent to 16 creditors, including Taurus, and to some 19 other companies. Mrs. Bailey did not receive notice except information furnished by her son-in-law. The rig was neither cleaned, painted nor dismantled. Liberty did not move it to a convenient site, but sold it at the place where it had been near Perryton, Texas. The sale was conducted by an attorney for Liberty who had never conducted an auction of an oil rig or oil field equipment and who lacked experience in the oil business. The attorney was assisted by a Liberty Bank officer who knew something about oil production, but was not acquainted with the drilling of wells. Some 40 or 50 people appeared for the sale, but few made bids. In fact, after the price reached $37,000, there were only two bidders. The final sale price, $42,000, was sufficient to pay off the Taurus note and pay the expenses of the sale, but left little for the other creditors. The rig had been appraised at $60,000 to $80,000.
>
> The successful bidder was Raymond Hefner of Bonray Oil Company and Miller & Miller Auctioneers. In June 1972, Miller & Miller sold the equipment for $77,705.50.

540 F.2d at 1377–78.

In deciding that the sale was not conducted in a commercially reasonable manner (it was held in a snowstorm in Perryton, Texas), the court quoted the District Court's findings of fact:

> 13. The proper way to sell the rig and related equipment would have been to contract with a professional auctioneer, or to follow the same steps and procedures a professional auctioneer follows in disposing of equipment of this type which is to clean and paint the equipment, prepare a brochure and mail it to the proper people; advertise in trade journals, regional newspapers and the *Wall Street Journal*; move the equipment to a convenient location, and offer the equipment on a piece by piece basis as well as in one lot.

The Court finds that the rig and related equipment were not sold by Liberty Bank in the usual manner in a recognized market, nor in conformity with reasonable commercial practices among oil field equipment dealers.

540 F.2d at 1378.

UCC § 9–501(1) allows a creditor to dispose of collateral "in its then condition *or* following any commercially reasonable preparation." (Emphasis added.) Doesn't this language give the creditor an option whether to repair and refurbish or to sell the collateral in its present state? Is this option taken away from the creditor in some situations by the dictate of UCC § 9–504(3) that every aspect of the disposition must be commercially reasonable? A leading credit lawyer, speaking of cases like *Liberty*, says, "Clearly the most significant development under part 5 of Article 9 has been the trend evidenced by a series of decisions to impose upon secured creditors a duty to make reasonable efforts to refurbish or repair repossessed collateral before sale." Burke, Uniform Commercial Code Annual Survey—Secured Transactions, 32 Bus.Law. 1133, 1161 (1977).

5. In the principal case the court sets out some of the cases bearing on the right of a creditor to obtain a deficiency judgment after noncompliance with UCC § 9–504(3). An update on this issue is found in Hoch v. Ellis, 627 P.2d 1060 (Alaska 1981), in which the dissenting opinion states that 47 jurisdictions have now passed on the question. The cases are collected. The dissenting judge says, "As can be seen from these cases, the majority of jurisdictions have chosen not to penalize creditors with automatic forfeitures of deficiency judgments. However, it is clear that there is a sharp and confusing split of authority on the issue. An excellent example of this frustrating split is presented by the New York courts where intermediate appellate courts have adopted all three positions on the issue." 627 P.2d at 1067. In Wilmington Trust Co. v. Conner, 415 A.2d 773 (Del. 1980), the court also collects the cases and concludes that the majority rule is that failure to comply strictly with the notice provisions of the Code acts as an absolute bar to recovery of a deficiency judgment.

PROBLEMS

1. On August 1 Debtor purchased a used car from Dealer for $1,595 plus finance charges, payable under an installment sale contract under which Dealer was granted a security interest in the car. The car immediately developed mechanical problems

and Debtor had to return the car several times for repairs. On August 25, after paying only one partial installment Debtor refused to make additional payments and surrendered the car to Dealer. After making a demand for payment which was ignored Dealer sent written notice to Debtor that after October 15 the car would be sold at private sale. The car was purchased by Dealer at a private sale with itself on October 16. The sale took place by means of an interoffice exchange of papers by which Debtor was credited with $900, the proceeds of the sale. Debtor was also credited with the amount of his down payment and first installment payment totalling $95. Dealer then brought an action against Debtor for a deficiency judgment of $600 ($1,595 − $995).

Dealer testified that the $900 value was based on the wholesale value for used cars of the same model, year etc. stated in the then current market reporter or "blue book" used by used car dealers in the area. Dealer resold the car to a retail customer for $1,495 a few weeks after Debtor surrendered the car.

How much is Dealer entitled to recover from Debtor? Would your answer differ if Dealer had sold the car surrendered by Debtor to another used car dealer for $900 and used that sale as the basis for its deficiency judgment claim? See Vic Hansen & Sons, Inc. v. Crowley, 57 Wis.2d 106, 203 N.W.2d 728 (1973).

In, In re Ford Motor Co., 27 UCC Rep. 1118 (1979), the Federal Trade Commission examined the practice of an automobile dealer with respect to repossessed automobiles of crediting the debtor with the wholesale value of the automobile and then reselling the car at retail. This practice was that normally followed in the used car business. It held that the debtor's right to any surplus realized by the secured party on resale of collateral under UCC § 9–504(2) must be measured by the retail resale price obtained by the dealer reduced only by the direct expenses incurred in the repossession and resale, with no allowance for overhead or lost profit. Failure of the auto dealer to calculate surpluses on that basis was held to be an unfair trade practice under Section 5 of the Federal Trade Commission Act. The decision was reversed on the basis that the Commission should have proceeded by rule making rather than adjudication. Ford Motor Co. v. Federal Trade Commission, 673 F.2d 1008 (9th Cir. 1981). See Professor Kripke's critique of the FTC position in 32 UCC Rep. 4 (1982).

2. Corporation granted Bank a security interest in all its equipment to secure a loan. Bank required Guarantors (Corpo-

ration's president and his wife) to sign a separate agreement providing in part: "The liability of Guarantors for the debt the Corporation owes to Bank is absolute and unconditional. Upon default by Corporation Bank may proceed immediately against the undersigned Guarantors without first proceeding against Corporation or any security given by Corporation. The Guarantors waive any right to notice regarding disposition of the collateral or regarding any amendment or extension of Corporation's debt to Bank."

Corporation defaulted and Bank sold the collateral at public sale after due written notice to Corporation. Guarantors knew of the notification to Corporation but Bank did not send written notification to Guarantors. Are Guarantors liable to Bank for the deficiency stemming from Bank's disposition of the property at less than the amount of the debt? See UCC § 9–105(1)(d) and § 9–501(3). Compare First National Park Bank v. Johnson, 553 F.2d 599 (9th Cir. 1977) with Commercial Discount Corp. v. King, 515 F.Supp. 988 (N.D.Ill.1981), and United States v. Chatlin's Department Store, Inc., 506 F.Supp. 108 (E.D.Pa.1980). What result if Bank had proceeded directly against Guarantors without repossessing the collateral? See UCC § 9–504(5).

REEVES v. FOUTZ AND TANNER, INC.

Supreme Court of New Mexico, 1980.
94 N.M. 760, 617 P.2d 149.

SOSA, CHIEF JUSTICE. These suits were brought as separate actions but were consolidated by the Court of Appeals because the issues were essentially the same. The trial court held for plaintiffs, the Court of Appeals reversed, and we reverse the Court of Appeals.

Plaintiffs Reeves and Begay are uneducated Navajo Indians whose ability to understand English and commercial matters are limited. Each of them pawned jewelry with the defendant whereby they received a money loan in return for a promise to repay the loan in thirty days with interest. The Indian jewelry left with defendant as collateral was worth several times the amount borrowed. The plaintiffs defaulted and defendant sent each of them a notice of intent to retain the collateral, though Reeves claimed she never received notice. The retention was not objected to by either plaintiff. Defendant then sold the jewelry in the regular course of its business.

The question we are presented with is whether a secured party who sends a notice of intent to retain collateral, in conformance with Section 9–505 of the Uniform Commercial Code, may sell the collateral in its regular course of business without complying with Section 9–504? We decide that the secured party in this case could not sell the collateral without complying with Section 9–504.

The Uniform Commercial Code provides a secured party in possession with two courses of action upon the default of the debtor. Section 9–504 provides generally that the secured party may sell the collateral, but if the security interest secures an indebtedness, he must account to the debtor for any surplus (and the debtor must account for any deficiency). Section 9–505(2) provides the secured party with the alternative of retaining the collateral in satisfaction of the obligation. Under this section, the secured party must give written notice to the debtor that he intends to keep the collateral in satisfaction of the debt. The debtor is then given thirty days to object to the proposed retention and require the sale of the property according to Section 9–504.

In the present case we will assume that defendant gave proper notice to both Reeves and Begay of its intention to retain the collateral and that neither objected within thirty days. The trial court found that the defendant, in accordance with its normal business practice, then moved the jewelry into its sale inventory where it was sold to Joe Tanner, president of defendant corporation, or to Joe Tanner, Inc., a corporation owned by Joe Tanner and engaged in the sale of Indian jewelry. There was no accounting to plaintiffs of any surplus. The trial court also found that the defendant did not act in good faith in disposing of the jewelry, taking into consideration the relative bargaining power of the parties.

The defendant argues that the trial court should be reversed because it applied Section 9–504. It essentially argues that once it complied with Section 9–505(2) and sent the notice of intent to retain, it could do as it pleased with the property once the thirty days had elapsed without objection. The debtor-creditor relationship terminates, they claim, and the creditor becomes owner of the collateral.

The plaintiffs argue that the trial court was correct in applying Section 9–504 to require that any surplus from the sale of collateral be returned to the debtor. They urge that the intention of the secured party should control and where he intended to sell the collateral and did sell the collateral in the normal course of business, he must comply with Section 9–504 which governs sales of such collateral.

Neither party to this action has cited a case which has dealt directly with the issue here, but amicus has referred us to a Federal Trade Commission case on the subject where it was stated:

In the Draftsmen's Statement of Reasons for 1972 Changes in Official Text, the Draftsmen summarized the purpose of Section 9–505 as follows:

"Under subsection (2) of this section the secured party may in lieu of sale give notice to the debtor and certain other persons that he proposes to retain the collateral in lieu of sale."

The foregoing language strongly suggests that waiver of surplus and deficiency rights under 9–505 is appropriate only when prompt resale of repossessed collateral in the ordinary course of business is not contemplated by the creditor * * *. That being so, use of Section 9–505 by an automobile dealer, particularly one not disposed to pursue deficiency judgments, would appear calculated solely to extinguish surplus rights of consumers, which we do not believe was the intended purpose of Section 9–505.

In the Matter of Ford Motor Company, Ford Motor Credit Company, and Francis Ford Inc., 93 F.T.C.Rep. ___, 3 CCH Trade Reg.Rep. 21756, 21767 (F.T.C. Docket No. 9073, Sept. 21, 1979). The Commission went on to say that a creditor of this type is not foreclosed from using Section 9–505(2) so long as he intends to retain the collateral for his own use for the immediately foreseeable future, rather than to resell the collateral in the ordinary course of business. We agree with the approach used by the Federal Trade Commission.

The Court of Appeals reasoned that once the creditor elected to retain the collateral, and followed the mechanics of Section 9–505, the property became his to keep or to sell. We do not find fault with this reasoning, but it misses the point. Defendant can do as he pleases with the property, but where he intends to sell the property in the regular course of his business, which is in substance selling the property as contemplated by Section 9–504, he must account for a surplus in conformity with Section 9–504.

The defendant also argues that plaintiffs could have objected to the retention, thus forcing a sale in compliance with Section 9–504. But because there was never any actual intent to retain under Section 9–505(2), the failure of plaintiffs to timely object does not foreclose their claim. Moreover, the fact that plaintiffs could have objected means nothing in this context; their objection would only have served to cause a sale of the goods, which sale was already intended by defendant.

The defendant also argues that the trial court erred in finding that it acted in bad faith. We need not reach this question because bad faith was not material to the trial court's conclusions of law and judgment, which we find to be proper.

The defendant next claims error in the fact that the trial court allowed interest on the judgment from November 1, 1974. The date is the approximate day on which the loss took place and is apparently not controverted. The amount due the plaintiffs was a sum certain once the jewelry was sold, as calculated according to the provisions of Section 9–504. It was not error for the court to allow prejudgment interest or to allow interest as a portion of the damages. Sundt v. Tobin Quarries, 50 N.M. 254, 265, 175 P.2d 684, 690–91 (1946).

The judgment of the trial court is affirmed.

EASLEY, FEDERICI and FELTER, JJ., concur.

PAYNE, J., dissenting, based upon the opinion of the Court of Appeals.

NOTES

1. The court in *Reeves* states that UCC § 9–505(2) cannot be used by a secured party that intends to resell the collateral. In effect that section could be used only by a secured party who "intends to retain the collateral for his own use for the immediately foreseeable future." Is this a reasonable interpretation of the intent of § 9–505(2)? How often do you think the secured party, that will normally be a financial institution or a seller of goods, would repossess the collateral for its own use? Compare the explanation of Professor Gilmore: "The best and simplest way of liquidating any secured transaction, default having occurred, is for the secured party to keep the collateral as his own free of the debtor's equity, waiving any claim to a deficiency judgment. This avoids the tricky and difficult problem of arriving at a fair valuation of the collateral as well as the expense and delay involved in sale or other methods of foreclosure, judicial or nonjudicial. The land mortgagee's right to a decree of strict foreclosure and the common law conditional seller's right to forfeit the buyer's equity on retaking of the goods (which au-

tomatically barred the seller's claim for the unpaid balance of
the price) were both illustrations of this approach." Gilmore,
Security Interests in Personal Property 1220 (1965).* The problem in *Reeves* was that the § 9–505(2) remedy was not used by
the secured party as a convenient way of squaring accounts with
the debtors but rather as a way of gaining an unconscionable
windfall. Since the trial court found that the secured party acted in bad faith in disposing of the collateral, what remedy is appropriate?

2. Professor Gilmore's prescience is shown by his comment
on UCC § 9–505(2). "Now what is to happen when a secured
party makes a proposal to retain, say, a million dollars' worth of
collateral in satisfaction of a hundred-thousand-dollar debt—or a
thousand dollars' worth of collateral in satisfaction of a hun-
dred-dollar debt—and, through oversight in the million-dollar
case or ignorance in the thousand-dollar case, no one who is
qualified to object does so within the statutory time limits? The
courts will do what they always have done and always will do.
If fraud is alleged by someone who has standing to complain of
it, the allegation will be inquired into. If the fraud is proved,
the offending transaction will be set aside and the court will de-
vise an appropriate remedy." Gilmore, Security Interests in
Personal Property 1226–27 (1965).*

3. Suppose the creditor repossesses and holds the property
for two years and then resells and sues the debtor for a deficiency judgment. Can the debtor defend on the theory that the
creditor has impliedly elected to retain the collateral in satisfaction of the debt? In Haufler v. Ardinger, 28 U.C.C. Rep. 893
(Mass. Dist. Ct., App.Div. 1979), the creditor repossessed machinery and used it in his business for 38 months before selling
it. A guarantor was allowed to defend against deficiency judgment liability on the ground that the creditor's delay constituted
an implied retention of the collateral in satisfaction of the debt-
or's obligation. National Equipment Rental, Ltd. v. Priority
Electronics Corp., 435 F.Supp. 236 (E.D. N.Y. 1977), is in accord.
For a well-reasoned decision holding that retention in satisfaction under UCC § 9–505(2) should not be implied from a delay in
disposing of the collateral, see S. M. Flickinger Co., Inc. v. 18
Genesee Corp., 71 A.D.2d 382, 423 N.Y.S.2d 73 (Sup.Ct. 1979).
First National Bank v. Cole, 291 Pa.Super. 391, 435 A.2d 1283
(1981), and Roylex, Inc. v. E. F. Johnson Co., 617 S.W.2d 760

* Published by Little, Brown &
Company. Reprinted with permission.

(Tex.Civ.App. 1981), are in accord. If the debtor cannot invoke implied retention in satisfaction under UCC § 9–505(2), what rights should he assert under Part 5 when the creditor holds property for a long period before disposing of it?

LOUIS ZAHN DRUG CO. v. BANK OF OAK BROOK TERRACE

Appellate Court of Illinois, 1981.
95 Ill.App.3d 435, 50 Ill.Dec. 959, 420 N.E.2d 276.

NASH, JUSTICE. In this appeal we consider whether plaintiff, a junior secured creditor, has stated a cause of action pursuant to sections 9–504(1)(c) or section 9–507(1) of the Uniform Commercial Code against defendant, a senior secured creditor, and others, to recover damages for the alleged improper disposition of the collateral which secured their respective loans to the debtor. * * * Defendants' motion to dismiss * * * the complaint was granted by the trial court and plaintiff appeals.

* * * plaintiff alleged that prior to June 6, 1977, defendant Bank of Oak Brook Terrace (Bank) loaned $25,000 to George Meringolo and GJM Enterprises, Inc. (debtor). According to a financing statement filed on June 6, 1977, the loan was secured by a security interest in "inventory, fixtures, equipment now owned or hereafter acquired [by the debtor]." On December 20, 1977, plaintiff loaned $82,282.82 to the debtor and, according to a financing statement filed on January 9, 1978, plaintiff was given a security interest in

"All fixtures, furnishings, fittings, utensils, tools and equipment signs, prescription records and files, stock in trade, inventory, pharmaceuticals, drugs, sundry products, lease hold improvements, accounts receivable, proceeds, franchises, contract rights, good will, assignment of store lease, including, but not limited to, all other goods, wares, merchandise, furniture, fixtures, equipment, appliances, prescriptions and miscellaneous items, now existing or hereafter acquired by debtor * * *."

The debtor subsequently defaulted on the obligations to both plaintiff and defendant.

After the debtor defaulted, plaintiff attempted to find purchasers for the business and defendants, Harold Shapiro and Donald Warsaw (Buyers), expressed an interest in purchasing it for $70,000. Plaintiff alleged that prior to October 20, 1978, it entered "into negotiations with the defendant [Bank], with an intent to obtain a settlement of the first lien position of the defendant [Bank] * * * by way of verbal and written communications with said Bank * * * ." At about the same time, plaintiff began negotiations with defendant American National Bank & Trust Co., as Trustee (Trustee) which held legal title to the debtor's premises, and its rental agent, defendant Triangle Management Co., in order to assure that the Buyers would be able to obtain a lease of the premises. James Guido was alleged to be the beneficial owner of the premises and also a major shareholder and chairman of the board of the defendant Bank. Plaintiff alleged it also received another offer to purchase the business for $100,000 and then invited the buyers to reconsider their previous bid. When plaintiff did not hear from them, it resumed its attempts to consummate a sale of the business to the high bidder.

Plaintiff alleges that on October 30, 1978, the bank had, without notice to plaintiff, obtained a renunciation of rights in the collateral from the debtor and sold the entire inventory assets, fixtures and equipment of the debtor's business for $70,000 to others. The complaint asserts that the sale was commercially unreasonable "in that, among other things, a higher price could have been obtained" and that the Bank, the Buyers, and Triangle Management Co. "did enter into a conspiracy" to defraud plaintiff. Plaintiff further alleged that the bank had failed to exercise good faith in its dealings with plaintiff concerning the sale, in failing to give notice of it, and in failing to disclose the relationship between the Bank, the beneficiaries of the trust under which title to the premises was held, and Triangle Management Co. Plaintiff also alleged that although the Bank had received payment in full for its loan, it had refused to account for the balance of the funds received or to pay over any excess amount to the plaintiff. Plaintiff prayed that the sale be held commercially unreasonable and that damages be awarded pursuant to [UCC §] 9–507(1).

* * *

Section 9–504(1) of the Uniform Commercial Code describes a secured party's right to dispose of collateral after default and provides that the proceeds of the disposition shall be applied first (a) to the expenses incurred, then (b) to satisfaction of the principal indebtedness secured, and then (c) to

"the satisfaction of indebtedness secured by any subordinate security interest in the collateral if written notification of demand therefor is received before distribution of the proceeds is completed. * * * " ([UCC §] 9–504(1)(c).)

With certain exceptions not pertinent here

" * * * notification shall be sent to any other secured party from whom the secured party [who is making the disposition] has received (before sending his notification to the debtor or before the debtor's renunciation of his rights) written notice of a claim of an interest in the collateral. * * * " ([UCC §], 9–504(3).)

Section 9–504(3) further provides that the "[s]ale or other disposition may be as a unit or in parcels and at any time and place and on any terms but every aspect of the disposition including the method, manner, time, place, and terms must be commercially reasonable." The Code also provides a remedy if a secured party fails to proceed in accordance with its provisions in the disposition of collateral:

"If it is established that the secured party is not proceeding in accordance with the provisions of this Part disposition may be ordered or restrained on appropriate terms and conditions. If the disposition has occurred the debtor or *any person* entitled to notification or *whose security interest has been made known to the secured party prior to the disposition* has a right to recover from the secured party any loss caused by a failure to comply with the provisions of this Part. * * * " ([UCC §] 9–507(1).) (Emphasis supplied.)

Thus, in seeking to impose liability upon a secured party under the remedies provided by section 9–507, plaintiff must allege facts showing it is "a person entitled to notification" or that its security interest was "made known" to defendant prior to disposition of the collateral.

The essential question presented by defendant's motion to dismiss the complaint in the trial court and by the arguments of the parties on appeal is whether plaintiff, as a secondary secured party, must allege it gave notice *in writing* to defendant in order to proceed under section 9–507, or whether allegations that plaintiff's security interest was otherwise "made known" to defendant before disposition are sufficient. Plaintiff relies upon the allegations in the complaint that plaintiff and defendant bank had negotiated in an attempt to settle the bank's first lien against the collateral and did so by both written and verbal communications. It contends that by these means plaintiff's security interest was made known to defendant prior to sale of the collateral giving plaintiff standing to now assert the sale was commercially unreasonable and to seek damages pursuant to section 9–507. Defendant contends, however, that a secondary secured party such as plaintiff may not complain about any aspect of the sale of the collateral unless it has given written notice of its claim or interest before sale and plaintiff's complaint failed to allege it did so.

Prior to the 1972 amendments of Article 9 of the Uniform Commercial Code, a secured party wishing to dispose of collateral was under a duty to give notice to any person who had a security interest in the collateral who had filed a financing statement with the Secretary of State. He was also required to give notice to any other person known to him to have a security interest in the collateral. Under the 1972 amendments the notice requirements were eased to the extent that a selling secured party need not notify other secured parties of a proposed disposition of collateral unless such parties had first given him written notice of a claim of interest in the collateral. It necessarily follows that a subordinate secured party who has failed to give the requisite written notice of his claim cannot be heard to complain if he is not notified in advance of the disposition of the collateral and may not seek satisfaction of his indebtedness from the proceeds of the disposition pursuant to section 9–504(1)(c). See Kolton v. K & L Furniture & Appliances, Inc. (1980), 82 Ill.App.3d 868, 875, 38 Ill.Dec. 247, 293, 403 N.E.2d 478, 484.

It does not necessarily follow, however, that the failure of a subordinate secured party to give written notice of a claim of interest in the collateral forecloses him from contesting the commercial reasonableness of the sale and seeking damages if proven. While the amendments to section 9–504(3) eased the notice requirements of the selling secured party, the provisions of section 9–507(1) giving a secured party whose security interest has been "made known" to the selling secured party an action for damages was not affected by the amendments. We note that the commentators to section 9–507 have reasoned that its language "whose security interest has been made known" to the other secured party may be read to mean "made known in writing", but that is not what it says. Had the legislature intended that an action for damages was to be limited to subordinate secured parties whose interest had been made known to the selling secured party "in writing", as it did so limit their rights under section 9–504(1)(c), it could easily have done so. The legislature clearly chose, however, to retain the existing remedy in favor of other secured parties whose interest was made known to the selling party prior to disposition of the collateral. Those subordinate secured parties who have given written notice of their claim against the collateral are entitled to receive notice of its proposed disposition and also to satisfaction of their claim from any surplus in the proceeds. The remedy sought by plaintiff arises after disposition and is granted to the debtor, any person entitled to notification (being those who have given written notice of their claim), or [any person] whose security interest has been made known to the selling party. If, as urged by defendant, the remedy extends only to those secured parties in the third category who have given notice in writing it would be redundant as such parties are already included within the second category.

One of the purposes of the Code requirement that a sale of collateral be conducted in a commercially reasonable manner is to protect the interests of other secured parties. The selling party is not required to search out and give notice of an intended disposition to all other secured parties, but as to those from whom it has received written notice of their claim of an interest in the collateral prior to the time distribution of the proceeds has been completed, the holder of the subordinate security interest would be entitled to seek satisfaction of its indebtedness from any surplus remaining of the proceeds of sale after payment of expenses and the primary indebtedness.

In the event the subordinate secured party has not given the notice required by section 9–504(3) then he would not be entitled to receive the notice provided by that section from the principal secured party. As we have noted, however, the subordinate secured party is not without remedy as section 9–507(1) provides that any person whose security interest has been made known to the secured party prior to disposition of the collateral may recover for losses caused by a failure to comply with the Act.

Under somewhat analogous circumstances, this court in Blackhawk Production Credit Association v. Meridian Implement Co. (1980), 82 Ill.App.3d 93, 37 Ill.Dec. 387, 402 N.E.2d 277, considered the rights of a secured party holding a subordinate security interest where the party with the superior security interest retained the collateral in full satisfaction of the debtor's obligation to it. Under section 9–505(2) if a secured party retains the collateral in satisfaction of its obligation, it is required to send notice to any other secured party from whom it has received written notice of a claim of an interest in the collateral and if another secured party objects in writing within 21 days thereafter, the collateral must be disposed of under section

9–504. In *Blackhawk* we held that a secured party was not authorized by section 9–505 to retain collateral in satisfaction of unsecured as well as secured debts and, therefore, the failure of the holder of a subordinate security interest to serve written notice on the senior secured party prior to the repossession of the collateral did not preclude his recovery since his security interest was *made known* to the senior secured party before the subsequent sale of the collateral. The wrongful disposition of the collateral in that case which gave rise to a claim under section 9–507(1) was the sale of the collateral after the primary secured party had received notification of the interest of the junior secured party.

Similarly, it has been said that mere knowledge by the selling secured party of the interest of another secured party in the collateral is sufficient to subject him to liability under section 9–507(1), if he fails to dispose of the collateral in a commercially reasonable manner. See Liberty National Bank & Trust Co. of Oklahoma City v. Acme Tool Division of the Rucker Co. (10th Cir. 1976), 540 F.2d 1375, 1382.

We conclude that a subordinate secured party's security interest in the collateral need not be made known in writing to the selling secured party in order to challenge a disposition under section 9–507 on the grounds it was commercially unreasonable where the interest was otherwise made known to the secured party prior to disposition.

While plaintiff does not and need not allege that its security interest was made known to the Bank in writing in order to maintain an action under section 9–507, its complaint must set forth facts which if proven show that the selling secured party had been informed of plaintiff's interest prior to the disposition of the collateral. It may not be inferred from plaintiff's allegation that it negotiated with the Bank seeking to settle the Bank's first lien that the Bank became aware of plaintiff's junior secured status. A complaint will not withstand a motion to dismiss under section 45 of the Civil Practice Act unless it at least minimally allege facts setting forth the essential elements of a cause of action (Kolton v. K & L Furniture & Appliances, Inc. (1980), 82 Ill.App.3d 868, 38 Ill.Dec. 247, 403 N.E.2d 478).

* * *

The trial court dismissed the complaint finding it lacked necessary allegations that plaintiff had given written notice to the Bank of its claim of an interest in the collateral. As we have determined written notice is not required to preserve a remedy pursuant to section 9–507(1), the court erred in dismissing [the complaint] on that ground. * * * A complaint should not be dismissed unless it clearly appears that no set of facts can be proved which will justify a recovery. (Fitzgerald v. Chicago Title & Trust Co. (1978), 72 Ill.2d 179, 20 Ill.Dec. 581, 380 N.E.2d 790; Edgar County Bank & Trust Co. v. Paris Hospital, Inc. (1974), 57 Ill.2d 298, 312 N.E.2d 259), and plaintiff may wish to amend its complaint in an effort to supply the deficiencies we have discussed.

For these reasons the judgment of the trial court will be reversed and the cause remanded for further proceedings in accordance with the views expressed herein.

Reversed and remanded.

NOTES

1. The court in *Zahn* discussed Blackhawk Production Credit Ass'n v. Meridian Implement Co. The facts were as follows: Seller sold Debtor a tractor and reserved a purchase money security interest for the balance of the price. Later Debtor granted Lender a security interest in the same tractor. Although Lender knew of Seller's senior interest, it did not send Seller written notice of its claim of an interest in the collateral. In July 1976 Seller repossessed the tractor and entered into an agreement with Debtor to retain the tractor in full satisfaction of both the remaining secured debt and an additional unsecured debt owed by Debtor to Seller. The two debts amounted to a total of over $20,000. Seller knew nothing of Lender's interest until the spring of 1977 when Lender demanded that Seller either sell the tractor pursuant to UCC § 9–504 or pay over to Lender the difference between the value of the tractor and the unpaid balance secured by Lender's senior security interest. Seller refused Lender's demand and sold the tractor in ordinary course of its business. Lender sued Seller under UCC § 9–507(1).

In allowing Lender to recover more than $11,000 from Seller the court stated that Seller could retain possession under UCC § 9–505(2) only in satisfaction of the secured debt. Any value of the tractor in excess of the secured debt had to be used to pay off Lender's security interest and not to satisfy Debtor's unsecured debt to Seller. The court acknowledged that Lender could have avoided the problem by promptly notifying Seller of its claim to the collateral. It held that the word "disposition" in the second sentence of UCC § 9–507(1)—" * * * any person entitled to notification or whose security interest has been made known to the secured party prior to the disposition has a right to recover from the secured party *   *   * "—refers to the eventual sale of the collateral by the secured party and not the act of strict foreclosure pursuant to UCC § 9–505(2). Do you agree with that interpretation? If that interpretation is correct what must a secured party do to protect himself against possible claims of unknown secured parties?

2. The rights of junior secured parties in personal property do not receive the degree of protection under Article 9 that like interests in real property receive. Perhaps this reflects the fact that junior security interests are not as important in personal property financing as in real property financing. Under Article 9, only if he makes his interest known to the senior secured party in writing may the junior secured party receive notification before the senior disposes of the collateral (UCC § 9–504(3)) or share in the proceeds of the disposition (UCC § 9–504(1)(c)). The junior secured party may recover from the senior for wrongful disposition of the collateral under UCC § 9–507(1) only if he has given the senior written notice of his interest or the senior knows of his interest.

A holder of a judicial lien enjoys none of these rights. UCC § 9–504(1)(c) applies only to holders of junior security interests. Although the definition of security interest in UCC § 1–201(37) is broad enough to include nonconsensual liens (e.g. the security interest of a buyer of goods under UCC § 2–711(3)) the holder of a judicial lien is not the holder of a security interest as the term is used in UCC § 9–504(1)(c). That section would appear to be restricted to Article 9 security interests which must be created by contract. UCC § 9–102(2). Judicial lienholders are treated separately under Article 9 as "lien creditors." UCC § 9–301(3). UCC § 9–311 provides that a lien creditor may reach the debtor's interest in collateral and UCC § 9–301(1)(b) subordinates a lien creditor's interest to a prior perfected security interest. Beyond that the rights of the lien creditor in the collateral as against those of the secured party are left to other state law. See Justice, Secured Parties and Judgment Creditors—The Courts and Section 9–311 of the Uniform Commercial Code, 30 Bus. Law. 433 (1975). Usually security agreements provide that default occurs when a debtor allows the collateral to become subject to a judicial lien. Under California Code of Civil Procedure § 689b the secured party, whether or not levy was an event of default, is entitled to have the levying officer release the property to him unless the lien creditor pays the claim of the secured party or posts a bond in lieu of payment. If the secured party gets possession of the collateral he can then dispose of it pursuant to UCC § 9–504 or § 9–505 without accounting to the holder of the judicial lien.

MAJOR'S FURNITURE MART, INC. v. CASTLE CREDIT CORP., INC.

United States Court of Appeals, Third Circuit, 1979.
602 F.2d 538.

GARTH, CIRCUIT JUDGE: This appeal requires us to answer the question: "When is a sale—not a sale, but rather a secured loan?" The district court held that despite the form of their Agreement, which purported to be, and hence was characterized as, a sale of accounts receivable, the parties' transactions did not constitute sales. Major's Furniture Mart, Inc. v. Castle Credit Corp., 449 F.Supp. 538 (E.D.Pa.1978). No facts are in dispute, and the issue presented on this appeal is purely a legal issue involving the interpretation of relevant sections of the Uniform Commercial Code and their proper application to the undisputed facts presented here.

The district court granted plaintiff Major's motion for summary judgment. Castle Credit Corporation appeals from that order. We affirm.

Major's is engaged in the retail sale of furniture. Castle is in the business of financing furniture dealers such as Major's. Count I of Major's amended complaint alleged that Major's and Castle had entered into an Agreement dated June 18, 1973 for the financing of Major's accounts receivable; that a large number of transactions pursuant to the Agreement took place between June 1973 and May 1975; that in March and October 1975 Castle declared Major's in default under the Agreement; and that from and after June 1973 Castle was in possession of monies which constituted a surplus over the accounts receivable transferred under the Agreement. Among other relief sought, Major's asked for an accounting of the surplus and all sums received by Castle since June 1, 1976 which had been collected from the Major's accounts receivable transferred under the Agreement (App. 64–65).

The provisions of the June 18, 1973 Agreement which are relevant to our discussion provide: that Major's shall from time to time "sell" accounts receivable to Castle (¶ 1), and that all accounts so "sold" shall be with full recourse against Major's (¶ 2).

Major's was required to warrant that each account receivable was based upon a written order or contract fully performed by Major's.[3] Castle in its sole discretion could refuse to "purchase" any account (¶ 7). The amount paid by Castle to Major's on any particular account was the unpaid face amount of the account exclusive of interest [4] less a fifteen percent "discount"[5] and less another ten percent of the unpaid face amount as a reserve against bad debts (¶ 8).[6]

Under the Agreement the reserve was to be held by Castle without interest and was to indemnify Castle against a customer's failure to pay the full amount of the account (which included interest and insurance premiums), as well as any other charges or losses sustained by Castle for any reason (¶ 9).

In addition, Major's was required to "repurchase" any account "sold" to Castle which was in default for more than 60 days. In such case Major's was obligated to pay to Castle

> an amount equal to the balance due by the customer on said Account plus any other expenses incurred by CASTLE as a result of such default or breach of warranty, less a rebate of interest on the account under the "Rule of the 78's."
> *   *   * [7]

3. The parties do not dispute that their rights are governed by the law of Pennsylvania. The Pennsylvania Uniform Commercial Code, and in particular § 9–105, classifies the accounts receivable which are the subject of the agreement as "chattel paper."

4. According to Major's brief, the "face amount" of its customers' installment payment agreements included (1) the retail cost of the furniture purchased (amount financed), (2) the total amount of interest payable by the customer over the life of the customer's installment payment agreement, and (3) insurance charges.

5. The 15% "discount" was subsequently increased unilaterally by Castle to 18% and thereafter was adjusted monthly to reflect changes in the prime rate (Appellee's Supplemental Appendix 3b–4b).

6. It becomes apparent from a review of the record that the amount which Castle actually paid to Major's on each account transferred was the unpaid face amount exclusive of interest *and* exclusive of insurance premiums less 28% (18% "discount" and 10% reserve).

In its brief on appeal, Castle sets out the following summary of the transactions that took place over the relevant period. It appears that the face amount of the accounts which were "sold" by Major's to Castle was $439,832.08, to which finance charges totalling $116,350.46 and insurance charges totalling $42,304.03 were added, bringing the total amount "purchased" by Castle to $598,486.57. For these "purchases" Castle paid Major's $316,107. Exclusive of any surplus as determined by the district court Castle has retained $528,176.13 which it has received as a result of customer collections and repurchases by Major's. Collection costs were found by the district court to be $1,627.81.

7. The Rule of 78 is "the predominant method used to determine refunds of unearned finance charges upon prepayment of consumer debts." Hunt, James H., "The Rule of 78: Hidden Penalty for Prepayment in Consumer Credit Transactions," 55

App. at 22, ¶ 10. Thus essentially, Major's was obligated to repurchase a defaulted account not for the discounted amount paid to it by Castle, but for a "repurchase" price based on the balance due by the customer, plus any costs incurred by Castle upon default.

As an example, applying the Agreement to a typical case, Major's in its brief on appeal summarized an account transaction of one of its customers (William Jones) as follows:

A customer [Jones] of Major's (later designated Account No. 15,915) purchased furniture from Major's worth $1700.00 (or more).* [H]e executed an installment payment agreement with Major's in the total face amount of $2549.88, including interest and insurance costs.   *   *   *   Using this piece of chattel paper,   *   *   *   Major's engaged in a financing transaction with Castle under the Agreement.   *   *   *   Major's delivered the Jones' chattel paper with a $2549.88 face amount of Castle together with an assignment of rights. Shortly thereafter, Castle delivered to Major's cash in the amount of $1224.00. The difference between this cash amount and the full face of the chattel paper in the amount of $2549.88, consisted of the following costs and deductions by Castle:

1. $180.00 discount credited to a "reserve" account of Major's.

2. $300.06 "discount" (actually a prepaid interest charge).

3. $30.85 for life insurance premium.

4. $77.77 for accident and health insurance premium.

5. $152.99 for property insurance premium.

6. $588.27 interest charged to Jones on the $1700 face of the note (App. 73a No. 15,915).

B.U.L.Rev. 331, 332 (1975). That article points out that the Rule of 78 allocates a disproportionately large portion of finance charges to the early months of a credit transaction which produces a hidden penalty for prepayment, although the extent of the penalty diminishes as the term of the debt nears expiration.

Apparently a rebate of insurance premiums was provided as well as a rebate of interest. *See* N.T. 6–94–99 and Appellant's Brief at 21.

* Some transactions involved cash downpayment to Major's, but this is not at issue in the law suit.

Thus, as to the Jones' account, Castle received and proceeded to collect a piece of chattel paper with a collectible face value of $2549.88. Major's received $1224.00 in cash.

Brief of Appellee at 5–6.

As we understand the Agreement, if Jones in the above example defaulted without having made any payments on account, the very least Major's would have been obliged to pay on repurchase would be $1,700 even though Major's had received only $1,224 in cash on transfer of the account and had been credited with a reserve of $180. The repurchase price was either charged fully to reserve or, as provided in the Agreement, 50% to reserve and 50% by cash payment from Major's (¶ 10). In the event of bankruptcy, default under the agreement or discontinuation of business, Major's was required to repurchase all outstanding accounts immediately (¶ 13). Finally, the Agreement provided that the law of Pennsylvania would govern and that the Agreement could not be modified except in writing signed by all the parties. (Apparently, no objection has ever been made to Castle's unilateral modification of the discount rate. That issue is not before us.)

Under the Agreement, over 600 accounts were transferred to Castle by Major's of which 73 became delinquent and subject to repurchase by Major's. On March 21, 1975, Castle notified Major's that Major's was in default in failing to repurchase delinquent accounts (App. 52). Apparently to remedy the default, Major's deposited an additional $10,000 into the reserve.[8] After June 30, 1975, Major's discontinued transferring accounts to Castle (App. 51). On October 7, 1975 Castle again declared Major's in default (App. 53).

Major's' action against Castle alleged that the transaction by which Major's transferred its accounts to Castle constituted a financing of accounts receivable and that Castle had collected a surplus of monies to which Major's was entitled. We are thus faced with the question which we posed at the outset of this opinion: did the June 18, 1973 Agreement create a *secured interest* in the accounts, or did the transaction constitute a *true sale* of the accounts? The district court, contrary to Castle's contention, refused to construe the Agreement as one giving rise to the sales of accounts receivable. Rather, it interpreted

---

8. This "deposit" was effected through the mechanism of a promissory note to Castle dated April 15, 1975 in the amount of $40,000, of which $10,000 was credited to reserve.

the Agreement as creating a security interest in the accounts which accordingly was subject to all the provisions of Article 9 of the U.C.C. It thereupon entered its order of June 13, 1977 granting Major's' motion for summary judgment and denying Castle's motion for summary judgment. This order was ultimately incorporated into the court's final judgment entered May 5, 1978 which specified the amount of surplus owed by Castle to Major's. It was from this final judgment that Castle appealed.

Castle on appeal argues (1) that the express language of the Agreement indicates that it was an agreement for the sale of accounts and (2) that the parties' course of performance and course of dealing compel an interpretation of the Agreement as one for the sale of accounts. Castle also asserts that the district court erred in "reforming" the Agreement and in concluding that the transaction was a loan. In substance these contentions do no more than reflect Castle's overall position that the Agreement was for an absolute sale of accounts.

Our analysis starts with Article 9 of the Uniform Commercial Code which encompasses both *sales* of accounts and *secured interests* in accounts. Thus, the Pennsylvania counterpart of the Code "applies * * * (a) to any transaction (regardless of its form) which is intended to create a security interest in * * * accounts * * *; and also (b) to any sale of accounts * * * " § 9–102. The official comments to that section make it evident that Article 9 is to govern *all* transactions in accounts. Comment 2 indicates that, because "[c]ommercial financing on the basis of accounts * * * is often so conducted that the distinction between a security transfer and a sale is blurred," that "sales" as well as transactions "intended to create a security interest" are subject to the provisions of Article 9. Moreover, a "security interest" is defined under the Act as "any interest of a buyer of accounts." § 1–201(37). Thus even an outright buyer of accounts, such as Castle claims to be, by definition has a "security interest" in the accounts which it purchases.

Article 9 of the Pennsylvania Code is subdivided into five parts. Our examination of Parts 1–4, §§ 9–101 to 9–410, reveals no distinction drawn between a sale and a security interest which is relevant to the issue on this appeal. However, the distinction between an outright sale and a transaction intended to create a security interest becomes highly significant with respect to certain provisions found in Part 5 of Article 9. That part pertains to default under a "security agreement." § 9–501, et seq.

The default section relevant here, which distinguishes between the consequences that follow on default when the transaction *secures an indebtedness* rather than a *sale*, provides:

A secured party who by agreement is entitled to charge back uncollected collateral or otherwise to full and limited recourse against the debtor and who undertakes to collect from the account debtors or obligors must proceed in a commercially reasonable manner and may deduct his reasonable expenses of realization from the collections. *If the security agreement secures an indebtedness, the secured party must account to the debtor for any surplus*, and unless otherwise agreed, the debtor is liable for any deficiency. But, *if the underlying transaction was a sale of accounts*, contract rights, or chattel paper, *the debtor is entitled to any surplus* or is liable for any deficiency *only if the security agreement so provides.*

§ 9–502(2) (emphasis added).

Thus, if the accounts were transferred to Castle *to secure Major's' indebtedness*, Castle was obligated to account for and pay over the surplus proceeds to Major's under § 9–502(2), as a debtor's (Major's') right to surplus in such a case cannot be waived even by an express agreement. § 9–501(3)(a). On the other hand, if a *sale of accounts* had been effected, then Castle was entitled to all proceeds received from all accounts because the June 18, 1973 Agreement does not provide otherwise.

However, while the Code instructs us as to the consequences that ensue as a result of the determination of "secured indebtedness" as contrasted with "sale," the Code does not provide assistance in distinguishing between the character of such transactions. This determination, as to whether a particular assignment constitutes a sale or a transfer for security, is left to the courts for decision. § 9–502, Comment 4. It is to that task that we now turn.

*   *   *

The comments to § 9–502(2) (and in particular Comment 4) make clear to us that the presence of recourse in a sale agreement without more will not automatically convert a sale into a security interest. Hence, one of Major's arguments which is predicated on such a *per se* principle attracts us no more than it attracted the district court. The Code comments however are consistent with and reflect the views expressed by courts and commentators that "[t]he determination of whether a particular assignment constitutes a [true] sale or a transfer for security is left to the courts." § 9–502, Comment 4. The question for the court then is whether the *nature* of the recourse, and the true nature of the transaction, are such that the legal rights and economic consequences of the agreement bear a greater similarity to a financing transaction or to a sale.

[The court's discussion of other cases is omitted.]

Hence, it appears that in each of the cases cited, despite the express language of the agreements, the respective courts examined the parties' practices, objectives, business activities and relationships and determined whether the transaction was a sale or a secured loan only after analysis of the evidence as to the true nature of the transaction. We noted earlier that here the parties, satisfied that there was nothing other than the Agreement and documents bearing on their relationship (Part III, supra), submitted to the court's determination on an agreed record. The district court thereupon reviewed the Agreement and the documents as they reflected the conduct of the parties to determine whether Castle treated the transactions as sales or transfers of a security interest. In referring to the extremely relevant factor of "recourse"[12] and to the risks allocated, the district court found:

> In the instant case the allocation of risks heavily favors Major's claim to be considered as an assignor with an interest in the collectibility of its accounts. It appears that Castle required Major's to retain all conceivable risks of uncollectibility of these accounts. It required warranties that retail account debtors—e.g., Major's customers—meet the criteria set forth by Castle, that Major's perform the credit check to verify that these criteria were satisfied, and that Major's warrant that the accounts were fully enforceable legally and were "fully and timely collectible." It also imposed an obligation to indemnify Castle out of a reserve account for losses resulting from a customer's failure to pay, or for any breach

---

12. Gilmore, in commenting on the Code's decision to leave the distinction between a security transfer and a sale to the courts, would place almost controlling significance on the one factor of recourse. He states:

If there is no right of charge-back or recourse with respect to uncollectible accounts and no right to claim for a deficiency, then the transaction should be held to be a sale, entirely outside the scope of Part 5. If there is a right to charge back uncollectible accounts (a right, as § 9–502 puts it, of "full or limited recourse") or a right to claim a deficiency, then the transaction should be held to be for security and thus subject to Part 5 as well as the other Parts of the Article.

II Gilmore, Security Interests in Personal Property, § 44.4 at 1230.

Here, of course, the Agreement provided Castle with full recourse against Major's.

of warranty, and an obligation to repurchase any account after the customer was in default for more than 60 days. Castle only assumed the risk that the assignor itself would be
unable to fulfill its obligations. Guaranties of quality alone,
or even guarantees of collectibility alone, might be consistent
with a true sale, but Castle attempted to shift all risks to
Major's, and incur none of the risks or obligations of ownership. It strains credulity to believe that this is the type of
situation, referred to in Comment 4, in which "there may be a
true sale of accounts   *   *   *   although recourse exists."
When we turn to the conduct of the parties to seek support
for this contention, we find instead that Castle, in fact, treated these transactions as a transfer of a security interest.

449 F.Supp. at 543.

Moreover, in looking ot the conduct of the parties, the district
court found one of the more significant documents to be an August 31, 1973 letter written by Irving Canter, President of Castle Credit, to Major's. As the district court characterized it, and
as we agree:

> This letter, in effect, announces the imposition of a floating
> interest rate on loans under a line of credit of $80,000 per
> month, based upon the fluctuating prime interest rate. The
> key portion of the letter states:
>
> > Accordingly, your volume for the month of September
> > cannot exceed $80,000. Any business above that amount
> > will have to be paid for in October. I think you'll agree
> > that your quota is quite liberal. The surcharge for the
> > month of September will be 3% of the principal amount
> > financed which is based upon a $9^{1}/_{2}\%$ prime rate. On Oc-
> > tober 1, and for each month thereafter, the surcharge will
> > be adjusted, based upon the prime rate in effect at that
> > time as it relates to a $6^{1}/_{2}\%$ base rate.   *   *   *
>
> This unilateral change in the terms of the Agreement makes
> it obvious that Castle treated the transaction as a line of
> credit to Major's—i.e., a loan situation. Were this a true
> sale, as Castle now argues, it would not have been able to
> impose these new conditions by fiat. Such changes in a sales
> contract would have modified the price term of the agree-
> ment, which could only be done by a writing signed by all the
> parties.

449 F.Supp. at 543.

It is apparent to us that on this record none of the risks present in a true sale is present here. Nor has the custom of the parties or their relationship, as found by the district court, given rise to more than a debtor/creditor relationship in which Major's' debt was secured by a transfer of Major's' customer accounts to Castle, thereby bringing the transaction within the ambit of § 9–502. To the extent that the district court determined that a surplus existed, Castle was obligated to account to Major's for that surplus and Major's' right to the surplus could not be waived, § 9–502(2). Accordingly, we hold that on this record the district court did not err in determining that the true nature of the transaction between Major's and Castle was a secured loan, not a sale.

* * *

The judgment of the district court will be affirmed.

NOTES

1. The only transaction covered by Article 9 which is not a true secured transaction is the sale of accounts and chattel paper. UCC § 1–201(37), § 9–102(1)(b). The fact that it is difficult to distinguish between an outright sale and a security transfer of accounts or chattel paper is one of the reasons the Code covers such sales. Comment 2 to UCC § 9–102. Another reason is that in some states some form of public notice was probably needed to protect the buyer of accounts or chattel paper against creditors of the seller and other buyers or transferees of the account or chattel paper, and Article 9's provisions on perfection and priority perform that function admirably. Gilmore, Security Interests in Personal Property § 8.7 (1965).

2. Comment 1 to UCC § 9–502 explains the advantage the accounts creditor has over the creditor whose collateral is tangible property in realizing on the collateral. We have seen the difficulties encountered in realizing on tangible personal property. The selling creditor must be concerned about refurbishing or repairing the property, selling it in the proper market, and getting a decent price even though the liquidation value of used goods may seem disproportionately low compared to their original cost. He must, in short, make sure that he has disposed of goods in a manner that a reviewing court years later will deign to call commercially reasonable. Contrast the position of the accounts or chattel paper creditor. If the financing arrangement calls for account debtors to pay him directly, he merely continues to collect after the default of the debtor-assignor. If the

financing arrangement calls for account debtors to pay the debtor-assignor, UCC § 9–502 (and invariably the security agreement) allows the creditor-assignee to notify the account debtors to make their payments directly to him in the future. Under UCC § 9–318(3) the account debtors must comply. If the accounts are good, the creditor-assignee collects one hundred cents on the dollar and does so virtually without additional expense.

If the assignment of accounts or chattel paper is a secured transaction, the collecting creditor-assignee must protect the debtor's interest in the collateral. He cannot settle with account debtors for just enough to pay off the secured debt; he must act in a commercially reasonable manner. But if an outright sale of accounts or chattel paper has taken place and the assignor is neither liable for a deficiency nor entitled to a surplus, Part 5 of Article 9 has no application. The assignee may deal with the accounts or chattel paper in any way he wishes; they are his property and the buyer has no interest in them. Gilmore, Security Interests in Personal Property § 44.4 (1965). The accounts or chattel paper creditor may dispose of the accounts by sale under UCC § 9–504 if he does not choose to collect them.

Chapter 5

PERSONAL GUARANTIES AND LETTERS OF CREDIT

A. INTRODUCTORY NOTE

We have examined the secured transaction in terms of the debtor's granting to the creditor an interest in property. But frequently creditors demand another form of security—a guaranty of the debt by some third party. A guaranty is often used as a substitute for, or a supplement to, an Article 9 security interest. In fact, a guaranty has much in common with some kinds of Article 9 security interests. For example, in accounts receivable financing the secured creditor's collateral is simply the account debtor's obligation to pay money to the debtor. In a guaranty transaction the secured creditor's security is the guarantor's obligation to pay the debt owed to the secured creditor. In both instances the security of the secured creditor lies in the creditworthiness of the third party. Although a guaranty transaction can properly be described as a secured transaction guaranties are not covered by Article 9.

We will examine some examples of guaranties in this Chapter. First we will examine direct guaranties of the debtor's obligation effected by having the guarantor sign the promissory note that evidences the obligation owed to the secured party. These guaranties are governed by Article 3 of the UCC which describes the guarantor as an accommodation party. Next we will examine letters of credit which are usually issued by a bank. The letter of credit, which has grown greatly in importance in recent years, is in effect, though not in form, a guaranty. Letters of credit are governed by Article 5 of the UCC.

B. ACCOMMODATION PARTIES

Usually the creditor takes a promissory note from the debtor as evidence of the debt, and obtains the guaranty of the debtor's obligation by having the guarantor sign the note. Sometimes

379

the guaranty is expressly stated. UCC § 3–416 sets forth rules defining the obligation when certain common forms of guaranty language are used. But in many cases a person who intends to act as guarantor does not expressly state that intention on the instrument. Instead he simply signs the instrument as co-maker or indorser. For example, Son wants to buy from Dealer equipment for use in Son's business venture. Dealer is willing to sell to Son on credit only if Mother signs the note as co-maker along with Son. An ambiguity results. Mother as a maker of the note is clearly liable as such. UCC § 3–413(1). But she may not have directly benefitted from the transaction in the sense that she has no interest either in Son's business venture or in the equipment for which the note was given. If the three parties to the transaction understand that Mother's signature simply represents her guaranty of payment of the note Mother is said to be an "accommodation party." She is liable on the note as maker. That is precisely what Dealer bargained for. But as accommodation party she has certain rights that Son, the other maker, does not have. For example, if Son doesn't pay the note when due and Mother has to pay, it is only fair that she should be able to recover from Son the amount that she has paid. He got the benefit of the transaction and ultimately should have to bear its burdens. UCC § 3–415(5) so provides. UCC § 3–415 is the only section of the UCC specifically dealing with accommodation parties and you should study it at this point.

An accommodation party or other surety, in addition to having rights against the person whose debt is guaranteed, also has certain rights against the creditor in the transaction. If Dealer by its actions reduces the likelihood that Son will pay the debt, Mother may be released from liability on her guaranty. For example, suppose the note is a four-year installment note for $5,000 plus finance charges and the resale value of the equipment at the time of sale is $10,000. Dealer normally takes a security interest in the equipment in a case of this kind. If Son defaults, Dealer can exercise its rights under the security interest to repossess the equipment and use the value it represents to pay Son's debt. The security interest benefits Dealer but it also benefits Mother because its existence makes it less likely that she will have to pay the debt. Indeed, if Mother pays the debt on Son's default, she is entitled to have the note and the security interest transferred to her. By subrogation, she succeeds to the rights that Dealer had against Son. See Comment 5 to UCC § 3–415, UCC § 9–504(5), and Reimann v. Hybertsen, 275 Or. 235, 550 P.2d 436 (1976). But Dealer's rights to repossess the equipment can be lost to other creditors of Son if Dealer doesn't perfect the security interest by filing a financing statement. Suppose Dealer doesn't file and one of Son's creditors seizes the equipment or Son goes into bankruptcy. Mother has been hurt by Dealer's negligence. See Farmers State Bank of Oakley v. Cooper, infra, p. 398. Or, suppose Dealer allows Son to miss many installment payments without insisting on payment or resorting to the collateral. Again, this action may make ultimate default by Son more likely thereby increasing Mother's risk. Pre-Code suretyship law provided that actions of this kind that adversely affected the surety could under some circumstances result in the surety's partial or complete release from the debt. This law as applied to negotiable instruments is set forth in UCC § 3–606, which, unfortunately, is not a model of clarity. It is important to note that these rights can be, and frequently are, waived by the guarantor by the terms of the instrument. In other words the creditor may bargain for liability of all makers of the note as principal debtors. The bargain should be clearly expressed.

Often accommodation party status is acquired by indorsement of the instrument. An indorsement usually is made to allow a negotiation of the instrument, but liability as an indorser may be avoided by an indorsement without recourse. UCC § 3–414(1). In that case the indorsement has a negotiation function but no liability function. The accommodation indorsement is the converse. It has no function in the negotiation process. Its sole purpose is to impose indorser's liability on the signer. An indorsement which on its face is not part of the process of negotiation is referred to as an "anomalous indorsement" or an indorsement not in the chain of title. See UCC § 3–415(4) and Comment 1 to § 3–415.

FITHIAN v. JAMAR

Court of Appeals of Maryland, 1979.
286 Md. 161, 410 A.2d 569.

COLE, JUDGE. The dispute in this case involves the rights and liabilities of co-makers of a note in a suit among themselves, where none of the disputants is a holder of the note. We granted certiorari to consider two questions, which simply stated are:

1. Whether a co-maker of a note was also an accommodation maker of the note and thus not liable to the party accommodated;

2. Whether the agreement of one co-maker to assume another co-maker's obligation on a note constitutes a defense to the latter when sued for contribution by the former.

In 1967 Walter Fithian (Walter) and Richard Jamar (Richard), who were employed as printers at Baltimore Business Forms, decided to form a partnership to carry on their own printing business. They applied to the People's Bank of Chestertown, Maryland (Bank) for an $11,000 business loan to enable them to purchase some equipment. The Bank agreed to lend the money to Walter and Richard only if Walter's wife, Connie, Richard's wife, Janet, and Walter's parents, Walter William (Bill) and Mildred Fithian would co-sign the note. The Executive Vice-President of the Bank explained that the additional signatures were required to make the Bank more secure. The note, which authorized confession of judgment in the event of default, was signed on its face in the bottom right-hand corner by these six parties. The monies loaned were deposited in Walter and Richard's business checking account and were used to purchase printing equipment.

By 1969, Walter and Richard were encountering business problems. They spoke with Frank Hogans (Hogans) and Gerald Bos (Bos) (who were interested in joining the business) about forming a corporation to be called J–F Printing Co., Inc. and refinancing the note so that it (the note) could become a corporate rather than an individual obligation. The business continued to falter and on March 23, 1972 Walter, Richard, Hogans and Bos met and entered into a written agreement in their individual capacities whereby Richard was to take over management and ownership of the business in exchange for his assumption of liability for the company's outstanding obligations, one of which was the note in question in this case. The agreement also provided that should Richard default in the performance of those obligations, Walter, Hogans, and Bos would have the right to terminate the agreement and resume ownership of the business.

Pursuant to the agreement Richard assumed control of the business but was unable to make any further payments on the note. Consequently, the Executive Vice-President of the Bank requested that Bill and Mildred Fithian pay the note in full. They did and the Bank assigned the note to them for whatever disposition they might choose. Bill demanded that Richard indemnify him for the total amount Bill paid on the note.

Receiving no satisfaction from Richard, Bill and Mildred sought judicial relief. On November 10, 1976, a confessed judgment against Richard and Janet of $8,953.95, the balance on the note paid by Bill and Mildred, with interest from January 18, 1974, court costs, and attorney's fees of $472.70, was entered in the Circuit Court for Kent County. Richard and Janet filed a motion to vacate the judgment, which the circuit court granted and ordered a hearing on the merits. Prior to trial, Richard and Janet filed a third party claim against Walter and Connie averring that as co-makers of the note, Walter and Connie were liable to Richard and Janet for any judgment that Bill and Mildred might recover against Richard and Janet. Walter and Connie counterclaimed contending that the agreement barred Richard's recovery.

The matter was brought to trial on August 25, 1977 before the circuit court, sitting without a jury. The court found that the J–F Printing Company, Inc. was never a de jure corporation and that those who attempted to act under that name were merely acting in their individual capacities; that the March 23, 1972 agreement was not material to the determination of the case; that Bill and Mildred were accommodation makers for Richard, Janet, Walter and Connnie and were entitled to collect from any one of the four.

Final judgment was entered on September 6, 1977 for Bill and Mildred against Richard and Janet in the amount of $8,953.95, the principal sum due, plus $2,288.95, representing interest from January 18, 1974 to August 25, 1977. The court denied Bill and Mildred's claim for collection fees specified in the note and also entered a judgment for Richard and Janet on Walter and Connie's counterclaim. In the third party claim of Richard and Janet against Walter and Connie, judgment was entered for Richard and Janet in the amount of $5,621.45, fifty percent of the total judgment. The costs of the case were to be divided equally between Richard and Janet and Walter and Connie.

Bill and Mildred Fithian filed a timely appeal to the Court of Special Appeals, complaining of the circuit court's adverse ruling as to the collection fees. Walter and Connie took their own appeal, challenging the lower court's findings concerning both Connie's status in relation to the note and the materiality of the March, 1972 agreement. These appeals were consolidated for oral argument in that court.

In an unreported per curiam decision filed on April 7, 1978, Fithian v. Jamar, No. 946, Sept. Term, 1977, the Court of Special Appeals affirmed the circuit court in part and reversed in part. The Court of Special Appeals reversed on the issue of collection fees, ruling that there was a "valid and enforceable contract right of Bill and Mildred to the payment of collection costs * * * ."; the Court of Special Appeals affirmed the circuit court's finding that Connie Fithian was a co-maker of the note, and not an accommodation party. The Court of Special Appeals also affirmed the trial court's finding that the March, 1972 agreement was not material to the case because it was "a private agreement between only two (2) of the six (6) makers of the note."

Walter and Connie (appellants) requested review of these rulings in this Court, and we granted their petition for certiorari on June 21, 1978 to consider the two questions presented: whether Connie Fithian was an accommodation maker of the note and thus not liable to the party accommodated; and whether the March, 1972 agreement constitutes a defense to Richard and Janet's (appellees) third party claim against Walter and Connie.

Our disposition of the questioned rulings requires us to reverse and remand. The error which occurred in the court below was caused in part by a failure to fully analyze the individual rights and obligations of Connie, Walter, Janet and Richard. Therefore, in the discussion which follows, in addition to examining the two questions presented, we will clarify the resulting rights and obligations of these parties.

Richard v. Connie

Since there is no dispute that Connie signed the note, the answer to the first question depends on her purpose in doing so. This is made clear by Maryland Code (1975), § 3–415(1) of the Commercial Law Article which provides that an accommodation party is "one who signs the instrument in any capacity for the purpose of lending his name to another party to it." The undisputed evidence as presented by the Executive Vice-President of the Bank was to the effect that the wives' signatures were required before the Bank would make the loan to Walter and Richard. Such practices are common among lending institutions which recognize that

> [o]ne with money to lend, goods to sell or services to render may have doubts about a prospective debtor's ability to pay. In such cases he is likely to demand more assurance than the debtor's bare promise of payment. The prospective creditor can reduce his risk by requiring some sort of security. One form of security is the Article 9 security interest in the debtor's goods. Another type of security takes the form

of joining a third person on the debtor's obligation. [J. White and R. Summers, Uniform Commercial Code § 13–12, at 425 (1972)].

It is readily apparent, therefore, that Connie lent her name to facilitate the loan transaction. As such she lent her name to two parties to the instrument, Richard and Walter, to enable them to receive a *joint* loan for the purchase of equipment for their printing business, thereby giving the Bank the added assurance of having another party to the obligation. Connie signed as an accommodation party as to both Walter and Richard.

Nor is there any merit in the argument advanced by Richard that Connie must be either a co-maker or an accommodation party, that she cannot be both. The actual language of § 3–415(1) indicates that an accommodation party also signs in a particular capacity, as maker, acceptor or indorser of an instrument. The Official Comment 1 to § 3–415 explains that

> [s]ubsection (1) recognizes that an accommodation party is always a surety (which includes a guarantor), and it is his only distinguishing feature. He differs from other sureties only in that his liability is on the instrument and he is a surety for another party to it. His obligation is therefore determined by the capacity in which he signs. An accommodation maker or acceptor is bound on the instrument without any resort to his principal, while an accommodation indorser may be liable only after presentment, notice of dishonor and protest.

Moreover, § 3–415(2) refers specifically to the liability of an accommodation party "in the capacity in which he has signed." It follows, therefore, that the fact that Connie was a co-maker of the note does not preclude her from also being an accommodation party.

Section 3–415(5) of the Commercial Law Article states that "[a]n accommodation party is not liable to the party accommodated"; thus, Connie is not liable to Richard. Our predecessors, prior to Maryland's adoption of the Uniform Commercial Code, explained the reasons for this proposition in Crothers v. National Bank, 158 Md. 587, 593, 149 A. 270, 273 (1930):

> Since the accommodating party lends his credit by request to the party accommodated upon the assumption that the latter will discharge the debt when due, it is an implied term of this agreement that the party accommodated cannot acquire any right of action against the accommodating party.

Richard contends, however, that Connie intended to accommodate only her husband, Walter. Even if there were evidence to this effect (and there is none), the subjective intent of a co-maker of a note is of little weight when objective facts and circumstances unambiguously demonstrate the capacity in which the note was signed. Seaboard Finance Co. of Connecticut, Inc. v. Dorman, 4 Conn.Cir. 154, 227 A.2d 441 (1966); Hover v. Magley, 116 App.Div. 84, 101 N.Y.S. 245 (1906). It is clear to us that the signatures of both wives were required to effect this joint business venture and thus Connie's signature was as much an accommodation to Richard as it was to Walter. We hold that Connie was an accommodation maker and that she cannot be liable to Richard, the party accommodated. The Court of Special Appeals erroneously held to the contrary.

Janet v. Connie

The preceding discussion of Connie's status demonstrates that each of the four parties, Walter, Connie, Richard, and Janet, has certain rights and obligations with respect to this note which are not affected by his or her marital status. The court below erred in not fully analyzing these separate rights and obligations. It follows that our finding that Connie has no liability to Richard in no way changes any obligation she may have to Janet. Janet, as well as Connie, is a co-accommodation maker on this note.

The question is therefore whether one co-accommodation maker who pays more than her proportionate share of the debt has a right of contribution against another co-accommodation maker. The Uniform Commercial Code contains no provision expressly dealing with the right of an accommodation party to contribution from another accommodation party. However, the Code does provide that the principles of the common law remain applicable "[u]nless displaced by the particular provisions" of the Code. Maryland Code (1975), § 1–103 of the Commercial Law Article.

That an accommodation maker has a right of contribution from a co-accommodation maker is a settled principle of the law. The Restatement of Security provides

A surety who in the performance of his own obligation discharges more than his proportionate share of the principal's duty is entitled to contribution from a co-surety. [Restatement of Security § 149 (1941)].

* * *

Maryland has followed this rule. Jackson v. Cupples, 239 Md. 637, 212 A.2d 273 (1965). *Jackson* was decided after the effective date of the U.C.C. in Maryland, but the note in question had been executed prior to that date. The Court held that a co-surety who pays a debt has a right of contribution from his co-sureties.

This Court has not addressed this question in regard to a note controlled by the U.C.C. Our research revealed only one case which directly confronted the effect of the U.C.C. on the common law rule. The court stated that the U.C.C. does not change the rule of suretyship law permitting contribution by one surety from a co-surety. McLochlin v. Miller, 139 Ind.App. 443, 217 N.E.2d 50 (1966).

Accordingly Janet has a right of contribution against Connie. But this right to contribution is an inchoate claim which does not ripen into being unless and until Janet pays more than her proportionate share to Bill and Mildred. Cotham and Maldonado v. Board, 260 Md. 556, 566–67, 273 A.2d 115 (1971). Judgment can be entered on behalf of Janet against Connie, but it must be fashioned so that it may not be enforced until Janet proves she actually paid more than her proportionate share to Bill and Mildred.[1] Baltimore County v. Stitzel, 26 Md.App. 175, 184–88, 337 A.2d 721 (1975).

Richard v. Walter

[Omitted is the portion of the opinion in which the court held that Richard's agreement in 1972 to assume all liabilities of the printing business, including the note, precluded any right of contribution that Richard would otherwise have against Walter, his joint obligor on the note.]

Janet v. Walter

That the 1972 agreement serves as a defense by Walter against Richard in no way serves to insulate Walter against Janet. Janet's status as an accommodation maker is unaffected by the agreement. As an accommodation maker, Janet has a right to look to any principal, including Walter for any amounts

---

1. A surety who is called upon to pay more than his proportionate share of the debt has a right of contribution from his co-sureties in an amount not to exceed each co-surety's proportionate share of the debt. See Schindel v. Danzer, 161 Md. 384, 157 A. 283 (1931); 72 C.J.S. Principal and Surety § 369 (1951). Here the note was signed by four sureties (Bill, Mildred, Connie and Janet); Janet's proportionate share of indebtedness to her co-sureties is 25% of the debt.

she actually pays.   Maryland Code (1975), § 3–415 of the Commercial Law Article.   Janet's status as Richard's wife does not affect her status as an accommodation maker.   She is entitled to judgment from either principal when she actually pays any amount of the debt.

In summary, Richard is not entitled to judgment against Walter because of the agreement.   Rather, Walter is entitled to indemnification from Richard for any amount Walter is forced to pay.   Richard is not entitled to judgment against Connie because an accommodation party is not liable to the party accommodated.   Janet is entitled to contribution from her co-surety, Connie, the judgment being unenforceable unless and until Janet proves she actually has paid more than her proportionate share of the debt to Bill and Mildred.   Similarly, Janet as a surety is entitled to judgment against Walter as a principal for any amount of the debt for which Janet proves payment.[3]

NOTE

In footnote 3 the court states that it does not decide whether Bill and Mildred were entitled to recover the full amount of the debt from Janet.   How much were Bill and Mildred entitled to recover from Janet?

PROBLEM

Manny owned 50% of the capital stock of Corporation and was its President.   Moe and Jack each owned 25%.   Corporation needed money for working capital and borrowed it from Bank which insisted as a condition to the loan that Manny sign the note because of the precarious financial condition of Corporation.   The note was signed as follows:

Corporation
By Manny, President
Manny, in his individual capacity.

The note contained the following clause.   "All signers of the note are principals and not accommodation parties, guarantors or other sureties."   The loan, which is unsecured, was made by crediting the entire principal amount to Corporation's account with Bank and was used entirely for corporate purposes.   Corporation has defaulted on the loan.   After Corporation's default on the loan to Bank, Manny paid Bank the entire unpaid balance

---

3.   Whether Bill and Mildred were entitled to judgment in the full amount of the debt against Janet we do not decide because Janet did not appeal from that judgment.

amounting to $10,000. Is Manny an accommodation party? Is Manny entitled to reimbursement from Corporation for the $10,000 paid to Bank or are his rights limited to a claim for contribution? Would Manny's rights be any different if he owned 100% of the stock of Corporation rather than 50%?

WILMINGTON TRUST CO. v. GESULLO

Delaware Superior Court, New Castle County, 1980.
29 U.C.C.Rep. 144.

O'HARA, J. Appellant Wilmington Trust Company ("W.T.C."), plaintiff below, brought suit against appellee Leonard Gesullo ("Gesullo"), defendant below, in the Justice of the Peace Court, seeking recovery on a note signed by appellee. Following a trial on the merits judgment was entered in favor of Gesullo on June 15, 1977. W.T.C. moved for a new trial, below, which was denied on September 7, 1977. Thereafter, this appeal was filed in the Superior Court.

* * *

I

Around the beginning of September, 1971, Vernon Steele (who was not made a party to the action below) desired to purchase a certain 1967 Brockway truck equipped with a diesel engine from Healthways Co., Inc. ("Healthways"). Gesullo was at that time the chief executive officer of Healthways, a fifty percent shareholder therein, and Healthways' sales representative in the negotiations with Steele. In order to finance this purchase Steele attempted to borrow $5,250, the purchase price, from W.T.C. However, W.T.C. insisted as a pre-condition to approval of the loan that Steele obtain Gesullo's signature on the note and that Steele grant to W.T.C. a security interest in the Brockway truck. On September 24, 1971, both Steele and Gesullo signed a note with W.T.C. The proceeds of this loan, in the amount of $5,250, were made payable by check to Steele and Healthways. None of the loan proceeds were payable to Gesullo. Also on September 24, 1971, Steele and W.T.C. entered an agreement, to which Gesullo was not a party, which granted W.T.C. a security interest in the Brockway truck as collateral for the loan. On this same date, Healthways transferred the truck to Steele and received the $5,250 check as payment. The security interest of W.T.C. in the truck was never entered on the certificate of title as required by 21 Del C §§ 2331–2332, and no other attempt to perfect, pursuant to 6 Del C § 9–302, was made.

Installment payments were apparently made on the loan as required until March 30, 1973. Steele contacted W.T.C. on or about May 18, 1973 and requested that the time for making the March 30 payment be extended to May 30, 1973. W.T.C. agreed to the extension for which Steele paid a separate consideration of $65. Gesullo was not contacted about this extension and did not consent thereto either before or after W.T.C. and Steele agreed upon the extension.

Sometime prior to September, 1974, the Brockway truck was involved in an accident. Steele brought the damaged truck to Healthways and requested Gesullo to have the major salvageable parts (i.e., engine, rear-end and transmission) removed and installed into a Mack truck cab and frame. The rebuilt Mack truck was then to be sold by Healthways on behalf of Steele. On or about June 13, 1974, Gesullo contacted W.T.C. and requested a payoff figure on the 1971 loan. At first he was advised that $500 was owed thereon, and Healthways paid this amount to W.T.C. On or about June 20, 1974, a W.T.C. employee contacted Gesullo and informed him that an additional $173.54 was needed to clear the loan account. Healthways also paid this additional amount to W.T.C. On or about September 13, 1974, Healthways, on behalf of Steele, sold the Mack truck containing the Brockway parts to a third person. No lien was noted on the certificate of title to this vehicle. On or about September 16, 1975, a W.T.C. representative wrote to Gesullo claiming that an additional $1,104.56 remained to be paid in the 1971 loan and requesting Gesullo to pay this amount. Gesullo refused and this suit followed.

* * *

III

The first substantive question to be resolved is whether Gesullo was an "accommodation party" on the note. The Delaware Commercial Code, 6 Del.C. § 3–415(1), provides:

"An accommodation party is one who signs the instrument in any capacity for the purpose of lending his name to another party to it."

The Delaware Study Comment to this section makes clear that an accommodation party is always a surety. This is important because a surety is entitled to certain special defenses under the Code. See 6 Del.C. § 3–606.

The most significant element in determining whether an individual is an accommodation party is the intention of the parties to the commercial transaction. 2 Anderson, Uniform Commercial Code § 3–415:9 (2d ed 1971). The most direct evidence of intention in this regard may be found where words of guarantee are expressly added to the signature of one claiming accommodation status on the face of the commercial instrument. See 6 Del.C. § 3–416(4). However, where there is no direct evidence of accommodation status on the face of the instrument, such status may nonetheless be shown by parol evidence if the rights of a holder in due course are not involved. 6 Del.C. § 3–415(3). In cases where parol evidence is admissible and necessary to a determination of the status of parties to a commercial instrument, the court will look to the facts and circumstances connected with the transaction and draw reasonable and logical inferences therefrom. MacArthur v. Cannon, Conn.App., 229 A2d 372 (1967).

Because receipt of proceeds from the instrument or other direct benefit will generally be inconsistent with accommodation status, courts have focused on this aspect of the transaction. Stockwell v. Bloomfield State Bank, Ind.App, 367 N.E.2d 42 [22 U.C.C.Rep. 726] (1977); White & Summers, Uniform Commercial Code § 13–13 at 431 (1972); 2 Anderson, supra § 3–415:9. Other important factors include the source of collateral used to secure the loan, Wilmington Trust Co. v. Sutton, Del.Super., C.A. No. 674, 1976 (unreported decision dated October 11, 1979), and the lender's motive in securing multiple signatures on the instrument. Id.; see also Stockwell v. Bloomfield State Bank, 367 N.E.2d at 44–45; and compare MacArthur v. Cannon, 229 A.2d at 377. The application of these factors in the case sub judice supports Gesullo's assertion that he was an accommodation party to Steele on the loan note.

First, the proceeds of the 1971 note were made payable to Steele and Healthways; none of the proceeds were payable to Gesullo. By turning the endorsed proceeds check over to Gesullo as Healthways' representative, Steele acquired possession of the Brockway truck. Thus, Steele received the full and direct benefit of the proceeds. By comparison, the benefit Gesullo derived from the proceeds was indirect and relatively small, i.e., as a fifty percent shareholder he had an interest in the profit (if any) which Healthways gained by sale of the truck to Steele.

See Stockwell v. Bloomfield State Bank, 367 N.E.2d at 45. Secondly, only Steele provided collateral, i.e., the Brockway truck, to secure payment of the note. Gesullo was not even a party to this security agreement. Thirdly, W.T.C. initially refused to make the loan to Steele and agreed to do so only if Steele could get Gesullo to co-sign the note. This is a strong indication that W.T.C. considered Steele to be the principal obligor on the note and Gesullo only secondarily liable. Compare MacArthur v. Cannon, above, with Stockwell v. Bloomfield State Bank, above. On this point, the court takes note of a letter dated September 16, 1975 from a W.T.C. representative to Gesullo which stated:

"On September 24, 1971, you cosigned a note * * * for Mr. Vernon P. Steele * * *

"As comaker, you are responsible for payment of the loan in the event the original maker fails to meet his obligation with us." [See attachment to appellee's answers to appellant's first interrogatories.]

Consideration of all of these factors leads the court to conclude that Gesullo signed the 1971 note as an accommodation party for the benefit of Steele.

IV

As an accommodation party to the 1971 note, Gesullo seeks to assert special suretyship defenses under 6 Del.C. § 3–606 which provides in pertinent part:

"(1) The holder discharges any party to the instrument to the extent that without such party's consent the holder

(a) without express reservation of rights releases or agrees not to sue any person against whom the party has to the knowledge of the holder a right of recourse or agrees to suspend the right to enforce against such person the instrument or collateral or otherwise discharges such person * * *; or

(b) unjustifiably impairs any collateral for the instrument given by or on behalf of the party or any person against whom he has a right of recourse."

Gesullo first argues that he is entitled to a full discharge from liability on the note because W.T.C. and Steele entered an agreement to extend the time for payment of an installment due on March 30, 1973 to May 30, 1973. The date of this agreement was May 18, 1973.

The Delaware Study Comment to § 3–606(1)(a) expressly states that "[a]n extension of time * * * [is] covered by the language 'agrees to suspend the right to enforce.' " This provision is consistent with the general rule in Delaware suretyship law that a binding agreement between the creditor and the principal debtor to extend time for payment will discharge a surety who has not consented thereto. Equitable Trust Co. v. Shaw, Del.Ch., 194 A. 24 (1937); Simpson, Handbook on the Law of Suretyship, § 73 (1950); Restatement of Security § 129 (1941).

W.T.C. does not argue that the 1973 extension agreement was not binding between itself and Steele. Also, the undisputed facts in this case clearly establish that Gesullo was, at all pertinent times, completely unaware of the 1973 extension agreement and never consented to it.[1] Moreover, there is nothing on the face of the 1971 loan note, or in the circumstances of its negotiation or the negotiation of the 1973 extension agreement, to indicate that W.T.C. expressly reserved its rights against Gesullo as permitted by § 3–606(2). Compare Parnes v. Celia's, Inc., N.J. Super.App.Div., 239 A.2d 19 (1968). Therefore, Gesullo, as an accommodation party on the 1971 note, is entitled to discharge from liability thereunder pursuant to § 3–606(1)(a).

W.T.C. has sought to avoid the discharge mandated by § 3–606(1)(a) in this case by focusing the court's attention on a provision in the 1971 security agreement executed in connection with the loan note.[2] W.T.C. claims that this provision somehow

---

1. It does no good to argue, as W.T.C. has done herein, that Gesullo would almost surely have agreed to the extension had he known of it. The simple fact is that Gesullo did not consent to the extension of time.

In reaching this conclusion, the court is mindful that an accommodation party's "consent" under the Code may be given in advance of an extension agreement between the creditor and the principal obligor, simultaneously with such agreement, or subsequent thereto. UCC § 3–606, Comment 2. Additionally, such "consent" may be expressed or may be implied from conduct of the accommodation party which shows assent to the creditor's action. White & Summers, supra § 13–15 at 436. There is simply no evidence in the record presented upon which the court could find that Gesullo had expressly or impliedly consented to the W.T.C.-Steele extension agreement either before or after its inception. To the contrary, Gesullo's unchallenged evidence indicates clearly that there was no consent clause in the 1971 note that he signed, and that he was completely unaware of the 1973 extension agreement and never discussed it with either W.T.C. or Steele at any time prior to the institution of these proceedings. Deposition of Leonard Gesullo at 20–21, 26–27. Consequently, Gesullo cannot be said to have impliedly consented to the 1973 extension agreement by making payments on the 1971 note subsequent to the agreement of which he was completely unaware.

2. The pertinent clause provides:

"Debtor further represents, warrants and agrees: (a) No delay or omission by Bank in exercising any right or remedy hereunder or with respect to any Indebtedness shall

removes the 1973 extension agreement from the purview of the statute. The only possible basis for such argument is that this provision constituted either a consent by Gesullo to extensions of time or a reservation of rights by W.T.C. as against Gesullo. As to the first basis, Gesullo cannot be said to have consented to anything under a document to which he was not a party. See UCC § 3–119, Comment 2. As to the second basis, while no special form of words is required to create a reservation of rights, a creditor must clearly manifest an intention to reserve its rights against the accommmodation party. 2 Anderson, supra § 3–606:11. The security agreement provision relied upon by W.T.C. provides no evidence of such intent. The only parties mentioned in the clause are W.T.C. ("Bank") and Steele ("Debtor"). There is no discussion whatsoever of rights or obligations as between W.T.C. and Gesullo. Therefore, on the facts presented it is impossible for the court to conclude that W.T.C. had expressly reserved its rights against Gesullo via the security agreement.

The only remaining issue to be resolved is the extent to which Gesullo is entitled to be discharged from liability. The language of § 3–606(1)(a) indicates that an accommodation party is entitled to discharge only "to the extent that" the creditor has agreed to suspend its right to enforce the instrument against the principal obligor. On the basis of this language an argument can be made in the instant case that Gesullo is entitled only to pro tanto discharge limited to the amount of the March, 1973 installment ($173.54). While reported cases discussing the application of this pro tanto language in the context of unjustifiable impairment of collateral under § 3–606(1)(b) are legion, counsel for the parties have not directed the court's attention to any extension-of-time cases discussing the issue; nor has the court's own research disclosed any such cases decided under the Code. Since the purpose of this statute was to "incorporate basic principles of suretyship law into the negotiable instruments law," Delaware Study Comment to § 3–606, the court will refer to that

operate as a waiver thereof or of any other right or remedy, and no single or partial exercise thereof shall preclude any other or further exercise thereof or the exercise of any other right or remedy. Bank may remedy any default by Debtor hereunder or with respect to any Indebtedness in any reasonable manner without waiving the default remedied and without waiving any other prior or subsequent default by Debtor. All rights and remedies of Bank hereunder are cumulative."

Interestingly, the argument based on this clause is not discussed in the parties' briefs on the cross-motions, and was only raised by W.T.C.'s counsel at oral argument.

body of law for assistance in determining the extent of discharge to which Gesullo is entitled on the instant note.

As stated above, the general rule in suretyship law is that a nonconsenting surety is discharged by a binding creditor-debtor agreement to extend time for payment. However, in cases where the principal debtor's obligation to pay arises in installments rather than at a single point in time, another rule comes into play. In such cases it has been held that where successive payments are to be made at fixed periods, a creditor's extension of time as to one payment will discharge the surety as to it, but not as to subsequent payments which have not yet become due at the time of the extension agreement. 74 Am.Jur.2d Suretyship § 50 (1974); 72 C.J.S. Principal and Surety § 170 (1951); 38 C.J.S. Guaranty § 75(a) (1943); Croydon Gas Co. v. Dickinson, 2 C.P.D. 46 (1876). The key element which triggers operation of this rule is a finding that the principal debtor's successive obligations to pay are divisible and severable from each other. If the principal's debt is not entirely divisible, then the rule of partial discharge does not apply, and an extension of time will fully discharge the surety. 10 Williston on Contracts § 1222 (3d ed. 1967); Stearn's Law of Suretyship § 6.26 (5th ed. 1951); I Brandt, Suretyship and Guaranty § 393 (3d ed. 1905); Compare Croydon Gas Co. v. Dickinson, above, with Midland Motor Showrooms, Ltd. v. Newman, 2 K.B. 256 (1929); but see 43 Harv.L. Rev. 503 (1930).

Examples of the kinds of situations in which the rule of partial discharge has most commonly been applied include: consignment contracts where the consignee, whose performance has been guaranteed by a surety, is obligated to make periodic remittances to the consignor based upon the amount of sales during each defined period of time, e.g., I. J. Cooper Rubber Co. v. Johnson, Tenn.Supr., 182 S.W. 593 (1916); indebtedness evidenced by multiple notes which mature at different times and on which payment has been guaranteed by the same surety, e.g., Owings v. MacKenzie, Mo.Supr., 33 S.W. 802 (1896); real estate lease agreements where the rents, payment of which have been guaranteed by a surety, are to be paid in periodic installments, e.g., Sutter v. Nenninger, N.Y. Cnty., 189 N.Y.S. 662 (1921). The rationale in these cases is that the successive obligations to pay are separate and independent of each other, so that an extension of time as to one payment does not extend time for performance as to future payments. In other words, each obligation to pay is treated as though it were a separate contract.

The case at bar does not fall into any of the above-mentioned categories. There is but a single installment loan contract here, and Steele's indebtedness thereunder, for which Gesullo guaranteed payment, is evidenced by a single note. Moreover, although the note specifies that repayment was to be made in thirty-six consecutive monthly installments, there was but one debt to be satisfied, not thirty-six separate and independent debts. In such a situation it strains logic to say that the principal's debt is entirely divisible. See Midland Motor Showrooms, Ltd. v. Newman, above. On this basis alone, the court might be warranted in holding that the rule of partial discharge has no application and Gesullo should be entitled to full discharge as a result of the extension of time granted on the March, 1973 payment. However, there is another significant factor in this case which the court believes deserves consideration.

The face of the 1971 note which Gesullo signed as an accommodation party contains a rather standard acceleration clause. This clause provided in pertinent part that "if any . . . installment shall remain unpaid for a period of thirty (30) days the entire unpaid balance may be declared due and payable." At the time W.T.C. and Steele entered the binding extension agreement (May 18, 1973), the March 30 installment was already forty-nine days overdue. But for that agreement, W.T.C. could have accelerated the entire debt immediately. More importantly, Gesullo could also have accelerated Steele's repayment obligation by way of subrogation to W.T.C.'s rights and remedies had Gesullo chosen to fully satisfy the debt after Steele's default continued into May, 1973.[3] See Stearn's Law of Suretyship, supra §§ 11.1, 11.2 and 11.5; see also Restatement on Security, supra § 141. However, the extension agreement destroyed this option. In addition to extending by two months the time within which Steele could make the March payment, the agreement also necessarily suspended W.T.C.'s rights under the acceleration clause, as well as Gesullo's potential rights via subrogation, to declare the entire remaining balance immediately due and payable. Therefore, because the extent to which W.T.C. agreed "to suspend the right to enforce" the note against Steele related to the entire unpaid balance, Gesullo is entitled to be fully discharged from liability on the note pursuant to § 3–606(1)(a).

3. This holding is fully supported by § 3–415(5) of the Code which provides:

"An accommodation party is not liable to the party accommodated, and if he pays the instrument has a right of recourse on the instrument against such party."

The court is aware that the decision herein is at least superficially at odds with the case of Cohn v. Spitzer, N.Y.Supr.App. Div., 129 N.Y.S. 104 (1911). Generally the facts in Cohn are not essentially dissimilar to the facts in the case at bar, and the acceleration clause in the Cohn debt instrument [4] is functionally equivalent to the instant acceleration clause. The Cohn court chose to apply the rule of partial discharge notwithstanding the presence of the acceleration clause, holding simply that the acceleration provision "was exclusively for the benefit of the obligee [i.e., the creditor] or its assigns." Id. at 106. By holding that the sureties had no rights under this provision, it appears that the court failed to give due deference to the sureties' potential rights by way of subrogation. Therefore, this Court respectfully declines to follow the Cohn rationale as to the effect of an acceleration provision on a surety's right to full or partial discharge.

The court is confident that the rules announced herein are entirely justifiable in today's commercial marketplace and will not impose unreasonable burdens on lending institutions. While it has often been said that sureties have been ancient favorites of the law, White & Summers, supra § 13–14 at 432, their position as compared to that of creditors is rather precarious as a practical matter. Generally, the creditor owes no duty to the surety to diligently pursue the principal debtor in order to directly enforce the debtor's obligations. Stearn's Law of Suretyship, supra § 6.35. Additionally, the creditor has no duty to notify the surety of default by the principal debtor, Simpson, supra § 41, or to notify the surety that an extension of time which also expressly reserves the creditor's rights against the surety has been granted to the principal debtor. U.C.C. § 3–606, Comment 4; 72 C.J.S. Principal and Surety, supra § 153. Given these inherent disadvantages with which sureties must cope, it cannot be seriously contended that the result reached herein is overly solicitous for these "ancient favorites of the law." Moreover, the prudent lender who seeks to avoid the impact of this decision can easily do so by obtaining the surety's prior consent to an extension of time or by including an express reservation of rights in the extension agreement.

4. The acceleration clause in Cohn provided that if default in the payment of any installment for principal or interest occurred and such installment remained unpaid for twenty days, the entire remaining balance "should, at the option of said obligee, its legal representatives or assigns, become and be due and payable immediately thereafter." 129 N.Y.S. at 105.

Lastly, the court notes that although most of the commentators to the Code have not addressed the impact of § 3–606 in the context of an installment loan contract which contains an acceleration provision, the one treatise which has recognized and discussed the problem appears to concur with the approach taken herein. See 2 Hart and Willier, Commercial Paper Under the U.C.C. § 13.21[3] (1976).

V

Because the court has determined that appellee is entitled to full discharge under § 3–606(1)(a), the court does not reach appellee's contention that he is also entitled to discharge under § 3–606(1)(b) allegedly because appellant unjustifiably impaired the collateral given by Steele to secure the loan. The court notes, however, that under the facts of this case Gesullo's impairment of collateral claim is not insubstantial.

VI

Based on the foregoing analysis, the court holds that summary judgment should be entered in favor of appellee Gesullo, and appellant's motion for summary judgment should be denied, and the appeal herein should be dismissed.

It is so ordered.

NOTE

In the principal case W.T.C. made the mistake of granting the extension to Steele "without express reservation of rights" against Gesullo. What should W.T.C. have done to protect itself when it granted the extension? If W.T.C. had reserved rights would Gesullo have been entitled to any notice? It W.T.C. reserved rights and Gesullo found out about it, what effect would the reservation of rights have had on Gesullo's rights? See UCC § 3–606(2).

FARMERS STATE BANK OF OAKLEY v. COOPER

Supreme Court of Kansas, 1980.
277 Kan. 547, 608 P.2d 929.

MILLER, JUSTICE:

*   *   *

The factual background is necessary to an understanding of the issues. In July, 1971, Dr. Michael P. Cooper, son of defendant Paul A. Cooper, Jr., moved with his wife Georgia to Oakley, Kansas. Michael, a chiropractor, intended to establish a practice in Oakley. He approached the bank for a loan in order to purchase equipment and remodel his office, rented from the bank and located on an upper floor of the bank building. The bank committed a line of credit of five thousand dollars. The president of the bank testified that when the original commitment was made, the professional equipment, household items, and automobile that were offered as security were not sufficient to completely secure the loan; therefore Paul Cooper's signature was necessary to protect the bank for the total amount.

The first promissory note in the amount of three thousand dollars was executed on August 12, 1971. It was signed by Michael P. Cooper, Georgia L. Cooper, and Paul A. Cooper, Jr. The note was secured by a security agreement of the same date, designating all equipment, instruments, and furnishings in the office and all household goods located in the Michael Cooper residence, and a 1967 Chevrolet, as security. Michael P. Cooper and Georgia Cooper, together with William B. Griffith as agent for the bank, signed the security agreement. The security agreement was never perfected.

Four additional notes for amounts under one thousand dollars, signed only by Michael P. Cooper, were made in subsequent months. The five notes were consolidated on February 12, 1972, when a note for five thousand dollars, secured by the security agreement of August 12, 1971, was executed. This note was signed by Michael, Georgia, and Paul Cooper. This note was renewed by the execution of new notes signed by all three persons on August 12, 1972, February 12, 1973, December 1, 1973, and July 1, 1974. Some payments of principal and interest were made; the face amount of the final renewal note, due January 1, 1975, was $4,550.63. The majority if not all of the payments on the notes were made by defendant Paul Cooper. The final note is on a form substantially different from the earlier notes
*   *   *

Michael's chiropractic practice did not prosper. During 1975 he moved from Oakley to the State of Washington. It then appeared that Dr. Cooper had a splendid opportunity in Washington, and the bank was hopeful that his practice would prosper there enabling him to satisfy the note. The bank gave permission to Dr. Cooper to remove the collateral to Washington. The move was not financially successful, and Dr. Cooper returned to Oakley for a short time during 1976. He then moved to Macksville, Kansas, and later returned to his home in Shawnee, Kansas. He has not practiced chiropractic medicine since his return to Kansas. Dr. Cooper disposed of some of the collateral; the only items the defendant has seen in his recent possession are a handheld vibrator, a sewing machine, and the automobile. The record does not indicate any attempt of the bank to obtain payment from Dr. Cooper or to foreclose on the remaining collateral.

On October 26, 1977, the bank filed suit against defendant Paul Cooper for the balance due on the note plus accrued interest. Paul Cooper filed an answer and counterclaim, and later filed a third-party petition against his son, Dr. Michael Cooper, and his son's wife, Georgia, for indemnity in the event a judgment is entered against Paul Cooper and in favor of the bank. Neither Michael nor Georgia Cooper have answered or otherwise appeared in this action.

* * *

The third and determinative issue is whether the bank, by failing to perfect its security agreement and by allowing the removal of the collateral from Kansas, unjustifiably impaired the collateral, thus discharging the defendant, an accommodation party. Defendant claims discharge under [U.C.C. § 3–606(1)(b)].

The discharge provisions of that statute apply only to signers who occupy the position of sureties, such as accommodation parties.

* * *

Is defendant released from part or all of his liability because the bank failed to perfect its security agreement and Dr. Cooper has since sold a part of the collateral? Defendant contends that the failure of the bank to perfect its security agreement constituted an unjustifiable impairment of collateral. A review of the principles involved may be helpful.

An unperfected security agreement is valid and effective between the parties to the agreement according to its terms. [U.C.C. §] 9–201; and see [U.C.C. §] 9–203. Ordinarily, a financing statement must be filed to perfect it. [U.C.C. §] 9–302. Except in the circumstances encompassed by [U.C.C. §] 9–307, a secured party's interest in collateral is prior to that of a purchaser if the security interest is perfected; however, if the interest is not perfected, a buyer for value without knowledge takes free of the security interest. [U.C.C. §] 9–301(1)(c).

Defendant relies on Redlon v. Heath, 59 Kan. 255, 52 P. 862 (1898). The creditor in *Heath* recorded the mortgage in the wrong county; the error was not discovered until other mortgages, exceeding the total value of the property, had been properly filed of record. We noted in that case that the evidence showed that the mortgaged land was of sufficient value to have paid prior encumbrances as well as the amount of the improperly filed one, but that other mortgages, later filed and "sufficient in amount to absorb the entire property, took precedence and swept his security away." We held that the person who signed the note as a surety or accommodation party was released from liability because of the failure of the creditor to record the mortgage in the right county and thus protect the collateral.

The U.C.C. has codified this rule in [U.C.C. §] 3–606(1)(*b*) which provides for discharge of any party *to the extent* that without such person's consent the holder unjustifiably impairs collateral. It is clear from the statute that the release is only *pro tanto*, and the cases so hold. See Langeveld v. L. R. Z. H. Corporation, 74 N.J. 45, 376 A.2d 931, 22 U.C.C.Rep. 106 (1977), and Mikanis Trading Corp. v. Block, 59 App.Div.2d 689, 398 N.Y.S.2d 679 (1977). The failure of the holder of a security agreement to perfect it, which failure results in a loss of available collateral to an accommodation party, is an impairment of the collateral. Here, the sale of collateral was wrongful, if not criminal (see K.S.A. 21–3734), and the failure of the bank to perfect its security agreement has resulted in a loss of some of the collateral, so far as the defendant is concerned. Part of the collateral is gone, and presumably is not subject to the security agreement.

Should the defendant be released from liability? We think not. No evidence of the value of the missing collateral, or of the value of the remaining collateral, was offered. No such evidence is contained within the record.

[UCC §] 3–307(2) provides:

"When signatures are admitted or established, production of the instrument entitles a holder to recover on it unless the defendant establishes a defense."

The official U.C.C. comment to this section reads in part:

"2. Once signatures are proved or admitted, a holder makes out his case by mere production of the instrument, and is entitled to recover in the absence of any further evidence. *The defendant has the burden of establishing any and all defenses*, not only in the first instance but by a preponderance of the total evidence." (Emphasis supplied.)

The bank did not know until trial of the sale or disposal; it did not know when, to whom, or for what price or on what terms it was sold or transferred. Defendant had all this evidence available; his son, the third party defendant, had the information; defendant knew of his son's whereabouts but the bank did not; defendant could have called his son as a witness had he wished to do so.

We conclude that the burden of proof was upon defendant to establish the extent to which the collateral was impaired. See Christensen v. McAtee, 256 Or. 333, 473 P.2d 659, 8 U.C.C.Rep. 66 (1970); Langeveld v. L. R. Z. H. Corporation, 74 N.J. 45, 376 A.2d 931 (1977); and Telpner v. Hogan, 17 Ill.App.3d 152, 308 N.E.2d 7 (1974). Having failed to establish the extent of the impairment, defendant is liable for the full amount of the note.

* * *

C. LETTERS OF CREDIT

Baird, Standby Letters of Credit in Bankruptcy

49 U. of Chi.L.Rev. 130, 133–135 (1982).*

I. THE LETTER-OF-CREDIT TRANSACTION

A. Background

As recently as twenty years ago, letters of credit were used principally in international sales. No seller willingly sends its goods across national borders unless it is confident it will be paid, because no seller welcomes the prospect of having its goods in the care of unknown parties in a foreign port, where finding a new buyer may be impossible and bringing a legal action extremely difficult. The letter of credit as we now know it arose in the middle of the nineteenth century in response to this problem.

Although letter-of-credit transactions vary, their basic structure can be stated briefly. In a typical letter-of-credit transaction, a seller specifies that payment be made with a letter of credit in its favor. The buyer (known as the "customer" in the

* Reprinted with the permission of the author and the University of Chicago Law Review. Some of the author's footnotes are omitted.

letter-of-credit transaction) contracts with the bank to issue the letter. The bank, knowing the creditworthiness of its customer, is willing to issue the letter for a small fee, typically some fraction of one per cent of the price of the goods. The bank sends the letter to the seller, promising to pay the full price of the goods when the seller presents it with a draft and the documents specified in the letter. These documents typically include a negotiable bill of lading.

This arrangement benefits all parties to the transaction. The seller can manufacture goods to the buyer's order, confident it will be paid regardless of what befalls the buyer, because it can rely on the bank's commitment. The buyer that secures the letter of credit is better off than if it had advanced cash to the seller, because it does not become liable for the price until a trustworthy party (the bank) has possession of a negotiable document of title. The bank, in turn, earns a fee for issuing the letter and exposes itself to only a small risk, because it can readily assess the creditworthiness of its customer and, as the holder of a negotiable bill of lading, it has a perfected security interest in the goods involved in the transaction.

The linchpin of the letter-of-credit transaction is the unique legal relationship between the bank and the beneficiary.[16] Unlike a guarantor, the bank is primarily liable whenever the beneficiary presents a draft and documents that conform to the letter. Unlike its counterpart in a third-party beneficiary contract, the bank may not invoke the defenses its customer might have on the underlying contract. Moreover, the status of a beneficiary of a letter of credit is radically different from that of a payee of a check, who has no right to compel payment from the drawee bank. In the letter-of-credit transaction, the beneficiary does have the right to compel payment, and once the letter of credit is issued, the customer is powerless to stop payment in the absence of fraud. This difference exists because a letter of credit, unlike a negotiable instrument such as a check, is a binding and irrevocable obligation of the bank itself, not of the cus-

---

16. In their discussion of the legal relationship created by the letter of credit, Professors White and Summers note that a letter of credit is not like other devices creating legal obligations, but rather that

a letter of credit is a letter of credit. As Bishop Butler once said, "Everything is what it is and not another thing." Thus, when a beneficiary sues an issuer for refusal to honor drafts drawn pursuant to a letter of credit, his theory is not that of breach of contract, nor does he sue "on a negotiable instrument." Rather, he sues "on a letter of credit."

J. White & R. Summers, supra note 15, § 18–2, at 715 (footnotes omitted).

tomer who procured it. The legal relationship between bank and beneficiary is governed by special principles which, like the law merchant in an earlier era, are nearly uniform throughout the world.

B. The Standby Letter of Credit

The archetypal letter-of-credit transaction described above is the means by which the parties pay one another if the underlying transaction takes place as planned. Standby letters of credit, in contrast, are never drawn upon if the transaction runs smoothly. For example, a builder might require a developer to have a bank issue a letter of credit in its behalf to ensure payment if the developer defaults. Such a letter of credit might require that the bank honor the builder's draft when accompanied by an architect's certificate that the building was finished and a statement by the builder that it had not been paid. In this kind of transaction, the bank usually will issue the letter only if the developer gives it a security interest in some property to which the bank will have recourse if the letter is drawn upon. If all goes well, the builder never presents its draft because it has been paid on schedule by the developer. If the developer defaults, however, the builder is still assured payment under the letter of credit. The bank then must seek reimbursement from the developer or enforce its security interest.

The parties to this transaction might employ a standby letter of credit in a different way. The developer might want to ensure that any money it advances to the builder is used to build the building. The developer could require the builder to have its bank issue a letter of credit in the developer's favor. Such a letter might provide that the developer's draft, accompanied by its statement that the builder had defaulted on its obligations, would be honored by the bank. Unlike the negotiable document of title specified in the usual commercial letter-of-credit transaction, the documents in the standby letter-of-credit transaction have no intrinsic value. For this reason, the bank is likely to insist that the builder give it a security interest as a condition of the letter's issuance.

Standby letters of credit also are used in transactions involving sales of goods. A supplier of raw materials, for example, might prefer to have a letter of credit in its favor from the buyer's bank rather than a security interest in the goods. Alternatively, a buyer of manufactured goods might want to protect itself when it advances money to finance its seller's purchase of raw materials. Such a buyer risks more in the event of default than one who sells on credit, because the buyer cannot easily acquire a purchase money security interest in the raw materials its seller uses. As the beneficiary of a standby letter of credit issued by the seller's bank, however, the buyer obtains equivalent protection.

A business that wishes to raise money may issue commercial paper backed by a standby letter of credit. This type of transaction involves larger dollar amounts than other uses of letters of credit. The business's bank may be more willing to accept the risk of its customer's insolvency than will the buyers of commercial paper. The buyers, however may be willing to extend cash to the business if they can rely on the bank to ensure repayment. The letter of credit makes it easy for all of the parties to allocate among themselves the risk of the business's failure. The business acquires the cash it needs, the bank lends its credit to the business without having to supply cash, and the buyers of commercial paper enjoy a relatively safe investment. As in the other letter-of-credit transactions, all parties directly involved benefit.

DATA GENERAL CORP., INC. v. CITIZENS NATIONAL BANK OF FAIRFIELD

United States District Court, D. Connecticut, 1980.
502 F.Supp. 776.

ELLEN B. BURNS, DISTRICT JUDGE. Plaintiff, a Delaware corporation with its principal place of business in Westboro, Massachusetts, designs and produces computer hardware and software. Plaintiff entered into a contract, dated November 13, 1976, with B.B.S. Systems, Inc. (hereinafter B.B.S.), located in Fairfield, Connecticut, to sell certain computer equipment to B.B.S., which equipment was to be used by the Town of North Haven. Some time thereafter, defendant, Citizens National Bank of Fairfield, a national banking corporation located in Fairfield, Connecticut, was contacted to serve as the issuing bank in a letter of credit in which plaintiff would be the beneficiary. A letter was written on April 4, 1977, by defendant's president, Mr. Raymond T. Bogert, to plaintiff, Bogert Affidavit, Exh. 1 (filed June 14, 1979), and a Mailgram was returned on April 13, 1977. On April 22, 1977, Bogert mailed two letters to plaintiff, with copies sent to B.B.S. One letter [Exhibit 2] read in full:

> Based on Assignment of funds to us by the subject and originating from the Town of North Haven, this Bank hereby

commits to honor your draft in an amount not to exceed $83,000 relative to the Data General–B.B.S. OEM contract of November 13, 1975, provided:

1) Said draft is in bankable form, and

2) Said draft is accompanied by a certification that the items called for in Town of North Haven purchase order No. 12991, dated 3/2/77, have been delivered and have successfully completed the Data General standard diagnostic test.

We have endeavored to cover all the essential elements in your Mailgram of April 13, but if there are any questions, please contact the undersigned.

* * * The other letter [Exhibit 3] read in full:

Based on Assignment of funds to us by the subject and originating from the Town of North Haven, this Bank hereby commits to honor your draft in an amount not to exceed $83,000, relative to the Data General–B.B.S. OEM contract of November 13, 1975, provided:

1) Said draft is in bankable form, and

2) Said draft is accompanied by a certification provided by Data General Corp. that all the equipment supplied by Data General Corp. as called for in B.B.S. Systems purchase order #TNH–01 dated 12–12–76, will have completed the running of the Data General Standard Diagnostic Test.

3) This amount will be paid directly to Data General Corp., Route 9, Westboro, Mass. 01591, no later than 30 days after receipt by Citizens National Bank of Fairfield, unless Data General Corp. has recieved [sic] payment in full from B.B.S. Systems Inc. Any partial payment from B.B.S. Systems, Inc. against referenced purchase order number will reduce the amount to be covered under this document.

* * *

On October 21, 1977, plaintiff mailed a letter to Mr. Robert Winstanley, of the defendant bank, certifying that the computer equipment had passed the required tests and also enclosing a draft, dated October 20, 1977, for payment in the amount of $82,070.50. * * * On February 16, 1978, Winstanley wrote a letter to plaintiff in which he denied the bank's obligation to make payment against the October 20, 1977 draft. * * * In this suit, based upon diversity jurisdiction, plaintiff claims it is entitled to payment of $82,070.50 plus attorneys fees and costs.

Defendant opposes plaintiff's motion for summary judgment on the grounds that there are genuine issues of material facts to be resolved, including questions whether there had been a valid contract between plaintiff and defendant, whether plaintiff had made its acceptance of the contract known to defendant, whether acceptance was a condition precedent to the letter of credit, whether the April 22, 1977, letter constituted the letter of credit, whether the assignment of funds from B.B.S. to defendant was a condition of the letter of credit, and whether all other conditions were met. The court disagrees, for suits concerning letters of credit are especially appropriate for determination by motions for summary judgment, whether on cross-motions by both parties, * * * motions for summary judgment by the defendant bank, * * * or motions for summary judgment by the plaintiff beneficiary * * *.

Letters of credit are governed by Article 5 of the Uniform Commercial Code [hereinafter U.C.C.] * * *. Letters of credit commonly are used to facilitate commercial transactions between reluctant sellers and buyers, both of whom hesitate to initiate the exchange of money for goods. In a letter of credit, one or more banks function as intermediaries to avoid such an impasse. * * * A letter of credit is designed to provide an assurance to the selling party of prompt payment upon presentation of documents, thereby substituting the credit of the bank for that of the buyer. * * * The particular letter of credit in this case falls within the ambit of U.C.C. § 5–102(1)(a) as a "credit issued by a bank if the credit requires a documentary draft or a documentary demand for payment." A letter of credit is defined as "an engagement by a bank or other person made at the request of a customer and of a kind within the scope of U.C.C. § 5–102 that the issuer will honor drafts or other demands for payment upon compliance with the conditions specified in the credit." U.C.C. § 5–103(1)(a). The defendant here is the issuer, i.e., the bank or other person issuing a credit. U.C.C. § 5–103(1)(c). The plaintiff, the seller of the computer equipment, is the beneficiary, for it is the "person who is entitled under its terms to draw or demand payment." U.C.C. § 5–103(1)(d). B.B.S., the buyer of the equipment, is the customer, as that company was the "buyer or other person who causes an issuer to issue a credit." U.C.C. § 5–103(1)(g). The U.C.C. provides that no particular form of phrasing be required for a letter of credit. The only requisites are that the letter of credit be in writing and signed by the issuer. U.C.C. § 5–104(1).

In a letter of credit situation, there are ordinarily three separate and distinct contracts involved: (1) the contract between a bank and its customer (usually the buyer) whereby the bank agrees to issue the letter of credit to the beneficiary (usually the seller); (2) the contract of sale between the buyer and the seller whereby, among other things, the seller agrees to obtain payment under the letter of credit by drawing drafts thereunder and presenting them to the bank accompanied by documents specified by the buyer; and (3) the letter of credit itself, which is a contract between the bank and the beneficiary (usually the seller) whereby the bank agrees to pay the drafts drawn under the letter of credit and presented to it by the beneficiary if they are accompanied by the requisite documents. * * * A letter of credit is entirely independent of the underlying contract of sale between the customer and beneficiary; as long as the documents of the beneficiary are in order, the issuing bank must honor the demand for payment, regardless of whether the goods conform to the contract of sale. U.C.C. § 5–114, comment 1; U.C.C. § 5–109(1)(a) and comment 1. * * * This independence is even true in cases in which the letter of credit specifically incorporated the underlying contract of sale, * * * or when an inadvertent error in the price was made. * * * The sole interest of the issuing bank in a letter of credit transaction is in the documents to be presented, unless the parties agree otherwise; those documents must be exactly as stated in the letter of credit and the bank is obligated to pay only if the beneficiary has strictly complied with the terms of the letter.[5] * * * The bank's function is "basically ministerial," * * * for the bank is deprived of any discretion not granted within the letter of credit itself. * * *

Defendant argues that the letter of credit was not binding upon it because plaintiff failed to "accept" the terms of the agreement. Such an acceptance was explicitly required in the letter of credit agreement in Okay Industries, Inc. v. Continental

---

5. Two different standards have developed: if the beneficiary sues an issuing bank for dishonoring a draft drawn pursuant to a letter of credit, "strict compliance" with the terms of the credit is required; however, if a customer sues an issuing bank for dishonor, [Ed.: The court may have used the word "dishonor" inadvertently. It probably meant "wrongful payment."] all that needs to be proven is "substantial compliance." Far Eastern Textile, Ltd. v. City National Bank & Trust, 430 F.Supp. 193, 196 (S.D. Ohio 1977); Marine Midland Grace Trust Co. v. Banco del Paris, S.A., 261 F.Supp. 884, 889 (S.D.N.Y.1966).

Bank of Harvey, Civil No. H78–342 (D.Conn. June 18, 1979), reprinted in 5 Conn.L.T., No. 34, at 9, col. 1 (Aug. 20, 1979), in which the defendant issuing bank requested the plaintiff beneficiary to indicate satisfaction with the letter of credit's provisions by signing acceptance on a copy of the letter and returning it to the defendant. Id. at 9 col. 2 and n. 1. No such explicit instructions were made here.

Defendant suggests that it cannot ascertain which letter of credit, if any, was accepted by plaintiff. It is clear that the April 4, 1977, letter was rejected as plaintiff asked for major revisions in its telex of April 13, 1977. A more difficult question would be to determine which of the letters of April 22, 1977, is the operable letter of credit. Plaintiff has proceeded on the assumption that the more detailed letter [Exhibit 3] is the applicable letter. The court is not troubled by this selection as [Exhibit 3] is more comprehensive and rigorous than [Exhibit 2]. The only material differences are that paragraph 2 of [Exhibit 3] specifies that the certification is to be supplied by the plaintiff and paragraph 3 specifies the manner of payment, a term which was lacking in [Exhibit 2]. Paragraph 3 of [Exhibit 3] is less favorable to plaintiff as it allows defendant to offset against the funds due plaintiff any partial or full payment from B.B.S. to plaintiff. As long as plaintiff voluntarily has chosen to abide by [Exhibit 3], a letter of credit which imposes upon plaintiff more rigorous and less favorable terms than those found in [Exhibit 2], the court has no problem finding that [Exhibit 3] constitutes the appropriate letter of credit.

There are a number of theories under which summary judgment for the plaintiff may be granted. The first theory requires the determination of whether the April 22, 1977, letter of credit was revocable or irrevocable. U.C.C. § 5–103(1)(a) states that a letter of credit "may be either revocable or irrevocable." No indication is given how to construe a letter of credit which fails to indicate its revocability or irrevocability. However, comment 1 states:

Neither the definition nor any other section of this Article deals with the issue of when a credit, not clearly labelled as either revocable or irrevocable falls within the one or other category although the Code settles this issue with respect to the sales contract (Section 2–325). This issue so far as it effects [sic] an issuer under the Article is intentionally left to the courts for decision in the light of the facts and general law (Section 1–103) with due regard to the general provisions of the Code in Article 1 particularly Section 1–205 on course of dealing and usage of trade.

Certain legal consequences flow from categorizing a letter of credit as revocable or irrevocable. U.C.C. § 5–106(1)(b) provides that, unless otherwise agreed, a letter of credit is "established" as regards a beneficiary "when he receives a letter of credit or an authorized written advice of its issuance." Receipt by the beneficiary, not acceptance, is the pivotal action. Once an irrevocable letter of credit is "established," unless otherwise agreed, as regards a beneficiary, it "can be modified or revoked only with his consent." U.C.C. § 5–106(2). Conversely, after a revocable letter of credit is "established," unless otherwise agreed, it "may be modified or revoked by the issuer without notice to or consent from the * * * beneficiary." U.C.C. § 5–106(3). Therefore, if the April 22 letter of credit were revocable, defendant had statutory authority to revoke and hence dishonor it; however, if the letter were irrevocable, defendant lacked such authority.

As the district court commented in Beathard v. Chicago Football Club, Inc., 419 F.Supp. 1133, at 1137, "(t)here is a dearth of case law on the question of what constitutes an irrevocable letter of credit." Some states have resolved this problem by appropriate legislation. For example, Fla.Stat. § 675.103 (1977) (U.C.C. § 5–103) requires a letter of credit to state whether it is revocable or irrevocable. Furthermore, the statute provides, "[I]n the absence of such statement [it] shall be presumed to be irrevocable." * * * Other states allow for reference to the Uniform Customs and Practices for Documentary Credits (hereinafter U.C.P.). New York, for example, is one of three states which added a subsection (4) to section 5–102, which reads:

> Unless otherwise agreed, this Article 5 does not apply to a letter of credit or a credit if by its terms or by agreement, course of dealing or usage of trade such letter of credit or credit is subject in whole or in part to the Uniform Customs and Practice for Commercial Documentary Credits fixed by the Thirteenth or by any subsequent Congress of the International Chamber of Commerce.

N.Y. Uniform Com.Law § 5–102(4) (McKinney). Therefore, if the parties provide that a letter of credit is subject to the U.C.P., the U.C.C. does not apply. J. White & R. Summers, supra, § 18–3, at 612. Article One of the U.C.P. provides that "all credits, therefore, should clearly indicate whether they are revocable or irrevocable. In the absence of such indication, the credit shall be deemed to be revocable even though an expiry date is stipulated." Prior to the adoption of the U.C.C., New York case law provided that an ambiguous letter of credit was to be construed as irrevocable, thus protecting the beneficiary. Laudisi v. American Exchange National Bank, 239 N.Y. 234, 146 N.E. 347 (1924). There is an interesting question concerning the extent to which the U.C.C. has replaced this prior law; White and Summers believes it has. "Now by virtue of the New York amendment to Article Five, it appears that the U.C.P. governs in New York and that the New York case law which would otherwise have dictated a different result has been superseded." J. White and R. Summers, supra, § 18–3, at 613. This could be true, however, only if the particular letter of credit specifies that only the U.C.P. applies, or both the U.C.C. and U.C.P., for the U.C.C. allows for reference to prior law if a situation or rule is not covered by the U.C.C., U.C.C. § 5–102(3) and comment 2. In Beathard v. Chicago Football Club, Inc., supra, the parties themselves stated that their letter of credit was "subject" to the U.C.P. In *Beathard*, plaintiffs were players for a new football team, the Chicago Winds, which arranged for payment of plaintiffs' salaries by a letter of credit with the Mid-City National Bank. The issuing bank failed to honor plaintiffs' drafts, stating that the credit had been revoked. The court ruled for the bank because, by incorporating the U.C.P. by reference, the players allowed the letter of credit to be construed as revocable, in the absence of any indication to the contrary. 419 F.Supp. at 1138.

The letter of credit here does not make any reference to the U.C.P., nor does the Connecticut version of the U.C.C. provide any guidance. White and Summers advise that the best way to ensure that a letter of credit will be construed as irrevocable is to state so explicitly,

> Article Five does not state that letters of credit are presumed to be irrevocable, yet it is a rare beneficiary who will look with delight upon a revocable credit. If the letter of credit is silent, the answer to whether it is irrevocable depends on case law. Thus, for practical purposes, it would appear that a further formal requirement for the issuance of an irrevocable letter of credit is that it expressly state that it is irrevocable.

J. White and R. Summers, supra, § 18–4, at 616.

A situation similar to the instant case arose in West Virginia Housing Development Fund v. Sroka, 415 F.Supp. 1107 (W.D.Pa.

1976), in which the customer, a developer and mortgagor, arranged for a letter of credit from the defendant issuing bank for the benefit of the plaintiff beneficiary, a mortgagor. The defendant dishonored the letter of credit, arguing that the letter was revocable and had been revoked properly. The court granted summary judgment for the plaintiff, finding that a revocable letter of credit is "in reality, an illusory contract" because of the issuing bank's ability to revoke it without the beneficiary's knowledge or consent. 415 F.Supp. at 1111. Construing an ambiguous letter of credit as revocable would impede the "purpose and function" of such letters. Id. at 1112.

This court finds the reasoning of the *West Virginia* case persuasive. The bank's role in a letter of credit is to facilitate commercial transactions between its customer and the beneficiary by creating an arrangement whereby the beneficiary seller can deal freely with the buyer without fear that payment will be withheld. A revocable letter of credit provides the beneficiary seller with little protection. Therefore, unless otherwise provided in the letter of credit itself, there should be a presumption in favor of irrevocability. The court finds the April 22, 1977, letter to be an irrevocable letter of credit. The credit was established upon its receipt, by plaintiff, U.C.C. § 5–106(1)(b), obviating the need for acceptance. Once an irrevocable letter of credit is established, the issuing bank cannot revoke or modify the letter without the beneficiary's consent, U.C.C. § 5–106(2). Therefore, the letter of credit here was still in effect when plaintiff presented its draft to the defendant bank. The bank having dishonored the draft at that time, plaintiff's motion for summary judgment is granted.

Summary judgment for plaintiff is also appropriate under a theory that letters of credit are not formal contracts which mandate the standard contractual requirements of offer, acceptance, and consideration. Indeed, the definitional section, section 5–103(1)(a), defines a letter of credit as an "engagement" to honor drafts, not a "contract." Similarly, section 5–105 provides that no consideration is necessary to establish a letter of credit. White and Summers agree:

> The obligations, particularly those of an issuer to a beneficiary, that arise under a letter of credit are not exclusively contractual in nature, and it is unfortunate that some of the Code comments suggest as much. It is true that the issuer's customer and the beneficiary will ordinarily have a contract, for instance, for the purchase and sale of goods, for the con-

struction of a ship, or the like, and it is also true that the issuer and the customer will ordinarily have a contract between them whereby the customer pays a fee and the issuer issues the letter of credit. But the resulting letter of credit is not itself a contract, and the issuer's obligation to honor drafts drawn by the beneficiary is not, strictly speaking, contractual. The beneficiary does not enter into any agreement with the issuer.

J. White and R. Summers, supra, § 18–2, at 607. Therefore, under such an analysis, no acceptance is necessary, and hence defendant's argument fails.

* * *

NOTES

1. One of the problems that has arisen with respect to standby letters of credit is whether the use of a letter of credit as a general guaranty device conflicts with federal and state laws forbidding banks from guaranteeing the obligations of others. For example, in New Jersey Bank v. Palladino, 77 N.J. 33, 389 A.2d 454 (1978), Palladino sought a loan from New Jersey Bank which was willing to make the loan only if the borrower produced "some sort of collateral or support for the note." Palladino obtained a letter from First State Bank addressed to New Jersey Bank which stated that First State Bank would "assume the obligation" arising from a note signed by Palladino in the amount of $50,000, and that First State Bank would honor the commitment upon notice that the loan had not been paid. The New Jersey statute denied power to First State Bank to "guarantee the obligations of others" subject to an exception which allowed it "to issue letters of credit authorizing holders thereof to draw drafts upon it." The court noted that Article 5 of the UCC applies "to a credit issued by a bank if the credit requires a documentary draft or a documentary demand for payment." UCC § 5–102(1)(a). "Documentary demand for payment" is defined as a demand "honor of which is conditioned upon the presentation of a document or documents" and "document" is defined as "any paper including * * * notice of default and the like." UCC § 5–103(1)(b). The court held that the letter of First State Bank was a letter of credit within these definitions, stating that the notice of default was intended by the parties to be a written notice and therefore was a "document." The court noted that this "standby letter of credit" was "akin to a guaranty, for the bank's sole function is to act as surety for

its customer's failure to pay," but it followed cases decided in other jurisdictions holding that standby letters of credit fall within the exception to the prohibition against banks acting as sureties. A dissenting opinion stated that the standby letter of credit was in substance identical to a guaranty and that to allow its use was to erode the statutory policy against bank guaranties. It also stated: "The difference between conventional letters of credit and the standby variety in terms of bank solvency is clear. In the former, typically used to finance sales of goods, the issuing bank's obligation arises only on the delivery of shipping documents evidencing title to the goods. The bank is therefore secure. In the standby letter of credit situation, by the time the bank is called upon to meet the demand of the beneficiary there has typically been a default of the bank customer to the beneficiary and there is no practicable recourse by the bank because of the insolvency of the customer." For a discussion of "standby" or "guaranty" letters of credit see, in addition to the Baird article cited above, Verkuil, Bank Solvency and Guaranty Letters of Credit, 25 Stan.L.Rev. 716 (1973).

2. UCC § 5–115 sets forth the remedies that are available to "the person entitled to honor" for breach of the issuer's obligation. Subsection (1) covers damages for wrongful dishonor while subsection (2) covers anticipatory repudiation. This section was drafted with the traditional sales transaction in mind. If the seller, as beneficiary of the letter of credit, presents a draft for payment and it is wrongfully dishonored he is entitled to the face amount of the draft plus the incidental damages specified in UCC § 2–710 less any amount that the seller realizes upon disposition of the goods in the underlying sales transaction. In the case of anticipatory repudiation the seller has the same rights against the issuer that he would have against the buyer under UCC § 2–610. In effect the seller is made whole by being able to recover from the issuer as guarantor of the obligation of the buyer. How does this section apply to transactions not involving sales of goods in which a letter of credit is used? This question was presented in In re F & T Contractors, Inc., 17 B.R. 966 (Bkrtcy.Mich.1982), which involved the anticipatory repudiation of a standby letter of credit guaranteeing certain obligations in connection with a real estate construction project. The plaintiff was not the beneficiary of the letter of credit but the contractor which the court held was a customer under the letter of credit. The plaintiff claimed consequential damages for loss of profits and increased costs as a result of delays in com-

pleting the project which were caused by the breach. The court stated:

> It is the opinion of this court that a letter of credit transaction which is authorized by Article 5 of the Uniform Commercial Code is not restricted to the damage provisions provided in Article 2 of the Uniform Commercial Code. If the underlying transaction concerns a sale of goods and the letter of credit is issued to insure payment to the seller upon breach by the buyer, then § 5–115 of the Uniform Commercial Code makes plain sense in referring to remedies provided under Article 2 of the Uniform Commercial Code. However, such is not the case in the present lawsuit. The letters of credit issued by NOB were procured for the purpose of securing a mortgage construction loan and not for the purpose of insuring payment under a contract for the sale of goods. In addition, the collateral used to secure the letters of credit also involved mortgages. Under such circumstances, this court is of the opinion that it should defer to the more general principles of law in supplementing the provisions of Article 5 of the Uniform Commercial Code. This view is expressly permitted by [§ 1–103 of] the Uniform Commercial Code itself * * *.

The court awarded more than $925,000 in damages. The face amount of the letter of credit was $275,000. The significance of the decision is not clear, however, because in addition to repudiating the letter of credit the issuer unreasonably delayed releasing the collateral which the customer gave to the issuer. Since testimony established that prompt release of the collateral would have allowed the plaintiff to obtain substitute letters of credit that would have avoided any delays in completing the project, it appears that the damages were caused by the delay in releasing the collateral rather than by the repudiation of the letter of credit.

COLORADO NATIONAL BANK OF DENVER v. BOARD OF COUNTY COMMISSIONERS

Supreme Court of Colorado, 1981.
634 P.2d 32.

HODGES, CHIEF JUSTICE. We granted certiorari to review the court of appeals' decision affirming a district court's judgment holding the petitioner, the Colorado National Bank of Denver (the Bank), liable for the face amounts of three letters of credit it issued to secure the completion of road improvements by its customer, the Woodmoor Corporation (Woodmoor). Board of County Commissioners of Routt County v. The Colorado National Bank of Denver, Colo.App., 607 P.2d 1010 (1979). We reverse the judgment as to letters of credit No. 1156 and No. 1157, and affirm the judgment as to letter of credit No. 1168.

Woodmoor planned to develop a mountain recreation community in Routt County, Colorado (the County), to be known as Stagecoach. Early in 1973, Woodmoor obtained plat approval from the Routt County Board of County Commissioners (the Commissioners) for several Stagecoach subdivisions. Pursuant to section 30–28–137; C.R.S.1973 (1977 Repl.Vol. 12), and county subdivision regulations, approval of three of these subdivision plats was conditioned upon Woodmoor's agreement to provide a bond or other undertaking to ensure the completion of roads in accordance with the subdivision design specifications. Accordingly, subdivision improvements agreements were executed between Woodmoor and the County.

At Woodmoor's request, the Bank issued three letters of credit to secure Woodmoor's obligations under the agreements. The first two letters of credit, No. 1156 and No. 1157, were issued January 23, 1973 in the respective amounts of $158,773 and $77,330 bearing expiry dates of December 31, 1975. The third letter of credit No. 1168 was issued March 7, 1973 in the amount of $113,732 bearing an expiry date of December 31, 1976. The face amounts of the letters of credit were identical to the estimated costs of the road and related improvements in the respective subdivision improvements agreements. The County was authorized by each letter of credit to draw directly on the Bank, for the account of Woodmoor, up to the face amount of each letter of credit. Each letter of credit required the County, in order to draw on the letters of credit, to submit fifteen-day sight drafts accompanied by:

"A duly-signed statement by the Routt County Board of Commissioners that improvements have not been made in compliance with a Subdivision Improvements Agreement between Routt County and the Woodmoor Corporation dated [either January 9, 1973 or March 7, 1973] and covering the [respective subdivisions] at Stagecoach and that payment is therefore demanded hereunder."

Woodmoor never commenced construction of the roads and related improvements. On December 31, 1975, the expiry date of letters of credit No. 1156 and No. 1157, the County presented two demand drafts to the Bank for the face amounts of $158,773 and $77,330. The demand drafts were accompanied by a resolution of the Commissioners stating that Woodmoor had failed to comply with the terms of the subdivision improvements agreements and demanded payment of the face amounts of the letters of credit. On January 5, 1976, within three banking days of the demand,[1] the Bank dishonored the drafts. The Bank did not specifically object to the County's presentation of demand drafts rather than fifteen-day sight drafts as required by the letters of credit.

On December 22, 1976, the County presented the Bank with a demand draft on letter of credit No. 1168 which was accompanied by the required resolution of the Commissioners. The Bank dishonored this draft because of the County's nonconforming demand, viz., that a demand draft was submitted rather than a fifteen-day sight draft. On December 29, 1976, the County presented a fifteen-day sight draft to the Bank. This draft was not accompanied by the resolution of the Commissioners. On December 31, 1976, the Bank dishonored this draft.

The County sued to recover the face amounts of the three letters of credit plus interest from the dates of the demands. The Bank answered the County's complaints alleging several affirmative defenses. The fundamental premise of the Bank's defenses was the assertion that the County would receive a windfall since it had not expended or committed to spend any funds to complete the road improvements specified in the subdivision improvements agreements.

The County filed a motion in limine seeking a determination by the trial court to exclude evidence concerning matters beyond the four corners of the letters of credit and demands made on the letters of credit. The Bank replied by filing a cross-motion in limine seeking a ruling that it would not be precluded at trial from offering evidence outside the four corners of the letters of credit. The trial court, after extensive briefing by the parties and a hearing, granted the County's motion to limit the admissibility of evidence to the letters of credit, documents and drafts presented thereunder, the demands on the letters of credit, and the Bank's refusals to honor the County's demands for payment.

The remaining issues were whether the County's demands conformed to the letters of credit or, if not, whether the Bank

---

1. Under [UCC §] 5–112(1)(a), a bank called upon to honor drafts under a letter of credit may defer until the close of the third banking day following receipt of the documents.

had waived nonconforming demands, and whether interest ought to be awarded. The parties agreed on a stipulated set of facts concerning these remaining issues. The Bank did, however, make an offer of proof as to the rejected affirmative defenses. The Bank would have attempted to prove that the subdivisions in question remained raw, undeveloped mountain property for which there was no viable market and that the County had neither constructed, made commitments to construct, nor planned to construct the roads or other improvements described in the subdivision improvements agreements secured by the letters of credit. These allegations were disputed by the County.

The trial court entered judgment against the Bank for the face amounts of the letters of credit plus accrued interest at the statutory rate from the date of the County's demands. Costs were awarded in favor of the County. The Bank's motion for new trial was denied, and the Bank appealed.

The court of appeals affirmed the judgment of the trial court ruling that standby letters of credit are governed by article 5 of the Uniform Commercial Code * * * and that an issuer must honor a draft or demand for payment which complies with the terms of the relevant credit regardless of whether the goods or documents conform to the underlying contract. The court of appeals affirmed the trial court's refusal to consider any evidence regarding the County's alleged windfall. The court of appeals also held that any defects in the form of the County's demands were waived by the Bank.

I.

We first address the question whether the trial court properly limited the evidence to be presented at trial to the letters of credit, the demands by the County, and the Bank's replies to the demands. The Bank has continually asserted during each stage of this action that it ought to be permitted to show that the County will receive a windfall if the County is permitted to recover against the letters of credit. The Bank requested an opportunity to prove that the County will utilize the funds it would receive in a manner other than that specified in the road improvements agreements. Fundamentally, the Bank seeks to litigate the question of the completion of the purpose of the underlying performance agreements between Woodmoor and the County. This the Bank cannot do.

An overview of the history and law concerning letters of credit is useful in the consideration of this issue. The letter of credit arose to facilitate international commercial transactions involving the sale of goods. * * * Today the commercial utility of the letter of credit in both international and domestic sale of goods transactions is unquestioned and closely guarded. * * * In recent years, the use of the letter of credit has expanded to include guaranteeing or securing a bank's customer's promised performance to a third party in a variety of situations. * * * This use is referred to as a standby letter of credit. Article five of the Uniform Commercial Code governs both traditional commercial letters of credit and standby letters of credit. * * *

Three contractual relationships exist in a letter of credit transaction. * * * Underlying the letter of credit transaction is the contract between the bank's customer and the beneficiary of the letter of credit, which consists of the business agreement between these parties. Then there is the contractual arrangement between the bank and its customer whereby the bank agrees to issue the letter of credit, and the customer agrees to repay the bank for the amounts paid under the letter of credit. See also [UCC §] 5–114(3). Finally, there is the contractual relationship between the bank and the beneficiary of the letter of credit created by the letter of credit itself. The bank agrees to honor the beneficiary's drafts or demands for payment which conform to the terms of the letter of credit. See generally [UCC §] 5–103(1)(a) and [UCC §] 5–114(1); White and Summers, Uniform Commercial Code § 18–6 (2d Ed. 1980).

It is fundamental that the letter of credit is separate and independent from the underlying business transaction between the bank's customer and the beneficiary of the letter of credit. * * * "The letter of credit is essentially a contract between the issuer and the beneficiary and is recognized by [article 5 of the Uniform Commercial Code] as independent of the underlying contract between the customer and the beneficiary. * * * In view of this independent nature of the letter of credit engagement the issuer is under a duty to honor the drafts for payment which in fact conform with the terms of the credit without reference to their compliance with the terms of the underlying contract." [UCC §] 5–114, Official Comment 1.

The independence of the letter of credit from the underlying contract has been called the key to the commercial vitality of the letter of credit. * * * The bank must honor drafts or demands for payment under the letter of credit when the documents required by the letter of credit appear on their face to comply with the terms of the credit. [UCC §] 5–114(2). An exception to the bank's obligation to honor an apparently conforming draft or demand for payment, * * * is when a required document is, *inter alia,* forged or fraudulent, or there is fraud in the transaction. [UCC §] 5–114(2). The application of this narrow exception is discussed in detail later in this opinion.

As mentioned above, letters of credit have recently come to be used to secure a bank's customer's performance to a third party. When a letter of credit is used to secure a bank's customer's promised performance to a third party, in whatever capacity that might be, the letter of credit is referred to as a "guaranty letter of credit," * * * Standby letters of credit are closely akin to a suretyship or guaranty contract. The bank promises to pay when there is a default on an obligation by the bank's customer. "If for any reason performance is not made, or is made defectively, the bank is liable without regard to the underlying rights of the contracting parties." Verkuil, Bank Solvency and Guaranty Letters of Credit, [25 Stan.L.Rev. 716, 723 (1973)].

While banks cannot, as a general rule, act as a surety or guarantor of another party's agreed performance, see generally Lord, The No-Guaranty Rule and the Standby Letter of Credit Controversy, 96 Banking L.J. 46 (1979), the legality of standby letters of credit has been uniformly recognized. * * * What distinguishes a standby letter of credit from a suretyship or guaranty contract is that the bank's liability rests upon the letter of credit contract rather than upon the underlying performance contract between the bank customer and the beneficiary of the letter of credit. * * *

The utilization by banks of standby letters of credit is now wide-spread, although some commentators suggest that bankers may not appreciate the legal obligations imposed by the standby letter of credit. Where the bank issues a standby letter of credit, the bank naturally expects that the credit will not be drawn on in the normal course of events, i.e., if the customer of the bank fulfills its agreed-upon performance, then the credit will not be drawn upon. This expectation of the bank must be compared to the bank's expectation with respect to a traditional letter of credit issued as a means of financing a sale of goods. In the latter situation, the bank expects that the credit will always be drawn upon.

* * *

We now turn to a discussion of the present case, and why the Bank cannot introduce evidence beyond that directly relating to its contract with the County. As discussed above, the letters of credit, and the Bank's obligations thereunder, are separate and independent from the underlying subdivision improvements agreements between Woodmoor and the County. The fact that the letters of credit issued by the Bank are standby letters of credit does not alter this general rule. The Bank is bound by its own contracts with the County.

Each of the letters of credit prepared and issued by the Bank in this case sets forth specifically the condition for payment, i.e., that Woodmoor failed to make the improvements in conformance with the respective subdivision improvements agreements. Had the Bank desired additional conditions for payment, such as the actual completion of the road improvements prior to payment under the letters of credit, it could have incorporated such a condition in the letters of credit. * * * To demand payment under the letters of credit, the County was only required to submit a "duly-designed statement by the [Commissioners] that improvements have not been made in compliance with [the] Subdivision Improvements Agreement[s]. * * * "

The Bank cannot litigate the performance of the underlying performance contracts. "[P]erformance of the underlying contract is irrelevant to the Bank's obligations under the letter of credit." West Virginia Housing Development Fund v. Sroka, [415 F.Supp. 1107] at 1114 (W.D.Pa.1976). * * * Likewise, the question of whether the beneficiary of the letter of credit has suffered any damage by the failure of the bank's customer to perform as agreed is of no concern. * * * Further, a bank cannot challenge the utilization of funds paid under a letter of credit. * * *

The Bank argues that it is entitled to dishonor the County's drafts under [UCC §] 5–114(2). * * * Under this section, the issuer of a letter of credit may in good faith honor a draft or demand for payment notwithstanding notice from its customer that documents are forged, or fraudulent, or there is fraud in the transaction. The issuer may, however, be enjoined from honoring such drafts or demands for payment. Impliedly, the issuer may also refuse to honor such drafts or demands for payment when it has been notified by its customer of these defects. [UCC §] 5–114, Official Comment 2.

In this case, the Bank has not argued, nor can it reasonably assert, that the documents presented by the County are forged or fraudulent. The Bank has not challenged the authenticity of the drafts and demands for payment by the County or the truthfulness of the statements that the requirements of the underlying subdivision improvements agreements have not been fulfilled. The Bank does assert, however, that there has been fraud in the transaction on the basis that the funds the County would receive would be utilized by the County other than to pay for the completion of the road improvements.

Fundamentally, "fraud in the transaction," as referred to in [UCC §] 5–114(2), must stem from conduct by the beneficiary of the letter of credit as against the customer of the bank. See generally White and Summers, Uniform Commercial Code § 18–6 (2d ed. 1980). It must be of such an egregious nature as to vitiate the entire underlying transaction so that the legitimate purposes of the independence of the bank's obligation would no longer be served. Intraworld Industries, Inc. v. Girard Trust Co., [461 Pa. 343, 336 A.2d 316 (1975)]; New York Life Insurance Co. v. Hartford National Bank & Trust Co., 173 Conn. 492, 378 A.2d 562 (1977); Sztejn v. Henry Schroder Banking Corp., [31 N.Y.Supp.2d 631 (Sup.Ct.1941)]. "[I]t is generally thought to include an element of intentional misrepresentation in order to profit from another. * * *" West Virginia Housing Development Fund v. Sroka, supra. This fraud is manifested in the documents themselves, and the statements therein, presented under the letter of credit. Dynamics Corporation of America v. Citizens & Southern National Bank, [356 F.Supp. 991 (N.D.Ga. 1973)]; Shaffer v. Brooklyn Park Garden Apartments, 311 Minn. 452, 250 N.W.2d 172 (1977). See generally Harfield, Enjoining Letter of Credit Transactions, 95 Banking L.J. 596 (1978); Verkuil, Bank Solvency and Guaranty Letters of Credit, supra. One court has gone so far as to say that only some defect in these documents would justify a bank's dishonor. O'Grady v. First Union National Bank of North Carolina, 296 N.C. 212, 250 S.E.2d 587 (1978).

In this case, the Bank has not asserted that there is fraud in the transaction between Woodmoor and the County, nor can it reasonably make such an argument. No facts have been pled to establish fraud which vitiated the entire agreement between the County and Woodmoor. No fraud has been asserted by the Bank's offer of proof which would entitle it to dishonor the County's drafts and demands for payment. * * * Thus, the trial court properly granted the County's motion in limine excluding all evidence beyond the four corners of the letters of credit, the demands thereunder, and the Bank's replies.

II.

We next consider whether the drafts and demands for payment by the County complied with the terms of the letters of credit, or if not, whether the Bank waived any nonconforming demands.

The Bank was obligated to examine the documents "with care so as to ascertain that on their face they appear[ed] to comply with the terms of the credit. * * * " [UCC §] 5–109(2). To maintain the commercial vitality of the letter of credit device, strict compliance with the terms of the letter of credit is required. * * * If the drafts or demands for payment on their face complied with the terms of the letters of credit, the Bank was obligated to honor the drafts. [UCC §] 5–114(1).

In this case, the Bank promised to pay the County, for the account of Woodmoor, upon the County's presentation of fifteen-day sight drafts accompanied by a "duly signed statement by the Routt County Board of Commissioners that improvements have not been made in compliance with [the respective Subdivision Improvements Agreements.]" In order to determine whether the County's drafts and demands for payment complied with the terms of the letters of credit, we must analyze the drafts on the first two letters of credit numbers 1156 and 1157 separately from the drafts on the third letter of credit number 1168.

Letters of credit No. 1156 and 1157 bore expiry dates of December 31, 1975. On that date, the County presented two demand drafts to the Bank in the full face amounts of the respective letters of credit. The drafts were accompanied by, as required by the letters of credit, a resolution of the Commissioners stating that Woodmoor failed to comply with the terms of the underlying subdivision improvements agreements and demanded payment under the terms of the respective letters of credit. On January 5, 1976, within three banking days of the demand, the Bank dishonored the drafts. The Bank did not object to the County's presentation of demand drafts as opposed to fifteen-day sight drafts.

A demand draft is not the same as a fifteen-day sight draft. A fifteen-day sight draft provides the issuer an additional period of time not conferred by a demand instrument to examine the draft and determine whether the conditions of payment, if any, have been fulfilled. Thus, the County's demand did not strictly conform to the terms of the letters of credit. * * *

The Bank did not, however, object to the form of the demands by the County. As a general rule, when an issuer of a letter of credit formally places its refusal to pay upon specified grounds, it is held to have waived all other grounds for dishonor. * * * "However, the application of the rule confining an issuer to its stated grounds for dishonor is limited to situations where the statements have misled the beneficiary who could have cured the defect but relied on the stated grounds to its injury * * *." Siderius, Inc. v. Wallace Co., [583 S.W.2d 852, 862 (Tex.Civ.App.1979)]. * * *

In this case, the County did not present its drafts and demands for payment on the letters of credit until the final day of their vitality. The Bank then had three banking days before it was required to honor or dishonor the drafts and demands for payment. Within this period the Bank dishonored the drafts. The County could not have cured the defect since the presentment would have then been untimely. * * * Consequently, the County did not detrimentally rely on the Bank's failure to state as one ground for its dishonor of the drafts that the County presented demand instruments rather than fifteen-day sight drafts. Accordingly, since the County could not have cured its nonconforming demand, we therefore hold that the Bank did not waive its objections to the County's nonconforming demands on letter of credit numbers 1156 and 1157. Therefore, the Bank is not liable on these letters of credit.

Letter of credit number 1168 bore an expiry date of December 31, 1976. On December 22, 1976, the County presented the Bank with a demand draft on this letter of credit accompanied by a resolution by the Commissioners that Woodmoor had not fulfilled its obligations on the underlying subdivision improvements agreement. The Bank timely dishonored this draft on the basis, *inter alia*, that the County submitted a demand draft rather than a fifteen-day sight draft. The County cured this defect by presenting a fifteen-day sight draft to the Bank on December 29, 1976. This fifteen-day sight draft was not accompanied by the required resolution of the Commissioners. On December 31, 1976, the Bank sent the County a letter notifying the County that this draft had also been dishonored.

The same rules of strict compliance discussed above must be applied to determine whether the County's drafts and demands for payment complied with the terms of letter of credit number 1168. The County's first draft on letter of credit number 1168 was nonconforming, since it was submitted as a demand instrument rather than a fifteen-day sight draft. On December 29, 1976, the County presented a fifteen-day sight draft which cured this defect. While the County failed to attach the required statement and demand for payment by the Commissioners with the fifteen-day sight draft, it was not required to do so. The County was merely curing a prior nonconforming demand. The two demands, taken together, consequently strictly complied with the terms of the letter of credit. The Bank therefore wrongfully dishonored this draft and demand for payment.

We reverse the judgment as to letters of credit No. 1156 and No. 1157, and affirm the judgment as to letter of credit No. 1168. This case is returned to the court of appeals for remand to the trial court for the entry of judgment in consonance with the views expressed in this opinion.

ROVIRA and LOHR, JJ., concur in part and dissent in part.

LOHR, JUSTICE, concurring in part and dissenting in part.

I concur in part I of the majority opinion and in that portion of part II which treats letter of credit number 1168 and affirms the court of appeals' opinion upholding the district court's judgment against the Colorado National Bank of Denver (Bank) on that letter of credit. I dissent to that portion of part II which reverses the judgment against the Bank on letters of credit numbers 1156 and 1157. I would affirm the decision of the court of appeals in its entirety.

The majority finds that the Bank justifiably dishonored letters of credit numbers 1156 and 1157 because the draft presented by Routt County (County) did not strictly comply with the terms of the credit. See [UCC §] 5–114(1). Because I conclude that this was an improper application of the rule of strict compliance to a non-material term of the letters of credit, I respectfully dissent.

As the majority indicates, the prevailing rule requires strict compliance with the terms of a letter of credit. * * * But the rule of strict compliance is not dictated by the language of the controlling statute, Uniform Commercial Code—Letters of Credit, * * * [UCC §] 5–114(1), merely requires that the issuer honor a draft or demand for payment "which complies with the terms of the relevant [letter of] credit * * *" Specifically, the code does not state whether strict compliance is necessary or "substantial performance" is sufficient. It was apparently a conscious decision of the drafters of the uniform act which is the source of our statute to leave this question unresolved. See

J. White and R. Summers, Uniform Commercial Code, section 18–6 at 729 (1980).

The prevailing view stated by the majority not only lacks statutory mandate but also has not been uniformly accepted. A minority position has been adopted by a number of courts, rejecting a formalistic application of the rule of strict compliance where this would not be consistent with the policies underlying the use of letters of credit. As stated by Judge Coffin in Banco Espanol de Credito v. State Street Bank and Trust Co., 385 F.2d 230 (1st Cir. 1967), cert. denied 390 U.S. 1013, 88 S.Ct. 1263, 20 L.Ed.2d 163 (1968):

> But we note some leaven in the loaf of strict construction. Not only does *haec verba* not control absolutely [citation omitted], but some courts now cast their eyes on a wider scene than a single document. We are mindful, also, of the admonition of several legal scholars that the integrity of international transactions (i.e., rigid adherence to material matters) must somehow strike a balance with the requirement of their fluidity (i.e., a reasonable flexibility as to ancillary matters) if the objective of increased dealings to the mutual satisfaction to all interested parties is to be enhanced. See e.g., Mentschicoff, How to Handle Letters of Credit, 19 Bus. Lawyer 107, 111 (1963).

Banco Espanol de Credito v. State Street Bank and Trust Co., supra, at 234.

Other cases have also recognized that non-material variations from the terms of a letter of credit do not justify the issuer in dishonoring a draft or demand for payment.

* * *

In the instant case, the majority found that the County's submission of a demand draft rather than the fifteen-day sight draft required by the letters of credit rendered the presentment defective.[2] In my opinion this is the sort of non-material, technical condition which should properly be treated under a standard of substantial rather than strict compliance.[3]

2. Although I conclude that substitution of a demand draft for the fifteen-day sight draft required by the letters of credit does not excuse the Bank from all liability, this is not to suggest that the County could demand immediate payment. As noted infra, the Bank had a right to insist upon the fifteen-day review period, and the County could not unilaterally impair that right.

3. It is of interest on the issue of materiality that the Bank made no mention of the fact that the drafts were demand drafts in its letter of January 5, 1976, dishonoring the drafts and stating its reasons.

There is no danger that the Bank would be misled by the use of the demand draft, nor did the use of that draft place the Bank at risk by providing a basis for its customer Woodmoor to refuse reimbursement. In this context, the Bank's contention is no more than a technical defense which frustrates equity without furthering the policies and purposes underlying the use of letters of credit.

I am not unmindful of the need for certainty in letter of credit transactions, where a bank's function is designed to be primarily ministerial *   *   *. However, I believe that upholding the county's claim in this case would require only a limited but beneficial exception to the general rule of strict compliance. The alleged nonconformance did not relate to the underlying transaction. Rather, the nonconformity concerned only a provision designed to assure the Bank adequate time to review and consider the adequacy of the demand for payment. Thus, I would hold only that non-material defects, independent of any requirements relating to the underlying transaction, do not excuse the duty to honor a letter of credit.[4] This would avoid placing the issuer in the undesirable position of choosing between a suit by the beneficiary of a letter of credit and the risk of refusal of reimbursement by the customer who obtained that letter, while simultaneously avoiding the assertion of a technical defense to defeat payment where that payment would not place the issuer at risk.

Of course, the Bank was free in this case to inform the County that the demand draft was improper and that payment would be made as if a fifteen-day sight draft had been submitted. The

---

4. That holding would not be inconsistent with those cases requiring strict compliance with letter of credit requirements necessary to ensure that a substantive condition precedent to payment has been met. See, e.g., Courtaulds North America, Inc. v. North Carolina Nat. Bank, [528 F.2d 802 (4th Cir. 1975)] (*packing lists* which were attached to invoices accompanying draft by beneficiary and which stated that the shipment was 100% acrylic yarn did not satisfy requirement that *invoices* specify shipment was 100% acrylic yarn); Far Eastern Textile, Ltd. v. City National Bank and Trust, [430 F.Supp. 193 (E.D.Ohio 1977)] (requirement that principal sign purchase orders evidencing underlying transaction not satisfied by the signature of an agent on those orders). When the disputed condition relates to the underlying transaction, a standard of strict compliance may well be preferable. Thus, if the nonconformance had related to the requirement that the County certify Woodmoor's failure to construct the agreed-upon improvements a different question would be presented. In this respect, it is not necessary to apply the rule of substantial compliance as broadly as some courts have. See, e.g., U.S. Industries, Inc. v. Second New Haven Bank, [462 F.Supp. 662 (D.Conn.1978)] (failure to certify expressly that payment for goods had been demanded as required by letter of credit excused where other documents satisfied the purpose of this requirement).

County could not unilaterally deprive the Bank of the fifteen-day period for payment prescribed by the letter of credit. But the Bank should not be able to elevate a minor nonconformance into a total exoneration from liability. Neither existing law nor sound policy requires this result.

I would affirm the decision of the court of appeals.

ROVIRA, J., joins in this opinion.

NOTE

As the principal case indicates the strict compliance rule has often allowed the issuer bank to avoid its liability under the letter of credit, but the cases are not uniform. Sometimes the beneficiary has won in spite of technical noncompliance. Several recent cases illustrate the problem.

Seller in accord with instructions from Buyer shipped goods to Columbus, Indiana. Payment was to be made under a letter of credit issued by Bank. The letter of credit mistakenly stated the place of delivery as Scottsdale, Arizona. Bank had issued the letter of credit without checking the financial status of Buyer. When Seller presented its demand for payment Bank refused on the ground that shipment was not made to the destination stated in the letter of credit. At that time Bank had reason to believe that Buyer would not be able to reimburse Bank for any payment made under the letter of credit. Both Buyer and Seller requested Bank to amend the letter of credit to reflect the correct destination point. Bank refused. The court stated: "In this action, [Seller] plainly relied upon the letter of credit issued by [Bank]. The point of delivery, [Seller] alleges, is of no concern to [Bank]. [Bank] did not have a security interest in the goods, and [Bank's] ability to collect from its customer will not be prejudiced by changing delivery from Arizona to Indiana. [Bank's] sole reason for refusal to amend the letter of credit was simply to rescue itself from its poor judgment when the letter was issued. On these facts, the conduct of [Bank] is inequitable." Nevertheless, the court found that Bank had no duty to amend the letter of credit and could refuse payment because the terms of the letter of credit had not been satisfied. AMF Head Sports Wear, Inc. v. Ray Scott's All-American Sports Club, 448 F.Supp. 222 (D.Ariz.1978).

In Board of Trade of San Francisco v. Swiss Credit Bank, 597 F.2d 146, 25 U.C.C.Rep. 1132 (U.S. Ct. of Appeals, 9th Cir. 1979), a letter of credit called for presentment of various documents including a "full set clean on board bills of lading" which according to expert testimony referred to ocean shipment. An initial shipment was made by air and an air way bill (bill of lading) was presented in support of the draft which was paid. Two subsequent shipments were also made by air and air way bills were again presented in support of the draft. This time the issuing bank refused to pay stating that the letter of credit required ocean shipment. The court held that if the expert testimony was correct the letter of credit required ocean shipment and the issuing bank did not wrongfully dishonor the credit.

In United States Industries, Inc. v. Second New Haven Bank, 462 F.Supp. 662 (D.Conn.1978), the letter of credit required a certificate that the demand for payment represented money owing for goods duly shipped to Buyer for which payment was demanded and not received within seven days of shipment. Seller, on the morning of the last day of the term of the credit, presented a certificate that the demand for payment represented money owing for goods duly shipped to Buyer for which payment was not received within seven days of shipment. The certificate did not expressly state that payment had been demanded; however, invoices accompanying the certificate clearly evidenced that demand had been made. (Compare *Courtaulds* discussed in footnote 4 to the dissenting opinion in *Colorado National Bank*.) When the certificate was received an officer of Issuer stated that "there did not appear to be any problems" with the documents and that if any problems arose Seller would be notified. Two days after the credit expired Issuer refused payment on the ground that the certificate did not state that demand was made. The court held that the documents presented complied with the credit because on their face they put Issuer "on notice that [Seller] had made the required demand for payment." The court also held that even if the documents did not meet the strict compliance rule Issuer was estopped to assert the noncompliance. "In the present case, [Seller], based on [Issuer's] assurances, reasonably assumed that Issuer would honor its obligation under the letter of credit. Since [Seller] acted in reliance and to its detriment, Issuer is estopped from asserting any defense it may have had concerning nonconformity of the documentary demand for payment without calling the discrepancy to the attention of [Seller] prior to the expiration of the letter of credit." The court found that Issuer in fact knew about the discrepancy prior to the expiration of the credit.

In First National Bank of Atlanta v. Wynne, 149 Ga.App. 811, 256 S.E.2d 383 (1979), the letter of credit required a draft marked "Drawn Under The First National Bank of Atlanta Credit No. S–3753." Beneficiary presented a draft without the quoted phrase but the letter transmitting the draft referred to Credit No. S–3753 and the original letter of credit No. S–3753 was enclosed. Issuer refused to pay. In holding in favor of Beneficiary the court stated: "Accordingly, we hold that if from all the documents presented to the issuer by the beneficiary there is substantial compliance *and* there is no possibility that the documents submitted could mislead the issuer to its detriment, there has been compliance with the letter of credit."

NMC ENTERPRISES, INC. v. COLUMBIA BROADCASTING SYSTEM, INC.

New York Supreme Court, New York County, 1974.
14 U.C.C.Rep. 1427.

FEIN, J. Plaintiff (NMC), a wholesaler of audio products and accessories seeks a preliminary injunction restraining defendant CBS from presenting for payment, enforcing or negotiating any drafts under or in accordance with a letter of credit in the sum of five hundred thousand dollars issued by the defendant bank (FNB) and further restraining FNB from honoring any draft drawn and presented for payment thereunder by CBS. Issuance of the letter in question was procured by NMC to engage the bank's credit and thus secure payment of NMC's obligations to CBS in connection with NMC's contract to purchase from CBS a large quantity of stereo receivers and related equipment. NMC has already received, accepted and paid for over two and a half million dollars worth of merchandise under this contract. NMC's obligation under two prior letters of credit has been satisfied.

In addition to seeking permanent injunctive relief with respect to the letter of credit, the complaint herein seeks substantial damages based upon, inter alia, claims of breach of warranty and fraud in the inducement of the portion of the contract relating to the sale of four different models of stereo receivers.

The affidavit of NMC's president avers that at the time the contract was negotiated NMC's representatives were provided with brochures containing the technical performance specifications for these receivers, including their continuous power output ratings. Such ratings, it is alleged, have a significant bearing upon the quality of the sound emitted and were a material factor in plaintiff's decision to purchase the models in question.

It is further stated that after the receivers were marketed NMC was advised by many of its customers that the continuous power output of the receivers was substantially below that specified in the brochures. It appears that such advice has since been confirmed by a testing laboratory. Of critical significance upon this application, however, is the alleged admission by one of CBS's officers that it was aware of such non-conformity prior to the execution of the contract and failed to disclose this to plaintiff.

These allegations clearly suffice to make out a substantial prima facie case of fraud in the inducement of the contract. The opposing affidavit submitted by the aforesaid CBS officer is vague and evasive. He fails to make any unequivocal denial that he made the admission in question. Indeed, the crux of the CBS defense seems to be that, though there may have been some degree of non-conformity, it was insubstantial and, in any event, NMC agreed to buy the receivers on the basis of samples previously provided to and tested by it and placed no reliance on the power specifications contained in the accompanying literature.

The papers demonstrate that (1) plaintiff's present financial status is precarious; (2) if CBS is permitted to draw upon or negotiate the letter of credit and thereby obtain payment at the contract price for receivers having a market value to NMC substantially less than it had originally counted on, NMC will be unable to realize sufficient profit from sale of the receivers to meet its obligations to reimburse the bank for the credit thus extended; and (3) in all likelihood NMC will be forced into bankruptcy. On the other hand, it is unlikely that a temporary restraint upon CBS's access to such credit will defeat or impair any of its rights to payment or have any serious impact upon its financial structure.

Plaintiff makes a sufficient showing to obtain temporary injunctive relief. Concededly, a commercial letter of credit is usually independent of the underlying sales contract between the issuing bank's customer and the beneficiary. As a general rule, the responsibility of the bank to honor the draft is not affected by an ordinary breach of warranty on the part of the seller as to the quality or condition of the goods involved (Maurice O'Meara Co. v. Nat. Park Bank, 239 N.Y. 386). In the usual course, the issuing bank must honor a draft or demand for payment which complies with the terms of the relevant credit, regardless of whether the goods or documents conform to such contract of sale (UCC § 5–114[1]). However, where no innocent third parties are involved and where the documents or the underlying transaction are tainted with intentional fraud, the draft need not be honored by the bank, even though the documents conform on their face (UCC § 5–114[2][b]; Sztejn v. Schroder Banking Corp., 177 Misc. 719; Banco Tornquist v. American Bank & Trust Co., 71 Misc.2d 874) and the court may grant injunctive relief restraining such honor (UCC § 5–114[2][b]; Sztejn v. Schroder Banking Corp., supra; Merchants Corp. of America v. Chase Manhattan Bank, N. A., NYLJ, Sup.Ct.N.Y.Co., March 5, 1968, p. 2, col. 7; Dynamics Corp. of America v. Citizens & Southern Nat. Bank, 356 F.Supp. 991.

On the papers plaintiff has made a sufficient prima facie showing of fraud in the transaction underlying the letter of credit and has further shown that it may be irreparably injured if an injunction restraining honor of the drafts is not granted. This is all that is required to justify preliminary equitable relief (Sztejn v. Schroder Banking Corp., supra; Tornquist v. Amer. Bank & Tr. Co., supra).

CBS's argument that the fraud referred to in *Sztejn* (supra), is "fraud intrinsic to the documents and not as to the sales contract between the buyer and seller" is specious. If the sales contract is tainted with fraud in its inducement, then any document or signed certificate which the letter of credit requires CBS to submit, as a condition to FNB's honoring the draft, that the amount covered by the draft "is due and owing to (CBS) under Agreement of Sale and Purchase made as of the 9th day of August, 1973, between (CBS) and N. M. C. Enterprises, Inc., as amended" is equally tainted.

Accordingly, the motion is granted   *   *   *.

*   *   *

PROBLEM

Buyer contracted to purchase fifty cases of bristles from Seller and arranged to have Bank issue an irrevocable letter of credit in favor of Seller. The credit required that the draft of Seller be accompanied by an invoice and bill of lading with respect to fifty cases of bristles. Seller had fifty cases of merchandise loaded on a steamship and obtained a bill of lading describing the merchandise as bristles. Seller then drew a draft and presented it, along with the bill of lading and invoices for 50 cases of bristles, to Bank. Before Bank paid the draft Buyer discovered that the fifty cases covered by the bill of lading did not contain bristles but "cowhair and other worthless material."

Buyer immediately notified Bank of the fraud and demanded that the draft not be paid. You, as counsel for Bank, are notified that the documents presented by Seller are all regular on their face and comply with the letter of credit. Bank wants to know (1) whether it is required to pay the draft; (2) whether it is required to refuse payment of the draft; or (3) whether it has discretion to pay or not pay; and (4) in the last case what course of conduct is most advisable. Give the requested advice. If you were counsel to Buyer what action would you advise on his behalf? See UCC § 5–114(1) and (2). This problem is based on the facts of Sztejn v. J. Henry Schroder Banking Corp., 177 Misc. 719, 31 N.Y.S.2d 631 (1941). For a detailed discussion of *Sztejn* and UCC § 5–114, see Note, Letters of Credit: Injunction as a Remedy for Fraud in UCC Section 5–114, 63 Minn.L.Rev. 487–516 (1979).

AMERICAN BELL INTERNATIONAL, INC. v. ISLAMIC REPUBLIC OF IRAN

United States District Court, S.D.New York, 1979.
474 F.Supp. 420.

MACMAHON, DISTRICT JUDGE. Plaintiff American Bell International, Inc. ("Bell") moves for a preliminary injunction pursuant to Rule 65(a), Fed.R.Civ.P. and the All Writs Act, 28 U.S.C. § 1651, enjoining defendant Manufacturers Hanover Trust Company ("Manufacturers") from making any payment under its Letter of Credit No. SC 170027 to defendants the Islamic Republic of Iran or Bank Iranshahr or their agents, instrumentalities, successors, employees and assigns. We held an evidentiary hearing and heard oral argument on August 3, 1979. The following facts appear from the evidence presented:

The action arises from the recent revolution in Iran and its impact upon contracts made with the ousted Imperial Government of Iran and upon banking arrangements incident to such contracts. Bell, a wholly-owned subsidiary of American Telephone & Telegraph Co. ("AT & T"), made a contract on July 23, 1978 (the "Contract") with the Imperial Government of Iran— Ministry of War ("Imperial Government") to provide consulting services and equipment to the Imperial Government as part of a program to improve Iran's international communications system.

The Contract provides a complex mechanism for payment to Bell totalling approximately $280,000,000, including a down payment of $38,800,000. The Imperial Government had the right to demand return of the down payment at any time. The amount so callable, however, was to be reduced by 20% of the amounts invoiced by Bell to which the Imperial Government did not object. Bell's liability for return of the down payment was reduced by application of this mechanism as the Contract was performed, with the result that approximately $30,200,000 of the down payment now remains callable.

In order to secure the return of the down payment on demand, Bell was required to establish an unconditional and irrevocable Letter of Guaranty, to be issued by Bank Iranshahr in the amount of $38,800,000 in favor of the Imperial Government. The Contract provides that it is to be governed by the laws of Iran and that all disputes arising under it are to be resolved by the Iranian courts.

Bell obtained a Letter of Guaranty from Bank Iranshahr. In turn, as required by Bank Iranshahr, Bell obtained a standby Letter of Credit, No. SC 170027, issued by Manufacturers in favor of Bank Iranshahr in the amount of $38,800,000 to secure reimbursement to Bank Iranshahr should it be required to pay the Imperial Government under its Letter of Guaranty.

The standby Letter of Credit provided for payment by Manufacturers to Bank Iranshahr upon receipt of:

"Your [Bank Iranshahr's] dated statement purportedly signed by an officer indicating name and title or your Tested Telex Reading: (A) 'Referring Manufacturers Hanover Trust Co. Credit No. SC170027, the amount of our claim $ represents funds due us as we have received a written request from the Imperial Government of Iran Ministry of War to pay them the sum of   under our Guarantee No.   issued for the account of American Bell International Inc. covering advance payment under Contract No. 138 dated July 23, 1978 and such payment has been made by us'
*   *   * .' "

In the application for the Letter of Credit, Bell agreed—guaranteed by AT & T—immediately to reimburse Manufacturers for all amounts paid by Manufacturers to Bank Iranshahr pursuant to the Letter of Credit.

Bell commenced performance of its Contract with the Imperial Government. It provided certain services and equipment to update Iran's communications system and submitted a number of invoices, some of which were paid.

In late 1978 and early 1979, Iran was wreaked with revolutionary turmoil culminating in the overthrow of the Iranian government and its replacement by the Islamic Republic. In the wake of this upheaval, Bell was left with substantial unpaid invoices and claims under the Contract and ceased its performance in January 1979. Bell claims that the Contract was breached by the Imperial Government, as well as repudiated by the Islamic Republic, in that it is owed substantial sums for services rendered under the Contract and its termination provisions.

On February 16, 1979, before a demand had been made by Bank Iranshahr for payment under the Letter of Credit, Bell and AT & T brought an action against Manufacturers in the Supreme Court, New York County, seeking a preliminary injunction prohibiting Manufacturers from honoring any demand for payment under the Letter of Credit. The motion for a preliminary injunction was denied in a thorough opinion by Justice Dontzin on March 26, 1979, and the denial was unanimously affirmed on appeal by the Appellate Division, First Department.

On July 25 and 29, 1979, Manufacturers received demands by Tested Telex from Bank Iranshahr for payment of $30,220,724 under the Letter of Credit, the remaining balance of the down payment. Asserting that the demand did not conform with the Letter of Credit, Manufacturers declined payment and so informed Bank Iranshahr. Informed of this, Bell responded by filing this action and an application by way of order to show cause for a temporary restraining order bringing on this motion for a preliminary injunction. Following argument, we granted a temporary restraining order on July 29 enjoining Manufacturers from making any payment to Bank Iranshahr until forty-eight hours after Manufacturers notified Bell of the receipt of a conforming demand, and this order has been extended pending decision of this motion.

On August 1, 1979, Manufacturers notified Bell that it had received a conforming demand from Bank Iranshahr. At the request of the parties, the court held an evidentiary hearing on August 3 on this motion for a preliminary injunction.

Criteria for Preliminary Injunctions

The current criteria in this circuit for determining whether to grant the extraordinary remedy of a preliminary injunction are set forth in Caulfield v. Board of Education, 583 F.2d 605, 610 (2d Cir. 1978):

> "[T]here must be a showing of possible irreparable injury *and* either (1) probable success on the merits *or* (2) sufficiently serious questions going to the merits to make them a fair ground for litigation *and* a balance of hardships tipping decidedly toward the party requesting the preliminary relief."

We are not persuaded that the plaintiff has met the criteria and therefore deny the motion.

A.   *Irreparable Injury*

Plaintiff has failed to show that irreparable injury may possibly ensue if a preliminary injunction is denied. Bell does not even claim, much less show, that it lacks an adequate remedy at law if Manufacturers makes a payment to Bank Iranshahr in violation of the Letter of Credit. It is too clear for argument that a suit for money damages could be based on any such violation, and surely Manufacturers would be able to pay any money judgment against it.

Bell falls back on a contention that it is without any effective remedy unless it can restrain payment. This contention is based on the fact that it agreed to be bound by the laws of Iran and to submit resolution of any disputes under the Contract to the courts of Iran. Bell claims that it now has no meaningful access to those courts.

There is credible evidence that the Islamic Republic is xenophobic and anti-American and that it has no regard for consulting service contracts such as the one here. Although Bell has made no effort to invoke the aid of the Iranian courts, we think the current situation in Iran, as shown by the evidence, warrants the conclusion that an attempt by Bell to resort to those courts would be futile. Cf. Stromberg-Carlson Corp. v. Bank Melli, 467 F.Supp. 530 (Weinfeld, J.) (S.D.N.Y.1979). However, Bell has not demonstrated that it is without adequate remedy in this court against the Iranian defendants under the Sovereign Immunity Act which it invokes in this very case. 28 U.S.C. §§ 1605(a)(2), 1610(b)(2) (Supp.1979).

Accordingly, we conclude that Bell has failed to demonstrate irreparable injury.

B. *Probable Success on the Merits*

Even assuming that plaintiff has shown possible irreparable injury, it has failed to show probable success on the merits. Caulfield v. Board of Education, supra, 583 F.2d at 610.

In order to succeed on the merits, Bell must prove, by a preponderance of the evidence, that either (1) a demand for payment of the Manufacturers Letter of Credit conforming to the terms of that Letter has not yet been made, see e.g., Venizelos, S.A. v. Chase Manhattan Bank, 425 F.2d 461, 465 (2d Cir. 1970); North American Foreign Trading Corp. v. General Electronics Ltd., App.Div., 413 N.Y.S.2d 700 (1st dep't 1979), or (2) a demand, even though in conformity, should not be honored because of fraud in the transaction, see, e.g., N.Y. UCC § 5–114(2); United Bank Ltd. v. Cambridge Sporting Goods Corp., 41 N.Y.2d 254, 392 N.Y.S.2d 265, 360 N.E.2d 943 (1976); Dynamics Corp. v. Citizens & Southern Nat'l Bank, 356 F.Supp. 991 (N.D.Ga.1973). It is not probable, in the sense of a greater than 50% likelihood, that Bell will be able to prove either nonconformity or fraud.

As to nonconformity, the August 1 demand by Bank Iranshahr is identical to the terms of the Manufacturers Letter of Credit in every respect except one: it names as payee the "Government of Iran Ministry of Defense, Successor to the Imperial Government of Iran Ministry of War" rather than the "Imperial Government of Iran Ministry of War." Compare defendants' Exhibit A with Complaint Exhibit C. It is, of course, a bedrock principle of letter of credit law that a demand must strictly comply with the letter in order to justify payment. See, e.g., Key Appliance, Inc. v. First Nat'l City Bank, 46 A.D.2d 622, 359 N.Y.S.2d 866 (1st dep't 1974), aff'd, 37 N.Y.2d 826, 377 N.Y.S.2d 482, 339 N.E.2d 888 (1975). Nevertheless, we deem it less than probable that a court, upon a full trial, would find nonconformity in the instant case.

At the outset, we notice, and the parties agree, that the United States now recognizes the present Government of Iran as the legal successor to the Imperial Government of Iran. That recognition is binding on American courts. Guaranty Trust Co. v. United States, 304 U.S. 126, 137–38, 58 S.Ct. 785, 82 L.Ed. 1224 (1938). Though we may decide for ourselves the consequences of such recognition upon the litigants in this case, id., we point out that American courts have traditionally viewed contract rights as vesting not in any particular government but in the state of which that government is an agent. Id.

Accordingly, the Government of Iran is the successor to the Imperial Government under the Letter of Guaranty. As legal successor, the Government of Iran may properly demand payment even though the terms of the Letter of Guaranty only provide for payment to the Government of Iran's predecessor, see Pastor v. National Republic Bank, 56 Ill.App.3d 421, 14 Ill.Dec. 74, 371 N.E.2d 1127 (1977), aff'd, 76 Ill.2d 139, 28 Ill.Dec. 535, 390 N.E.2d 894 (1979), and a demand for payment under the Letter of Credit reciting that payment has been made by Bank Iranshahr to the new government is sufficient. * * *

If conformity is established, as here, the issuer of an irrevocable, unconditional letter of credit, such as Manufacturers normally has an absolute duty to transfer the requisite funds. This duty is wholly independent of the underlying contractual relationship that gives rise to the letter of credit. Shanghai Commercial Bank, Ltd. v. Bank of Boston Int'l, 53 A.D.2d 830, 385 N.Y.S.2d 548 (1st dep't 1976). Nevertheless, both the Uniform Commercial Code of New York, which the parties concede governs here, and the courts state that payment is enjoinable where a germane document is forged or fraudulent or there is "fraud in the transaction." N.Y.U.C.C. § 5–114(2); United Bank Ltd. v. Cambridge Sporting Goods Corp., supra. Bell does not contend that any documents are fraudulent by virtue of misstatements or omissions. Instead, it argues there is "fraud in the transaction."

The parties disagree over the scope to be given as a matter of law to the term "transaction." Manufacturers, citing voluminous authorities, argues that the term refers only to the Letter of Credit transaction, not to the underlying commercial transaction or to the totality of dealings among the banks, the Iranian government and Bell. On this view of the law, Bell must fail to establish a probability of success, for it does not claim that the Imperial Government or Bank Iranshahr induced Manufacturers to extend the Letter by lies or half-truths, that the Letter contained any false representations by the Imperial Government or Bank Iranshahr, or that they intended misdeeds with it. Nor does Bell claim that the demand contains any misstatements.

Bell argues, citing equally voluminous authorities, that the term "transaction" refers to the totality of circumstances. On this view, Bell has some chance of success on the merits, for a court can consider Bell's allegations that the Government of Iran's behavior in connection with the consulting contract suffices to make its demand on the Letter of Guaranty fraudulent and that the ensuing demand on the Letter of Credit by Bank Iranshahr is tainted with the fraud.

There is some question whether these divergent understandings of the law are wholly incompatible since it would seem impossible to keep the Letter of Credit transaction conceptually distinct. A demand which facially conforms to the Letter of Credit and which contains no misstatements may, nevertheless, be considered fraudulent if made with the goal of mulcting the party who caused the Letter of Credit to be issued. Be that as it may, we need not decide this thorny issue of law. For, even on the construction most favorable to Bell, we find that success on the merits is not probable. Many of the facts alleged, even if proven, would not constitute fraud. As to others, the proof is insufficient to indicate a probability of success on the merits.

Bell, while never delineating with precision the contours of the purported fraud, sets forth five contentions which, in its view, support the issuance of an injunction. Bell asserts that (1) both the old and new Governments failed to approve invoices for services fully performed; (2) both failed to fund contracted-for independent Letters of Credit in Bell's favor; (3) the new Government has taken steps to renounce altogether its obligations under the Contract; (4) the new Government has made it impossible to assert contract rights in Iranian courts; and (5) the new Government has caused Bank Iranshahr to demand payment on the Manufacturers Letter of Credit, thus asserting rights in a transaction it has otherwise repudiated. Plaintiff's Memorandum (Aug. 2, 1979) at 17–18.

As to contention (4), it is not immediately apparent how denial of Bell's opportunity to assert rights under the Contract makes a demand on an independent letter of credit fraudulent.

Contentions (1), (2), (3) and the latter part of (5) all state essentially the same proposition—that the Government of Iran is currently repudiating all its contractual obligations with American companies, including those with Bell. Again, the evidence on this point is uncompelling.

Bell points to (1) an intragovernmental order of July 2, 1979 ordering the termination of Iran's contract with Bell, and (2) hearsay discussions between Bell's president and Iranian officials to the effect that Iran would not pay on the Contract until it had determined whether the services under it had benefited the country. Complaint Exhibit E; Kerts Affidavit ¶ 3. Manufacturers, for its part, points to a public statement in the Wall Street Journal of July 16, 1979, under the name of the present

Iranian Government, to the effect that Iran intends to honor all legitimate contracts. Defendant's Exhibit C. Taken together, this evidence does not suggest that Iran has finally and irrevocably decided to repudiate the Bell contract. It suggests equally that Iran is still considering the question whether to perform that contract.

Even if we accept the proposition that the evidence does show repudiation, plaintiff is still far from demonstrating the kind of evil intent necessary to support a claim of fraud. Surely, plaintiff cannot contend that every party who breaches or repudiates his contract is for that reason culpable of fraud. The law of contract damages is adequate to repay the economic harm caused by repudiation, and the law presumes that one who repudiates has done so because of a calculation that such damages are cheaper than performance. Absent any showing that Iran would refuse to pay damages upon a contract action here or in Iran, much less a showing that Bell has even attempted to obtain such a remedy, the evidence is ambivalent as to whether the purported repudiation results from nonfraudulent economic calculation or from fraudulent intent to mulct Bell.

Plaintiff contends that the alleged repudiation, viewed in connection with its demand for payment on the Letter of Credit, supplies the basis from which only one inference—fraud—can be drawn. Again, we remain unpersuaded.

Plaintiff's argument requires us to presume bad faith on the part of the Iranian government. It requires us further to hold that that government may not rely on the plain terms of the consulting contract and the Letter of Credit arrangements with Bank Iranshahr and Manufacturers providing for immediate repayment of the down payment upon demand, without regard to cause. On the evidence before us, fraud is no more inferable than an economically rational decision by the government to recoup its down payment, as it is entitled to do under the consulting contract and still dispute its liability under that Contract.

While fraud in the transaction is doubtless a possibility, plaintiff has not shown it to be a probability and thus fails to satisfy this branch of the *Caulfield* test.

C. *Serious Questions and Balance of Hardships*

If plaintiff fails to demonstrate probable success, he may still obtain relief by showing, in addition to the possibility of irreparable injury, both (1) sufficiently serious questions going to the merits to make them a fair ground for litigation, and (2) a balance of hardships tipping decidedly toward plaintiff. Caulfield v. Board of Education, supra. Both Bell and Manufacturers appear to concede the existence of serious questions, and the complexity and novelty of this matter lead us to find they exist. Nevertheless, we hold that plaintiff is not entitled to relief under this branch of the *Caulfield* test because the balance of hardships does not tip *decidedly* toward Bell, if indeed it tips that way at all.

To be sure, Bell faces substantial hardships upon denial of its motion. Should Manufacturers pay the demand, Bell will immediately become liable to Manufacturers for $30.2 million, with no assurance of recouping those funds from Iran for the services performed. While counsel represented in graphic detail the other losses Bell faces at the hands of the current Iranian government, these would flow regardless of whether we ordered the relief sought. The hardship imposed from a denial of relief is limited to the admittedly substantial sum of $30.2 million.

But Manufacturers would face at least as great a loss, and perhaps a greater one, were we to grant relief. Upon Manufacturers' failure to pay, Bank Iranshahr could initiate a suit on the Letter of Credit and attach $30.2 million of Manufacturers' assets in Iran. In addition, it could seek to hold Manufacturers liable for consequential damages beyond that sum resulting from the failure to make timely payment. Finally, there is not guarantee that Bank Iranshahr or the government, in retaliation for Manufacturers' recalcitrance, will not nationalize additional Manufacturers' assets in Iran in amounts which counsel, at oral argument, represented to be far in excess of the amount in controversy here.

Apart from a greater monetary exposure flowing from an adverse decision, Manufacturers faces a loss of credibility in the international banking community that could result from its failure to make good on a letter of credit.

Conclusion

Finally, apart from questions of relative hardship and the specific criteria of the *Caulfield* test, general considerations of equity counsel us to deny the motion for injunctive relief. Bell, a sophisticated multinational enterprise well advised by competent counsel, entered into these arrangements with its corporate eyes open. It knowingly and voluntarily signed a contract allowing the Iranian government to recoup its down payment on demand, without regard to cause. It caused Manufacturers to enter into an arrangement whereby Manufacturers became obligated to pay Bank Iranshahr the unamortized down payment balance upon receipt of conforming documents, again without regard to cause.

Both of these arrangements redounded tangibly to the benefit of Bell. The Contract with Iran, with its prospect of designing and installing from scratch a nationwide and international communications system, was certain to bring to Bell both monetary profit and prestige and good will in the global communications industry. The agreement to indemnify Manufacturers on its Letter of Credit provided the means by which these benefits could be achieved.

One who reaps the rewards of commercial arrangements must also accept their burdens. One such burden in this case, voluntarily accepted by Bell, was the risk that demand might be made without cause on the funds constituting the down payment. To be sure, the sequence of events that led up to that demand may well have been unforeseeable when the contracts were signed. To this extent, both Bell and Manufacturers have been made the unwitting and innocent victims of tumultuous events beyond their control. But, as between two innocents, the party who undertakes by contract the risk of political uncertainty and governmental caprice must bear the consequences when the risk comes home to roost.

Manufacturers also contends that, in view of the action apparently still pending in the state courts, we should abstain from deciding the issues before us and that Bell is engaging in forum-shopping which dirties its hands so as to require a denial of injunctive relief. In view of our findings and conclusions based on the *Caulfield* test, we find it unnecessary to consider these contentions.

The foregoing opinion constitutes this court's findings of fact and conclusions of law, pursuant to Rule 52(a), Fed.R.Civ.P.

Accordingly, plaintiff's motion for a preliminary injunction, pursuant to Rule 65(a), Fed.R.Civ.P., is denied. However, Manufacturers Hanover Trust Company, its officers and agents are hereby enjoined from making any payments to Bank Iranshahr or the Islamic Republic of Iran, pursuant to the subject Letter of Credit, until August 6, 1979, at 3:00 P.M., to permit plaintiff to apply to the Court of Appeals for a stay pending appeal, if it is so advised.

So ordered.

Chapter 6

ARTICLE 2 SECURITY INTERESTS

A. INTRODUCTORY NOTE

Security interest, as defined in UCC § 1-201(37), is a very broad term. It encompasses Article 9 security interests which, by virtue of UCC § 9-102(2), must be created by contract, i.e., by the agreement of the person owing the obligation secured. But it also includes security interests in the goods arising out of Article 2 sales transactions. These security interests are not consensual in nature, i.e., they may arise without the consent of the debtor or even against his wishes. The Article 2 security interest may arise in favor of either the buyer or the seller. We can cite two examples:

1. An unpaid seller may ship goods to a buyer "under reservation." See § 2-505. Although title to the goods may pass to the buyer upon shipment (see § 2-401(2)(a)) the seller may reserve a security interest in the goods by shipping them under a negotiable bill of lading to his own order. The security interest arises solely by the act of the seller.

2. If a buyer takes delivery of goods from the seller and rightfully rejects or revokes acceptance he gets, by operation of law, a security interest in the goods which continues during his possession to secure his claim against the seller for any payment made for the goods or for various expenses of the buyer with respect to the goods. See UCC § 2-711(3).

By virtue of UCC § 9-113 these Article 2 security interests become subject to Article 9, but with important exceptions. Their creation depends on Article 2. Furthermore, so long as the debtor does not lawfully obtain possession of the goods the security interest is perfected without filing, and the rights of the secured party on default are governed by Article 2. Consider the Problem that follows:

PROBLEM

Dealer is a retailer of appliances that granted to Bank a security interest in all of Dealer's inventory whether then owned or after-acquired. Inventory was defined in the security agreement as including all goods received by a common carrier for shipment to Dealer as buyer under a contract of sale. Bank filed a financing statement adequately describing the collateral. Dealer then contracted to buy 10 refrigerators from Seller. Seller shipped the refrigerators by common carrier to Dealer under a negotiable bill of lading to the order of Seller. When the refrigerators arrived Dealer could not pay for them as required by the contract. Seller thereupon ordered the carrier to hold the refrigerators subject to Seller's further instructions. Two days later Dealer filed in bankruptcy. Who is entitled to the 10 refrigerators? See UCC § 2–401(2)(a), § 2–505(1)(a) and § 9–113.

There are other rights of sellers under Article 2 that are not described as security interests but which resemble security interests. The right of an unpaid seller to withhold delivery of the goods even though title has passed to the buyer, recognized in UCC § 2–703(a), is based on Uniform Sales Act § 53(a) which described the right as "a lien on the goods," a reference to the common law seller's lien which the unpaid seller had so long as he did not give up possession of the goods. The right of stoppage in transit, recognized in UCC § 2–705(1), is also based on common law rights and the seller's lien. Finally, UCC § 2–702 and § 2–507(2) allow the seller to reclaim goods delivered to the buyer under the circumstances described in those provisions. It is not clear whether these rights are "security interests arising solely under Article 2" and thus subject to Article 9 by virtue of UCC § 9–113. Jackson & Peters in their article, Quest for Uncertainty: A Proposal for Flexible Resolution of Inherent Conflicts Between Article 2 and Article 9 of the Uniform Commercial Code, 87 Yale L.J. 907 (1978), argue that these rights are Article 2 security interests. These rights, akin to Article 2 security interests, are discussed in the cases that follow.

B. STOPPAGE IN TRANSIT AND SELLER'S RIGHTS TO RECLAIM GOODS UNDER UCC § 2–702 AND § 2–507(2)

IN RE MURDOCK MACHINE & ENGINEERING CO. OF UTAH

United States Court of Appeals, Tenth Circuit, 1980.
620 F.2d 767.

BARRETT, CIRCUIT JUDGE. The United States appeals from a judgment of the District Court, which affirmed the judgment of the Bankruptcy Court. The Bankruptcy Court dismissed the government's counterclaim for possession of certain cold drawn bar steel and awarded possession of the steel to appellee Ramco Steel, Inc. (Ramco).

Factual and Procedural Background

Ramco sold the steel on credit to Murdock Machine and Engineering Company of Utah (Murdock), delivery F.O.B. Buffalo, New York, the place of shipment. The steel was shipped to a warehouse in Indiana for reshipment to Murdock at Clearfield, Utah, the final destination.

The last shipment of steel left Ramco's plant on May 22, 1975. The Bankruptcy Court made no findings about the dates on which other shipments occurred. Murdock had become insolvent on May 13, 1975. Ramco learned of this fact on May 23, 1975. On that same day, Ramco stopped delivery of that steel which was then being held at the Indiana warehouse. In addition, Ramco stopped delivery of one truckload of steel on June 11, 1975.

Unknown to Ramco, Murdock had ordered the steel to fulfill a contractual obligation to the United States to supply fins and nozzles for missiles. The contract between Murdock and the United States contained a title-vesting clause reading as follows:

Title. Immediately upon the date of this contract, title to all parts; materials; * * * acquired or produced by the contractor [Murdock] and allocated or properly chargeable to this contract under sound and generally accepted accounting principles and practices shall forthwith vest in the Government; and title to all like property thereafter acquired or produced by the contractor and properly chargeable to this contract as aforesaid, shall forthwith vest in the Government upon said acquisition, production, or allocation.

After Murdock filed its petition to be adjudged a bankrupt, Ramco filed a complaint with the Bankruptcy Court seeking reclamation of the steel it had shipped to Murdock on credit. Ramco joined both the trustee in bankruptcy and the United States as defendants. The United States filed a counterclaim, asserting its ownership of the steel by virtue of the contract it had entered into with Murdock.

The Bankruptcy Court conducted a hearing on the conflicting claims of Ramco and the United States. The Bankruptcy Court ruled that Ramco was entitled to reclaim the steel based upon the "applicable law [of] * * * the Uniform Commercial Code" whereby Ramco had exercised its right to stop delivery in transit of the steel following its discovery of Murdock's insolvency. (R., Vol. II, p. 69). The Bankruptcy Court concluded that "the provisions of the contract between the United States of America and the bankrupt are not binding upon the plaintiff [Ramco]." (R., Vol. II, p. 70). The District Court affirmed the judgment of the Bankruptcy Court in all respects.

The government has informed us that, "Pursuant to the agreement of all parties, the steel (which was deteriorating in the warehouse) has been sold, and it is the proceeds from this sale which are at issue here." (Brief of appellant, p. 5, n. 6).

Contentions on Appeal

On appeal, the United States contends that the District Court erred, in that: (1) Ramco's right (as seller) to stop delivery of the steel in transit under state law is subject to the superior right of the United States to the steel inasmuch as title to the steel passed to the United States, pursuant to its contract with Murdock, immediately after Murdock "acquired" title to the steel, and (2) Ramco's right to stop delivery of the steel in transit pursuant to § 2–705 of the Uniform Commercial Code was not effective against the United States, because the United States was a bona fide purchaser of the steel for value.

Discussion and Disposition

I.

The United States contends that Ramco's right to stop delivery of the steel in transit under state law is subject to the superior right of the United States to the steel because title to the steel vested in the United States, pursuant to its contract with Murdock, immediately after Murdock "acquired" the steel.

The United States, of course, relies upon the "title-vesting clause", heretofore quoted verbatim, in advancing its contention that it obtained title to the steel immediately after Murdock acquired *title* to it at the point of shipment, inasmuch as under U.C.C. § 2–401(2) the effect of the delivery term between Ramco and Murdock, i.e., F.O.B. Buffalo, New York, the place of shipment, was to pass title to the steel from Ramco to Murdock at the time and place of shipment. Ramco, however, reasons that because Murdock did not acquire *possession* of the steel, the United States did not obtain title to it.

The Bankruptcy Court made no finding relative to the contract term "acquired." However, for purposes of this opinion only, we will assume that the interpretation urged by the United States is correct.

"The validity and construction of contracts through which the United States is exercising its constitutional functions, their consequences on the rights and obligations of the parties, the titles or liens which they create or permit, all present questions of federal law not controlled by the law of any state." United States v. Allegheny County, 322 U.S. 174, 183, 64 S.Ct. 908, 913–914, 88 L.Ed.2d 1209 (1944), overruled in part by United States v. City of Detroit, 355 U.S. 466, 78 S.Ct. 474, 2 L.Ed.2d 424 (1958), and companion cases. "In [the] absence of an applicable Act of Congress it is for the federal courts to fashion the governing rule of law according to their own standards." Clearfield Trust Co. v. United States, 318 U.S. 363, 367, 63 S.Ct. 573, 575, 87 L.Ed. 838 (1943); accord, United States v. Kimbell Foods, Inc., 440 U.S. 715, 726, 99 S.Ct. 1448, 1457, 59 L.Ed.2d 711 (1979). The government asserts that the United States must be awarded the proceeds of the sale of steel to which it had legally obtained title. The government urges us not to follow the Uniform Commercial Code.

The government's argument is tied to the principle that no creditor "may obtain a lien, without the consent of the United States, against any public work * * * to which the United States has taken title." (Brief of appellant, pp. 5–6). See: United States v. Ansonia Brass & Copper Co., 218 U.S. 452, 31 S.Ct. 49, 54 L.Ed. 1107 (1910); Armstrong v. United States, 364 U.S. 40, 80 S.Ct. 1563, 4 L.Ed.2d 1554 (1960). The critical inquiry which the government ignores is *when* Ramco obtained its "lien." Ramco's right to withhold possession of the steel attached when Murdock became insolvent. (U.C.C. § 2–702(1)). Title to the steel did not vest in the government until immediately after it was shipped from Buffalo, New York.

(a).

As to steel not yet shipped when Murdock became insolvent, Ramco's right was prior in time to the government's. Ramco is entitled to the proceeds of that steel if the analysis of Armstrong v. United States, supra, is applied. In Armstrong v. United States, supra, the Court held that state-created materialmen's liens which attached to, but had not been enforced against, a privately owned vessel under construction for the government, remained valid after title to the vessel vested in the government under its contract with the shipbuilder.

*   *   *

In *Armstrong* the Court flatly rejected the argument that the government's contract with the shipbuilder affected the validity of the materialmen's liens:

> The Government also seems to suggest that because the contract between Rice and the United States expressly gave the Government the option of requiring a conveyance of title upon default, petitioners' liens attached subject to that limitation. Petitioners, however, were not parties to the contract. Furthermore, their liens attached by operation of law and nothing in the record indicates that the scope of such liens is affected by contractual arrangements into which the owner of the property may have entered. 364 U.S. at pp. 45–46, 80 S.Ct. at 1567.

In Armstrong v. United States, supra, because the United States already had posssesion of the vessel, the doctrine of sovereign immunity prevented the materialmen from enforcing their liens. Thus, while the liens were legally valid, in fact the United States' immunity from suit rendered the liens inoperative. The Court held that the United States had destroyed the liens and must compensate the materialmen for their value.

*   *   *

We believe that *Armstrong* squarely supports Ramco's claim to at least that steel in which Ramco's state created right in the nature of a lien attached before the United States obtained title. As we have noted, any steel which had not been shipped when Murdock became insolvent belongs in that category. Ramco's right to refuse delivery and to stop delivery of that steel attached when Murdock became insolvent and before that steel was shipped. The United States obtained title from Murdock to that steel after shipment, subject to Ramco's prior right to withhold possession.

(b).

Although the Bankruptcy Court's findings are incomplete with respect to when shipments of steel occurred, the evidence shows that Ramco shipped some of the steel before Murdock became insolvent. By contract with Murdock, the United States obtained title to the steel "forthwith" after shipment and before Ramco had any right to refuse or to stop delivery. Under the general federal decisional rule, implicit both in United States v. Alabama, supra, and United States v. Armstrong, supra, Ramco's "liens" could not attach once the United States took title to the steel. We are convinced, however, that federal law in cases such as this must incorporate the commercial laws of the several states, and we so hold.

In United States v. Kimbell Foods, Inc., 440 U.S. 715, 99 S.Ct. 1448, 59 L.Ed.2d 711 (1979), the Supreme Court decided two cases of competing liens or security interests. In one case, the issue was whether a contractual security interest, held by the Small Business Administration (SBA), was superior to that of a private wholesaler which was not yet choate when the SBA's interest was created. In the other case, the issue was whether a security interest of the Farmers Home Administration (FHA) was superior to a subsequent repairman's lien. The government argued for the federal "first in time, first in right" and "choateness" tests which federal courts traditionally applied in tax lien cases. The SBA and FHA interests would have defeated the competing private interests had the Court applied those tests.

The Court rejected a uniform federal common law based on the "first in time, first in right" and "choateness" principles. Instead, it held that the relative priority of private liens and liens arising from the SBA and FHA lending programs is to be determined by reference to "nondiscriminatory state laws." 440 U.S. at p. 740, 99 S.Ct. at p. 1464. The Court noted that in forty-nine of the fifty states, those laws are variants of the Uniform Commercial Code. 440 U.S. at p. 732, n. 28, 99 S.Ct. at p. 1460, n. 28.

Many of the reasons which support the holding in *Kimbell Foods* persuade us that we must adopt state law as the rule of decision in this case. State commercial codes control the mainstream of business life in this country. These codified rights and duties allow business to work within the framework of a settled, predictable environment. Thus, businessmen reasonably rely on the availability of those rights and duties unless otherwise agreed. See: United States v. Kimbell Foods, Inc., supra at 739–740, 99 S.Ct. at 1464.

By contract with Murdock, the government interposed its title to the steel as early as possible without contractual obligation to Ramco. Ramco had no knowledge that Murdock was simply a conduit for passing title to the United States. In the government's view, this is of no significance. The government believes its hidden title overrode rights of Ramco to which others are subject. The government thus argues that Ramco cannot look to it for payment, and that Ramco has no rights of stoppage as against the government.

In our view, if the government is allowed greater rights in the marketplace than others, then in every sale, including those between private parties, it becomes for the seller relevant, and perhaps critical, to probe whether the government is somehow secretly involved. Once government involvement is discovered, the peculiar legal effect of such involvement as it bears on the seller's risks must be ascertained. In some instances, sellers, in spite of investigation, will fail to discover the government involvement until it is too late to take protective measures. Mindful of the burdens of time and expense such investigations would impose on our nation's commerce, and the injustice which would result by dealing government "wild cards" to businessmen at random, we are not inclined to create a special commercial law for the government's benefit.

*   *   *

II.

The United States contends that the District Court erred in finding that Ramco, as seller, had a superior right to that of the government pursuant to § 2–705 of the Uniform Commercial Code. Section 2–705, of course, was the predicate for the Court's ruling that Ramco's right to stop delivery of the steel in transit upon learning of Murdock's insolvency was not rendered ineffective or terminated by virtue of the government's claim that prior to the stoppage it had become a good faith purchaser for value from Murdock. The government argues that even under the Uniform Commercial Code the United States must be awarded the proceeds from the sale of the steel. The government contends that it is a good faith purchaser for value of the steel, and although the Bankruptcy Court made no findings on the matter, we assume, *arguendo*, that the contention is correct.

Section 2–705 of the Uniform Commercial Code states that, "The seller may stop delivery of goods in the possession of a carrier or other bailee when he discovers the buyer to be insolvent * * *" This provision descends from the equitable right of stoppage *in transitu* which, by the preponderance of authority, "was the assertion of a right in the nature of a lien against property whereof another held title." Northern Grain Co. v. Wiffler, 223 N.Y. 169, 119 N.E. 393, 394, 7 A.L.R. 1370 (1918). "The right of stoppage in transitu [was] merely an extension of the lien for the price which the vendor [had] after contract of sale and before delivery of goods sold on credit." Johnson v. Eveleth, 93 Me. 306, 45 A. 35, 37 (1899); accord, Letts-Spencer Grocer Co. v. Missouri Pac. Ry. Co., 138 Mo.App. 352, 122 S.W. 10, 11 (1909). See: U.C.C. § 9–113 (Official Comment).

Under the Uniform Commercial Code, the seller's refusal to deliver goods in his possession to an insolvent buyer, and the seller's order to stop delivery of goods in the possession of a carrier or warehouseman, remain dual aspects of the seller's right to withhold possession of goods from an insolvent buyer. (U.C.C. § 2–702(1)). That right attaches when the buyer becomes insolvent, but generally speaking, it is enforceable at any time until the goods have come into the buyer's actual or constructive possession. (U.C.C. § 2–705(2)). Who has "title" to the goods is a matter of no relevance whatsoever. (U.C.C. § 2–401). Our view is that a seller's right of stoppage is not cut off by the intervention of a third party good faith purchaser.

Although it is true that "[a] person with voidable title has power to transfer a good title to a good faith purchaser for value" (U.C.C. § 2–403(1)), we see no relevance in this language. In § 2–702 ("Seller's Remedies on Discovery of Buyer's Insolvency") we find a significant difference of treatment between the seller's right to reclaim goods that an insolvent buyer has already received (§ 2–702(2)), and the seller's right of stoppage with respect to goods not yet received by the buyer (§ 2–702(1)). The seller's right to reclaim goods in the buyer's possession is expressly made subject to "the rights of a buyer in ordinary course or other good faith purchaser under this Article (Section 2–403)." (§ 2–702(3)). The reference to § 2–403 is a reference to the title which the good faith purchaser for value obtains from a transferor with a voidable title. Thus, the Code provision on the seller's right to reclaim goods in the insolvent buyer's possession appears to present an exception to the general rule that a seller's remedies are not affected by matters of title.[3]

In contrast, the provision on the seller's right to stop delivery of goods in transit (§ 2–702(1)) makes no reference to title or the rights of good faith purchasers. The case for protecting a good faith purchaser from the seller's right of stoppage is, if anything, weaker and more in need of specific support in the language of the Code than is the case for protecting such a purchaser from the seller's right of reclamation. Since § 2–702 explicitly does protect the good faith purchaser from the seller's right of reclamation, that section, in equally explicit terms, would protect a good faith purchaser from the seller's right of stoppage were such protection intended. Cf. Amoco Pipeline Co. v. Admiral Crude Oil Corp., 490 F.2d 114, 117 (10th Cir. 1974), holding that a seller's stoppage of goods in transit under New Mexico's commercial code was effective regardless of whether title passed to the buyer.

The only decision we have found which has addressed the question of whether a seller may stop delivery of goods under § 2–705 as against a good faith purchaser for value is Ceres, Inc. v. ACLI Metal & Ore Co., 451 F.Supp. 921, 925 (N.D.Ill., E.D.1978). There the Court held that the rights of a good faith purchaser for value are subject to the seller's right of stoppage until delivery of the goods to the buyer or good faith purchaser. The Court further held that an attornment of a bailee of the goods to the buyer or good faith purchaser, as well as a physical transfer of the goods to the buyer or good faith purchaser, constitutes "delivery." According to *Ceres*, the events that cut off the seller's right of stoppage as against the buyer (§ 2–705(2)(a), (b), (c)), also cut off such right as against the good faith purchaser for value.

No contention has been made that the steel was delivered to the government. In the Bankruptcy Court, the trustee cross-examined an officer from the Indiana warehouse in an attempt to establish that the steel came into Murdock's physical or constructive possession in Indiana, and that the warehouse had attorned to Murdock in writing or by telephone. That effort

---

3. Section 2–401 of the Uniform Commercial Code provides:

[E]ach provision of this Article with regard to the rights, obligations and remedies of the seller, the buyer, purchasers or other third parties applies irrespective of title to the goods except where the provision refers to such title.

failed. The testimony of the witness does not support a finding that the steel was in any sense "delivered" to Murdock. Although the government argued on appeal to the District Court that Murdock obtained physical possession of the steel in Indiana, it no longer contends that the steel was delivered to Murdock.

The provisions of the Code concerning documents of title support our conclusion that a good faith purchaser for value does not cut off the seller's right to stop delivery of goods in transit. Goods in transit, and "in the possession of a carrier or other bailee" (U.C.C. § 2–705(1)), invariably are consigned under a document of title, such as a bill of lading. There was evidence in this case that the steel was consigned under non-negotiable straight bills of lading.

The federal statute dealing with bills of lading for the movement of interstate commerce (39 Stat. 538, 49 U.S.C. §§ 81–124), states that, "Where an *order* bill has been issued for goods no seller's lien or right of stoppage in transitu shall defeat the rights of any purchaser for value in good faith *to whom such bill has been negotiated*" (49 U.S.C. § 119) (Emphasis supplied). But "[a] straight [i.e., non–negotiable] bill can not be negotiated free from existing equities, and the indorsement of such a bill gives the transferee no additional right." (49 U.S.C. § 109). Thus, even if the government were a transferee of the straight bills of lading covering the steel (and there is no evidence that the government was such a transferee), the government would be subject to Ramco's right of stoppage. See: Weyerhaeuser Timber Co. v. First Nat. Bank, 150 Or. 172, 38 P.2d 48 (1934); and Kasden v. New York, N.H. & H.R. Co., 104 Conn. 479, 133 A. 573 (1926). See also: Clock v. Missouri-Kansas-Texas R. Co., 407 F.Supp. 448 (E.D.Mo., E.D.1976), affirmed without opinion, 553 F.2d 102 (8th Cir. 1977), where the Court held that a seller was entitled to goods stopped in transit as against the third party transferee of a straight bill of lading. Answering the transferee's contention that it was a bona fide purchaser for value, the Court stated, "Under the authority of 49 U.S.C. § 81 et seq., there cannot be such status where one is a transferee under a straight bill of lading." 407 F.Supp. at p. 450. These decisions and statutes are consistent with the Uniform Commercial Code, which provides that the seller's right of stoppage is cut off as against the buyer upon "negotiation to the buyer of any negotiable document of title covering the goods." (§ 2–705(2)(d)). There was no evidence that negotiable documents of title for the steel were issued, let alone that such documents were negotiated to Murdock or the government.

The old equitable right of stoppage *in transitu* has been repeatedly held to defeat rights of good faith purchasers for value. See, e.g., Branan v. Atlanta & W.P.R. Co., 108 Ga. 70, 33 S.E. 836 (1899); Ocean S.S. Co. v. Ehrlich, 88 Ga. 502, 14 S.E. 707 (1892); Pattison v. Culton, 33 Ind. 240 (Ind.1870); and Chandler v. Fulton, 10 Tex. 2 (1853). Section 62 of the Uniform Sales Act provided that the unpaid seller's right of stoppage in transit "is not affected by any sale or other disposition of goods which the buyer may have made, unless the seller has assented thereto." Regrettably, the Uniform Commercial Code is not explicit on this point. However, if the drafters of the Code had intended to give third party purchasers greater rights than under previous law, we believe that the official comments to the Code provisions on stoppage in transit would reflect that intention. Instead, the official comments do not indicate a change from prior law. See U.C.C. § 1–103.

Paragraph 2 of the official comments to § 2–705 explains that receipt of goods by a "subpurchaser" bars the seller from stopping the goods in transit. The rationale given is that in such circumstances the seller has "acquiesced" in the third party's purchase from the insolvent buyer. The rationale implies that without "acquiescence" in the sale to the third party, the seller retains his right of stoppage just as he did under § 62 of the Uniform Sales Act. Ramco did not acquiesce in the transfer of steel from Murdock to the government. Ramco was unaware of the transfer.

We affirm.

NOTES

1. At common law the right to stop goods in transit could be exercised only by an unpaid vendor against his vendee and only in cases in which title to the goods had passed to the vendee. If the vendor had reserved title in himself, there was no need for the right because his title allowed him to fully control the goods. See Williston on Sales § 521 (Rev. ed. 1948). The right arose only in the event of the insolvency of the vendee and it terminated when the transit ended, which in most cases occurred when goods were delivered to the vendee or into his control through possession by an agent holding for him. The right originated in equity and was designed to avoid the injustice of allowing the buyer, who owned the goods, to acquire possession of them

when he had not paid for them and could not pay for them because of his insolvency. See Williston on Sales § 518 (Rev. ed. 1948). The right provided by UCC § 2–705(1) is broader than the common-law right. Examine that section as well as UCC § 2–703 and § 2–609. Events that terminate the right are stated in UCC § 2–705(2).

2. Although the UCC does not specifically deal with the question of how the right of stoppage is affected by bona fide purchasers of the goods, the common-law cases distinguished between unilateral action by the buyer in reselling the goods and cases in which the seller assented to the resale and shipment of the goods to the subpurchaser. A typical case in which the right was lost is as follows: Buyer orders goods from Merchant who to fill the order buys the goods on credit from Manufacturer. At Merchant's request, Manufacturer ships the goods on a straight bill of lading directly to Buyer. Before the goods arrive Manufacturer learns of the insolvency of Merchant. The only right of Manufacturer is to stop delivery to his buyer, Merchant, but in this case no delivery to Merchant was contemplated so that right never arose. The shipment by Manufacturer to Buyer was treated by the courts as the equivalent of a delivery to Merchant and a reshipment by Merchant to Buyer. See A. J. Niemeyer Lumber Co. v. Burlington & Missouri River Railroad Co., 54 Neb. 321 (1898) and M. & L. R. Railroad Co. v. Freed, 38 Ark. 614 (1882). If the seller shipped to his buyer the buyer could not unilaterally defeat the seller's right of stoppage by reselling the goods to a subpurchaser, but the seller by his own action could give up the right. "* * * when the vendor contemplates a transit to his purchaser, and ships accordingly, he cannot be defeated of his right by the conduct of the purchaser during the transit, without his assent, either express, or implied * * * Here he assents to a different destination before parting with his property; and if he thereby loses his right of stoppage, it is his voluntary act." M. & L. R.R.R. Co. v. Freed, supra at p. 623. This law was codified in Uniform Sales Act § 62 quoted by the court in *Murdock*. Comment 2 to UCC § 2–705 which addresses the question of direct shipment to subpurchasers is ambiguous with respect to the question of whether the right of stoppage is terminated 1) when the goods are received by the subpurchaser or 2) when the goods are shipped. *Murdock*, in its last paragraph, suggests the first interpretation, but that conclusion conflicts with its further statement that the UCC carries forward Uniform Sales Act § 62 which clearly incorporated the second interpretation.

3.   Suppose in the example given in Note 2 it is Buyer rather than Merchant who becomes insolvent.   Does Merchant have a right to stop delivery?   Is he able to stop delivery?   See UCC § 2–705(1) and (3)(d).

MATTER OF FLAGSTAFF FOODSERVICE CORP.

United States Bankruptcy Court, S.D. New York, 1981.
14 B.R. 462.

ROY BABITT, BANKRUPTCY JUDGE.   This dispute between Flagstaff Foodservice Company New England, Inc. (Flagstaff or debtor), a Chapter 11 debtor and McCain Foods, Inc. (McCain) centers on the reach of Section 546(c) of the 1978 Bankruptcy Code, 11 U.S.C. (1976 ed. Supp. III) § 546(c), involving the rights Congress gave in that section to a seller of goods on credit to an insolvent purchaser.

Flagstaff, a distributor of food to institutional customers, filed its petition in this court on July 21, 1981 for the relief afforded by Chapter 11 of the 1978 Code.   Sections 109(d) and 1101 et seq.   Upon learning of this filing, McCain, a seller on credit of $11,610 worth of frozen french fried potatoes, made a timely demand to reclaim these foodstuffs in accordance with Section 2–702(2) of New York's Uniform Commercial Code (U.C.C.).   As this demand proved fruitless, McCain sought judicial aid in recovering the property sold to Flagstaff.   McCain began an adversary proceeding under Rule 701(1) of Part VII of the Bankruptcy Rules, 411 U.S. 1068.

McCain filed a complaint seeking reclamation, Rule 703, and alleged the sale on credit, the delivery of the potatoes, the debtor's insolvency, the filing of Flagstaff's Chapter 11 petition, the demand required by Section 2–702(2) of the U.C.C. and by Section 546(c)(1) of the Code, and the timeliness of the demand as prescribed by both of these sections.

Although Flagstaff's answer facially put some of these allegations in issue, its main defense was bottomed on the premise that McCain could reclaim only those potatoes in the debtor's possession and that, in any event, McCain could not receive payment for the value of such goods but would have to settle for priority status as an administrative expense creditor.[3]

---

3.   Section 503 of the Code prescribes those claims, usually arising after a bankruptcy petition has been filed, which are given adminis- trative expense status.   As such, first priority is accorded in the Code's scheme of priorities spelled out by Section 507(a).   Section 726(a)(1) then

At the hearing, both sides agreed that there were no controlling facts in dispute save for the quantity of the potatoes from the specific sale still in the debtor's possession when the petition was filed, and as to that the parties could readily ascertain the quantity without the need for testimony. (pp. 22, 29 of the August 13, 1981 transcript).

* * * McCain insists that it is entitled to an administrative claim under Section 546(c)(2)(A) for the full amount of its $11,610 shipment or a lien to that extent under Section 546(c)(2) (B), both without regard to whether any or all of the shipped foodstuffs could be retrieved by reclamation. The debtor insists that the discretion conferred by those sections may be exercised only to the extent it holds property which McCain could reclaim under applicable teachings.

For the reasons which follow the court concludes that the reading given to Section 546(c) of the 1978 Bankruptcy Code by the debtor is the proper one and that the plaintiff, McCain, is entitled to the administrative claim priority given by the scheme of the Code, but only to the extent of that portion of the foodstuffs delivered on July 13, 1981 which was in the debtor's possession on the date of McCain's demand.

I.

A SELLER'S PRE–1978 BANKRUPTCY CODE RIGHTS

Section 546(c) of the Code knows no antecedents in bankruptcy statutes as it appears to be Congress' first expression in the area it touches. But it cannot be said that Congress was unaware of non-federal statutes on the subject of the rights of sellers to recover property sold to insolvent purchasers and of the interfacing of those statutes with Congress' bankruptcy enactments as taught by federal judges. As so much is clear from the words of Section 546(c) itself and from its legislative history, the court does more than just assume that Congress knew of the state of the law before it wrote as it did. Compare Erlenbaugh v. United States, 409 U.S. 239, 243–4, 93 S.Ct. 477, 480, 34 L.Ed. 2d 446 (1972). See S.Rep. No. 95–989, 95th Cong., 2d Sess. 86–7 (1978); H.Rep. No. 95–595, 95th Cong., 1st Sess. 371–2 (1977).

Section 546(c) reads this way:

"The rights and powers of the trustee under sections 544(a), 545, 547 and 549 of this title are subject to any statutory

provides for the distribution of the estate's property first to the Section 507 priorities "in the order specified" in that section.

right or common-law right of a seller, in the ordinary course of such seller's business, of goods to the debtor to reclaim such goods if the debtor has received such goods while insolvent, but—(1) such a seller may not reclaim any such goods unless such seller demands in writing reclamation of such goods before ten days after receipt of such goods by the debtor; and (2) the court may deny reclamation to a seller with such a right of reclamation that has made such a demand only if court—(A) grants the claim of such a seller priority as an administrative expense; or (B) secures such claim by a lien."

As the section clearly recognizes a common law or nonbankruptcy statutory right of a seller to reclaim goods received by an insolvent, it is not inappropriate to consider what those rights were first at common law and, later, by statute. See Frankfurter, Some Reflections on the Reading of Statutes, 47 Colum.L. Rev. No. 4 at 537 (1947).

A. *AT COMMON LAW*

At common law, the right of a seller to reclaim his goods was governed by the law of contracts which permitted rescission by a seller who was induced to enter into a sales contract by a fraudulent or innocent misrepresentation. There were essentially four kinds of conduct which gave a seller at common law the right to rescind a sale based on the buyer's insolvency: (1) the buyer's concealment of insolvency with a demonstrable intent not to pay for the goods; (2) the buyer's concealment of insolvency where intent not to pay cannot be demonstrated; (3) the buyer's insolvency did not have to be proved but the buyer had materially misrepresented his financial status; and (4) the buyer's innocent misrepresentation. But, see 4A Collier on Bankruptcy (14th ed.) ¶ 70.41 for the treatment of this fourth common law basis for rescission on the coming of bankruptcy.

But the reach of the remedies flowing from rescission from the standpoint of the seller's ability to retrieve the property sold on application of common law principles yielded a melange of state court rulings. These turned on identification of the goods, their fungibility, commingling and the like where reclamation was not possible under applicable law because of problems of identification, the tracing of funds specifically allocable to the seller's goods yielded some solace in some places.

The lack of consistent and predictable handling of the dialogue between a seller and an insolvent purchaser and the absence of a standard which could harmonize the interests of both in an expanding economy has been noted, *inter alia*, in Weintraub & Edelman, Seller's Right to Reclaim Property Under Section 20702(2) of the Code Under the Bankruptcy Act: Fact or Fancy, 32 Bus.Law 1165, 1167 (1977).

B. *UNDER SECTION 2–702(2) OF THE UNIFORM COMMERCIAL CODE*

In large measure, the Uniform Commercial Code, and particularly relevant in this dispute, Section 2–702(2), were designed to afford certainty and completeness in preference to "those sources of 'general law' to which we were accustomed to resort in the days of Swift v. Tyson", to borrow the words of Judge Learned Hand in New York, N.H. & H.R. Co. v. Reconstruction Finance Corp., 180 F.2d 241, 244 (2d Cir. 1950). Today, 15 years after Judge Friendly made the observation in United States v. Wegematic Corp., 360 F.2d 674, 676 (2d Cir. 1966), the Uniform Commercial Code is with us as "a truly national law of commerce."

Section 2–702(2) of the U.C.C. is as follows:

"(2) Where the seller discovers that the buyer has received goods on credit while insolvent he may reclaim the goods upon demand made within ten days after the receipt, but if misrepresentation of solvency has been made to the particular seller in writing within three months before delivery the ten day limitation does not apply. Except as provided in this subsection the seller may not base a right to reclaim goods on the buyer's fraudulent or innocent misrepresentation of solvency or of intent to pay."

As the Official Uniform Comment discloses, Section 2–702(2)

"takes as its base line the proposition that any receipt of goods on credit by an insolvent buyer amounts to a tacit business misrepresentation of solvency and therefore is fraudulent as against the particular seller. This Article makes discovery of the buyer's insolvency and demand within a ten day period a condition of the right to reclaim goods on this ground. The ten day limitation period operates from the time of receipt of the goods. An exception to this time limitation is made when a written misrepresentation of solvency has been made to the particular seller within three months prior to the delivery. To fall within the exception the statement of solvency must be in writing, addressed to the particular seller and dated within three months of the delivery".

And as to the goods involved in the seller's Section 2–702(2) quest, the rights there given bar all other remedies.

What emerges plainly from the section is that its predicate is the existence of the goods in the seller's possession and therefore able to be reclaimed. These must not have left the seller's possession as is clear from Section 2–702(3) making the rights of the seller seeking to recover subject to the rights of the purchasers there described.

Given the limitations on the seller's right to recover the goods and the problems inherent in tracing specific fungibles among others from the standpoints of the time of delivery of a given lot, it came as no surprise that the proceeds of a seller's identifiable goods would become the object of a seller's Section 2–702(2) claim. See 4A Collier on Bankruptcy (14th ed.) ¶ 70.39. That such a remedy going beyond Section 2–702(2) would cause problems is nowhere made more clear than in the several opinions coming from the Fifth Circuit Court of Appeals in Matter of Samuels & Co., Inc. There, after an earlier reversal and remand on other grounds by the Supreme Court, sub nom. Mahon v. Stowers, 416 U.S. 100, 94 S.Ct. 1626, 40 L.Ed.2d 79 (1974), the Court of Appeals divided in a dispute between a trustee in bankruptcy and a seller of cattle seeking to reclaim that which he could not get as the cattle had been slaughtered and butchered or, alternatively, seeking the proceeds attributable to the sale of the meat. 510 F.2d 139 (1975). Although the presence of a secured creditor loomed large, the majority opinion recognized that the cash seller's right to reclaim should not rest on the identity of the cattle as sold. 510 F.2d at 148. In short, reclamation on the facts there, was found to be "a futile gesture" contrary to "reason or logic." *Ibid.* Circuit Judge Godbold dissented, 510 F.2d at 154. Among other chidings, Judge Godbold took Section 2–702 of the Texas version of the U.C.C. to confer a right to reclaim and not a "right to go after proceeds." 510 F.2d at 157. Rehearing *en banc* was granted and the Court of Appeals, dividing 9–5, reversed the panel decision and adopted "as its opinion the dissenting opinion of Judge Godbold * * *". 526 F.2d 1238, 1240 (1976), reh. den. April 1, 1976, cert. denied sub nom. Stowers v. Mahon, 429 U.S. 834, 97 S.Ct. 98, 50 L.Ed.2d 99 (1976).

It would seem to follow, therefore, just from the tenor of the disparate views in the *Samuels* case itself and in others which need not be cited that the remedy of reclamation to a seller bringing himself within the plain language of U.C.C. Section

2–702(2) is secure as to the identifiable goods in the possession of the purchaser but much less so as to the proceeds yielded by the sale of those goods, for the tracing of specific funds attributable to specific sales is a formidable obstacle at best.

C. *BANKRUPTCY UNDER THE 1898 ACT AND ITS IMPACT ON U.C.C. SECTION 2–702(2)*

While the cup of the Section 2–702(2) seller was apparently full given the strictures of the section as to the goods sold and the questionable right to recover proceeds if they could be properly traced, a line of cases emerged where the purchaser's bankruptcy intervened which brought the seller's cup to overflowing.

In re Good Deal Supermarkets, 384 F.Supp. 887 (D.C.N.J. 1974); In re Giltex, 17 U.C.C.Rep. 887 (D.C.S.D.N.Y.1975), and In re Weston's Corp., 17 U.C.C.Rep. 423 (Bkrtcy.Ct.S.D.N.Y. 1975) all held for one reason or another that the right given by U.C.C. Section 2–702 collided impermissibly with rights given trustees in bankruptcy to denounce disguised priorities which looked like liens under state law. See Section 67(c)(1)(A) of the Act, 11 U.S.C. (1976 ed.) § 107(c)(1)(A). Other courts however, sustained the vitality of Section 2–702(2) as against trustees in bankruptcy although they reached these results by different lines of reasoning. Compare In re Telemart, 524 F.2d 761 (9th Cir. 1975), cert. denied 424 U.S. 969, 96 S.Ct. 1466, 47 L.Ed.2d 736 (1976), and In re Daylin, Inc., 596 F.2d 853 (9th Cir. 1979), with In re Federals, 553 F.2d 509 (6th Cir. 1977), with In re Mel Golde Shoes, Inc. 403 F.2d 658 (6th Cir. 1968). See also In re Jaylaw Drug, Inc., 2 B.C.D. 867 (Bkrtcy.Ct.S.D.N.Y.1976) where the seller sought and found refuge in his common law right to rescind on the purchaser's bankruptcy, thereby eschewing U.C.C. Section 2–702(2).

II.

A SELLER'S RIGHTS UNDER SECTION 546(c) OF THE 1978 BANKRUPTCY CODE

It is against this setting that Congress expressed itself in Section 546(c) of the Code in the matter of a seller's right to reclaim its goods where the purchaser had become subject to the provisions of the Bankruptcy Code.

What emerges plainly from the rather sparse legislative comments to Section 546 is that Congress was aware of the tension between U.C.C. Section 2–702 and the several rights given bankruptcy trustees by the 1898 Act to denounce certain pre-petition transactions. Swiftly and surely, Section 546(c) in its lead-in sentence resolves the disparate views of federal courts concerning the effect of bankruptcy on a reclaiming seller's U.C.C. or common law rights. Whatever weapons a bankruptcy trustee might have in his arsenal to gather the estate are subject to the U.C.C. statutory right or common law right of a seller to retrieve his goods.[8]

Congress explained this purpose of enacted Section 546(c) this way:

"The purpose of the provision is to recognize, in part, the validity of section 2–702 of the Uniform Commercial Code, which has generated much litigation, confusion, and divergent decisions in different circuits.

S.Rep. No. 95–989, 95th Cong., 2d Sess. 86–7 (1978); H.Rep. No. 95–595, 95th Cong., 1st Sess. 371–2 (1977), U.S.Code Cong. & Admin.News 1978, pp. 5872–5873, 6328.

It is not necessary in the context of the specific dispute here to appraise Section 546(c) against Section 2–702(2) to determine whether a seller's right to seek reclamation depends on different conditions precedent where bankruptcy has come. See In re Auto Parts Distributors, Inc., 9 B.R. 469, 7 B.C.D. 490 (Bkrtcy. S.D.N.Y.1981).

Here the issue is whether, if reclamation is denied, and the court exercises its judgment to grant the seller a priority administrative claim or a lien, both authorized by Section 546(c)(2), the extent of either will exceed the value of the property which could be retrieved so that the full value of the goods sold will fix the reach of the priority or the lien.

Insofar as the discretion conferred on the court by Section 546(c)(2) expands the careful priority scheme outlined by Congress in Section 507(a) in which administrative claims under Section 503(b) lead all the rest, a legislative purpose to achieve greater expansion should be plainly expressed.

The conclusion emerging plainly is that the legislative history falls far short of what would be needed for the definitive answer that Section 546(c)(2) intended to give more to a reclaiming seller than he ever had either at common law or under U.C.C. Section

---

8. The rights of the trustee given by bankruptcy law which are specifically defined to be subordinate to a reclaiming creditor's rights are those conferred by Section 544 of the Code—the trustee as lien creditor (the strong-arm power); by Section 545—avoidance of statutory liens; by Section 547—avoidance of preferential transfers; and by Section 549—avoidance of post-petition transfers.

2–702(2). See Maine v. Thiboutot, 448 U.S. 1, 7, 100 S.Ct. 2502, 2505, 65 L.Ed.2d 555 (1980). To the contrary, the identical statements by Congressman Edwards, the House sponsor of H.R. 8200, and by Senator DeConcini, on the Senate side, support this court's conclusion that the administrative claim or lien which could be granted are in lieu of the goods which the seller could retrieve and not in lieu of the total invoiced shipment. Both legislators saw Section 546(c)(2) as permitting the bankruptcy court to grant an administrative expense claim or a lien

"in lieu of turning over the property"

124 Cong.Rec.H. 11097 (daily ed. September 28, 1978); 124 Cong. Rec.S. 17414 (daily ed. October 6, 1978).

"These remarks, offered in lieu of a conference report by the principal sponsors of the Act, are entitled to great weight."

In re Spong; Pauley v. Spong, 661 F.2d 6 at 10 (2d Cir. 1981).

To be sure, the identical comments by both the House and the Senate relevant to an earlier version of enacted Section 546(c)(2) are ambiguous and could support plaintiff's argument were it not for the much surer comments made on the eve of passage of a revised bill, H.R. 8200, introduced on September 28, 1978. Both statements, which recognize the right given by U.C.C. Section 2–702, observe that that right (to reclaim) is subject to the court's power to grant an administrative expense priority in lieu of reclamation

"for his [the seller's] claim arising out of the sale of the goods."

S.Rep. No. 95–989, supra, at 87; H.Rep. No. 95–595, supra, at 372, U.S.Code Cong. & Admin.News 1978, pp. 5878, 6328.

At first blush, these quoted words suggest that a seller could be given his priority for the invoiced amount rather than for the value of the goods which he could actually recover. But this reading of these few words would require the court to ignore their context and to put at nought strong policy considerations which underlie bankruptcy principles.

The context of which the above statement is a part recognizes the continuing vitality of U.C.C. Section 2–702 or common law rights given reclaiming sellers. All Section 546(c)(1) does is assess a somewhat different procedural mode by requiring a written demand for reclamation within 10 days of the receipt of the goods by the debtor in a bankruptcy proceeding. There is absolutely nothing to show that Congress meant to expand rights given, absent bankruptcy, by state law or the common law. The plain language of all the legislative coments makes this clear.

All this aside, bankruptcy is governed by its own truths and those truths relevant here also require the court to construe Section 546(c)(2) in favor of the debtor and the overwhelming mass of the debtor's unsecured creditors for whom neither U.C.C. Section 2–702, the common law, nor Section 546(c) works.

First it must be recognized that Congress' scheme of priority creditors, while designed to achieve important policy aims thought relevant, nevertheless distorts one of the dominant schemes of bankruptcy—equality of distribution. See, *inter alia*, Nathanson v. N.L.R.B., 344 U.S. 25, 29, 73 S.Ct. 80, 83, 97 L.Ed. 23 (1952). It follows, therefore, that if Congress meant to give the 10-day seller so much more than he ever had under non-bankruptcy law to the exclusion and detriment of the 11-day seller, it would have expressed itself far more clearly. Because any system of priorities ultimately attenuates the yield for those for whom Congress was less solicitous, the expressions of those priorities should be strictly read and not expanded unless plainly mandated.

The second truth is that reorganization under Chapter 11 is one of the desired aims of Congress for the financially pressed but honest debtor. The care Congress took in enacting Chapter 11 as "a carefully matured enactment", Guessefeldt v. McGrath, 342 U.S. 308, 319, 72 S.Ct. 338, 344, 96 L.Ed. 342 (1952), is reflected in the exhaustive discussions and numerous changes made before enactment of the final version. To achieve reorganization for the benefit of debtors and creditors alike, Congress gave the court the latitude Section 546(c)(2) gives it to ensure that the debtor's continued operation would not be adversely affected by the improvident grant to a seller of the right to retrieve its goods in the debtor's possession.

Section 546(c)(2) must therefore be read as striking a balance so that the debtor has the use of the goods it needs for its ongoing business while the seller has their value. To give the seller more, absent a clear indication that this should be so, cuts against the grain of compelling bankruptcy themes. In short, Congress' coverage of the reclaiming seller is vital to the Chapter 11 mission. See Powell v. U. S. Cartridge Co., 339 U.S. 497, 516, 70 S.Ct. 755, 765, 94 L.Ed. 1017 (1950).

*   *   *

IV.

THE JUDGMENT

Judgment is rendered for the plaintiff to the extent its goods were in the debtor's possession on the filing date. The amount of that judgment is allowed as an administrative priority within the meaning of Section 503 of the Code. Unless it is paid within a reasonable period, the court will entertain a motion for an order directing it be paid pursuant to Section 503(a).

* * *

MATTER OF SAMUELS & CO., INC.

United States Court of Appeals, Fifth Circuit, 1975.
510 F.2d 139.

INGRAHAM, CIRCUIT JUDGE.

* * *

To briefly reiterate, the relevant facts are as follows. Samuels & Co., Inc., is a Texas meatpacking firm that purchases, processes and packages meat and sells the meat within and without the State of Texas. Since 1963 Samuels' operations, including its cattle purchases, have been financed on a weekly basis by C.I.T. Corporation. To secure its financing, C.I.T. has properly perfected a lien on Samuels' assets, inventory and all after-acquired property, including livestock that is from time to time purchased for slaughter and processing.

From May 12 through May 23, 1969, the appellants, fifteen cattle farmers, delivered their cattle to Samuels. Although the sellers did not receive payment for the sale simultaneously with delivery of the cattle, checks were subsequently issued to the sellers. On May 23, 1969, before these checks had been paid, C.I.T., believing itself to be insecure, refused to advance any more funds to Samuels for the operation of the packing plant. On that same day Samuels filed a petition in bankruptcy. Since C.I.T. refused to advance more funds, although apparently aware that there were unpaid checks outstanding, the appellants' checks issued in payment for cattle were dishonored by the drawee bank.

Because of the fungible nature of the cattle, the beef has long since been butchered and processed and sold through the normal course of business. The proceeds from the cattle sales have been deposited with the trustee in bankruptcy pending the outcome of this litigation. The issues in this case concern the priority of interest in these proceeds between a creditor of the debtor, which holds a perfected security interest in the debtor's after-acquired property, and a seller of goods to the debtor. Since the sellers have not been paid, they claim a superior right to the deposited proceeds and argue that they are now entitled to payment out of these proceeds. The finance corporation, on the other hand, contends that the sellers are merely unsecured creditors of the bankrupt and are not entitled to a prior claim to the funds, and alternatively that the finance corporation qualified as a good faith purchaser of the cattle and is therefore immune to the sellers' claims of non-payment. For the reasons that follow, we conclude that the sellers should prevail.

I.

In order to determine which provisions of the Texas Business & Commerce Code govern the relationships among the parties, the first question that must be resolved is whether this commercial venture was a cash or credit transaction. The significance of classifying a sale as a cash or credit transaction relates back to the common law and the historical passing of title concept. Under the common law, a sale for cash, as opposed to a sale on credit, meant that the seller of goods implicitly reserved the incidents of ownership or title to the goods until payment was made in full. If the buyer failed to make payment, the seller could regain possession of the goods by instituting an action in replevin. Additionally, since the buyer of goods for cash did not obtain title to the goods until the seller was paid, the defaulting buyer was incapable of passing title to a third party. Based on the cash sale doctrine, an unpaid seller could even reclaim goods sold by an intermediary to one who otherwise qualified as a bona fide purchaser.

When the owner of goods sold them on credit, however, all the incidents of ownership, including title, passed to the buyer. If the buyer subsequently failed to make payment, the seller's rights were only those of a creditor for the purchase price, and he had no right against the merchandise. Since in a sale on credit the buyer obtained all the incidents of ownership in the goods, including title, he was able to convey his interest in the goods, absolute ownership, to a third party without recourse on behalf of the seller. Corman, Cash Sales, Worthless Checks and the Bona Fide Purchaser, 10 Vanderbilt Law Review 55 (1956);

Gilmore, The Commercial Doctrine of Good Faith Purchaser, 63 Yale L.J. 1057, 1060 & n. 10 (1954).

Underlying the different characteristics and consequences of cash and credit sales are the expectations and intentions of the three parties concerned. When goods are sold for cash, the seller is assuming virtually no risk of loss because he believes that he has full payment for the goods in his hands. When the sale is for credit, however, the seller assumes a far more substantial risk and voluntarily relinquishes the incidents of ownership to the buyer. The buyer, possessed of these incidents of ownership, is capable of conveying title to a bona fide purchaser, completely terminating the rights of the seller in the goods. The credit seller recognizes that he will receive full payment for his merchandise only if the business of the buyer progresses normally and sales are made to third parties in the normal course of business. Note, The Owner's Intent and the Negotiability of Chattels: A Critique of Section 2–403 of the Uniform Commercial Code, 72 Yale L.J. 1205, 1220 (1963). Although commercial transactions and the law governing such relationships has developed significantly since the conception of these doctrines, this reasoning with respect to the different risks assumed by the different sellers underlie and differentiate the two concepts and is as valid a distinction today as it was when the doctrines were originally conceived.

The Uniform Commercial Code as adopted by the State of Texas has to some extent modified the common law doctrines of cash and credit sales. It is clear that the historical concept of passing title to goods is not emphasized in the Code, and the location of title generally is not regarded as being determinative of the rights of adverse parties. Helstad, Deemphasis of Title Under the Uniform Commercial Code, 1964, Wisconsin L.R. 362. Instead of implementing the fictional concept of title, the countervailing interests of the parties are sometimes defined in terms of various rights, privileges, powers and immunities.

But even though the title concept is so reduced in significance, the Code recognizes and adopts the fundamental distinctions of the common law between cash and credit sales, at least with respect to the rights of the unpaid seller against the defaulting buyer. The Code deals with a sale on credit in provisions separate from those dealing with cash sales. Section 2–702 specifically sets forth the credit seller's remedy and provides that when "the seller discovers that the buyer has received goods on credit while insolvent, he may reclaim the goods upon demand made within ten days after receipt * * *." UCC § 2–702(2). This provision goes on to define the seller's priority rights against other specific parties, providing that "[t]he seller's right to reclaim under Subsection (2) is subject to the rights of a buyer in the ordinary course or other good faith purchaser or lien creditor under this chapter (Section 2–403)." Id. § 2–702(3). Although this section authorizes a limited right against the goods, it generally recognizes that when the sale is on a credit basis, all the incidents of ownership pass to the buyer who may then convey this interest to certain third parties. The seller stands merely as a general creditor for the purchase price.

With respect to cash sales, however, § 2–507 of the Code explicitly recognizes that "unless otherwise agreed," "[w]here payment is due and demanded on the delivery to the buyer of goods * * *, [the buyer's] right as against the seller to retain or dispose of them is conditional upon his making payment due." Like the cash sale doctrine at common law, § 2–507 provides that when the buyer is to pay cash for the goods, the validity of the transaction is dependent upon his making payment, and when the buyer fails to pay, he does not even have the right to possess the goods. Absolute ownership does not pass to the buyer until payment is complete.

The limited interest conveyed to the buyer prior to payment under § 2–507(2) is reemphasized in § 2–511(3), which deals specifically with the situation where payment for goods is made by check that is later dishonored. Section 2–511(3) provides that payment by check "is conditional and is defeated as between the parties by dishonor of the check on due presentment." Underlying this provision is the principle that, in order to encourage and facilitate commercial sales and economic growth generally, the recipient of a check in payment for goods "is not to be penalized in any way" for accepting this commercially acceptable mode of payment. Id. Comment 4.

Even though the Code deemphasizes the title concept of the common law, these two provisions strongly suggest that the underlying philosophy of the common law cash sale doctrine has been embodied here. Like the traditional cash sale doctrine, the existence of a valid contractual relationship between the buyer and seller is dependent upon the buyer's completing his part of the bargain and paying for the merchandise. When the buyer fails to pay, he no longer has even the right to possess the goods.

Mindful of these principles we turn to the facts of the instant case to determine whether the sale of the cattle to the packing house was on a cash or credit basis. This sale of goods must be regarded as a cash transaction rather than a credit transaction because of the established course of dealing between the buyer and sellers. A course of dealing, as defined by the Texas Commercial Code, is a "sequence of previous conduct between the parties to a particular transaction which is fairly to be regarded as establishing a common basis of understanding for interpreting their expressions and other conduct." UCC § 1–205(1). As suggested by the Supreme Court in *Stowers*, supra, the Packers and Stockyards Act and the regulations issued thereunder so outline the course of conduct to be followed as between the cattle seller and the purchasing meat packer.

According to the Act and regulations, when a cattle grower sells his livestock on what is termed a "grade and yield" basis, the contract price to be paid is left open because it has yet to be determined. Before the purchase price can be determined, the cattle must be slaughtered and the carcasses chilled for twenty-four hours. After the meat is chilled, the Department of Agriculture grades it and determines the yield, and at that time the contract price can be set. When the price is set, a point sometime after delivery, a check is issued to the seller. 9 CFR §§ 201.43(b),—.99.

While a lapse of time occurring between delivery of the cattle and payment, even if only a day, might be considered an extension of credit, the course of dealing between the parties establishes that this was a sale for cash. The delay between delivery and payment was not credit, but rather was the result of a procedure mandated by the Act and regulations that governed the relationship between the buyer and seller when cattle are sold on a grade and yield basis. This procedure apparently had been followed since the inception of the regulations requiring such conduct. Moreover, not only do the Act and regulations prescribe such a course of conduct, all the cattle sellers regarded this commercial venture as a cash transaction, and there is nothing in the record to suggest that the buyer regarded the delay in issuing the check as credit. The course of conduct prescribed by the Act and regulations, coupled with the undisputed intent of the cattle sellers, compels the conclusion that this was a cash and not a credit affair. Engstrom v. Wiley, 191 F.2d 684 (9th Cir., 1951); In re Helms Veneer Corp., 287 F.Supp. 840 (W.D.Va., 1968).

* * *

Nor does the seller's ultimate reclamation of the cattle, or rather proceeds from sale of the cattle, prejudice the rights of any creditors. When a sale is made on credit, the purchased merchandise belongs to the estate of the bankrupt and all the seller has is a security interest in the property. If the seller failed to perfect his interest, he stands as a general creditor with the rest of the unsecured creditors and is entitled only to his proportionate share of the bankrupt's estate. To allow him to recover his loss in full from the estate would prejudice the rights of the other creditors. In re Colacci's of America, Inc., Bar Control of Colorado v. Gifford, 13 U.C.C.Rep. 1023 (10th Cir., 1973); Engstrom v. Wiley, supra, 191 F.2d at 689; Engelkes v. Farmers Co-op Co., 194 F.Supp. 319 (N.D.Iowa, 1961).

But when the sale is for cash, the merchandise belongs to the bankrupt's estate only if the buyer pays for the goods. If payment is not made, the seller is not a mere creditor and therefore is not compelled to share proportionately with the general creditors of the estate. The general creditors are not entitled to any portion of these assets because the goods do not belong to the bankrupt estate. The seller's reclamation of the goods does not remove any assets of the bankrupt in which general creditors would share and thus does not prejudice the rights of the seller on credit. Since the seller for cash is not a creditor and is not required to share with the general creditors in the estate as a creditor, he is entitled to his merchandise.

* * *

III.

The third question is whether C.I.T. qualifies as a good faith purchaser. Under § 2–403 of the Code, the buyer of goods from a seller is vested with a limited interest that it can convey to a good faith purchaser and thus create in the purchaser a greater right to the goods than the buyer itself had. This is possible even when the buyer obtains the goods as a result of giving a check that is later dishonored or when the purchase was made for cash. But in order to attain this status, the proponent must be a *purchaser* that gives *value* and acts in *good faith*. While C.I.T. gave value for the goods within the meaning of the Code, it failed to meet the test of a purchaser or one acting in good faith.

With regard to C.I.T.'s status as a purchaser, the Code broadly defines this term as one who take "by sale, discount, negotiation, mortgage, pledge, lien, issue or reissue, gift or any other voluntary transaction creating an interest in property." UCC § 1–201(32); see id. § 1–201(33). As noted earlier, C.I.T. does not have an interest in the cattle because its rights in the collateral are derivative of its debtor's rights in it. When Samuels failed to pay for the cattle, its rights in the cattle terminated and thus so did C.I.T.'s. C.I.T.'s status as a good faith purchaser is also defeated with regard to its acting in good faith. The Code defines good faith as "honesty in fact in the conduct or transaction concerned." UCC § 1–201(19). Implicit in the term "good faith" is the requirement that C.I.T. take its interest in the cattle without notice of the outstanding claims of others. See Greater Louisville Auto Auction v. Ogle Buick, Inc., supra, 387 S.W.2d at 21. See also Fidelity and Casualty Co. v. Key Biscayne Bank, 501 F.2d 1322, 1326 (5th Cir. 1974).

It is true that the evidence does not reveal any breach of an express obligation on C.I.T.'s behalf to continue financing the packing house after Samuels filed a petition in bankruptcy. Nor does the good faith element require the creditor to continue to finance the operation of a business when it is apparent that the business is unprofitable and is going bankrupt. But because of the integral relationship between C.I.T. and Samuels, we do not see how C.I.T. could have kept from knowing of the outstanding claims of others. C.I.T. maintained close scrutiny over the financial affairs of Samuels' operations. C.I.T. had been financing Samuels' packing house operations for at least six years, and the financing involved the flow of millions of dollars. The amount of cash advances made to Samuels was not predetermined or determined arbitrarily, but was calculated only after C.I.T. examined weekly the outstanding accounts and the current inventory of the business. From such a continuous and prolonged study of the business to determine the amount of each weekly advance, C.I.T. must have been intricately aware of the operations and financial status of the business.

Since C.I.T. was so intimately involved in Samuels' financial affairs, it must have known that when it refused to advance additional funds, unpaid checks issued to cattle sellers by Samuels would be dishonored. Samuels' operations were totally dependent on the financing of C.I.T. and both parties knew it. From its enduring involvement in the weekly financing, C.I.T. apparently knew that Samuels was purchasing and processing cattle up until the very time of filing the petition. Knowing that cattle had been purchased and processed immediately preceding its refusal to advance more money, C.I.T. must have known as a result of this refusal that some cattle sellers who had recently de-

livered their cattle to Samuels would not be paid. Because
C.I.T. and Samuels were so intertwined in the management of
the financial affairs of the business, we do not think that C.I.T.
can plausibly claim, in complete honesty, that it was unaware of
the claims of the unpaid cattle sellers. Since C.I.T. was aware
of these outstanding claims, it does not qualify as a good faith
purchaser.

* * *

V.

We believe it inequitable to deny the claims of the stock
farmers who produced and delivered the cattle, in favor of the
mortgagee who refused to advance the money before bankruptcy.

* * *

It is our firm belief that the approach to the Code outlined
above is eminently reasonable and conforms with the Code's express provisions and underlying policies. We do not believe that
the drafters of the Code intended for the unpaid sellers to walk
away from this transaction with nothing, neither their goods nor
the purchase price, while the mortgagee enjoys a preferred lien
on that for which it refused to advance payment. Based on our
understanding of the Code, such a result is insupportable.

We again reverse the judgment of the district court.

GODBOLD, CIRCUIT JUDGE (dissenting):

I dissent.

This case raises one primary question: under the Uniform
Commercial Code as adopted in Texas, is the interest of an unpaid cash seller in goods already delivered to a buyer superior or
subordinate to the interest of a holder of a perfected security
interest in those same goods? In my opinion, under Article
Nine, the perfected security interest is unquestionably superior
to the interest of the seller. Moreover, the perfected lender is
protected from the seller's claims by two independent and theoretically distinct Article Two provisions. My result is not the
product of revealed truth, but rather of a meticulous and dispas-
sionate reading of Articles Two and Nine and an understanding
that the Code is an integrated statute whose Articles and Sections overlap and flow into one another in an effort to encourage
specific types of commercial behavior. The Code's overall plan,
which typically favors good faith purchasers, and which encourages notice filing of nonpossessory security interests in person-

alty through the imposition of stringent penalties for nonfiling, compels a finding that the perfected secured party here should prevail.

My brothers have not concealed that their orientation in the case before us is to somehow reach a result in favor of the sellers of cattle, assumed by them to be "little fellows," and against a large corporate lender, because it seems the "fair" thing to do. We do not sit as federal chancellors confecting ways to escape the state law of commercial transactions when that law produces a result not to our tastes. Doing what seems fair is heady stuff. But the next seller may be a tremendous corporate conglomerate engaged in the cattle feeding business, and the next lender a small town Texas bank. Today's heady draught may give the majority a euphoric feeling, but it can produce tomorrow's hangover.

I.   Rights under § 2–403

My analysis begins with an examination of the relative rights of seller and secured party under § 2–403(1).

Section 2–403 gives certain transferors power to pass greater title than they can themselves claim. Section 2–403(1) gives good faith purchasers of even fraudulent buyers-transferors greater rights than the defrauded seller can assert. This harsh rule is designed to promote the greatest range of freedom possible to commercial vendors and purchasers.

The provision anticipates a situation where (1) a cash seller has delivered goods to a buyer who has paid by a check which is subsequently dishonored, § 2–403(1)(b), (c), and where (2) the defaulting buyer transfers title to a Code-defined "good faith purchaser." The interest of the good faith purchaser is protected *pro tanto* against the claims of the aggrieved seller. §§ 2–403(1); 2–403, Comment 1. The Code expressly recognizes the power of the defaulting buyer to transfer good title to such a purchaser even though the transfer is wrongful as against the seller. The buyer is granted the *power* to transfer good title despite the fact that under § 2–507 he lacks the *right* to do so.

The Code definition of "purchaser" is broad, and includes not only one taking by sale but also covers persons taking by gift or by voluntary mortgage, pledge or lien. § 1–201(32), (33). It is therefore broad enough to include an Article Nine secured party. §§ 1–201(37); 9–101, Comment; 9–102(1), (2). Thus, if C.I.T. holds a valid Article Nine security interest, it is by virtue of that status also a purchaser under § 2–403(1). See First Citizens

Bank and Trust Co. v. Academic Archives, Inc., 10 N.C.App. 619, 179 S.E.2d 850 (1971); Stumbo v. Paul B. Hult Lumber Co., 251 Or. 20, 444 P.2d 564 (1968); In re Hayward Woolen Co., 3 U.C.C. Rep. 1107 (D.Mass.1967).

While I shall discuss in detail infra, the implications of C.I.T.'s security interest under Article Nine and under other Article Two provisions, I here note that C.I.T. is the holder of a perfected Article Nine interest which extends to the goods claimed by the seller Stowers.

Attachment of an Article Nine interest takes place when (1) there is agreement that the interest attach to the collateral; (2) the secured party has given value; and (3) the debtor has rights in the collateral sufficient to permit attachment. [1962 UCC] § 9–204(1).

(1) *The agreement:* In 1963, Samuels initially authorized C.I.T.'s lien in its after-acquired inventory. The agreement between these parties remained in effect throughout the period of delivery of Stowers' cattle to Samuels.

(2) *Value:* At the time of Stowers' delivery, Samuels' indebtedness to C.I.T. exceeded $1.8 million. This pre-existing indebtedness to the lender constituted "value" under the Code. § 1–201(44).

(3) *Rights in the collateral:* Finally, upon delivery, Samuels acquired rights in the cattle sufficient to allow attachment of C.I.T.'s lien. The fact that the holder of a voluntary lien—including an Article Nine interest—is a "purchaser" under the Code is of great significance to a proper understanding and resolution of this case under Article Two and Article Nine. The Code establishes that purchasers can take from a defaulting cash buyer, § 2–403(1). Lien creditors are included in the definition of purchasers, § 1–201(32), (33). A lien *is* an Article Nine interest, §§ 9–101, Comment; 9–102(2); 9–102, Comment. The existence of an Article Nine interest presupposes the debtor's having rights in the collateral sufficient to permit attachment, [1962 UCC] § 9–204(1). Therefore, since a defaulting cash buyer has the power to transfer a security interest to a lien creditor, including an Article Nine secured party, the buyer's rights in the property, however marginal, must be sufficient to allow attachment of a lien. And this is true even if, *arguendo*, I were to agree that the cash seller is granted reclamation rights under Article Two. See First National Bank of Elkhart Cty. v. Smoker, 11 U.C.C. Rept.Serv. 10, 19 (Ind.Ct.App., 1972); Evans Products Co. v. Jorgensen, 245 Or. 362, 421 P.2d 978 (1966).

If the Article Nine secured party acted in good faith, it is prior under § 2–403(1) to an aggrieved seller. Under the facts before us, I think that C.I.T. acted in good faith.

* * *

MATTER OF SAMUELS & CO., INC.

United States Court of Appeals, Fifth Circuit, 1976.
526 F.2d 1238.

Before BROWN,* CHIEF JUDGE, WISDOM, GEWIN, BELL, THORNBERRY, COLEMAN, GOLDBERG, AINSWORTH, GODBOLD, DYER, MORGAN, CLARK, INGRAHAM, RONEY and GEE, CIRCUIT JUDGES.

PER CURIAM. The action of the panel [1] is reversed and the judgment of the District Court is affirmed.

The court en banc adopts as its opinion the dissenting opinion of Judge Godbold with the additional comments which we set out in the margin. [3]

The judgment of the District Court is affirmed.

GEE, CIRCUIT JUDGE (specially concurring):

Troubled by the seeming harshness of the result, I nevertheless concur, despite its effect to force a cash seller to act like a credit seller to protect his interest. It asks much of these small cattle dealers, selling their cattle for cash, that they wrangle with the complicated provisions of art. 9 to protect themselves against an insufficient funds check, but this seems to be the clear demand of the Texas Code. In the normal course of deal-

---

* Chief Judge Brown did not participate in the decision of this case.

1. 510 F.2d 139 (C.A.5, 1975).

3. In remanding the case to this court the Supreme Court left open for our determination the question of whether "a course of conduct mandated by the Act or regulations might not, just as any other course of conduct, be relevant or even dispositive under state law." Mahon v. Stowers, 416 U.S. 100, 113–114, 94 S.Ct. 1626, 1633, 40 L.Ed.2d 79, 89 (1974). The evidence of course of dealings, see Texas Business and Commercial Code, § 1.205(a), shows that the plaintiffs and Samuels had a history of dealing in the manner mandated by the Act and the regulations. That course of dealing is the basis for the view, shared by the majority members and the dissenting member of the panel, that the sales of livestock to Samuels by plaintiffs were cash sales.

Also we note a matter not mentioned in the dissenting opinion of Judge Godbold. The District Court, which accepted the Referee's findings of fact but rejected his conclusions of law, held that C.I.T. and the trustee in Bankruptcy were good faith purchasers for value, and the Supreme Court in its opinion referred to them as such. 416 U.S. at 104, 94 S.Ct. at 1628, 40 L.Ed.2d at 84.

ing, such a check will give a seller an action on the instrument as well as for breach of the contract of sale, all in addition to the remedy of reclamation read into the Code by some courts. This protection is adequate except in cases such as this, where the buyer writes a bad check and subsequently declares bankruptcy. All sellers who accept checks run the same risk—some take out insurance against such a loss by the simple procedure of drawing up and filing a security agreement giving them rights in the goods sold to secure the purchase price.

Such an agreement can be filed in advance, so there is no need to wait until one receives a check to fill out a security agreement and race to file it before the bank dishonors the check. The very nature of this transaction recommended taking this simple additional precaution of filing a purchase money security interest—the cows were immediately slaughtered, making it impossible to recover the "goods" if the deal fell through, and, too, the delayed pricing arrangement transformed the "cash sale" into a credit transaction for all commercial purposes regardless of how the two parties characterized it. Comment 6 to art. 2–511 says acceptance of a check postdated by even one day "insofar as *third parties* are concerned, amounts to a delivery on credit and the [seller's] remedies are set forth in the section on buyer's insolvency (§ 2–702)." As Judge Hughes pointed out in the district court opinion, Stowers' delivery of livestock to the bankrupt without perfecting a security interest therein placed the bankrupt in such a position that it could transfer good title to a good faith purchaser for value, which is precisely what Samuels did.

NOTE

The Packers and Stockyards Act was amended in 1976 to protect unpaid cash sellers from the result reached in *Samuels*. See 7 U.S.C. § 196.

BURK v. EMMICK

United States Court of Appeals, Eighth Circuit, 1980.
637 F.2d 1172.

HEANEY, CIRCUIT JUDGE.

I

This appeal arises out of a transaction in which plaintiff Willard Burk contracted to sell approximately 950 head of yearling steers to defendant Bob Emmick, d/b/a Emmick Cattle Company. The terms of the sales contract provided that the buyer would make a $15,000 down payment and tender the balance upon delivery.

The contract was amended, postponing the delivery date and modifying the manner in which payment would be made. The amended agreement called for payment of a major portion of the purchase price at delivery by sight draft drawn upon the codefendant, Northwestern National Bank of Sioux City. The balance of the purchase price was to be covered by the buyer's personal note. Just prior to delivery, the defendant Bank orally guaranteed to the seller that funds were available to cover the sight draft so that delivery could be made. The seller made delivery, but the sight draft was not accepted by the Bank and the buyer's personal note was never honored.

Subsequent to these transactions, the seller reclaimed the cattle and resold them for less than the original contract price. Thereafter, the seller sued the buyer in the United States District Court for the Northern District of Iowa, alleging breach of contract and fraud. The seller also sued the Bank on a promissory estoppel theory, reasoning that he detrimentally relied upon the Bank's oral assurance that funds were available to cover the sight draft, thus inducing the seller to make delivery and suffer pecuniary injury. The case was tried to a jury and a verdict was returned on the seller's breach of contract claim against the buyer in the amount of $19,300. The jury also returned a verdict in the seller's favor against the Bank on the promissory estoppel claim in the amount of $24,700.

All parties filed post trial motions. The seller moved to amend the judgment by increasing the amount of the award. The buyer and the Bank moved for judgment notwithstanding the verdict, for a new trial, and to amend the judgment. All motions were denied, and all parties appealed. We affirm.

II

The buyer and the Bank argue that [UCC § 2–702] controls this case. The buyer contends this section bars a seller who successfully reclaims goods from further recovering a deficiency judgment. The Bank agrees that section 2–702 applies, but asserts that because the seller failed to demand return of the goods within ten days of delivery, the reclamation was improper. The Bank asserts that it has an interest in the cattle superior to the unpaid seller based upon a preexisting security interest covering after-acquired property of the defendant buyer.

In resolving the question posed by this appeal, we first determine the relative rights of the parties involved in this sales transaction.

A. *The rights of the secured party under section 2–403*

Section 2–403 gives a transferor power to pass good title to certain transferees even though the transferor does not possess good title. This section contemplates the situation in which a cash seller delivers goods to a buyer who pays by a draft that is subsequently dishonored, and then transfers title to a good faith purchaser. U.C.C. §§ 2–403(1)(b) & (c). In such a situation, as between the good faith purchaser and the unpaid seller, the former's claim is clearly superior. Swets Motor Sales, Inc. v. Pruisner, 236 N.W.2d 299, 304–305 (Iowa 1975).

Furthermore, section 2–403 does not limit the power of a transferor to pass good title only through sales transactions. The language of the Code specifically provides that "purchasers" may take good title from transferors. The term purchaser is broadly defined in the Code to include an Article IX secured party. See U.C.C. §§ 1–201(32) & (33); Swets Motor Sales, Inc. v. Pruisner, supra, 236 N.W.2d at 304. See also In re Samuels & Co., 526 F.2d 1238, 1242 (5th Cir.), cert. denied, 429 U.S. 834, 97 S.Ct. 98, 50 L.Ed.2d 99 (1976). Here, if the Bank had acted in good faith, its interest in the cattle would be superior to the aggrieved seller. However, as the district court noted, the issue was properly submitted to the jury and the jury determined that the Bank did not exercise good faith. Accordingly, the Bank does not qualify as a good faith purchaser under section 2–403. As between the seller and the Bank, the seller's interest in the cattle is superior.

B. *The rights of the cash seller under the U.C.C.*

Section 2–703 indexes the remedies available to a seller upon the buyer's breach. The right of reclamation is not specifically mentioned there. The cash seller's right to reclaim has been drawn from the language of sections 2–507 and 2–511.

Section 2–507(2) gave the seller in this case the right to reclaim the cattle which were sold and not paid for. The buyer's main contention is that once the seller had successfully reclaimed the goods, he could not also seek a deficiency judgment. The buyer asserts the election of remedies provision in section 2–702(3) is applicable to a cash seller's section 2–507 right of reclamation. We do not agree. There is nothing in the language of the Code or the Comments to suggest that the election of remedies provision applies to a cash seller's reclamation under section 2–507. In fact, the concept of election of remedies is foreign to the liberal remedial provisions intended by the drafters of the U.C.C. See § 2–703 Comment 1. See also 2 R. Anderson, Uniform Commercial Code, § 2–703:5 at 337 (1971).

The buyer also asserts that the seller failed to demand reclamation within ten days of delivery of the cattle. Some courts have decided that a cash seller's reclamation right is subject to the ten-day limitation provision covering credit sale transactions involving insolvent buyers under section 2–702, but those decisions are factually dissimilar.[5] The courts that have imposed the ten-day limitation have concerned the respective rights of a

---

5. See, e.g., In re Samuels, supra, 526 F.2d at 1245; In re Colacci's of America, Inc., 490 F.2d 1118, 1120 (10th Cir. 1974); In re Helms Veneer Corp., supra, 287 F.Supp. at 846. See also In re Fairfield Elevator Co., 14 U.C.C.Rep.Serv. 96, 106–108 (S.D.Iowa 1973) (Bky.Ct.)

The Code does not expressly require that § 2–702's ten-day limitation be applied to cash sale transactions not involving insolvent buyers. J. White & R. Summers, Uniform Commercial Code § 3–6 at 115 (2d Ed. 1980). Several factors militate against grafting § 2–702's limitation to cash sale transactions: (1) § 2–702 by its terms applies only to credit sales. (2) The seller's reclamation right is not dependent upon Comment 3 to § 2–507. The right to reclaim is inherent in the language of the statute. See Dugan, Cash Sale Sellers Under Articles 2 and 9 of the Uniform Commercial Code, 8 U.C.C.L.J. 330, 345–349 (1976); Mann & Phillips, The Cash Seller Under the Uniform Commercial Code, 20 B.C.L. Rev. 370, 383 & n.68 (1979). The limitation, at best, is only suggested by the Comment; the Comments to the Code cannot impose restrictions unwarranted by the statutory language. See Thompson v. United States, 408 F.2d 1075, 1084 n. 15 (8th Cir. 1969); Dugan, supra at 341–342. (3) The legislative history of § 2–507 indicates that this section was intended to reflect the common law of cash sale transactions; the common law tradition includes the seller's right to reclamation. See generally Mann & Phillips, supra at 376–380, 383–384, & nn. 46–50 (1979).

good faith purchaser or trustee in bankruptcy and an unpaid seller.[6] But here, a good faith purchaser is not involved. Nor are we faced with the conflicting interests of an unpaid seller and a trustee in bankruptcy representing the interests of a bankrupt's creditors. Rather, the conflict is between the unpaid cash seller and the breaching buyer, and the question is whether the seller may reclaim and recover a deficiency judgment from that buyer.

It is instructive to note that the buyer in the case at bar has never forcefully opposed the seller's right to reclaim; rather, it has focused its primary attention upon the seller's right to a deficiency. This is understandable in light of the fact that the buyer was not prejudiced by the seller's reclamation, improper or not. Had the seller not reclaimed the goods, he could have sued for the full contract price. See U.C.C. §§ 2–703, 2–709.

Our holding is quite limited. We determine that as between the seller and the buyer, where a cash seller reclaims goods sold to a breaching buyer, the only limitation imposed upon the seller's right is a reasonableness requirement. Since we determine that the buyer was not prejudiced by the seller's delay in reclaiming the cattle, we find the seller's reclamation was not unreasonable.

Furthermore, the district court was correct in determining that section 2–702 did not properly apply to the instant case. By its very terms, that section applies when the seller discovers the buyer to be insolvent *and* when the underlying transaction is a

---

6. But see Szabo v. Vinton Motors, Inc., 630 F.2d 1, (1st Cir., 1980). In *Szabo*, the First Circuit characterized the case before it as simply a question involving the relative rights of a reclaiming cash seller and a breaching buyer under § 2–507. Essentially, the Appeals Court ruled that the seller could only reclaim where the seller's demand for reclamation was made upon the buyer within ten days of delivery.

Szabo v. Vinton Motors, Inc., supra, concerned an appeal taken by the trustee in bankruptcy of the breaching buyer. Mr. Szabo, the trustee, argued that since the seller did not make a demand for reclamation within ten days after it sold an automobile to the buyer, it lost any special right to reclamation and stood before the court in the shoes of a general credi-

tor. The First Circuit, moved by the trustee's argument, reversed the lower court order ruling otherwise.

The Court's reasoning was simple; it stated that §§ 2–507 and 2–511 provide the cash seller the right to reclaim. The Court then noted that Official Comment 3 to § 2–507 imposed a ten-day limitation upon the cash seller's statutory right. Szabo v. Vinton Motors, Inc., supra 630 F.2d at 3–4, citing In re Samuels & Co., supra, and In re Helms Veneer Corp., supra.

We reject this reasoning. In our view, it would tend to coerce the cash seller who reasonably expects the buyer to tender payment at delivery to go through the cautious motions of a credit seller dealing with an economically unstable buyer. This we are not prepared to do.

credit sale. The transaction that gave rise to this lawsuit was a cash sale. As the district court reasoned, the fact that payment was made by a draft that was subsequently dishonored does not alter the nature of the underlying transaction. See In re Helms Veneer Corp., 287 F.Supp. 840, 844 (W.D.Va.1968).

The district court properly determined that section 2–703 controls this case. This section declares the right of the aggrieved seller to: (1) withhold delivery; (2) stop delivery by any bailee; (3) proceed under section 2–704; (4) *resell and recover damages as provided in section 2–706*; (5) recover damages for nonacceptance or the price; or (6) cancel. In this case, the seller properly chose the fourth alternative. This section's applicability to this case is highlighted by Official Comment 3, which provides: "In addition to the typical case of refusal to pay or default in payment, the language in the preamble, 'fails to make a payment due,' is intended to cover the dishonor of a check on due presentment, or the non-acceptance of a draft * * *." U.C.C. § 2–703 Official Comment 3.

In this case, when the draft was not accepted by the Bank, the seller chose to reclaim the cattle pursuant to section 2–507 and resell them. Section 2–703(d) allows the seller to recover a deficiency judgment upon a reasonable resale.

*   *   *

NOTES

1. In *Szabo*, discussed in footnote 6 of the principal case, the court stated:

> The reference in the last sentence of Comment 3 [to UCC § 2–507] is to the limitation contained in section 2–702(2) requiring a credit seller to reclaim goods within ten days of receipt. See note 1 supra. Based on this reference, courts have invariably held that a cash seller must make a demand for the return of the goods within ten days after the goods are received by the buyer. E.g., In re Samuels & Co., 526 F.2d 1238, 1245 (5th Cir.) (en banc), cert. denied, 429 U.S. 834, 97 S.Ct. 98, 60 L.Ed.2d 99 (1976); In re Helms Veneer Corp., 287 F.Supp. 840, at 846 (W.D.Va.1968).

> Appellee urges us to disregard the limitation contained in Comment 3 on the ground that it directly contradicts the language of the Code. Although Official Code Comments do not have the force of law, they are helpful in explaining the Code provisions and their purpose is to promote uniformity in

construction. Mass.Gen.Laws ch. 106, Comment to Title; Thompson v. United States, 408 F.2d 1075, 1084 n.15 (8th Cir. 1969). See generally Skilton, Some Comments on the Comments to the Uniform Commercial Code, 1966 Wisc.L.Rev. 597. It has been stated that the Official Comments "are powerful dicta." In re Yale Express System, Inc., 370 F.2d 433, 437 (2d Cir. 1966). Nevertheless, it is the Code provisions and not the Comments which control. We do not, however, accept appellee's argument that there is a direct conflict between the cash sale provisions of the Code and Comment 3 to section 2–507. As noted above, Comment 3 supports a reclamation right which is only implicit in Sections 2–507(2) and 2–511(3), and limits that right by reference to another Code provision, section 2–702(2), dealing with credit sales. Comment 3 does not contradict, but merely complements and explains the Code. We decline to disregard it.

Although, as the district court noted, the rule we embrace today may on occasion work a hardship on the cash seller since he may lose his right to reclaim before receiving notice that the buyer's check has been dishonored, the cash seller is not defenseless. A seller is free to require payment by certified check, see section 3–411, Mass.Gen.Laws ch. 106, § 3–411; and he can take and perfect a purchase money security interest in the goods, section 9–107(a), 9–312(3). A cash seller who declines to take these precautions does so at his own risk. Moreover, even at common law a cash seller's right to reclaim was not unlimited and could be lost as the result of an unreasonable delay in exercising that right. Frech v. Lewis, 218 Pa. 141, 67 A. 45 (1907). See Note, The Rights of Reclaiming Cash Sellers When Contested by Secured Creditors of the Buyer, 77 Colum.L.Rev. 934, 942 & n. 53 (1977). We hold that the ten day limitation period contained in Comment 3 provides a more certain guide for conducting commercial transactions than the common law yardstick of "reasonableness," and that it will encourage cash sellers to make prompt presentment. Any extension of the ten day limitation period based on the realities of the commercial banking world is for the legislature, not this Court.

2. Under pre-UCC law the right of the unpaid cash seller to reclaim the goods from the buyer in bankruptcy was recognized. See, for example, In re Perpall, 256 F. 758 (2d Cir. 1919). The seller's right under UCC § 2–507(2) to reclaim from a bankrupt buyer under bankruptcy law in effect prior to the effective date of the Bankruptcy Code was uncertain. Some decisions recog-

nized the right and others denied it on various theories. See Mann & Phillips, The Cash Seller Under the Uniform Commercial Code, 20 Boston Coll.L.Rev. 370, 395–406 (1979). The principal purpose of Bankruptcy Code § 546(c) was to validate the right of reclamation of the credit seller under UCC § 2–702, but its legislative history indicates that it was meant to apply as well to unpaid cash sellers and it literally applies to any seller with a right of reclamation. See Collier on Bankruptcy ¶ 546.04 (15th ed.). Since the primary importance of the right of reclamation is in bankruptcy the effect of Bankruptcy Code § 546(c) is, in most cases, to make the rights of the reclaiming credit seller and unpaid cash seller against the buyer subject to the same restrictions. In both cases the seller must demand reclamation in writing before ten days after receipt of the goods by the buyer and the right is exercisable only if the buyer was insolvent in the bankruptcy sense (i.e., his liabilities exceeded his assets) when he received the goods. See Orr & Klee, Secured Creditors Under the New Bankruptcy Act, 11 U.C.C.L.J. 312, 342–345 (1979). The rights of the reclaiming credit seller and unpaid cash seller vis-à-vis subsequent purchasers of the goods are identical under UCC § 2–403(1).

PROBLEMS

1. Seller sold a boat to Buyer, a retailer of boats. Seller was entitled to and demanded cash on delivery. Buyer gave Seller a check for the price and received delivery of the boat. Buyer knew that there were insufficient funds to cover the check, and it was dishonored when presented. Before Seller was able to repossess the boat Buyer borrowed money from Finance Co., and to secure the debt granted to Finance Co. a security interest in the boat. Buyer kept possession of the boat as part of his inventory. Finance Co. had no knowledge of Buyer's fraud on Seller. Neither Seller nor Finance Co. made any filing of a financing statement under Article 9 of the UCC. Seller then repossessed the boat from Buyer, who voluntarily gave up possession. Finance Co. then brought an action against Seller for conversion. Seller argues that its rights are determined by UCC § 2–507(2), § 9–113, § 9–305 and § 9–312(5). Finance Co. argues that its rights are determined by UCC § 2–403(1). What result? See Hardick v. Hill, 403 So.2d 1125 (Fla.App.1981).

2. Assume the same facts as in Problem 1 except for the following changes: Under the contract of sale Buyer was to pay 10% of the purchase price on delivery with the balance payable

in 90 days. The contract of sale signed by the parties reserved a security interest in the boat in favor of Seller to secure payment of the price. Buyer gave Seller a check for the down payment and received delivery of the boat. Buyer believed that there were sufficient funds to cover the check but he was mistaken. The check was dishonored when presented. Seller argues that its rights are determined by UCC § 9–203, § 9–503, § 9–305 and § 9–312(5).   Who is entitled to the boat? Compare UCC § 2–403(1) and § 9–301(1)(a).

INDEX

†